Antibody Patenting

AIPPI Law Series

VOLUME 5

Series Editors

AIPPI

Introduction & Contents/Subjects

Books in this series are developed within the framework of the International Association for the Protection of Intellectual Property (AIPPI), a non-affiliated non-profit organization dedicated to the development and improvement of legal regimes for the protection of intellectual property at both national and international levels.

Objective & Readership

The aim is to publish innovative work appealing to practitioners, other users of IP systems and academics.

The titles in this series are listed at the back of this volume.

Antibody Patenting

A Practitioner's Guide to Drafting, Prosecution and Enforcement

Edited by

Jürgen Meier

Oswin Ridderbusch

Wolters Kluwer

Published by:
Kluwer Law International B.V.
PO Box 316
2400 AH Alphen aan den Rijn
The Netherlands
Website: www.wolterskluwerlr.com

Sold and distributed in North, Central and South America by:
Wolters Kluwer Legal & Regulatory U.S.
7201 McKinney Circle
Frederick, MD 21704
United States of America
Email: customer.service@wolterskluwer.com

Sold and distributed in all other countries by:
Air Business Subscriptions
Rockwood House
Haywards Heath
West Sussex
RH16 3DH
United Kingdom
Email: international-customerservice@wolterskluwer.com

ISBN: 978-94-035-1073-6

Web PDF ISBN: 978-94-035-1081-1
e-ISBN: 978-94-035-1080-4

AIPPI Law Series ISBN 98-888-8020-8

About the Editors

Jürgen Meier

Dr. Jürgen Meier is a European and German Patent Attorney, and a partner at Vossius & Partner, Munich. He has extensive experience representing clients before both national German courts, including the Federal Supreme Court, and the EPO. He primarily focuses on the fields of biotechnology, (bio-)pharmaceuticals, and employees' inventions. In the antibody field, he handles cases relating, *inter alia*, to 'next generation' antibodies, bi- and multispecific binders, antibody modification/ purification technologies, and therapeutic antibodies, like Herceptin®, Stelara®, Actemra®, Avastin®, Mabthera®, anti-Aβ, anti-PD-1 or anti-PD-L1. Jürgen currently serves as the Chairman of the AIPPI Sub-Committee for Biotechnology and Plant Varieties and has been an active member of this committee for many years. He also actively participates in the AIPPI Study Questions and Surveys. In addition to his frequent publications in the IP field, he is present at conferences and IP associations like AIPPI, JIPA or AIPLA. He is co-author of the sixth edition of 'From Clones to Claims' on the EPO's jurisdiction in the field of biotechnology in comparison to the US and Japanese practice as well as the annually revised AIPPI Law Series book 'Patent Protection for Second Medical Uses'. Jürgen regularly lectures at academic institutions, including the CEIPI/Strasbourg, the LMU and TU Munich, University Würzburg and the Medical University Vienna.

Oswin Ridderbusch

Oswin Ridderbusch is a German and European patent attorney and a partner at the IP law firm Vossius & Partner. He graduated in biochemistry from the University of Tübingen, focusing on medicinal chemistry and protein biochemistry, and conducted research at the Max Planck Institute for Developmental Biology. His practice includes the drafting and prosecution of patent applications, mainly in the fields of antibodies and biologics, small molecular pharmaceuticals, formulations, drug delivery technologies, functional foods and diagnostics, as well as contentious post-grant proceedings including opposition, revocation and infringement actions, and the filing of supplementary protection certificates (SPCs). He further provides counsel in the strategic management of patent portfolios and prepares freedom-to-operate and due diligence opinions. Oswin is an editor and author of the handbook 'European SPCs Unravelled: A Practitioner's Guide to Supplementary Protection Certificates in Europe'. He has been a member of the Executive Committee of AIPPI since 2017, and engages in AIPPI's Standing Committee on the Unitary Patent and the Unified Patent Court.

About the Contributors

Sergio Arboleda

Sergio Arboleda is a senior associate at Cavelier Abogados in Colombia. Arboleda is a data driven and business focused Chemist and Chemical Engineer from Universidad de los Andes (Bogotá, Colombia) with a particular interest in exact sciences, organic synthesis, computational chemistry, polymer production, marketing and business relations. He has more than 5 years of experience in prosecuting and litigating patents in the areas of biotechnology, chemistry, pharmacy, mechanical engineering, chemical engineering and software-implemented inventions; as well as a passion for teaching and training new team members. His experience and knowledge related to patent prosecution extends throughout more than 12 Latam jurisdictions.

Juan Arias

Juan Arias, MSc Chemistry, European Patent Attorney and Spanish Patent & Trademark Agent, is founding and managing partner of ABG Intellectual Property. His practice focuses on patent prosecution, including EPO oppositions and SPCs prosecution; opinion work, including freedom to operate, validity opinions and litigation support in the areas of organic chemistry, biotechnology and pharmaceuticals. Before founding ABG Intellectual property, Juan was an examiner at the European Patent Office in Munich. Prior to his patent career, Juan performed research on protein chemistry at the Max-Planck-Institut für Biochemie in Munich. Juan is member of the European Patent Institute (EPI) Council, and member of its Patent Litigation Committee, as well as of the Biotech Committee of the AIPPI.

Claire Baldock

Claire Baldock is a Chartered Patent Attorney and European Patent Attorney and a Consultant for the Biotechnology and Life Sciences practice group at Boult Wade

Tennant. Claire has special expertise in patent work in the chemical, pharmacological and biotechnological fields, particularly in relation to oppositions and appeals at the European Patent Office. She is a specialist in patent due diligence exercises. She possesses technical expertise in the areas of drug delivery systems, herbal medicines, vaccines, diagnostics, fermentation technology, DNA sequencing techniques, therapeutic antibodies, biologics and pharmaceuticals. Claire has a BSc in Biochemistry and Microbiology from the University of Leeds and an MSc in Biotechnology. She is a current member of the AIPPI sub-committee for Biotechnology and Plant Varieties, and a former longstanding member of the Chartered Institute of Patent Attorneys Life Sciences Committee. She has also recently been elected to the AIPPI Council for the UK group. Claire has written numerous articles and spoken extensively on biotechnology and due diligence matters.

Martín Bensadon

Martín Bensadon joined Marval, O'Farrell & Mairal in 1991 and has been a partner of the firm since 1998. He specializes in industrial property and more particularly in patent law, having advised many national and foreign firms in this area. He graduated as a lawyer from the Universidad de Buenos Aires in 1991 and obtained a Master in Laws at the University of Illinois at Urbana-Champaign in 1996. He has participated in seminars on industrial property and has written various articles on subjects related to his area of specialty in national and international publications as well as a book on Argentine Patent Law. He currently teaches at the Universidad Austral and Universidad de San Andrés. He was a Guest Researcher of the Max Planck Institute for Intellectual Property, Competition and Tax Law and a Visiting Scholar at The George Washington University Law School.

Cristian D. Bittel

Cristian Daniel Bittel joined Marval, O'Farrell & Mairal in 2004 and became a partner in 2016. He is currently a member of the Intellectual Property department, specializing in Patents. In particular, his areas of expertise include biotechnology, pharmaceuticals and chemistry. Before joining the firm, he was a scholar of the CONICET (National Council of Science) for the Instituto de Biología Molecular y Celular de Rosario. He graduated in Biotechnology from the Universidad Nacional de Rosario in 1996 and later completed three post-graduate studies: a PhD in Biological Sciences at the same university, a specialization in Environmental Management at Universidad Católica Argentina and the third in Industrial Property at the INPI. Cristian has worked as a teaching assistant at the biology department of Universidad Nacional de Rosario and has written many articles in his practice area.

Graeme Boocock

Graeme Boocock is a Senior Patent Agent in the Ottawa office of Borden Ladner Gervais LLP. He specializes in drafting and prosecution of patent applications in the life sciences, including personalized medicine and antibody technologies. He holds a PhD in Molecular and Medical Genetics (University of Toronto). His doctoral research was carried out at The Hospital for Sick Children, and culminated in the discovery of the human gene that is mutated in Shwachman-Diamond syndrome – an inherited disease involving bone marrow failure, leukemia risk, and pancreatic exocrine insufficiency. Graeme then worked for three years at the Medical Research Counsel Laboratory of Molecular Biology in Cambridge, UK, focusing on synthetic biology and protein engineering. He is an amateur plant breeder and holder of a pending Plant Breeders' Rights application.

Pedro Henrique Borges de Figueiredo

Pedro holds a BSc in Biological Sciences and MSc in Molecular Biology from the Federal University of Rio de Janeiro. Since joining Dannemann Siemsen firm in 2010, he has worked in drafting, prosecuting patent applications and obtaining effective protection for a diverse portfolio of inventions in the field of biotechnology, serving clients in the agricultural, food, cosmetics, pharmaceutical and industrial biotechnology segments, among others. Pedro also assists clients in plant variety protection, access to genetic resources, traditional knowledge and as technical assistant in biotech patent lawsuits and is a member of International Association for the Protection of Intellectual Property (AIPPI) and Brazilian Association of Industrial Property Agents (ABAPI).

Charles Boulakia

Charles Boulakia is a partner of Ridout & Maybee LLP in the firm's Toronto office. His practice is principally directed towards the preparation and prosecution of patent applications in the biotechnology, chemistry, biofuel, oil and gas and pharmaceutical areas. Charles provides his clients with IP due diligence, validity, and freedom to operate opinions. Charles also drafts and negotiates license agreements. Charles is currently the Vice-Chair of the AIPPI Standing Committee on Pharma and Biotechnology and the Treasurer of the Royal Canadian Institute for Science. He provides pro bono advice on IP law for the Law and Business Clinic at Ryerson University, volunteers on the selection committee for the Norman Esch Engineering Innovation and Entrepreneurship Award and is a mentor at the University of Toronto Entrepreneurship Hatchery. He is an avid sailor and watch collector, and is fluent in French.

Olga Capasso

Dr. Olga Capasso, European and Italian Patent Attorney, Master Diploma in European Patent Litigation, is a founding partner of De Simone & Partners IP in Rome, Italy. She was formerly a molecular and cell biology scientist. She is responsible of the patent department of the Firm and mainly assists national and international clients in matters relating to patent strategy and litigation, mostly in pharmaceutical and biotech areas; in fact, Olga was involved in many patent litigations in such fields. She also acts as Court Expert in national patent litigations. Olga has lectured extensively in Italy, published articles about current aspects of IP law and drafted a commentary of relevant Italian provision on protection of biotech inventions.

Hector E. Chagoya-Cortes

Hector E. Chagoya-Cortes has a Chemical Engineering background and is Partner and Patents & Technology Director at BC&B. With IP experience since 1997, he has been recognized consistently as a leading patent practitioner in several international surveys including IP Stars, Patents 1000, IAM Strategy 300, and Leaders League among others since 2005. He has past experience in the scale-up of biotechnology processes at an immunochemistry lab and is currently in charge of the whole patent practice of his firm, as well as of consulting services for leveraging value from IP assets. He is currently President of LES Mexico, Past Vice-president of LES International, among other leadership positions in other professional associations including AIPPI where he represents the Mexican group in the Pharmaceutical Patents and Trade Secrets Committees and where is part of the Information Technologies Committee and the Patents Committee within the Mexican group.

Michael Christie

Michael Christie is a senior patent attorney at MinterEllison in Sydney, Australia. He has a PhD in biochemistry and has worked as a post-doctoral scientist at the Max Planck Institute for Developmental Biology in Tuebingen, Germany. He represents universities, research institutes and start-ups through to multinational biotech and pharmaceutical companies. Michael is a member of the AIPPI Standing Committee for Pharma and Biotechnology.

Takashi Fujita

Takashi Fujita is a patent attorney, and the Vice President responsible for biotechnology and chemistry at Hiraki & Associates. He works each day to ensure that the firm's Biotechnology & Chemistry Group will be able to provide the most comprehensive services possible for IP-related matters at every step of the way, from the research and development stage to the registration of patent rights. He served as a patent examiner and an appeal examiner at the Japan Patent Office (JPO), working in the fields of biotechnology, food processing, and chemical engineering. Furthermore, while at the Examination Standards Office of the JPO, he was involved in the drafting of Examination Guidelines and Trilateral Office comparative studies. He was also sent to Washington, D.C. in the United States as a visiting scholar to study US patent practice, and later he was dispatched to Munich, where his tasks included acting as a liaison between the JPO and the EPO.

David Gilat

Adv. and patent attorney David Gilat is a Senior Partner at Gilat Bareket & Co., Reinhold Cohn Group in Israel. He has extensive professional experience in various fields of IP: patents, trademarks, designs, copyrights, plant breeders' rights, distribution agreements and competition law. David appeared before the Knesset Committee (Israeli Parliament) in charge of the new Designs law. He teaches patent law at the Tel Aviv University and lectures in various forums. He served as a research fellow at the

Max Planck Institute for Foreign and International Patent, Copyright and Competition Laws and has written books, articles and manuals in the field of Intellectual Property.

Khoo Kian Hoe

Khoo Kian Hoe is a senior associate at the Singapore office of Davies Collison Cave. He specialises in the drafting and prosecution of patent applications, particularly in the areas of life sciences and biotechnology. He also provides advice to clients on validity and infringement matters. Kian Hoe was a recipient of the Agency for Science, Technology and Research (A*STAR) National Science Scholarship award. He earned his PhD in Protein Engineering from the University of Cambridge and BSc in Biochemistry from Imperial College London. He has previously worked as a cancer researcher at A*STAR and has taught at the Lee Kong Chian School of Medicine at Nanyang Technological University (NTU) in Singapore.

Gesheng Huang

Gesheng Huang's practice focuses on patent prosecution and litigation, and related matters. Mr. Huang started his practice in 1986. He has extensive experience in drafting and prosecuting patent applications, in patent reexamination, appeal, invalidation and litigation. Mr. Huang represents foreign and domestic clients, mainly in the fields of biotechnology, pharmaceuticals, crop science, organic chemistry, and polymer chemistry. In addition, Mr. Huang has expertise in the protection of new plant varieties. Mr. Huang has a BSc degree in microbiology in 1986 from Wuhan University. He joined CCPIT in 1986. From 1995 to 1996, he studied US patent law and practice in New York City. Mr. Huang joined Beijing Zhongzi Law Office in 2001. He is now a senior partner of Zhongzi and head of Biotech and Pharmaceutical group of the firm. Mr. Huang is the author and contributor of a number of articles on intellectual property practice in China and in U.S. He is a member of AIPPI and LES. He is now the Chair of Pharma/Biotech committee of AIPPI China.

Hans-Rainer Jaenichen

Dr. Hans-Rainer Jaenichen is a German patent attorney, a registered European patent attorney and a European Trademark and Design attorney. He has been a partner in the IP law firm of Vossius & Partner in Munich, Germany since 1990. He studied biology and holds a PhD in molecular immunology. Hans-Rainer has frequently lectured internationally, has chaired numerous conferences and has authored many publications on biotech intellectual property. The sixth edition of his book 'From Clones to Claims' on the European Patent Office's jurisdiction in the field of biotechnology in comparison to the US and Japanese practice was published together with Jürgen Meier, James F. Haley, Leslie McDonell and Yoshinori Hosoda in January 2016. Hans-Rainer has handled cases in the entire field of biotechnology and biopharmaceuticals, e.g. PCR, RNAi and CRISPR. Many of them related to antibody inventions (monoclonal, single chain, humanized, recombinant, Actemra®, Herceptin®, Rituximab®, Simponi®, Benlysta®, anti-PD1-antibodies, anti-PD-L1 antibodies, anti-CD27-antibodies, anti-TNF-antibodies, etc.). He is an AIPPI and GRUR member, a supporting member of the Max-Planck-Society (Max-Planck-Gesellschaft) and a member of the Board of Trustees of the Munich Intellectual Property Law Center (MIPLC). He has been invited to the 2012 and 2016 Banbury Conferences on patenting genes.

Mamta Rani Jha

Mamta Rani Jha is the Senior Partner and currently heads the litigation and opposition practice at Inttl Advocare, one of India's leading IP law firms. With over 20 years of litigation experience, her expertise lies in advising and strategizing effective enforcement in field of IP. She has been involved in over 100 patent litigation cases in the last four years, representing leading global pharmaceutical, electronic and telecom giants. She has also been actively involved in handling issues pertaining to IT, telecom, media and antitrust law. Apart from litigation, Mamta actively advises clients on IP licensing, auditing, contract drafting and negotiation, business venture evaluation and due diligence, anti-counterfeiting and border-control measures. Mamta is a Gold Medalist in BSc (Zoology) and a regular speaker at various IP fora. She is a member of the INTA Enforcement Committee. She is also member of the AIPPI, APAA and IACC participant.

Israel Jiménez

Israel is one of the founding partners of BREAKTHROUGH IP INTELLIGENCE S. Before starting his IP practice, he oversaw several projects of Environmental Assessments in various Industries in Mexico, and he began his practice in Intellectual and Industrial Property in 1992. Israel has contributed to various studying committees with the local IP association and presently, he is the chair of the Patent Committee of AMPPI. He has written several Articles related to the IP practice in Mexico and foreign countries. Israel is a member of several National and International Associations such as AMPPI; INTA; AIPPI (Biotech-Pharma Committee and Mexican Delegate); PTMG; APAA (as Observer), AIPLA. He has participated in Patent Litigation cases in Mexico, mainly on Chemical and Pharmaceutical matters, where he has acted as a technical Expert before Mexican courts in those areas. He is an advisor both in Intellectual Property and in Technological Intelligence for several National and International Companies.

Marta Kawczyńska

Marta Kawczyńska is a Polish patent and trademark attorney, qualified European patent attorney and professional representative before the EUIPO. She is a shareholder of POLSERVICE Patent and Trademark Attorneys Office in Warsaw, Poland, and member of the company's Supervisory Board. Marta specializes in drafting, filing and prosecuting patent applications in the fields of biotechnology, pharma, molecular medicine and diagnostics, both in the national, regional and international procedures. She also has vast experience in representing clients in all matters relating to Supplementary Protection Certificates (SPCs), as well as in patent ligation proceedings. Marta is currently Council Member of the European Patent Institute (epi), and Vice-President of the AIPPI Poland.

Martin Klok

Martin Klok is a Dutch and European patent attorney at V.O. Patents & Trademarks, working from the firm's head office in The Hague, the Netherlands. Martin has a PhD degree in chemistry and extensive research experience in the fields of molecular nanotechnology and the relationship food/health. As a member of V.O.'s litigation support team, a large part of his time is spent on providing technical assistance in litigation cases. Also, he is active as a representative at the EPO in opposition cases, as well as in the drafting and prosecution of patent applications. He specializes in the fields of pharmaceuticals, biomedical technology and food. Martin is also a vice-chair in the AIPPI Standing Committee on Pharmaceuticals.

Isabelle Labarre

Isabelle holds a BSc degree in Life Sciences from the University of Paris V. She also holds a MSc degree in Biotechnology & Law from the University of Tours. Isabelle is a Graduate of the CEIPI, European Patent Attorney and French *Conseil en propriété industrielle*. She joined Cabinet Plasseraud in 2017. Her practice focuses on patent filing and prosecution, as well as opposition proceedings. Her practice also focuses on Supplementary Protection Certificates. Isabelle is a member of several professional associations (CNCPI; AIPPI).

Daniel Lim

Daniel is a partner in Kirkland & Ellis' IP litigation team in London, where his practice is focused on complex and high-value life science patent litigation. He frequently acts for clients involved in pharmaceuticals, diagnostics and the emerging fields of cell and gene therapy, bringing his dual qualifications in law and biochemistry to bear. In addition to UK litigation, Daniel often assists clients in devising and coordinating complex patent litigation strategy at a pan-European and global level, working closely with local lawyers around the world. Daniel writes and speaks regularly on a wide range of life sciences and IP topics including precision medicine, CRISPR and biologics. He is a member of EPLAW, the AIPPI Standing Committee on IP and genetic resources/traditional knowledge and an observer on the AIPPI Standing Committee on Biotechnology.

Mirit Lotan

Mirit Lotan, PhD is an Israeli patent attorney at Reinhold Cohn and Partners, an intellectual property firm based in Tel Aviv, Israel. She focuses her practice on drafting and prosecuting patent applications, conducting opinion work and due diligence investigations, and advising on intellectual property protection strategies mainly in the life sciences area, with special expertise in antibodies. She earned her Doctor of Philosophy in Biology from the Weizmann Institute of Science. Before joining Reinhold Cohn and Partners she worked for more than ten years in the Biotechnology industry combining IP practice with licensing and business development activities.

Philipp Marchand

Philipp Marchand is a German and European Patent Attorney and the managing director of the Swiss office of Vossius and Partner in Basel. He is a trained biochemist with a PhD in biophysical chemistry. His practice focuses on advising companies of all sizes with respect to patent prosecution, opposition and litigation. He is also involved in due diligence matters for various investment companies. He has been accredited by the Swiss government as IP coach for the Swiss Innovation Agency (Innosuisse) where he works with young startup companies on developing global IP strategies. Philipp is an active AIPPI member and has been involved in AIPPI working groups on various study questions in the past.

Rodrigo Marré Grez

Rodrigo Marré Grez is a partner in the Mackenna, Irarrázaval, Cuchacovich y Paz, Law firm in Chile, where he leads the Intellectual Property practice. Rodrigo has vast experience on IP issues concentrating on patents, prosecution, litigation and contracts. He also has deep knowledge on regulatory issues concerning pharmaceutical and cosmetic health registration and administrative litigation. He is a member of the Chilean Bar Association, International Trademark Association (INTA), Interamerican Association of Intellectual Property (ASIPI), Chilean Association of Intellectual Property (ACHIPI), International Association for the Protection of Intellectual Property (AIPPI), as well as an observer at Asian Patent Attorney Association (APAA). Rodrigo has multiple professional acknowledgements and publications.

Cyra Nargolwalla

Cyra Nargolwalla is one of four Managing Partners at Plasseraud IP and Head of the Chemistry and Life Sciences Department. Her practice focuses on advising and assisting clients in patent matters, specialising in EPO Opposition/Appeal Proceedings and patent litigation matters in France. She also coordinates patent litigation in other countries. Cyra holds BSc and MSc degrees in Biochemistry from the University of Toronto. She also holds LLB and BCL (Bachelor of Civil Laws) degrees from McGill University and a Maîtrise de Droit privé et droit international privé from Université Paris II (Assas). Cyra is a Graduate of the CEIPI, European Patent Attorney and French *Conseil en propriété industrielle*. She joined Cabinet Plasseraud in 1994 and became a partner in 2004. Cyra is an active member of several professional associations (CNCPI – Treasurer from 2007 to 2011; AIPPI – Secretary of the French National Group since 2017; IPO – Active member of the European Practice Committee; LES).

Allison Ortega del Valle

Allison Ortega del Valle is a Biochemist and Master in Biochemistry at Mackenna, Irarrázaval, Cuchacovich & Paz, Intellectual Property Law firm in Chile. Her practice focuses on drafting, prosecuting invention patent applications and advising on intellectual property protection strategies of new technologies. She earned her Post-graduate in Intellectual Property, at Pontifical Catholic University of Chile, and her Master in Biochemistry at University Andres Bello in Chile. Allison is a member of the Association Chilean of the Intellectual Property (ACHIPI) and member International Association for the Protection of Intellectual Property (AIPPI).

Andres Rincon

Andres Rincon is a Colombian Patent Attorney and barrister. Partner at Cavelier Abogados and with 19 years experience in patents, plant breeding rights and regulatory affairs related to chemical synthesis and biological pharmaceutical and agrochemical products. JD in Law from the Pontimcia Universidad Javeriana (Colombia 1998), with specialized studies in IP of the Universidad Externado de Colombia (2002), scholarship holder from the AlßAN program of the European Commission (2006) and LLM in IP from the Max Planck Institute and the George Washington University, through the Munich Intellectual Property Law Center, Germany (2007). Rincon has successfully intervened in the most important cases of compulsory licenses, patent validity and infringement, both before Colombian and Andean courts, and is an active member of different patent committees at AIPLA, ASIPI and AIPPI, last in which he is the current representative from Colombia before the Biotechnology committee.

Min Son

Min Son is a founder and a president of Hanol Intellectual Property Law firm in Korea. With a PhD in biochemistry, Dr. Son focuses on prosecuting patent applications and managing international patent portfolios for biotechnology and pharmaceutical companies. Dr. Son has led her firm to achieve the 'Best in Class' status in the fields of life science and chemistry. Before founding the firm, Dr. Son worked as a patent examiner of KIPO in the fields of biotechnology, organic, and inorganic chemistry and contributed to the preparation of the Examination Guidelines for Biotechnology Inventions. Dr. Son is recognized in the 2018 edition of Managing Intellectual Property's Top 250 Women in IP and she is an active member of AIPPI, AIPLA, INTA, APAA and FICPI.

Maria Carmen de Souza Brito

Chemical engineer graduated from the State University of Rio de Janeiro. Patent specialist in the areas of chemistry, pharmaceutical, cosmetics, agribusiness, biotechnology and traditional knowledge, amongst others. Partner at the Dannemann Siemsen firm where she started her career in 1988. President of the Brazilian Intellectual Property Association (ABPI) for the 2016–2017 term and also member of International Association for the Protection of Intellectual Property (AIPPI), Inter-American Association of Intellectual Property (ASIPI) and Brazilian Association of Industrial Property Agents (ABAPI).

John C. Todaro

John Todaro is an Executive Director in the Intellectual Property Group of the Office of General Counsel of Merck & Co., Inc., Kenilworth, New Jersey, USA. John leads a group of attorneys who support Merck research in the fields of neuroscience, oncology and infectious diseases. John has been with Merck since 2003. Prior to joining Merck, John worked as an associate and senior counsel at patent law firms in New York. John is currently the Chair of the AIPPI Pharma & Biotech Standing Committee.

Michele M. Wales

The founder of InHouse Patent Counsel, Michele focuses on providing exceptional biotech legal advice on flexible and affordable financial terms for start-ups and emerging biotech clients. Before starting her firm, Michele was the head of Litigation and Intellectual Property at Human Genome Sciences where she worked for over fifteen years. Under her direction, HGS' IP portfolio was repeatedly recognized by the Wall Street Journal as one of the 'Top 10 Biotech Portfolios' and covered over 10,000 human genes, proteins and antibodies. She also successfully managed the team that established the Utility Standard for gene-based patents at the United Kingdom's Supreme Court and European Patent Office. The International Law Office nominated her team in 2012 as 'In-House Litigation Team of the Year.' Michele received her J.D. from George Washington National Law Center, her PhD in Human Genetics and Molecular Biology from Johns Hopkins Medical School, and is an inventor on multiple patents.

Osamu Yamamoto

Osamu Yamamoto is a patent attorney, and a partner of YUASA and HARA in Japan. Osamu is the acting Chief of the Chemical Section of the Patent Division of the firm. He has nineteen years of experience in intellectual property, focusing on patents, including drafting patent applications, dealing with Office Actions, providing expert opinions, defending or attacking patent rights in invalidation trials and oppositions, and infringement litigation. He frequently gives lectures on patents, especially in the fields of pharmaceuticals and biotech. Before specializing in intellectual property, he gained ten years of experience working in pharmaceutical and biotechnology research and development for a chemical company.

Summary of Contents

Table of Contents

Foreword

Renata Righetti Pelosi, President of AIPPI

AIPPI has been improving and promoting the protection of intellectual property (IP) since 1897, celebrating its 120th anniversary in 2017. A truly global association, today it has 70 national and regional groups, and over 9000 members from more than 125 countries and regions in Europe, the Americas, Asia, Oceania and Africa.

AIPPI is a non-affiliated, non-profit organization. Its members include lawyers, attorneys and agents working across all fields of IP in corporate and private practice throughout the world, as well as academics, judges, government officials and other persons interested in IP.

AIPPI promotes the value of all types of IP through its comprehensive analyses of existing and proposed IP laws and policies; working with government and non-government organizations to develop and improve international and regional treaties and agreements, and national laws; and hosting conferences and seminars. AIPPI is delighted to partner now again with Wolters Kluwer to deliver the fifth volume of the 'AIPPI Law Series' – another way to promote the protection of IP.

Modern medicine and diagnostics can no longer be imagined without antibodies. As a matter of fact, therapeutic antibodies are nowadays always in the top ten of best-selling drugs. Correspondingly, since the early 1980s, the patenting of antibodies all over the world has been a success story, and antibody claims have been – and still are – important assets for inventors in the pharma and biotech sector. However, recent case law in the U.S. and other jurisdictions on antibody patents has led to discussions on the scope of protection of antibody claims and the 'written description' requirement in relation to corresponding patent applications. These developments and worldwide discussions have spurred the Pharma and Biotech Committee of AIPPI on a joint project, namely a global survey of the status of antibody patents.

The current volume of the AIPPI Law Series is, *inter alia*, based on this survey. It provides a global review of the patenting of antibodies in 23 jurisdictions and, as such, will prove a valuable tool for IP practitioners working in the pharma and life science sector. More than 30 authors have contributed to this comparative law study and compendium. All contributors are well-established experts in the life science sector and have succeeded in delivering a worldwide overview and in-depth analysis of the current antibody patenting and litigation landscape. The clear explanations and close attention to details, both in relation to prosecution matters before the different patent offices and in the review of national infringement and litigation cases, render this book an indispensible resource for patent attorneys and litigators in the life science and pharma fields. All contributors rely on very recent case law, as also reflected in the appended table of cases which, by itself, will be a valuable resource for IP professionals, not only for the prosecution of antibody cases before the national and regional patent offices but also for corresponding litigations in court.

AIPPI would like to cordially thank the volume editors of this book, Jürgen Meier and Oswin Ridderbusch. Jürgen currently serves as Chairman of the AIPPI Biotech Committee (Sub-Committee of Pharma and Biotechnology), and Oswin is a member of the Standing Committee on the Unitary Patent and the Unified Patent Court, a member of the Executive Committee, and a delegate of the German national group. Furthermore, AIPPI also expressly thanks the chapter contributors, all of whom are active AIPPI members, for their dedication and diligence without which this impressive global law review would not have been possible. Wolters Kluwer has again partnered with AIPPI for this book, and AIPPI gratefully acknowledges this ongoing support and fruitful partnership.

Renata Righetti Pelosi
President of AIPPI
July 2019

Acknowledgments

We are grateful to Dr. Friederike Stolzenburg, Dr. Richard Enmon and Dr. Georg Andreas Rauh of Vossius & Partner for their valuable support and stimulating discussions.

We would also like to thank our co-authors Sergio Arboleda, Juan Arias, Claire Baldock, Martín Bensadon, Dr. Cristian D. Bittel, Dr. Graeme Boocock, Pedro Henrique Borges de Figueiredo, Charles Boulakia, Dr. Olga Capasso, Hector E. Chagoya-Cortes, Dr. Michael Christie, Takashi Fujita, David Gilat, Dr. Khoo Kian Hoe, Gesheng Huang, Dr. Hans-Rainer Jaenichen, Mamta Rani Jha, Israel Jiménez, Marta Kawczyńska, Dr. Martin Klok, Isabelle Labarre, Daniel Lim, Dr. Mirit Lotan, Dr. Philipp Marchand, Rodrigo Marré Grez, Cyra Nargolwalla, Allison Ortega del Valle, Dr. Andres Rincon, Dr. Min Son, Maria Carmen de Souza Brito, John C. Todaro, Dr. Michele M. Wales and Osamu Yamamoto for their thorough and dedicated contributions to this book, and for generously sharing their knowledge on the patenting of antibodies.

We further wish to thank Steve Lambley and Christine Robben of Wolters Kluwer for their valued support in the preparation of this book.

Dr. Jürgen Meier
Oswin Ridderbusch

Introduction

Jürgen Meier & Oswin Ridderbusch

Antibodies, it may fairly be said, have been an unprecedented success story. Since it became possible to generate monoclonal antibodies having a predefined target specificity using the hybridoma technology developed by César Milstein and Georges J.F. Köhler in 1975,[1] antibodies have revolutionized medicine and biotechnology, and have become indispensable tools in therapy, diagnostics, analytical methods, and research. The number of antibodies among newly approved medicinal products has seen a steady increase over the last decades, and therapeutic antibodies have become ever more prominent in the ranks of blockbuster drugs. Indeed, monoclonal antibodies and antibody constructs account for 10 out of the top 15 pharmaceutical products by worldwide sales in 2018, including the number one best-selling drug Humira® (containing the antibody adalimumab).[2]

The growing commercial success of antibodies has been accompanied by patent disputes in most major jurisdictions, which have resulted in a formidable body of case law dealing specifically with the patentability of antibody-related inventions and the enforcement of antibody patents. In principle, the necessity to grant patents in order to foster innovation in this important technical field has been universally acknowledged. It therefore came as a shock when the US Supreme Court in 2013 found

1. *See* Köhler G & Milstein C, Continuous cultures of fused cells secreting antibody of predefined specificity, *Nature*, 1975, 256(5517): 495–497. César Milstein and Georges J.F. Köhler, together with Niels K. Jerne, were awarded the Nobel Prize in Physiology or Medicine in 1984 for this contribution.
2. *See*, e.g., Philippidis A, Top 15 Best-Selling Drugs of 2018, *Genetic Engineering & Biotechnology News*, 2019, 39(4):16–17 (accessible online at: https://www.genengnews.com/a-lists/top-15-best-selling-drugs-of-2018/). Among the top 15 best-selling drugs by worldwide sales in 2018, the following 10 drugs are monoclonal antibodies or antibody constructs: Humira® (adalimumab), Opdivo® (nivolumab), Keytruda® (pembrolizumab), Enbrel® (etanercept), Herceptin® (trastuzumab), Avastin® (bevacizumab), Rituxan®/MabThera® (rituximab), Eylea® (aflibercept), Remicade® (infliximab), and Stelara® (ustekinumab).

naturally occurring molecules to be excluded from patentability,[3] and when the US Court of Appeals for the Federal Circuit in 2017 raised the 'written description' bar for antibody inventions so outrageously high as to effectively make patent protection unattainable even for slightly generalized classes of antibodies.[4] Under this new restrictive approach, only antibodies that do not occur in nature can be patented in the United States, and only if their relevant amino acid sequences are specified in the claims (or if a cell line producing the respective antibody has been deposited) whereas purely functional definitions of antibodies are no longer accepted. These decisions have been heavily criticized and stand in stark contrast to the valid practice and the established case law in Europe and many other countries worldwide. Yet, they have also raised awareness of the at times considerable divergences in the assessment of patents claiming antibody inventions in different jurisdictions.

In the IP community, and not least within AIPPI, these disruptive US decisions have prompted major discussions. During the AIPPI World Congress in Sydney in October 2017, the Federal Circuit's decision in *Amgen v. Sanofi*, which had been handed down just one week before, became subject of controversial discussions among participants, not only in panels and in the congress halls but also in the corridors of the conference center. These vivid discussions encouraged AIPPI's Pharma and Biotechnology Committees to jointly conduct a worldwide survey on antibody patenting. While this survey cast a spotlight on recent alarming developments in the United States and a few other jurisdictions which put highly valuable patents protecting antibody inventions at risk, it also made apparent that an increasing number of antibody cases were being litigated before national patent infringement courts and that an impressive amount of case law had already been generated in many different jurisdictions. The desire to make this knowledge available to patent professionals in a structured and practice-oriented form laid the groundwork for the conception of the present volume of the AIPPI Law Series.

This book is designed to provide practitioners with a comprehensive and up-to-date resource elucidating all aspects of the patenting of antibodies from drafting and prosecution to enforcement, and covering more than 20 of the most important jurisdictions worldwide. All chapters follow the same structure, which makes this book easily accessible and allows a direct comparison between different jurisdictions. This is complemented by a detailed table of cases referencing all decisions discussed in the various chapters. The 35 distinguished authors of this book have been carefully selected and are all renowned experts in the patenting of antibodies in their respective countries.

---

3. *Association for Molecular Pathology v. Myriad Genetics, Inc.*, 569 U.S. 576 (2013). The US Supreme Court in this judgment strongly relied on its previous decision in *Mayo Collaborative Services v. Prometheus Laboratories, Inc.*, 566 U.S. 66 (2012).
4. *Amgen v. Sanofi*, 872 F.3d 1367 (Fed. Cir. 2017).

Chapter 1

European Patent Office

Jürgen Meier & Hans-Rainer Jaenichen

§1.01 ANTIBODIES AS PATENTABLE SUBJECT-MATTER

[A] Legal Framework

European patents are granted by the European Patent Office (EPO) which was established on the basis of an international treaty, the European Patent Convention (EPC), in 1973. There are currently 38 'Contracting States' to the EPC, i.e. Albania, Austria, Belgium, Bulgaria, Croatia, Cyprus, the Czech Republic, Denmark, Estonia, Finland, France, Germany, Greece, Hungary, Iceland, Ireland, Italy, Latvia, Liechtenstein, Lithuania, Luxembourg, Malta, Monaco, the Netherlands, North Macedonia, Norway, Poland, Portugal, Romania, San Marino, Serbia, Slovakia, Slovenia, Spain, Sweden, Switzerland, Turkey, and the United Kingdom.

European patents can further be extended to take effect in a number of 'Extension States' and 'Validation States' located both within and outside of Europe, i.e. Bosnia and Herzegovina, Montenegro, Morocco, Moldova, Tunisia, and Cambodia, on the basis of bilateral agreements concluded between the European Patent Organization and these countries.[1] The EPO/European Patent Organization currently negotiates new validation agreements with various African and Asian countries, including Angola, Brunei, Jordan, Laos, and Malaysia, as well as the African Intellectual Property Organization (OAPI).[2] In addition, European patents granted with effect

1. While the existing extension and validation agreements are very similar in substance, a principal difference is that the Extension States (Bosnia and Herzegovina, as well as Montenegro) are expected to eventually accede to the EPC whereas the Validation States (Morocco, Moldova, Tunisia, and Cambodia) have not been offered any accession perspective. Note that under Art. 166(1)(b) EPC, only European states may accede to the EPC.
2. See, e.g., the keynote presentation of former EPO president Benoît Battistelli given at the FICPI Open Forum in 2017 (available online at: https://ficpi.org/_/uploads/files/

for the United Kingdom can be extended to several further countries and territories, including Hong Kong[3] as well as Brunei, Fiji, Gambia, Grenada and others.[4]

The EPO has the exclusive competence to grant European patents (after substantive examination proceedings) and to conduct centralized post-grant opposition proceedings. While the EPO will also become responsible for the registration of European unitary patents – if and when the Unified Patent Court Agreement comes into force, the EPO and the EPC remain outside of the legal framework of the European Union.

Once a European patent is granted, it confers the same rights in each designated Contracting State as would be conferred by a corresponding national patent, which in some of the Contracting States is subject to the filing of a translation of the claims or the complete patent specification.[5] After grant, a European patent thus disintegrates into a bundle of separate national parts, each of which can be individually maintained or allowed to lapse, enforced, and become the subject of national revocation actions.

The *Guidelines for Examination in the European Patent Office*[6] ('Guidelines'), provide detailed guidance on the substantive and procedural aspects of all proceedings before the EPO. They are binding for the departments of first instance but not for the Boards of Appeal which serve as an independent judicial instance that can be called upon to review decisions of the Examining Divisions, the Opposition Divisions, the Legal Division and the Receiving Section of the EPO.

The provisions of the EPC have been interpreted in the case law of the Boards of Appeal of the EPO,[7] including the decisions of the Technical Boards of Appeal ('T-decisions') and the Legal Board of Appeal ('J-decisions'). Of particular relevance is the case law of the Enlarged Board of Appeal ('G-decisions') which addresses important questions of law and ensures a uniform interpretation and application of the EPC. The EPO has also published a reference book entitled *Case Law of the Boards of Appeal of the European Patent Office*, which provides a comprehensive summary of the most important Board of Appeal decisions and is currently available in its eighth edition from 2016.[8]

The original European Patent Convention of 1973 was revised by the Act revising Article 63 EPC of 17 December 1991 and the Act revising the EPC of 29 November 2000. The revised EPC (known as 'EPC2000') entered into force on 13 December 2007.

FICPI_2017_-_Keynote_-_Recent_Developments_at_the_EPO.pdf), and the official EPO news of 5 April 2019 referring to six new validation agreements being negotiated (accessible online at: https://www.epo.org/news-issues/news/2019/20190405a.html).

3. See OJ EPO 2009, 546 for further details on the patent registration procedure in Hong Kong.
4. See the UK IPO guidance document on the 'Extension of UK intellectual property rights abroad' which is accessible online at: https://www.gov.uk/government/publications/extension-of-uk-intellectual-property-rights-abroad.
5. Articles 64 and 65 EPC.
6. The Guidelines are updated every year in November and are available online in English, French and German at: https://www.epo.org/law-practice/legal-texts/guidelines.html.
7. All decisions of the Boards of Appeal can be accessed online at: https://www.epo.org/law-practice/case-law-appeals/advanced-search.html.
8. The most recent edition of the *Case Law of the Boards of Appeal* is available online in English, French and German at: https://www.epo.org/law-practice/case-law-appeals/case-law.html.

The general requirements for patentability are set forth in Article 52(1) EPC:

> 'European patents shall be granted for *any inventions*, in all fields of technology, provided that they are *new*, involve an *inventive step* and are susceptible of *industrial application*.' (emphasis added)

Novelty and inventive step are governed by Article 54 EPC and Article 56 EPC, respectively. Furthermore, patentable subject matter must also fulfil the requirement of industrial applicability (Article 57 EPC) and it must be sufficiently disclosed/enabled (Article 83 EPC). Particularly in the biotech and antibody field, issues under Article 83 EPC arise often and are discussed before the EPO in both examination and opposition proceedings.

The admissibility of amendments to European patents and European patent applications is governed by the 'disclosure requirement' of Article 123(2) EPC. This provision requires that amendments must not introduce any subject-matter which extends beyond the content of the application as originally filed, and it is applied by the EPO in a notoriously strict manner.

The patentability of surgical and therapeutic methods of treatment as well as *in vivo* diagnostic methods is explicitly excluded in Article 53(c) EPC:

> 'European patents *shall not* be granted in respect of: ...
>
> (c) *methods for treatment of the human or animal body by surgery or therapy* and *diagnostic methods practised on the human or animal body*; this provision shall not apply to products, in particular substances or compositions, for use in any of these methods.' (emphasis added)

At the same time, Article 54(4) and (5) EPC allow purpose-limited product protection for substances and compositions 'for use' in any such method referred to in Article 53(c) EPC, provided that the corresponding use is novel. These provisions thus form the legal basis for the grant of first, second and further medical use claims, codifying an exception to the 'absolute novelty' requirement defined in Article 54(1) to (3) EPC. Medical use claims are of utmost importance in the antibody field, particularly where antibodies to a given target/epitope are already known in the art whereas their concrete therapeutic and/or diagnostic value is only elucidated and invented later.

In accordance with the Guidelines (part G-VI, 7.1.2), an independent claim directed to a further therapeutic use of an antibody should be formulated as illustrated in Table 1.1 (adapted from the Guidelines).

Table 1.1

ANTIBODY X or Composition comprising ANTIBODY X	for use	in a method for the treatment of Y, or in the therapy of Y, or in a method of treating Y, or in a method of therapy of Y, or as a medicament defined by its function (e.g. as an anti-inflammatory medicament)

Further examples of allowable and unallowable claim language can be found in part G-VI, 7.1.2 of the Guidelines. Notably, the presence of the term 'for use', which mirrors the wording of Article 54(5) EPC, is considered to be mandatory in medical use claims.

Swiss-type claims, however, which typically relate to the use of a known substance for the manufacture of a medicament for a specific (novel and inventive) therapeutic application, are no longer accepted by the EPO in applications having a filing date or earliest priority date of 29 January 2011 or later, which means that the specific therapeutic use recited in such claims is no longer taken into account for the assessment of novelty. This is a consequence of the Enlarged Board of Appeal decision G 2/08 *Dosage regime/ABBOTT RESPIRATORY*[9] wherein it is stated that 'where the subject matter of a claim is rendered novel only by a new therapeutic use of a medicament, such claim may no longer have the format of a so called Swiss-type claim as instituted by decision G 5/83'.

Since antibodies are also of high relevance in the diagnostic field, it is notable that *in vivo* diagnostic applications (on the human or animal body) must likewise be claimed in the purpose-limited product format in accordance with Article 54(5) EPC. The Guidelines in part G-VI, 7.1.3 provide examples of suitable claim formulations which are illustrated in Table 1.2 (adapted from the Guidelines).

Table 1.2

ANTIBODY X or Composition comprising ANTIBODY X	for use in a method of diagnosis	'*in vivo*'	of disease Y

It must be borne in mind that diagnostic methods practiced *in vitro* or *ex vivo* are not excluded from patentability under Article 53(c) EPC, and can therefore not be claimed in the purpose-limited product claim format according to Article 54(5) EPC. Accordingly, a claim reading

> 'ANTIBODY X for use in the diagnosis of disease Y or for use in the *in vitro/ex vivo* diagnosis of disease Y'

would be construed as relating to antibody X per se, and would thus *not* be allowable due to a lack novelty if antibody X is already disclosed in the prior art in a form which could be considered suitable for the claimed use.

The Guidelines (in part G-VI, 7.1.3) recommend rephrasing such contestable claims to, e.g., the following formats:

> 'Use of ANTIBODY X in the *in vitro/ex vivo* diagnosis of disease Y'; or

9. Enlarged Board of Appeal, decision in G 2/08 of 19 February 2010, *Dosage regime/ ABBOTT RESPIRATORY*, Headnote 3 and Reasons 7.1.3 to 7.1.4. See also the Notice from the European Patent Office dated 20 September 2010 concerning the non-acceptance of Swiss-type claims (OJ EPO 2010, 514).

'A method for *in vitro/ex vivo* diagnosing disease Y using ANTIBODY X ...'

Biotechnological inventions and biological material, including antibodies and fragments thereof as well as nucleic acid sequences encoding the same, are *not* excluded from patentability under the EPC (see also §1.01[B], *infra*).

For European patent applications and patents concerning biotechnological inventions, the relevant provisions of the EPC are to be applied and interpreted in accordance with Rules 26 to 29 EPC which mirror the provisions of European Union Directive 98/44/EC of 6 July 1998 on the legal protection of biotechnological inventions (the 'Biotech Directive'[10]). The Biotech Directive itself is to be used as a supplementary means of interpretation, as prescribed in the Guidelines, part G-II, 5.2.

Biological deposits have lately seen a renaissance at the EPO, not only in order to safeguard reproducibility of inventions but also when, for example, sequences of relevant antibodies/hybridomas are not available at the filing or priority date to fully enable the invention or when the invention is based on specific secondary modifications of the antibody, such as glycosylation patterns originating from a given production cell line/clone.

The EPO regulates the deposit of biological material in Rules 31 to 34 EPC. In contrast to other jurisdictions, with the EPO an applicant/patentee can only rely on deposited material if the biological material has been deposited with a recognized depositary institution on the same terms as those laid down in the Budapest Treaty on the International Recognition of the Deposit of Microorganisms for the Purposes of Patent Procedure of 28 April 1977 (the 'Budapest Treaty'[11]). Furthermore, and again in contrast to other jurisdictions, with the EPO such a deposit must have been completed at the relevant date of filing of the application, i.e. the filing date of the European patent application or, if priority is claimed, the priority date (see Rule 31(1) EPC).

Importantly, Rule 31 EPC also requires that the deposit be made in the name of the applicant or that evidence is made available that at the filing date the depositor authorized the applicant to reference the deposited material (among other conditions). Failing this, the deposit will be deemed invalid pursuant to the EPC, potentially destroying enablement. Moreover, if a deposit has been made in the name of two persons, it may not suffice if a patent application referencing the deposited material designates only one of the two depositors as an applicant, as found in T 1338/12 *Depôt micro-organisme/SEDERMA*.[12]

With the EPO, it is thus critical that the determination of whether a deposit is valid is made at the priority or filing date, and that the deposit is made in the name of the applicant or that the applicant provides written evidence that the depositor has authorized the applicant to refer to the deposited biological material in the EP

10. Available online at: https://eur-lex.europa.eu/legal-content/EN/TXT/?uri=CELEX:31998L0044.
11. Budapest Treaty on the International Recognition of the Deposit of Microorganisms for the Purposes of Patent Procedure. Practical information on the making of deposits under the Budapest Treaty is provided in the 'Guide to the Deposit of Microorganisms under the Budapest Treaty' published by WIPO, which is accessible online at: https://www.wipo.int/treaties/en/registration/budapest/guide/.
12. Technical Board of Appeal, decision in T 1338/12 of 14 December 2018, *Depôt micro-organisme/SEDERMA*, Reason 26.

application. These formal requirements for deposits *cannot* normally be remedied by subsequent action after the filing or priority date. Even attempts to rectify such issues by adding the depositor as a co-applicant via the procedure for correcting obvious errors under Rule 139 EPC are rarely successful, as illustrated by the aforementioned decision T 1338/12.

[B] General Amenability or Exclusion of Antibodies from Patentability

As briefly discussed in §1.01[A], *supra*, biological and biotechnological inventions, including antibodies, are in principle patentable under the EPC. For European patent applications and patents concerning biotechnological inventions, the relevant provisions of the EPC are to be applied and interpreted in accordance with the provisions of Rules 26 to 29 EPC.

Rule 28 EPC relates to exceptions to patentability. Under this provision, European patents shall not be granted in respect of biotechnological inventions which concern either the cloning of human beings, modifying the germ line genetic identity of human beings, the use of human embryos for industrial or commercial purposes, or modifying the genetic identity of animals which are likely to cause them suffering without any substantial medical benefit to man or animal. Accordingly, neither nucleic acids nor proteins, including antibodies, are affected by the exclusions established in Rule 28 EPC.

Furthermore, Rule 29(2) EPC makes it clear that an element isolated from the human body or otherwise produced by means of a technical process, including the sequence or partial sequence of a gene, may constitute a patentable invention, even if the structure of said element is identical to that of a natural element. In T 272/95 *Relaxin/HOWARD FLOREY INSTITUTE,*[13] it was confirmed that inventions falling under this category, i.e. even naturally occurring elements, are not excluded from patentability. This was also acknowledged, *inter alia*, in T 1213/05 *Breast and ovarian cancer/UNIVERSITY OF UTAH.*[14]

[C] Required Distinction from Naturally Occurring Antibodies

In accordance with §1.01[B], *supra*, antibodies are not excluded from patentability before the EPO and there is no need for distinguishing even naturally occurring antibodies from recombinantly produced antibodies, from antibodies obtained via biotechnological processes and/or engineered antibody constructs, such as bispecific antibodies, scFvs or nanobodies. Rule 27(a) EPC explicitly confirms that biotechnological inventions are patentable if they concern biological material which is isolated from its natural environment or produced by means of a technical process even if it previously occurred in nature. It is not necessary that the term 'isolated' is recited in the claims.

---

13. Technical Board of Appeal, decision in T 272/95 of 23 October 2002, *Relaxin/HOWARD FLOREY INSTITUTE*, Reasons 6 to 9.
14. Technical Board of Appeal, decision in T 1213/05 of September 2007, *Breast and ovarian cancer/UNIVERSITY OF UTAH*, Reasons 46 to 57.

In contrast to the approach taken by the US Supreme Court in *Mayo v. Prometheus*,[15] a technical teaching that utilizes the discovery of a law of nature does not require any additional 'inventive surplus' to be patent eligible with the EPO.

§1.02 ACCEPTABLE CLAIM FEATURES FOR DEFINING ANTIBODIES

[A] Functional Features

There is no legal provision in the EPC which would prevent an applicant/patentee from claiming an antibody defined exclusively by functional features. The allowability of functional features was considered and confirmed in very early decisions of the Technical Boards of Appeal, such as *inter alia* in T 430/92 *Growth of Tulips/SUMITOMO*[16] and T 412/06 *Proteinase inhibitor/MAX-PLANCK-GESELLSCHAFT*.[17] Already in T 68/85 *Synergistic herbicides/CIBA*,[18] the Board provided guidance when 'functional features' are acceptable, namely when two conditions are met:

(1) the features provide instructions for the skilled person to reduce the invention to practice without undue burden; and
(2) such features could not otherwise be defined more precisely without restricting the scope of the invention.[19]

Even very broadly defined antibody claims can meet these conditions so long as the description in the application and the knowledge already available in the prior art allow the skilled person to find such antibodies, no matter how long it takes to obtain, screen for and/or make corresponding antibodies. It is decisive in this regard that the application as filed comprises all the technical guidance 'to reduce the invention to practice without undue burden'. This was confirmed in several decisions of the Technical Boards of Appeal, such as T 617/07 *Monoclonal NGF-antagonist antibodies/LAY Line*[20] or T 1300/05 *RET screening assay/PROGENICS*[21] discussed herein below, and in the *Case Law of the Boards of Appeal*, 8th edition of 2016, at II.A.3.4 (on functional features) and II.C.4.4/II.C.6.3 (on the required disclosure).

15. U.S. Supreme Court, *Mayo Collaborative Services v. Prometheus Laboratories, Inc.*, 566 U.S. 66 (2012).
16. Technical Board of Appeal, decision in T 430/92 of 29 September 1994, *Growth of Tulips/SUMITOMO*, Reason 3.2.
17. Technical Board of Appeal, decision in T 412/06 of 12 October 2006, *Proteinase inhibitor/MAX-PLANCK-GESELLSCHAFT*, Reason 2.1.
18. Technical Board of Appeal, decision in T 68/85 of 27 November 1986, *Synergistic herbicides/CIBA*, Reasons 8.4.2 to 8.4.3.
19. The EPO and opponents often argue that such functional features (i.e., claim limitations) can be defined more precisely by recitation of a specific antibody sequence. This argument is premised on the position that an antibody's activity is an *inherent* function of its structure, i.e. sequence.
20. Technical Board of Appeal, decision in T 617/07 of 4 August 2009, *Monoclonal NGF-antagonist antibodies/LAY Line*.
21. Technical Board of Appeal, decision in T 1300/05 of 11 July 2006, *RET screening assay/PROGENICS*.

Yet, in particular when antibodies against a given target/epitope are already known in the art, it is preferable either to combine such functional features with additional structural features, such as for example concrete sequences, or to define the functional feature in a manner that renders the claimed antibody absolutely unique.

On the other hand, antibody claims reciting functional features that do not limit the antibody to any particular structure, but potentially distinguish the claimed antibody from those already known in the art are normally based on one or more specific and unique activities. Such distinguishing and potentially superior functional features can comprise any feature identified by the applicant/patentee. In this context, the reader is reminded that the EPO applies, at least since decision T 1329/04 *Factor IX/JOHNS HOPKINS*,[22] the now very popular 'plausibility approach' in the assessment of patentability. It is notable that the requirement of plausibility is not expressly recited in the European Patent Convention but is now widely accepted as part of the assessment of inventive step, enablement and industrial applicability.[23]

In light of this plausibility approach, but also in order to potentially delimit the claimed antibodies from the prior art, claiming antibodies by functional features should be based on conclusive and repeatable experimental data supporting the invention and/or on the relevant knowledge in the corresponding field at the time of filing. Only in cases where the application as originally filed documents that the invention was already made and the application does indeed solve a technical problem, may the applicant rely on post-published evidence. Accordingly, in order to avoid having to limit the claim scope by, for example, inclusion of the primary antibody structure (e.g., concrete amino acid sequences of variable regions), it is advisable for European applications, wherever possible, to include in the original specification experimental evidence and/or test systems documenting that the claimed functional features are not inherently tied to one specific antibody but are, for example, the result of a certain biological feature of the claimed antibodies, such as the binding to a specific epitope. If feasible, the application should provide several working examples of antibodies with the claimed functional features, whereby the exemplified antibodies should comprise structural differences, for example in the complementarity determining regions (CDRs), within selected CDRs and/or in their variable regions. It would also be important to disclosing functional features that render the relevant genus of antibodies distinguishable from antibodies of the prior art. In order to be able to use such 'functional features' for drafting claims, they should not only be disclosed in the examples/experimental part of the patent application but they should also be discussed and be explained in the general patent specification.

Especially in light of the plausibility concept of the EPO, functionally defined antibody claims are often contested as allegedly attempting to monopolize antibodies that have certain properties 'to be achieved' ('*desiderata*'). On the other hand, the

---

22. Technical Board of Appeal, decision in T 1329/04 of 28 June 2005, *Factor IX/Johns Hopkins*, was the first decision by the EPO where the 'plausibility approach' was applied in the assessment of inventive step. The Board held in Reason 12 that '[t]he definition of an invention as being a contribution to the art, i.e. as solving a technical problem and not merely putting forward one, requires that it is at least made plausible by the disclosure in the application that its teaching solves indeed the problem it purports to solve.'
23. See also the discussion of T 18/09 *Neutrokine/HUMAN GENOME SCIENCES* herein below.

Technical Boards of Appeal have scrutinized functional claims and have considered them permissible as long as the patentability requirements of novelty, inventive step, enablement and industrial applicability were met and the teachings provided by the applicant were 'plausible' at the relevant filing date. This will be discussed and illustrated herein below.

[1] Target/Antigen

Generally, the EPO accepts antibody claims wherein the antibody is directed (specifically) to a certain epitope or a target molecule which is not known in the prior art and which is inventive. If an antibody to such a target is provided for the first time, a very broad protection may be obtained with the EPO. In such cases where the discovery of a novel target/antigen constitutes an inventive contribution to the art, the EPO also accepts claims directed to any antibodies binding to the novel target/antigen.[24] The broadest possible claim could read:

> 'Antibody specifically binding target X.'[25]

Such a claim covers not only one particular antibody, but any antibody that specifically binds to the target antigen, for example a protein X.

The EPO considers the generation of antibodies a matter of routine and takes into account that the corresponding technology is highly advanced. Therefore, the EPO normally accepts that once a (novel and inventive) antigen and a particular antibody have been provided, it will be a routine matter to identify and/or develop other antibodies having the same specificity.[26] Consequently, in the case of a newly identified antigen, the acknowledgment of novelty and inventive step for the antigen means that an antibody to that antigen will likewise be considered novel and inventive, even without the disclosure of any actual exemplary antibody.[27]

For instance, in the case underlying decision T 18/09 *Neutrokine/HUMAN GENOME SCIENCES*,[28] the polypeptide Neutrokine-alpha as provided and claimed

---

24. See, e.g., Technical Board of Appeal, decision in T 1902/11 of 11 December 2014, *Human IL-23/MERCK SHARP & DOHME*, Reason 56.
25. It is of note that the term 'specifically' is not always necessary since a novel and inventive antibody may also interact with orthologues and/or close family members. The notion of specificity does not exclude that an antibody may cross-react with other polypeptides than that against which it has been raised; see, *inter alia*, Technical Board of Appeal, decision in T 189/01 of 15 June 2004, *IFN-beta 2/IL-6R/YEDA RESEARCH AND DEVELOPMENT CO., LTD.*; Reasons 12 and 14.
26. See, e.g., Technical Board of Appeal, decision in T 2045/09 of 14 May 2014, *Anti-ErbB3 antibody/GENENTECH*, Reason 21.
27. See, e.g., Technical Board of Appeal, decision in T 2101/09 of 26 February 2013, *Human Delta3 – Notch/MILLENNIUM*, particularly Reason 17.
28. Technical Board of Appeal, decision in T 18/09 of 21 October 2009, *Neutrokine/HUMAN GENOME SCIENCES*. This decision establishes that the 'serious doubts substantiated by verifiable facts' requirement originally established for enablement objections in T 19/90 *Oncomouse/HARVARD* also applies to the assessment of industrial applicability; see Reasons 31 to 33 and Catchword 2 of T 18/09, reading: 'An objection of lack of industrial application

in the respective patent was considered novel, inventive and industrially applicable. The contested patent also comprised an antibody claim that read:

> 'An antibody or portion thereof that binds specifically to the Neutrokine-alpha portion of a Neutrokine-alpha polypeptide having the amino acid sequence encoded by the nucleic acid molecule of any one of claims 1(a) through 1(f) or 7 or the Neutrokine-alpha portion of a Neutrokine-alpha polypeptide of claim 15 or 16'

This claim belongs to the broadest class of antibody claims, and it was maintained in opposition appeal proceedings since the contested patent provided a novel and inventive polypeptide (Neutrokine-alpha) and the invention rendered the new class of antibodies available for the first time. Also enablement and industrial applicability were accepted.

Also T 1300/05 *RET screening assay/PROGENICS*[29] illustrates that functional features, in particular specific binding, can characterize a claimed antibody. The patent under discussion in T 1300/05 claimed a monoclonal antibody generated against a cell line susceptible to infection by macrophage-tropic HIV-1 isolates (HuT 78 lymphoblastoid). This antibody was defined in the main claim by functional features, namely of inhibiting a given HIV-1 envelope glycoprotein mediated membrane fusion of the cell line it was generated against, and of not inhibiting such a membrane-fusion between other specific cell lines recited in the main claim.

Whereas the Examining Division of the EPO refused the grant of the patent for lack of clarity and lack of sufficient disclosure, the Technical Board of Appeal held that the antibody was unambiguously defined in terms of its origin and its properties. As stated in Reason 4 of T 1300/05, the antibody features were described in a clear manner, the characteristics of the cells to which the antibody is raised were unambiguous and its binding capacities were identified by reference to specific cell lines. The Board held that the skilled person would have no difficulties in finding out whether or not an antibody 'answers to the terms of the claim', not least because the application as filed comprised an experimental protocol leading to the isolation and characterization of four monoclonal antibodies having the relevant properties. Furthermore, in Reason 8 of T 1300/05, the Board held that the requirement of sufficiency of disclosure was also fulfilled since it was common general knowledge at the filing date to raise antibodies against a given antigen – such as the cell line specified in the claim – and since there existed at least three methods to quantify HIV-1 envelope protein-mediated membrane fusions. As the cell lines involved were either available to the skilled artisan or could be isolated without undue burden, the Board came to the conclusion that, at the filing date, all cell lines necessary for the isolation and characterization of the claimed antibody were available or reproducible without undue burden. The Board made clear that the potential undue burden of isolating all antibodies falling within the scope of the claim would not stem from

(Article 57 EPC) requires the same standard of proof as an objection of insufficient disclosure (Article 83 EPC), namely serious doubts substantiated by verifiable facts'.

29. Technical Board of Appeal, decision in T 1300/05 of 11 July 2006, *RET screening assay/ PROGENICS*.

deficiencies in the way the invention was described but rather from the task of isolating all antibodies, i.e. from the task which the skilled artisan chose to accomplish.

This decision nicely highlights the thinking of the EPO when it comes to functional features in claims. As long as there is enough evidence in the application as filed that the skilled artisan has all the means and methods to carry out a characterization of these functional features, the requirements of clarity and sufficiency are fulfilled. Yet, it is of importance that corresponding reliable and performable tests and assays are provided in the original application. Details and corresponding technical information can not only safeguard clarity and sufficiency of a given (antibody) claim but can also help in potential plausibility discussions during the prosecution phase before the EPO and in later oppositions/appeals.

In decision T 2238/11 *Antibody against the extracellular domain of canine CD20/IDEXX*[30] an antibody or an antibody binding portion thereof that specifically binds canine CD20 positive B-lymphocytes was claimed. The Technical Board of Appeal denied inventive step of the corresponding claim, since the closest prior art already disclosed therapeutically effective, but cross-reactive anti-CD20 antibodies for treating B-cell lymphomas and the prior art explicitly suggested that animal equivalents of (human) antigens are 'readily identifiable and their use is preferred'. Therefore, in Reason 21 the Technical Board of Appeal came to the conclusion that the skilled person has in light of the teachings of the prior art 'ample motivation to provide as alternative antibodies those which are specifically directed against extracellular epitopes of canine CD20'. The Technical Board of Appeal was also of the opinion that due to the fact that the sequences of at least human and mouse CD20 genes were known in the art, the skilled person would have been readily in a position to identify species-specific extracellular domains simply by using standard sequence alignment procedures. Accordingly, whereas this decision confirms that antibodies against novel and inventive epitopes may be claimed with the EPO, it also documents that avoiding cross-species reactivity might not require inventive efforts.

T 1433/14 *Peptide Influenza Vaccine/BOGOCH*[31] is based on an opposition case, wherein the contested patent claimed a specific (novel) influenza virus peptide ('Replikin'). The patent also comprised claims relating to antibodies that specifically bind to said 'Replikin' for use in the treatment of the human or animal body by therapy, 'wherein said antibody is comprised in a composition, and wherein said composition comprises a pharmaceutically acceptable carrier and/or adjuvant'. Accordingly, the opposed patent contained claims relating to the 'Replikin' peptide itself as well as to antibodies directed against this peptide in the form of a purpose-limited product claim as provided for by Article 54(4) EPC, i.e. in the 'first medical use' format.

The Board of Appeal came to the conclusion that the 'Replikin' peptide as claimed does not fulfil the requirement of inventive step. With reference to the plausibility case law of the EPO, the Board noted that the patent discloses that the 'Replikin' amino acid concentration in a hemagglutinin protein may be correlated to influenza epidemics. However, in the eyes of the Board there was no evidence that

30. Technical Board of Appeal, decision in T 2238/11 of 8 October 2015, *Antibody against the extracellular domain of canine CD20/IDEXX*.
31. Technical Board of Appeal, decision in T 1433/14 of 2 October 2018, *Peptide Influenza Vaccine/BOGOCH*.

the 'Replikin' peptide may act as a vaccine against influenza virus infection, neither in the patent nor in the state of the art. The Board concluded in T 1433/14[32] that 'the patent itself contains *no evidence of any kind, in the form of results from either in vivo or in vitro experiments or otherwise* to show that any "Replikin" peptide [...] is capable of acting as a vaccine against H1N1 influenza virus'. Accordingly, the Board came to the conclusion that the skilled person would not have considered it credible that the claimed peptide could be used as a vaccine against influenza and refers in this context again to the plausibility case law, and particularly the *Case Law of the Boards of Appeal*, 8th edition of 2016, part I.D.4.6.

In light of this assessment, the provision of 'Replikin' was simply seen as an arbitrary selection from various equally suitable prior art proteins and, therefore, was considered to be obvious. As far as the medical use claims directed to anti-Replikin antibodies were concerned, the Board came to the conclusion that the skilled person reading the application and taking into account the general knowledge in the art would not have considered it credible that 'Replikin' could be used as a vaccine against H1N1 influenza, and found that this conclusion applies also to the antibodies against 'Replikin'. Furthermore, the patent does not disclose the suitability of antibodies raised against 'Replikin' for the claimed therapeutic application, i.e. a vaccination (see Reasons 13 to 15 and 33 to 35 of T 1433/14). Accordingly, the Technical Board of Appeal denied patentability of the antibody medical use claim under the requirements of Article 83 EPC (enablement).

This case again illustrates how the EPO considers the plausibility approach as a tool in the assessment not only of industrial applicability, but also of inventive step and/or enablement. Also in such cases, however, it should be borne in mind that the pertinent test whether a patent application or a granted patent discloses the claimed subject-matter in a plausible and/or credible fashion – as established by T 18/09[33] – remains that 'serious doubts' need to be raised, and that these serious doubts need to be 'substantiated by verifiable facts'. This test corresponds to the 'enablement' test established by T 19/90.[34]

In T 503/12 *Tumour marker/DIADEXUS*,[35] antibodies which specifically bind 'to the protein encoded by polynucleotide sequence SEQ ID NO: 1' for use in *in vivo* imaging of a selection from a breast, ovarian, endometrial and uterine cancer were claimed. The patent in suit defined three proteins encoded by the gene having the sequence SEQ ID NO: 1 as 'Ovr110'. Yet, neither the patent in suit nor the prior art disclosed experimental evidence that anti-Ovr110 antibodies detect the claimed cancers by *in vivo* imaging. As laid down in Reasons 23 to 26 of T 503/12, the Board denounced the lack of information in the application as filed: neither the location of the Ovr110 protein nor the existence of an extracellular domain of the protein was disclosed. While the application reported in the examples an increased gene expression of Ovr110 in various cancer tissues, the Board held that the skilled

32. *Ibid.*, Reason 15 (emphasis added).
33. Technical Board of Appeal, decision in T 18/09 of 21 October 2009, *Neutrokine/HUMAN GENOME SCIENCES*.
34. Technical Board of Appeal, decision in T 19/90 of 3 October 1990, *Oncomouse/HARVARD*.
35. Technical Board of Appeal, decision in T 503/12 of 7 September 2018, *Tumour marker/DIADEXUS*.

person still had to find out by trial and error which of the claimed anti-Ovr110 antibodies would be suitable for the claimed *in vivo* diagnostic use. The Board thus concluded that even when assuming in the patentee's favour that a protein based on the disclosed DNA sequence of Ovr110 could be obtained and antibodies could be generated against such a protein, the skilled person would have no guidance how to generate antibodies that are necessarily suitable for the claimed diagnostic use. To put the skilled person in a position to perform the invention across the whole of the claimed scope would amount to a research program and would constitute an undue burden. Accordingly, the Board denied sufficiency of disclosure.

A detailed description of technical means and methods in a European patent application is of importance not only during the prosecution phase before the EPO but also in potential oppositions. This also holds true for routine experimentations and tests as well as for further technical advances. For example, which routine methods can be employed without further effort should be described to verify even a working hypothesis. Such tests and experiments should be described in a manner that the skilled person can readily carry out the corresponding experiments 'without undue burden'. In this context, the EPO has repeatedly acknowledged that even cumbersome and labour- or time-consuming routine (screening) methods can be accepted as long as the claimed and/or described technology can be reproduced without needing inventive skill. These methods should not merely consist in a 'trial-and-error approach' and they should not consist in a 'call for a research programme'. The Boards have also clarified that even 'tedious' work of testing is nothing out of the ordinary since the techniques for the production and selection of, for example, classical antibodies or hybridomas are common routine techniques (see also T 431/96 *Monoclonal antibody/AGEN*,[36] T 877/03 *Anti-CD30 antibodies/ROCHE*,[37] T 617/07 *Monoclonal NGF-antagonist antibodies/LAY LINE*,[38] T 2045/09 *Anti-ErbB3 antibody/GENENTECH*,[39] T 2101/09 *Human Delta3 – Notch/MILLENNIUM*[40] and *Case Law of the Boards of Appeal*, 8th edition of 2016, II.C.6.3 and II.C.6.4).

[2] *Mode of Binding: Target Affinity, Binding Specificity, Epitope, Definitions via Reference Antibodies and Competitive Binding*

In general, the EPO does not bar the patenting of antibodies by reference to functional features, including affinities to the target molecule, avidity, inhibitory or activating functions, binding specificities and the like. Yet, such technical features are often contested by examiners (or opponents) as not having been demonstrated for the

36. Technical Board of Appeal, decision in T 431/96 of 23 February 1999, *Monoclonal antibody/ AGEN*, Reason 12.
37. Technical Board of Appeal, decision in T 877/03 of 7 April 2005, *Anti-CD30 antibodies/ ROCHE*, Reasons 20 to 23.
38. Technical Board of Appeal, decision in T 617/07 of 4 August 2009, *Monoclonal NGF-antagonist antibodies/LAY LINE*, Reasons 21 to 33.
39. Technical Board of Appeal, decision in T 2045/09 of 14 May 2014, *Anti-ErbB3 antibody/ GENENTECH*, Reason 21.
40. Technical Board of Appeal, decision in T 2101/09 of 26 February 2013, *Human Delta3 – Notch/MILLENNIUM*, Reason 17.

entire class of antibodies covered by the claims, unless the claims comprise additional (limiting) structural features. Such claims may be contested as mere '*desiderata*', in particular if no antibody is provided in the application which fulfils the required functional feature beyond any doubt.

When it comes to the assessment of novelty and inventive step, comparative data to prior art antibodies may be of high value. Here, the reader is reminded that the EPO follows a very strict approach when such comparative data is only provided by applicant/patentee in the form of post-filed evidence. Such data is allowed only if the EPO is convinced that the application as filed rendered the invention plausible/credible (see, *inter alia*, T 1329/04 *Factor IX/JOHNS HOPKINS*,[41] T 415/11 *Lyophilized Neisseria meningococcus vaccine/NOVARTIS*,[42] T 601/05 *Anti-TNF alpha human monoclonal antibodies/BAYER II*,[43] and *Case Law of the Boards of Appeal*, 8th edition of 2016, I.D.4.6).

Furthermore, such functional features in the claims are scrutinized for clarity and completeness of disclosure. Technical features expressed in functional terms must be able to be verified by tests or procedures adequately specified in the description or generally known to the skilled person. Such tests and/or screening assays further need to be absolutely reproducible, and the specification has to provide means and methods allowing a skilled person to reliably obtain the corresponding parameters and/or concrete comparative values, such as binding or affinity constants (see also *Case Law of the Boards of Appeal*, 8th edition of 2016, II.A.3.4 and II.C.6.3).

Accordingly, when the applicant/patentee relies on functional features, it is strongly recommended that the application as filed comprises enough guidance for the skilled person to rework the invention and to obtain the claimed antibody reliably and without having to 'embark on a research program' (see also T 1466/05 *Pyridinoline/SEREX*[44]).

Also 'negative functional features' in antibody claims can suffice to characterize the claimed subject matter clearly and to delimit the claimed antibodies from the prior art. For example, claim 1 of the main request discussed in T 2332/10 *Antibody to C5 and C5a/GENENTECH*[45] reads as follows:

> 'An antibody or fragment thereof that binds to C5 and C5a, but does not prevent the activation of C5 and does not prevent formation of or inhibit the activity of C5b.'

The claimed anti-C5/C5a antibody enables the treatment of diseases caused by an excessive activation of the (immune) complement system through both the classical and the alternative pathway but without compromising the complement system's bactericidal activity. This antibody was considered by the Board to be sufficiently

41. Technical Board of Appeal, decision in T 1329/04 of 28 June 2005, *Factor IX/Johns Hopkins*.
42. Technical Board of Appeal, decision in T 415/11 of 12 January 2012, *Lyophilized Neisseria meningococcus vaccine/NOVARTIS*.
43. Technical Board of Appeal, decision in T 601/05 of 24 April 2008, *Anti-TNF alpha human monoclonal antibodies/BAYER II*.
44. Technical Board of Appeal, decision in T 1466/05 of 27 July 2007, *Pyridinoline/SEREX*.
45. Technical Board of Appeal, decision in T 2332/10 of 24 February 2015, *Antibody to C5 and C5a/GENENTECH*.

disclosed and also to fulfil the requirements of novelty and inventive step since the anti-C5/C5a antibodies of the prior art were not unambiguously disclosed as not interfering with both complement systems/pathways.

Competitive binding or binding to a correspondence epitope as a feature of a claimed antibody is in principle patentable with the EPO. However, in cases where the 'competition or correspondence molecule' is another antibody, issues of either inventive step or enablement may arise. This is, for example, illustrated in T 1681/11 *Mucosal endothelial receptor MAdCAM-1/MILLENIUM.*[46] In the patent under discussion, *inter alia*, the medical use of an antibody having 'the epitopic specificity of the ACT-1 monoclonal antibody' was claimed. The Board understood the reference to 'epitopic specificity' to require that the claimed antibodies bind the same epitope of a given integrin as the 'ACT-1 monoclonal antibody' recited in the contested claim. However, none of the epitopes bound by this reference antibody were known in the art and what was even worse, the monoclonal antibody ACT-1 was deposited only after the filing date of the contested patent (which falls short of the requirements for deposits laid down in Rule 31(1)(a) EPC; see also §1.01[A], *supra*). Accordingly, the Board came to the conclusion that, at the date of filing, the reference antibody was not available to the skilled person for comparative experiments and the contested patent was therefore revoked under Article 83 EPC (enablement).

The EPO also accepts claims defining an antibody by its target epitope. Such claims retain a broad scope in that they do not specify a primary antibody structure (i.e., sequence of the CDRs or of the variable chains), but nevertheless further limit the scope by specifying a particular *antibody binding site*. The scientific basis for such a claim limitation is that certain antibody functionalities are determined not only by the antigen to which the antibody binds, but also by *where* it binds the antigen. Such a claim may have the following exemplary form:

> 'Antibody X binding protein X within the sequence corresponding to from residue XX to residue YY of SEQ ID NO: 1234.'

It is also feasible to claim antibodies directed against a specific secondary and tertiary structure with the EPO. However, in such a case the applicant must document that prior art antibodies do not interact with the corresponding 'folded' structure. For example, in T 1318/13 *Anti-PTH antibodies/QUEST*[47] the claim under dispute reads:

> 'An isolated antibody that recognizes and selectively binds a three-dimensional epitope of parathyroid hormone, wherein the three-dimensional epitope of parathyroid hormone comprises amino acids located between amino acids 1–13 of SEQ ID NO: 1 and includes the first amino terminal amino acid of native PTH along with the intact helix of the amino terminus.'

Whereas this claim was formally accepted and also considered enabled, the Board came to the conclusion that the claim lacked novelty over polyclonal antisera of the prior art. The prior art antibodies recognized $hPTH_{1-10}$, $hPTH_{2-10}$ and $hPTH_{4-12}$ and

46. Technical Board of Appeal, decision in T 1681/11 of 12 July 2017, *Mucosal endothelial receptor MAdCAM-1/MILLENIUM*.
47. Technical Board of Appeal, decision in T 1318/13 of 18 January 2018, *Anti-PTH antibodies/QUEST*.

thus recognized and selectively bound an epitope comprising amino acids located within residues 1 to 13 of hPTH, i.e. the same three-dimensional epitope present in natural human parathyroid hormone that is recognized by the claimed antibodies.

It is generally accepted that a certain antibody activity is mediated by the epitope to which the antibody binds. Epitope-limited claims thus seek to encompass an entire class of newly identified antibodies, i.e. exhibiting the same functionality as that demonstrated by the exemplary antibody. However, as the field becomes more crowded, epitope claims are increasingly attacked by opponents for lack of clarity and/or enablement in European opposition proceedings. It is, if technically feasible, recommended to identify given epitopes by their concrete amino acid portion of the target protein.

[3] Effect on Target

As already discussed herein above, defining antibodies by functional features is allowed with the EPO. This also holds true for features defining a specific effect on the target whereby even 'negative technical features' are considered allowable with the EPO (see also T 2332/10 *Antibody to C5 and C5a/GENENTECH* discussed in §1.02[A][2] above).

However, also in antibody claims relying on functional effects on the target, the basic principles as laid down in T 68/85 *Synergistic herbicides/CIBA*[48] (see §1.02[A] above) need to be observed. In particular, such claims are only permissible in cases where (i) the technical features could not be defined more precisely without restricting the scope of the invention and (ii) these features provide instructions which are sufficiently clear for the expert to reduce them to practice without undue burden (see also *Case Law of the Boards of Appeal*, 8th edition of 2016, II.A.3.4).

In particular in cases where the functional feature is a 'target effect', the requirements on the disclosure content of the application as filed are high with the EPO. This is in particular the case if the applicant provides only one working example but expects the EPO to grant a claim that encompasses a large group of antibodies with this functional property. Accordingly, the requirements of in particular Article 83 EPC (enablement) and Article 56 EPC (inventive step) but also of Article 123 EPC (impermissible broadening/claim amendments) are often discussed in the context of such functional features.

In the recent decision T 2488/12 *Cas genes/DUPONT NUTRITION BIOSCIENCES*,[49] the Board stressed that a reasonable amount of trial and error is permissible when it comes to sufficiency of disclosure. However, as laid down in Reason 25 of T 2488/12, the skilled person has to have at their disposal, either in the specification of the patent/the patent application or on the basis of his common general knowledge, adequate information leading necessarily and directly towards success through the evaluation of initial failures.

48. Technical Board of Appeal, decision in T 68/85 of 27 November 1986, *Synergistic herbicides/CIBA*.
49. Technical Board of Appeal, decision in T 2488/12 of 26 January 2016, *Cas genes/DUPONT NUTRITION BIOSCIENCES*.

Accordingly, it is always recommended to include in the specification ample data as well as test systems and experimental protocols how particular structural and functional features can be readily tested and how reproducible results can be obtained. Here details may be of the utmost importance. The same holds in particular true for biological or biochemical functions recited in the claims as 'effect' of the antibody interaction with its target. Examples of such effects may be the activation or inhibition of the target molecule or of receptor/ligand systems, protease inhibition or activation on the targets (for example, the avoidance or the augmentation of shedding), stabilization of receptor molecules, rendering cells sensitive or insensitive to drugs or irradiation, inhibition or activation of cellular dimerization events, the activation of apoptotic events, cytotoxicity, cytostasis, etc. When such effects are attributed to the claimed antibodies, the specification as filed needs to provide ample evidence that the skilled person is readily in a position to test these functional features, either based on the disclosure content of the application or on the basis of the accessible knowledge in the prior art.

But experimental evidence is also advantageous when biophysical parameters as discussed in §1.02[A] and [B], *supra,* are recited in the claims. Some of these biophysical parameters or functions comprise 'dissociation/association constants' or concentration values, e.g. 'IC_{50}' (half maximal inhibitory concentration). Should it be necessary to define the claimed antibody by such biological, biochemical and/or biophysical features, the application as filed should provide all details how to measure and to verify these functional features/parameters. A very detailed description in the specification is highly recommended in this respect. For example, buffer concentrations, assay temperature and even details on analysis software and instruments to be used should be described. Moreover, when it comes to functional features defining a specific effect on the target, corresponding *in vitro* and/or *in vivo* experiments should be provided in the originally filed application.

It is highly recommended to ensure that the specification as filed does not contain inconsistencies or technical contradictions, and that the (structural and functional) technical features are linked and combined in the same context. As mentioned above, the EPO tends to follow a very strict approach when determining the disclosure content of a patent application and assessing the admissibility of amendments to the claims during prosecution or in opposition proceedings (Article 123 EPC). This is illustrated by the recent decision T 776/12 *RSV infection/GOVERNMENT OF THE UNITED STATES OF AMERICA.*[50] The relevant, amended claim under discussion read:

> 'A composition comprising an anti-RSV G glycoprotein antibody, which antibody *blocks* binding of respiratory syncytial virus G glycoprotein to a CX3CR1 receptor, for use in treating respiratory syncytial virus infection in a subject infected with respiratory syncytial virus, *wherein the antibody inhibits the biological activity of a CX3C motif of a RSV G glycoprotein, wherein the biological activity is cell migration.*' (emphasis in the original)

In Reasons 21 and 26 of this decision the Board considered, however, that such antibodies are not disclosed in the original patent application in a form which

50. Technical Board of Appeal, decision in T 776/12 of 29 January 2018, *RSV infection/ GOVERNMENT OF THE UNITED STATES OF AMERICA*.

would allow the combination of these features. The Board was of the opinion that the antibody with the recited functional features is not defined in the application as being specific for the RSV G protein (i.e. an anti-RSV G glycoprotein) and the biological activity is specified *not as inhibited* (as recited in the claim) *but rather as blocked*. Further sections in the application relate to monoclonal antibodies, while another paragraph relates to, *inter alia*, antibodies that are specific for the RSV G glycoprotein CX3C motif but do not necessarily block binding between the motif and the receptor. The Board came to the conclusion that the application as filed provided functional alternatives which are 'opposed to binding to the G glycoprotein in general, as allowed in the claim' and considered the presented claim as being impermissibly broadened in violation of Article 123(2) EPC.

However, issues under enablement may also arise if the applicant/patentee relies on functional features and if the application as filed/the granted patent is considered to comprise inconsistencies or the filed specification does not provide for distinguishing test/assay systems. An example of such a situation is T 1389/13 'YKL-40 monoclonal antibodies/BIO-Y'.[51] Claim 1 of the patent as granted (main request) read:

> 'An antibody, antigen binding fragment or recombinant protein thereof, which is specific for human YKL-40 (SEQ ID NO: 1), said antibody, binding fragment or recombinant protein thereof capable of inhibiting growth of a cell upon binding to an epitope on YKL-40, wherein the cell is an YKL-40 expressing cancer cell.'

Accordingly, the antibody against YKL-40 was merely defined by its function, namely being 'capable of inhibiting growth of a cell upon binding to an epitope on YKL-40'. The opponent argued that the patent failed to provide a single (reliable) analytical measuring method allowing the person skilled in the art to carry out the invention as claimed, i.e. to arrive at an anti-YKL-40 antibody which *inhibits* growth of a cell. The Board followed this argumentation and held in Reason 19 that a number of passages throughout the description of the patent in suit emphasize and distinguish different possible biological activities of the compounds of the invention, including the inhibition of growth of cells (which is the functional feature comprised in the claim), induction of apoptosis of cells, and a 'growth repressive effect'. However, the methods in the patent were considered as failing to distinguish between *inhibition of the growth of cells* and the *induction of apoptosis*. Accordingly, the Board in Reason 25 concluded that the patent in suit does not provide the skilled person with suitable methods for obtaining the compounds of the claim, i.e. such compounds which are capable of inhibiting growth of a cell. The patent therefore does not disclose the invention in a manner sufficiently clear and complete for it to be carried out by a person skilled in the art (Article 83 EPC).

51. Technical Board of Appeal, decision in T 1389/13 of 10 July 2018, *YKL-40 monoclonal antibodies/BIO-Y*.

[B] Structural Features

[1] Molecular Topology: Antibody Types, Fragments and Antibody Constructs

Under the precondition that the patentability requirements are met, the EPO accepts claims directed to antibody types, antibody isotypes, fragments and antibody constructs. In particular, recombinantly produced/'engineered' constructs, such as bispecific constructs, modified immunoglobulins, single-domain antibodies, fusion constructs, nanobodies, tribodies and the like have been granted. It is notable that the source of a given antibody/antibody construct may also be of relevance to delimit the claimed antibody from the prior art (see *inter alia* IgNAR domains from cartilaginous fish or the now routinely employed camelid single-domain antibodies).

[2] Amino Acid Sequences

[a] Full-Length Sequences of Antibodies

Focusing claims on full-length sequences of antibodies is normally not required by the EPO as long as the application as filed identifies the antibody fragments (e.g., CDRs or variable regions) that are responsible for the technical properties or effects supporting patentability.

However, it is notable that in some cases the EPO (and opponents) allege that the definition of CDRs alone is 'not enough' since the framework regions also have an influence on the binding features or the specificity of a given antibody. This discussion surfaced in the context of humanization approaches, e.g., in T 500/01 *Humanized immunoglobulins/PROTEIN DEIGN LABS, INC.*[52]

In order to counter such objections, it can be very helpful to have evidence in the application as filed, which demonstrates that the technical properties or effects relied upon by the applicant/patentee in the discussion of patentability are independent of the full variable part of an antibody (as long as the required CDRs are present) and that, for example, the framework regions are irrelevant. Wherever possible, experimental data for several exemplary antibodies having differences, for example in their framework sequences should therefore be included when drafting new patent applications.

[b] Sequences of Fragments, CDRs and Framework Regions

The EPO routinely accepts claims that define the recited antibodies by partial sequences of antibodies or sequences of antibody fragments that confer binding and/or specificity to the corresponding antigen. These sequences need to be unambiguously disclosed in the application as filed and may comprise, for example, (i) the variable regions of the light and the heavy chain comprising the CDRs and framework regions,

52. Technical Board of Appeal, decision in T 500/01 of 12 November 2003, *Humanized immunoglobulins/PROTEIN DEIGN LABS, INC.*

(ii) individual CDRs (in most cases six CDRs, three from the heavy chain and three from the light chain), and (iii) CDRs with additional framework regions.

It is important that the applicant provides the correct sequences, typically in the form of amino acid sequences or nucleic acid sequences encoding the same. A correction of sequences after the filing date is in most cases impossible; in this regard, the requirements of Rule 139 EPC (relating to the correction of errors in documents filed with the EPO) need to be considered, which have been elucidated by the Enlarged Board of Appeal in G 11/91 *Glu-Gln/CELTRIX*.[53] Accordingly, sequences may be corrected after the filing date only if the skilled person directly and unambiguously understands that a mistake has occurred and how the mistake is to be corrected without any ambiguity. Problems arising from changes in sequence data, particularly between priority and filing dates, are illustrated by T 1213/05 *Breast and ovarian cancer/UNIVERSITY OF UTAH*.[54]

The sequences should also be provided to the EPO in the form of an acceptable sequence listing which, if submitted on the filing date, will be considered as forming part of the description.[55] The EPO generally requests sequence listings for any sequence comprising more than four amino acids and/or ten nucleotides, and the sequence listing must comply with WIPO Standard ST.25.[56]

The definition of antibodies by CDRs, however, is not without danger, in particular when the CDRs are defined as partial sequences of the variable region(s) and/or when the CDRs and the framework regions are not clearly separated in the specification.

The determination of CDR sequences is not straightforward. There are multiple well known and routinely used numbering systems for variable domains (e.g., the Kabat and Chothia numbering systems), each setting slightly different borders for the CDR regions. Thus, the specific amino acid residues constituting a particular CDR as defined by one system will not necessarily correspond identically to the CDR residues defined by another system. To add to the confusion, only the Kabat system references the term 'CDR' while other systems use different terms. For example, the Chothia system references 'hypervariable regions or loops'.

Although these terms are recognized to functionally relate to the same antibody structures, opponents have often used the difference in terminology and the slight differences in specified residues to create the appearance of a lack of clarity and/or a lack of support for the CDRs in question. That is, they typically argue that the mere

53. Enlarged Board of Appeal, decision in G 11/91 of 19 November 1992, *Glu-Gln/CELTRIX*.
54. Technical Board of Appeal, decision in T 1213/05 of 27 September 2007, *Breast and ovarian cancer/UNIVERSITY OF UTAH*.
55. See Rule 30 EPC, as well as the 'Decision of the President of the European Patent Office dated 28 April 2011 on the filing of sequence listings' (published in OJ EPO 2011, 372) and the 'Notice from the European Patent Office dated 18 October 2013 concerning the filing of sequence listings' (published in OJ EPO 2013, 542).
56. The standardized presentation of nucleotide and amino acid sequences in accordance with WIPO Standard ST.25 can be achieved by using corresponding programs, such as BiSSAP (version 1.3) from the EPO (https://www.epo.org/applying/online-services/online-filing/auxiliary/bissap.html) or PatentIn from the USPTO (https://www.uspto.gov/patents-getting-started/patent-basics/types-patent-applications/utility-patent/checker/patentin).

recitation of the term 'CDR' without further information is unclear or non-enabling because the skilled person cannot know with certainty the exact bounds of the claim and/or cannot with certainty practice the claimed invention. This can become very problematic because it is common practice to cite to more than one variable domain numbering system in an antibody application.

Antibody variable domain sequences and their definition in the claims also need to be carefully considered by the applicant. Since the variable domain of an antibody can in particular tolerate some degree of modification (e.g., substitution, insertion and/or deletion of amino acid residues) while still maintaining functional activity, the applicant should seek to obtain claims that recite the specific variable domain sequences but allow for an adequate degree of sequence variability. Indeed, the necessity to allow applicants/patentees to protect their inventions by claiming a certain degree of sequence variability has been expressly acknowledged by the Boards of Appeal, for example, in T 2101/09 *Human Delta3 – Notch/MILLENNIUM.*[57]

Typically, the variability of antibody sequences (and also of the variable domains) is described in patent applications in a list format, such as 'the invention also encompasses variable domains having 85%, 90% or 95% identity to the variable domain of SEQ ID NO: X, SEQ ID NO: Y or SEQ ID NO: Z.' With such definitions, however, there can be a risk that the EPO might consider them as two separate lists of alternatives, namely a first list of percentage identities and a second list of variable domain sequences, and might question whether any particular 'combination' of a specific percentage identity and a specific variable domain sequence is directly and unambiguously derivable from the corresponding definition.

This problem is illustrated by decision T 583/09 *Novel genes/MILLENNIUM,*[58] in which the competent Board of Appeal regarded a specific 'combination' of sequence identity and sequence number as not being disclosed in individualized form, and ultimately refused the corresponding application. In subsequent decisions the Boards of Appeal have taken a more sensible approach to assessing the technical information actually conveyed by such definitions in list format, as reflected by T 2134/10 *S. pneumoniae antigen/HUMAN GENOME SCIENCES*[59] and T 1581/12 *Outer membrane protein immunogen Neisseria/GLAXOSMITHKLINE.*[60] Nevertheless, care should be taken when defining sequence variabilities in new patent applications in order to ensure that potentially desirable fallback lines can later be incorporated into the claims, if necessary, without having to make any selections and combinations.

Normally, providing the mere structure, i.e. the relevant sequences, of new antibodies is not considered inventive by the EPO where antibodies to the same target are already known in the art. Exceptionally, the EPO grants patents on antibodies that are merely defined by their relevant structural sequences if these antibodies

57. Technical Board of Appeal, decision in T 2101/09 of 26 February 2013, *Human Delta3 – Notch/MILLENNIUM*, Reason 13.
58. Technical Board of Appeal, decision in T 583/09 of 13 December 2011, *Novel genes/ MILLENNIUM.*
59. Technical Board of Appeal, decision in T 2134/10 of 14 November 2013, *S. pneumoniae antigen/HUMAN GENOME SCIENCES.*
60. Technical Board of Appeal, decision in T 1581/12 of 15 September 2016, *Outer membrane protein immunogen Neisseria/GLAXOSMITHKLINE.*

are obtainable only via unconventional methods or if the corresponding sequences confer unexpected and advantageous properties on the claimed antibodies. In contrast to the USPTO, novel antibody sequences (full length, variable regions, CDRs, etc.) do not render the claimed antibodies inventive since the principle of 'structural non-obviousness' is not accepted by the EPO.[61]

It is rather common for applicants to combine structural with functional features. An illustrative example of a corresponding claim was discussed in T 648/13 *Anti-αOPGL-1 antibody/AMGEN*[62] where the claim under discussion read:

> 'An antibody, comprising a heavy chain and a light chain, wherein: the heavy chain comprises: an amino acid sequence as set forth in SEQ ID NO: 13; and the light chain comprises: an amino acid sequence as set forth in SEQ ID NO: 14; and wherein the antibody binds to an osteoprotegerin ligand (OPGL) and inhibits binding of OPGL to an osteoclast differentiation and activation receptor (ODAR).'

In this opposition/appeal case, it was held that whereas the cited prior art had disclosed antibodies that block the interaction between OPGL and its receptor ODAR, these prior art antibodies do not unambiguously and inevitably have the same amino acid sequences as those of the claims. Accordingly, the claimed antibody was considered novel, and the Board went on to assess whether the claimed antibody, comprising concrete heavy and light chains, was inventive over the prior art. In T 648/13, the Board maintained the claim in light of the fact that the claimed antibody exhibited an unexpected and surprisingly high affinity and binding specificity for OPGL, concluding that the skilled person would not have arrived at this antibody in an obvious manner. The opponent did not file any counterevidence and merely argued that the claimed antibodies were an obvious alternative to the prior art antibodies without discussing their alleged properties. Again, in this case it was also to the advantage of the patentee that the application as filed provided ample scientific information which was considered plausible and credible. It would have been the burden of proof of the opponent to demonstrate that the claimed antibodies do not possess the alleged advantageous technical effects.

The claims under discussion in T 511/14 *DKK-1 antibodies/MEDIMMUNE*[63] related to an antibody or immunological fragment thereof, wherein said antibody or immunological fragment specifically binds a Dkk-1 polypeptide. The corresponding antibodies/immunological fragments were defined in the claims as comprising *either six CDRs* (three light chain CDRs and three heavy chain CDRs) *with at least 80% sequence identity* to given specific sequences (main request) *or as comprising three concrete CDR sequences of the light chain and 'one or more heavy chain CDR(s)'* as defined by concrete sequences (auxiliary request). Accordingly, these antibodies were defined by partial structural elements and the claims allowed less than 100% sequence identity.

61. See, e.g., Technical Board of Appeal, decision in T 605/14 of 7 June 2018, *Anti-angiopoietin-2 antibodies/MEDIMMUNE*, Reason 24, and Technical Board of Appeal, decision in T 187/04 of 11 January 2007, *Antikörper/KREBSFORSCHUNGSZENTRUM*, Reason 11.
62. Technical Board of Appeal, decision in T 648/13 of 15 February 2018, *Anti-αOPGL-1 antibody/AMGEN*.
63. Technical Board of Appeal, decision in T 511/14 of 12 June 2018, *DKK-1 antibodies/MEDIMMUNE*.

Whereas this decision shows that the EPO readily accepts antibody definitions by CDRs, in that specific case the Board came to the conclusion that the claimed antibody/immunological functional fragments thereof lack inventive step. As a matter of fact, anti-Dkk-1 antibodies were already known in the art. The appellant (applicant) had argued that the anti-Dkk-1 antibodies provided with the application as filed have superior properties over the antibodies of the prior art. However, the Technical Board of Appeal reasoned that even if the claimed antibody were accepted as having demonstratively superior properties compared to the antibody of the prior art, these properties would have been demonstrated for only one particular embodiment of the claimed antibodies, namely an antibody with six concrete CDR sequences. Furthermore, the structural reason for the superior property of the antibody is not disclosed in the application as filed. The Technical Board of Appeal in T 511/11 therefore came to the conclusion that it cannot be inferred that any favourable properties of the concretely described anti-Dkk-1 antibodies are inevitably also properties of every embodiment of the claimed subject-matter.[64]

When less than six concrete CDRs are recited in the claims or when the binding sequences, such as the variable regions, allow for a certain flexibility by requiring less than 100% sequence identity, the claims should comprise at least one functional limitation. In decision T 617/07 *Monoclonal NGF-antagonist antibodies/LAY Line*[65] the Board held an antibody patentable wherein the antibody was characterized (i) by *functional limitations*, namely antagonizing the binding of nerve growth factor (NGF) to a high affinity tyrosine kinase receptor (TrkA) and prevention of the corresponding activation of TrkA by NGF, and (ii) by the *structural feature of having at least one CDR from a list of six concretely recited CDRs*.

Accordingly, even very broadly defined claims may be patentable when they meet the condition that the skilled person can readily test and find with routine methods or methods provided in the specification the broadly defined antibodies, no matter how long it takes to make such antibodies (see T 617/07, Reasons 25 to 28, T 1300/05,[66] Reasons 8 to 17, and *Case Law of the Boards of Appeal*, 8th edition of 2016, II.C.6.3).

Decision T 617/07 made clear that the application must demonstrate that at least the specifically exemplified antibody can be tested for the claimed feature using common knowledge and/or routine methods known in the art, and the application must demonstrate that at least the exemplary antibody exhibits the claimed functional feature. The provision of such an exemplary antibody and antigen has been recognized by the Technical Boards of Appeal to theoretically allow the skilled person to produce further antibodies sharing the same technical features without undue burden.

This is illustrated, e.g., by decision T 877/03 *Anti-CD30 antibodies/ROCHE*,[67] in which the claim under discussion read:

---

64. *Ibid.*, Reasons 3 and 4.
65. Technical Board of Appeal, decision in T 617/07 of 4 August 2009, *Monoclonal NGF-antagonist antibodies/LAY LINE*.
66. Technical Board of Appeal, decision in T 1300/05 of 11 July 2006, *RET screening assay/PROGENICS*.
67. Technical Board of Appeal, decision in T 877/03 of 7 April 2005, *Anti-CD30 antibodies/ROCHE*.

> 'An antibody which binds to the CD30 antigen and
> a) releases sCD30 from Hodgkin's disease cells to an amount of, or less than, 10%, referred to the release found without an addition of antibody;
> b) does not bind to B cell non-Hodgkin's lymphomas or plasma cells in a manner which can be detected by immune precipitation.'

In Reasons 21 and 23 of T 877/03, the Board held that as the claimed monoclonal antibody is characterized by features readily testable in an assay, the skilled person seeking to reproduce the invention and to produce antibodies different from the exemplified one (which was also deposited) will have to produce antibodies by routine methods and test them individually in an assay. This may possibly involve some tedious and time-consuming work, but it is nothing out of the ordinary since the techniques for the production and selection of antibodies were common routine techniques at the priority date of the patent in suit and since the patent described at least one screening process for the recited functional features.

Thus, the provision of at least the one exemplary antibody should support the entire breadth of the claim (i.e., as also directed to other antibodies structurally unrelated to the exemplary antibody). Moreover, if assays for the determination of the functional features are described in the application, then it has been found that encompassing non-functional antibodies in the scope of the claim is irrelevant as a scientist would know how to exclude such antibodies; see also *Case Law of the Boards of Appeal*, 8th edition of 2016, II.C.6.3.

Decision T 605/14 *Anti-angiopoietin-2 antibodies/MEDIMMUNE*[68] provides a further example how important technical details and reliable information in the patent specification are. The claim at stake related to:

> 'An antibody or antigen binding fragment thereof comprising a variable light chain having a sequence defined by SEQ ID NO:81 and a variable heavy chain having a sequence defined by SEQ ID NO:79.'

Accordingly, this claim was directed to an antibody comprising specific variable light and heavy chains, which were those of the specific, singled-out monoclonal antibody (mAb) 3.19.3, an anti-Ang-2 antibody provided in the patent. The patentee relied in the defence of this antibody, *inter alia*, on Biacore binding affinity data as originally disclosed in the patent specification and argued that the single antibody claimed shows a higher (advantageous) preferential binding for Ang-2 versus Ang-1.

However, in Reason 11 of T 605/14, the Board considered that, while according to the application as filed, the high-resolution Biacore measurements are reproducible, the values themselves are not considered reliable in the application. Indeed, the Board concluded that the technical effect of a higher preferential binding affinity of mAb 3.19.3 for Ang-2 versus Ang-1 is not derivable from the application as filed. In light of this finding and based on the now established 'plausibility case law', the Board did not accept any post-filed evidence and data which were generated only after the filing date of the application. The Board came to the final conclusion that the specific structure of the variable heavy and light chain amino acid sequences

68. Technical Board of Appeal, decision in T 605/14 of 7 June 2018, *Anti-angiopoietin-2 antibodies/MEDIMMUNE*.

of mAb 3.19.3 does not impart an additional property to the antibody which differs from the property screened for and which could be regarded as surprising. The Board referred to established jurisprudence in the field of antibodies, in particular decision T 735/00 *Anti-CRP antibodies/IATRON LABORATORIES, INC.*,[69] Reason 26 (see §1.05[B], *infra*), and considered the claimed mAb 3.19.3 as obvious.

Again, this decision illustrates how important technical details are in the jurisprudence of the EPO and that technical ambiguities need to be avoided in a patent specification. T 605/14, at Reason 11, also reminded the parties that, in accordance with established jurisprudence, any effect provided by the invention may be used as a basis for reformulating the technical problem, for example in oppositions, as long as that effect is derivable from the application as filed. Only if this has been established can evidence (produced after the effective date of the application) be used in support of such an effect (see also *Case Law of the Boards of Appeal*, 8th edition of 2016, I.D.4.4.1 and I.D.4.6).

The disclosure requirements for antibodies with the EPO is also discussed in detail in the *Case Law of the Boards of Appeal*, 8th edition of 2016, at II.C.6.3.

[3] Chemical Modifications, Conjugation and Glycosylation

Claims defining antibodies by specific chemical modifications, conjugations and glycosylations are also accepted by the EPO. For instance, antibodies with a specific glyosylation pattern and methods for their production have been found to be patentable with the EPO (see e.g. T 1784/15 *Glycosylated antibodies/HOFFMANN-LA ROCHE*[70]). Another example of a patented antibody modification is EP-B1 1308455, wherein compositions of antibodies with limited deamidated, acidic variants are claimed. This patent was maintained in opposition appeal proceedings with decision T 2522/10 *Anti-HER2 antibodies/GENENTECH.*[71]

[C] Cell Line Deposits and Process of Production

It is highly recommended to provide ample information in a European patent application how the claimed antibody can be obtained/produced without further effort. In this context, a 'deposit' for example of a production cell line, may be of benefit. Accordingly, at least one method that is intended to be used to produce the desired antibody should be disclosed in the application. Such a method of production may also be novel and inventive and may merit a patent before the EPO. The description of a corresponding method may further allow to claim the resulting antibody in the form of a 'product-by-process claim'. Furthermore, the deposition of a production cell line may also be of high value when secondary modifications of an antibody (such as cell-specific glycosylations) are of relevance.

69. Technical Board of Appeal, decision in T 735/00 of 23 March 2004, *Anti-CRP antibodies/ IATRON LABORATORIES, INC.*
70. Technical Board of Appeal, decision in T 1784/15 of 22 June 2017, *Glycosylated antibodies/ HOFFMANN-LA ROCHE.*
71. Technical Board of Appeal, decision in T 2522/10 of 16 April 2015, *Anti-HER2 antibodies/ GENENTECH.*

It is also permissible to refer in the patent application to hypothetical methods, including hypothetical production methods. Yet, care must be taken that the description of these methods is detailed enough to be readily performable by a skilled person without further effort (see, e.g., T 1080/01 *Thermostable enzyme/F. HOFFMANN-LA ROCHE*[72]), Reasons 29 to 37. Should the hypothetical method not work as described in the application or should it not be performable, enablement may be found to be lacking. Furthermore, it is now established that if the patent or the application as filed contains only an example with a hypothetical experimental protocol, and if this example is to be relied on for showing sufficiency of disclosure, then the burden of proof lies with the patentee to demonstrate that in practice this protocol does indeed work as stated. Evidence that a variation of the protocol works is unlikely to be enough (see, e.g., T 792/00 *Varied binding proteins/DYAX*,[73] Headnotes and Reasons 9 to 11).

However, care must be taken that the application as filed provides enough guidance as to how the claimed antibodies can be obtained. For example, in T 1466/05 *Pyridinoline/SEREX*[74] the question arose as to whether the availability of a hybidoma producing one specific antibody together with a *general description of the epitope* recognized by the antibody put the skilled person in the position to obtain further antibodies with the same specificity. Since the application did not provide a specific antigen, the Board considered that the skilled person seeking to prepare the claimed antibody would have had to embark on a 'research program' without any teaching in the application as filed as to how the desired specificity could be achieved. This amounts to an 'undue burden' and thus a lack of sufficient disclosure (see also *Case Law of the Boards of Appeal*, 8th edition of 2016, II.C.6.3).

Also methods for the production and/or purification of antibodies/antibody variants are patentable with the EPO, as, *inter alia*, confirmed in T 458/07 *Ion exchange chromatography method/GENENTECH*.[75] Furthermore, specific formulations comprising antibodies may likewise be patentable with the EPO. For example, in T 159/16 *High Concentration Antibody Formulation/CHUGAI*[76] a stable antibody-containing liquid formulation was confirmed to be patentable since the claimed formulation exhibits improved stability against both dimerization and deamidation. In a recent decision, T 139/16 *Anti-HER2 antibody formulations/HOFFMANN-LA ROCHE*,[77] the Board confirmed the patentability of a stable pharmaceutical antibody formulation for subcutaneous injection.

---

72. Technical Board of Appeal, decision in T 1080/01 of 24 October 2003, *Thermostable enzyme/F. HOFFMANN-LA ROCHE*.
73. Technical Board of Appeal, decision in T 792/00 of 2 July 2002, *Varied binding proteins/DYAX*.
74. Technical Board of Appeal, decision in T 1466/05 of 27 July 2007, *Pyridinoline/SEREX*.
75. Technical Board of Appeal, decision in T 458/07 of 23 September 2009, *Ion exchange chromatography method/GENENTECH*.
76. Technical Board of Appeal, decision in T 159/16 of 11 December 2018, *High Concentration Antibody Formulation/CHUGAI*.
77. Technical Board of Appeal, decision in T 139/16 of 7 February 2019, *Anti-HER2 antibody formulations/HOFFMANN-LA ROCHE*.

§1.03 BREADTH OF CLAIMS AND SUPPORT BY EXAMPLES

[A] Acceptable Breadth of Claims to Antibodies

The breadth of the claims is considered by the EPO on a case-by-case basis and depends on the teachings in the prior art and the distinct technical contribution disclosed in the patent application/the patent under discussion. Broad claims can only be defended over their full scope if they are novel and inventive over the prior art and if it is made plausible in the application as filed that the taught technical effect can readily be obtained for the whole range of embodiments claimed.

Especially in the life science field, it will be assessed how far the provision of one example or even merely of an inventive idea can be extrapolated to other, broader embodiments without further effort. Furthermore, the EPO and also potential opponents will scrutinize whether the application as filed comprises enough evidence and technical details that enable the person skilled in the art to reliably achieve, without undue burden, all embodiments claimed. It is, however, to be borne in mind that an application or the 'breadth' of a claim can only be objected to for the lack of sufficiency (for example, over the full scope as claimed) if there are serious doubts, substantiated by verifiable facts.[78]

[B] Required Experimental Support for Claims to Functionally Defined Antibodies

Compound claims reciting functional features maintain a broad scope of protection because they do not limit the claimed antibody to any particular structure (thus potentially encompassing a wide variety of amino acid sequences), but potentially distinguish the claimed antibody from those already known based on their specific (biological/biophysical) activity. Such distinguishing functional features can potentially include any feature identified by the inventor. Such features may correspond to *in vivo* and/or *in vitro* activities and also include those determined in cell-free assays (e.g., antibody affinity, cross-reactivity) and/or in cell cultures (e.g., anti-proliferative or stimulatory activity).

The required experimental support for corresponding functionally claimed antibodies depends again on the technical contribution of the inventor. For example, if the inventor provides a novel and inventive antigen or epitope, the inventor is also entitled to obtain patent protection for an 'antibody specifically binding to said antigen/epitope' since the EPO considers the preparation of antibodies, such as polyclonals or monoclonals, as a routine technique readily mastered by the skilled person. However, if functionally defined antibodies are claimed and the claimed function goes beyond 'specifically binding', additional support in the experimental part of the application will be required.

If the methods used in the invention could not be practised at the priority date, then it is critical that the specification describes the invention in such a way that

78. The corresponding principle laid down in T 19/90, Reason 3.3 for enablement also applies to inventive step and industrial applicability.

the skilled person will succeed in putting the invention into practice (see, *inter alia*, T 792/00 *Varied binding proteins/DYAX*[79]). Likewise, if any potentially important methods are disclosed in a merely hypothetical manner, the hypothetical methods will actually need to work in order to be successfully relied upon (see T 1080/01 *Thermostable enzyme/F. HOFFMANN-LA ROCHE*[80] or T 792/00[81]). The Boards have consistently held that it is the patentee's burden to prove that such hypothetically described methods achieve the intended result as specifically described in the application.

As discussed in detail herein above in §1.02, the information relied on to establish plausibility by the EPO is information that is available to the skilled person in the form of either (1) existing general knowledge or (2) new experimental evidence disclosed in the patent. Accordingly, the experiments provided in the specification/application are of particular importance if the inventor embarked on an absolutely novel field of research and there was no existing knowledge to build on. In such a case, the requirements of the disclosure content of the patent application and of the scientific/experimental evidence are higher. Simply put, the lack of experimental evidence may be to the detriment of the applicant in the assessment of enablement and/or may endanger inventive step with the EPO.

The reliance on what was already known and a lack of any new data in the application creates a tension between enablement and inventive step because the same knowledge that is relied upon to establish the enablement of the invention is then also applied to the prior art under inventive step (see, for example, T 532/06 *Use of Sertraline/PFIZER INC.*[82]). In such a case, the existing knowledge, rather than new data, supports enablement. However, the same standard and the same 'existing knowledge' is also applied to the prior art. Accordingly, if enablement is established by existing knowledge, there is a substantial risk that the invention will be found to lack inventive step (see T 1306/08 *Needles coated with vaccine/SMITHKLINE BEECHAM*[83]).

[C] Required Experimental Support for Claims to Structurally Defined Antibodies

Antibodies defined by structural features, for example by relevant sequences of the CDRs and/or the variable regions, are readily accepted by the EPO as long as these antibodies are novel and inventive, i.e. the general patentability requirements are fulfilled, see also §1.05[B], *infra*.

---

79. Technical Board of Appeal, decision in T 792/00 of 2 July 2002, *Varied binding proteins/DYAX*, Reason 3.
80. Technical Board of Appeal, decision in T 1080/01 of 24 October 2003, *Thermostable enzyme/F. HOFFMANN-LA ROCHE*, Reasons 29 to 37.
81. Technical Board of Appeal, decision in T 792/00 of 2 July 2002, *Varied binding proteins/DYAX*, Reasons 9 to 11 and 17 to 26.
82. Technical Board of Appeal, decision in T 532/06 of 4 June 2009, *Use of Sertraline/PFIZER INC.*, Reason 3.1.3.
83. Technical Board of Appeal, decision in T 1306/08 of 12 September 2012, *Needles coated with vaccine/SMITHKLINE BEECHAM*, Reason 9.2.

Testing structurally defined features is normally a matter of routine and readily acceptable. In particular this holds true for antibody definitions by amino acid sequences (or by nucleic acid sequences encoding such relevant sequences, such as CDRs or variable regions). It is notable that a certain variability in the claimed sequences ('x % identify to the concrete sequence provided') will also be allowed depending again on the teachings in the prior art (namely in comparison to the sequences of the corresponding prior art antibodies) and whether it is plausible that these sequence variants also result in an antibody with the novel and inventive features.[84] Accordingly, it is of importance that the application as filed renders such variants plausible, either by corresponding experimental data or by a detailed technical reasoning.

When claiming antibodies which are structurally defined by specific biochemical modifications, such as certain glycosylation patterns, it is of importance that the patent specification provides enough information on (a) how such modifications can be obtained and (b) how their presence or absence can be assessed and verified. In this respect, the same (high) standard as described in §1.03[B] applies.

Again, if a corresponding plausible teaching is provided by the application as filed, the applicant/patentee may also rely on evidence available after the filing date in order to document that antibodies with the claimed structure or structural modification can indeed be obtained by the skilled person without further effort.

In general, when drafting a new patent application, it is advisable to include meaningful experimental data supporting the claimed invention even if, for example, the claims relate to an antibody that is comprehensively defined by structural features, such as by its full length sequence. The need for meaningful data is well illustrated by the recent decision T 488/16 *Dasatinib/BRISTOL-MYERS SQUIB*,[85] in which the claim under consideration was a product claim directed to a single chemical compound (the blockbuster drug dasatinib). This claim was found to lack inventive step because, simply put, the pharmacological activity of dasatinib relied upon by the patentee was not considered to be rendered plausible in the complete absence of any corresponding data in the original application. Under these circumstances, the patentee's attempts to rely on post-published supporting data were swept aside by the Board. This decision once again demonstrates the importance of providing a credible and plausible disclosure of the claimed invention in the patent application as originally filed.

§1.04 SPECIFIC MEDICAL APPLICATIONS AND OTHER FOLLOW-UP INVENTIONS

Claims relating to therapeutic methods of treatment are not allowable before the EPO under Article 53(c) EPC. This is also discussed in detail in the Guidelines, and the pertinent case law of the Technical Boards has very early on confirmed this exception from patentability.

84. See, e.g., Technical Board of Appeal, decision in T 2101/09 of 26 February 2013, *Human Delta3 – Notch/MILLENNIUM*, Reasons 13 and 16.
85. Technical Board of Appeal, decision in T 488/16 of 1 February 2017, *Dasatinib/BRISTOL-MYERS SQUIB*.

In cases where the claim under consideration comprises *at least one feature* defining a physical activity or action that constitutes a 'method step for treatment of the human or animal body by surgery or therapy', the claim will be rejected by the EPO under said Article 53(c) EPC. This prompted controversial discussions before the Boards of Appeal regarding claims that comprised as a mandatory feature a dosage regime or that comprised language such as 'wherein substance/compound X *is administered* to a subject in need of treatment'. However, since the advent of the EPC2000 (including the new provisions of Article 54(4)/(5) EPC; see §1.01[A], *supra*) and the corresponding relevant case law (e.g., T 1020/03, *Method of administration of IGF-1/GENENTECH INC.*[86] and G 2/08, *Dosage regime/ABBOTT RESPIRATORY*[87] it has been clarified that inventions relating to, for example, dosage regimes can be protected in the 'medical use claim format'.

Accordingly, not only are new indications for known drugs amenable to patent protection, also the 'uses' of such drugs in new patient groups, new administration regimes, new technical effects, etc. are patentable as long as these technical features lead to a 'truly novel medical or clinical situation'. The same applies to therapeutic antibodies. In cases where the invention lies in a truly novel medical or clinical situation, known therapeutic antibodies can also be claimed in the form of a 'purpose-limited compound claim', such as:

> 'Antibody X for use in treating specific disease Y.'

Such a claim is considered as a 'second' or 'further' medical use claim.

If a known antibody is described for the first time as being useful as a pharmaceutical, even broader, general protection is possible, for example in the form of:

> 'Antibody X for use as a pharmaceutical.'

In this case, the claim is not limited to the treatment of any particular disease and, therefore, *any and all* medical uses will be protected. Such a claim is considered as a 'first' medical use claim.

Both first and second (further) medical use claims in the format accepted by the EPO are also referred to as 'purpose-limited product claims'.

Since the Enlarged Board of Appeal handed down its decision G 2/08, acknowledging that a medical use claim reciting a specific dosage regime is patent eligible and that the dosage regime can indeed confer novelty, the Boards of Appeal have (rightly) adopted a liberal approach when assessing features of medical use claims that define specific aspects of the claimed therapeutic treatment. Thus, for example, in T 285/14 *–/INTERMUNE*[88] the competent Board acknowledged novelty of a second medical use claim reciting a specific contraindication:

> 'Pirfenidone for use in treating a patient in need of pirfenidone therapy and in need of fluvoxamine therapy, characterized in that the treating comprises

---

86. Technical Board of Appeal, decision in T 1020/03 of 29 October 2004, *Method of administration of IGF-1/GENENTECH INC.*
87. Enlarged Board of Appeal, decision in G 2/08 of 19 February 2010, *Dosage regime/ABBOTT RESPIRATORY*.
88. Technical Board of Appeal, decision in T 285/14 of 18 December 2018, *–/INTERMUNE*.

> *avoiding, contraindicating or discontinuing concomitant use of fluvoxamine.'* (emphasis added)

Remarkably, the Board acknowledged that the feature of 'avoiding, contraindicating or discontinuing concomitant use of fluvoxamine' does indeed constitute a technical feature that distinguishes the claimed medical use from the prior art.[89] This decision illustrates that virtually any aspects relating to the therapeutic use of a substance or composition can, in principle, be claimed in the form of a second medical use claim in a European patent application.

It is furthermore notable that the EPO routinely accepts medical use claims in the form of subordinate or dependent claims in applications where a novel and inventive antibody is claimed, provided that the application as filed renders such a medical use at least plausible. A corresponding claim could read as follows:

> 'Antibody X according to claim 1 for use in the treatment of disease Y.'

The above-discussed decision T 1300/05[90] may serve as an example here. The main claims related to antibodies generated against a cell-line susceptible to infection by macrophage-tropic HIV-1 isolates. The subordinate medical use claim (still in the EPC 1973/Swiss-type format) read:

> 'Use of a monoclonal antibody according to claim 1 for the preparation of a medicament for the treatment of HIV-1 infections'[91]

Yet, in the absence of an exemplary antibody and some experimental data linking the antigen/antibody to the biological mechanism of a specific disease, medical use claims may not be considered by the EPO as 'supported' (see *inter alia* T 604/04 *PF4A receptors/GENENTECH*[92]). In this decision it was held that 'the patent in suit provides no evidence at all that an antibody blocking the receptor would thereby produce a useful physiological effect of therapeutic potential'. Accordingly, the provision of even a *single* antibody with the desired feature will likely *enable* the entire scope of a medical use claim, i.e., will render it plausible that, using the information in the application (which was not previously available in the prior art), other antibodies falling within the scope of the claim can be readily developed. Corresponding evidence in the specification may even support a broad first medical use claim in the form 'Antibody X for use as a medicament' or 'Antibody X for use in therapy'.

In T 609/02 *AP-1 complex/SALT INSTITUTE*[93] the Board recalled that attaining the therapeutic effect recited in a claim is a functional technical feature of that claim (see also G 2/88). As a consequence, under Article 83 EPC (enablement), unless this is already known to the skilled person at the priority/filing date, the application

89. *Ibid.*, Reasons 2.3 and 3.5.
90. Technical Board of Appeal, decision in T 1300/05 of 11 July 2006, *RET screening assay/PROGENICS*.
91. The claim would nowadays read: 'The antibody according to claim 1 for use in the treatment of HIV-1 infections'.
92. Technical Board of Appeal, decision in T 604/04 of 16 March 2006, *PF4A receptors/GENENTECH*, Reasons 20 to 28.
93. Technical Board of Appeal, decision in T 609/02 of 27 October 2004, *AP-1 complex/SALT INSTITUTE*.

must disclose the suitability of the product for the claimed therapeutic use (see also *Case Law of the Boards of Appeal*, 8th edition of 2016, II.C.6.2). T 609/02 further confirmed that showing pharmaceutical effects *in vitro* may be sufficient if for the skilled person the observed effect directly and unambiguously reflects the corresponding therapeutic application.

Once evidence is available from the patent application which makes it plausible that there is an established relationship between the *in vitro* experiments and the disease to be treated by the claimed antibody, even post-published evidence may be taken into account (but only to back up the findings in the patent application in relation to the use of the antibody as a pharmaceutical and not to establish sufficiency of disclosure on its own); see, e.g. T 1329/04 and T 18/09.

Accordingly, in T 609/02 it was held that if the description in a patent specification provides no more than a vague indication of a possible medical use for a chemical compound (or an antibody) yet to be identified, more detailed evidence cannot be used later to remedy the fundamental insufficiency of disclosure of such subject-matter. This was also confirmed in T 433/05 *Fusion Peptide Inhibitors/ CONJUCHEM*[94] in which it was recalled that where a therapeutic application was claimed in a Swiss-type form (i.e., a medical use claim in the format of EPC1973), attaining the claimed therapeutic effect was a functional technical feature of the claim. In T 895/13 *Meningococcal/NOVARTIS*[95] it was also confirmed that attaining the claimed therapeutic effect was a functional technical feature of a 'medical use claim'. Accordingly, the therapeutic effect provided by the claimed subject-matter is to be examined in the context of the assessment of sufficiency of disclosure/enablement.

In accordance with the above, as for small molecules or other pharmaceuticals/ bioceuticals, also for medical uses of antibodies, the patent specification should comprise a plausible and credible teaching as to why the claimed second medical use should be therapeutically feasible and the specification must disclose the suitability of the product (the antibody) for the claimed therapeutic application. These requirements on (further) medical uses have been handled rather strictly in some decisions of the Technical Boards.

For example, T 1150/09 *–/VLAAMS INTERUNIVERSITAIR INSTITUUT VOOR BIOTECHNOLOGIE*[96] related to the medical use of an 'angiogenesis inhibitor consisting of an antibody or a fragment thereof specifically binding to placental growth factor (PIGF)' in the treatment of several diseases including, *inter alia*, cancer. The patent in suit did not indicate which criteria the skilled person should apply for identifying a cancer that is to be treated with the claimed angiogenesis inhibitor (an antibody directed against PIGF). The Board recalled that it has been established by the case law relating to 'sufficiency of disclosure with regard to claims to a second medical use' that a claimed therapeutic effect may be proven by any kind of data as long as they directly and unambiguously reflect the therapeutic application. The experiments

94. Technical Board of Appeal, decision in T 433/05 of 14 June 2007, *Fusion Peptide Inhibitors/ CONJUCHEM*.
95. Technical Board of Appeal, decision in T 895/13 of 28 March 2014, *Meningococcal/ NOVARTIS*.
96. Technical Board of Appeal, decision in T 1150/09 of 14 November 2013, *–/VLAAMS INTERUNIVERSITAIR INSTITUUT VOOR BIOTECHNOLOGIE*, Reasons 5 to 13.

in the contested patent were carried out in PlGF 'knock-out' mice, and the Board held that the mere fact that these experiments were carried out in knock-out mice (and not with the claimed anti-PlGF antibody in a test system in which PlGF is actually present) 'does not in itself suffice to deny sufficiency of disclosure'. Rather, the question to be addressed, in the eyes of the Board, is 'whether or not the data provided in the patent in suit reflect the claimed therapeutic application'. Since the skilled person was not in a position to predict, on the basis of the information contained in the specification and taking into account the relevant common general knowledge, which diseases/cancers can be treated, the Board came to the conclusion in Reason 13 that:

> 'The patent in suit does not indicate which criteria the skilled person should apply for identifying *a cancer* which can be treated with an angiogenesis inhibitor consisting of an antibody or a fragment thereof specifically binding to PlGF. The specification of the patent merely addresses the treatment of tumour formation in the general part of the description to the extent that a generic list of various types of tumours is provided (cf paragraphs [0016] and [0017]) however no indication is given regarding which of the tumours are actually suitable for treatment using anti-PlGF antibodies in accordance with the invention and whether or not PlGF is actually involved in the formation of any of these tumours.' (emphasis added)

Therefore, in the eyes of the competent Board in T 1150/09, the requirements of Article 83 EPC (enablement) were not fulfilled.

Similarly, in decision T 1602/10 *Anti-TIM-3 antibodies for the treatment of cancer/BRIGHAM*,[97] a medical use claim was under discussion wherein an antibody specific for TIM-3 (a transmembrane protein preferentially expressed on differentiated Th1 cells) was claimed for use in the treatment of cancer. The experimental evidence provided in the application as filed related to administering an antibody *in vivo* in a mouse model of experimental autoimmune encephalitis (EAE) which is a model for human multiple sclerosis. In this mouse model, the administration of an antibody against TIM-3 resulted in more severe clinical disease and increased mortality in the EAE model.

The Board denied sufficiency of disclosure of the medical use claim by reasoning that, based on the evidence provided in the application, the person would have considered 'it plausible that an extant immune reaction could be amplified with anti-TIM-3 antibodies'. However, the Board did not find it plausible that a *de novo* immune response to cancers could be generated with anti-TIM-3 antibodies since the skilled person 'would not have believed that substantially all cancer types inherently generate a TH1, TIM-3 mediated immune response' and that all cancers are treatable by administration of anti-TIM-3 antibodies. Furthermore, the Board criticized the antibodies used in the examples of the application had not been deposited with a recognized depositary institution according to Rule 31(1)(a) EPC and the application did not disclose whether the interaction of TIM-3 with its (not yet identified) ligand was to be blocked or activated by the antibody in order to achieve the claimed

97. Technical Board of Appeal, decision in T 1602/10 of 17 March 2015, *Anti-TIM-3 antibodies for the treatment of cancer/BRIGHAM*, Reasons 13 to 16.

therapeutic effect. Thus, no verification of the proposed and/or tentative mechanism of action was possible.

In both decisions, T 1150/09 and T 1602/10, the Boards applied the plausibility test very strictly. If further or more detailed technical information and evidence had already been provided in the application as filed, this would have certainly been of advantage for the applicant/patentee. Therefore, under the strict 'plausibility approach' of the EPO, it is advantageous if the application as filed provides serious and clear-cut scientific evidence, either in the form of experimental data or in the form of credible explanations of the desired technical effect based on teachings of the prior art. Such experimental data and/or credible explanations may (even) support superior effects of the claimed subject matter or may render a claimed medical use sufficiently disclosed.

Last but not least, decisions such as the above-discussed T 1602/10, indicating the relevance of formal biological 'deposits', are one of the reasons why such deposits under the Budapest Treaty have lately seen a certain renaissance. For specific antibodies, individually claimed antibodies or cell systems/cell lines producing such antibodies with particular modifications (for example glycosylations), a deposit under the Budapest Treaty is always of advantage to ensure enablement and reproducibility before the EPO. For instance, in cases where such an antibody cannot easily be described and characterized by structural and/or functional features, where structural information, such as sequence information of CDRs. is not available at the priority/filing date, or where particular advantageous production cell lines are obtained via elaborate screening and selection methods, a biological deposit may be opportune.

It should be noted that 'functional limitations/features' as a definition of the disorder to be treated may come to a limit even when antibodies with a distinct function or precise structural features are claimed in such medical uses. These 'functionally defined disorders' are often based on the discovery of biological relationships or the description of biological events occurring *in vitro* or *in vivo*. Such functional limitations/features of diseases are routinely considered as 'unclear' by the EPO. Accordingly, the disease proposed to be treated in the claim must also be, from an objective viewpoint, sufficiently clear.

For example, in T 241/95 *Serotonin receptor/ELI LILLY AND COMPANY*[98] a Swiss-type second medical use claim defined the disease or disorder to be treated as 'a condition which can be improved or prevented by selective occupation of the serotonin receptor'. Here the Board held that this functional definition was unclear because no test was provided to determine whether therapeutic effects were a result of the newly discovered property of the corresponding substance or any other known or unknown property of that substance.

Also in decision T 830/08 *Rimcazole/DUNDEE*[99] it was confirmed that a second medical use claim can only be considered as clear if the disease to be treated is clearly defined. Accordingly, as far as medical use claims are concerned, not only does the antibody to be employed need to be clearly and unambiguously characterized in the

---

98. Technical Board of Appeal, decision in T 241/95 of 14 June 2000, *Serotonin receptor/ELI LILLY AND COMPANY*.
99. Technical Board of Appeal, decision in T 830/08 of 11 October 2010, *Rimcazole/DUNDEE*.

claims, the disorder to be treated (or in some cases to be diagnosed) should also be clearly defined and should preferably not comprise functional terms.

This was again confirmed in a recent decision, T 2321/13 *Hyperproliferative diseases/MAX-PLANCK-GESELLSCHAFT,*[100] wherein the use of an anti-HER3 antibody capable of inhibiting HER3 kinase activity was claimed for 'the diagnosis, prevention or treatment of a MAP kinase pathway associated hyperproliferative disease associated with HER3 kinase activity directly phosphorylating PYK2'. Thus, the condition to be treated was not defined in terms of a specific disease, but in functional terms with two requirements, namely that the hyperproliferative disease is associated with (i) the MAP kinase pathway and (ii) HER3 kinase activity directly phosphorylating PYK2. The Board concluded that the use of the term 'associated' in the functional definition of the hyperproliferative disease in relation to the MAP kinase pathway and the lack of any guidance in the form of experimental tests or any testable criteria (in the patent documents and the common general knowledge, which would allow the skilled person to recognize which conditions fall within the functional definition and accordingly within the scope of the claim) leads to a lack of clarity of the claim. This finding is in line with the established jurisprudence of the Boards of Appeal, and the Board referred to the above-discussed 'serotonin receptor' case T 241/95.[101]

In accordance with these decisions as well as the *Case Law of the Boards of Appeal*, 8th edition of 2016, I.B.4.4.1, a medical use claim should relate to a 'defined, real treatment of a pathological condition', i.e. a clearly defined disease. The skilled person should be able to recognize which conditions fall within the functional definition and, consequently, within the scope of the claim.

Accordingly, the Technical Boards of Appeal have routinely pointed out that the effort to define a feature in functional terms had to stop short where it jeopardizes the clarity of a claim as required by Article 84 EPC (clarity) (see also *Case Law of the Boards of Appeal,* 8th edition of 2016, II.A.3.4).

[A] Treatment of Specific Diseases

Medical use claims relating to antibodies for use in the treatment of specific diseases are readily accepted by the EPO as long as the requirements of novelty, inventive step and sufficiency are met (there is hardly any issue under 'industrial applicability' with the EPO when the medical use claim is correctly drafted as a 'purpose-limited product claim' in accordance with Article 54 (4)/(5) EPC). As discussed herein above, claims to second or further medical uses of a known therapeutic antibody are accepted by the EPO if the claimed use relates to a 'truly new clinical/therapeutic situation'. Such a truly new clinical situation is certainly given when the therapeutic antibody is to be used in the context of a completely different disease, for example when the prior art used the antibody in the treatment of a specific lung cancer and the novel proposed use is in the therapy of Alzheimer's disease.

100. Technical Board of Appeal, decision in T 2321/13 of 13 September 2018, *Hyperproliferative diseases/MAX-PLANCK-GESELLSCHAFT*, Reason 17.
101. Technical Board of Appeal, decision in T 241/95 of 14 June 2000, *Serotonin receptor /ELI LILLY AND COMPANY.*

Very broad claims to medical uses of antibodies appear to have a high hurdle to clear with the EPO when it comes to assessing inventive step. For example, in decision T 171/11 *Blockade of CTLA-4/UNIVERSITY OF CALIFORNIA*[102] the claim under discussion read:

> 'An anti-CTLA-4 antibody or a fragment thereof for use in a method of treatment of melanoma.'

Whereas the claim was formally allowable and novel, inventive step of this second medical use claim, relating (very broadly) to any anti-CTLA-4 antibody in the treatment of a specific cancer, was denied. The prior art in this case already disclosed experiments in which the *in vitro* administration of antibodies directed to CTLA to mice resulted in the rejection of tumours including pre-established ones. The authors of this prior art document concluded that CTLA-4 blockade enhances anti-tumour responses. The Board combined this teaching with a further document which referred to the closest prior art and stated that in mouse models anti-CTLA-4 antibodies could successfully be applied to tumors without overt toxicity. It was also taught that the success of an anti-CTLA-4 antibody depends on the presence of pre-existing T cell responses against the tumour antigens which, under normal circumstances, 'fail to develop enough amplitude to win the battle against the tumor'. Tumors that were known to elicit a T cell response would therefore have been considered good candidates for treatment by CTLA-4 blockade by an anti-CTLA-4 antibody already successfully used to treat carcinomas and fibrosarcomas. The fact that a melanoma was such a type of tumour was known from the prior art. Whereas the patentee/appellant had argued that the blocking activity of CTLA-4 in the prior art was for carcinomas and fibrosarcomas and that it was not generally established that blocking of the binding of CTLA-4 to its receptor would always lead to an immune boost, the Board came to the conclusion that the skilled person would have had an incentive to apply CTLA-4 blockade therapy using (blocking) anti-CTLA-4 antibodies to treat melanomas. The prior art also provided for a reasonable expectation of success for the treatment of melanomas in light of the fact that the closest prior art already referred to a potentially successful treatment of melanomas and that the person skilled in the art would have at least been motivated to repeat the experimental treatments as provided for carcinoma or sarcoma cell lines.

In this context, it is notable that the EPO accepts the concept of 'selection inventions'. It is possible to obtain European patent protection for specific (often narrow) embodiments. These specific selections may be considered inventive if, *inter alia*, it can be documented in the application as filed that the particular selection (for example a *specific* anti-CTLA antibody) has an unexpected, advantageous effect in the treatment of a *specific* disease (for example in the treatment of melanomas even considering that the treatment of carcinomas and sarcomas was already known in the art). Selection inventions are also made in the antibody space and the *Guidelines for Examination in the EPO* as of November 2018 provide corresponding detailed guidance and information in G.VI.8, in G.VII.12 and in G.VII, Annex 3.

102. Technical Board of Appeal, decision in T 171/11 of 9 June 2016, *Blockade of CTLA-4/UNIVERSITY OF CALIFORNIA*, Reasons 5, 6, 10 and 13.

Along the lines of 'selection inventions' and a more restricted claim scope, for example the use of a *specific* (surprisingly advantageous) antibody in the treatment of a *specific* disease, there are also circumstances where even the *same* therapeutic antibody could be claimed in the use of the *same* disease as disclosed in the prior art. This is the case, for example, when the new clinical situation is based on a new, previously not elucidated technical effect. Relevant decisions in this context are T 836/01 *Interferon-beta2/YEDA RESEARCH AND DEVELOPMENT CO. LTD.*[103] and T 1642/06 *Sigma receptor/SPRUCE/BARBARA, et al.*,[104] in which it was discussed whether a new technical effect alone is sufficient to establish novelty for a second/ further medical use of a known substance.

For example, in the patent underlying T 836/01 the use of interferon-β2 to directly influence tumour cell growth and (terminal) differentiation was considered novel over the prior art that discloses the use of interferon-β2 for the purpose of activating mature lymphoid cells exerting cytolytic T cell activity on cancer cells. Accordingly, here the novel clinical situation was based on a 'new technical effect'. Again, a claim based on a new technical effect of a known therapeutic antibody can only be considered novel if the new technical effect leads to a truly novel (and also inventive) industrial/commercial application arising from, for example, the opening of a new field of application, the healing of a different pathology/clinical situation or the creation of a distinct group or sub-group of subjects, or if the new use has to involve new physical means/measures for its practice.

The same approach was taken in T 406/06 *Stimulation of beta cell proliferation/ NOVO NORDISK*[105] and T 1955/09, *Antimicrobial peptides/OCTOPLUS SCIENCES*[106] (see also *Case Law of the Boards of Appeal*, 8th edition of 2016, I.C.7.2.4c, as well as the discussion in §1.04[E], *infra*).

[B] Mode of Administration

Enlarged Board of Appeal decision G 2/08 *Dosage regime/ABBOTT RESPIRATORY* clarified that novelty of claims directed to therapeutic uses of a known substance/ composition may be based not only on the treatment of a different disease but also on the treatment of the same disease by a different therapeutic method, e.g., different administration modes, different dosage regimens, different mechanisms or modes of action, or patient/subject selection. All that is required is that the distinction from the known treatment, for example the administration mode, is novel, inventive and sufficiently disclosed.

Also in the context of further technical features of medical use claims (administration schemes, dosages, patient groups, etc.), the most recent Guidelines of

---

103. Technical Board of Appeal, decision in T 836/01 of 7 October 2003, Interferon-*beta2/ YEDA RESEARCH AND DEVELOPMENT CO. LTD.*
104. Technical Board of Appeal, decision in T 1642/06 of 3 March 2009, *Sigma receptor/ SPRUCE/BARBARA, et al.*
105. Technical Board of Appeal, decision in T 406/06 of 16 January 2008, *Stimulation of beta cell proliferation/NOVO NORDISK.*
106. Technical Board of Appeal, decision in T 1955/09 of 12 June 2013, *Antimicrobial peptides/ OCTOPLUS SCIENCES.*

2018 propose formulations for claims (see part G-VI, 7.1.2). Table 1.3 indicates the corresponding antibody claims.

Table 1.3

Antibody X for use or Composition comprising Antibody X for use	in a method for the treatment of Y, or in the therapy of Y, or in a method of treating Y, or in a method of therapy of Y, or as a medicament defined by its function (e.g. as an anti-inflammatory medicament)	characterized in that or wherein	other features, for example: said Antibody X is administered topically, or three times daily or [...]

[C] Dosage Regimens

An important milestone in claiming second medical uses before the EPO was the acknowledgment that claims relating to treatment/dosage regimes are not merely an instruction to the attending physician how to perform his art and that they are not excluded from patentability by Article 53(c) EPC (corresponding to former Article 52(4) EPC1973). In particular, it was intensively discussed whether such treatment regimes could even confer patentability where the medical use of a given compound was already known.

In the early landmark decision T 1020/03 *Method of administration of IGF-1/ GENENTECH INC.*[107] it was held that 'any use to which Article 52(4) EPC[1973] first sentence applies in circumstances where the composition has already been suggested for some therapeutic use, allows a second medical use claim to the preparation of the composition for that second medical use, irrespective of in what detail that use was specified, subject to the use being novel and inventive. For the purposes of novelty also under Article 54(5) EPC this depends on whether use for therapy is novel, irrespective of the detail with which the therapy is stated in the claim' (Headnote).

Accordingly, this decision and also T 36/04 *DNA damaging agents and p53/ UNIVERSITY OF TEXAS*[108] from the same Board acknowledged that claim features

107. Technical Board of Appeal, decision in T 1020/03 of 29 October 2004, *Method of administration of IGF-1/GENENTECH INC.*, Headnote.
108. Technical Board of Appeal, decision in T 36/04 of 16 February 2006, *DNA damaging agents and p53/UNIVERSITY OF TEXAS.*

relating to a treatment regimen can establish novelty (and inventive step) and are not generally excluded from patentability. However, the Board in T 1319/04 *Dosage regimen/KOS LIFE SCIENCES*[109] was reluctant to share this view and referred corresponding questions to the Enlarged Board of Appeal. The resulting decision G 2/08 *Dosage regime/ABBOTT RESPIRATORY*[110] confirmed the patentability of treatment regimens. In particular, it was confirmed that dosage regimes may relate to a different technical teaching and may lead to a truly new (medical) situation.

Potential claim language for a 'dosage second medical use claim' as proposed in the Guidelines, part G-VI, 7.12 may be:

> 'Antibody X for use in the treatment of [specific] disease Y, whereby X is administered by the dosage regime Z'

Inventive step of such novel dosage regimes can also be based on better patient compliance. For example, in T 1074/06 *Infertility/ARS*[111] it was held that a new dosage regimen is novel and inventive over the prior art, since the proposed dosage regimen for FSH (follicle stimulating hormone) is more user friendly than the regimens of the prior art and that the corresponding regimen maintains good follicle growth.

[D] Specific Patient Groups

The first positive decision by the EPO on 'patient groups' was T 19/86 *Pigs/DUPHAR*[112] and several important cases followed, such as T 893/90 *Controlling bleeding/QUEEN'S UNIVERSITY KINGSTON,*[113] T 233/96 *Adrenaline/*MEDCO RESEARCH,[114] T 1399/04 *Combination therapy HCV/SCHERING,*[115] and T 734/12 *Arthritis patients with an inadequate response to a TNF-alpha/GENENTECH,*[116] in which the Boards confirmed that the use of the same compound in the treatment of the same disease for a particular group of subjects can nevertheless constitute a novel therapeutic application, provided that it is carried out in a new group of subjects which is distinguished from the former by its physiological or pathological status (see *Case Law of the Boards of Appeal*, 8th edition of 2016, I.C.7.2).

Accordingly, the Boards have found medical inventions in which a new group of subjects or a new sub-group of patients have been identified for medical intervention of a given disease with a known compound as patentable as long as the treatment of

109. Technical Board of Appeal, decision in T 1319/04 of 22 April 2008, *Dosage regimen/KOS LIFE SCIENCES*.
110. Enlarged Board of Appeal, decision in G 2/08 of 19 February 2010, *Dosage regime/ABBOTT RESPIRATORY*.
111. Technical Board of Appeal, decision in T 1074/06 of 9 August 2007, *Infertility/ARS*.
112. Technical Board of Appeal, decision in T 19/86 of 15 October 1987,*Pigs/DUPHAR*.
113. Technical Board of Appeal, decision in T 893/90 of 22 July 1993, *Controlling bleeding/ QUEEN'S UNIVERSITY KINGSTON*.
114. Technical Board of Appeal, decision in T 233/96 of 4 May 2000, *Adrenaline/MEDCO RESEARCH*.
115. Technical Board of Appeal, decision in T 1399/04 of 25 October 2006, *Combination therapy HCV/SCHERING*.
116. Technical Board of Appeal, decision in T 734/12 of 17 May 2013, *Arthritis patients with an inadequate response to a TNF-alpha/GENENTECH*.

this new (sub-) group of patients is novel and inventive. The new patient group to be treated should be clearly distinct from subjects treated in the prior art and it was held in several decisions of the EPO that the two groups must not overlap.

However, since T 1399/04,[117] the prior art patient groups may overlap to a certain extent with the patient group recited in the claim on condition that the pathological and physiological status of the novel patient group is different from the status of the patient group disclosed in the prior art (see also T 1044/14 *Method of treating prostate cancer/FERRING*[118] and T 734/12, discussed above).

Furthermore, it has been routinely held by the Boards that the distinction in the patient groups must not be arbitrary (whereby an 'arbitrary selection' would mean that no functional relationship exists between the particular physiological or pathological status of the selected, distinct group of subjects recited in the claim and the therapeutic or pharmacological effect achieved). Accordingly, the selection of the specific patient group must be based on a (plausible/credible) functional relationship between the physiological or pathological characteristics of the novel patient group to be treated and the obtained therapeutic effect.

It is recommended that the medical use claim before the EPO clearly and unambiguously defines the patient group to be treated. An interesting special case is the 'definition' of the patient to be treated as a specific *genetic* sub-population of individuals to be treated in accordance with the invention. Here, a method for the selection of the individualized patient group should be claimed and, furthermore, the genetic definition/molecular markers should be comprised in a corresponding 'use' claim. Such a claim could, for example, read as follows:

> 'Antibody X for use in the treatment/therapy of [specific] disease Y *in patients carrying allele/genetic marker Z*.'

However, it has to be noted that certain Examining Divisions of the EPO have raised novelty objections against medical use claims with such wordings.

[E] Specific Mode of Action

Also a medical use claim reciting a novel 'mode of action' or a novel technical effect may be considered as inventive by the EPO. For example, T 1229/03 *Estrogen compositions for neuroprotection/UNI FLORIDA*[119] concerned the use of estrogen compounds for treating a neurodegenerative disorder by protecting a population of nerve cells from death. The specific technical effect 'protecting nerve cells from death' was considered a novel feature. This protection was shown in the patent application as being directly linked to the claimed therapeutic use as well as to the estrogen compound(s). The Board was satisfied that the intended technical effect

117. Technical Board of Appeal, decision in T 1399/04 of 25 October 2006, *Combination therapy HCV/SCHERING*, Reason 35.
118. Technical Board of Appeal, decision in T 1044/14 of 1 February 2018, *Method of treating prostate cancer/FERRING*, Reason 7.
119. Technical Board of Appeal, decision in T 1229/03 of 23 November 2006, *Estrogen compositions for neuroprotection/UNI FLORIDA*.

was credibly disclosed in the application in a meaningful and plausible manner and had been proven by technical data obtained from several *in vitro* and *in vivo* tests.

Similarly, in T 1955/09 *Antimicrobial peptides/OCTOPLUS SCIENCES,*[120] the discussed claim related to the medical use of a specific peptide in the treatment of a bacterial or fungal infection 'by killing said bacteria or fungi' whereas the prior art disclosed the same peptide to 'neutralize toxins produced by bacteria or fungi'. Accordingly, the difference was a direct effect versus an indirect effect of the same peptide in the treatment of the same infections. The Board held that the attaining of a new technical effect ('killing of bacteria or fungi') is considered as a functional technical feature of a claim, referring to the new use of a known substance. Since this technical feature had not been previously made available to the public, the claim was considered novel even though such technical effect may have inherently taken place in the course of carrying out what was previously made available to the public.

Similar conclusions were also reached in a number of further decisions, including T 290/86 *Cleaning plaque/ICI,*[121] T 542/96 *Xylitol-Fluoride/COLGATE-PALMOLIVE,*[122] and T 1127/05 *Inhibition of angiogenesis/SCRIPPS RESEARCH INSTITUTE.*[123]

However, as illustrated and clarified in several decisions of the Technical Boards, such as in T 433/13 *Increasing neurogenesis/NEWRON,*[124] a new technical effect alone is not sufficient to establish novelty of a second medical use claim. The claimed therapeutic use may only be considered as novel if the new technical effect also leads to a truly new industrial/commercial application or activity, i.e. a truly novel clinical/medical situation such as the healing of a different pathology or the treatment of the same disease with the same compound in a new patient group (see also T 836/01 *Interferon-beta2/YEDA RESEARCH AND DEVELOPMENT CO. LTD.,*[125] T 486/01 *IGF-1/GENENTECH, INC., et al.,*[126] T 384/03 *Use of a carbonic anhydrase inhibitor/ADVANCED RESEARCH,*[127] T 406/06 *Stimulation of beta cell proliferation/ NOVO NORDISK,*[128] and T 1642/06, *Sigma receptor/SPRUCE/BARBARA, et al.*[129]).

---

120. Technical Board of Appeal, decision in T 1955/09 of 13 June 2013, *Antimicrobial peptides/ OCTOPLUS SCIENCES*, Reason 6.
121. Technical Board of Appeal, decision in T 290/86 of 13 November 1990, *Cleaning plaque/ ICI.*
122. Technical Board of Appeal, decision in T 542/96 of 11 May 2000, *Xylitol-Fluoride/ COLGATE-PALMOLIVE.*
123. Technical Board of Appeal, decision in T 1127/05 of 15 January 2008, *Inhibition of angiogenesis/SCRIPPS RESEARCH INSTITUTE.*
124. Technical Board of Appeal, decision in T 433/13 of 11 July 2017, *Increasing neurogenesis/ NEWRON.*
125. Technical Board of Appeal, decision in T 836/01 of 7 October 2003, *Interferon-beta2/ YEDA RESEARCH AND DEVELOPMENT CO. LTD.*
126. Technical Board of Appeal, decision in T 486/01 of 3 September 2003, *IGF-1/GENENTECH, INC., et al.*
127. Technical Board of Appeal, decision in T 384/03 of 17 January 2006, *Use of a carbonic anhydrase inhibitor/ADVANCED RESEARCH.*
128. Technical Board of Appeal, decision in T 406/06 of 16 January 2008, *Stimulation of beta cell proliferation/NOVO NORDISK.*
129. Technical Board of Appeal, decision in T 1642/06 of 23 August 2007, *Sigma receptor/ SPRUCE/BARBARA, et al.*

[F] Combinations with Other Active Ingredients

Medical use claims comprising the use of antibodies and further active ingredients are allowable by the EPO as long as the patentability requirements are fulfilled. Also these claims should be drafted in the 'medical use' format and a corresponding claim may read:

> 'Antibody X for use in treating disease Y, whereby antibody X is to be administered in combination with a medicament Z.'

However, the invention may also have its basis in the disclosure of 'medicament Z', and a corresponding claim would read:

> 'Medicament Z for use in treating disease Y, whereby medicament Z is to be administered in combination with antibody X.'

This different claim language may be of importance in national litigation proceedings, namely when a potential infringer markets a monopreparation of antibody X with a package leaflet prescribing its administration together with medicament Z which is separately offered by a different undertaking. In particular, it would seem that direct infringement could be asserted on the basis of the above-mentioned claim directed to antibody X, whereas there might only be indirect (contributory) infringement if the claim were directed to the 'combination of antibody X with medicament Z for use in treating disease Y' (see also the corresponding discussion in §3.04[F] in relation to Germany).

An antibody may also be claimed for a specific therapeutic use requiring the (co-) administration of physical means, such as irradiation. It is self-evident that for such a claimed combination the general patentability requirements of novelty, inventive step and enablement also need to be fulfilled.

In general, for inventions relating to combination approaches comprising antibodies, it is also highly recommended that the original specification comprises ample evidence for the technical effect achieved. The compounds (including the antibody) to be used should also be clearly defined and it should be disclosed how further embodiments can be obtained and/or how such potential embodiments can be tested.

For example, in T 352/07 *IL-6 Antagonist/CHUGAI SEIYAKU*,[130] an interleukin-6 (IL-6) antagonist/antibody was claimed 'for the use in enhancing the effect of an antitumor agent'. Examples of specific anti-IL-6 antibodies were provided in the specification, and as specific embodiment for the antitumour agent platinum compounds, such as cisplatinum, were mentioned. Yet, the Board contested the functional characterizations in the claim as not enabled and held that the 'functional feature of "platinum compound having antitumor effects" characterises a full research programme in itself and, therefore, cannot constitute a feature characterising a teaching which is sufficiently disclosed for the skilled person to carry it out'. Also the functional antibody characterization was considered as 'too broad' and there

130. Technical Board of Appeal, decision in T 352/07 of 4 February 2010, *IL-6 Antagonist/CHUGAI SEIYAKU*, Reasons 4.2 and 4.5.1.

was not enough 'guidance' on how to derive from the structural knowledge of the disclosed antibodies further 'antibodies within the meaning of the claimed teaching'. In particular in context of combination therapies with antibodies further decisions of the Technical Boards, like, e.g. T 542/03 *Combination/BERLEX*[131] or T 1243/12 *Treatment of autoimmune diseases/GENENTECH*[132] are of interest.

[G] Specific Diagnostic Applications

There are no specific limitations for claims relating to antibodies for *in vitro* uses or as *in vitro* diagnostics. Accordingly, novel and inventive diagnostic *in vitro* uses of antibodies conducted on (isolated) patient samples or corresponding screening/ analysis methods are patent eligible.[133] In contrast to the restrictive approach adopted in the USA, the fact that such methods may rely on 'laws of nature' (such as a relationship existing in nature between a specific genetic mutation and a predisposition for a certain disease) does not generally result in any exclusion from patentability, as also confirmed in T 80/05 *Method of diagnosis/UNIVERSITY OF UTAH*.[134]

However, it is notable that the corresponding claims should not comprise a recitation or a 'method step' of 'obtaining a sample from a patient'. This is considered by the EPO as a contravention of Article 53(c) EPC which provides that European patents shall not be granted for diagnostic methods practised on the human or animal body.

Yet, as for therapeutic/medical uses, a claim to a known antibody for the first (or second/further) use in a diagnostic method is allowable and must be drafted in the purpose-limited product format, such as:

> 'Antibody X for use in *in vivo* diagnostics'
>
> (the antibody is proposed for the first time as an *in vivo* diagnostic);

or

> 'Antibody X for use in the *in vivo* diagnosis of disease Y'
>
> (the antibody was already known in the art as an *in vivo* diagnostic but not for the specific diagnostic use specified in the claim; for example, novelty and inventive step may be based on a different physiological status/disease).[135]

---

131. Technical Board of Appeal, decision in T 542/03 of 14 July 2005, *Combination/BERLEX*.
132. Technical Board of Appeal, decision in T 1243/12 *Treatment of autoimmune diseases/ GENENTECH*.
133. The patent eligibility of *in vitro* diagnostic methods has been confirmed in a number of Board of Appeal decisions, including: Technical Board of Appeal, decision in T 666/05 of 13 November 2008, *Mutation/UNIVERSITY OF UTAH*; Technical Board of Appeal, decision in T 80/05 of 19 November 2008, *Method of diagnosis/UNIVERSITY OF UTAH*; and Technical Board of Appeal, decision in T 1328/08 of 10 May 2012, *Allergen-Microarray/ PHADIA*.
134. Technical Board of Appeal, decision in T 80/05 of 19 November 2008, *Method of diagnosis/ UNIVERSITY OF UTAH*.
135. For further information on the wording of diagnostic use claims see *Guidelines for Examination in the EPO*, parts G-II, 4.2 as well as G-VI, 7.1 and G-VI, 7.1.3. An exemplary decision in which second diagnostic use claims have been accepted is the Technical Board

For *in vitro* diagnostics, the 'for use' language is not necessary and not even accepted by the EPO. In cases where an antibody was previously known and where the invention lies in a novel *in vitro* method, the corresponding claim should *not* be formulated in the purpose-limited product format (as for medical uses), i.e. the claim should *not* read:

> 'Antibody X for use in the diagnosis of disease Y, or for use in the *in vitro/ex vivo* diagnosis of disease Y.'

As the Guidelines point out in part G-VI, 7.1.3, the claim recited above would lack novelty over the prior art disclosing either the antibody per se in a form which could be considered suitable for the claimed use, or disclosing its first medical/diagnostic application.

Such a claim could be reformulated as:

> 'Use of antibody X in the *in vitro/ex vivo* diagnosis of disease Y.'

If the application as filed discloses, either explicitly or implicitly, that the claimed diagnostic methods are to be carried out *in vivo*, the wording of the claims could also be limited to encompass only corresponding *in vivo* methods, as described above.

§1.05 ASSESSMENT OF INVENTIVENESS

[A] General Approach

Article 56 EPC stipulates that 'an invention shall be considered as involving an inventive step if, having regard to the state of the art, it is not obvious to a person skilled in the art'.

Whereas the assessment of inventive step is considered to be more subjective than the 'novelty test' by the EPO, the Boards of Appeal have developed the so-called 'problem-solution approach'[136] as a guidance tool, which is now widely applied in examination and opposition proceedings before the EPO.

Here, the closest prior art is determined, the technical effect resulting from the feature(s) distinguishing the claimed subject-matter from the closest prior art is established, and on this basis the corresponding objective technical problem solved by the claimed invention is formulated. It is then assessed whether or not the claimed invention, starting from the closest prior art, would have been obvious to a person skilled in the art attempting to solve the objective technical problem.

The problem-solution approach has been summarized in T 2438/09 *Detergent products/PROCTER*[137] as follows:

---

of Appeal decision in T 34/95 of 26 February 1999, *Diagnostic reagents/CALIFORNIA INSTITUTE OF TECHNOLOGY*.

136. For further guidance on the problem-solution approach, see *Guidelines for Examination in the EPO*, part G.VII.3.

137. Technical Board of Appeal decision in T 2438/09 of 16 March 2012, *Detergent products/PROCTER*, Reason 3, last paragraph.

> '[T]he problem solution-approach [is] normally applied by the Boards of Appeal for the assessment of inventive step. According to this approach inventiveness is assessed on the basis of a suitable piece of prior art and the effects actually achieved by the claimed invention when compared with that prior art, hence the effects achieved by those features which distinguish the claimed subject-matter from the prior art. These effects constitute the technical problem solved by the claimed invention in view of that prior art and it has to be examined whether it was obvious for a skilled person to solve that technical problem by those distinguishing features.'

Thus, in the assessment of inventive step, structural or functional differences between the claimed invention and the closest prior art are taken into account and it is elucidated whether or not the technical effect resulting from these differences would have been obvious. For this assessment, normally only one additional prior art document[138] and the common general knowledge of the skilled person may be taken into account.

[B] Particularities Regarding Claims to Antibodies

The general principles of the 'problem-solution approach' as discussed in §1.05[A] are also applied in the assessment of inventive step of antibody inventions. One of the decisive questions in this assessment is always whether the person skilled in the art would have had, on basis of the prior art, (a) an '*incentive to try*' the claimed technical solution with (b) a '*reasonable expectation of success*'.

As illustrated above, for example in the discussion of T 18/09 *Neutrokine/HUMAN GENOME SCIENCES*[139] in §1.02[A][1], when a novel and inventive antigen is provided in an invention, the applicant is also entitled to obtain protection of antibodies targeting said novel antigen.[140] However, this approach finds its limitations where it is not plausible from the application as filed that specific antibodies to said antigen may be obtained with 'routine methods known in the art'. On the other hand, inventive step of a claim to a novel antibody to a known antigen is typically contested by the EPO if there is no tangible reason to doubt that the novel antibody would have been obtainable by routine methods. Accordingly, and considering that the EPO does not accept a 'structural non-obviousness approach'[141] as applied in the USPTO, the mere provision of further antibodies with novel CDRs or novel

138. When assessing inventive step, the Divisions and Boards of the EPO typically consider only one further document in combination with the closest prior art. Note, however, that the possibility of combining more than two documents in the examination of inventive step is not generally excluded, as confirmed in: Technical Board of Appeal, decision in T 1149/09 of 24 October 2013, *Vaccinia virus formulation/BAVARIAN NORDIC*, Reason 43; and Technical Board of Appeal, decision in T 413/10 of 29 November 2012, *–/KAO*, Reason 7.9.
139. Technical Board of Appeal, decision in T 18/09 of 21 October 2009, *Neutrokine/HUMAN GENOME SCIENCES*.
140. See also, e.g., Technical Board of Appeal, decision in T 1902/11 of 11 December 2014, *Human IL-23/MERCK SHARP & DOHME*, Reason 56.
141. The EPO does not accept the principle of 'structural non-obviousness'; see, e.g., Technical Board of Appeal, decision in T 605/14 of 7 June 2018, *Anti-angiopoietin-2 antibodies/*

variable regions (such as humanized antibodies)[142] is not normally considered as inventive. It rather needs to be made plausible that these novel antibodies have an unexpected technical effect and/or superior properties for inventive step to be acknowledged. This principle was summarized in T 735/00 *Anti-CRP antibodies/ IATRON LABORATORIES, INC.*[143] as follows:

> 'The case law in this field acknowledges inventive step if and when there is evidence that a claimed monoclonal antibody prepared by routine methods shows unexpected properties (cf decision T 645/02[144] of 16 July 2003). If, however, there are no unexpected effects achieved with a further monoclonal antibody compared with a [prior art] monoclonal antibody with essentially the same properties as desired the case law denies inventive step (cf decision T 512/94[145] of 23 June 1998).'

The (technical) complexity of a task in the antibody or immunoglobulin field may also contribute to the evaluation of inventive step. This particularly holds true for production and purification processes. For example, in T 1280/08 *Immunoglobulin products/STATENS SERUM INSTITUT*,[146] the Board considered a process for purifying immunoglobulin G (IgG) from a crude immunoglobulin-containing plasma protein fraction and followed the patentee's argumentation for patentability in that the provision of a new process for purifying IgG from plasma was not an easy task due to the high complexity of the starting material and the fragility of the immunoglobulins. In particular, the Board was of the opinion that the claimed combination of various chromatographic steps was inventive since the effects caused by the presence of varying amounts of different dominant contaminants which have to be removed at an early stage, by the competition between higher charged proteins and IgG for the binding sites of ion exchange resins, and by the presence of lipoproteins were hard to predict.

MEDIMMUNE, Reason 24, and Technical Board of Appeal, decision in T 187/04 of 11 January 2007, *Antikörper/KREBSFORSCHUNGSZENTRUM*, Reason 11.

142. See, e.g., Technical Board of Appeal, decision in T 67/11 of 26 May 2014, *Humanized antibodies/CENTRO DE INMUNOLOGIA MOLECULAR*, Reason 19, where the Board of Appeal noted that a skilled person would have had an incentive to attempt the humanization of a potentially interesting therapeutic antibody. In the specific case at hand, however, the Board found that achieving this while maintaining the affinity and specificity of the original antibody would not have been straightforward and acknowledged inventive step.
143. Technical Board of Appeal, decision in T 735/00 of 23 March 2004, *Anti-CRP antibodies/ IATRON LABORATORIES, INC.*, Reason 26. Note that the corresponding findings of the Board in T 735/00 have been acknowledged to be 'established jurisprudence in the field of antibodies'; see Technical Board of Appeal, decision in T 605/14 of 7 June 2018, *Anti-angiopoietin-2 antibodies/MEDIMMUNE*, Reason 25.
144. Technical Board of Appeal, decision in T 645/02 of 16 July 2003, *Antikörper/ EBERHARD-KARLS-UNIVERSITÄT*.
145. Technical Board of Appeal, decision in T 512/94 of 23 June 1998, *Monoclonal antibody (OKT10)/ORTHO*.
146. Technical Board of Appeal, decision in T 1280/08 of 29 September 2010, *Immunoglobulin products/STATENS SERUM INSTITUT*, Reason 15.

In the opposition appeal decision T 386/08 *Humanized antibodies to the amyloid beta peptide/WASHINGTON UNIVERSITY*,[147] the experimental data provided in the opposed patent for a mouse antibody were considered sufficient to prove that corresponding humanized antibodies, as claimed in the patent at issue, exhibit the same biological functions and therefore solve the technical problem underlying the invention. The opponent's argument that binding affinity and biological function do not always correlate and that the existing data for a mouse antibody could therefore not be transferred to the claimed humanized antibodies was not accepted by the Board in the absence of any actual evidence relating specifically to the claimed antibodies.

In medical use claims not only the used compound/the antibody will be scrutinized in the context of inventive step but also the disease to be treated will be assessed. For example, in T 1317/13 *anti-IL-1β therapy/NOVARTIS*[148] the Board denied inventive step of a (second) medical use claim relating to a human IL-1β binding antibody as defined by concrete sequences in the treatment of an auto-inflammatory syndrome, in particular gout. The appellant/applicant held that the technical problem to be solved by the claimed invention was the provision of an improved medicament, as compared to colchicine, for the treatment of gout, gouty arthritis and pseudogout in a patient. Yet, the Board held that the closest prior art already taught the skilled person that: (i) increased production of IL-1β is the trigger for the autoinflammation in gout as in other auto-inflammatory diseases; (ii) administration of colchicine completely blocks the crystal-induced production of IL-1β and leads to greatly reduced inflammation; and (iii) gout patients were anticipated to benefit from treatments designed to block IL-1β. Accordingly, the Board concluded that the closest prior art suggests to the skilled person to treat gout by blocking IL-1β. The appellant further argued that anti-IL-1β antibodies had an additional effect on pain perception which was not reported in any of the cited prior art documents, which was however an effect that was indeed achieved by the antibody recited in the claim as demonstrated by post-published evidence. The Board was not convinced by this argument and held that the effect on pain perception, even if it may be an extra effect and may be unforeseen when implementing the treatment, is not an effect which contributes to the non-obviousness of the claimed treatment, also in light of the fact that the antibody recited in the claims had been known in the art and was described for blocking IL-1β in patients suffering in general from auto-inflammatory syndromes and the effect of this known antibody on pain perception cannot be considered as unexpected.

Attesting to the importance of antibodies in the medical sciences and in therapy, an impressive number of clinical trials with antibodies are ongoing and such trials are publicly announced very early.[149] Indeed, the public announcement of clinical trials is a legal requirement in most countries. The Boards of Appeal have now had

147. Technical Board of Appeal, decision in T 386/08 of 22 November 2010, *Humanized antibodies to the amyloid beta peptide/WASHINGTON UNIVERSITY*, Reasons 79 to 85.
148. Technical Board of Appeal, decision in T 1317/13 of 9 February 2018, *anti-IL-1β therapy/NOVARTIS*, Reasons 10 to 13.
149. See, for example, the webpage www.clinicaltrials.gov which is a database provided by the U.S. National Library of Medicine, documenting publicly and privately funded clinical studies conducted anywhere in the world.

several occasions to comment on the disclosure content of such announcements and have considered these publications in most cases as not detrimental for novelty. However, such announcements are seriously considered in the assessment of inventive step. In T 715/03 *Use of ziprasidone for treating Tourette's syndrome/PFIZER*[150] the prior art had mentioned that the compound to be used for the treatment of Tourette syndrome (ziprasidone) is undergoing clinical trials. However, the Board held that such an announcement of clinical trials or even mentioning that clinical trials are ongoing cannot be considered to anticipate the claimed second medical use. This is in line with decision T 1859/08 *Anti-ErbB2 antibodies/GENENTECH*[151] wherein it is confirmed that the mentioning of a clinical phase evaluation for a specific therapeutic application is not prejudicial to the novelty of a claim if the content of said mentioning does not allow any conclusion to be drawn with regard to the actual existence of a therapeutic effect or a pharmacological effect which directly and unambiguously underlies the claimed therapeutic application. Accordingly, the therapeutic effect is an important part of such 'second or further' medical use claims.

Accordingly, in light of the pertinent case law of the Technical Boards, if a prior art document discloses clinical investigations, such as phase I, II or III studies (or it is stated in the prior art that these investigations are ongoing), but fails to disclose the final result of these studies, it will normally not be novelty-destroying. However, such a disclosure is often considered as a relevant prior art reference for the assessment of inventive step. Therefore, it is recommended that, at the filing/priority date, a corresponding EP patent application should go beyond the content of clinical trial announcements and comprise data/information which documents surprising results of the clinical trial. Such results may, *inter alia*, be a specific combination therapy comprising the relevant antibody or a dosage regimen specifying how and/or when the antibody should be administered to the respective patient.

§1.06 ENFORCEMENT AND SCOPE OF PROTECTION

The EPO is the executive of the European Patent Organization and grants European patents for the Contracting States to the European Patent Convention (see also §1.01[A], *supra*). However, the EPO has neither jurisdiction on patent infringement nor on the revocation of national patents in the Contracting States. A granted European patent, being validated in the designated Contracting States in the form of 'national parts of a European patent', has to be separately litigated before the respective national courts, in accordance with Article 64(3) EPC.[152] This can be a costly and time consuming exercise.

However, the EPO possesses with its high quality opposition and appeal system a very attractive system to contest the validity of a granted European patent, providing the opportunity to have a European patent centrally revoked (or limited) with effect

150. Technical Board of Appeal, decision in T 715/03 of 16 January 2006, *Use of ziprasidone for treating Tourette's syndrome/PFIZER*.
151. Technical Board of Appeal, decision in T 1859/08 of 5 June 2012, *Anti-ErbB2 antibodies/ GENENTECH*, Reason 21.
152. Article 64(3) EPC provides that: 'Any infringement of a European patent shall be dealt with by national law.'

for all designated states, and without the considerable cost risk associated with national revocation actions in many Contracting States.

Thus, in accordance with Article 99 EPC, '[w]ithin nine months of the publication of the mention of the grant of the European patent in the European Patent Bulletin, any person may give notice to the European Patent Office of opposition to that patent'. This gives third parties the chance to question and contest the validity of a granted patent in one single proceeding for all designated states. In case the time period of nine months has been missed by third parties, separate national nullity or revocation proceedings, if appropriate and necessary, have to be instigated in the individual designated states.

The validity of a European patent that has undergone and 'survived' the opposition/appeal procedure before the EPO may again be challenged in one or more of the designated states via national revocation actions or invalidity counterclaims (where available), which typically occurs when the corresponding patent is enforced against an alleged infringer. In such cases, the Technical Board of Appeal decision with which the corresponding patent was maintained in opposition/appeal proceedings will typically be carefully considered by the national courts deciding on patent validity, particularly if the same arguments and/or the same prior art references are relied upon. To give but one example, in Germany it is established case law that a German court deciding on the validity of a patent is obliged to take into consideration any decision of a Division or Board of the EPO or of a national court in another Contracting State to the EPC, in which substantially the same issues have already been dealt with, and to scrutinize the reasoning underlying the corresponding decision, as confirmed by the German Federal Supreme Court in *Walzenformgebungsmaschine*.[153] Similarly, the UK Supreme Court in *Human Genome Sciences v. Eli Lilly* acknowledged that 'in a number of recent decisions of the House of Lords, attention has been drawn to "the importance of UK patent law aligning itself, so far as possible, with the jurisprudence of the EPO (and especially decisions of its Enlarged Boards of Appeal)"', and it further emphasized that 'where the Board has adopted a consistent approach to an issue in a number of decisions, it would require very unusual facts to justify a national court not following that approach'.[154]

Conversely, the EPO should, in principle, likewise consider the case law of its Contracting States in order to strive for a harmonized interpretation of the largely harmonized European patent laws. Indeed, when the Enlarged Board of Appeal rendered its very first decision[155] in G 5/83 *Second medical indication/EISAI* a few years after the EPO started operating, it emphasized that 'it is incumbent upon the European Patent Office, and particularly its Boards of Appeal, to take into consideration the decisions and expressions of opinion of courts and industrial property

153. German Federal Supreme Court, decision in Xa ZB 10/09 of 15 April 2010 – *Walzenformgebungsmaschine*.
154. UK Supreme Court, judgment in *Human Genome Sciences v. Eli Lilly* of 2 November 2011, [2011] UKSC 51.
155. The first seven referrals made to the Enlarged Board of Appeal, i.e. G 1/83 to G 7/83, all related to the patentability of second medical use claims and were decided together on 5 December 1984. Contrary to the current practice of the EPO, only the decisions in G 1/83 (in German), G 5/83 (in English) and G 6/83 (in French) have been published. They are substantially identical in content.

offices in the Contracting States'.[156] In practice, however, the Divisions and Boards of the EPO can at times be rather reluctant to study and consider national decisions cited by the parties to examination or opposition proceedings, often noting that the case law of different Contracting States is divergent and, therefore, 'the boards of appeal would be at a loss as to which interpretation to follow'.[157]

[A] Biosimilars

As explained above, the centralized opposition and appeal proceedings before the EPO provide a very attractive means to challenge the validity of any granted European patent with effect for all designated states. Therefore, and due to the cost-effectiveness of this system, companies developing biosimilars frequently make great efforts to attack originators' antibody patents in European opposition proceedings.

[B] Equivalence

Since the EPO is not involved in the national litigation of granted European patents, it is less concerned with the interpretation of the granted claims for the purpose of determining the 'scope of protection'. Yet, as a patent office entrusted primarily with search and examination, the EPO also scrutinizes the clarity of the claims (Article 84 EPC) and examines whether the wording of the claims goes beyond the scope of the original disclosure in the application as filed in order to ascertain that the claims are not impermissibly broadened (Article 123(2) EPC). In opposition proceedings before the EPO, the Opposition Divisions and the Technical Boards of Appeal furthermore ascertain that any amendments to the granted claims do not lead to a broadening of the scope of protection conferred by the patent (Article 123(3) EPC). This can be overly restrictive at times; see, e.g. T 972/04 *Arsenic trioxide formulations/SLOAN-KETTERING*[158] or T 223/11 *Ibandronic acid/HOFFMANN – LA ROCHE.*[159]

As laid down in Article 69(1) EPC, the extent of protection conferred by a European patent or a European patent application shall be determined by the claims. Nevertheless, the description and drawings shall be used to interpret the claims. Such an interpretation of the claims is necessary during search and examination but also in opposition and appeal proceedings. For example, when interpreting claims for the purpose of the search, the search will also take into consideration prior art incorporating technical features which are well-known equivalents to the technical features of the claimed invention, which may undermine inventive step.

Although the infringement of a European patent is generally dealt with under national law (Article 64(3) EPC), it is important to note that the consideration of

156. Enlarged Board of Appeal, decision in G 5/83 of 5 December 1984, *Second medical indication/EISAI*, Reason 6.
157. Technical Board of Appeal, decision in T 154/04 of 15 November 2006, *Estimating sales activity/DUNS LICENSING ASSOCIATES*, Reason 3.
158. Technical Board of Appeal, decision in T 972/04 of 11 May 2010, *Arsenic trioxide formulations/SLOAN-KETTERING*.
159. Technical Board of Appeal, decision in T 223/11 of 22 May 2012, *Ibandronic acid/HOFFMANN - LA ROCHE*.

'equivalents' in the determination of the scope of protection conferred by a granted European patent is explicitly prescribed in the European Patent Convention itself and is therefore mandatory for all Contracting States. Specifically, Article 2 of the 'Protocol on the Interpretation of Article 69 EPC', which forms an integral part of the EPC (see Article 164(1) EPC), provides that:

> *Equivalents*
>
> For the purpose of determining the extent of protection conferred by a European patent, due account shall be taken of any element which is equivalent to an element specified in the claims.

How exactly equivalents are to be considered when determining the scope of protection differs significantly between the different Contracting States and is discussed in more detail in the subsequent chapters on individual European states.

It may further be noted that the consideration of equivalents in the determination of the scope of protection is a matter of law and should therefore not require any clarifying statement in the patent specification. In line with this, when it comes to the adaptation of the description, the EPO typically requests that statements relating to equivalents should be deleted. This is also reflected in the Guidelines, which explain in part F-IV, 4.4 that general statements in the description which imply that the extent of protection may be expanded in some vague and not precisely defined way are not allowed. In particular, any statement which refers to the extent of protection being expanded to cover the 'spirit of the invention' or 'all equivalents' of the claims must be deleted.

In opposition proceedings, the EPO does not determine the extent of protection of a granted European patent, albeit in the context of the above-mentioned assessment whether an amendment to a granted claim results in an extension of the scope of protection conferred by the patent as originally granted (Article 123(3) EPC) or whether the scope established by claim construction encompasses embodiments which are not novel, enabled or inventive. The consideration of 'equivalents', however, is entirely in the hands of the national courts.

Chapter 2

France

Cyra Nargolwalla & Isabelle Labarre

§2.01 ANTIBODIES AS PATENTABLE SUBJECT-MATTER

[A] Legal Framework

In France, Article L611-18 of the Intellectual Property Code (IPC) was amended in 2004 to implement Directive 98/44/EC of 6 July 1998 regarding legal protection of biotechnological inventions. Article L611-18 IPC restricts the protection of inventions relating to an element of the human body to the extent necessary for the implementation and exploitation of the particular use disclosed in the patent application. The particular use must be disclosed in a concrete and precise manner. The scope of protection of patent claims to human sequences is thus limited to the specific uses which are disclosed in the patent application.

There is no specific legal framework relative to the patentability of antibodies in France. The criteria applied by examiners of the French Patent & Trademark Office (INPI, French PTO) are usually the same criteria applied by the examiners of the European Patent Office (EPO).

Antibodies are considered to be patentable subject-matter in France. Therefore, the term 'isolated', 'chimeric', 'humanized', 'human' 'monoclonal' and/or 'polyclonal' is not necessary to distinguish the claimed antibody from a 'product of nature', i.e. naturally occurring antibodies. Such terms may however be necessary to distinguish the claimed antibody from the prior art, e.g. 'chimeric', 'humanized', or 'human', when a murine antibody against the same antigen is already known.

It is also possible to claim the use of an antibody. When the use concerns the treatment or the diagnosis of a disease, the wording of the claims must be in a specific form. Article L611-16 IPC specifically excludes from patentability the methods for treatment of the human or animal body and diagnostic methods practised on the human or animal body. However, this provision does not apply to products, in particular substances or compositions, for use in any of these methods. Hence, said use claims must be drafted in the following format: 'An antibody X for its use for [treatment/diagnosis]'.

[B] General Amenability or Exclusion of Antibodies from Patentability

Antibodies are not excluded from patentability in France.

[C] Required Distinction from Naturally Occurring Antibodies

There is no need for such a distinction in France.

§2.02 ACCEPTABLE CLAIM FEATURES FOR DEFINING ANTIBODIES

Antibodies can be defined by functional and/or structural features. For example, an antibody can be defined by antigen specificity, a target epitope, an activity, CDRs, sequences, a hybridoma or by a process of production.

Such features can be used to confer novelty on an antibody claimed *per se*. Sufficiency of disclosure and inventiveness of such claims are discussed respectively in §2.03 and §2.05 *infra*. Novelty of claims pertaining to the use of antibodies are discussed in §2.04 *infra*.

[A] Functional Features

[1] Target/Antigen

If the target/antigen X is new, an antibody can be defined by its binding to this new target. Such claims usually read as follows: 'An antibody which binds to the target X', 'An antibody directed against antigen X', or 'An antibody that is reactive to antigen X'.

[2] Mode of Binding: Target Affinity, Binding Specificity, Epitope, Definitions via Reference Antibodies and Competitive Binding

Generally speaking, it is possible to claim an antibody by indicating a specific property, as long as this specific property is not known from the prior art. There is no need to define the antibody by another feature, notably a structural feature, for example by also referring to the sequence of CDRs. The specific property can be a high affinity, a reduced cross-reactivity, a cross-reaction with multiple antigens, an unexpected physiological activity (e.g. internalization of the antibody), antibody's reactivity, biological properties, competition for binding with another antibody, agonist/antagonist properties due to the binding to a specific epitope, selective binding one antigen rather than another, *in vivo* effects, and so on.

Therefore, it may be possible to claim a general group of antibodies which possess a specific property by defining them solely in functional terms, provided that the functional features are clear.

It is also possible to claim an antibody by indicating the epitope to which the antibody binds. An epitope is generally defined by reference to its amino acid sequence within the antigen sequence. Such epitope can be linear or discontinuous/conformational. When the epitope is linear, the claim usually reads as follows: 'An antibody that specifically binds to a peptide of amino acid sequence of SEQ ID NO: 1'. When the epitope is discontinuous/conformational, the claim may read as follows: 'An antibody that specifically binds to antigen X, wherein the epitope comprises amino acid residues from position [to be identified] to position [to be identified], and amino acid residues from position [to be identified] to position [to be identified], the positions being identified by reference to the amino acid sequence of antigen X as represented in SEQ ID NO: 1'.

The epitope may also be defined functionally., For example, an antibody can thus be claimed by reference to a specific monoclonal antibody which binds to the same epitope. Such claims may read as follows: 'A monoclonal antibody that competes with monoclonal antibody Y for binding to antigen/epitope X' or 'A monoclonal antibody that specifically binds to the same epitope on antigen X as monoclonal antibody Y', provided that these antibodies are novel.

[3] Effect on Target

An antibody can be defined by its effect on a target. Moreover, it may be possible to claim a general group of antibodies which achieve a specific effect, provided that this specific effect is clear. Indeed, allowance of such a claim depends on how the specific effect is disclosed. The effect on the target has to be clearly described in the patent application for a claim to be considered allowable. For example, if the claim reads 'An antibody that neutralizes at least 70% of the binding of the protein X and its ligand Y', such a claim is usually considered allowable, provided that the patent application clearly describes the ligand. On the contrary, if the claim reads 'An antibody that neutralizes at least 70% of the binding of the protein X and its ligand', such a claim would be considered unallowable, because the ligand is not clearly identified or unknown. The same applies to a claim reading 'An antibody that neutralizes at least 95% of the biological activity of the protein X'. Such a claim might be considered as unclear because the biological activity is not explicit, and because a protein may possess different biological activities.

Antibodies can also be defined by agonistic or antagonistic effects. However it is necessary to define a specific method to determine whether or not an antibody possesses said agonistic or antagonistic effect.

[B] Structural Features

[1] Molecular Topology: Antibody Types, Fragments and Antibody Constructs

Even if a polyclonal antibody against a target X is known in the prior art, it is still possible to claim a monoclonal antibody against the same target (provided that unexpected properties are associated with the monoclonal antibody).

Antibody types are well-known and it is acceptable to define an antibody by simply referring to 'a murine', 'a chimeric', 'a humanized' or 'a human' antibody against an antigen X.

Fragments such as Fab, F(ab)'$_2$, and their obtention, is usually considered a routine method. Therefore, it is possible to claim a fragment Fab or F(ab)'$_2$, as long as the full antibody is not required to achieve the technical effect (notably due to the presence of the Fc fragment).

Other fragments, such as scFv, or antibody constructs such as diabody, or triabody are patentable, but a specific sequence seems to be required (otherwise, examiners consider that the claim is unclear and/or lacks technical features).

[2] Amino Acid Sequences

[a] Full-Length Sequences of Antibodies

An antibody can be defined by its full-length sequences. The novelty of such an antibody is recognized if the sequences are unknown in the prior art. Such a claim usually reads as follows: 'An antibody against X comprising a heavy chain of SEQ ID NO: 1 and a light chain of SEQ ID NO: 2'.

[b] Sequences of Fragments, CDRs and Framework Regions

When an antibody is characterized by its CDRs, the provision of the six CDRs is often considered as a minimum requirement, unless a specific technical effect may be shown to be associated with fewer CDRs.

In some cases, the mention of the framework regions in the claims may be necessary, e.g. when the mention of the six CDRs is not considered as a minimum requirement (it is generally the case when the framework region also plays a role in the binding affinity).

In such cases it may be relevant to define the antibody by referring to –at least- the sequences of the variable domains. The novelty of such an antibody is recognized if the sequences are unknown in the prior art. Such a claim usually reads as follows: 'An antibody against X comprising a heavy chain variable domain of SEQ ID NO: 1 and a light chain variable domain of SEQ ID NO: 2'.

[3] Chemical Modifications, Conjugation and Glycosylation

It is possible to claim an antibody comprising a chemical modification (e.g. a chemical modification of a residue to modify the stability of the antibody), or an antibody conjugate (such as an antibody drug conjugate or an antibody-toxin conjugate).

It is also possible to claim antibodies with specific levels of fucosylation (from 0 to 100%) or specific glycosylation patterns. However, there seems to be a tendency in France where examiners often raise an objection when the antibody is defined by a specific level of fucosylation. Examiners often consider that a 'result to be achieved' is claimed. Such an objection can usually be contested by arguing that a fucosylation level is a technical feature, provided that a specific method of measurement of the fucosylation level is disclosed in the patent application.

[C] Cell Line Deposits and Process of Production

An antibody can be defined by reference to a hybridoma. However, the hybridoma must be deposited at a recognized international depositary institution, according to the Budapest Treaty, before the filing date of the patent application (Article L612-5 IPC). Such a claim usually reads as follows: 'An antibody against antigen X as produced by the hybridoma cell deposited at [name of the recognized international depositary institution] on [date of filing] under [accession number]'.

An antibody can also be defined by a process of production. Such a claim may read as follows: 'An antibody against antigen X produced by the immunization of [an animal, usually a rabbit]' with the antigen X'.

§2.03 BREADTH OF CLAIMS AND SUPPORT BY EXAMPLES

[A] Acceptable Breadth of Claims to Antibodies

Generally speaking, patentability of antibodies mainly depends on the prior art at the date of filing the patent application. When the target X is new, as well as the antibody against this target, a broad scope of protection is usually allowable. On the contrary, the scope of protection decreases, sometimes to protect only one specific antibody, when antibodies against the same antigen are already disclosed in the prior art.

[B] Required Experimental Support for Claims to Functionally Defined Antibodies

When the target X is new, an antibody against X is usually considered sufficiently disclosed, so long as the antigen is sufficiently identified and/or disclosed in the patent application. The French PTO does not require such antibodies to be exemplified, because it is now considered routine to obtain antibodies.

When an antibody is defined by a specific property, it is highly recommended to provide in the specification of the patent application an assay that can be used to screen for the property, and to provide at least one example of an antibody possessing this specific (and unexpected) property. For example, when an antibody is defined by a specific affinity, the patent application should provide at least one method of measurement of the affinity, as well as a process of production of such antibodies.

When an antibody is defined by an effect, it is necessary to define a specific method to determine whether or not an antibody possesses said effect. The patent application must also describe a process for obtaining antibodies having this effect, which can be performed without undue burden for the person skilled in the art.

When an antibody is defined by a specific function, such as 'An antibody that neutralizes at least 70% of the activity of the protein X', the patent application should provide experimental data that support the claimed function, as well as a process of production of such antibodies. Otherwise the invention may be considered as being insufficiently disclosed.

When an antibody is defined by reference to an epitope, such an epitope must be clearly identified. This is easier when the epitope is linear because the specific sequence of the epitope can be fully identified. Indeed, a linear epitope is usually a small sequence, well defined within the full-length sequence of the antigen. On the contrary, when the epitope is discontinuous/conformational, the full characterization of the epitope is difficult to achieve. For the discontinuous/conformational epitope to be considered sufficiently disclosed, the different parts of the epitope must be clearly identified, as well as their positions within the full-length sequence of the antigen.

When an antibody is defined by a process of production, comprising notably an immunization step with an antigen, the process must be reproducible to obtain the claimed antibody without undue burden (meaning, for example, that the antigen is sufficiently immunogenic).

[C] Required Experimental Support for Claims to Structurally Defined Antibodies

When an antibody is defined by sequences, the sequences which are considered essential for binding to the target have to be claimed. Usually the mention of at least all six CDRs is required. Sometimes, another feature may, in addition, be required.

When the patentability of the antibodies relies on unexpected properties, it is usually required to provide experimental data with several antibodies possessing these unexpected properties in order to obtain a broad scope of protection.

§2.04 SPECIFIC MEDICAL APPLICATIONS AND OTHER FOLLOW-UP INVENTIONS

[A] Treatment of Specific Diseases

The use of an antibody against X for the treatment of a specific disease is patentable, whether or not the antigen X is known, and whether or not the antibody against X is already known. In order for the claim not to be considered as applying to a method of treatment, such claim must be drafted in the following format: 'Antibody against X for use in the treatment of Y [i.e. specific disease]'.

[B] Mode of Administration

INPI considers that a mode of administration of a substance is a method of treatment and is therefore unpatentable.

[C] Dosage Regimens

The patentability of dosage regimens in France is uncertain. In a 2010 decision, the first instance court (TGI of Paris) held that a Swiss claim directed to a specific dosage was excluded from patentability, since it concerned a method for treatment by therapy (TGI of Paris, 3rd chamber, 1st section, 28 September 2010, No. 07/16296, *Actavis v. Merck*). However, this decision was reversed on appeal (Appeal Court of Paris, 30 January 2015, No. 10/19659, *Merck v. Actavis*). In this case, the patent was revoked for lack of novelty, but the appeal judgement positively acknowledged the possibility to obtain a patent for a second medical use, even if this medical use relates to a new dosage.

[D] Specific Patient Groups

French case law admits the patentability of claims limited to a specific patient group. Therefore, the use of an antibody against X for the treatment of a specific group of patients is patentable, provided that the new group of patients is distinguished from the former by its physiological or pathological status. The identification of a new specific group of patients is considered as a novel therapeutic application.

[E] Specific Mode of Action

When the specific mode of action merely explains the mechanism behind the use of the antibody already disclosed in the prior art, it is not possible to patent an antibody by reference to its specific mode of action.

However, the knowledge of a specific mode of action can lead to a patentable invention, for example when it makes it possible to identify a specific patient group. Claims should then refer to this specific group of patients in order to be patentable.

[F] Combinations with Other Active Ingredients

It is possible to claim a combination of an antibody with other active ingredients, such as specific drugs. Such a claim may read as follows: 'Composition comprising an antibody against X and another active ingredient, such as [to be completed]'. When the antibody *per se* is new and inventive, the patentability applies *mutatis mutandis* to a composition comprising such antibody. Patentability of such compositions may also result from a technical effect, e.g. due to the synergy/advantageous effect between the antibody and another drug.

[G] Specific Diagnostic Applications

The use of an antibody against X for the diagnosis of a specific disease is patentable, whether or not the antigen X is known, and whether or not the antibody against X is already known. In order for the claim not to be considered as applying to a method of diagnosis, such claim must be drafted in the following format: 'Antibody against X for use in the diagnosis of Y [i.e. specific disease]'. An antibody can also be claimed for *in vitro* diagnostics.

§2.05 ASSESSMENT OF INVENTIVENESS

[A] General Approach

The provisions regarding inventiveness at INPI are similar to those applied at the EPO. An important difference is that the French PTO can only reject a patent application for lack of novelty but not for lack of inventiveness. Indeed, inventiveness is not examined during the substantive examination before the French PTO. However, lack of inventiveness still remains a ground for revocation of the patent in France, e.g. in a law suit before a French court.

The situation may evolve in the near future. Indeed, a bill called 'PACTE', (i.e. 'Plan d'Action pour la Croissance et la Transformation des Entreprises', meaning 'Action Plan for Business Growth and Transformation') was passed on in April 2019. This Bill proposes to modify the French Intellectual Property Code to extend the scope of examination by the French PTO, by giving it the possibility to reject a patent application for lack of inventiveness. This bill also introduces opposition proceedings before French PTO.

[B] Particularities Regarding Claims to Antibodies

An antibody directed against a new antigen X is usually considered to be inventive. In this situation both the antigen X and the antibody against X were unknown before filing of the patent application.

When the antigen X is known but the antibody against X is not known *per se*, the inventiveness is more difficult to argue. Indeed, it is now considered straightforward to obtain antibodies, so no inventiveness is recognized for providing a new antibody, unless:

1. it can be proven that the antibody against X was in fact difficult to obtain (e.g. low expectation of success), and/or
2. if the antibody against X possesses an unexpected property.

When an antibody is defined by simply referring to a specific property, this property must be unexpected for the inventiveness to be recognized. Unexpected properties may be for example: an unexpected affinity, a low cross-reactivity, a cross-reaction with multiple antigens, an unexpected physiological activity, antibody's reactivity, biological properties, competition for binding with another antibody, agonist/antagonist properties due to the binding to a specific epitope, selective binding of one antigen rather than another, *in vivo* effects, and so on. For example, if an antibody is defined by a specific affinity, it is highly recommended to provide experimental data that compare an antibody according to the invention *versus* an antibody having a lower affinity.

In the case of an antibody defined by its epitope, the provision of the sequence of the epitope is usually not sufficient to recognize inventiveness. It is necessary to demonstrate that some unexpected and/or advantageous property is associated with the binding to this epitope.

When an antibody is defined by its sequences (full-length, variable domain, CDRs, etc.), acknowledgement of inventiveness usually depends on whether an unexpected effect or property is achieved by an antibody having these specific sequences. Usually the provision of new sequences is not sufficient for inventiveness to be recognized.

When the antigen X and the antibody against X are both known, it is still possible to protect the use of the antibody against X. Inventiveness can be recognized for the treatment of a specific disease, for use in a vaccine, for use in a diagnosis method, and so on.

§2.06 ENFORCEMENT AND SCOPE OF PROTECTION

[A] Biosimilars

To date there is no case law in France relative to the biosimilar of an antibody.

Anyway, a (valid) patent covering the reference biological medicinal of the biosimilar should preclude the marketing of the biosimilar medicinal product before the expiry of a patent, without prior agreement of the patent holder.

[B] Equivalence

The doctrine of equivalents is generally recognized in France. Even if there is no literal infringement of the claims, due to (minor) differences between the allegedly infringing product and the subject matter of the claims, the patentee may argue that there is infringement by equivalence.

According to French doctrine, means having a different structure are equivalent when they perform the same function to achieve the same result, provided that said function performed by the claimed means is novel.

The doctrine of equivalents applies to all categories of inventions, including pharmaceutical cases. Therefore the doctrine of equivalents could be applied to a claim relative to an antibody or its use.

Chapter 3

Germany

Oswin Ridderbusch

§3.01 ANTIBODIES AS PATENTABLE SUBJECT-MATTER

[A] Legal Framework

In Germany, the most important national laws on patents and utility models are provided in the German Patent Act (Patentgesetz, 'PatG')[1] and the German Utility Model Act (Gebrauchsmustergesetz, 'GebrMG'), respectively. Further pertinent provisions can be found in the German Patent Ordinance (Patentverordnung, 'PatV'), including the formal requirements for sequence listings which are set out in Section 11 PatV and the corresponding Annex 1 PatV. While European patents are governed by the European Patent Convention (*see* §1.01[A] above), additional legal provisions on the German part of European patents are provided in the German Act on International Patent Treaties (Gesetz über internationale Patentübereinkommen, 'IntPatÜG'). Practical information and guidance can furthermore be found in the Guidelines for the Examination Procedure[2] issued by the German Patent and Trademark Office in German and English.

There are no German national legal provisions dealing specifically with antibodies. The patentability of biological material and elements of the human body, however, has been regulated in the European Union by Directive 98/44/EC on biotechnological inventions (the 'Biotech Directive'), which came into force in 1998 and was transposed into German national law in 2005.

1. An English translation of the German Patent Act and related German legislation can be found online at: https://www.dpma.de/english/our_office/law/index.html.
2. The most recent edition of the Guidelines for the Examination Procedure (P 2796/3.19) was issued by the German Patent and Trademark Office on 11 January 2019 and entered into force on 1 March 2019.

With respect to antibodies, Sections 1a(1) and 1a(2) PatG are particularly relevant, which implement Articles 5(1) and 5(2) of the Biotech Directive and provide that:

(1) The human body, at the various stages of its formation and development, including germ cells, and the simple discovery of one of its elements, including the sequence or partial sequence of a gene, cannot constitute patentable inventions.

(2) An element isolated from the human body or otherwise produced by means of a technical process, including the sequence or partial sequence of a gene, may constitute a patentable invention even if the structure of that element is identical to the structure of a natural element.

These provisions have primarily clarifying character,[3] as German law does not exclude any elements of the human body or any biomolecules from patentability.[4] The notion in Section 1a(1) PatG that the 'simple discovery' of elements of the human body cannot constitute a patentable invention merely reflects the general distinction between unpatentable discoveries and patentable inventions.[5]

The German Patent Act includes further legal provisions on genetic material, which have been introduced in order to implement the Biotech Directive, including in particular Section 1(2) PatG,[6] Section 1a(3),[7] Section 1a(4) PatG,[8] and Sections 9a to 9c PatG.[9] It should be noted that the term 'biological material' as used in these provisions does not relate to any material of biological origin but rather to genetic material as well as cells, tissues and organisms containing genetic material, as it is defined in Section 2a(3)(1) PatG to mean 'any material containing genetic information and capable of reproducing itself or being reproduced in a biological system'. The

---

3. *See* also recital 20 of the Biotech Directive 98/44/EC.
4. This is also reflected in recital 15 of the Biotech Directive 98/44/EC, which acknowledges that 'no prohibition or exclusion exists in national or European patent law (Munich Convention) which precludes a priori the patentability of biological matter'.
5. *See* also recital 16 of the Biotech Directive 98/44/EC.
6. Section 1(2) PatG provides that:

   Patents shall be granted for inventions within the meaning of subsection (1) even if they concern a product consisting of or containing biological material or a process by means of which biological material is produced, processed or used. Biological material which is isolated from its natural environment or produced by means of a technical process can also be the subject of an invention even if it previously occurred in nature.
7. Section 1a(3) PatG provides that:

   The industrial application of a sequence or partial sequence of a gene shall be disclosed in the application specifying the function performed by the sequence or partial sequence.
8. Section 1a(4) PatG provides that:

   If the invention concerns a sequence or partial sequence of a gene whose structure corresponds to that of a natural sequence or partial sequence of a human gene, the patent claim shall include its use for which industrial application is disclosed pursuant to subsection (3).
9. Sections 9a to 9c PatG further specify the effects of the patent as defined in Sec. 9 PatG. In particular, Sec. 9a(3) PatG provides that:

   Where the patent concerns a product which contains or consists of genetic information as a result of an invention, the effects of section 9 shall extend to all material in which the product is incorporated and in which the genetic information is contained and performs its function. Section 1a (1) shall remain unaffected.

Higher Regional Court of Düsseldorf in its judgment in I-2 U 98/11[10] found that the amino acid lysine does not contain any genetic information and does therefore not constitute 'biological material' within the meaning of the Patent Act (and the Biotech Directive). This finding should likewise hold true for antibodies which do not contain genetic information and should therefore not be regarded as 'biological material' within the specific meaning of Section 2a(3)(1) PatG.

Notably, for inventions concerning the natural sequence (or partial sequence) of a human gene, Section 1a(4) PatG requires that the corresponding claims must recite the use of that sequence for an industrial application.[11] Since the recitation of a use feature in a product claim is normally interpreted to mean that the claimed product must merely be *suitable* for the recited use but that the claim is not actually limited to that specific use,[12] it could be held that the recitation of an industrial application of a human gene in a product claim should not necessarily result in a limitation of the claim. On the other hand, it has to be taken into account that the German legislator's intention underlying the introduction of Section 1a(4) PatG was precisely to abolish absolute product protection for human gene sequences and to limit the protection conferred by a corresponding patent to the specific use recited in the claim.[13]

The requirement under Section 1a(4) PatG is highly controversial and does not have any direct counterpart in the Biotech Directive, which merely requires in Article 5(3) that the industrial application of a sequence or partial sequence of a gene must be disclosed in the patent application but does not require that the claims should be limited accordingly. Since the European Patent Convention does not impose any requirement corresponding to Section 1a(4) PatG (*see* §1.01[A] above, and Rule 29 EPC), it may seem preferable to file a European patent rather than a German national patent in order to secure absolute product protection for nucleic acids corresponding to the natural sequence or partial sequence of a human gene without having to recite a specific use of such nucleic acids in the claims.

There is, however, an important caveat to such an approach. Under Section 9a(3) PatG (which implements Article 9 of the Biotech Directive and is applicable to both German national patents and the German parts of European patents[14]), where a patent concerns a product that contains or consists of genetic information, the effects of the patent extend to all materials in which the product is incorporated and in which the genetic information is contained *and performs its function*. Conversely, as confirmed by the CJEU in *Monsanto v. Cefetra* (C-428/08),[15] the effects of a patent

10. Higher Regional Court of Düsseldorf, decision in I-2 U 98/11 of 18 July 2013.
11. It is arguable whether the use that must be recited in the claims can simply be the indication that the claimed gene sequence encodes a specific polypeptide, or whether an actual industrial application of the encoded polypeptide must also be recited in the claims.
12. *See*, e.g., German Federal Supreme Court, decision in Xa ZR 140/05 of 28 May 2009 – *Bauschalungsstütze*; and German Federal Supreme Court, decision in X ZR 121/88 of 12 July 1990 – *Befestigungsvorrichtung II*.
13. *See* printed document 15/4417 of the German Federal Parliament (*Bundestag*) of 1 December 2004 (available online at: http://dipbt.bundestag.de/doc/btd/15/044/1504417.pdf).
14. Articles 2(2) and 64 EPC.
15. Court of Justice of the European Union, *Monsanto Technology LLC v. Cefetra BV and others*, C-428/08 of 6 July 2010.

with a product claim reciting a gene sequence do not extend to a corresponding product in which the gene sequence does not perform its function (as disclosed in the patent specification), which also applies to European patents with product claims for gene sequences that do not expressly recite any use limitation. Arguably, it would thus seem that the presumed advantage of obtaining a European patent having product claims reciting nucleic acids without any specific use limitation, rather than a German national patent with a corresponding use limitation, might not translate into any actual difference in the protection conferred by such patents, given that their effects are limited in the same manner by Section 9a(3) PatG.

The deposit of biological material is regulated by Section 34(8) PatG and specifically by the German Ordinance on the Deposit of Biological Material in Patent and Utility Model Proceedings (Verordnung über die Hinterlegung von biologischem Material in Patent- und Gebrauchsmusterverfahren, 'BioMatHintV'), which was issued in 2005 and is partly based on the Biotech Directive. Germany is also a contracting party to the Budapest Treaty.[16]

Under Section 2a(1) no. 2 PatG,[17] methods for the treatment of the human or animal body by therapy or surgery as well as diagnostic methods practised on the human or animal body are excluded from patentability; this exclusion, however, does not apply to products for use in any one of these methods. For a claim directed to a substance or composition for use in one of these methods, the corresponding specific use recited in the claim is taken into account for the assessment of novelty and inventive step, which follows from Sections 3(3) and 3(4) PatG.[18] The German national provisions of Sections 2a(1) no. 2, 3(3) and 3(4) PatG are equivalent to the corresponding European provisions of Articles 53(c), 54(4) and 54(5) EPC (*see* §1.01[A] above).

Not only patents but also German national utility models are available for second medical uses.[19] German utility models are granted without prior substantive examination and offer a maximum term of protection of only ten years.

---

16. Budapest Treaty on the International Recognition of the Deposit of Microorganisms for the Purposes of Patent Procedure. Practical information on the making of deposits under the Budapest Treaty is provided in the 'Guide to the Deposit of Microorganisms under the Budapest Treaty' published by WIPO, which is accessible online at: https://www.wipo.int/treaties/en/registration/budapest/guide/.
17. Section 2a(1) no. 2 PatG provides that:

    [Patents shall not be granted for] methods for the treatment of the human or animal body by surgery or therapy and diagnostic methods practised on the human or animal body. This shall not apply to products, in particular to substances or compositions, for use in one of these methods.
18. Sections 3(3) and 3(4) PatG provide that:

    (3) Subsections (1) and (2) shall not exclude the patentability of any substance or composition, comprised in the state of the art, for use in a method referred to in section 2a (1) no. 2, provided that its use for any such method is not comprised in the state of the art.

    (4) Subsections (1) and (2) shall also not exclude the patentability of any substance or composition referred to in subsection (3) for any specific use in a method referred to in section 2a (1) no. 2, provided that such use is not comprised in the state of the art.
19. German Federal Supreme Court, decision in X ZB 7/03 of 5 October 2005 – *Arzneimittelgebrauchsmuster*.

[B] General Amenability or Exclusion of Antibodies from Patentability

Antibodies as well as other biomolecules, including nucleic acids and proteins, are generally patentable in Germany.

This is in accordance with Sections 1(2) and 1a(2) PatG (*see* §3.01[A] above) and has been expressly confirmed by the German Federal Supreme Court in *Rezeptortyrosinkinase*[20] for product claims directed to certain nucleic acids of human origin, the polypeptides encoded by these nucleic acids, and antibodies which are specific for the corresponding polypeptides. According to the Federal Supreme Court, even if the provision of these molecules is the only technical teaching embodied by the respective product claims, this is sufficient to render these claims patent-eligible. Notably, the Court rejected the notion that the claimed biomolecules should have to be characterized as 'isolated' or as being obtained by a technical process in the corresponding product claims. It also stressed that, contrary to the approach adopted by the US Supreme Court in *Mayo v. Prometheus*,[21] a technical teaching that utilizes the discovery of a law of nature does not require any additional 'inventive surplus' to be patent-eligible.

Therefore, the question of whether claims directed to antibodies or other biomolecules are patent-eligible is typically entirely unproblematic in Germany.

[C] Required Distinction from Naturally Occurring Antibodies

There is no provision in German law that would, in general, render naturally occurring antibodies or any other naturally occurring biomolecules unpatentable.

On the contrary, Section 1a(2) PatG expressly clarifies that an element isolated from the human body or otherwise produced by means of a technical process can indeed constitute a patentable invention 'even if the structure of that element is identical to the structure of a natural element'. Similarly, Section 1(2) PatG acknowledges that biological material which is isolated from its natural environment or produced by means of a technical process can be a patentable invention 'even if it previously occurred in nature'. These legal provisions have mainly clarifying character as there is no corresponding statutory exclusion from patentability (*see* also §3.01[A] above).

While Sections 1(2) and 1a(2) PatG acknowledge the patentability of biological material and elements of the human body that are 'isolated' or 'produced by means of a technical process', the German courts have not considered it necessary to explicitly recite a corresponding qualifier in products claims directed to such biomolecules. Thus, for example, the German Federal Supreme Court in *Rezeptortyrosinkinase*[22] confirmed that a claimed nucleic acid does not need to be explicitly characterized as being 'isolated' or produced by a technical process in order to be patent-eligible, and that this same reasoning likewise applies to claims directed to antibodies.

20. German Federal Supreme Court, decision in X ZR 141/13 of 19 January 2016 – *Rezeptortyrosinkinase*, headnote and paragraphs 49–53.
21. US Supreme Court, *Mayo Collaborative Services v. Prometheus Laboratories, Inc.*, 566 U.S. 66 (2012).
22. German Federal Supreme Court, decision in X ZR 141/13 of 19 January 2016 – *Rezeptortyrosinkinase*, headnote and paragraph 49–53.

Also in the context of the examination of novelty, a claim directed to an antibody is normally not found to be anticipated by the prior occurrence of a corresponding antibody in nature, unless the antibody has been actually disclosed or otherwise made available to the public.

In line with this, the German Federal Patent Court in a decision on a revocation action found that a product claim directed to 'a purified antibody that specifically binds to' a certain polypeptide was not anticipated by a prior art document describing corresponding human serum antibodies detecting protein bands of Borrelia antigens in Western blots.[23] In reaching this conclusion, the Court emphasized that the presence of such antibodies in the serum sample could only be demonstrated in knowledge of the patent but was not derivable from the prior art document itself. On appeal, the Federal Supreme Court in *Borrelioseassay*[24] confirmed this conclusion. This case illustrates that the merely inherent occurrence of an antibody in the prior art does not necessarily anticipate a claim directed to that antibody. This holds true all the more for the occurrence of an antibody in nature that is in no way communicated to the public.

§3.02 ACCEPTABLE CLAIM FEATURES FOR DEFINING ANTIBODIES

[A] Functional Features

The definition of antibodies by functional features alone, or by functional features in combination with structural features, is in principle acceptable in Germany.

Notably, even if a claim already defines a class of antibodies by structural features, it can still be advantageous to additionally include functional limitations, at least in dependent claims and in the description, that focus on antibodies having certain desired properties or effects and thereby exclude any potentially disadvantageous or ineffective embodiments. For this same reason, even if a class of antibodies is already defined extensively by structural features, it may nevertheless be advisable to additionally specify at least the target/antigen of the claimed antibodies in the corresponding claim.

[1] Target/Antigen

Claims directed to antibodies defined solely by their target are, in principle, considered acceptable in Germany, provided of course that they are novel and inventive.

As an example illustrating this practice, the German Federal Supreme Court in *Rezeptortyrosinkinase*[25] maintained a patent in second-instance revocation proceedings, having a product claim directed to an antibody defined exclusively by its target, i.e. 'an antibody which is specific for' a certain receptor tyrosine kinase.

---

23. German Federal Patent Court, decision in 3 Ni 6/13 (EP) of 30 September 2014, section III.1.4 of the reasons.
24. German Federal Supreme Court, decision in X ZR 11/15 of 17 January 2017 – *Borrelioseassay*, paragraphs 40–42, 44 and 48.
25. German Federal Supreme Court, decision in X ZR 141/13 of 19 January 2016 – *Rezeptortyrosinkinase*.

Similarly, the Federal Supreme Court in *Borrelioseassay*[26] upheld a patent with a product claim to 'a purified antibody that specifically binds to' a certain immunogenic polypeptide, and the Federal Patent Court in 3 Ni 14/13 (EP)[27] maintained a patent with a second medical use claim directed to 'an anti-interleukin-12 antibody', wherein the claimed antibody was not defined by any further functional or structural features. Moreover, in the opposition appeal decision 14 W (pat) 8/06,[28] the Federal Patent Court maintained a patent with a product claim directed to 'antibodies having a biospecific affinity to at least one peptide according to claim 1 to 6', wherein the corresponding peptides were defined by their amino acid sequences.

Claims that define the target of an antibody will normally be interpreted as requiring that the antibody binds specifically via its antigen-binding site(s) (paratope) to the corresponding target molecule. For example, the Federal Patent Court in 3 Ni 14/13 (EP) found that the claim at issue, reciting an 'anti-interleukin-12 antibody', was to be interpreted as encompassing all antibodies that undergo an 'immunological interaction' with the target interleukin-12.[29]

The meaning of the feature that a claimed antibody 'specifically binds' to a certain antigen was also extensively discussed by the Higher Regional Court of Düsseldorf in the context of an infringement action in I-15 U 35/14.[30] While the patent asserted in this case did not contain any definition of the term 'specific' or 'specific binding', the Higher Regional Court found that a person skilled in the art would understand this to be a relative term, which means that an antibody is 'specific' for a certain antigen if it is complementary to the surface of the antigen, i.e. if it matches or recognizes the antigen, so that the binding between antibody and antigen occurs regularly and reliably. Importantly, this specificity of an antibody for its antigen is not changed if the antibody cross-reacts with other antigens, i.e. if it also recognizes other antigens.[31] The occurrence of cross-reactivity would therefore not prevent a skilled person from considering an antibody as 'specific' for its antigen. The Court considered these findings to be in accordance with the position of the Boards of Appeal of the European Patent Office, which in decision T 189/01[32] explained that specific binding does not exclude cross-reactivity with other antigens, as such cross-reactivity

26. German Federal Supreme Court, decision in X ZR 11/15 of 17 January 2017 – *Borrelioseassay*.
27. German Federal Patent Court, decision in 3 Ni 14/13 (EP) of 1 July 2014.
28. German Federal Patent Court, decision in 14 W (pat) 8/06 of 14 April 2011.
29. German Federal Patent Court, decision in 3 Ni 14/13 (EP) of 1 July 2014, section III.1 of the reasons.
30. Higher Regional Court of Düsseldorf, decision in I-15 U 35/14 of 15 July 2014.
31. *Ibid.*, section II.B.1a) of the reasons.
32. Technical Board of Appeal of the European Patent Office, decision in T 189/01 of 15 June 2004. In section 14 of the reasons of this decision, the Board provided the following explanations:

    The notion of specificity, which is an expression of the high affinity of a given antibody for the antigen against which it has been raised, is inherent to the nature of the antibodies and, hence, already contained in the denomination 'antibody', so that reference to the specificity can be, but does not need to be explicitly made. … The notion of specificity does not exclude that an antibody may cross-react with other polypeptides than that against which it has been raised. This is because the cross-reaction is in fact not a feature of an antibody, but much more a feature of the antigenic epitope, against which the antibody has been raised, which can be present on several different molecules.

is not a property of the antibody but rather of the epitope which may be present on different antigens.[33]

A different meaning may, of course, be assigned to the expression 'specific binding' if a patent provides a corresponding definition or disclosure. By way of example, the Higher Regional Court of Düsseldorf in several related judgments[34] concerning pregnancy test devices found that the expression 'specific binding', as construed on the basis of the respective patent specification, does not have a single uniform meaning. Rather, in these particular cases, the required specificity of each of several antibodies used in the claimed immunoassay was found to depend on the degree of specificity of the other antibodies used.

In general, it is recommendable to include a definition of the term 'specifically binds' or 'specific binding' in the description when drafting a new patent application, and also to include adequate fallback lines specifying, e.g., a preferred minimum binding strength for the corresponding antigen, as further discussed in §3.02[A][2] below.

[2] Mode of Binding: Target Affinity, Binding Specificity, Epitope, Definitions via Reference Antibodies and Competitive Binding

Functional features that specify the mode of binding of a claimed antibody are generally acceptable in Germany. Such features include, in particular, the definition of an antibody's binding strength (affinity or avidity) for a certain target/antigen, its binding specificity or selectivity for that antigen, and the definition of the specific region of the antigen (epitope[35]) that is bound by the antibody. These features can be defined in absolute terms (e.g., by specifying the equilibrium dissociation constant K_d as a measure of the antibody's affinity for a certain antigen, or by specifying the amino acid sequence of the epitope) or in relative terms (e.g., by comparison to a reference antibody with which the claimed antibody competes in binding).

For example, the German Federal Patent Court in 3 Ni 19/02 (EU)[36] decided on a revocation action against the German part of a European patent granted for 'a murine

---

33. Higher Regional Court of Düsseldorf, decision in I-15 U 35/14 of 15 July 2014, section II.B.1c) of the reasons.
34. Higher Regional Court of Düsseldorf, decision in I-2 U 62/04 of 24 June 2011; Higher Regional Court of Düsseldorf, decision in I-2 U 26/10 of 24 June 2011; Higher Regional Court of Düsseldorf, decision in I-2 U 53/04 of 17 December 2015; Higher Regional Court of Düsseldorf, decision in I-2 U 54/04 of 17 December 2015; Higher Regional Court of Düsseldorf, decision in I-2 U 87/04 of 17 December 2015; Higher Regional Court of Düsseldorf, decision in I-2 U 25/10 of 17 December 2015; Higher Regional Court of Düsseldorf, decision in I-2 U 30/10 of 17 December 2015; Higher Regional Court of Düsseldorf, decision in I-2 U 31/10 of 17 December 2015; Higher Regional Court of Düsseldorf, decision in I-2 U 33/10 of 17 December 2015; and Higher Regional Court of Düsseldorf, decision in I-2 U 34/10 of 17 December 2015.
35. A definition of the commonly accepted meaning of the term 'epitope', in the absence of a corresponding explicit definition in the patent specification, has been provided by the German Federal Patent Court in its decision in 3 Ni 66/00 (EU) of 13 August 2002, section III.5 of the reasons.
36. German Federal Patent Court, decision in 3 Ni 19/02 (EU) of 9 March 2004.

monoclonal antibody' which was defined primarily by functional features, i.e. in that it 'binds a human breast cancer antigen that is also bound by a reference antibody selected from those produced by the hybridomas obtainable from [various specific cell lines identified by their ATCC number]' and by its cytotoxicity against certain cancer cells (expressed as a minimum 50% Tissue Culture Infectious Dose, TCID 50%) when conjugated to ricin A chain (a cytotoxic N-glycosidase), while the only structural feature defining the claimed antibody in the granted independent product claim was that it 'has a G or M isotype'. This patent was maintained by the Federal Patent Court after the product claim had been restricted, in particular, by requiring that the antibody 'selectively binds to human breast cancer cells' and either 'binds to a protein of approximately 210,000 daltons found in cancerous breast tissue' or 'is produced by the hybridoma ATCC HB8484' (as recited in two independent product claims drafted on the basis of originally granted claim 1). This case illustrates that antibodies can be validly claimed on the basis of a functional definition, wherein the antigen of the claimed antibody is characterized merely by its molecular weight and by the binding of a reference antibody produced from a deposited hybridoma. In this regard, the Federal Patent Court explicitly acknowledged that the definition of the antigen of the claimed antibody via the binding of a reference antibody produced from a deposited hybridoma is a valid qualitative feature which, in order to be sufficiently disclosed, does not require any further quantitative specification of the corresponding binding strength.[37]

In general, in order to broadly claim antibodies that bind to a specific antigen which has not yet been fully characterized (or antibodies having functional features that are difficult to define in absolute terms), in cases where at least one such antibody has been obtained, it may thus be feasible to deposit the hybridoma producing the corresponding antibody and define the antigen (or the other functional features) of the claimed antibodies by reference to the antibody produced from deposited hybridoma.

Whenever a functional definition is used to characterize the binding properties of the claimed antibody, it is advisable to describe in detail the experiments required to verify the respective feature, including a preferred choice for a suitable binding assay (e.g., a surface plasmon resonance technique[38]) and the corresponding specific materials, techniques and conditions to be employed. It would appear safest to define even presumably trivial details, such as whether an antigen is to be employed in native or denatured state, and to additionally provide an actual working example of a corresponding assay with a complete description of all details.

Claims directed to antibodies can also be focused, e.g., on monospecific antibodies (which have only one type of antigen-binding site) or bispecific antibodies (which have two different types of antigen-binding sites and can thus bind to different targets). Unless a corresponding explicit limitation is made in the claims, a general expression such as 'IgG antibody' will normally be interpreted as encompassing both

37. *Ibid.*, section II.2.1 of the reasons.
38. *See*, e.g., Hearty S et al., Measuring Antibody-Antigen Binding Kinetics Using Surface Plasmon Resonance, *Methods Mol Biol*, 2018, 1827:421–455.

monospecific and bispecific antibodies. This has been acknowledged, for example, by the Federal Patent Court in 3 Ni 44/10 (EP).[39]

[3] Effect on Target

In addition to defining the target of a claimed antibody, the effect of the antibody's binding to that target can also be specified in a claim.

In particular, in claims directed to an antibody binding to a certain receptor or ligand, it is often specified that the claimed antibody acts as an agonist or antagonist on the corresponding target signalling pathway. Reciting more specific effects in a claim, such as defining the claimed antibody not only as 'antagonistic' but, beyond that, as being capable of blocking a certain ligand/receptor interaction, inhibiting receptor dimerization or stabilizing a certain receptor conformation may also be feasible, particularly in cases where the prior art already describes antibodies binding to the same target but eliciting a different effect. Other effects may also be specified, for example, that the claimed antibody is capable of sensitizing cells carrying a specific cell-surface antigen to radio- or chemotherapy, or that it is capable of inducing apoptosis or eliciting antibody-dependent cellular cytotoxicity (ADCC), complement-dependent cytotoxicity (CDC) or antibody-dependent cellular phagocytosis (ADCP).

The German courts typically take a more liberal approach to the assessment of sufficiency of disclosure than the European Patent Office, as further explained in §3.03[A] below. In this regard, when assessing whether a claim specifying a therapeutic agent by defining its effect is sufficiently disclosed, particular importance is also attached to the actual technical contribution of the claimed invention and the question of whether the generalized definition used in the claim is commensurate with the broadest technical teaching of the patent that solves the problem underlying the claimed invention.

For example, the German Federal Supreme Court in a judicial review decision in *Dipeptidyl-Peptidase-Inhibitoren*[40] overturned the preceding negative decision of the Federal Patent Court on sufficiency of disclosure for a medical use claim relating effectively to any inhibitor of the enzyme dipeptidyl peptidase IV (DP IV) for lowering the blood sugar level in diabetes patients. In this decision, the Federal Supreme Court held that the most general form of the technical teaching of the patent did not merely consist in the provision of the specific DP IV inhibitors disclosed in the patent specification but, rather, in the fundamental finding that any substance having DP IV inhibitory activity can be used for the specific therapeutic application claimed, with the consequence that sufficiency of disclosure could not be denied for the generalized definition of the therapeutic agent in the claim. While this decision was not specifically

---

39. German Federal Patent Court, decision in 3 Ni 44/10 (EP) of 5 June 2012, section II.2.1 of the reasons. Note that this finding was not reassessed in the subsequent appeal judgment; *see* German Federal Supreme Court, decision in X ZR 133/12 of 13 May 2014, paragraphs 25, 28, 32 and 36.
40. German Federal Supreme Court, decision in X ZB 8/12 of 11 September 2013 – *Dipeptidyl-Peptidase-Inhibitoren*.

concerned with antibodies, it would seem that the same principle should likewise apply to claims relating generically to an antibody having a specific effect on its target.

[B] Structural Features

[1] Molecular Topology: Antibody Types, Fragments and Antibody Constructs

Claims directed to antibodies can be focused on specific immunoglobulin classes/ isotypes (such as IgA, IgD, IgE, IgG or IgM) or even on specific immunoglobulin subclasses (such as IgG1, IgG2, IgG3 or IgG4 in the case of human IgG). If, however, such a limitation is made in order to delimit the claimed antibodies from the prior art, it should be carefully assessed whether the antibodies thus defined are truly different from the ones described in the prior art.

For example, the German Federal Patent Court in a judgment on a revocation action in 3 Ni 3/00 (EU)[41] found that a product claim directed to 'a stabilized pharmaceutical formulation comprising an IgG_1 immunoglobulin and an amount of a chelator of copper ions sufficient to prevent degradation of the immunoglobulin' was anticipated by a prior art document disclosing a corresponding stabilized pharmaceutical formulation of human IgG, even though the prior art document did not expressly mention the presence of the claimed IgG1 subtype. The Federal Patent Court held that human IgG was known to contain about 70% of the subtype IgG1, so that this feature was fulfilled by the prior art document despite the lack of a corresponding explicit disclosure. When denying novelty, the Court also rejected the patentee's argument that the claim at issue should be interpreted as excluding mixtures of IgG1 with other IgG subtypes, pointing out that no such limitation was derivable from the wording of the claim or the patent specification.

Besides regular intact antibodies, a wide range of antibody fragments have been explored and have increasingly obtained regulatory approval, offering advantages for certain applications. This includes antibody fragments such as Fab, Fab', $F(ab')_2$, mono- or bispecific Fab dimers (Fab_2), trispecific Fab trimers (Fab_3), Fv, single-chain variable fragments (scFv), diabodies, triabodies, tetrabodies, bispecific scFv (bis-scFv), scFv-Fc, minibodies, camelid VhH domains, shark V-NAR domains, nanobodies, and one-armed antibodies.

While the claims of a patent may be focused deliberately on a particular type of antibody fragment where an invention specifically relates to such a fragment, it is often desirable to secure patent protection for all conceivable antibody types and fragments. To this end, an adequately broad definition of the term 'antibody' – listing all of the above-mentioned types of antibody fragments as examples – should be provided in the patent specification (which should be authoritative for the interpretation of the granted claims[42]), and the claims can also be drafted to include an explicit reference

41. German Federal Patent Court, decision in 3 Ni 3/00 (EU) of 24 July 2001.
42. In accordance with established case law, a patent can be its own dictionary, and if a patent ascribes a specific meaning to a technical term, this meaning alone is decisive. *See*, e.g., German Federal Supreme Court, decision in X ZR 85/96 of 2 March 1999 – *Spannschraube*, headnotes 1–2; German Federal Supreme Court, decision in X ZR 103/13 of 2 June 2015

to functional antibody fragments. In this latter case, the use of an expression like 'or an antigen-binding fragment thereof' can clarify that only fragments capable of binding to the respective antigen are encompassed. It is furthermore advisable to explicitly recite functional limitations reflecting the desired properties and effects of the claimed antibodies and antibody fragments, at least in the dependent claims and in the description, in order to exclude any potentially ineffective or disadvantageous embodiments.

[2] Amino Acid Sequences

Under German patent law and practice, it is possible but not generally required to define an antibody (or any part thereof) in terms of its amino acid sequence.

While this may be seen as the most definite structural characterization, the scope of a corresponding definition can be broadened by requiring only a certain minimum percent identity to a defined amino acid sequence.

[a] Full-Length Sequences of Antibodies

Antibodies can be defined by their full-length amino acid sequence (and also by their variable region or CDR sequences, as further discussed in §3.02[B][2][b] below).

When drafting a new patent application that covers one or more potential clinical candidate antibodies, it is advisable to include, as a preferred embodiment, the full sequence of each such antibody in the application and to file corresponding individual claims.

In order to avoid an overly narrow claim scope and to mitigate the risk of sequencing errors, it can further be considered to allow at least slight deviations from the corresponding specific amino acid sequence, e.g., by requiring at least 90% (or at least 95%) sequence identity or by permitting a certain maximum number of amino acid additions, deletions and replacements, particularly conservative amino acid replacements, in combination with a functional characterization of the claimed antibody. In this regard, it may be particularly interesting to draft claims allowing only the framework sequences of the claimed antibody to be varied to a certain extent, while requiring identical CDR sequences (and a defined function).

[b] Sequences of Fragments, CDRs and Framework Regions

It is also possible to define the amino acid sequences of specific parts of an antibody in a claim, including its complementarity determining regions (CDRs), its framework regions, or its variable domains.

– *Kreuzgestänge*, headnote 2 and paragraph 22; German Federal Supreme Court, decision in X ZR 11/13 of 27 October 2015 – *Fugenband*, paragraph 14; German Federal Supreme Court, decision in X ZR 145/98 of 7 November 2000 – *Brieflocher*, headnote; German Federal Supreme Court, decision in X ZR 102/15 of 9 May 2017, paragraph 12; and German Federal Supreme Court, decision in X ZR 44/16 of 13 March 2018, paragraph 25.

In the past, it used to be considered acceptable to define the sequences of only some of the CDRs of an antibody but not necessarily the sequences of all six CDRs that together form an antigen-binding site. Nowadays, however, objections against the definition of less than six CDRs seem to have become more common, particularly on the grounds that the antigen-binding site is incompletely characterized by only one (or fewer than six) CDR sequences. While there is no definite guidance from the German courts as to which structural definitions of the antigen-binding site of an antibody should normally be acceptable, it is advisable at least to include adequate fallback lines in a patent application that allow specifying the sequences of all six CDRs and the corresponding framework regions, or even the sequences of the complete variable regions, if that should become necessary.

Since the definition of the CDR sequences of an antibody implies a specific location and attributes a specific function to the corresponding amino acid sequences, it is recommendable to also specify, at least in the patent description, the precise method used for the identification and numbering of the CDRs thus defined, e.g., any of the Kabat, Chothia, Martin, IMGT, or Honneger (AHo) numbering schemes.[43] In order to avoid any potential issues with respect to the definition of CDR sequences, it may also be considered to recite both the CDR sequences and the corresponding variable region sequences as alternatives in the claims.

[3] Chemical Modifications, Conjugation and Glycosylation

Claims relating to antibodies can define specific chemical modifications, such as the attachment of polyethylene glycol (PEG) chains to the claimed antibody, as well as the conjugation of cytotoxic drugs or other functional moieties. In principle, there are numerous valid approaches for defining such modifications.

Claims directed to antibody-drug conjugates that broadly define the drug moiety conjugated to the antibody have been considered acceptable in Germany. For example, the Federal Patent Court in 3 Ni 19/02 (EU)[44] maintained a patent with a product claim directed to an 'immunotoxin, which is a conjugate of a monoclonal antibody according to any one of claims 1 to 3 and a cytotoxic moiety'.

The glycosylation profile of an antibody can be defined with respect to the location of sugar chains as well as their qualitative and quantitative composition. Thus, the presence and content of specific sugars like glucose, galactose, mannose, fucose, N-acetylglucosamine, sialic acid and N-acetylneuraminic acid can be defined for the entire antibody or for sugar chains at individual glycosylation sites. Moreover, it can also be specified that the claimed antibody is devoid of certain (or all) sugars. Afucosylated antibodies, for example, have attracted considerable attention for their increased antibody-dependent cellular cytotoxicity. Virtually completely fucosylated antibodies, however, are also pharmaceutically important. Focusing on aglycosylated antibodies, on the other hand, may be preferable if antibody effector functions are not required or undesirable.

---

43. *See*, e.g., Dondelinger M et al., Understanding the Significance and Implications of Antibody Numbering and Antigen-Binding Surface/Residue Definition, *Front Immunol*, 2018, 9:2278.
44. German Federal Patent Court, decision in 3 Ni 19/02 (EU) of 9 March 2004.

[C] Cell Line Deposits and Process of Production

Besides functional and structural features, a further important possibility to define an antibody is by reference to a deposited hybridoma that produces the claimed antibody.

This may be the best possibility to comprehensively define a specific antibody, and it can also serve as a safety net to avoid any risk of errors in the structural and functional characterization of the claimed antibody, including in particular sequencing errors. The deposit of a hybridoma can further be used to define a reference antibody, and to specify various functional properties of the claimed antibodies in relation to the reference antibody (*see* §3.02[A][2] above).

Importantly, for German patent applications, if a deposited hybridoma (or any other deposited biological material) is to be relied upon to ensure sufficiency of disclosure, the corresponding deposit must have been made with a recognized depositary institution no later than the priority or filing date of the patent application, and the patent application must state the name of the depositary institution and the accession number.[45] If the patent application as originally filed allows an unambiguous assignment to the deposited material, the accession number can also be supplemented after the filing date of the application, but this must be done within 16 months from the earliest priority date; this term is deemed to be observed if the accession number is supplied before the termination of the technical preparations for the publication of the patent application.[46]

Under German law, the deposit does not necessarily have to be made at an international depositary authority according to the Budapest Treaty but can also be made at certain other recognized scientific institutions which are legally, economically and organizationally independent from the depositor and from the patent applicant.[47] If the deposit has been made outside the Budapest Treaty, the patent applicant has to furnish an irrevocable declaration of release, making the deposited biological material available without reservation to the depositary institution from the filing date of the patent until the end of the required storage period for the purpose of issuing samples in accordance with Section 5 BioMatHintV; if the deposit is made by a third party different from the patent applicant, the applicant must furnish documentary evidence that the deposited material has been made available by the actual depositor in a corresponding manner.[48] To be on the safe side, the requirements for relying on deposits made by third parties should be observed even if the deposit is made by a subsidiary or associate company of the patent applicant.

Claims defining an antibody as being produced by a specific deposited hybridoma are generally accepted in Germany. For example, the German Federal Patent Court in 3 Ni 19/02 (EU)[49] maintained a patent in revocation proceedings after one of its independent product claims directed to a murine monoclonal antibody had been amended to require, inter alia, that the claimed antibody 'is produced by the hybridoma ATCC HB8484'.

45. Section 1(1) BioMatHintV.
46. Section 3 BioMatHintV.
47. Section 2 BioMatHintV.
48. Section 4(1) BioMatHintV.
49. German Federal Patent Court, decision in 3 Ni 19/02 (EU) of 9 March 2004.

In relation to the above-mentioned case 3 Ni 19/02 (EU), it is noteworthy that although the nullity plaintiff had filed experimental data showing that the claimed murine monoclonal antibody could not be produced from a sample of the hybridoma ATCC HB8484 obtained from the depositary institution, the Federal Patent Court did not consider this finding sufficient to demonstrate a lack of enablement. According to the Court, when samples of cell line deposits are requested, it can often happen that one or another sample thus obtained does not give the desired results. Therefore, the failure of a single attempt to reproduce the claimed antibody from the deposited hybridoma cannot prove that the deposited cells as a whole are incapable of allowing the claimed invention to be put into practice. In the Court's view, the nullity plaintiff should have requested further samples of the deposited hybridoma and should have made further attempts to produce the corresponding antibody in order to demonstrate a lack of sufficient disclosure.[50]

The definition of a claimed antibody as being produced from a deposited hybridoma can be regarded as a specific example of a product-by-process feature.

In Germany, the definition of a claimed product by its process of production is, in principle, considered acceptable.[51] This also applies to antibodies and other proteins, as illustrated, e.g., by the German Federal Patent Court decision in 3 Ni 35/99 (EU).[52] In this decision, a patent with a product claim directed to a purified follicle stimulating hormone characterized by the amino acid sequence of one of its two subunits, its enzymatic activity, and its purity, was maintained in revocation proceedings – but only after the claimed hormone had been further defined to be obtainable by a specific process of purification.

In line with this, antibodies can, in principle, also be defined by process features relating to their production or purification.

§3.03 BREADTH OF CLAIMS AND SUPPORT BY EXAMPLES

[A] Acceptable Breadth of Claims to Antibodies

The German Patent Office and the German courts are typically more inclined than the European Patent Office to acknowledge claims directed to broadly defined antibodies as clear and sufficiently disclosed (enabled).

This rather liberal approach rests, inter alia, on the principle established in the case law of the German Federal Supreme Court that the disclosure of at least one way to carry out a claimed invention is normally enough to acknowledge sufficiency of disclosure (enablement) while even a 'disproportionate breadth' of the claims is not a ground for revocation,[53] as well as the established principle that sufficiency of

50. *Ibid.*, section II.2.1 of the reasons.
51. *See*, e.g., German Federal Supreme Court, decision in X ZB 13/90 of 30 March 1993 – *Tetraploide Kamille*; German Federal Supreme Court, decision in X ZB 9/70 of 6 July 1971 – *Trioxan*; and German Federal Supreme Court, decision in X ZR 159/98 of 19 June 2001 – *Zipfelfreies Stahlband*.
52. German Federal Patent Court, decision in 3 Ni 35/99 (EU) of 8 November 2000.
53. *See*, e.g., German Federal Supreme Court, decision in X ZR 168/97 of 3 May 2001 – *Taxol*; German Federal Supreme Court, decision in X ZR 51/06 of 11 May 2010 – *Polymerisierbare*

disclosure can be acknowledged even if the claim under consideration encompasses both workable and unworkable embodiments, provided that a person skilled in the art can identify workable embodiments without undue burden.[54]

These principles have also been applied specifically in antibody cases. For example, the Federal Supreme Court in *Borrelioseassay* (X ZR 11/15)[55] acknowledged sufficiency of disclosure for a diagnostic method claim employing either a functionally defined antibody or a polypeptide that binds to such an antibody as a diagnostic reagent, and in this respect endorsed the position taken by the Federal Patent Court in the corresponding first-instance judgment that sufficiency of disclosure was not impaired by the fact that this diagnostic method claim embraced both workable and unworkable variants because a person skilled in the field of immunology could determine suitable pairs of antibodies and epitopes on the basis of their common general knowledge.[56]

The German Federal Patent Court in 3 Ni 5/01[57] maintained a patent with a claim to an immunoassay for detecting antibodies against an HCV antigen, in which a polypeptide probe containing an HCV epitope was to be employed as a reagent. The Court rejected the argument that the claim was not sufficiently disclosed within its full scope, emphasizing that the disclosure of at least one way to carry out the claimed invention, i.e. at least one polypeptide probe, is enough to acknowledge sufficiency of disclosure, and that a disproportionate breadth of the claims is not in itself a ground for revocation. For this same reason, also the nullity plaintiff's objection that certain embodiments covered by the claims of the patent did not work, as presumably demonstrated by post-published evidence, was dismissed by the Court as irrelevant.

Moreover, the Federal Patent Court in 3 Ni 14/13 (EP)[58] maintained a patent in revocation proceedings with a second medical use claim directed to 'an anti-interleukin-12 antibody' for a specific treatment of psoriasis, wherein the claimed antibody was not defined by any further structural or functional features. Regarding the breadth of this claim, the Court held that even if it is true, as argued by the nullity plaintiff, that not all anti-interleukin-12 antibodies are effective in the claimed treatment of psoriasis, this does not result in a lack of enablement as long as the skilled person can identify effective antibodies without undue difficulties.[59] This was acknowledged to be the case because the skilled person was aware of the identity and structural properties of the antigen of the claimed antibody, i.e. interleukin-12, as well as the structure and the production of antibodies in general, so that the claim at issue could

Zementmischung; German Federal Supreme Court, decision in X ZR 88/13 of 10 November 2015; German Federal Supreme Court, decision in X ZR 148/11 of 19 April 2016 – *Zöliakiediagnoseverfahren*; and German Federal Patent Court, decision in 3 Ni 4/01 of 7 August 2002.

54. *See*, e.g., German Federal Supreme Court, decision in X ZB 13/89 of 9 October 1990 – *Polyesterfäden*; German Federal Supreme Court, decision in X ZB 8/12 of 11 September 2013 – *Dipeptidyl-Peptidase-Inhibitoren*; and German Federal Patent Court, decision in 4 Ni 16/17 (EP) of 17 December 2018.
55. German Federal Supreme Court, decision in X ZR 11/15 of 17 January 2017 – *Borrelioseassay*.
56. *Ibid.*, paragraphs 31, 33 and 37.
57. German Federal Patent Court, decision in 3 Ni 5/01 of 14 August 2002.
58. German Federal Patent Court, decision in 3 Ni 14/13 (EP) of 1 July 2014.
59. *Ibid.*, section IV.4 of the reasons.

not be regarded as encompassing an unmanageable number of antibodies which the skilled person could identify only by trial and error. The fact that the experiments required to determine particular effective antibodies could take years was considered to be expectable in the field of immunology.

Similarly, the German Federal Patent Court in the examination appeal decision in 15 W (pat) 7/13[60] found that a patent could be granted for a second diagnostic use claim directed to 'a diagnostic substance for use in a method of determining the aggressiveness of a prostate tumour', wherein the diagnostic substance is administered via the blood stream to the prostate and comprises (i) a biomarker binding specifically to a VEGF molecule and carrying a detectable first label, and (ii) a biomarker binding specifically to a target molecule which is present in the endothelium of blood vessels of the prostate tumour and which carries a detectable second label. Both biomarkers contained in the claimed diagnostic substance could be, in particular, antibodies. The Federal Patent Court expressly acknowledged that the claimed diagnostic substance was sufficiently disclosed, noting that the lack of any details regarding the chemical structure of the diagnostic substance and of the biomarkers contained therein does not justify an enablement objection.[61]

Furthermore, while the description of at least one way to carry out the claimed invention is normally enough to acknowledge sufficiency of disclosure, it is not generally necessary to provide any working examples. This is in line with established case law of the German Federal Supreme Court,[62] and has also been affirmed by the Federal Patent Court in 3 Ni 5/10 (EU)[63] in relation to a method for producing antibodies by phage display.

As illustrated by the above-discussed decisions, the German courts typically take a relatively liberal approach with respect to the question of which breadth of claims is acceptable for antibody inventions, provided that novelty and inventive step can be acknowledged. In practice, however, unless the invention relates to a novel target or a novel medical use, it will normally be necessary to define the claimed antibody by further features, often by the structure of its antigen-binding site and/ or by additional functional features pertaining to a particular binding mode or effect.

[B] Required Experimental Support for Claims to Functionally Defined Antibodies

There are no general rules regarding the required experimental support for claims relating to functionally defined antibodies. As set out in §3.03[A] above, the German Patent Office and the German courts typically adopt a rather liberal approach when assessing the compliance of such claims with the requirements of clarity and sufficiency of disclosure.

60. German Federal Patent Court, decision in 15 W (pat) 7/13 of 23 March 2015.
61. *Ibid.*, section II.3 of the reasons.
62. *See*, e.g., German Federal Supreme Court, decision in Xa ZR 126/07 of 13 July 2010 – *Klammernahtgerät*, headnote and paragraph 17; and German Federal Supreme Court, decision in X ZR 58/14 of 29 September 2016, paragraph 32.
63. German Federal Patent Court, decision in 3 Ni 5/10 (EU) of 24 January 2012, section II.1c of the reasons.

If the claimed invention relates to a novel and inventive antigen, it is normally also possible to claim any antibodies directed against this antigen, without having to provide any actual example or experimental data for a corresponding antibody.

In all other cases, however, it is clearly advisable to provide at least one example of an antibody having the claimed functional features as well as experimental data showing a surprising advantageous effect. The provision of at least two examples exhibiting the claimed functional features can also be helpful to confirm that these functional features are indeed responsible for the advantageous effect relied upon in the discussion of inventive step.

[C] Required Experimental Support for Claims to Structurally Defined Antibodies

There are no general rules governing the required experimental support for claims directed to structurally defined antibodies. In this regard, the same basic principles explained in §3.03[A] and §3.03[B] above apply.

If a claimed antibody is defined by its sequence, e.g., by the amino acid sequence of its CDRs, there will normally be at least one actual example of an antibody having this specific sequence. In such a case, the description of at least one example of the claimed antibody should normally be considered sufficient. It may nevertheless be advantageous to provide several actual examples of the claimed antibodies, such as exemplary antibodies having the same CDR sequences but different framework regions, which can be very helpful in supporting claims directed to antibodies defined by their CDR sequences (ideally in combination with functional features, as discussed in §3.02[A] above).

§3.04 SPECIFIC MEDICAL APPLICATIONS AND OTHER FOLLOW-UP INVENTIONS

As explained in §3.01[A] above, methods for the treatment of the human or animal body by therapy or surgery as well as diagnostic methods practised on the human or animal body are excluded from patentability. Claims directed to a substance or composition for use in any of these methods, however, are patentable.

While the German Patent Act includes a statutory provision (Section 3(4) PatG) expressly allowing such second medical use claims in the purpose-limited product format (e.g., 'Substance X for use in treating disease Y'), second medical use claims are also accepted in the Swiss-type format (e.g., 'Use of substance X for the preparation of a medicament for treating disease Y') and in the German-type format[64] (e.g., 'Use of substance X for treating disease Y').

64. The so-called German-type claim format was accepted by the German Federal Supreme Court on the grounds that the claimed use of an active ingredient in the treatment of a disease not only encompasses the actual use or the prescription of a medicament by a medical practitioner, which was deemed to be devoid of industrial application and therefore unpatentable, but also a number of preceding activities such as formulating, confectioning and packaging the medicament, which were regarded to be clearly susceptible to industrial application. In consequence, the use claim as a whole was found to be patentable as it

Although the admissibility of second medical use claims in the German-type and the Swiss-type formats was originally established by the judiciary under the 'old' German Patent Act, which until 13 December 2007 provided that therapeutic methods of treatment were by legal fiction deemed to be devoid of industrial application, these claim formats are still considered acceptable under the current law.[65] This is in contrast to the approach taken by the European Patent Office which no longer accepts Swiss-type claims as second medical use claims in any patent applications having a filing date or earliest priority date of 29 January 2011 or later.[66]

[A] Treatment of Specific Diseases

Claims directed to an antibody (or any other active agent) for use in the treatment or prevention of a specific disease are the classical example of second medical use claims and can indeed constitute patentable inventions in Germany.

While this is now expressly codified in Section 3(4) PatG, the patentability of second medical use claims relating to the treatment of a new disease with a known therapeutic agent had already been established by the German Federal Supreme Court in the 1970s.[67]

[B] Mode of Administration

Second medical use claims requiring a specific mode of administration (e.g., oral administration) can constitute patentable inventions in Germany.[68]

[C] Dosage Regimens

Second medical use claims requiring a specific dosage regimen can likewise constitute patentable inventions in Germany.

---

encompasses industrial applications besides non-industrial applications; *see* German Federal Supreme Court, decision in X ZB 13/75 of 20 January 1977 – *Benzolsulfonylharnstoff*, section II.3.b)bb) of the reasons. This is in stark contrast to the position adopted by the European Patent Office which considers claims directly relating to a therapeutic treatment to be excluded from patentability, regardless of whether they are drafted as method or use claims.

65. German Federal Supreme Court, decision in X ZB 5/13 of 25 February 2014 – *Kollagenase I*, headnote 1 and paragraph 17; and German Federal Supreme Court, decision in X ZB 6/13 of 25 February 2014 – *Kollagenase II*, paragraph 17.
66. Enlarged Board of Appeal of the European Patent Office, decision in G 2/08 of 19 February 2010, headnote 3; and Notice from the European Patent Office dated 20 September 2010 concerning the non-acceptance of Swiss-type claims (Official Journal EPO, 2010, 514).
67. German Federal Supreme Court, decision in X ZB 13/75 of 20 January 1977 – *Benzolsulfonylharnstoff*; German Federal Supreme Court, decision in X ZB 21/81 of 3 June 1982 – *Sitosterylglykoside*; and German Federal Supreme Court, decision in X ZB 4/83 of 20 September 1983 – *Hydropyridin*.
68. *See*, e.g., German Federal Supreme Court, decision in X ZB 5/13 of 25 February 2014 – *Kollagenase I*, paragraph 27; and German Federal Supreme Court, decision in X ZB 6/13 of 25 February 2014 – *Kollagenase II*, paragraph 27.

Before the introduction of Section 3(4) PatG into the German Patent Act in 2007, which allows second medical use claims in the purpose-limited product format, the German Federal Supreme Court in *Carvedilol II* (X ZR 236/01)[69] held that a feature in a Swiss-type claim requiring a specific dosing schedule in the form of an active administration step ('wherein the medicament is administered in an initial dose of ... per day for a period of 7 to 28 days ...') was an unpatentable treatment suggestion and, as such, could not be taken into account for the assessment of novelty and inventive step; in this same judgment, however, the Federal Supreme Court found that the corresponding dosing schedule could be validly claimed in the form of a manifest preparation feature ('wherein the medicament is prepared for administration of an initial dose of ... per day for a period of 7 to 28 days ...').

Since the patentability of second medical use claims has been codified in Section 3(4) PatG, it seems to be clear that dosage regimen features can be validly recited in second medical use claims as part of the specific therapeutic use claimed, both as an active administration step and as a manifest preparation feature. Indeed, this has been expressly confirmed by the Federal Supreme Court in *Kollagenase I* (X ZB 5/13)[70] and *Kollagenase II* (X ZB 6/13)[71] in relation to second medical use claims in the purpose-limited product format.

It is also noteworthy that the Federal Supreme Court in the aforementioned decisions *Kollagenase I* and *Kollagenase II* went further and found that any and all features specifying the modalities of a claimed therapeutic use are patentable, as long as they influence the properties or effects of the claimed therapeutic substance on the human or animal body, i.e. as long as they objectively aim at facilitating, enhancing, accelerating or otherwise improving the effects of the claimed therapeutic substance.[72] This was acknowledged to be the case for the specific second medical use claims at issue, which in *Kollagenase II* were directed to 'collagenase for use in the treatment of Peyronie's disease in a subject ... wherein the collagenase is prepared for injection into a fibrous plaque in the penis of the subject ... and for immobilization of the penis directly after injection for several hours'. The feature requiring the immobilization of the penis directly after injection was found to improve the effectiveness of the claimed therapeutic agent collagenase and, therefore, to be a feature closely related to the claimed therapeutic use that has to be taken into account for the assessment of novelty and inventive step.[73]

69. German Federal Supreme Court, decision in X ZR 236/01 of 19 December 2006 – *Carvedilol II*.
70. German Federal Supreme Court, decision in X ZB 5/13 of 25 February 2014 – *Kollagenase I*, paragraph 20.
71. German Federal Supreme Court, decision in X ZB 6/13 of 25 February 2014 – *Kollagenase II*, paragraph 20.
72. German Federal Supreme Court, decision in X ZB 5/13 of 25 February 2014 – *Kollagenase I*, headnotes 2–3 and paragraphs 27–31; and German Federal Supreme Court, decision in X ZB 6/13 of 25 February 2014 – *Kollagenase II*, paragraphs 27–31.
73. German Federal Supreme Court, decision in X ZB 6/13 of 25 February 2014 – *Kollagenase II*, paragraphs 32–35. Note that the Federal Supreme Court in the parallel decision *Kollagenase I* came to the same conclusion for the corresponding second medical use claim directed to 'collagenase for use in the treatment of Dupuytren's disease, wherein the collagenase is prepared for injection into a fibrous strand of a hand ... and for immobilization of the hand

[D] Specific Patient Groups

Second medical use claims relating to the treatment of a specific patient group, which is clearly distinguished from any patient group already treated in the prior art, can constitute patentable inventions in Germany.[74]

In principle, the corresponding approach established by the European Patent Office, as explained in §1.04[D] above, should likewise apply in Germany.

[E] Specific Mode of Action

The approach established in the case law of the Boards of Appeal of the European Patent Office, which have under certain conditions acknowledged novelty of second medical use claims on the basis of a specific novel mechanism of action (*see* §1.04[E] above),[75] has so far not been followed by the German courts.

Thus, where the same active ingredient has already been disclosed for the treatment of the same disease in the same patient group via the same mode of administration, the mere discovery of the underlying biological mechanism of action which also inherently takes place in the treatment described in the prior art does not constitute a novel technical teaching. This principle has been endorsed by the German Federal Supreme Court in *Memantin* (X ZR 68/08)[76] and *Fettsäuren* (X ZR 40/12),[77] and has also been affirmed by the Federal Patent Court specifically in connection with the claimed therapeutic use of an antibody in 3 Ni 25/16 (EP).[78]

Nevertheless, it remains to be seen whether the German courts might still acknowledge patentability of second medical use claims on the basis of a novel mechanism of action, possibly in such cases where the claimed mechanism of action is distinct and independent from the one described in the prior art, and where the novel mechanism allows the use of the corresponding active ingredient in clinical circumstances under which this active ingredient would not have previously been used. It will also be interesting to see how such patents granted by the European Patent Office will be dealt with by the German courts in enforcement and revocation proceedings.

---

directly after injection for several hours'; *see* German Federal Supreme Court, decision in X ZB 5/13 of 25 February 2014 – *Kollagenase I*, paragraphs 32–35.

74. *See*, e.g., German Federal Supreme Court, decision in X ZB 5/13 of 25 February 2014 – *Kollagenase I*, paragraph 27; and German Federal Supreme Court, decision in X ZB 6/13 of 25 February 2014 – *Kollagenase II*, paragraph 27.
75. *See* also: Wachenfeld & Ridderbusch, A second bite at the cherry, Life Sciences Intellectual Property Review (LSIPR), 24 March 2016 (accessible online at: https://www.lifesciences ipreview.com/article/a-second-bite-at-the-cherry).
76. German Federal Supreme Court, decision in X ZR 68/08 of 9 June 2011 – *Memantin*.
77. German Federal Supreme Court, decision in X ZR 40/12 of 24 September 2013 – *Fettsäuren*.
78. German Federal Patent Court, decision in 3 Ni 25/16 (EP) of 16 January 2018, section III.1.1 of the reasons.

[F] Combinations with Other Active Ingredients

The combination of an antibody with one or more further active ingredients can constitute a patentable invention.

For such inventions, it is generally advisable to draft claims that allow the antibody and the further active ingredient(s) to be formulated in the same or in separate pharmaceutical compositions. It is also permissible to draft second medical use claims relating to the antibody alone, wherein the combined administration of the further active ingredient(s) is required as part of the claimed specific therapeutic use, and vice versa:

> 'An antibody X for use in treating disease D, wherein the antibody X is to be administered in combination with an active ingredient Y.'

> 'Active ingredient Y for use in treating disease D, wherein the active ingredient Y is to be administered in combination with an antibody X.'

These claim formats should be advantageous in enforcement, for example if an alleged infringer offers a monopreparation of antibody X with a package leaflet prescribing its administration together with active ingredient Y which is separately offered by a different undertaking. In particular, it would seem that direct infringement could be asserted in this case, whereas there might only be indirect (contributory) infringement if the claim were directed to the 'combination of antibody X with active ingredient Y for use in treating disease D'.

It should also be borne in mind that not only the combination with additional therapeutic agents may constitute a patentable invention, but also the limitation of a medical use claim to a monotherapeutic treatment. Thus, for example, the Federal Patent Court in 3 Ni 14/13 (EP)[79] acknowledged the presence of an inventive step for a second medical use claim relating to an anti-interleukin-12 antibody for the treatment of psoriasis only after the claim had been limited to require that this antibody is the sole active agent used in the claimed treatment of psoriasis. While such cases are rather exceptional, it may be worthwhile to consider including fallback lines that focus on monotherapy when drafting new patent applications.

[G] Specific Diagnostic Applications

Analogous to second medical use claims, Section 3(4) PatG also provides for so-called second diagnostic use claims which typically relate to a substance or composition for use in a specific diagnostic method practised on the human or animal body.

An exemplary decision acknowledging the patentability of a second diagnostic use claim in the field of antibodies was rendered by the German Federal Patent Court in 15 W (pat) 7/13.[80] In this examination appeal decision, the Court acknowledged the patentability of a second diagnostic use claim directed to 'a diagnostic substance for use in a method of determining the aggressiveness of a prostate tumour', wherein the diagnostic substance is administered via the blood stream to the prostate and

79. German Federal Patent Court, decision in 3 Ni 14/13 (EP) of 1 July 2014.
80. German Federal Patent Court, decision in 15 W (pat) 7/13 of 23 March 2015.

comprises (i) a biomarker binding specifically to a VEGF molecule and carrying a detectable first label, and (ii) a biomarker binding specifically to a target molecule which is present in the endothelium of blood vessels of the prostate tumour and which carries a detectable second label; both biomarkers comprised in the claimed diagnostic substance could be antibodies, as also recited in a dependent claim.

It should further be noted that only diagnostic methods practised on the human or animal body are excluded from patentability under Section 2a(1) no. 2 PatG, whereas *in vitro* diagnostic methods conducted with a patient sample as well as analytical methods practised on the human or animal body that do not encompass the making of a diagnosis are patentable.[81] The purpose-limited product format is therefore not available to claim substances or compositions for use in such *in vitro* diagnostic methods or mere analytical methods.

§3.05 ASSESSMENT OF INVENTIVENESS

[A] General Approach

The general approach of the German Patent Office and the German courts to the assessment of inventive step is quite similar to the problem-solution approach developed by the European Patent Office (as discussed in §1.05[A] above) although there are some significant differences in the details.

In particular, the German courts do not adhere to the EPO's concept of choosing a single 'closest' prior art document but often consider any one or more documents that a skilled person working in the technical field of the invention would have reasonably consulted as a valid starting point for the assessment of inventive step.[82] In this regard, great importance is attached to the definition of the notional person skilled in the art.

The technical 'problem' that the claimed invention solves must be determined in an objective manner on the basis of what the invention actually achieves in view of the pertinent state of the art.[83] In contrast to the EPO, however, the German courts often refuse to consider the attainment of a specific advantageous effect or property of the claimed invention as part of the definition of the technical problem to be solved, and rather tend to choose a more general definition of the technical problem

81. German Federal Supreme Court, decision in X ZB 9/09 of 31 August 2010 – *Bildunterstützung bei Katheternavigation*; German Federal Patent Court, decision in 3 Ni 68/16 (EP) of 24 April 2018, section III.1 of the reasons; and German Federal Patent Court, decision in 21 W (pat) 88/83 of 19 January 1984 – *Diagnostizierverfahren*.

82. German Federal Patent Court, decision in 20 W (pat) 46/01 of 26 February 2003 – *Programmartmitteilung*; and German Federal Supreme Court, decision in Xa ZR 138/05 of 18 June 2009 – *Fischbissanzeiger*.

83. German Federal Supreme Court, decision in X ZB 33/03 of 19 October 2004 – *Anbieten interaktiver Hilfe*, section II.4.b of the reasons; German Federal Supreme Court, decision in X ZR 200/99 of 12 February 2003 – *Hochdruckreiniger*, section 3, penultimate paragraph of the reasons; and German Federal Supreme Court, decision in X ZR 41/13 of 13 January 2015 – *Quetiapin*, paragraph 11.

which the skilled person would 'realistically' have tried to tackle.[84] As a consequence, at least in some cases it can be more difficult to rely on surprising advantages in support of inventive step in German proceedings than before the EPO. Moreover, in comparison to the EPO, the German courts rarely question of whether the problem thus defined has indeed been credibly solved within the full scope of the claims.

When assessing whether it would have been obvious for the skilled person to come to the claimed invention when trying to solve the objective technical problem, it is typically decisive whether the prior art provides a specific suggestion, pointer, stimulus or incentive leading the skilled person to the specific solution claimed,[85] and whether the skilled person would have had a reasonable expectation of success when embarking on a route leading to the claimed invention.[86]

Although surprising advantageous effects can, in principle, be relied upon as indicators of an inventive step, the German courts frequently take the position that an additional unexpected and advantageous effect, including even an unexpected synergistic effect, cannot render a technical teaching inventive if the skilled person already had an incentive to come to the claimed teaching, even without the expectation of achieving this particular advantageous effect.[87] While this is similar to the 'bonus effect' or 'one-way-street situation' sometimes invoked by the Boards of Appeal of the EPO,[88] this concept appears to be applied more often by the German courts than by the EPO. Therefore, and due to the often more general definition of the technical problem, the reliance on comparative experimental data showing a surprising advantageous effect or property in support of inventive step tends to be less successful in Germany than before the EPO.

---

84. German Federal Supreme Court, decision in X ZR 128/09 of 11 November 2014 – *Repaglinid*; German Federal Supreme Court, decision in X ZR 41/13 of 13 January 2015 – *Quetiapin*; German Federal Supreme Court, decision in X ZR 72/08 of 1 March 2011 – *kosmetisches Sonnenschutzmittel III*; and German Federal Patent Court, decision in 3 Ni 23/14 (EP) of 1 December 2015.
85. German Federal Supreme Court, decision in Xa ZR 92/05 of 30 April 2009 – *Betrieb einer Sicherheitseinrichtung*; German Federal Supreme Court, decision in X ZB 6/10 of 20 December 2011 – *Installiereinrichtung II*; German Federal Supreme Court, decision in X ZR 65/05 of 8 December 2009 – *einteilige Öse*; German Federal Supreme Court, decision in X ZR 27/04 of 11 September 2007 – *Stahlblech*; German Federal Supreme Court, decision in X ZR 59/16 of 27 March 2018 – *Kinderbett*; German Federal Supreme Court, decision in X ZR 134/11 of 12 December 2012 – *Polymerzusammensetzung*; and German Federal Patent Court, decision in 3 Ni 36/11 (EP) of 23 July 2013.
86. German Federal Supreme Court, decision in X ZR 98/09 of 15 May 2012 – *Calcipotriol-Monohydrat*; German Federal Supreme Court, decision in Xa ZR 130/07 of 10 September 2009 – *Escitalopram*; German Federal Supreme Court, decision in X ZR 148/11 of 19 April 2016 – *Zöliakiediagnoseverfahren*; German Federal Supreme Court, decision in X ZR 50/09 of 6 March 2012; and German Federal Supreme Court, decision in X ZR 50/14 of 28 June 2016.
87. German Federal Supreme Court, decision in X ZR 128/09 of 11 November 2014 – *Repaglinid*; German Federal Supreme Court, decision in X ZR 68/99 of 10 December 2002 – *Kosmetisches Sonnenschutzmittel*; German Federal Supreme Court, decision in Xa ZR 130/07 of 10 September 2009 – *Escitalopram*; and German Federal Supreme Court, decision in Xa ZR 28/08 of 15 April 2010 – *Fettsäurezusammensetzung*.
88. Case Law of the Boards of Appeal of the European Patent Office, 8th Edition, 2016, ISBN-978-3-89605-154-7, chapter I.D.10.8.

In spite of the differences outlined above, the German approach to assessing inventive step is altogether very similar to the problem-solution approach established by the EPO, and in most cases the same lines of argument can be used.

Further indicators of inventive step are considered by the German courts in a similar manner as by the EPO. In particular, a prejudice in the prior art against the approach leading to the claimed invention ('teaching away') can be an indicator of inventive step, but only if such a prejudice was technically founded and widely accepted in the prior art, whereas this may not be the case if doubts are asserted only in a single document or if the invention merely accepts the known drawbacks of the corresponding approach.[89]

When arguing in defence of inventive step before the German Patent Office or the German courts, it would seem promising to explain, where possible, why the skilled person would not have found any *incentive* in the prior art to come to the claimed invention, why the skilled person would not have had any *reasonable expectation of success* or would have encountered *undue difficulties* when trying to embark on a path leading to the claimed invention, and why potential *alternative approaches* to the claimed solution would have seemed more promising to the skilled person (provided, of course, that the claimed solution does not merely accept known disadvantages). Moreover, although the mere 'agglomeration' of distinguishing features does normally not render the claimed subject-matter inventive, it can be helpful to point out that the skilled person would have had to make several modifications to the prior art in order to arrive at the claimed invention.[90]

[B] Particularities Regarding Claims to Antibodies

The same general approach to the assessment of inventive step as outlined in §3.05[A] above also applies to antibody inventions, whereby particular importance is typically attached to the question of whether the skilled person would have been motivated to modify the prior art in such a manner as to arrive at the claimed subject-matter with a reasonable expectation of success.

In the case of a novel and inventive antigen, it should normally not be necessary to separately discuss inventive step for a claim directed to any antibodies against this novel and inventive antigen. For example, the Federal Patent Court in the opposition appeal decision 14 W (pat) 8/06[91] acknowledged novelty and inventive step for a main product claim directed to certain peptides, and concluded without further ado that this favourable assessment of patentability likewise applies to another independent

---

89. German Federal Supreme Court, decision in X ZR 24/82 of 13 March 1984 – *Chlortoluron*, section II.3.a of the reasons; German Federal Supreme Court, decision in X ZR 49/94 of 4 June 1996 – *Rauchgasklappe*, section III.2.c of the reasons; German Federal Supreme Court, decision in X ZR 115/96 of 12 May 1998 – *Stoßwellen-Lithotripter*, section III.2 of the reasons; German Federal Supreme Court, decision in Xa ZR 34/08 of 25 February 2010, paragraph 86; German Federal Supreme Court, decision in X ZR 29/07 of 13 April 2010, paragraph 36; and German Federal Supreme Court, decision in X ZR 104/07 of 11 January 2011, paragraph 29.
90. German Federal Supreme Court, decision in X ZR 24/03 of 3 May 2006 – *Mikrotom*.
91. German Federal Patent Court, decision in 14 W (pat) 8/06 of 14 April 2011, section II.5 of the reasons.

product claim relating to antibodies having an affinity to these peptides, noting that the claimed antibodies are derivable from the claimed peptides on the basis of 'biochemical principles'.

Conversely, where the antigen of the claimed antibody is already known and the provision of antibodies against this antigen would have been possible by routine approaches, the mere provision of a further novel antibody is typically not considered to be inventive. Under such circumstances, a specific amino acid sequence may render the claimed antibody novel but does not normally confer inventive step. In this sense, there is no concept of 'structural non-obviousness' for antibody inventions in Germany.

In cases where the prior art already discloses an antibody against the same antigen as the claimed antibodies, it will usually be necessary to show an unexpected advantageous or improved property or a particular suitability for a certain application in order to establish the presence of an inventive step. To this end, comparative experimental tests with prior art antibodies can be very helpful. If tests with a specific antibody disclosed in a prior art document are not feasible, e.g. due to the non-availability of the corresponding antibody, it may alternatively be considered to provide comparative experimental data for other antibodies binding to the same target. In particular, if other antibodies against the same antigen have been obtained in the course of the research and development activities leading to the claimed invention, which do not exhibit the same advantageous properties as the claimed antibodies and do not fall within the scope of the claims in suit, the filing of experimental data for these other antibodies may be used to demonstrate that the provision of the claimed antibodies having the corresponding advantageous properties was not straightforward but rather an achievement that could not have reasonably been expected.

In this regard, it should also be noted that if a prior art document discloses an antibody without identifying its sequence and without making available the hybridoma producing this antibody (by depositing it with a depository institution), it follows that the prior art document does not provide an enabling disclosure of the corresponding specific antibody. This was acknowledged, for example, by the German Federal Patent Court in 3 Ni 19/02 (EU).[92]

As explained in §3.05[A] above, if the prior art is found to provide an incentive that would have led a skilled person to the claimed subject-matter, then even the demonstration of an unexpected advantageous effect of the claimed subject-matter may not justify the presence of an inventive step.[93]

This principle has also been applied specifically to antibody cases. For example, the German Federal Patent Court in 3 Ni 53/08 (EU)[94] denied inventive step for a claim directed to the combination of a specific therapeutic antibody (trastuzumab) with a

92. German Federal Patent Court, decision in 3 Ni 19/02 (EU) of 9 March 2004, section II.2.2.1 of the reasons.

93. German Federal Supreme Court, decision in X ZR 68/99 of 10 December 2002 – *Kosmetisches Sonnenschutzmittel*, headnote; German Federal Supreme Court, decision in Xa ZR 130/07 of 10 September 2009 – *Escitalopram*, paragraph 41; and German Federal Supreme Court, decision in Xa ZR 28/08 of 15 April 2010 – *Fettsäurezusammensetzung*, paragraph 80.

94. German Federal Patent Court, decision in 3 Ni 53/08 (EU) of 1 March 2011, section III.2.2.1 of the reasons.

specific small molecule active ingredient (docetaxel), taking the position that, in line with the principles established in *Kosmetisches Sonnenschutzmittel* (X ZR 68/99),[95] if the skilled person would have been motivated to come to the claimed combination of active ingredients in knowledge of the prior art, then even the finding of a surprising synergistic effect does not render this combination inventive.

Further specific examples of cases in which the question of inventive step was discussed in detail for antibody-related inventions can be found, for example, in the Federal Patent Court decisions 3 Ni 14/13 (EP)[96] (relating to a second medical use claim for a functionally defined antibody), 15 W (pat) 29/05[97] (concerning a claim directed to a competitive receptor binding assay for determining thyroid-stimulating hormone (TSH) receptor autoantibodies, in which a labelled TSH receptor antibody is employed as a reagent), 3 Ni 5/10 (EU)[98] (regarding claims directed to a method for producing antibodies via phage display) and 3 Ni 37/17 (EP)[99] (concerning a claim to a composition comprising a specific therapeutic antibody and a defined maximum amount of certain undesired variants), as well as the Federal Supreme Court decision in X ZR 133/12[100] (dealing with claims to a method for the purification of antibodies).

§3.06 ENFORCEMENT AND SCOPE OF PROTECTION

Germany has a bifurcated patent litigation system, whereby patent infringement and revocation actions are tried in different courts.

Patent Infringement

For patent infringement actions, there are twelve District Courts (*Landgerichte*) that have exclusive jurisdiction.[101] Since the infringing acts in the case of biologics and antibody-related inventions are typically not locally restricted within the territory of Germany, plaintiffs can file infringement actions with any of the twelve District Courts at their own choice. Most popular among plaintiffs and therefore most frequented are the District Courts of Düsseldorf, Munich, Mannheim, and Hamburg.

Both the court fees and the statutory attorney's fees for an infringement action are calculated on the basis of a theoretical value of the matter in dispute, which is fixed by the court. The losing party is liable to pay the court fees and reimburse the statutory attorney's fees incurred by the prevailing party. A decision in first-instance patent infringement proceedings is typically rendered by the competent District Court

95. German Federal Supreme Court, decision in X ZR 68/99 of 10 December 2002 – *Kosmetisches Sonnenschutzmittel*.
96. German Federal Patent Court, decision in 3 Ni 14/13 (EP) of 1 July 2014.
97. German Federal Patent Court, decision in 15 W (pat) 29/05 of 11 February 2010.
98. German Federal Patent Court, decision in 3 Ni 5/10 (EU) of 24 January 2012.
99. German Federal Patent Court, decision in 3 Ni 37/17 (EP) of 19 February 2019.
100. German Federal Supreme Court, decision in X ZR 133/12 of 13 May 2014.
101. Section 143(1) PatG. The twelve District Courts that have jurisdiction to hear patent infringement cases in Germany are the District Courts of Berlin, Braunschweig, Düsseldorf, Erfurt, Frankfurt am Main, Hamburg, Leipzig, Magdeburg, Mannheim, Munich I, Nuremberg-Fürth, and Saarbrücken.

within 9 to 20 months from the filing of the infringement action, depending on the court that is chosen.

The decision of a District Court in an infringement case can be appealed before the corresponding competent Higher Regional Court (*Oberlandesgericht*).[102] In both instances, the case will be heard by a panel of three legally qualified judges who do not have a technical background. An appeal decision is typically handed down by the Higher Regional Court within 12 to 24 months from the filing of the appeal.

As a further remedy, an appeal on points of law may be lodged with the German Federal Supreme Court against the final judgment of a Higher Regional Court,[103] but only if the competent Higher Regional Court has granted leave to appeal in its judgment. Otherwise, the losing party may file a complaint against the refusal of leave to appeal with the Federal Supreme Court which shall allow the complaint if the case is of fundamental legal importance or if a judicial review decision is required for the further development of the law or for ensuring uniform jurisprudence.[104] If an appeal on points of law is admitted, the Federal Supreme Court will render a judgment after an oral hearing, which may take approximately one to four years from the filing of the appeal.

Preliminary Injunctions

In urgent cases, a patentee (plaintiff) may also obtain preliminary injunctive relief, which can be granted ex parte (without first hearing the other party) within a few days, particularly if there is an evident case of infringement, if there is sufficient certainty for the patent to be valid, and if a prompt decision is required to avert irreparable damage. In this regard, different standards are applied by the twelve District Courts competent to hear patent cases,[105] which should be carefully considered for a strategic choice of court venue.[106] If, however, the District Court seized for a preliminary injunction has doubts about the alleged infringement, the validity of

102. Section 511 German Code of Civil Procedure (Zivilprozessordnung, 'ZPO').
103. Sections 542 et seqq. ZPO.
104. Section 543 ZPO.
105. The decisions of the different District Courts can be appealed before the respective competent Higher Regional Courts. There is, however, no possibility to file an appeal on points of law against the decisions of the Higher Regional Courts in preliminary injunction proceedings (Sec. 542(2) ZPO), which is why the case law of the different Higher Regional Courts (and their subordinate District Courts) relating specifically to preliminary injunctions is not harmonized.
106. For example, the District Court of Düsseldorf and the Higher Regional Court of Düsseldorf as well as the District Court of Mannheim and the Higher Regional Court of Karlsruhe take the position that a patent must normally have survived first-instance opposition or revocation proceedings in order to be assumed to be valid with a sufficient degree of certainty in preliminary injunction proceedings (*see*, e.g., Higher Regional Court of Düsseldorf, decision in I-2 U 6/17 of 31 August 2017; Higher Regional Court of Düsseldorf, decision in I-2 U 126/09 of 29 April 2010 – *Harnkatheterset*; and Higher Regional Court of Karlsruhe, decision in 6 U 52/15 of 23 September 2015 – *Ausrüstungssatz*), whereas the District Court of Munich and the Higher Regional Court of Munich do not consider this to be necessary (*see*, e.g., Higher Regional Court of Munich, decision in 6 U 3039/16 of 18 May 2017).

the patent or the required urgency, it will summon the plaintiff and the defendant to an oral hearing which may take place within two weeks to four months from the filing of the request for preliminary injunction, or alternatively it may immediately reject the request.

The defendant in preliminary injunction proceedings can file an opposition if a preliminary injunction is issued ex parte without an oral hearing, which will then be dealt with by the District Court that issued the preliminary injunction. If a decision granting the preliminary injunction is issued after an oral hearing, the defendant can file an appeal to the competent Higher Regional Court. The plaintiff can likewise file an appeal if the District Court rejects its request for a preliminary injunction. The corresponding appeal proceedings before the Higher Regional Court typically take about two to six months until a decision is rendered.

If a potential preliminary injunction based on a competitor's patent is anticipated (e.g., if a warning letter has been received), the defendant may choose to deposit a protective brief setting out its defence in an electronic central register. The protective brief is thereby made available to all District Courts for a period of six months from deposit, while the patentee or plaintiff will remain unaware of the protective brief until they file a request for a preliminary injunction. The filing of a protective brief is advisable particularly if there are strong arguments against the validity of the corresponding patent, whereas a weak defence may entail the risk that the District Court seized by the plaintiff could even be more inclined to grant an ex parte preliminary injunction without first hearing the defendant.

Patent Revocation

In patent infringement proceedings, alleged infringers cannot defend themselves by arguing that the asserted patent is invalid, as this is beyond the competence of the District Courts and Higher Regional Courts. If they wish to challenge the validity of a patent, a separate revocation action must be filed with the German Federal Patent Court, which has exclusive jurisdiction in this regard,[107] or an opposition must be lodged with the German or European Patent Office (in case this is still possible). A revocation action cannot be filed as long as an opposition can still be lodged or opposition proceedings are still pending.[108]

While parallel proceedings relating to the infringement and revocation of the same patent will, in principle, proceed independently from one another, alleged infringers can request the court dealing with the infringement action to stay the proceedings until the parallel revocation or opposition proceedings are resolved.[109] This normally requires the demonstration of a predominant likelihood that the patent will be found invalid, at least in the scope in which it is asserted in the infringement proceedings.[110]

107. Section 81 PatG.
108. Section 81(2) PatG.
109. Section 148(1) ZPO.
110. German Federal Supreme Court, decision in X ZR 61/13 of 16 September 2014 – *Kurznachrichten*, paragraph 4; and German Federal Supreme Court, decision in X ZR 56/85 of 11 November 1986 – *Transportfahrzeug*, headnote. This same standard has also been applied

Conversely, if a patent has been invalidated in first-instance revocation or opposition proceedings, any parallel infringement or preliminary injunction proceedings will be stayed until the revocation of the patent is overturned or unless the court deciding on infringement determines that the first-instance decision revoking the patent is 'evidently wrong',[111] which has also been affirmed specifically in antibody litigation.[112] According to the District Court of Munich, this principle should apply not only to first-instance revocation decisions but also to reasoned negative preliminary opinions issued by the Federal Patent Court in revocation proceedings.[113]

Patent revocation actions filed with the Federal Patent Court are typically decided within one to three years, following an oral hearing before a panel of three technically qualified and two legally qualified judges. The losing party is liable to pay the court fees and reimburse the statutory attorney's fees of the prevailing party, both of which are calculated on the basis of a theoretical value of the patent in dispute, as determined by the court.

The decision of the Federal Patent Court in first-instance patent revocation proceedings can be appealed before the Federal Supreme Court. The corresponding appeal proceedings usually take about two to three years.

[A] Biosimilars

A biosimilar is a biological medicine that is 'highly similar' to another already approved biological medicine in terms of its structure, biological activity and efficacy, safety, and immunogenicity.[114] In contrast to chemical small molecular medicines, it is practically impossible for competitors to exactly replicate an approved reference biological medicine without access to the originator's production process and cell lines, which is why biosimilars are treated differently from generics under European regulatory law.[115]

---

to antibody-related patents; *see*, e.g., District Court of Düsseldorf, decision in 4a O 73/15 of 28 July 2016, section V of the reasons; District Court of Düsseldorf, decision in 4a O 143/10 of 10 November 2011, section VI.1 of the reasons; District Court of Düsseldorf, decision in 4a O 331/03 of 6 April 2006, section IV of the reasons; and District Court of Düsseldorf, decision in 4 O 320/97 of 29 April 1999, section B.VII of the reasons.

111. Higher Regional Court of Düsseldorf, decision in I-2 W 47/07 of 29 May 2008 – *Olanzapin*; Higher Regional Court of Düsseldorf, decision in I-2 U 126/09 of 29 April 2010 – *Harnkatheterset*; and District Court of Munich, decision in 7 O 9443/12 of 12 February 2015 – *Google Maps*.
112. District Court of Munich, decision in 7 O 11152/17 of 17 August 2017.
113. *Ibid.*, section B.II of the reasons.
114. European Medicines Agency, Biosimilar medicines: Overview (accessible online at: https://www.ema.europa.eu/en/human-regulatory/overview/biosimilar-medicines-overview).
115. Article 10(4) of Directive 2001/83/EC (Community code relating to medicinal products for human use). For practical guidance, *see* European Medicines Agency, Guideline on similar biological medicinal products (CHMP/437/04 Rev 1) of 23 October 2014; and European Medicines Agency, Guideline on similar biological medicinal products containing monoclonal antibodies – non-clinical and clinical issues (EMA/CHMP/BMWP/403543/2010) of 30 May 2012.

The European Union was the first region worldwide to regulate biosimilars, and the first approval of a biosimilar in the EU occurred in 2006 when Sandoz obtained a marketing authorization for Omnitrope®, a biosimilar of Pfizer's Genotropin® containing the peptide hormone somatropin. The first biosimilar of a monoclonal antibody was approved in the EU in 2013, when two biosimilar copies of Janssen's Remicade® containing the antibody infliximab were authorized, i.e. Celltrion's Remsima® and Pfizer's Inflectra®. Since then, the number of antibody biosimilar approvals in the EU has been growing rapidly, as various biosimilars of Enbrel® (etanercept), MabThera® (rituximab), Humira® (adalimumab), Herceptin® (trastuzumab) and Avastin® (bevacizumab) were authorized in the period from 2016 to 2018.

The entry of antibody biosimilars to the European market has been accompanied by a number of patent litigations in Germany, not all of which, however, have been terminated with court decisions.

Thus, for example, Korean biosimilar producer Celltrion obtained regulatory approval of Truxima®, a biosimilar of Roche/Biogen's medicament MabThera®/ Rituxan® containing the antibody rituximab, in the European Union in 2017. When Mundipharma set out to distribute this biosimilar in Germany, Biogen filed a request for a preliminary injunction based on their patent EP 2 055 313 B1 against Mundipharma with the District Court of Munich. These proceedings, however, were terminated without a decision from the District Court, as Biogen withdrew their request for a preliminary injunction.[116]

A further biosimilar patent litigation in Germany concerned the therapeutic antibody trastuzumab. The District Court of Düsseldorf in its judgment 4a O 36/18[117] decided on a request for a preliminary injunction filed by F. Hoffmann-La Roche against Celltrion and their German distributor Mundipharma in respect of Herzuma®, a biosimilar of Roche's blockbuster medicament Herceptin® containing the antibody trastuzumab.

The patent asserted by Roche described how trastuzumab could be purified to reduce the amount of undesirable 'acidic variants' of this antibody. The granted claims related, simply put,[118] to a mixture of trastuzumab and particular acidic variants thereof, wherein the amount of the acidic variants is less than 25%.

What makes this case intriguing are the consequences of the technological advance in the development of analytical methods over the course of the 20 years from the patent's priority date (1998) to the approval of the allegedly infringing

---

116. The preliminary injunction proceedings before the District Court of Munich are discussed in a parallel Dutch decision; *see* District Court of The Hague, decision in *Biogen v. Hoffman La Roche*, C/09/531270 / KG ZA 17-519 of 12 May 2017 (ECLI:NL:RBDHA:2017:5035), paragraph 2.10.
117. District Court of Düsseldorf, decision in 4a O 36/18 of 12 July 2018.
118. The full wording of claim 1 of the patent EP 1 308 455 B9 as granted (and as maintained in European opposition appeal proceedings) reads as follows:

    A composition comprising a mixture of anti-HER2 antibody and one or more acidic variants thereof, wherein the amount of the acidic variant(s) is less than about 25%, and wherein the acidic variant(s) are predominantly deamidated variants wherein one or more asparagine residues of the anti-HER2 antibody have been deamidated, and wherein the anti-HER2 antibody is humMAb4D5-8, and wherein the deamidated variants have Asn30 in CDR1 of either or both VL regions of humMAb4D5-8 converted to aspartate.

biosimilar Herzuma® in the European Union in 2018. In principle, one and the same purified trastuzumab preparation may be determined to contain less than 25% acidic variants if examined with analytical methods available at the priority date of the patent, but to contain more than 25% if tested with the more advanced analytical techniques available at the time when the allegedly infringing biosimilar entered the EU market 20 years later.

Thus, the patent described the determination of the content of acidic variants in the examples using a specific type of cation exchange chromatography column. This column, however, was no longer available when the patent was asserted. Comparable columns which had been developed by the corresponding manufacturers in the meantime, and which were also used by the patentee in regulatory approval proceedings, showed a higher resolution of charged variants. This higher resolution led to an additional peak representing an acidic variant in the ion exchange chromatogram, thereby increasing the content of acidic variants in comparison to the use of the column described in the patent. The patentee argued in the infringement proceedings that this peak would have to be disregarded since it would not have been detectable by the cation exchange column used in the patent for the determination of the acidic variants.

The District Court of Düsseldorf in its judgment found that the claim feature requiring less than 25% acidic variants had to be construed from the perspective of a person skilled in the art at the priority date of the patent, using their common general knowledge available at that date, whereas later-gained knowledge could not be taken into account for determining the scope of protection of the patent.[119] In line with this principle, the Court acknowledged that the skilled person would understand that any suitable analytical method available at the priority date of the patent could be used for determining the content of acidic variants of the antibody.

The District Court thus agreed with the patentee insofar as the determination of the content of acidic variants would have to be done with a technique that was available at the priority date of the patent.

Based on the fact that the granted claims did not prescribe the use of any particular measurement method, however, the District Court concluded that the finding of less than 25% acidic variants with only one single analytical method (which had been exemplified in the patent specification) would not suffice to demonstrate that the patent is infringed.[120] Rather, the skilled person would consider all of the analytical methods available at the priority date of the patent and would choose those methods that are particularly accurate. Only if such measurements had shown a content of acidic variants of less than 25%, would the corresponding product have been found to infringe the patent, even in the case that more recent techniques would demonstrate an actual content of acidic variants above 25%.[121] The Court ultimately denied infringement, noting that the realization of this claim feature had not been adequately proven.

---

119. District Court of Düsseldorf, decision in 4a O 36/18 of 12 July 2018, section I.4.b)bb) of the reasons.
120. *Ibid.*, section I.4.b)dd) of the reasons.
121. *Ibid.*, sections I.4.b)cc), I.4.b)dd) and I.4.b)ff) of the reasons.

While, at the time of writing, these findings of the District Court might still be overturned,[122] this case illustrates that reciting in the claims a single specific measurement method for determining a parameter such as the content of acidic variants, at least in a dependent claim, could be advantageous for the enforcement of the corresponding patent. This would seem to be particularly interesting in the case of 'negative' features requiring the absence of certain components or setting an upper limit for their content, because in such cases it might otherwise become a matter of dispute whether the use of a single specific measurement method is sufficient to demonstrate the absence (or low content) of the respective components.

[B] Equivalence

General Principles of Equivalent Patent Infringement

In Germany, the extent of protection conferred by a patent is determined by the claims, whereby the description and the drawings shall be used to interpret the claims.[123]

What is decisive in this regard is not the literal sense of the terms used in the patent claims but rather their technical meaning, which must be purposively construed from the perspective of the notional person skilled in the art and in consideration of the patent description, taking into account which function the patent attributes to the respective claim features.[124] In accordance with this principle, where a patent ascribes a specific meaning to a technical term (which may deviate from or even contradict the usual meaning of that term in the art), this specific meaning alone is decisive, i.e. a patent can be its own dictionary in this sense.[125]

Importantly, the scope of protection of a patent is not limited to the specific subject-matter defined in the granted claims (corresponding to 'literal infringement') but also extends to equivalent embodiments. There are no corresponding statutory provisions in German law, except for the Protocol on the Interpretation of Article 69 EPC,[126] which the German Federal Supreme Court has found to be applicable not

122. Note that the patent was subsequently revoked in parallel first-instance revocation proceedings; *see* German Federal Patent Court, decision in 3 Ni 37/17 (EP) of 19 February 2019. This decision was open to appeal at the time of writing.
123. Section 14 PatG and Art. 69(1) EPC.
124. German Federal Supreme Court, decision in X ZR 29/15 of 14 June 2016 – *Pemetrexed*; and German Federal Supreme Court, decision in X ZR 176/02 of 12 October 2004 – *Staubsaugersaugrohr*.
125. German Federal Supreme Court, decision in X ZR 85/96 of 2 March 1999 – *Spannschraube*, headnotes 1–2; German Federal Supreme Court, decision in X ZR 103/13 of 2 June 2015 – *Kreuzgestänge*, headnote 2 and paragraph 22; German Federal Supreme Court, decision in X ZR 11/13 of 27 October 2015 – *Fugenband*, paragraph 14; German Federal Supreme Court, decision in X ZR 145/98 of 7 November 2000 – *Brieflocher*, headnote; German Federal Supreme Court, decision in X ZR 102/15 of 9 May 2017, paragraph 12; and German Federal Supreme Court, decision in X ZR 44/16 of 13 March 2018, paragraph 25.
126. Pursuant to Art. 164(1) EPC, the Protocol on the Interpretation of Art. 69 EPC forms an integral part of the European Patent Convention.

only to European patents but also to German national patents.[127] Article 2 of the Protocol on the Interpretation of Article 69 EPC reads as follows:

> *Equivalents*
>
> For the purpose of determining the extent of protection conferred by a European patent, due account shall be taken of any element which is equivalent to an element specified in the claims.

Thus, even an embodiment that deviates from the specific features required by the granted claims of a patent may still be found to infringe the patent under the doctrine of equivalence.

In line with established case law of the German Federal Supreme Court,[128] the infringement of a patent by equivalent means requires that the following three conditions are cumulatively fulfilled:

1. The equivalent embodiment must solve the technical problem underlying the claimed invention by means which, although modified, have objectively the same effect as the means required in the granted claims.
2. The person skilled in the art must be able to infer the equivalent embodiment from the disclosure-content of the patent and their common general knowledge at the priority or filing date of the patent without inventive activity.
3. The considerations required to find the equivalent embodiment must be oriented towards the technical teaching of the claimed invention, so that the skilled person would recognize the respective embodiments, i.e. the literally claimed one and the allegedly infringing one, as being equivalent.

An important limitation to the equivalent scope of protection, however, results from the 'Formstein defence' (or 'free prior art defence'),[129] which allows alleged infringers to defend themselves by showing that an allegedly equivalent embodiment was anticipated or rendered obvious by the prior art available at the relevant priority or filing date of the patent. This effectively ensures that the equivalent scope of protection conferred by a patent does not extend to embodiments that would have been anticipated or obvious in view of the prior art. The Formstein defence can be

127. German Federal Supreme Court, decision in X ZR 28/85 of 29 April 1986 – *Formstein*, section I.5.b) of the reasons.
128. German Federal Supreme Court, decision in X ZR 28/85 of 29 April 1986 – *Formstein*; German Federal Supreme Court, decision in X ZR 43/01 of 12 March 2002 – *Kunststoffrohrteil*; German Federal Supreme Court, decision in X ZR 168/00 of 12 March 2002 – *Schneidmesser I*; German Federal Supreme Court, decision in X ZR 135/01 of 12 March 2002 – *Schneidmesser II*; German Federal Supreme Court, decision in X ZB 12/00 of 12 March 2002 – *Custodiol I*; German Federal Supreme Court, decision in X ZR 73/01 of 12 March 2002 – *Custodiol II*; German Federal Supreme Court, decision in X ZR 81/13 of 13 January 2015 – *Kochgefäß*; German Federal Supreme Court, decision in X ZR 114/13 of 10 May 2016 – *Wärmetauscher*; and German Federal Supreme Court, decision in X ZR 76/14 of 23 August 2016 – *V-förmige Führungsanordnung*.
129. German Federal Supreme Court, decision in X ZR 28/85 of 29 April 1986 – *Formstein*, section I.5.b) of the reasons.

invoked only against equivalent infringement but not against literal infringement,[130] because in this latter case the validity of the patent would be challenged, which is not a permissible defence in infringement proceedings under the bifurcated litigation system in Germany.

A further notable limitation to the equivalent scope of protection applies if the patent specification explicitly describes several alternative technical means but the granted claims selectively relate to only one of these alternative means, while the others have been deliberately excluded. Under such circumstances, an embodiment making use of those alternative technical means which have been deliberately excluded from the claims cannot be covered by the equivalent scope of protection.[131]

Equivalent Infringement of Antibody Patents

A fundamental decision relating to the equivalent infringement of an antibody patent was rendered in the second instance by the Higher Regional Court of Düsseldorf in I-2 U 80/02[132] in 2005.

In the case underlying this decision, Roche had been sued for infringement of the patent EP 0 153 114 B1 held by Chiron Corp. due to the marketing of Herceptin®, a medicament containing the humanized monoclonal anti-HER2 antibody trastuzumab. Claim 1 of this patent (as maintained by the Federal Patent Court in parallel revocation proceedings[133]) related, simply put, to a murine monoclonal antibody which binds a human breast cancer antigen that is also bound by a reference antibody produced by a specific deposited hybridoma; the functionally defined antigen bound by the claimed murine antibody was the same antigen (HER2) that is also bound by Roche's antibody trastuzumab. The claims of the asserted patent thus related specifically to a *murine* (mouse) monoclonal antibody whereas the allegedly infringing trastuzumab was a *humanized* monoclonal antibody, i.e. trastuzumab had been obtained by inserting the CDRs of a murine precursor antibody into the framework of a human IgG1 antibody.

The Higher Regional Court of Düsseldorf in its judgment in I-2 U 80/02 upheld the preceding first-instance decision[134] and denied both literal and equivalent infringement of Chiron's patent. In reaching this decision, the Higher Regional Court found that in light of the entire disclosure of the patent, the claimed 'murine' monoclonal antibody had to be interpreted as meaning an antibody that has exclusively murine sequences. The patent was therefore not literally infringed by the humanized antibody trastuzumab.

---

130. German Federal Supreme Court, decision in X ZR 22/97 of 17 February 1999 - *Kontaktfederblock*.
131. German Federal Supreme Court, decision in X ZR 16/09 of 10 May 2011 – *Okklusionsvorrichtung*; German Federal Supreme Court, decision in X ZR 69/10 of 13 September 2011 - *Diglycidverbindung*; German Federal Supreme Court, decision in X ZR 29/15 of 14 June 2016 - *Pemetrexed*; and Higher Regional Court of Düsseldorf, decision in I-2 U 29/12 of 7 November 2013 – *WC-Sitzgelenk*.
132. Higher Regional Court of Düsseldorf, decision in I-2 U 80/02 of 10 February 2005.
133. German Federal Patent Court, decision in 3 Ni 19/02 (EU) of 9 March 2004.
134. District Court of Düsseldorf, decision in 4a O 125/01 of 14 May 2002.

With respect to the question of equivalent infringement, the Court held that even if the humanized antibody trastuzumab could be regarded as having objectively the same effect as the murine antibody claimed in the asserted patent, and even if a skilled person could have inferred trastuzumab from the disclosure of the patent and their common general knowledge at the effective date of the patent without inventive ingenuity, the skilled person could only have inferred trastuzumab by making considerations that are precisely *not* oriented towards the claimed technical teaching of the patent. In particular, the skilled person would have had to depart from the sole approach disclosed in the patent for obtaining the claimed antibodies (i.e., Köhler and Milstein's hybridoma technology) without a clear expectation of success. Moreover, the plaintiff itself asserted that approaches for the production of chimeric murine antibodies, in which sequences not required for antigen binding are replaced by human sequences, had already been known to the skilled person from scientific literature published several months before the effective date of the patent; according to the Court, precisely in this case would the skilled person have expected explicit indications in the patent that protection was also sought for corresponding antibodies. Therefore, at least the third criterion required to establish a case of equivalent infringement, i.e. that the considerations required to find the equivalent embodiment must be oriented towards the technical teaching of the claimed invention, was clearly not fulfilled.

Chapter 4

Italy

Olga Capasso

§4.01 ANTIBODIES AS PATENTABLE SUBJECT-MATTER

[A] Legal Framework

Reference law is the Italian Code of Industrial Property (ICIP) (Legislative Decree No. 30 of 10 February 2005 and further implementations and modifications). Specific provisions for biotech inventions are contained at Section IV*bis* of ICIP, including Articles from 81*bis* to 81*octies*, added with Legislative Decree No. 131 of 13 August 2010.

Given that an antibody is a biological material, the following provisions are of relevance.

Article 81*quater*(a) confirms that a biological material, isolated from its natural environment or produced through a technical process, even if pre-existing in a natural state may be patentable provided that it meets the requirements of novelty and inventive step and is susceptible to industrial application.

Analogously, Article 81*quater*(b) and c) affirm the patentability of technical processes through which biological material is produced, processed or used, even if pre-existing in a natural state, and of any new utilization of a biological material or of a technical process relating to biological material, respectively.

Article 81*quater*(d) stipulates that an invention relating to an element isolated from the human body or produced otherwise, through a technical process, even if its structure is identical to that of a natural element, may be patentable provided that its function and industrial application are concretely indicated and described.

Antibodies are commonly used for medical treatments and/or diagnosis methods.

Consequently, of relevance for patentability of antibodies are also provisions dealing with methods of diagnosis and treatment, namely at Article 45.4, which excludes from patentability methods for surgical or therapeutic treatment of the human or animal bodies and diagnostic methods applied to human or animal bodies. Further Article 45.5 clarifies that such provision does not apply to products, and in particular to substances or compositions, for the use of one of the specified methods.

There is no direct applicability of the G02/08 decision of the Enlarged Board of Appeal on the so-called Swiss-type second medical use claims. Then a claim wording such us 'Use of mAB X for the treatment of pathology Y' is still acceptable. It is advisable to include also claims drafted as 'mAB X for use in the treatment of pathology Y'.

[B] General Amenability or Exclusion of Antibodies from Patentability

As mentioned above Article 45.1 states that patents may be granted in all sectors of technology, provided that patentability requirements (novelty, inventive step and industrial applicability) are fulfilled.

No specific barrier to patentability of products of nature is present in the biotech related provisions. In fact Article 81*quater* clarifies that any biological material, isolated from its natural environment or produced through a technical process even if pre-existing in a natural state, may be patentable.

[C] Required Distinction from Naturally Occurring Antibodies

Article 81*quater*.1(d) may be of relevance as to human antibodies. In fact it states that an invention relating to an element isolated from the human body or produced otherwise, through a technical process, even if its structure is identical to that of a natural element, may be patentable provided that its function and industrial application are concretely indicated and described. Then a claim directed to a full human antibody requires a disclosure of its function and applicability at least in the patent text.

§4.02 ACCEPTABLE CLAIM FEATURES FOR DEFINING ANTIBODIES

In principle, no limitations are present in Italian law and practice as to characterizing features to be included in a claim directed to an antibody. Either functional or structural features may be used, even in combination. Certainly, special care should be given in properly limiting the claim over the prior art disclosing antibodies directed towards the same antigen, and in mentioning functional features in a clear and univocal manner. All of the following functional and structural features are acceptable.

[A] Functional Features

[1] Target/Antigen

As to the target, the mention of the antigen epitope amino acid sequence is admissible. For some particular cases i.e. in case of discontinuous epitopes, further information on spatial structure thereof may also be of support.

[2] Mode of Binding: Target Affinity, Binding Specificity, Epitope, Definitions via Reference Antibodies and Competitive Binding

In principle, all of the above features may be used to define an antibody. In such circumstance special attention should be given to a clear disclosure of the methods of measurement.

[3] Effect on Target

An antibody may also be defined as to its effects, e.g. agonistic or antagonistic activity, requiring special care as to the definition of such effect (e.g. agonistic for binding and/or for activity?). Due attention should be given to providing a clear definition of such activity, and methods of measurement as well.

The Tribunal of Milan Decision No. 6778/2017 (*Roche v. Amgen*) accepted a functional feature of the antibody in the claim wording, namely the ability of the antibody itself to induce apoptosis, to define the scope of claim.

[B] Structural Features

[1] Molecular Topology: Antibody Types, Fragments and Antibody Constructs

All of above features may be used to define an antibody and may be essential to properly define the claimed matter with respect to prior art. To overcome potential clarity problems, generic mention in the claims of antibody fragments should be properly supported by definitions in the patent text.

[2] Amino Acid Sequences

[a] Full-Length Sequences of Antibodies

Full length sequence of antibodies may be used to define claimed matter, though the scope of protection may as a result be very limited.

[b] Sequences of Fragments, CDRs and Framework Regions

All of the above features may be used to define an antibody, though such features might not be sufficient to support inventive step with respect to a prior art disclosing a generic antibody against a known antigen or even the only antigen.

[3] Chemical Modifications, Conjugation and Glycosylation

All of the above features may be used to define an antibody, giving proper attention to the disclosure of methods of measurement.

[C] Cell Line Deposits and Process of Production

Both of the above features may be used to define an antibody. ICIP Article 51.2 provides that the description of a patent application should be sufficient to be performed by an expert in the art. In the case of an invention relating to an antibody, depositing a cell line able to produce the antibody, namely an hybridoma cell line, may be necessary to fulfil such a requirement. The deposit should be performed according to the Budapest Treaty, pursuant to Article 162 ICIP. The material must be deposited on or before the patent application filing date, or priority if claimed, and relevant information may be provided within 16 months from the earliest priority date.

§4.03 BREADTH OF CLAIMS AND SUPPORT BY EXAMPLES

[A] Acceptable Breadth of Claims to Antibodies

The scope of a claim directed to an antibody strictly depends on available prior art disclosing related antibodies and on the actual contribution of the inventors. Then it is advisable to create in the patent disclosure some fallback positions to properly limit the scope of the claims, if needed.

A claim directed to an antibody binding to antigen X, antigen X being a novel and inventive pharmacological target, may in principle be accepted even if the patent application does not provide any actual example of an antibody binding to antigen X. In fact experimental data are not strictly required. However it could be difficult to support a wide scope of protection, for example by claiming a specific activity, with no support of some exemplificative antibodies falling within the claimed definition.

The Tribunal of Milan Decision No. 6778/2017 (*Roche v. Amgen*) confirmed that a functional feature, namely the ability of the claimed antibody itself to induce apoptosis, present in the claim wording and properly supported by examples in the patent text, was able to limit the scope of protection of the claim and distinguish it from the prior art.

[B] Required Experimental Support for Claims to Functionally Defined Antibodies

Though experimental data are not strictly required, it could be difficult to support a claim directed to an antibody defined (also) by its specific activity, without the aid of some exemplificative antibodies falling within the claimed definition.

[C] Required Experimental Support for Claims to Structurally Defined Antibodies

Though experimental data are not strictly required, it could be difficult to support a wide scope of protection, for example by claiming not all CDR sequences, without the support of some exemplificative antibodies showing that unclaimed CDRs are irrelevant for the claimed use. The same reasoning may apply to claims referring to the sequence identity (%) with no proper support that antibody features are maintained.

§4.04 SPECIFIC MEDICAL APPLICATIONS AND OTHER FOLLOW-UP INVENTIONS

In general antibodies may be treated as molecules having medical and/or diagnostic applications. Then all of the following applications may in principle be claimed, by using proper claim wording, as discussed in §4.01[A].

[A] Treatment of Specific Diseases

Subject to fulfilment of patentability requirements, a claim directed to an antibody X for treatment of a specific pathology is acceptable.

[B] Mode of Administration

Subject to fulfilment of patentability requirements, a claim directed to an antibody X for treatment of a pathology and further including a mode of administration is in principle acceptable. National case law would be needed to confirm that such affirmation is adopted at juridical level.

[C] Dosage Regimens

Subject to fulfilment of patentability requirements, a claim directed to an antibody X for treatment of a pathology and further including a specific dosage regimen is in principle acceptable. Inventive step fulfilment may be an issue for such claims. National case law would be needed to confirm that such affirmation is adopted at juridical level.

[D] Specific Patient Groups

Subject to fulfilment of patentability requirements, a claim directed to an antibody X for treatment of a pathology and further including specific patient groups is in principle acceptable. Novelty and/or inventive step fulfilment may be an issue for such claims in case the prior art discloses treatments with partial overlapping group of patients. National case law would be needed to confirm that such affirmation is adopted at juridical level.

[E] Specific Mode of Action

Medical use claims referring to a known antibody for a known treatment distinguished merely by a different mode of action may be considered not novel. A specific mode of action may be interpreted as an inherent feature of the claimed antibody and/or as disclosing an effect and not a means to achieve it. National case law would be needed to confirm that such affirmation is adopted at juridical level.

[F] Combinations with Other Active Ingredients

Antibodies may well be claimed in combination with further active ingredients. Special care is advisable to include in the text specific ingredients that may be part of the combination, possibly with formulation examples.

[G] Specific Diagnostic Applications

The Tribunal of Rome Decision No. 16509/2013 (*DiaSorin v. Eurospital et al.*) confirmed the patentability of a diagnostic method making use of specific antigen to detect anti-tTG antibodies in a biological sample.

§4.05 ASSESSMENT OF INVENTIVENESS

[A] General Approach

Though not bound to any provisions, usually EPO criteria to assess inventive step are increasingly adopted by Italian tribunals. Then the problem-solution approach is very often utilized during patent litigations.

[B] Particularities Regarding Claims to Antibodies

No peculiarities as to antibodies is relevant.

§4.06 ENFORCEMENT AND SCOPE OF PROTECTION

[A] Biosimilars

Italian tribunals do not seem to have issued decisions specifically dealing with antibodies related to biosimilars.

However the recent Supreme Court Decision No. 24658/2016 on infringement by equivalents of a chemical drug may be of relevance in approaching the infringement, direct or by equivalence, of a biosimilar. The Supreme Court stated that:

> 'In terms of patent infringement by equivalence, in order to assess whether the disputed realization can be considered equivalent to the patented one, so as to constitute an infringement, it must be ascertained whether, in allowing the same final result, it presents original character, offering a non-trivial or repetitive answer to the previous one'.

The Supreme Court also pointed out that

> 'in order to exclude an infringement by equivalence, the variation, even if original, made to a single element of the patented invention is not of relevance, if such variation does not allow to exclude the use, even partial, of the prior patent'.

It is tempting to foresee that such reasoning might well be adopted in biosimilar cases, too.

[B] Equivalence

Italian tribunals do not seem to have issued decisions specifically dealing with antibodies related to infringement by equivalents.

Of some relevance recently the Tribunal of Milan issued the order of 15 October 2018, in the context of a complaint to an order issued during preliminary proceedings of RG 45209/2017 (*Eli Lilly v. Fresenius*), stating that a limitation adopted during an examination procedure with the EPO may not represent a bar to apply the doctrine of infringement by equivalents.

Chapter 5

The Netherlands

Martin Klok

§5.01 ANTIBODIES AS PATENTABLE SUBJECT-MATTER

[A] Legal Framework

Patent law in the Netherlands follows European patent law as defined in the European Patent Convention and the case law based thereon. For a detailed analysis of the European Patent Convention as applied to the subject of antibodies, reference is made to Chapter 1.

The Dutch Patent Act of 1995 (DPA) provides the legal provisions which govern validity of, and infringement of, claims related to antibodies. The DPA has been amended in 2004 to implement Directive 98/44/EC of 6 July 1998 on the legal protection of biotechnological inventions. With this amendment, a new Article 2a was introduced, which explicitly allows patents directed to biological material:

> *Article 2a(1) DPA*:
>
> The inventions referred to in Article 2(1) ['that are new, that involve an inventive step and that are susceptible of industrial application'] are also taken to mean inventions that relate to a product that consists of or contains biological material or that relates to a process through which biological material is obtained, processed or used. [unofficial translation, RVO, 2009]

Article 2a (2) DPA defines in a non-limitative manner situations which should in principle be considered patentable:

> *Article 2a(2) DPA*:
>
> Inventions within the meaning of the first paragraph in any event include inventions with respect to:
>
> a. biological material that is isolated from its natural environment or is obtained using a technical process, even if that material occurs in nature;

b. a part of the human body that is isolated or that is otherwise obtained using a technical process, including a sequence or partial sequence of a gene, even if the structure of that part is identical to that of a natural part;
c. plants or animals, provided that the practicability of that invention is not technically limited to certain plant or animal varieties; or
d. a microbiological or other technical process through which biological material is obtained, processed or used, or a product obtained using such a process. [unofficial translation, RVO, 2009]

It follows from Article 2a(2) DPA that inventions which are directed to a particular antibody, or which encompass use of a particular antibody, should in principle be considered patentable, regardless of whether the antibody in question occurs in nature, or has been created in a laboratory environment.

Regarding medical application of antibodies, the provisions of the DPA provide, in line with Article 53(c) EPC, that:

Article 3(1) DPA:

No patent shall be issued for:

...

(f) methods of treating the human or animal body by means of surgery or medical treatment and diagnostic methods that are applied to the human or animal body, with the exception of products, in particular substances or compositions, for the application of such methods. [unofficial translation, RVO, 2009]

Antibodies are treated in the case law as a 'product ... for the application of such methods' according to Article 3(1)(f) DPA, and no distinction has been made between biological molecules such as antibodies and other products such as small molecules. Consequently, medical use of antibodies can validly invoke patent protection in the Netherlands, subject to the general provisions regarding valid patent protection, and subject to the specific formulation of first or second medical use claims as follows from Article 3(1)(f) DPA and Article 54(4) and (5) EPC.

The above provisions from the DPA follow the corresponding provisions from the EPC, and the case law on these provisions takes into account both European and Dutch case law. The discussion in Chapter 1 on antibodies as patentable subject-matter should be considered a valid representation of the Dutch situation as regards the validity of claims directed to antibodies.

[B] General Amenability or Exclusion of Antibodies from Patentability

Patent law in the Netherlands follows European patent law as defined in the European Patent Convention and the case law based thereon. For a detailed analysis of the European Patent Convention as applied to the subject of antibodies, reference is made to Chapter 1.

[C] Required Distinction from Naturally Occurring Antibodies

Patent law in the Netherlands follows European patent law as defined in the European Patent Convention and the case law based thereon. For a detailed analysis of the

European Patent Convention as applied to the subject of antibodies, reference is made to Chapter 1.

As mentioned in §5.01[A], the DPA explicitly allows for claims directed to a particular antibody, or which encompass use of a particular antibody, regardless of whether the antibody in question occurs in nature, or has been created in a laboratory environment.

§5.02 ACCEPTABLE CLAIM FEATURES FOR DEFINING ANTIBODIES

[A] Functional Features

[1] Target/Antigen

Patent law in the Netherlands follows European patent law as defined in the European Patent Convention and the case law based thereon. For a detailed analysis of the European Patent Convention as applied to the subject of antibodies, reference is made to Chapter 1.

In first instance main proceedings, the District Court of The Hague held that the term 'antibody' is to be understood in line with common general knowledge on the nature of an antibody (*MSD v. Ono* of 29 June 2016, C/09/489180/ HA ZA 15-623). That is, an antibody to a particular antigen (in this case, PD-1), should bind to its antigen. The argument that an antibody is merely a functional definition expressing that the signal conveyed by the recited antigen is suppressed by an antibody, regardless of whether it binds the antigen, was rejected. Thus, an antibody which inhibits the PD-1 pathway by binding to for instance PD-L1 was not considered an anti-PD-1 antibody.

In another case (*Roche v. Chiron*, 23 March 2005, 04/2384), the District Court of The Hague held in relation to a claim directed to an antibody, that the feature 'binds selectively to human breast cancer cells' would not lead to an insufficient disclosure. The Court considered that the general description could be relied on to assess whether binding should be considered selective. It was considered of particular importance that the antibodies in question were distinguished by their selectivity in binding to living material. This property, according to the Court, in its nature results in considerable scattering and inaccuracy. Molecular microbiology was on this aspect considered not an exact science relying on hard data. According to the Court, the feature of selective binding should be considered an in essence negative definition of the claimed antibodies, in the sense that antibodies should not be considered part of the invention if they bind to normal tissue 'too much'.

[2] Mode of Binding: Target Affinity, Binding Specificity, Epitope, Definitions via Reference Antibodies and Competitive Binding

Patent law in the Netherlands follows European patent law as defined in the European Patent Convention and the case law based thereon. For a detailed analysis of the European Patent Convention as applied to the subject of antibodies, reference is made to Chapter 1.

In the case between Roche and Chiron (*Roche v. Chiron*, 23 March 2005, 04/2384), the District Court of The Hague held that the claim feature that the claimed antibody 'when conjugated to a ricin A chain, exhibits a TCID 50% against MCF-7 cells of less than about 10 nM' did not lead to an insufficient disclosure. The Court recognized that TCID values by their nature may fluctuate between various determinations, and considered that if the skilled person would find a value relatively close to 10 nM, he could redo the determination in order to determine whether there would be infringement. The Court held that molecular microbiology is not a science which is based on strict numbers, and considered that this in particular applied to cytotoxicity tests to determine TCID. Therefore, the feature did not lead to an insufficient disclosure.

[3] Effect on Target

Patent law in the Netherlands follows European patent law as defined in the European Patent Convention and the case law based thereon. For a detailed analysis of the European Patent Convention as applied to the subject of antibodies, reference is made to Chapter 1.

[B] Structural Features

[1] Molecular Topology: Antibody Types, Fragments and Antibody Constructs

Patent law in the Netherlands follows European patent law as defined in the European Patent Convention and the case law based thereon. For a detailed analysis of the European Patent Convention as applied to the subject of antibodies, reference is made to Chapter 1.

[2] Amino Acid Sequences

[a] Full-Length Sequences of Antibodies

Patent law in the Netherlands follows European patent law as defined in the European Patent Convention and the case law based thereon. For a detailed analysis of the European Patent Convention as applied to the subject of antibodies, reference is made to Chapter 1.

[b] Sequences of Fragments, CDRs and Framework Regions

Patent law in the Netherlands follows European patent law as defined in the European Patent Convention and the case law based thereon. For a detailed analysis of the European Patent Convention as applied to the subject of antibodies, reference is made to Chapter 1.

[3] *Chemical Modifications, Conjugation and Glycosylation*

Patent law in the Netherlands follows European patent law as defined in the European Patent Convention and the case law based thereon. For a detailed analysis of the European Patent Convention as applied to the subject of antibodies, reference is made to Chapter 1.

[C] Cell Line Deposits and Process of Production

Patent law in the Netherlands follows European patent law as defined in the European Patent Convention and the case law based thereon. For a detailed analysis of the European Patent Convention as applied to the subject of antibodies, reference is made to Chapter 1.

In a case between Hoffmann-La Roche and Chiron Corporation (23 March 2005, 04/2384), the District Court of The Hague held that allegedly anticipatory documents were not enabled. The claim in question was directed to an antibody which was defined by a combination of functional and structural features. The prior art comprised allegedly anticipatory documents, but the proprietor argued that the antibodies/hybridomas described in those documents had not been made publicly available. The Court agreed.

According to the Court, it is in principle insufficient for public availability of an antibody or an antibody-producing hybridoma that the author indicates to provide said antibody/hybridoma on request. The reason was that it had not been sufficiently proven that the authors would indeed have provided the antibody or hybridoma to everyone who asked for it (for example, to a researcher of a competitor). In addition, the Court considered there could be various reasons which would make it impossible to provide the antibody or hybridoma, for example because the culture had been infected or had otherwise been lost. The Court also held that public availability of an antibody/hybridoma could not be proven by a single example that the antibody/hybridoma had been provided to a third party, because this was not sufficient to prove that it would have been available to everyone, without restrictions.

§5.03 BREADTH OF CLAIMS AND SUPPORT BY EXAMPLES

[A] Acceptable Breadth of Claims to Antibodies

Patent law in the Netherlands follows European patent law as defined in the European Patent Convention and the case law based thereon. For a detailed analysis of the European Patent Convention as applied to the subject of antibodies, reference is made to Chapter 1.

An apparent divergence between Dutch and EPO case law occurred in the proceedings between Bayer and Abbott (*Bayer Healthcare v. Abbott* of 20 October 2010, 356145 / HA ZA 10-57). In this case, the court held a claim to a pharmaceutical composition containing a human monoclonal antibody that binds to human necrosis factor alpha insufficiently disclosed. The Boards of Appeal at the EPO however considered the same claim sufficiently disclosed in decision T 601/05 of 2 December 2009.

The claim in question was directed to

> 'a pharmaceutical composition containing a human monoclonal antibody that binds to human necrosis factor alpha and is capable of inhibiting LPS-induced human tumor necrosis factor alpha secretion by human monocyte cells.'

The Dutch court considered this claim to comprise any type of human monoclonal antibody that binds to human necrosis factor alpha and had the recited effect. This included high affinity antibodies, as the claim was asserted against an allegedly infringing product which was an antibody of the high affinity type. However, the methods given in the patent to provide the claimed antibodies were not suitable to obtain high-affinity antibodies. For this reason, the Dutch court held the claim to be too broad; because the claim placed under protection high affinity antibodies, which could not be obtained using the methods disclosed in the patent, claim 1 was considered insufficiently disclosed.

The EPO held the same claim to be sufficiently disclosed. However, the competent Board of Appeal at the EPO decided that high affinity antibodies did not fall under the scope of claim 1, because the Board was not convinced that high affinity antibodies were capable of inhibiting LPS-induced TNF secretion by human monocyte cells. The Dutch court and the EPO were in agreement that the patent was insufficiently disclosed in so far as it placed under protection high-affinity antibodies. Ultimately therefore, the divergence arose from the finding at the Dutch court that high-affinity antibodies were comprised under the scope of the claims, whereas the EPO considered high-affinity antibodies not comprised under the scope of the same claims (or at least, did not consider this sufficiently proven).

[B] Required Experimental Support for Claims to Functionally Defined Antibodies

Patent law in the Netherlands follows European patent law as defined in the European Patent Convention and the case law based thereon. For a detailed analysis of the European Patent Convention as applied to the subject of antibodies, reference is made to Chapter 1.

In a case between MSD and Ono (District Court of The Hague, *MSD v. Ono* of 29 June 2016, C/09/489180/ HA ZA 15-623), the claim related to (medical use of) a functionally defined antibody: 'an anti-PD-1 antibody which inhibits the immunosuppressive signal of PD-1 ...'. Neither the first priority document nor the filed application contained an example of such an antibody. The examples on which the proprietor relied to support a sufficient disclosure of the claimed medical use relied on results obtained with a PD-1 knock-out mouse. The Court held that use of an anti-PD-1 antibody would be expected to give essentially the same results as those obtained with a knock-out mouse, and held the results in the patent to render sufficiently plausible the medical use of the claimed anti-PD-1 antibody. From this case, it can be derived that a claim to a medical use of a functionally defined antibody does not necessarily require support from results obtained with an exemplary antibody; other means of support are conceivable.

[C] Required Experimental Support for Claims to Structurally Defined Antibodies

Patent law in the Netherlands follows European patent law as defined in the European Patent Convention and the case law based thereon. For a detailed analysis of the European Patent Convention as applied to the subject of antibodies, reference is made to Chapter 1.

§5.04 SPECIFIC MEDICAL APPLICATIONS AND OTHER FOLLOW-UP INVENTIONS

[A] Treatment of Specific Diseases

Patent law in the Netherlands follows European patent law as defined in the European Patent Convention and the case law based thereon. For a summary, reference is made to Chapter 1.

[B] Mode of Administration

Patent law in the Netherlands follows European patent law as defined in the European Patent Convention and the case law based thereon. For a summary, reference is made to Chapter 1.

[C] Dosage Regimens

Patent law in the Netherlands follows European patent law as defined in the European Patent Convention and the case law based thereon. For a summary, reference is made to Chapter 1.

[D] Specific Patient Groups

Patent law in the Netherlands follows European patent law as defined in the European Patent Convention and the case law based thereon. For a summary, reference is made to Chapter 1.

[E] Specific Mode of Action

Patent law in the Netherlands follows European patent law as defined in the European Patent Convention and the case law based thereon. For a summary, reference is made to Chapter 1.

[F] Combinations with Other Active Ingredients

Patent law in the Netherlands follows European patent law as defined in the European Patent Convention and the case law based thereon. For a summary, reference is made to Chapter 1.

[G] Specific Diagnostic Applications

Patent law in the Netherlands follows European patent law as defined in the European Patent Convention and the case law based thereon. For a summary, reference is made to Chapter 1.

§5.05 ASSESSMENT OF INVENTIVENESS

[A] General Approach

Patent law in the Netherlands follows European patent law as defined in the European Patent Convention and the case law based thereon. Thus, the problem-solution approach as applied customarily at the EPO is common at the Dutch courts. For a summary on this topic, reference is made to Chapter 1.

However, the Dutch High Court has held explicitly that courts are not bound by the problem-solution approach (Dutch High Court, *Lundbeck v. Tiefenbacher*, 7 June 2013, 12/00888). In addition, the Court has held on multiple occasions that a patent must be inventive when starting from any document which would be a reasonable starting point, and consequently, it is not always relevant to determine which document is the closest prior art.

As an example in relation to (medical use of) an antibody, reference is made to the case between MSD and Ono (District Court of The Hague, *MSD v. Ono* of 29 June 2016, C/09/489180/ HA ZA 15-623). When analysing inventive step, the Court explicitly refrained from deciding which document should be considered the closest prior art. Inventive step was analysed from what was considered 'a realistic starting point', and it was considered irrelevant whether this starting point was in fact the closest prior art. The Court held that the document was a realistic starting point, and that even if this document would not be the closest prior art, the patent should be inventive when starting from it.

This also follows from a case between Celltrion and Biogen (District Court of The Hague, 21 February 2018, C/09/517753 / HA ZA 16-1056) on (medical use of) an anti-CD20 antibody. Although the Court agreed that the document which served as starting point for the inventive step analysis did not describe the treatment of patients with chronic lymphocytic leukemia (CLL; the document was directed to the treatment of a type of lymphoma and explicitly excluded CLL patients), the court held that a patent in principle should be inventive in view of any document which could be considered a realistic starting point. The Court considered the document on SLL treatment a realistic starting point, and held the patent not inventive.

In a case on a small molecule therapeutic substance (*Accord Healthcare v. Research Corporation Technologies* of 23 January 2019, C/09/548431 / HA ZA 18-205), the District Court of The Hague held that the problem-solution approach is merely an aid to analyse inventive step, based on the assumption that if a claim is inventive starting from the closest prior art, it should in principle be inventive starting from the prior art as a whole. The Court in this case held that the closest prior art does not necessarily have to be a realistic starting point for the skilled person. In the case in question, a document in the same technical area, which was directed to the same purpose, and had the most structural features in common with the claim, did not provide a realistic starting point, according to the Court. The claim was held inventive, among other things because there were 'secondary indicia' that pointed toward inventive merit, including the time between the publication of the document and the start of the research, the high need for the claimed compounds, and the commercial success thereof.

[B] Particularities Regarding Claims to Antibodies

Patent law in the Netherlands follows European patent law as defined in the European Patent Convention and the case law based thereon. For a summary, reference is made to Chapter 1.

§5.06 ENFORCEMENT AND SCOPE OF PROTECTION

[A] Biosimilars

In a case involving a claim directed to a murine monoclonal antibody, characterized by a combination of functional and structural features, the Court held that chimeric or humanized antibodies could not be considered to fall under the scope of protection (District Court of The Hague, *Hoffmann-La Roche v. Chiron Corporation*, 23 March 2005, 04/2384). The Court considered that the essential insight underlying the invention was the identification of an antibody which bound an antigen in human breast cancer cells later identified to be HER2; the fact that the claimed antibodies were of murine origin was not in itself an essential aspect of the invention. Nonetheless, the Court considered it not reasonable toward third parties to consider chimeric and humanized antibodies comprised in the scope of protection. The reason was that the description only disclosed the preparation of murine antibodies, and although preparation of chimeric antibodies had recently become known at the relevant date, the description did not refer to this possibility. In addition, the technology to humanize a murine monoclonal antibody had only been developed after the priority date. For these reasons, the Court considered that the claim was restricted exclusively to murine antibodies, and did not extend to chimeric or humanized antibodies. Thus, the claim did not place under its scope the allegedly infringing product, the humanized monoclonal antibody trastuzumab.

In another case, the claim was directed to a composition comprising the native antibody trastuzumab as well as a specified maximum of acidic variants thereof (District Court of The Hague, *F. Hoffmann-La Roche AG v. Mundipharma Pharmaceuticals*, 20 February 2019, C/09/565454 / KG 18-1345). In the case in question, the specification disclosed, as an example, a specific measurement method to determine the quantity of acidic variants. This measurement method was not included in the claim. An important aspect of the case was that after filing of the patent application, it was found that a different measurement method was able to resolve a higher quantity of acidic variants than the quantity specified in the claim. The proprietor argued that the claim should be read from the perspective of the skilled person at the priority date, and that hence, the measurement method from the specification was to be considered a limiting definition of what constituted an acidic variant.

The Court did not agree. The Court was of the (preliminary) opinion that the specification allowed for other methods to determine the quantity of acidic variants, and that the method from the example should not be considered limiting for the definition of an acidic variant. The Court thus reached the (preliminary) view that under the given circumstances, the definition in a claim of a quantity which depends on a measurement method should be interpreted as a claim to an absolute quantity, independent of the measurement method.

[B] Equivalence

Patent law in the Netherlands follows European patent law as defined in the European Patent Convention and the case law based thereon. This includes Article 69 EPC on the extent of protection of a European patent, and the protocol on its interpretation. For a summary, reference is made to Chapter 1. On this basis, Dutch courts must take into account any element which is equivalent to an element specified in the claims.

In the case between Hoffmann-La Roche and Chiron Corporation (District Court of The Hague, 23 March 2005, 04/2384), the subject of infringement by equivalence was considered. The claim in question was directed to a murine monoclonal antibody characterized by a combination of structural and functional features. The question was whether the humanized monoclonal antibody trastuzumab could be considered to fall under the scope of protection of claim 1 as an equivalent product.

In answering this question, the Court applied both the 'insubstantial differences' test and the 'function-way-result' test, and held that trastuzumab could not be considered to fall under the scope of claim 1 as an equivalent product. The reason was that the claim was directed to a murine monoclonal antibody, which by its nature causes the human immune system to respond to the foreign (murine) threat, leading to a severe immune reaction and sometimes death. This response of the human immune system to murine antibodies is called the HAMA (Human Anti-Mouse Antibody) response.

A humanized antibody such as trastuzumab is designed to avoid the HAMA response. In addition, a murine antibody is not capable of inducing effector-functions, something which a humanized antibody such as trastuzumab can. The Court held that these differences are not 'insubstantial', for which reason trastuzumab could not be considered to fall under the scope of the claim as an equivalent product.

The same conclusion was reached under the 'function-way-result' test. After all, the result achieved with trastuzumab is different, according to the Court. Trastuzumab is a humanized antibody which does not invoke a HAMA response, which makes it suitable for long-term treatment of humans. In addition, trastuzumab has a different 'way' of operation. Trastuzumab can be used to treat cancer by activating the human immune system against the cancer, whereas the murine monoclonal antibody can only be used for this treatment by coupling it to a cytotoxine. Therapeutically therefore, trastuzumab was considered to work in a different way than the claimed murine antibody.

For the above reasons, the Dutch Court held that in this case, a humanized antibody could not be considered equivalent to a murine monoclonal antibody.

Chapter 6

Poland

Marta Kawczyńska

§6.01 ANTIBODIES AS PATENTABLE SUBJECT-MATTER

[A] Legal Framework

Poland is a signatory to all major international treaties, agreements and conventions regarding the protection of intellectual property, in particular industrial property, including the Paris Convention for the Protection of Industrial Property, the Agreement on Trade-Related Aspects of Intellectual Property Rights (TRIPS), the Budapest Treaty on the International Recognition of the Deposit of Microorganisms for the Purposes of Patent Procedure (Budapest Treaty) and the Convention on Biological Diversity (CBD). Poland is also a contracting state of the European Patent Organization. Since Poland is also a Member State of the European Union (EU), its legal system is bound by the EU judicial system and Poland is obliged to harmonize its national law with EU laws, such as EU directives, e.g. Directive 98/44/EC of the European Parliament and of the Council on the legal protection of biotechnological inventions (The Biotech Directive).

The sources of law in Poland are as follows: the Polish Constitution, ratified international agreements, regulations, directives and decisions of the European Union, statutes, orders and acts of local authorities. The Polish legal provisions are either entirely or at least to a great extent harmonized with the above-mentioned treaties, agreements and conventions. However, if there are discrepancies, Article 91(2) and (3) of the Polish Constitution provides that the respective international or European law provisions shall prevail over any norms of the national law.

Polish patent litigation system is bifurcated, what means that patent invalidity and infringement cases are examined in separate proceedings. The Polish Patent Office has exclusive competence to adjudge disputes on patent invalidity cases, whereas the common courts have competence to decide on patent infringement suits.

The Polish Patent Office (PPO) conducts a full examination of patent applications. When performing its tasks in this regard it utilizes its own guidelines entitled The Inventor's Manual (The Patent Office of the Republic of Poland, 2017, 3rd edition, legal status as of 1 January 2017), which is generally analogous to the European Patent Office's (EPO) Guidelines for Examination. As the The Inventor's Manual of the PPO is not legally binding, it serves mainly for illustrative purposes.

Statutory provisions on the protection of biotechnological inventions, such as antibodies, are set forth in the Act of 30 June 2000 – Industrial Property Law (IPL), in particular in Chapter 9, Title II of the IPL, entitled 'Special Provisions Governing Biotechnological Inventions'.

It is important to note that the Polish legal system is based on statutory law. This means that the case law of Polish courts or administrative authorities, such as the PPO, has no binding force except for the specific case under consideration. Nevertheless, it may be a useful and potent source of argumentation in analogous factual and legal circumstances. In view of the limited amount of Polish case law relating to the biotechnological inventions based on the IPL, disputes arising are and shall be decided with reference to the case law developed by the EPO based on the European Patent Convention (EPC), taking into account the EPO's Guidelines for Examination. Such standpoint is confirmed in the judgment of the Supreme Administrative Court in Warsaw (NSA) No. II GSK 1140/11.

[B] General Amenability or Exclusion of Antibodies from Patentability

The IPL does not provide a definition of an invention, in particular it does not define a biotechnological invention. The IPL specifies however what kind of inventions are excluded from patent protection. These exclusions are stipulated in Article 29 of the IPL:

> *Article 29*
>
> 1. Patents shall not be granted for:
>
> (i) inventions exploitation of which would be contrary to public order or morality; the exploitation shall not be deemed to be so contrary merely because it is prohibited by law,
>
> (ii) plant varieties or animal breeds and purely biological processes for the production of plants or animals; this provision does not apply to microbiological production processes or the products obtained by the processes,
>
> (iii) methods for treatment of the human or animal body by surgery or therapy and diagnostic methods applied on human or animal bodies; this provision shall not apply to products, and in particular to substances or compositions applied in diagnostics or treatment.
>
> 2. The process for the production of plants or animals, referred to in Article 29.1, item ii) is purely biological if it consists entirely of natural phenomena such as crossing or selection.

The above–mentioned part of the IPL entitled 'Special Provisions Governing Biotechnological Inventions' provides in Article 93^2 a non-exhaustive list of biotechnological inventions for which patents may be granted a patent.

Article 93[2]

1. The following, in particular, shall be considered as biotechnological inventions eligible for patent protection:
(i) inventions, the subject of which is biological material which is isolated from its natural environment or produced by means of a technical process, even if it previously occurred in nature,
(ii) elements isolated from the human body or otherwise produced by means of a technical process, including the sequence or partial sequence of a gene, even if the structure of that element is identical to that of a natural element,
(iii) inventions which concern plants or animals, if the technical feasibility of the invention is not confined to a particular plant or animal variety.

2. In a patent application containing a sequence or a partial sequence of a gene, the industrial application of the sequence shall be disclosed in the description of the patent, while an independent patent claim shall indicate the function performed by the sequence.

3. In order to fulfil the industrial application criterion in the case of the sequence or a partial sequence of a gene being used to produce protein or protein component, the description of the invention shall determine which protein or which protein component is produced and what functions it performs.

[C] Required Distinction from Naturally Occurring Antibodies

The IPL excludes granting patents on all biological materials that naturally occur in nature. This exclusion does not apply however to biological materials isolated from their natural environment, even if they are identical in structure to materials present in nature, i.e. materials not isolated from elements accompanying them in their natural environment. It does not exclude from patent protection biological materials produced by means of a technical process even if they previously occurred in nature. Therefore, antibodies that have been isolated by technical means from their natural environment are considered as eligible for patent protection since such antibodies do not occur in an isolated form in nature. Thus, isolated antibodies, like polyclonal antibodies, are not a priori excluded from patent protection, but are eligible for patent protection, provided that they fulfil other patentability requirements, namely novelty, inventive step and industrial application. Similarly, monoclonal, chimeric or humanized antibodies, which are produced using technical means, are not a priori excluded from patent protection, and may be granted a patent, provided that they fulfil the other patentability requirements as mentioned above. Their method of production has to be documented, as well as their usefulness in any industrial field, i.e. industrial applicability.

§6.02 ACCEPTABLE CLAIM FEATURES FOR DEFINING ANTIBODIES

[A] Functional Features

In Poland it is generally required to define an invention in a product category by its structure, i.e. by structural features. According to The Inventor's Manual a patent claim may define a technical feature as a functional feature, even if there is only one working example for that feature, if the skilled person would be in a position to assess that other technical means may be applied to achieve the same function. Functional features are not allowable, however, if they negatively affect the clarity of the claims. Furthermore, according to The Inventor's Manual, functional features as such defining a technical effect may supplement patent claims, if, from an objective point of view, such features cannot be expressed more precisely in a different manner without limiting the scope of protection and provided that such functional supplement provides a skilled person with a sufficiently clear guidance to carry out the invention without undue burden. Therefore, although in principle products should not be defined by functional features, there are some exceptions to this general rule and under some conditions it may be allowable to define a product by a combination of both structural and functional features. The functional features in such case serve mainly as additional information specifying the product, such as an antibody, but these functional features as such are not considered to be sufficient to define the product on their own.

[1] Target/Antigen

In some instances it may be allowable to define an antibody solely by its target, i.e. an antigen to which it binds or a specific novel epitope of a known antigen, but only if the target is new and precisely described in structural terms, i.e. by its specific amino acid sequence. Although it is generally possible in the case of linear, relatively small, epitopes, the situation seems to be more complex when it comes to conformational, three-dimensional epitopes. One has to bear in mind that in the case of a new epitope of a known antigen, establishing an inventive step might be an issue if it is considered that such a new epitope was obtained in a routine manner. In such case it is also required to present in the description at least one working example showing that the antibody was indeed obtained and proving the antibody's binding with the target. If however the antibody's target is known, then, as Polish practice teaches, development of an antibody, against the known target e.g. by immunizing an animal using the known antigen or obtaining a hybridoma cell line producing a specific monoclonal antibody against the known target, is in principle considered as lying within routine skills of a person skilled in the art, thus the antibody so defined is considered as lacking inventive step, unless an unexpected technical effect is obtained and is documented in at least one working example. Thus, if the antibody's target is not new and/or is not sufficiently defined by its structure, it is unlikely that a patent would be granted for an antibody defined solely by such a feature.

[2] Mode of Binding: Target Affinity, Binding Specificity, Epitope, Definitions via Reference Antibodies and Competitive Binding

In some instances functional parameters of an antibody, such as target affinity or binding specificity, are important distinguishing technical features. In such cases it is allowable to define an antibody using such functional features but all of them must be clear and it necessary to provide a detailed description of a specific method of their measurement or a screening assay for the claimed activity. Other functional features, such as selectively of binding to a specific, structurally well-defined target, e.g. by its relevant sequence, or competing for binding with another (reference) antibody may also be claimed, as explained above, but usually in addition to structural features. In such cases the reference antibody must be disclosed and structurally well-defined, e.g. by its relevant amino acid sequences. It may be possible to define the reference antibody by referring to a biological material deposit, provided the deposit is made in accordance with the Budapest Treaty at the latest at the filing date and the required certificate of deposit is duly submitted. In all the cases the description should provide at least one working example (for each claim category) showing that the antibody having the functional features claimed was indeed obtained, for example using specific affinity measurement methods, competitive binding assays, or immunoreactivity tests, i.e. documenting the obtained competitive binding, immunoreactivity or affinity as claimed. Whether one example is recognized as sufficient support for the claimed scope of protection depends on the merits of the case and specific breadth of the claim and is examined on a case-by-case basis.

[3] Effect on Target

As explained above, it is not allowable, as of principle, to define an antibody merely by its functional features. Functional features may however be used to supplement the antibody's definition by structural terms. Such a supplementary functional feature might be the antibody's activity, such as its agonistic or antagonistic activity. The description has to disclose a method of measurement of such activity and should present at least one working example proving that the antibody exerted the claimed agonistic or antagonistic activity. The PPO's practice in this regard is quite strict and it may be said that there is a tendency to limit the scope of the protection to the exemplified antibodies, but each case is decided on its own merits.

[B] Structural Features

In product claims, like claims directed to isolated antibodies, it is usually required to define the antibody/antibodies by structural features, for example by relevant amino acid sequences. Polish practice in this area teaches that a minimum allowable antibody structural definition describes at least the amino acid sequences of each of the antibody's light and heavy chain complementarity determining regions (CDRs), unless the inventive properties of the antibody rely on fewer CDRs (if clearly shown in the application). In cases where the inventive properties of the claimed antibody are based on other features, e.g. modification(s) of framework region(s) conferring an antibody desirable, new and inventive properties such as improved antigen binding affinity or stability, these modifications need to be recited in the claims. However, in such cases it is crucial to provide appropriate support by at least one working example documenting such properties since patent protection might be granted only for the actually obtained products (provided they fulfil all other patentability criteria). Prosecution of applications directed to non-exemplified antibodies is very complicated and the outcome is at least uncertain, depending on the merits of the case.

[1] *Molecular Topology: Antibody Types, Fragments and Antibody Constructs*

Different antibody types, such as chimeric antibodies, bi-specific antibodies, humanized antibodies, as well as fragments thereof, and antibody constructs may be patentable in Poland, provided that they are sufficiently disclosed and supported by the description. It is of crucial importance to provide sufficient experimental data showing that such products were indeed obtained and that they exerted the claimed properties.

[2] *Amino Acid Sequences*

[a] *Full-Length Sequences of Antibodies*

Antibodies may be claimed by their full-length amino acid sequences, however definitions of full-length sequences of both the heavy and light chains are usually not required. The minimum structural definition seems to encompass amino acid sequences of three light chain CDRs and three heavy chain CDRs. In specific circumstances, in the case of novel antibodies (not known in the art), a definition solely by their CDRs might not be sufficient, and then full sequences of both heavy and light chain variable domains might be required.

[b] *Sequences of Fragments, CDRs and Framework Regions*

As indicated above, a product should generally be defined in principle by its respective structural features that enable a realization of the invention in the whole claimed scope without undue burden. In case of product claims relating to antibody fragments their respective amino acid sequences are expected. If the inventive properties of the antibody clearly rely on modification(s) of framework region(s), the sequences thereof might be sufficient, if the description makes it clear and provides an adequate experimental support in a working example. If the inventive properties of the antibody rely on fewer than six CDRs and the description makes it clear as well as provides appropriate (in particular experimental) support, then it might be allowable to define an antibody by amino acid sequences of less than six CDRs.

[3] *Chemical Modifications, Conjugation and Glycosylation*

It is a general rule that the PPO does not recognize antibodies defined solely by a chemical or enzymatic modification in general as sufficiently disclosed, i.e. in a manner enabling their realization by a skilled person without undue burden. In such cases the PPO is of the opinion that the product should be defined by its structural features, univocally describing the invention and enabling its realization. Any modification should be defined precisely, as otherwise in the PPO's opinion the skilled person not knowing the antibody's amino acid sequence and the specific modification would not be able to carry out the invention without performing an inventive activity, as even a minor change or modification may affect, in some cases, the antibody's function. Additionally, it is of crucial importance to provide experimental data confirming how the antibody was obtained and that it exerted properties necessary to obtain the technical effect of the invention, because, as mentioned above, only for inventions really so realized may patent protection be granted. A sole indication of a possibility of producing modified antibodies is not sufficient disclosure, because a skilled person has not obtained a proof in a form of an experimental verification that such modified antibody can be obtained and that it exerts the desired properties. Similar consideration would be applicable to conjugated, glycosylated or fucosylated forms of antibodies. Absent any specific working example, a derivative or modified form is not likely to be allowable. However, a specific, well-defined and documented variant or a modified form may be allowable. In view of harmonization of the Polish patent law and the EPC, as well as taking into account the limited guidelines and case law in Poland in this regard, both the Guidelines for Examination and case law developed by the EPO would be applicable for examination of an application pertaining to such solutions.

[C] Cell Line Deposits and Process of Production

In accordance with the Polish regulations, an antibody may be defined by a reference to a deposit of a biological material, such as a hybridoma cell line producing it. In such case the deposit has to be declared at the latest at the filing date, and a depositor, accession number and depositary authority have to be indicated. The deposit has to be made in accordance with the Budapest Treaty in a depositary institution recognized under an international agreement or in a national depositary institution, which is mentioned by the President of the Patent Office in an announcement published in the Official Gazette of the Republic of Poland, *Monitor Polski*. Further to that an appropriate certificate of deposit has to be duly submitted within three months as of the filing date. The term is not restorable.

Furthermore, antibodies may be defined by the method of their production. A patentable production method has to precisely define specific process steps, such as conditions, reagents or parameters used. According to Article 64 of the IPL, products, such as antibodies, obtained directly by the claimed process are also covered by the patent protection. In the case of new products or where the patentee shows that despite all due efforts it was not possible to ascertain an actual product production process applied by another person it is deemed that the product that may be produced by the process, and was in fact obtained by the process. One has to bear in mind, however, that in such a disproval the legally justified interest of a defendant in the area of his trade and production secrets has to be taken into account.

§6.03 BREADTH OF CLAIMS AND SUPPORT BY EXAMPLES

[A] Acceptable Breadth of Claims to Antibodies

According to the executory provisions of the IPL, a description shall describe in detail at least one way of carrying out the invention (working example) with the reference to the drawings, if any. The Inventor's Manual indicates that one part of an application's description should be examples, which should exemplify in detail at least one example of a realization or using the invention. If an application comprises more than one invention, then the number of examples provided in the description should correspond to the number of inventions contained in the application, including also variants of these inventions. If an application comprises inventions in different categories, at least one example should be provided for each category claimed. If an invention in one category comprises different variants, then it is recommended to provide examples corresponding to such variants. For example, if an application relates to different derivatives or variants of an antibody, then examples documenting obtainment of such derivatives or variants, and their properties, should be provided in the description. In such a situation one example, corresponding to one variant or derivative, is usually not recognized as providing sufficient support for all the claimed variants or derivatives. If an application pertains to a production method defined by broad process parameters, then the description should provide examples of realization using end and intermediate parameters. There is no clear line to define generally acceptable breadth of allowable antibody claims. Applications are examined on a case-by-case basis and the examiners try to find a fair balance between the patentee's interests and the interests of the public. There is a trend however for strict interpretation of the sufficiency of disclosure criterion, which in practice means a tendency to require a working example for every claimed solution or a variant thereof. Thus, for a broad scope of protection to be allowable, more than one working example is usually required. However, where there is no reasonable doubt that variants, other than specifically exemplified, would also exert the claimed activity, then such solutions should also be allowable. Therefore, although it might be possible, as explained above, to claim 'an antibody binding to antigen X', i.e. if antigen X is a novel and inventive (e.g. pharmacological) target, structurally well-characterized, but the description has to comprise at least one working example of such an antibody, proving its inventive properties by pharmacological and/or biological test results showing its efficacy. According to the judgment of the Administrative Court in Warsaw (WSA) No. VI SA/Wa 252/12 the results of clinical studies cannot constitute a supplement to the application. Furthermore, it is worth mentioning that according to the judgment of the Administrative Court in Warsaw No. VI SA/Wa 112/08 in the case of inventions having medical nature it is important that the disclosure shows not only the invention's applicability but also that its realization is safe for recipients. Following the guidance from this judgment The Inventor's Manual teaches that the obtained technical effect should be documented by results of internationally recognized tests, and preferably accompanied by statistical analysis, as well as benefit-risk assessment. An indication of potential applicability deduced from the prior art does not constitute a solution to a specific technical problem (the judgment of the Administrative Court in Warsaw No. VI SA/Wa 1474/04). Further to that it is worth noting that a lack of a specific example of realization may lead to an objection as to a lack of industrial applicability.

[B] Required Experimental Support for Claims to Functionally Defined Antibodies

As explained above, solutions in a product category, such as antibodies, shall be defined structurally. Moreover, according to The Inventor's Manual if the subject of an application is a product, examples should not only document its structural features, optionally in combination with functional features, but also provide a method of its production. If the claimed product is defined by both structural and functional terms, these terms have to be clear and the product defined sufficiently supported by the description. There are no specific rules defining exactly how many examples are required to support a claim to a functionally defined antibody. As explained above applications pertaining to antibodies are analysed on case-by-case basis. As there is a general trend for a strict interpretation of sufficiency of disclosure criterion, therefore, for a broad scope of protection to be allowable, more than one working example might be required.

[C] Required Experimental Support for Claims to Structurally Defined Antibodies

As explained above, solutions in a product category, such as antibodies, shall, as of principle, be defined structurally. In case of a claim directed to a structurally defined antibody, usually a minimum definition requires disclosure of at least six CDRs of the claimed antibody. Additionally, for solutions in a product category, the description has to provide a working example showing how exactly it was produced. It is of great importance to provide sufficient support, meaning experimental data, for the products as claimed, either structurally and/or functionally. Such data have to show that the claimed antibody was really obtained, as well as to document how it was obtained, i.e. a method of the production of the claimed product should be exemplified. If for example the claimed antibody is defined by both structural and functional features, at least one example should document that the antibody having the claimed structure was indeed obtained and at least one example should document that the functional properties have been achieved, i.e. proving that the obtained antibody exerted the claimed functional properties. Although some additional, comparative experimental data might generally be submitted later than on the filing date, i.e. during a prosecution of an application, such as with a reply to office action, whether they will be accepted is however analysed on a case-by-case basis and depends on the examiner. According to a general principle however, the application's description cannot be supplemented after the date of filing, e.g. by results of experimental or clinical tests, as confirmed in the judgment of the Administrative Court in Warsaw No. VI SA/Wa 252/12.

§6.04 SPECIFIC MEDICAL APPLICATIONS AND OTHER FOLLOW-UP INVENTIONS

[A] Treatment of Specific Diseases

According to statutory provisions in force in Poland (Article 24 of the IPL) patents shall be granted – regardless of the field of technology – for any inventions which are new, which involve an inventive step and which are susceptible of industrial application. Nevertheless methods for treatment of the human or animal body by surgery or therapy and diagnostic methods applied to human or animal bodies are excluded from patent protection; this provision shall not apply to products, and in particular to substances or compositions applied in diagnostics or treatment methods (Article 29.1 (iii) of the IPL). An invention is considered to be new if it does not form part of the state of the art. The state of the art comprises everything made available to the public by any means before the date according to which priority to obtain a patent is determined (Article 25.1 to 3 IPL). This does not apply however to inventions concerning a substance or compositions comprised in the state of the art for use of such substance or for the use of such substance in a specific manner for the purpose of treatment or diagnostics methods (Article 25.4 of the IPL). This exception applies only to substances or compositions and not to other products, such as medical devices. Therefore, second (and further) medical use claims are allowable in Poland. The PPO generally also applies in this regard rules of examination developed by the EPO, in particular the teaching from the EPO's Decision G 5/83 and parts of the EPO's guidelines for examination are mentioned in The Inventor's Manual. The new medical use should be supported by the description, i.e. it should provide results of detailed biochemical and/or pharmacological studies, proving the claimed medical properties. In particular the obtained technical effect should be documented by results of internationally recognized tests, and preferably accompanied by statistical analysis, as well as a benefit-risk assessment.

[B] Mode of Administration

Generally there is no specific regulation in the Polish law that allows granting patent protection for inventions in use category regarding a new mode of administration. However according to The Inventor's Manual medical use claims relating to mode of administration are understood as a new dosing of a known medicament. They are allowable, provided an unexpected technical effect is achieved and documented. In such case the invention relates to a new form of a medicament, which is responsible for its better efficacy. For example, if an intramuscular mode of administration was known, an invention relating to a subdermal administration might be patentable, as long as an unexpected technical effect is obtained as a consequence of such administration, e.g. an improved therapeutic efficacy, or elimination or alleviation of adverse effects and/or side effects. As the Polish law in this regard is harmonized with the EPC and the EPO's practice, its rules of examination of such application would be applicable. Similarly, as before, the EPO patentability of such inventions relies on a specific wording of a claim, as well as a sufficient support in the description. The description must disclose that the claimed mode of administration is new and provides for an unexpected technical effect, which has to be documented in at least one working example. It has to be clear that the inventive technical effect can be achieved only using the claimed mode of administration.

[C] Dosage Regimens

Generally there is no specific regulation in the Polish law that allows granting patent protection for inventions in use category regarding a new dosage regimen. There is no specific regulation in the Polish law that excludes granting patent protection for inventions in use category regarding a new dosage regimen either. As The Inventor's

Manual teaches it is not possible to define a new medical use by a medicament's dosage regimen, meaning dosing scheme, because in reality no medicaments are developed in this way. A new dosage regimen does not have a technical character, because it reflects a doctor's activity, which is not industrial by nature. The doctor's activity consists in defining a beneficial dosage regimen, which means that a doctor performs this activity based on his professional experience. Therefore, there is lack of a technical effect connected with the medicament's dosage regimen. According to the judgment of the Administrative Court in Warsaw No. VI SA/Wa 252/12 it is not allowable to distinguish an invention from the prior art solely by the effect to be achieved, e.g. its efficacy. In accordance with this judgment in the case of a change of a dosage regimen only, a solution relates in fact to a method of treatment, which is excluded from patent protection by the law and belongs to the medicine domain practiced by doctors. As a new dosing method (dosing scheme) is however understood by the PPO as a new mode (route) of administration, which is recognized as a potentially patentable invention in a new medical use category according to The Inventor's Manual, therefore it might be possible to obtain patent protection for inventions relating in essence to a new dosage regimen, provided that other patentability criteria are met, especially that the technical effect of such new dosage regimen is documented in the examples, in particular it is proved that claimed doses and frequencies of their administration are effective.

[D] Specific Patient Groups

Generally there is no specific regulation in the Polish law that allows granting patent protection for inventions in use category regarding a new specific patient group. However, according to The Inventor's Manual such claims to be allowable have to meet general patentability criteria as in the case of other claim categories. Patentability of such inventions also relies on a specific claim construction and sufficient support in the description. Furthermore, the description must clearly disclose that the claimed use in a specific patient group is new and inventive, i.e. it provides for an unexpected technical effect, understood in this case in such a way that the claimed patient group is distinguishable from the known patient group and not overlapping in any physiological or pathological manner with the known patient group, as well as that the effect does not arise in the known group of patients (e.g. judgment of the Administrative Court in Warsaw No. VI SA/Wa 1997/09 and judgment of the Supreme Administrative Court in Warsaw No. II GSK 52/10). This means that if the effect is also present within the previously known patient group, such invention cannot be recognized as patentable.

[E] Specific Mode of Action

Generally there is no specific regulation in the Polish law that allows granting patent protection for inventions in use category regarding a new specific mode of action. According to The Inventor's Manual a discovery of mechanism of action of a known compound used in a known therapeutic application is not considered to be an invention in a second medical use category. Similarly, an identification of a reason why certain side effects appear when using a known medicament in a known way is not considered to be a solution eligible for patent protection in the second medical use category either. If there are no testable criteria enabling a decision to be made as to whether a disease or a condition, which improved and/or was alleviated, is a result of the use under examination, an application relating to such use cannot be granted a patent, because of lack of clarity (Article 33.3 of the IPL), lack of disclosure or lack of novelty, when it relates to the same disease or condition.

[F] Combinations with Other Active Ingredients

Combination products are patentable in Poland. Their patentability is examined analogously as in the case of other inventions. A new combination of a new active ingredient, e.g. a new antibody with another active substance, either new or already known, may constitute an allowable invention. Similarly, a new combination of known active ingredients, e.g. a known antibody with another known active substance, may constitute a patentable invention, provided all other patentability criteria are met. In case of a new combination of known active ingredients having known therapeutic effects it is particularly important to document that the combination provides for an synergistic (therapeutic) effect, i.e. the effect so obtained is improved in comparison to a sum of effects of the single active ingredients. According to the judgment of the Supreme Administrative Court in Warsaw No. II GSK 405/13 patentability criteria shall be examined as of the date of filing, therefore experimental data confirming a synergistic activity of a claimed combination shall be submitted at the date of filing and should be comprised in the application.

[G] Specific Diagnostic Applications

According to The Inventor's Manual second (and further) medical use claims are only allowable in the case of substances used in methods excluded from patent protection. Therefore, if the specific diagnostic method is excluded from patent protection according to Article 29.1 (iii), i.e. it is applied to human or animal bodies, a substance for a specific use in such method shall not be excluded as such from patent protection according to Article 25.4 of the IPL, provided that other patentability criteria are met. As diagnostic methods performed in vitro are not excluded from the patent protection, these rules pertaining to second medical uses are not applicable thereto, consequently known products for use in such in vitro methods are not eligible for patent protection pursuant to Article 25.4 of the IPL. The Inventor's Manual presents examples of allowable claims directed to diagnostic applications. An allowable claim format would be 'Antibody X for diagnosing disease Y in vitro' (the antibody has to be new as the scope of protection covers also the product as such), 'Antibody X for use in diagnosis of disease Y', 'Use of antibody X for diagnosing disease Y in vitro', while a claim format 'Antibody X for diagnosing disease Y' would be considered as directed to a diagnostic method excluded from the patent protection.

§6.05 ASSESSMENT OF INVENTIVENESS

[A] General Approach

Pursuant to Article 26 of the IPL an invention shall be considered as involving an inventive step if, having regard to the state of the art, it is not obvious to a person skilled in the art. In deciding whether an inventive step has been involved, the patent applications or utility model applications which enjoy an earlier priority, not made available to the public, shall not be taken into an inventive step consideration as they are not considered as comprised in the state of the art for this purpose, contrary to the purpose of novelty assessment, where such applications are considered to form part of the state of the art. An inventive step can be acknowledged only for an invention, considered as a whole, which is not derivable in an obvious manner from the state of the art.

The Polish statutory provisions do not stipulate any particular method or means for an assessment of the inventive step. The Inventor's Manual does however provide some guidance on how the PPO approaches an inventive step analysis. According to the judgment of the Administrative Court in Warsaw No. VI SA/Wa 89/08 an assessment of inventive step should comprise three steps, first the definition of the closest prior art, secondly definition of a problem that should be solved by the invention, and finally analysis of whether a skilled person knowing the closest prior art when considering the technical problem solved by the invention would have arrived at the claimed solution of the problem without inventive activity and in a professional and routine manner. The PPO's inventive step analysis corresponds generally to the problem-solution approach for inventive step examination developed by the EPO. According to the judgment of the Supreme Administrative Court in Warsaw No. II GSK 1140/11 while interpreting the Polish regulations regarding patentability criteria one should apply European interpretation of the corresponding European regulations, in particular in accordance with the practice of the EPO expressed in its Guidelines for Examination. It means therefore that inventive step should be assessed in a uniform manner based both on the Polish regulations and the EPC.

The Polish case law regarding assessment of inventive step is rather consistent and teaches that an invention should be examined in its entirety, therefore the fact that separate elements constituting the invention are known as such does not automatically render the invention as a whole obvious, because a new combination of known features may result in a new surprising and unexpected technical effect. From the judgment of the Administrative Court in Warsaw No. VI Sa/Wa 2183/04 it results that for an invention to fulfil the inventive step criterion it is sufficient that it is not derivable for a skilled person in an obvious manner from the state of the art, i.e. that the invention goes beyond routine technical development in the field of the invention, so to achieve the invention an inventive activity is necessary.

As far as the assessment of the closest prior art is concerned The Inventor's Manual states that an invention is analysed in the light of one or more prior art documents considered together. Such standpoint, that the closest prior art does not necessarily refer to one document, is confirmed by various judgments of the Polish Administrative Courts, e.g. the judgment of the Supreme Administrative Court in Warsaw No. II GSK 163/12 or the judgment Administrative Court in Warsaw No. VI

SA/Wa 318/14, wherein it was stated that the closest prior art does not pertain to one cited solution but rather to a specific technical field. Such approach seems to be slightly different from the EPO's practice in this regard, according to which the closest prior art is that which in one single reference discloses the combination of technical features which constitutes the most promising starting point for a development leading to the invention (EPO' s GL VII 5.1).

As to the definition of the technical problem solved by the invention The Inventor's Manual teaches that the technical problem solved by the invention at issue should be defined in an objective manner, based on established facts from the prior art, without taking into consideration non-essential features.

As regards the analysis of inventive step, The Inventor's Manual teaches that once the objective technical problem has been formulated it is necessary to establish whether, based on the information from the prior art, a skilled person would have achieved the claimed invention in a professional and routine manner, i.e. without undue burden or without any inventive activity. According to the judgment of the Administrative Court in Warsaw No. VI SA/Wa 251/12 an invention consisting in transfer of a solution known in one technical field to another field may constitute a non-obvious solution. However according to the judgment of the Administrative Court in Warsaw No. VI SA/Wa 685/07 in such case the field should be sufficiently remote. As in view of the judgment of the Administrative Court in Warsaw No. VI SA/Wa 1545/07 non-obviousness is considered to be a vague term, therefore its assessment should be performed using all the information from the prior art and not only specific, known solutions.

[B] Particularities Regarding Claims to Antibodies

An analysis of the Polish case law regarding an inventive step teaches that it is of crucial importance to provide examples of realization documenting that the specific product was prepared and that the technical problem underlying the invention was solved, so the technical effect was achieved in the entire scope of requested patent protection defined by the claims. In case of antibodies it is therefore extremely important to provide working examples proving that the claimed antibodies were indeed produced and in the case of antibodies defined by functional features it is very critical to provide also examples documenting that the obtained antibodies exerted the claimed functional properties, so that the technical effect was achieved. If there are no examples, the PPO is of the opinion that the essence of the invention has not been disclosed, therefore automatically the invention under consideration lacks inventive step. For example, from the judgment of the Administrative Court in Warsaw No. II SA 3658/03, the lack of comparative data between antibodies according to the application at issue and the prior art ones makes it impossible for the PPO to assess the inventive step, therefore the antibodies according to the application at issue were recognized by the PPO as lacking inventive step.

Furthermore, another potentially problematic issue in the case of assessment of patentability of antibodies is the industrial applicability criterion. The industrial applicability criterion is most often interpreted in Poland as a possibility to use a technical solution in a reliable, repeated manner, meaning the possibility to obtain repeatedly the same desired result without a necessity to perform any additional inventive actions going beyond the routine adaptation or development in the field. An invention is considered to be industrially applicable if a specific technical solution is, at the date of filing complete (according to the judgment of the Administrative Court in Warsaw No. VI SA/Wa 2059/04 or No. VI SA/Wa 545/14), duly disclosed (according to the judgment of the Administrative Court in Warsaw No. VI SA/Wa 982/12), socially useful (according to the judgment of the Administrative Court in Warsaw No. VI SA/Wa 1474/04) and guarantees a repeatability of a result. Therefore, the lack of a specific example of a claimed solution may be interpreted as the lack of possibility to carry out the invention without undue burden, wherein such lack constitutes a deficiency that cannot be removed, so in such circumstances a grant of a patent should be refused.

§6.06 ENFORCEMENT AND SCOPE OF PROTECTION

As stated above, in Poland patent invalidity and infringement cases are dealt with separately and independently by different authorities. Disputes on patent invalidity are decided by the Polish Patent Office, while infringement of exclusive patent rights and principles of unfair competition are dealt with by common civil courts.

Furthermore, in Poland there are no specialized patent courts, so the cases are recognized by different regional courts. A need for specialized IP courts, in particular patent courts, has been discussed for a long time in Poland. Although the number of patent infringement disputes per year is rather low in comparison to other jurisdictions, it has been increasing for several years, thus it seems that the need for an implementation of specialized IP courts in Poland increases. It is worth noting that legislative works in this area initiated by the Polish Ministry of Justice are now well advanced and further developments may be expected in the near future.

[A] Biosimilars

Since their development biosimilar products, in short biosimilars, are attracting more attention and are gaining more and more interest in the field of biologics, in particular antibodies. Appropriate patent protection is therefore raising a lot of interest. A strict requirement for a structural antibody product definition or a combined definition by both structural and functional features raises a possibility for obtaining patent protection for biosimilar products. On the one hand, structurally defined antibody claims are usually quite easy to obtain and defend. However, their scope is restricted and therefore can easily be circumvented by antibodies retaining similar function but having some sequence differences. Even though restricted, such structurally defined antibody claims may still be extremely useful as a protection tool against generic competitors trying to launch biosimilar products using the same antibody sequence. On the other hand, functionally defined antibody claims provide for a broader scope of protection, but they may be more difficult both in the prosecution and enforcement.

One important aspect of the revocation proceedings in Poland is a requirement to document a legitimate interest in claiming revocation of a patent. Both the PPO and the Polish Administrative Courts are quite strict in assessment of this requirement. A legitimate interest must be direct, concrete and real. When the legitimate interest is derived from as general legal norm as the norm creating the freedom of economic activity, the petitioner must demonstrate particular, concrete factual circumstances due to which another party's exclusive right 'interferes with' the exercise of his freedom to an extent that justifies granting him the right to seek legal protection. Therefore, not all persons involved in trade who must respect the exclusive right of another party have a legitimate interest and standing to demand that said exclusive right be eliminated (the judgment of the Supreme Administrative Court in Warsaw No. II GSK 335/09). Producers of biosimilar products may be considered as persons having legitimate interest in claiming revocation of a patent (judgment of the Supreme Administrative Court in Warsaw No. II GSK 2942/15) provided that all the other general criteria for recognition of legitimate interest are met.

For enabling an appropriate assessment of the breadth of claims a so-called doctrine of equivalents has been developed, as it is of crucial importance to know how 'equivalents' shall be assessed in order to be in a position to decide what exactly is embraced by antibody claims.

[B] Equivalence

Article 63.2 of the IPL specifies that the scope of the protection sought shall be determined by the claims contained in the patent specification, while the patent specification and drawings may be used to interpret the claims.

According to Article 69 of the EPC the scope of the protection conferred by a European patent or a European patent application shall be determined by the claims. Nevertheless, the description and drawings shall be used to interpret the claims. Article 69 of the EPC should be interpreted in accordance with the Protocol on the Interpretation of Article 69 EPC, which is an integral part of the EPC. The Protocol stipulates that for the purpose of determining the extent of protection conferred by a European patent, due account shall be taken of any element which is equivalent to an element specified in the claims. In Poland however there is generally lack of an analogous legal norm allowing, based on the national regulations, broadening the interpretation of the scope of protection to equivalent solutions, i.e. beyond the literal meaning of the claims. Polish case law provides some guidance in this regard. For example, in judgment No. I ACa 612/12 of the Court of Appeal in Łódź it was indicated that in patent infringement suits Polish national courts are obliged to apply interpretation rules stipulated in The Protocol on the Interpretation of Article 69 EPC also in the case of national patents granted by the PPO, i.e. wherein the EPC does not apply. This judgment also formulated guidance for assessment of obviousness of equivalent features used in the patented invention, according to which a feature cannot be considered obvious if for a skilled person in the art it is not known that a replacement of one technical means covered by the claim with another, equivalent, means results in the same end effect and only the same end effect. However neither the Polish national provisions, nor international ones, provide for a normative definition of the skilled person (in Polish regulations 'expert'). Therefore, also in this case only the case law may provide some guidance in this regard. According to the judgment of the Administrative Court in Warsaw No. VI SA/Wa 1847/14 and the judgment of the Supreme Administrative Court in Warsaw No. II GSK 3482/15 a skilled person is an average practitioner having average, commonly available knowledge in the relevant art concerned at the relevant date, e.g. filing date of an application, having access to everything in the state of the art, in particular the cited documents, and having at his disposal the typical means and capacity for routine work and experimentation.

Another important issue in the assessment of the scope of patent protection in infringement suits in some jurisdictions, such as the US, is a doctrine of 'file wrapper estoppel'. It seems however that there is lack of normative basis for using this doctrine in patent infringement disputes on the ground of the IPL or EPC in Poland. Furthermore, files of a case are in Poland, as of principle, not publicly available, therefore history of the file cannot be easily accessed even after publication of an application or a patent grant.

Chapter 7

Spain

Juan Arias

§7.01 ANTIBODIES AS PATENTABLE SUBJECT-MATTER

[A] Legal Framework

On 1 April 2017, the new Spanish Patent Law 24/2015, approved in July 2015, entered into force replacing the previous Law 11/1986. This new law intends to update Spanish patent law to adapt it to international standards and, in particular, to bring it further into line with European legislation. In addition, new Guidelines for Examination of the Spanish Patent and Trademark Office (SPTO) have been published on 6 February 2019.

Since the previous Law was approved in 1986, several agreements have been signed by Spain on industrial property, such as the Agreement on Trade-Related Aspects of Intellectual Property Rights (TRIPS), the Patent Law Treaty (PLT), in addition to the creation of Supplementary Protection Certificates (SPCs) for medicines and phytosanitary products. These developments have made a renovation of the patent system in Spain necessary.

Main Changes in the new Spanish Patent Law 24/2015

The main changes of the Law 24/2015 relate to patent prosecution and patent litigation. In relation to patent prosecution, the new Law prescribes that patent applications concerning inventions developed in Spain must first be filed at the SPTO. In the absence of said compliance, unless the patent application claims priority from a previous application filed at the SPTO, the patent application will have no effect in Spain (Articles 152(2) and 163(2)). An authorization from the SPTO enabling the first filing in a country different from Spain may be obtained for those inventions that do not have interest to national defence unless expressly authorized by the Ministry of Defence (Article 115(1)).

Among the main changes incorporated in this new Law, the most notable aspect is the establishment of a single grant procedure for patent applications, which requires a substantive examination to be carried out, in order to assess novelty and inventive step among others requirements. Thus, the previously available option allowing for a general grant procedure (registration procedure without examination), irrespective of compliance with patentability requirements, no longer applies. The aim is to establish a more robust patent system that avoids unjustified monopolies.

Another important change is that the search report must be requested at the time of filing the patent application. This entails an increase in the initial cost of the patent application; however, it is to be expected that the search report and the written opinion on patentability will be issued in advance of the expiry of the priority term (before 12 months), thus allowing a more objective assessment of the convenience of extending the application to other countries within the priority year.

For the evaluation of the novelty requirement, European patent applications designating Spain, as well as PCT applications that have entered into the national phase in Spain, whose filing date is prior to the filing of the patent application and have been published in Spanish on or after that date, are also considered as prior art documents.

In relation to medical use patents, the amendments adopted in the Revision of the European Patent Convention made in 2000, which entered into force in 2007, by allowing the patentability of substances or compositions already known in a first medical use or for new therapeutic indications are also incorporated in the new Spanish Patent Law. Therefore, the wording of second medical use claims in Swiss-type form no longer applies.

Opposition prior to grant is replaced by a post-grant procedure comparable to that of the European system, with the difference that this opposition will have to be submitted within six months, instead of the nine-month period applicable at the European Patent Office.

In the new Patent Law, Supplementary Protection Certificates (SPCs) are expressly included among the protection titles.

The declaration of partial nullity of a claim is now allowed under the new Spanish Patent Law. Furthermore, the patentee may limit the patent by modifying the claims, or even revoke it in its entirety. The revocation or limitation procedure at the request of the proprietor of the patent may be initiated at any time during the validity of the patent and will be retroactive as in the case of total or partial nullity.

An additional change relates to the possibility of filling protective letters, and thus any person who foresees the filing of a request for a preliminary injunction without prior hearing against him, may appear in legal form before the judicial body or bodies that he considers competent to hear such possible measures and justify his position by means of a protective letter.

Patent Prosecution

The prosecution of a patent according to the new Patent Law is covered in Articles 22 to 44. In general terms, this procedure is very similar to the prosecution of a European patent.

Formal Examination

After filing the patent application if deficiencies are found during the formal examination period, the applicant shall be requested to overcome them within the established term of two months. In the case that the deficiencies are not overcome within the established term, the application will be refused/rejected by the SPTO.

Search Report

Once the patent application is filed, the SPTO will proceed to prepare the search report (IET). The presence of formal defects will not interrupt the drawing up of the search report unless their nature precludes the issuance of said search report.

If the deficiencies relate to lack of unity of invention, the applicant will be requested to divide the application or to pay additional search fees. If the applicant fails to reply, the prosecution will continue for the first invention, the remaining inventions being deemed to be withdrawn.

The applicant will receive the search report together with a written opinion and all documents cited therein.

According to Article 36(5) of Spanish Patent Law, a search report will not be issued for PCT national stage applications which designated the SPTO as International Search Authority during the PCT phase.

Publication

The application shall be made available to the public after the expiry of a period of 18 months from the filing date and will be published in the Official Industrial Property Gazette (BOPI). The search report can also be published along with the application or independently after the publication of the application.

Observations by Third Parties

In proceedings before the SPTO, and following the publication of the Spanish patent application, any third party may, in accordance with Article 38 of the Spanish Patent Law, present observations concerning the patentability of the invention to which the application relates until examination is finished. That person will not be a party to the proceedings.

The applicant has the opportunity to reply to any allegations concerning third party observations.

Request for Examination

The request for examination can be submitted from the moment the Spanish patent application is filed up to three months from the publication of the search report in the BOPI, or when applicable, from the mention of the publication of the International search report.

The request for examination can be accompanied by a written response to the search report, and if applicable, to any third party observations, along with an amended application (including claims, description and figures). The claim amendments cannot introduce technical features which were not searched and may not contain subject-matter which extends beyond the content of the application as filed.

Examination

The SPTO shall do an in-depth examination of patentability requirements. The patent will be granted only if these requirements are fulfilled. If examination reveals that the application does not meet the patentability requirements, the SPTO will issue a communication inviting the applicant to file a response to the objections raised by the examiner within a period of two months. The claims and description may be amended, if deemed necessary.

If any requirements are still not met, the SPTO may issue further communications giving new opportunities to the applicant to reply within the same time limit. Said new opportunities may consist of one or more communications, or resulting in a single oral hearing when deemed appropriate or requested by the applicant.

Opposition

Within the period of six months of the publication of the mention of the grant of the patent in the BOPI, any person is entitled to file an opposition to said patent on the grounds that the subject-matter of the patent does not fulfil the patentability requirements, there is lack of sufficiency of disclosure and/or the subject-matter extends beyond the content of the application as originally filed.

All documents deemed relevant for the assessment of the opposition must be filed in Spanish or, in the case of prior art documents, at least the most relevant parts thereof.

If the notice of opposition is admissible, the SPTO will inform the patent proprietor accordingly who, within three months of the publication of the opposition, can file a response and, if appropriate, modify the claims and description.

Once the response has been filed, the opponent(s) will have a right of reply within two months of the publication of the response to the opposition. In such a reply, the incorporation of additional grounds, documents or facts that were not alleged in the notice of opposition will not be allowed.

A Commission composed of three technically qualified experts from the SPTO will be constituted, which may further be completed with a legal expert from the same office if required.

If it is considered that no opposition reason prevents the maintenance of the patent as it was granted, the opposition will be rejected. The resolution of dismissal will be notified to the patent proprietor and opponents and said resolution will be published in the BOPI with a mention regarding the maintenance of the patent.

If it is considered that the patent can be maintained in the amended form proposed by the patent proprietor, the oppositions will be fully or partially admitted, maintaining the patent as amended.

If, despite the allegations or modifications made by the patent proprietor, the reasons for revoking the patent persist, a new period of one month from the publication of said reasons in the BOPI will be given to the patent proprietor to submit new allegations or modifications.

New opportunities for replying will be granted, which may consist of one or more written procedures or of a single oral hearing when deemed appropriate or at the request of the patent proprietor or of the opponent(s).

If, during the oral hearing, the patent is deemed to be maintained as amended, the patent proprietor must provide the amended description and claims, as agreed at the oral hearing, within ten working days from the day following the publication of the minutes of the oral hearing.

If the SPTO decides to revoke the patent, it will notify the patent proprietor and opponent(s), indicating the grounds for revocation. The decision shall be published in the BOPI.

Appeal

An administrative appeal may be filed against the resolution of the opposition division by those who have been party to the opposition procedure.

Likewise, the applicant may file an administrative appeal against a decision of refusal of the patent application. In the appeal procedure, the patent application can be modified.

Revocation or Limitation

The proprietor of a patent may request the revocation or limitation of the patent as it was granted or limited in opposition proceedings. This process entails the payment of the corresponding fee.

[B] General Amenability or Exclusion of Antibodies from Patentability

The general requirements for patentability under the Spanish Patent Law are set forth in Articles 4 to 9 and in the Guidelines for Examination of the SPTO 2019 part G. The SPTO as well as the Spanish courts tend to follow the provisions of the European Patent Office and the European case law. Therefore, although mandatory substantive examination at the SPTO is a relatively new procedure and there is no really hands-on experience on how the SPTO will act, we anticipate that the examination of inventions directed to antibodies will be carried out essentially following the same principles as in the EPO.

[C] Required Distinction from Naturally Occurring Antibodies

Antibodies are considered biological material. Biological material isolated from its natural environment or produced by means of a technical procedure may be the subject of an invention, even if it already exists previously in its natural state (Article 4.2 of the Spanish Patent Law).

For the purposes of this Article, the term 'biological material' means any material containing genetic information itself or being reproduced in a biological system, and 'microbiological process' means any process involving or performed upon or resulting in microbiological material. Although the human body at the various stages of its formation and development as well as the simple discovery of one of its elements, including the total or partial sequence of a gene, is excluded from patentability (Article 5.5 of the Spanish Patent Law), an element isolated from the human body or otherwise produced by a technical process, including the sequence or partial sequence of a gene, may constitute a patentable invention, even if the structure of that element is identical to a natural element.

§7.02 ACCEPTABLE CLAIM FEATURES FOR DEFINING ANTIBODIES

As in the case of the EPO, the SPTO typically accepts defining an antibody in the claims in terms of its structure, its function or a combination of structural and functional features. Alternatively, an antibody may also be defined by the method of its production or by the hybridoma that can produce said antibody. Antibody claims can be drafted in several ways mentioned below, where references to the corresponding case law of the EPO have been included.

[A] Functional Features

A functional definition of an antibody would be accepted if the person skilled in the art would be capable of isolating or making such antibody without an undue burden of experimentation. Said functional definition may consist of one or more features relating to aspects of antigen binding, competition abilities or cross-reactivity.

[1] Target/Antigen

Several situations occur when the antibody is defined by reference to the antigen or epitope, such as 'Antibody specific for the X antigen':

a) If the antigen is new, the novelty and inventive step of the antibody could be acknowledged. In this case, the antibody claim would be accepted even if said antibody has not been developed (T 542/95). To avoid lack of clarity and sufficiency of disclosure, the antigen must be well defined (by its structure, formula, chemical name or deposit in a recognized depositary authority).
b) If the antigen is known and there are no other antibodies to that antigen, the antibody would be new but would lack inventive step unless it showed an unexpected property (T 735/00) or if there were previously difficulties to obtain said antibody.
c) If the antigen is known and antibodies exist against that antigen, the antibody may be new if it binds to a different epitope. If some epitopes are known, the antibody should be defined in the claim, e.g., by difference in cross-reactivity or by depositing the hybridoma. In that case, the claimed antibody may not be inventive unless it exhibits an unexpected activity or property or different cross-reactivity or other functions (T 355/92; T 478/92).

Antibodies to non-linear or conformational epitopes are not patentable if the different parts and their positions are not clearly defined.

If an antibody against a conformational epitope of an antigen is known, an antibody exclusively against a linear epitope within the known conformational epitope is considered new (following decision T 30/09).

[2] Mode of Binding: Target Affinity, Binding Specificity, Epitope, Definitions via Reference Antibodies and Competitive Binding

Antibodies may be claimed by defining features relating to aspects of antigen binding or competing for binding with another antibody.

In the wording 'Antibody specific for the X antigen', the term 'specific' can generate problems of interpretation. According to the decision T 189/01, the term is interpreted in a general sense, without representing a technical limitation of the antibody, but simply indicates that it binds with high affinity and is inherent in the nature of the antibody so that it does not exclude cross-reaction with other antigens.

[3] Effect on Target

Antibodies may be functionally defined by their inhibitory/antagonistic or agonistic activities, biological effects in assays involving the target antigen and *in vivo* effects.

[B] Structural Features

If a particular structural feature is responsible for an effect that can be seen as inventive, the definition of an antibody exclusively by structural features should be acceptable.

[1] Molecular Topology: Antibody Types, Fragments and Antibody Constructs

A chimerized or humanized antibody or an antibody defined by its antigen binding fragments (Fab) and single chain variable fragments (scFv) may be considered patentable if said antibody has a new function or property relative to the already known antibody.

See also §1.02[B][1] in relation to molecular topology of antibodies in Europe.

[2] Amino Acid Sequences

Broad claim language could be used for first protection of a new antibody. However, if a particular antibody is already known, further protections require more restrictive language (e.g. by specifying the amino acid/DNA sequence).

[a] Full-Length Sequences of Antibodies

In general, the definition of an antibody by its structural features (sequence of the whole antibody or parts thereof), such as 'Antibody with the sequence shown in SEQ ID NO: 1', meets the requirement of sufficiency of disclosure.

[b] Sequences of Fragments, CDRs and Framework Regions

There may be a lack of sufficiency of disclosure when only one of the antibody chains is shown, or according to decision T 626/00 if less than six CDRs are shown. If all six CDRs are shown but if the framework region is considered to play a role in the binding affinity or in any other relevant feature, then showing the six CDRs alone will not be enough to comply with the disclosure requirement.

[3] Chemical Modifications, Conjugation and Glycosylation

See §1.02[B][3] in relation to chemical modifications, conjugations and glycosylation of antibodies in Europe.

[C] Cell Line Deposits and Process of Production

Antibodies may be defined by reference to a hybridoma, such as 'Antibody produced by the hybridoma with access number X'. It is necessary to deposit the hybridoma according to the Budapest Treaty to avoid a lack of sufficiency of the description. With this type of drafting, the protection obtained is relatively narrow since it refers specifically to the antibody produced by the deposited hybridoma. However, one could still include additional claims directed to an antibody as defined in the previous claim which exhibits certain modifications, e.g., which has been humanized. We do not anticipate that this will cause a problem before the SPTO, as humanization is a routine procedure nowadays.

§7.03 BREADTH OF CLAIMS AND SUPPORT BY EXAMPLES

[A] Acceptable Breadth of Claims to Antibodies

The Guidelines for Examination of the SPTO in section F4 indicate that although a single example may provide sufficient information for an expert to put the invention into practice, in the case of inventions defined by broad claims it cannot be assumed that the requirement of sufficiency of disclosure is met unless the description provides a large number of examples or alternative embodiments or variations to demonstrate that the technical effect is achieved over the whole scope of the claims.

The sufficiency of the disclosure is met if a person skilled in the art, taking into account the information provided in the application and common general knowledge, reaches the claimed invention without undue burden of experimentation and without exercise of any inventive skill. The SPTO determines the undue experimentation takes into account i) the breadth of the claims, ii) the nature of the invention, iii) common general knowledge, iv) the level of predictability of the technique, iv) the indications provided in the description, and v) the required level of experimentation. Thus, sufficiency of disclosure is linked to the reproducibility of the invention.

[B] Required Experimental Support for Claims to Functionally Defined Antibodies

As in the case of the EPO, the SPTO considers it straightforward to obtain an antibody against a new target and therefore does not usually require such antibodies to be exemplified.

The level of disclosure and experimental support required for antibodies in the SPTO is usually the same as required in the EPO (Guidelines for Examination EPO, II. C.6.3)

The need for the description of the patent to allow the object of the claim to be applied in its entire scope is likewise reinforced by the jurisprudence of the Boards of Appeal of the EPO. In particular, the Case Law of the Boards of Appeal, section II.C.4.4 applies regardless of whether the invention is described by means of functional or structural technical characteristics. However, since the use of functional technical characteristics comprises an undefined and abstract number of possible alternatives, the definition of the invention by means of this type of functional features is acceptable as long as all the alternatives are available and reach the desired result (T 1121/03 and T 369/05). A similar approach is expected to be taken by the SPTO.

[C] Required Experimental Support for Claims to Structurally Defined Antibodies

In order to fully satisfy the requirements of Article 27 of the Spanish Patent Law, it is required that the invention is described not only in terms of its structure but also in terms of its function, unless the function of any of its elements is immediately appreciated.

Variants of structurally defined antibodies may be allowed in the claims, when coupled to functional limitations or when examples of said variants are included in the experimental part of the description.

§7.04 SPECIFIC MEDICAL APPLICATIONS AND OTHER FOLLOW-UP INVENTIONS

[A] Treatment of Specific Diseases

According to the SPTO, antibodies are considered as any other pharmaceutical product. Therefore, even if an antibody has been disclosed in the prior art as suitable for the treatment of a specific indication, claims to second or further medical uses of the same antibody may be allowed. As previously mentioned, one of the most important changes in the new Patent Law is that the first medical use of compounds is now patentable and the second medical uses are to be drafted as purpose related product claims as in the EPO practice. Therefore, claims directed to second medical uses of antibodies should be properly drafted.

[B] Mode of Administration

Second medical use claims of an antibody are allowed if the claimed therapeutic method differs from the known method in the route of administration (Article 6.5 of the Spanish Patent Law and Guidelines for Examination of the SPTO G7.6.1).

[C] Dosage Regimens

Second medical use claims of an antibody are allowed if the claimed therapeutic method differs from the known method in the dosage regimen (Article 6.5 of the Spanish Patent Law and Guidelines for Examination of the SPTO G7.6.1).

[D] Specific Patient Groups

Second medical use claims of an antibody are allowed if the claimed therapeutic method differs from the known method in relation to the specific patients to be treated (Article 6.5 of the Spanish Patent Law and Guidelines for Examination of the SPTO G7.6.1).

[E] Specific Mode of Action

Second medical use claims of an antibody are allowed if the claimed therapeutic method differs from the known method in the specific mode of action that allows the application to a particular group of patients (Article 6.5 of the Spanish Patent Law and Guidelines for Examination of the SPTO G7.6.1).

[F] Combinations with Other Active Ingredients

Second medical use claims of an antibody are allowed if the claimed therapeutic method differs from the known method in the formulation of the pharmaceutical composition comprising the antibody (Article 6.5 of the Spanish Patent Law and Guidelines for Examination of the SPTO G7.6.1).

[G] Specific Diagnostic Applications

Diagnostic methods involving antibodies may be patentable. As in the case of the EPO, diagnostic methods applied to the human or animal body are excluded from patentability under the SPTO (Article 5.4 of the Spanish Patent Law and Guidelines for Examination of the SPTO G4.4.3). Notably, only such methods where all the technical steps of the method require the presence of the human or animal body are excluded from patentability.

See also §1.04[G] in relation to patentability of diagnostic methods involving antibodies in Europe.

§7.05 ASSESSMENT OF INVENTIVENESS

[A] General Approach

The SPTO applies the same patentability criteria of inventiveness as adopted by the EPO (Article 8 of the Spanish Patent Law and Guidelines for Examination of the SPTO G8).

[B] Particularities Regarding Claims to Antibodies

In order to avoid an objection of lack of inventive step of an antibody defined by its function, it is advisable to show evidence of an unexpected advantage of the antibody or technical reasons why the preparation of the antibody had no reasonable expectation of success.

If the antigen is known and there are no other antibodies to that antigen, the antibody would lack inventive step unless it showed an unexpected property (T 735/00) or if there were previously difficulties to obtain said antibody.

If polyclonal antibodies are known for an antigen, the monoclonal antibodies against the same antigen lack inventive step according to decision T 906/91, in the absence of a surprising advantage or of an unexpected effect.

See also §1.05 in relation to patentability of antibodies in Europe.

§7.06 ENFORCEMENT AND SCOPE OF PROTECTION

The Spanish IP specialist courts are currently in Madrid, Barcelona, Valencia, Bilbao, La Coruña and Las Palmas de Gran Canaria, which deal with infringement and invalidity issues.

Until now there have been no litigation cases in Spain of patents related to antibodies. However, due to the fact that new antibody-based medicaments are being approved on a regular basis, we believe that the first litigation on antibody patents will begin in the near future.

The only case where a patent containing claims referring to antibodies and uses thereof for the determination of the levels of the corresponding antigen was brought forward in an infringement action was the case *Fibrostatin S.L. v. Channel*, Commercial Court No. 2, Valencia, Spain, 12 April 2017 (Ref. 000085/2017). The claimant argued that the commercialization by Channel Corporation of a cosmetic product which contained a natural extract resulted in the infringement of certain claims of a patent owned by Fibrostatin S.L. The grounds for this allegation were that the assay used by Channel Corp. to measure the effect of the natural extract involved supposedly the detection of a protein using an immunodetection method which was covered by a claim in the patent. The only evidence for asserting this alleged infringing use was the description in a patent owned by Channel of a screening method which could be seen as falling under the scope of the patent owned by Fibrostatin. As it could be expected, both the request for a preliminary injunction as well as the main infringement action were dismissed among other reasons because there was no evidence that said method for detecting the expression of the protein using the protected method had been carried out in Spain, which is the only place where it would be relevant for the purposes of infringement of a patent in Spain in accordance with Article 59(b) of the Spanish Patent Law. The decision was confirmed in the second instance (Provincial Court of Valencia, Spain, 7 November 2017, Ref. 581/2017).

[A] Biosimilars

See §1.06[A] in relation to biosimilars in Europe.

[B] Equivalence

See §1.06[B] in relation to the doctrine of equivalents in Europe.

Chapter 8

Switzerland

Philipp Marchand

§8.01 ANTIBODIES AS PATENTABLE SUBJECT-MATTER

[A] Legal Framework

In Switzerland, patents for inventions are governed by the Swiss Patent Act ('Bundesgesetz über die Erfindungspatente', also referred to as Patentgesetz (PatG)) as amended up to 1 April 2019.[1] Further provisions can be found in the Swiss Patent Ordinance (Patentverordnung (PatV)). The Swiss Federal Institute of Intellectual Property (IPI) additionally issues Guidelines for Examination, which are, however, not legally binding in matters related to third parties, yet constitute binding instructions for patent examiners.

In general, claimed subject-matter is patentable if it fulfils the requirements of technicality (Article 1 PatG), repeatability (Article 1 PatG), novelty (Article 7 PatG), inventive step (Article 1 PatG) and if it is industrially applicable (Article 1 PatG). However, there are specific provisions with respect to elements of the human body and genetic sequences.

Specifically, as a non-EU member, Switzerland has chosen to base its relation with the EU on a series of bilateral agreements aimed at maintaining or establishing a harmonized legal framework. This includes provisions related to intellectual property. Thus, following the EU Directive 98/44/EC, the Swiss legislator has amended large parts of the Patent Act including amendments relevant to patenting of biotechnological

1. German, French and Italian are official languages in Switzerland and all legal texts are provided in these three languages as equally legally binding versions. An English version 'for information purposes only' is provided by the Swiss government at https://www.admin.ch/opc/en/classified-compilation/19540108/index.html.

inventions, which came into force on 1 July 2008. Specifically, Article 1a PatG provides with respect to the human body and its elements:

(1) The human body as such, at all stages of its formation and development, including the embryo, is not patentable.
(2) Elements of the human body in their natural environment are not patentable. An element of the human body is, however, patentable as an invention if it is produced by means of a technical process, a beneficial technical effect is indicated and the further requirements of Article 1 are fulfilled; Article 2 remains reserved.

With respect to gene sequences, Article 1b PatG governs that:

(1) A naturally occurring sequence or partial sequence of a gene is not patentable as such.
(2) Sequences that are derived from a naturally occurring sequence or partial sequence of a gene may, however, be patented as an invention if they are produced by means of a technical process, their function is specifically indicated, and the further requirements of Article 1 are fulfilled;[2] Article 2 remains reserved.[3]

---

2. Article 1 PatG provides that:
   (1) Patents for inventions are granted for new inventions applicable in industry.
   (2) Anything that is obvious having regard to the state of the art (Art. 7 para. 2) is not patentable as an invention.
   (3) Patents are granted without the guarantee of the State.
3. Article 2 PatG relates to exclusions from patentability:
   (1) Inventions whose exploitation is contrary to human dignity or that disregard the integrity of living organisms or that are in any other way contrary to public policy or morality are not patentable. In particular, no patent may be granted for:
      a. processes for cloning human beings and the clones obtained thereby;
      b. processes for forming hybrid organisms by using human germ cells, human totipotent cells or human embryonic stem cells and the entities obtained thereby;
      c. processes of parthenogenesis by using human germinal material and the parthenogenetic entities obtained thereby;
      d. processes for modifying the germ line genetic identity of human beings and the germ line cells obtained thereby;
      e. unmodified human embryonic stem cells and stem cell lines;
      f. the use of human embryos for non-medical purposes;
      g. processes for modifying the genetic identity of animals which are likely to cause them suffering without being justified by overriding interests worthy of protection, and also animals resulting from such processes.
   (2) Also excluded from patentability are:
      a. methods for treatment by surgery or therapy and diagnostic methods practised on the human or animal body;
      b. plant varieties and animal varieties or essentially biological processes for the production of plants or animals; however, subject to the reservation of paragraph 1, microbiological or other technical processes and the products obtained thereby as well as inventions that concern plants or animals are patentable provided that their application is not technically confined to a single plant or animal variety.

Further relevant provisions which were introduced following the Biotech Directive 98/44/EC are Article 8b[4] and 8c[5] PatG.

It is generally understood that the provisions extend to amino acid sequences, i.e. a sequence as a product of a genetic sequence.[6]

Accordingly, the mere discovery of elements of the human body or genetic (including polypeptide) sequences is not patentable unless they have been isolated by technical means and their function is indicated. The same holds true for a process related to its production.[7]

Since the above-discussed changes to the Swiss Patent Act entered into force in 2008, the provisions relevant for antibody patenting are harmonized with provisions of most EU member states.

However, there are still notable discrepancies between the patent laws in Switzerland and most EU states, such as Germany.

First, national patent applications in Switzerland are only examined with respect to the presence of patentable subject-matter or non-presence of subject-matter excluded from patentability, respectively, i.e. Articles 1, 1a, 1b and 2, and formal requirements including sufficiency of disclosure and clarity; *see* Article 59 PatG. According to Article 59(4) PatG, patent applications are not examined for novelty or inventive step. Therefore, a granted patent can be obtained in Switzerland via the national route irrespective of prior art disclosures.

Novelty and inventive step of a granted patent can be challenged in nullity proceedings pursuant to Article 26 PatG. There is also the possibility for third parties to file an opposition against the grant of a Swiss patent, however only based on lack of patentability pursuant to Articles 1a, 1b and 2; *see* Article 59c PatG.

Yet, the vast majority of granted patents in Switzerland are filed and prosecuted before the EPO and later validated in Switzerland as a contracting state of the European Patent Convention (EPC). The procedure related to European patents is governed by the provisions of the fifth Title of the PatG. Such patents are examined in accordance with the relevant provisions of the EPC and have thus undergone substantive examination.

In this respect, a further notable difference between the provisions of the EPC and Swiss patent law lies in the acceptable claim format for second or further medical uses. Following decision G2/08 of the Enlarged Board of Appeal of the EPO, for any patent application having a filing date (or earliest priority date) after 28 January 2011,

---

4. Article 8b PatG provides that:

   If the invention concerns a product that consists of or contains genetic information, the effects of the patent extend to any material in which the product is incorporated and in which the genetic information is contained and performs its function. Articles 1a paragraph 1 and 9a paragraph 3 remain reserved.

5. Article 8c PatG provides that:

   The protection conferred by a claim to a nucleotide sequence that is derived from a naturally occurring sequence or partial sequence of a gene is limited to the sequence segments that perform the function specifically described in the patent.

6. Ernsthaler Jürgen/Zech Herbert, GRUR 2006, 529 ff.
7. Commercial Court (HG) Zurich (ZH) in ZH HG of 18.10.2005, published in Case-law bulletin Zurich (ZR) 106 (2007); Swiss Federal Supreme Court (BGer) in 'Decisions of the BGer' (BGE) 97 I 423 of 25.05.1971 'Kristallform'.

the EPO grants second or further medical use claims in the format of purpose-limited product claims (Compound X for use in treating disease Y) and does not allow Swiss-type claims (Use of compound X in the manufacture of a medicament for treating disease Y). In contrast, the IPI continues to allow Swiss-type claims.

[B] General Amenability or Exclusion of Antibodies from Patentability

Antibodies are patentable in Switzerland under the provisions outlined above.

[C] Required Distinction from Naturally Occurring Antibodies

Naturally occurring sequences, including derived sequences such as cDNA, RNA or amino acid sequences, without a function are not patentable pursuant to Article 1b PatG.

Isolation of a sequence which is still identical to the naturally occurring sequence does not lead to a patentable claim.[8]

However, according to Article 1a(2) PatG an element of the human body is patentable if it is produced by means of a technical process and a beneficial technical effect is indicated. Of note, human embryonic stem cells or stem cell lines are expressly excluded from patentability according to Article 2(1)(e) PatG.

During the legislative process leading to the amendments to the Swiss Patent Act that implement the regulations of EU Directive 98/44/EC, the Federal Council clarified that only those elements of the human body are patentable for which a beneficial effect beyond the mere technical provision has been shown.[9] In the absence of a beneficial technical effect, the subject-matter would lack technicality irrespective of whether it has industrial applicability. The latter can, however, prevent grant of corresponding applications pursuant to Article 2 PatG, namely if the exploitation of the claimed invention is contrary to human dignity or it disregards the integrity of living organisms or it is in any other way contrary to public policy or morality.

A 'function' within the meaning of Article 1b PatG is a feature of the nucleotide or amino acid sequence which leads to a technically useable result. It is generally understood that the beneficial effect of Article 1a(2) PatG is identical to the function. This is often but not necessarily the biological function of the corresponding nucleotide or amino acid sequence.

§8.02 ACCEPTABLE CLAIM FEATURES FOR DEFINING ANTIBODIES

According to Swiss patent law, namely Article 51(1) PatG, an invention is defined by the claims. The claims also determine the scope of protection conferred by a Swiss patent (Article 51(2) PatG). In order to precisely determine the intended scope of protection, the claims must comprise the technical features of the invention in a clear and concise manner (Article 29(1) and (2) PatV). The description and the drawings must be used to interpret the claims (Article 51(3) PatG).

8. Message of the Federal Council of 23 November 2005, page 49.
9. Message of the Federal Council of 23 November 2005.

[A] Functional Features

As has been made clear by Swiss courts, claims directed to products/compounds can comprise functional features if a structural definition without undue limitation is impossible.[10]

Thus, broad claims relating to functionally defined antibodies should be acceptable pursuant to Swiss patent law provided that the above requirement is met.

However, it is of note that with respect to elements of the human body, such as human antibodies, it is required that a technical beneficial effect is indicated. According to the Guidelines for Examination at item 11.2.1 the technical effect must be part of the application documents as originally filed. In the case of functionally defined subject-matter, this may pose problems under Article 50(1) PatG, requiring that the invention must be described in such a manner that it can be carried out by a person skilled in the art. This is because general and speculative statements with respect to a function of a claimed antibody are considered insufficient (see Guidelines at item 11.2.2). The disclosure must be sufficiently precise, substantiated and plausible.

Moreover, it should be noted that other than a functional feature a purpose as part of a product claim is not considered limiting on the claimed scope. A claimed product must merely be suitable for the indicated purpose, as was repeatedly found by the Technical Boards of Appeal of the EPO and as was confirmed by the Swiss Federal Patent Court (Bundespatentgericht) in decision S2012_004 of 24 March 2012 (*Schneidvorrichtung für eine Stickmaschine*).

[1] Target/Antigen

There are no provisions in Swiss patent law which would prevent patentability of claims directed to antibodies defined by their target/antigen. As detailed above, as long as a beneficial effect is indicated in the application and the effect is made plausible over the claimed scope, such claims can be granted without the necessity to establish novelty and/or inventive step.

It is of note, however, that broad claims must not encompass embodiments which cannot be put into practice by the average skilled person or for which the function provided in the application is not fulfilled for a substantial part of the claimed embodiments.

If the skilled person cannot put the invention into practice, the patent may be revoked pursuant to Article 50 PatG in combination with Article 26(1)(b) PatG (lack of enablement). If the function is not fulfilled by a substantial part of the claimed embodiments, it lacks patentability pursuant to Article 1b PatG in combination with Article 26(1)(a) PatG.

10. Examples for allowable claims comprising functional features in BGE 92 II 48, 49 and BGE 92 II 280, *see* also Guidelines for Examination of the IPI at page 53, last paragraph.

[2] *Mode of Binding: Target Affinity, Binding Specificity, Epitope, Definitions via Reference Antibodies and Competitive Binding*

The explanations in §8.02[A][1] above also hold true with respect to antibodies defined by their mode of binding.

[3] *Effect on Target*

The explanations in §8.02[A][1] above also hold true with respect to antibodies defined by the effect on their target.

[B] Structural Features

[1] *Molecular Topology: Antibody Types, Fragments and Antibody Constructs*

Claims directed to structurally defined antibodies are generally admissible pursuant to Swiss patent law. There is no provision which would generally prevent admissibility of claims directed to partial sequences of antibodies such as CDR sequences or fragments.

However, Article 50 PatG requires that the invention must be described in such a manner that it can be carried out by a person skilled in the art. This is generally understood as comprising details with respect to the production and identification of products falling within the claim. According to the Guidelines, item 11.4, it is usually required that the application comprises at least one example demonstrating the provision of a specific product falling within the claim and the identification of further products in a reproducible manner. Moreover, if a claim relates to a group of products, the applicability of the disclosed methods to embodiments outside of the specific example but within the claimed scope must be credible.

Of note, disclosed nucleotide or amino acid sequences must be part of a sequence listing fulfilling the requirements of Article 27 PatV. If absent, the IPI will request submission of the same. However, a late-filed sequence listing is not part of the application documents as filed. Whether a claimed invention is sufficiently disclosed will thus be assessed based on the documents available at the date of filing without regard to the late-filed sequence listing.

[2] *Amino Acid Sequences*

[a] *Full-Length Sequences of Antibodies*

As detailed in §8.02[B][1] above, claiming an antibody by its full sequence is allowable under Swiss patent law.

[b] *Sequences of Fragments, CDRs and Framework Regions*

Fragments, CDRs and framework regions, thus parts of antibodies, lead to a broader scope than claiming an antibody by its full sequence. Therefore, one has to consider the requirements described in §8.02[B][1] above when pursuing such claims.

[3] Chemical Modifications, Conjugation and Glycosylation

Chemically modified sequences can also be claimed in Switzerland.[11] Such sequences may not fall under the provisions of Article 1b (1) or (2) PatG. However, the general requirements of patentability have to be met. Therefore, such sequences are patentable only if their industrial applicability has been shown.

[C] Cell Line Deposits and Process of Production

Additionally or alternatively to the above, claims directed to antibodies may be based on depositions of biological material, such as hybridoma cells. In such cases, the description exceptionally can be considered complete by reference to a deposit.[12] Article 50a PatG provides:

(1) If an invention that relates to the manufacture or use of biological material cannot be sufficiently described, then the description must be completed by depositing a sample of the biological material and, in the description, by providing details of the essential characteristics of the biological material as well as a reference to the deposit.
(2) If, in the case of an invention that relates to biological material as a product, the production process cannot be sufficiently described, then the description must be completed or replaced by depositing a sample of the biological material and, in the description, by a reference to the deposit.
(3) The invention is deemed to be disclosed in accordance with Article 50 only if the sample of the biological material has been deposited at the latest on the filing date with a recognized depositary institution and the patent application as originally filed contains details of the biological material and reference to its deposit.
(4) The Federal Council shall regulate in detail the requirements for depositing samples, for the details of biological material and for the reference to the deposit, together with access to the samples deposited.

According to Article 45b PatV the application as filed must disclose the depository and the reference number. However, the latter can be provided within 16 months from the filing date (Article 45d PatV).

§8.03 BREADTH OF CLAIMS AND SUPPORT BY EXAMPLES

[A] Acceptable Breadth of Claims to Antibodies

The allowable breadth of a claim is generally determined as part of the assessment of whether a claimed invention is sufficiently disclosed in accordance with Article 50 PatG. Accordingly, the claimed invention must be disclosed in such a manner that a

11. Ernsthaler Jürgen / Zech Herbert, GRUR 2006, 533.
12. ZH HG 15.12.1969, published in Communications related to Swiss law on intangible goods (SMI) 1970, 71.

person skilled in the art can put it into practice without undue burden and without inventive efforts.[13] A person skilled in the art or a group of persons skilled in the art have profound knowledge in the respective technical field.[14]

With respect to broad claims, in particular claims comprising prima facie ambiguous technical terms, Article 51(3) PatG governs that the description and the drawings must be used to determine their scope. Late-filed explanations can be considered to impermissibly broaden the claimed scope and can thus be found inadmissible pursuant to Article 58(2) PatG and Article 64(3) PatV.

Importantly, the Guidelines for Examination before the IPI, which are however not legally binding, make clear that definitions of terms used in the claims which are not in line with the general understanding in the art can be found impermissible (see Guidelines at item 4.3). The applicant can be asked to amend the term used in the claim or its definition in the application documents as filed. However, this may cause problems under Article 58(2) PatG requiring that the technical documents may not be modified such that their content extends beyond the content of the documents as filed. The responsibility for unclear definitions and potential consequences lies with the applicant.[15]

[B] Required Experimental Support for Claims to Functionally Defined Antibodies

With respect to examples supporting the claimed invention, it is generally accepted under Swiss patent law that at least one example is required which provides one way how a skilled person can provide the claimed subject-matter or identify compounds falling within the boundaries of the claim.[16] No further requirements have been defined. However, it is generally accepted that reach through claims do not fulfil the requirements of Article 50 PatG. Moreover, such claims are not understood as relating to methods of producing a product. Therefore, their scope does not extend to the immediate product resulting from practising the claimed method as is the case for production methods pursuant to Article 8a(1) PatG.

[C] Required Experimental Support for Claims to Structurally Defined Antibodies

The same as explained in §8.03[B] above also holds true with respect to structurally defined antibodies.

---

13. Swiss Federal Supreme Court (BGer) on 17.11.1970, published in SMI 1972; Cantonal High Court (OG) of Zurich (ZH) on 21.9.1990, published in SMI 1992, 269.
14. Swiss Federal Supreme Court in BGE 120 II 71.
15. Swiss Federal Supreme Court in BGE 85 II 131.
16. Swiss Federal Supreme Court (BGer) on 18.3.2006 – *Anschlaghalter II*.

§8.04 SPECIFIC MEDICAL APPLICATIONS AND OTHER FOLLOW-UP INVENTIONS

With respect to medical applications, Article 7c PatG holds that:

> Any substance or composition that forms part of the state of the art as such, but not in relation to its use in a surgical, therapeutic or diagnostic method specified in Article 2 paragraph 2 letter a is deemed to be new provided it is intended solely for such use.

Furthermore, Article 7d PatG holds that:

> Any substance or composition that forms part of the state of the art as such, but not in relation to a specific use in a surgical, therapeutic or diagnostic method specified in Article 2 paragraph 2 letter a that is distinct from the first medical use specified in Article 7c is deemed to be new provided it is intended for use in the manufacture of a means to a surgical, therapeutic or diagnostic end.

Accordingly, Swiss patent law allows medical use claims in the form 'substance X for use as a medicament' as well as Swiss-type claims in the form 'Use of substance X in the manufacture of a medicament for treating disease Y'. The latter is generally used for second or further medical uses claimed before the IPI. As noted above, this represents a major discrepancy between practice before the EPO and the IPI. Before the EPO, pursuant to decision G2/08, Swiss-type claims are not allowed for patent applications with a filing date (or earliest priority date) after 28 January 2011. Second or further medical uses have instead to be claimed in the format of purpose-limited product claims.

This discrepancy has led to further revisions of the Swiss Patent Act, which came into force on 1 January 2019. These revisions were found necessary since the vast majority of granted patents in Switzerland come into force via the European route and have thus undergone substantive examination before the EPO. Second or further medical uses are thus covered by purpose-limited product claims instead of the Swiss-type claim format. The Enlarged Board of Appeal of the EPO discussed potential implications, but reasoned that consequences with respect to the freedom of medical practitioners should be governed by national law.[17] The Swiss Federal Supreme Court subsequently suggested that corresponding provisions should be included as further exceptions from the effect of a granted patent in Article 9 PatG,[18] which has now been implemented with the revisions that have taken effect on 1 January 2019.

[A] Treatment of Specific Diseases

Second medical use claims in the EPC2000 format or as Swiss-type claims should include a reference to a specific disease. The disease must be defined such that it is clear to the skilled person how to determine whether a patient suffers from the indicated disease.

17. G2/08 at item 6.5.
18. BGE 137 III 170.

[B] Mode of Administration

The mode of administration can be included in a patentable claim in Switzerland.

[C] Dosage Regimens

Dosage regimens can be a basis for patentable claims in Switzerland. This has been clarified by the Swiss Federal Supreme Court following an appeal to a ruling of the Commercial Court in Zürich. Specifically, in HG 080018 of 14 April 2010, the Commercial Court had decided that dosage instructions represent an unallowable method of treatment. In BGE 137 III 170, the Swiss Federal Supreme Court overruled the previous finding and followed the German case-law on this matter.

[D] Specific Patient Groups

There is no provision or court case which would prevent second medical use claims including a specific patient group.

[E] Specific Mode of Action

There is also no provision which would prevent claims directed to a specific mode of action. However, it is of note that the Technical Boards of Appeal of the EPO have found that the mere explanation of a mode of action is not sufficient to restore novelty of a claim.[19]

[F] Combinations with Other Active Ingredients

Combinations or compositions comprising two or more active ingredients are patentable in Switzerland.

[G] Specific Diagnostic Applications

Diagnostic applications are also covered by the provisions of Articles 7c and 7d PatG. Accordingly, claims directed to the use of a substance in a diagnostic method are allowable in the Swiss-type format.

§8.05 ASSESSMENT OF INVENTIVENESS

[A] General Approach

According to Article 1(2) PatG anything that is obvious with regard to the state of the art as defined in Article 7(2) PatG is not patentable. The state of the art comprises everything made available to the public. Since Article 7(3) PatG only makes reference

19. T 254/93.

to novelty, unpublished applications are not considered in the assessment of inventive step, as is the case before the EPO. In principle, the skilled person has access to everything that was made available without restrictions.[20] The skilled person is considered a fictitious person without intuition or inventive activity.[21] It can also be a group of persons.[22] Moreover, the skilled person is defined based on the problem to be solved without regard to the proposed solution.[23]

In order to determine whether the claimed solution was obvious for the skilled person, the EPO has developed the problem-solution approach. A very similar approach is applied in Switzerland, which has been defined by the Swiss Federal Patent Court as comprising the following steps:[24]

- determining the closest prior art;
- determining the objective technical problem to be solved;
- determining whether an incentive was provided in the state of the art, which would have motivated the skilled person to amend the closest prior art in such a way as to arrive at the claimed subject-matter.

Although this approach is considered the 'normal' approach,[25] it is not the only approach which can be used in Swiss patent law.[26] Notably, using this approach, the EPO has also allowed claims directed to problem-inventions, i.e. claims including parts of the problem to be solved. Such claims have, however, been denied by Swiss courts.[27]

With respect to the last step of the approach, Swiss courts have issued a number of notable decisions. For example, it has been made clear that the skilled person does not ignore remote technical fields when looking for a solution to the underlying technical problem. Instead, the skilled person can even be motivated to search for solutions in remote technical fields depending on the specific problem.[28]

[B] Particularities Regarding Claims to Antibodies

It has been explicitly denied that special rules for different technical fields should apply.[29] However, Peter Heinrich is of the opinion that this principle has not always been followed in the past.[30] Specifically, in biotechnological inventions it has often been practised to base inventive activity on unexpected technical effects, e.g. the surprising function of a claimed sequence, rather than a strict assessment of whether the skilled person would have arrived at the claimed subject-matter. However,

20. Swiss Federal Supreme Court in BGE 89 II 109.
21. Swiss Federal Supreme Court in BGE 120 II 312.
22. Swiss Federal Supreme Court in BGE 120 II 71.
23. Swiss Federal Supreme Court in BGer 4C.52/2005 – *Kunststoffdübel*.
24. Swiss Federal Patent Court in S2014_001 of 11 February 2015.
25. Swiss Federal Patent Court in O2015_001 of 12 July 2016.
26. Swiss Federal Supreme Court in BGE 138 III 111.
27. Swiss Federal Supreme Court in BGE 114 II 82 – *Schneehalter*.
28. Swiss Federal Supreme Court in BGE 89 II 108 – *Lackschleier*.
29. Swiss Federal Labor Court (BAG) in BAGE 5.6.1968, SMI 1969, 38.
30. P. Heinrich, PatG/EPÜ, 3rd edition, Art. 1 PatG, 120 ff.

there is no Swiss case law available which specifically deals with inventive step of antibody-related claims.

§8.06 ENFORCEMENT AND SCOPE OF PROTECTION

As of 1 January 2012, the newly formed Swiss Federal Patent Court has been responsible for all disputes concerning patents as a first instance court. This includes patent infringement and validity as well as civil disputes relating to the right to a patent and licences. Decisions by the Federal Patent Court can be appealed. The second instance is the Swiss Federal Supreme Court (Bundesgericht).

The effects of a granted patent as basis for infringement proceedings are governed by Article 8 PatG, reading:

(1) The patent confers on its proprietor the right to prohibit others from commercially using the invention.
(2) Use includes, in particular, manufacturing, storage, offering, placing on the market, importing, exporting and carrying in transit, as well as possession for any of these purposes.
(3) Carrying in transit may only be prohibited if the proprietor of the patent is permitted to prohibit importation into the country of destination.

Moreover, it is held by Article 8a PatG that:

(1) If the invention concerns a manufacturing process, the effects of the patent also extend to the products directly obtained by that process.
(2) If the products directly obtained by the process concern biological material, the effects of the patent also extend to products obtained by propagating the biological material and which demonstrate the same characteristics. Article 9a paragraph 3 remains reserved.

With respect to genetic material, it is further specified in Article 8b PatG that:

> If the invention concerns a product that consists of or contains genetic information, the effects of the patent extend to any material in which the product is incorporated and in which the genetic information is contained and performs its function. Article 1a paragraph 1 and 9a paragraph 3 remain reserved.

Lastly, Article 8c PatG deals with nucleotide sequences:

> The protection conferred by a claim to a nucleotide sequence that is derived from a naturally occurring sequence or partial sequence of a gene is limited to the sequence segments that perform the function specifically described in the patent.

Accordingly, with respect to claims covering antibodies defined by deposited biological material, it is made clear that protection extends to propagated material having the same functional characteristics.[31] Moreover, for antibody patents also including claims directed to nucleotide sequences, it is important to consider that such claims only extend to segments that perform the function described in the patent.

---

31. *See* also Message from the Federal Council of 23 November 2005 at page 67 ff.

In general, however, claims including those directed to antibodies are subject to claim construction, potentially leading to a scope of protection extending beyond the literal understanding of the claim.[32]

[A] Biosimilars

Various biosimilars, i.e. biological products that are highly similar but not identical to existing biologics, e.g. antibodies, have received marketing approval in Switzerland. The first was a biosimilar of filgrastim approved in 2009. Since then other biosimilars have been approved, e.g. Erelzi® (Etanercept biosimilar), also including biosimilars of antibodies such as biosimilars of Remicade®. As such, the first biosimilar has been approved in Switzerland about three years after the first market approval granted by the European Medicines Agency (EMA).

With respect to receiving market approval for biosimilars in Switzerland, it should be noted that according to Article 9(1)(c) PatG the protection conferred by a patent does not extend to activities related to receiving market approval. This provision was introduced in 2008 in response to EU Directive 2004/27/EC. Previously, Swiss court practice lacked harmonization, finding that such activities infringed Swiss patents[33] or were allowed.[34]

[B] Equivalence

According to Article 51 PatG the invention is defined by the claims while the description and drawings are used for their interpretation. While the protocol on the interpretation of Article 69 EPC is not part of Swiss patent law, it has been repeatedly applied by Swiss courts.[35]

As such, it is accepted that equivalence is determined following the steps set by the *Schneidmesser* decisions of the German Federal Supreme Court,[36] namely:

1. The equivalent embodiment must solve the technical problem underlying the claimed invention by means which, although modified, have objectively the same effect as the means required in the granted claims.
2. The person skilled in the art must be able to infer the equivalent embodiment from the disclosure content of the patent and their common general knowledge at the priority or filing date of the patent without inventive activity.
3. The considerations required to find the equivalent embodiment must be oriented towards the technical teaching of the claimed invention, so that the

32. Exemplified by the Swiss Federal Patent Court in O2013_008 of 25 August 2015 - *Pulversprühpistole.*
33. *See* for example Commercial court (HG) of the canton of St. Gallen (SG) of 31 August 2004 (HG.2004.49) - *Simvastatin.*
34. High Court of the canton of Basel-Land of 1 October 1997, sic! 1/1998, 78 - *Acyclovir.*
35. P. Heinrich, PatG/EPÜ, 3rd edition, Art. 51 PatG, 62.
36. German Federal Supreme Court, decision in X ZR 168/00 of 12 March 2002 - *Schneidmesser I*; German Federal Supreme Court, decision in X ZR 135/01 of 12 March 2002 - *Schneidmesser II.*

skilled person would recognize the respective embodiments, i.e. the literally claimed one and the allegedly infringing one, as being equivalent.

The third part of the above assessment has been controversially discussed by Swiss courts. In a number of cases, first instance decisions followed the above approach but issued decisions that contradicted those of German or British courts.[37] However, the Swiss Federal Court has overturned those decisions and repeatedly followed German and British courts, which has led to a substantial degree of harmonization.[38]

This became also evident in the matter related to 'pemetrexed'. Although the Swiss Federal Supreme Court did not exactly follow the reasoning of courts deciding in parallel cases in other jurisdictions, the final outcome was identical. Specifically, in the underlying case, the Federal Supreme Court focused on the question of the infringement of Eli Lilly's patent by equivalent means and did not deal with the issue of direct and indirect infringement. Yet, the Swiss Supreme Court sided with the parallel German decision X ZR 29/15 and the UK Supreme Court decision [2017] UKSC 48 and came to the final conclusion that the fact that the wording of the claims of Eli Lilly's patent had been narrowed down during prosecution from the broad term 'antifolate' to 'pemetrexed' and finally to 'pemetrexed disodium' does not exclude that these claims are infringed by equivalent means by Actavis' pharmaceutical product Amtiris®, which comprises pemetrexed diacid. Accordingly, the three courts decided that in this specific case the argumentation of *Okklusionsvorrichtung*[39] does not apply (see §3.06[B]).

In a further case related to an appeal against the rejection of an SPC application for 'panitumumab', it was confirmed by the Federal Administrative Court that a claim to a therapeutic composition comprising a specific antibody in combination with an antineoplastic agent is not infringed under the doctrine of equivalence by the use of the corresponding antibody alone.[40]

In sum, it can be concluded that Swiss court practice has been largely harmonized with the court practice in other European jurisdictions such as Germany or the UK.

37. *See* for example Swiss Federal Patent Court in O2014_002, E – 6.5.2.5.
38. *See* Swiss Federal Supreme Court (BGer) in 4A_131/2016 overturning the above decision.
39. German Federal Supreme Court, decision in X ZR 16/09 of 10 May 2011 – *Okklusionsvorrichtung*.
40. Swiss Federal Administrative Court, decision in B-3245/2010 of 18 August 2011.

Chapter 9

United Kingdom

Daniel Lim & Claire Baldock

§9.01 ANTIBODIES AS PATENTABLE SUBJECT-MATTER

[A] Legal Framework

Patents for inventions in the UK are governed by the Patents Act 1977 (Patents Act) as amended up to 1 October 2017. Biological inventions are specifically addressed in section 76A and schedule A2, which reproduce the provisions of EU Directive 98/448/EC on the legal protection of biotechnological inventions.[1] At the time of writing the UK Government has confirmed that it is intended that these provisions will be maintained in UK law following the departure of the UK from the European Union.

Schedule A2(1) confirms that an invention shall not be considered unpatentable solely on the ground that it concerns:

a) a product consisting of or containing biological material; or
b) a process by which a biological material is produced, processed or used.

Schedule A2(2) confirms that biological material that is isolated from its natural environment or produced by means of a technical process may be the subject of an invention even if it previously occurred in nature.

An antibody, being a biological material, can therefore be patentable subject matter in the UK providing all other criteria for patentability of an invention are met. In this respect section 1 of the Patents Act provides that a patent may be granted for an invention which is new, involves an inventive step and is capable of an industrial application. In addition, section 14(3) requires the specification for a patent application to be clear enough and complete enough for the invention to be performed

1. EU Directive 98/448/EC (https://eur-lex.europa.eu/legal-content/EN/TXT/?uri=CELEX:31998L0044).

by a person skilled in the art, often referred to as the requirement for sufficiency of disclosure. Under section 14(5) a patent claim in an application must also:

a) define the matter for which the applicant seeks protection;
b) be clear and concise; and
c) be supported by the description.

Section 4A of the Patents Act is relevant to the patentability of practical applications of antibodies. Section 4A(1) provides that a patent shall not be granted for the invention of:

a) a method of treatment of the human or animal body by surgery or therapy; or
b) a method of diagnosis practiced on the human or animal body.

However, subsections 4A(2) to (4) confirm that substances and compositions may nevertheless be patented where they are for use in such excluded methods of treatment or diagnosis. Thus, antibodies may be the subject of therapeutic and diagnostic use claims, for example, in the form 'Antibody X for use in treating disease Y'.

Since 26 May 2010, following the reasoning of the Enlarged Board of Appeal of the European Patent Office (EPO) in Decision G 02/08,[2] claims in the Swiss style 'Use of antibody X for the manufacture of a medicament for treatment of disease Y' are no longer permitted to be granted in the UK regardless of the priority date of the application.

Finally, it should be noted that, when examining patent applications for all kinds of inventions, the UK Intellectual Property Office (UKIPO) will generally follow legal principles established by the Boards of Appeal of the EPO, although judgments of the English courts will take precedence where there is divergence from the EPO position. Reference may be had to the Manual of Patent Practice (MOPP)[3] produced by the UKIPO which includes separate supplements on medical[4] and biological inventions.[5]

[B] General Amenability or Exclusion of Antibodies from Patentability

As discussed in §9.01[A] above, antibodies and their applications are patentable subject matter in the UK providing the requirements of novelty, inventive step, industrial application and sufficiency of disclosure are met. There are no general exclusions from patentability based upon their status as antibodies *per se*.

2. G 0002/08 *ABBOTT RESPIRATORY*/Dosage regime OJEPO 2010, 456.
3. Manual of Patent Practice (MOPP) https://www.gov.uk/government/publications/patents-manual-of-patent-practice.
4. MOPP Medical inventions. https://www.gov.uk/government/publications/examining-patent-applications-for-medical-inventions.
5. MOPP Biological inventions. https://www.gov.uk/government/publications/examining-patent-applications-for-biotechnological-inventions.

[C] Required Distinction from Naturally Occurring Antibodies

The patentability requirements can be met for a naturally occurring antibody, in particular, where its existence in nature was not previously recognised and it has been isolated from that environment or produced by means of a technical process. The principle that a naturally occurring product may be found novel so long as its existence was not previously recognised was established in a Decision of the EPO Technical Board of Appeal (T 0272/95)[6] concerning an application in the name of the Howard Florey Institute for the newly identified human relaxin gene. The principle still prevails and is affirmed by the UKIPO in the Manual of Patent Practice.

§9.02 ACCEPTABLE CLAIM FEATURES FOR DEFINING ANTIBODIES

[A] Functional Features

[1] Target/Antigen

It is possible in specific circumstances to secure a claim to an antibody defined solely by the antigen which it specifically recognises, without any further structural or functional definition being present. Those circumstances are where the antigen itself is identified for the first time in the patent application and is recognised as novel, inventive and industrially applicable.

While patent applications for inventions involving new antigens had for many years been allowed to have claims which 'reach through' to antibodies specifically binding that antigen at the UKIPO, this practice received judicial approval from the Court of Appeal in *Human Genome Sciences v. Eli Lilly and Co.*[7] The patent in issue claimed a newly identified member of the TNF ligand superfamily called Neutrokine-α. Also included was a claim directed to any antibody specifically binding the claimed protein (claim 13). The claims to Neutrokine-α had been previously held to be valid by the Supreme Court but that decision did not address the validity of the antibody claim. Lilly had attacked that claim for insufficiency on the basis that:

> 'Even though individual antibodies could be isolated and made, it would take undue effort to determine which of the millions of antibodies covered had any use.'

In a hearing before the Court of Appeal the Court rejected this attack because:

> 'At the level of generality of this patent, all the antibodies have a "use" ... Each member is susceptible of industrial application... and that was enough. All the claim calls for is an antibody which specifically binds to Neutrokine-α: that in itself is its potential utility.'

6. T0272/95 *Howard Florey Institute's Application / Relaxin* OJEPO 1995, 590.
7. *Human Genome Sciences v. Eli Lilly and Co* [2012] EWCA Civ 1185.

The Court also held:

> 'The argument that claim 13 was not enabling across its breadth because it included within it antibodies which could not be identified without undue effort fails because of the fundamental fact that all the antibodies of claim 13 can be made.'

Accordingly, an antibody defined solely by the antigen to which it specifically binds but for which no other functional or structural definition can be provided at the time of filing is, in principle, patentable in the UK provided the antigen is itself novel, inventive and industrially applicable.

In practice however, such claims can be vulnerable to other attacks in some cases. Definition is important. The UKIPO MOPP for Biological Inventions confirms that where a claim relates to an antibody 'specific' for an identified polypeptide, specificity cannot be accepted if there is evidence that the antibody reacts against a different polypeptide.

In addition, a claim of this type can be found to lack novelty in a situation where a prior art antibody binds to the same epitope on a related protein and will therefore cross-react with the claimed antigen.

[2] Mode of Binding: Target Affinity, Binding Specificity, Epitope, Definitions via Reference Antibodies and Competitive Binding

At the UKIPO there is no formal barrier to defining an antibody by a functional feature such as its binding affinity, or specificity for a particular antigen or epitope providing that the functional definition is clear, as required by section 14(5) of the Patents Act.

It is important to note that, unlike the situation discussed under [1] above where the antigen is new, an antibody raised against a known protein would, in principle, be found not inventive as immunizing an animal with an antigen and/or preparation of a hybridoma cell line is considered a routine procedure. However, methods for generating new antibodies that involve a skill that is beyond routine laboratory practice may nevertheless result in an antibody against a known antigen being recognised as inventive. Similarly, an antibody with unexpected properties may also be considered capable of patent protection. It follows that if the functional feature(s) are ones which are obvious *desiterata* (e.g. higher affinity for a given target than prior art antibodies for that target) and if merely routine procedures are used to achieve it, then inventive step is unlikely to be acknowledged for the antibody on the basis of that feature. Generally something more exceptional would need to have been done and/or the functional feature would need to confer an unexpected technical effect.

As regards the recognition of a new epitope, this might also be used to define an antibody in a claim but the new epitope would need to be clearly defined. Again, inventive step might not be recognised in such a feature, where the identification of the epitope had been achieved by routine epitope mapping techniques. Specific technical problems might need to have been overcome and/or the antibody would need to display unexpected properties which arise from the choice of epitope.

As to definitions using reference antibodies and competitive binding, (the so called cross-blocking or cross-competing claim), for example 'An antibody which competes with (known) antibody XYZ for binding to antigen A', such a claim is not specifically considered in MOPP, nor has it received any judicial consideration in the UK. Based upon general principles applied in examination to biological inventions, a clarity and support objection under section 14(5) could arise as the breadth of such a claim may not be commensurate with the applicant's contribution to the art. The allowance of such a claim would clearly be governed by the technical disclosure in the specification. For further discussion of support and exemplification see §9.03 below.

[3] *Effect on Target*

An antibody defined solely by the functional effect it has upon the target it recognises is likely to be considered a claim defining the invention merely by the result to be achieved. In the MOPP it is stated that, as a general rule, claims which attempt to define the invention, or a feature thereof, by a result to be achieved should not be allowed. However, they may be permitted in certain circumstances where (1) the invention can only be defined in such terms or cannot be defined more precisely without unduly restricting the scope of the claims, and (2) the result is one which can be directly and positively verified by tests adequately specified in the description and involving nothing more than trial and error. A similar approach to 'result to be achieved' claims is taken by the EPO.

Thus, patentability of any antibody defined solely by its effect on the target will fall to be considered under sections 14(3) and 14(5). In particular, the following two questions will be asked (1) can the invention be carried out across the breadth of the claim without undue burden? and (2) is the scope of the claim commensurate with the applicant's contribution to the art? As noted in [2] above, the allowance of such a claim would clearly be governed by the technical disclosure in the specification. For example, a single example of an antibody exhibiting the claimed technical effect is unlikely to be sufficient to support a claim to any antibody with that property. For further discussion see §9.03 below.

[B] Structural Features

[1] *Molecular Topology: Antibody Types, Fragments and Antibody Constructs*

As discussed in §9.02[A] above, given the clarity and support problems which can arise with purely functional definitions of antibodies, some level of structural definition may be needed to confer patentability. For example, definition by idiotype (IgG, IgM, IgD, IgE, IgA) would be permissible and useful insofar as this will confer certain further structural and functional features on the antibody which may distinguish it from prior art antibodies. Source of antibody (e.g. camelid, shark) where this implies a certain 3D structure, may also distinguish an antibody over prior art antibodies to the same target.

There are many known structural artificial fragments of antibodies, for example F(ab), F$(ab)_2$, Fv, Fc, scFv, diabodies, triabodies, tetrabodies, bis-scFv, minibodies and others. All such fragments may independently be patentable subject matter in the

UK provided the requirements of patentability are met. It should be noted however that difficulties under section 14(5) concerning clarity may arise where a patent claim defines a complete antibody but includes the generic language 'or a fragment thereof' without clear definition of the fragment by structure or limitation by function. Acceptable scope of antibody claims is discussed further under §9.03[A] below.

Artificial antibody-like constructs, for example a molecule comprising an antibody Fc portion and a receptor portion recognising a specific ligand which replaces the antibody variable region, could be patentable subject matter in the UK.

In practice, because elucidation of sequence alone does not generally confer inventive step, antibody claims are often presented with both functional and sequence features.

[2] Amino Acid Sequences

[a] Full-Length Sequences of Antibodies

There is no statutory requirement in the UK to define an antibody by the amino acid sequences of its heavy and light chains; but there is no bar to doing so either. The UKIPO considers the mere production of an antibody against a known antigen to be entirely routine and therefore obvious in the absence of any special or unexpected features arising. Similarly, the sequencing of such an antibody is considered equally routine and lacking in inventive step unless that sequence or part thereof confers an advantageous property compared with known antibodies to that same antigen. The UKIPO does not recognise inventive step based upon structure alone. The generation of humanised antibodies against a known target is also unlikely to involve an inventive step if non-humanised antibodies against the same target are already known, as such modifications are well known in the art and so it would be obvious to perform them. However, if the applicant can demonstrate a particularly useful property of their antibody that is not realised by those disclosed in the prior art then it may be possible to demonstrate an inventive step; for example, perhaps the selection of specific beneficial point mutations in antibody framework regions during antibody humanisation.

It must be noted that, according to rule 13 of The Patent Rules 2007 (as amended),[8] where the specification of an application for a patent discloses a sequence, it must include a sequence listing. The requirements for such a listing are set out in that rule.

[b] Sequences of Fragments, CDRs and Framework Regions

It is common practice when defining a specific antibody in a patent claim to provide the amino acid sequence of only part of the antibody, in particular those parts which confer specificity to a known antigen. These are the entire variable regions of the heavy and light chains or, more commonly, the complementarity determining regions

8. The Patents (Amendment) Rules 2007 (https://www.gov.uk/government/publications/the-patents-rules-2007-and-patents-fees-rules-2007).

(CDRs). As discussed under §9.02[A] above, the mere structure of these sections cannot of itself confer inventive step upon an antibody to a known antigen unless some special, non-routine technique were used to obtain them or they confer an advantageous property on the claimed antibody not exhibited by known antibodies against that target. A similar position arises in the case of sequences of framework or other constant regions of the antibody. Where mutations to these cause an advantageous property in the antibody then such sequences could confer patentability.

[3] Chemical Modifications, Conjugation and Glycosylation

Naturally occurring antibodies produced by a process conferring an unusual glycosylation pattern, or converted to an artificial molecule by chemical modification or by conjugation to another molecule can all, respectively, be patentable subject matter in the UK. This is the case even if the unmodified antibody is known, provided that something more than routine laboratory procedures have been used to generate the modified product and/or an advantageous and unexpected technical effect is conferred on the antibody by virtue of the modifications.

[C] Cell Line Deposits and Process of Production

The need for deposit of biological material for the purpose of meeting the sufficiency of disclosure requirement under section 14(3) is governed by rule 13(1) and schedule 1 of The Patents Rules 2007. These rules relate to the deposit, access and re-deposit of biological material.

The disclosure requirements for patent protection are satisfied if, in the case where biological material is not available to the public at the date of filing, a sample of the material is deposited in a culture collection on or before the date of filing, the application as filed gives such information on the characteristics of the biological material as is available to the applicant and the specification gives the name of the culture collection and the accession number of the deposit. The information about the two latter requirements may be added to the application within a period of 16 months from the earliest priority date. Giving the necessary information in the specification signifies consent to the availability of the biological material to the public as of the date of publication of the application, unless a request is made that the material should only be made available to an expert (see below). It should be noted that where a priority date for the subject matter, made sufficient by the deposition of biological material, is relied upon, it is necessary that the material must have been deposited on or before that priority date.[9]

As already discussed, section 14(3) requires that the description in an application should be sufficient for the invention to be performed by the person skilled in the art. In the case of an invention relating to an antibody, depositing a cell line capable of reproducing the antibody might be only one way in which the requirement may be met.

9. MOPP Biological inventions at [137].

The choice of a suitable depositary institution is up to the applicant. In the UK the depositary institution does not have to be one recognised under the Budapest Treaty but may be unacceptable if it is not clearly independent of the applicant and/ or does not seem capable of furnishing samples of the deposited material when a valid request for release of the sample is made to the UKIPO by a third party.

The release of a sample of the deposited material is governed by paragraphs 4 and 5 of schedule 1 of the Patents Rules to which reference should be made concerning undertakings required from the requester.

Where, in spite of the undertaking required to be given by requesters, an applicant has concerns about misuse of the sample once released it is possible to request that the availability of samples of the deposited material upon request should be restricted an expert. Before the end of a period of one month after the date on which a request for release to a nominated expert has been made, the applicant may give notice of objection to the particular expert, and where this happens the Comptroller of Patents shall determine the matter.

A request to restrict availability of any sample of deposited material to experts must be made before the preparations for the application's publication have been completed by the UKIPO. A notice will then be included in the publication to the effect that the expert access regime applies.

Paragraph 8 of schedule 1 also sets forth procedures for furnishing replacement samples at the depository institution in the event that the sample should become non-viable or cannot be released or maintained for other reasons.

Where an antibody producing cell line has been deposited in accordance with the provisions of schedule 1 it is acceptable to refer to the deposited material by accession number in a patent claim concerning a specific antibody produced by the cell line or a process for making the antibody.

§9.03 BREADTH OF CLAIMS AND SUPPORT BY EXAMPLES

[A] Acceptable Breadth of Claims to Antibodies

When a patent application is examined at the UKIPO an acceptable scope of claim will be determined by considerations of clarity and technical support (section 14(5)), sufficiency of disclosure (section 14(3)) and inventive step (section 3). In particular, in the case of a claim to a chemical or biological molecule or a pharmaceutical, the questions to be asked will be:

1) Is the scope of claim commensurate with the applicant's technical contribution to the art?
2) Can the invention be reproduced across the scope of the claim without undue burden?
3) Is the technical effect of the invention credible or plausible across the scope of the claim?

These considerations will apply to an antibody claim just as they would any other invention. A precise, narrow definition of an antibody will not always be required for these questions to be answered in the affirmative. The individual facts of any particular case will be relevant. It should also be observed that these are interrelated questions that in practice can be difficult to separate into discrete categories of objection. For present purposes it is more useful to consider the topic of claim breadth through these practical questions and the central theme of the technical contribution of the patent that underpins the issue.

In determining appropriate claim scope, the UKIPO relies on judicial precedent from both the EPO and the English courts.

A leading English authority is the decision of the House of Lords in *Biogen Inc v. Medeva plc* [1997] RPC 1.[10] The invention concerned a DNA molecule encoding an antigen of hepatitis B. In that decision their Lordships held:

> 'the specification must enable the invention to be performed to the full extent of the monopoly claimed. If the invention discloses a principle of general application, the claims may be in correspondingly general terms. The patentee need not show that he has proved its application in every individual instance. On the other hand, if the claims include a number of discrete methods or products, the patentee must enable the invention to be performed in respect of each of them.'

The Manual of Patent Practice also discusses other general principles in accordance with EPO Technical Board of Appeal Decision T 0292/85 (*Genentech/Polypeptide expression*).[11] It is stated that:

> 'At least one embodiment of the invention or at least one method for performing the invention must be described so that it can be reproduced without the need for inventive ingenuity. If a skilled person following the directions given in the specification has to find out something that is new in order to reproduce the invention, the disclosure is insufficient.

The non-availability of some unspecified variants of a functionally defined component feature of the invention is immaterial to sufficiency so long as there are suitable variants known to the skilled person as common general knowledge which provide the same effect for the invention. In other words, an application should provide enough information to allow a person skilled in the art to carry out substantially all that which falls within the ambit of what is claimed.'

This case should not be interpreted as suggesting that disclosure of only one way to realise an invention will be sufficient to allow a claim of broad scope. Circumstances will dictate whether one way will suffice and frequently only the disclosure of several ways will justify a broad claim. Arnold J in *Medimmune v. Novartis*,[12] commenting on the decision in *Biogen v. Medeva*, noted that:

> 'i) A claim will be invalid for insufficiency if the breadth of the claim exceeds the technical contribution to the art made by the invention. It follows that it is not necessarily enough to disclose one way of performing the invention in the specification.
>
> ii) The breadth of the claim will exceed the technical contribution if the claim covers ways of achieving the desired result which owe nothing to the patent or

10. *Biogen Inc v. Medeva plc [1997] RPC 1.*
11. T 0292/85 (*Genentech/Polypeptide expression*) OJEPO 1989, 275 (T 0292/85).
12. [2011] EWHC 1699 (Pat).

> any principle it discloses. Two classes of this are where the patent claims results which it does not enable, such as making a wider class of products when it enables only one and discloses no principle to enable the others to be made, and where the patent claims every way of achieving a result when it enables only one way and it is possible to envisage other ways of achieving that result which make no use of the invention.'

Where the patent has disclosed a principle of general application, this may constitute a technical contribution capable of justifying claims of broad scope. In *Regeneron v. Genentech*,[13] the Court of Appeal noted that:

> 'It must therefore be possible to make a reasonable prediction the invention will work with substantially everything falling within the scope of the claim or, put another way, the assertion that the invention will work across the scope of the claim must be plausible or credible. The products and methods within the claim are then tied together by a unifying characteristic or a common principle. If it is possible to make such a prediction then it cannot be said the claim is insufficient simply because the patentee has not demonstrated the invention works in every case.'

While the above precedents are applicable to assessment of sufficiency of disclosure at the UKIPO, the scope of claim may also be influenced by principles for determining inventive step.

For example, like the EPO, the UKIPO applies an underlying principle when assessing inventive step that the scope of the patent monopoly must be justified by the patentee's contribution to the art. Where the alleged contribution is a technical effect which is not common to substantially everything covered by a claim, it cannot be used for the purposes of judging obviousness.[14] Furthermore, a technical effect which is not rendered plausible by the patent specification may not be taken into account in assessing inventive step. The MOPP approves this 'plausibility' approach based upon EPO Technical Board of Appeal Decision T 1329/04 (*Johns Hopkins / Factor-9*).[15]

In this case it was held that the protein GDF-9 could not be 'clearly and unambiguously identified as a member of the TGF-β superfamily based upon the structure disclosed for it as there was no experimental data to support this conclusion'. The technical problem of finding a new member of the TGF-β had thus not been plausibly solved, thus no technical contribution was made and no inventive step was present.

It is fair to say that the law in respect of plausibility and what is an acceptable breadth of claim has developed significantly over the last decade or so. The Decisions of the UK Supreme Court in *Human Genome Sciences v. Eli Lilly*[16] and *Co* and *Warner-Lambert v. Generics UK Ltd and Mylan*[17] suggest that the concept of plausibility, despite having no direct statutory basis, is here to stay as an influential force in UK patent law.

---

13. [2013] RPC 28.
14. See Floyd LJ at [39] of *Generics v. Yeda* [2013] EWCA Civ 925.
15. T 1329/04 (*Johns Hopkins /Factor-9*).
16. *Human Genome Sciences v. Eli Lilly* [2011] UKSC 51, [2012] RPC 6 (UK Supreme Court).
17. *Warner-Lambert v. Generics UK Ltd t/a Mylan* [2018] UKSC 56.

The UK Supreme Court's consideration of plausibility in relation to second medical use claims in *Warner-Lambert v. Generics UK Ltd t/a Mylan* is discussed in §9.04 below.

Notably, the UK Supreme Court is due to grapple further with the issue of acceptable claim breadth and enablement across the scope of the claims in the appeal from the Court of Appeal's decision in *Regeneron v. Kymab*,[18] to be heard in the course of 2019. The fact that the Supreme Court granted permission for the appeal demonstrates the importance of the issue as a matter of public interest and suggests the law in this area will continue to develop.

In summary, although there is no one single principle to be applied to establish an acceptable scope of an antibody claim the question of the technical contribution of the patent is a common theme that cuts across the issue. In practice, the state of the art, common general knowledge of one skilled in the art and the extent of the technical disclosure of the application will all be determinative.

[B] Required Experimental Support for Claims to Functionally Defined Antibodies

As discussed in §9.02[A][1], where a patent application discloses for the first time a new and inventive antigen, a claim to an antibody which specifically binds to the antigen can also be granted by the UKIPO. Because it is considered routine to generate an antibody to a known antigen, the claim can be considered to meet the requirements of sufficiency of disclosure without a single example of such an antibody being present in the specification. This has been confirmed by the Court of Appeal in *Human Genome Sciences v. Eli Lilly and Co.* However, as will be apparent from §9.03[A] above, the burden of exemplification will be rather higher in other circumstances when the various principles set forth will be applied. Depending on the nature and breadth of the claims, and other disclosures of the patent, significant support in the form of experimental data may be required (for example) to render the claims plausible across their scope. On the other hand, if the patent discloses a plausible principle of general application that applies across the scope of the claims and represents a significant technical contribution, those claims may be sufficient despite minimal experimental data in the specification.

Where an unexpected technical effect and/or an exceptional effort associated with a functional feature is relied upon to confer inventiveness, data may be required to show the production of an antibody with the claimed feature, as well as the presence of the unexpected technical effect to that feature and/or why the attainment of that feature was noteworthy and inventive.

[C] Required Experimental Support for Claims to Structurally Defined Antibodies

When the principles set forth in §9.03[A] are applied it will not always be the case that an antibody must be defined by its exact amino acid sequence or partial sequence.

18. [2018] EWCA Civ 671.

Variants with a defined degree of homology or similarity to the exact sequence may be permitted. Similarly in the case of an antibody defined by its encoding nucleic acid, nucleic acid sequences which hybridise under particular conditions of stringency to the defined sequences may, in principle, expand the scope of the claim. However, in either case the claim must be limited to sequences which have the activity of the reference sequence. The acceptable level of sequence variation will be governed by the closeness of the prior art and whether it is credible or plausible that all the sequences within the scope of the claim would have the stated activity. The level of exemplification in the specification will, of course, play a significant part in this assessment.

§9.04 SPECIFIC MEDICAL APPLICATIONS AND OTHER FOLLOW-UP INVENTIONS

[A] Treatment of Specific Diseases

As noted in §9.01[A] above, section 4A(1) of the Patents Act establishes a general exclusion from patentability for methods of treatment or diagnosis, subject to a specific exception for inventions consisting of a substance or composition for use in such a method. Thus, antibodies, being such a substance or composition, may be the subject of therapeutic and diagnostic use claims, for example, in the form 'Antibody X for use as a medicament' (first medical use) or alternatively 'Antibody X for treating disease Y' (second medical use). The former type of claim is reserved for the situation where no previous medical use has been disclosed for an antibody against that target; and the latter for situations where other medical uses are already known and the new use must be specified to confer novelty.

It should be noted that this style of claim is only permitted at the UKIPO for use of a substance in methods which fall under the specific exclusion set forth in section 4A(1) following the reasoning of the Enlarged Board of Appeal of the European Patent Office (EPO) in Decision G02/08. For example, where the use is cosmetic or in an *in vitro* diagnostic method, this style of claim would not be permitted.

In the case of a medical use claim, in the UK, assessing novelty of the use over the prior art is not always straightforward. If the claimed antibody has previously been used in the treatment of the specified disease, then this will still anticipate the claim even if the beneficial effect was not shown for all patients. Furthermore, the prior art must provide an enabling disclosure. In this respect authorities relied upon by the UKIPO include T 0241/95,[19] *Regeneron Pharmaceuticals v. Genentech, Merck Sharp & Dohme v. Ono*[20] and T 715/03.[21] In particular it should be noted that a disclosure that the agent in question merely *might* have the claimed therapeutic effect does not enable the skilled person to directly and unambiguously deduce that it will have the claimed effect and so this does not meet the disclosure requirement for anticipation. Nor does the disclosure that an agent is being evaluated in clinical

19. T 0241/95 *Eli Lilly* OJEPO 2001, 103.
20. *Merck Sharp & Dohme v. Ono* [2015] EWHC 2973.
21. T 715/03 Pfizer.

trials for a condition if the therapeutic efficacy has not yet been determined and published. Further, the disclosure of the prior art must make the therapeutic use plausible to the skilled person.

Concerning the breadth of a claim to a medical use of an antibody, assessment of clarity and support, sufficiency of disclosure and inventive step will govern the appropriate scope based upon the same principles and authorities set out in §9.03 above. In the English courts it has been established that the therapeutic effect must be plausible across the scope for a finding that the invention is sufficiently disclosed. Two of the leading authorities are *Regeneron v. Genentech* and *Warner-Lambert v. Generics(UK) Ltd t/a Mylan.*

The Regeneron case concerned a medical use claim involving an antibody as follows:

> 'Use of a hVEGF antagonist in the preparation of a medicament for the treatment of a non-neoplastic disease or disorder characterised by undesirable excessive neovascularisation, wherein the hVEGF antagonist is: (a) an anti-VEGF antibody or antibody fragment; (b) an anti-VEGF receptor antibody or antibody fragment; or (c) an isolated hVEGF receptor.'

The broad definition of the diseases to be treated as '*a non-neoplastic disease or disorder characterised by undesirable excessive neovascularisation*', attracted an attack of insufficiency of disclosure under section 14.3. The Court of Appeal held that:

> 'It must be possible to make a reasonable prediction the invention will work with substantially everything falling within the scope of the claim or, put another way, the assertion that the invention will work across the scope of the claim must be plausible or credible.'

The Court did find the assertion plausible in this case.

The standard to be applied in assessing whether a claimed technical effect is plausible in relation to sufficiency of disclosure was also considered in great detail by the Supreme Court in the *Warner-Lambert* case in 2018. The claim at issue in the proceedings was a Swiss form claim directed to the use of the drug pregabalin for treating neuropathic pain. The claim had been held partially valid by the Court of Appeal because expert evidence suggested that only one category of neuropathic pain, peripheral neuropathic pain, was rendered plausible to the skilled person from the animal experiments presented in the specification. The Supreme Court was expressly asked to consider whether a plausibility assessment should play any part in determining sufficiency of disclosure.

In a 3:2 split judgment their Lordships held that it should, and arguably raised the bar on what has previously been considered a low threshold test by the English courts. In the prevailing judgment it was held that the proposition that a product is efficacious for the treatment of a given condition must be *plausible*. It is not made plausible by bare assertion as such a low threshold would not serve the purpose of barring speculative or armchair claims. There must be something to cause the skilled person to think there is a reasonable prospect the assertion is true and the 'reasonable prospect' requires showing that the claimed substance has a direct effect on a metabolic mechanism specifically involved in the disease. This test was established by the Technical Board of Appeal of the EPO in T 0609/02

Salk Institute[22] in 2004. As the application in the *Warner-Lambert* case did not disclose any mechanism by which pregabalin may be effective in treating any form of neuropathic pain, the claim as a whole was held insufficient.

The principles established by the Supreme Court in this case will be applied to claims directed to the medical use of an antibody and so efforts to disclose a plausible mechanism of action in future applications will be important even if only *in vitro* tests are available. Indeed, such principles have already been followed by the High Court in March 2019, in the case of *Eli Lilly v. Genentech.*[23] The patent at issue had claims (in both Swiss and EPC2000 format) to an antibody which specifically binds to the interleukin heterodimeric complex IL-17A/F and to the medical use thereof for treating, among other things, psoriasis. Insofar as the claims were directed to the treatment of psoriasis they were held insufficient because the patent provided neither experimental data, nor any discussion to the effect that IL-17A/F had any role in the development of psoriasis. Neither could this be deduced from the scientific papers referenced in the patent. Thus, it was held by Arnold J that the skilled person would not regard it as plausible that anti IL17A/F antibody would have any discernible effect on psoriasis. Notably, although Arnold J acknowledged (at [523]) that the claims were concerned with a 'first medical use', given that the claimed antibodies were not known, there was no dispute that the guidance given by Lord Sumption in *Warner-Lambert* was applicable. Despite accepting Genentech's submission that this fact must be borne in mind when applying such guidance, it did not appear to have any significant bearing on the result.

[B] Mode of Administration

The English courts have historically taken a more conservative view of what constitutes a 'new therapeutic use' than the EPO. Thus, claims couched in the medical use format which related to a known substance for its known use and in which the novelty resided only in the mode of administration (route of delivery or dosage regime) were rejected as disguised methods of treatment. This position was taken by the UKIPO following its approval by the Court of Appeal in *Bristol-Myers Squibb v. Baker Norton Pharmaceuticals.*[24]

This practice has now been superseded following the position established by the EPO in Technical Board of Appeal Decision T 1020/03[25] in which it was held that a new therapeutic use may relate to any new and inventive use falling within an otherwise excluded method of treatment or diagnosis. The principle set out in T 1020/03 was then approved by the Court of Appeal in *Actavis v. Merck.*[26] Thereafter, a medical use claim where novelty resides in a mode of administration can be permitted at the UKIPO providing that it does not impinge on the activities of the doctor and the requirements of sufficiency, inventive step and industrial application are met. In this

22. T 0609/02 *Salk Institute.*
23. [2019] EWHC 387 (Pat).
24. *Bristol-Myers Squibb v. Baker Norton Pharmaceuticals* [2001] RPC 1.
25. T1020/03 *Genentech* OJEPO 2007,204.
26. *Actavis v. Merck* [2008] RPC 26.

respect it will be noted that the inventive step hurdle is likely to be a high one for such claims (see §9.04[C] below).

[C] Dosage Regimens

Based upon the principles discussed above, in particular the authority of *Actavis v. Merck*, a medical use claim where novelty resides solely in a new dosage regimen may be permitted at the UKIPO.[27] However, a decision of 27 March 2019 from the Supreme Court establishes a very high bar for such claims to meet the inventive step requirement.[28]

In 2017 in *Actavis v. ICOS*[29] the Court of Appeal considered a claim to a composition comprising 1 to 5 mg tadalafil in a unit dosage form suitable for oral administration up to a maximum total dose of 5 mg per day for use in treating sexual dysfunction.

Prior art uses of tadalafil involved much higher doses than 5 mg and thus the efficacy of just 5 mg was not to be expected. While acknowledging this the Court of Appeal found that:

> 'a patent will not be granted for an invention which, though not obvious in this a priori sense, is nevertheless an invention which would be arrived at by a line of routine and uninventive enquiry which would be carried out by a skilled team.'

Clinical research into a new or known drug will always involve investigation of an optimum dosage regime. In the prevailing Judgment penned by Lord Hodge (with whom each of the other Supreme Court judges hearing the case agreed), the Supreme Court upheld the finding of the Court of Appeal that the claimed low dosage regime was obvious. Assisted by the expert evidence before him, Birss J at first instance had made factual findings that in a standard clinical research regime, a phase IIb trial is aimed at finding a dose/response relationship of the drug being investigated. Faced with experimental results indicating that doses of tadalafil between 25 and 100 mg lay on the plateau of therapeutic efficacy, the expert evidence suggested those skilled in the art would test lower doses, including 5 mg, in order to meet the aims of such a trial. The fact that the skilled team would not have had an expectation of the effectiveness at a 5 mg dose did not militate against a finding of obviousness if the skilled person was likely to study such a dose to establish the dose response relationship.

However, despite upholding the Court of Appeal's decision in this instance, Lord Hodge made it clear (at [103]) that he did not support any general proposition that the product of well-established or routine enquiries cannot be inventive. In particular, as established in *Actavis v. Merck*, there is no policy reason why a novel and inventive dosage regime should not be rewarded by a patent.

It is perhaps comforting that the Supreme Court confined its findings to the facts of the case in question but it nevertheless uses reasoning in relation to novel

27. See, however, Jacob LJ's qualification at [32] of *Actavis v. Merck*.
28. *Actavis v. ICOS Corporation* [2019] UKSC 15.
29. *Actavis v. ICOS Corporation* [2017] EWCA Civ 1671.

dosage regimes which may be difficult to overcome in future cases when inventive step is considered.

[D] Specific Patient Groups

A second medical use claim may rely for novelty and inventive step solely on the type of patient to be treated, despite the fact that the active agent and disease treated have already been associated in the prior art. However, practice at the UKIPO is divergent from the EPO approach in respect of this type of claim. Such claims have been considered in EPO Technical Board of Appeal Decisions T 0019/86,[30] T 0893/90,[31] T 0233/96,[32] T 0108/09[33] and T 1399/04.[34] In particular, T 0233/96 set out the conditions to be applied.

According to the principles in that decision, first, the new patient group must be clearly distinct from the subjects treated in the prior art, and the two groups must not overlap. Secondly, the distinction must not be arbitrary, but must be based on a functional relationship between the physiological or pathological characteristics of the new group and the therapeutic effect. However, in T 1399/04 the condition that the two patient groups must not overlap was removed from the assessment at the EPO.

Nevertheless, UKIPO practice remains that a second medical use claim to an agent for use in the treatment of a disease in a specific patient group is not new if the agent has already been used to treat the same group of patients, with the same disease. Overlap is not permitted. This position is based on the decision of the Patents Court in *Bristol-Myers Squibb v. Baker Norton Pharmaceuticals*, that a new piece of information about an advantage, or how a treatment worked, did not constitute an invention if it did not lead to a new use. The discovery that the treatment works particularly well for a group of patients does not therefore render such a claim novel if that same group of patients has already in fact been treated for the disease with the same agent, whether explicitly, implicitly or inherently.

[E] Specific Mode of Action

Second medical use claims which relate to the same therapeutic purpose as the prior art, but which are solely distinguished by claiming a different technical effect or mechanism of action, are generally rejected as lacking novelty at the UKIPO. This question was considered by the Patents Court in *Bristol-Myers Squibb v. Baker Norton Pharmaceuticals*.[35] It was held that a new piece of information about how a treatment worked did not constitute an invention if it did not lead to a new use. This principle has been upheld by the Court of Appeal.[36]

30. T 0019/86 *Duphar* OJEPO 1989, 13.
31. T 0893/90, *Queens's University Kingston*.
32. T 0233/96, *Medco Research*.
33. T 0108/09, *AstraZeneca*.
34. T 1399/04 *Schering*.
35. *Bristol-Myers Squibb v. Baker Norton Pharmaceuticals* [1998] EWHC Patents 300.
36. *Bristol-Myers Squibb v. Baker Norton Pharmaceuticals* [2001] RPC 1.

[F] Combinations with Other Active Ingredients

Second medical use claims to the use of a composition comprising two or more agents together for the treatment of a disease are allowable providing the combination has not previously been used for the same purpose. Such a claim will not be inventive if it represents a mere collocation of known elements, each only providing their known function. The absence of an unexpected technical effect (such as synergism) as a result of the combination of two known agents is likely to lead to a finding of lack of inventive step; but if some efficacy in the claimed treatment is shown, then a lack of synergistic effect does not give rise to an objection on grounds of sufficiency or support.

[G] Specific Diagnostic Applications

Antibodies are frequently an essential reagent in tests for the diagnosis of disease. Section 4A(1) states that methods of diagnosis practised on the human or animal body are not patentable subject matter. Since the exclusion applies only to diagnostic methods carried out on the living human or animal body, a method carried out on a dead body, for example to determine the cause of death, would not be objectionable. Furthermore, of course, *in vitro* diagnostic tests, performed on blood or other samples removed from the body are patentable at the UKIPO. The practical application, in a claimed *in vitro* diagnostic test, of the discovery of a naturally arising relationship between a particular indicator or marker and disease or predisposition to disease is also patentable subject matter providing other criteria for patentability are met.

§9.05 ASSESSMENT OF INVENTIVENESS

[A] General Approach

The test in the UK for whether a patent involves an inventive step is no more and no less than the statutory test laid down in section 3 of the Patents Act, i.e.:

> 'An invention shall be taken to involve an inventive step if it is not obvious to a person skilled in the art, having regard to any matter which forms part of the state of the art by virtue only of [having been made available to the public before the priority date of the invention].'

Unlike in the EPO, where the 'problem-solution' approach will applied to the assessment of inventiveness as a matter of course, courts in the UK have time and time again (and often in quite strident terms) emphasised the fact that such approaches merely serve as tools to assist in the application of the statutory test and should by no means be regarded as a substitute for it.[37] Along with the problem-solution approach,

37. See e.g. Jacob LJ in *Actavis UK Limited v. Novartis AG* [2010] EWCA Civ 82 at [17] (in which he then goes on to discuss various approaches and the limitations in his view of the problem-solution approach); and Lewison LJ in *Novartis v. Medimmune* [2012] EWCA Civ 1234 at [178]-[182].

the *Windsurfing/Pozzoli*[38] test and 'obvious to try with reasonable expectation of success'[39] question are frameworks that have proved influential in the UK.

As with any tool, there will be certain cases for which one or other of the approaches that have been developed to assist in the assessment of obviousness will be well suited and helpful, but other cases in which a rigid application of one of those frameworks will only serve as a distraction from the ultimate statutory test to be applied and could lead to error. For example, the problem-solution approach is regarded as useful where the patent addresses a real problem faced by the inventor, but not where part of the invention would be said to lie in the identification of the existence of a problem in the first place.

This is particularly the case given that obviousness is considered to be a 'multi-factorial question' which must be considered on the particular facts in each case. Some of the relevant factors were set out (non-exhaustively) by Kitchin J in *Generics v. Lundbeck*[40] as approved by Lord Hoffman in *Conor v. Angiotech*:[41]

> 'The question of obviousness must be considered on the facts of each case. The court must consider the weight to be attached to any particular factor in the light of all the relevant circumstances. These may include such matters as the motive to find a solution to the problem the patent addresses, the number and extent of the possible avenues of research, the effort involved in pursuing them and the expectation of success.'

It should also be borne in mind that the UK takes a stricter approach to the 'mosaicing' of prior art references than some other tribunals and jurisdictions. It will not be permissible to combine separate prior art documents for the purposes of an obviousness attack unless it can be shown, as a matter of fact, that upon reading the first citation the skilled person would have turned to the further reference(s) to supplement the information in the first. In practice this is difficult to establish in the UK, and will generally require the existence of a direct reference and/or some other pointer or instruction in the first reference that would encourage the skilled person to do so.

The series of decisions in the dispute between Actavis and ICOS Corporation heard in the High Court,[42] Court of Appeal[43] and Supreme Court[44] represent a potentially very significant development in the UK approach to inventive step, and in particular the approach to inventions relying on unexpected or surprising results and lack of expectation of success to support inventive step. The relevant patent in issue was a dosage regime patent for 'low dose' 5 mg tadalafil. Birss J at first instance had considered that tadalafil was obvious to take forward into a routine pre-clinical and clinical trial programme including routine phase II dose ranging studies and

38. *Windsurfing International Inc v. Tabur Marine (Great Britain) Ltd* [1985] R.P.C. 59; *Pozzoli v. BDMO SA* [2007] F.S.R. 37.
39. See e.g. *Johns-Manville Corporation's Patent* [1967] RPC 479, *Conor v. Angiotech; Novartis AG v. Generics* [2012] EWCA Civ 1623 at [55].
40. [2007] RPC 32.
41. *Conor v. Angiotech* [2009] UKHL 49 at [42].
42. *Actavis v. ICOS Corporation* [2016] EWHC 1955 (Pat).
43. *Actavis v. ICOS Corporation* [2017] EWCA Civ 1671.
44. *Actavis v. ICOS Corporation* [2019] UKSC 15.

had made clear that he had taken into consideration a broad range of factors[45] (as described in *Conor v. Angiotech*) in his assessment of obviousness. Nonetheless, he appeared to be ultimately swayed by his view that the skilled team, when carrying out the clinical programme, would not have a reasonable expectation of success at the claimed dose.[46]

The Court of Appeal considered that, given the judge's findings and expert evidence on the routine steps that would be taken in phase II trials to investigate the dose-response curve, the absence of an expectation of success as to the efficacy of the claimed low dose was not relevant. Their view was that Birss J had rather 'lost sight of the fact that, on his own findings, the claimed invention lies at the end of the familiar path through the routine pre-clinical and clinical trials' process'[47] and 'allowed himself to be side-tracked by his undoubtedly correct conclusion that the skilled team would not have been able to predict that the 5 mg/day dose would be effective'.[48] This decision by the Court of Appeal constitutes a rare instance where a first instance decision on obviousness in the UK has been overturned. In the past it has generally been considered that it will not be possible to overturn a first instance decision on obviousness unless an appellant can identify at least one point of principle in respect of which the judge erred.[49]

In a unanimous judgment from the Supreme Court upholding the decision of the Court of Appeal, Lord Hodge considered the issue of what a question of principle is in this context (at [80]-[81]):

> 'What is a question of principle in this context? An error of principle is not confined to an error as to the law but extends to certain types of error in the application of a legal standard to the facts in an evaluation of those facts. What is the nature of such an evaluative error? In this case we are not concerned with any challenge to the trial judge's conclusions of primary fact but with the correctness of the judge's evaluation of the facts which he has found, in which he weighs a number of different factors against each other. This evaluative process is often a matter of degree upon which different judges can legitimately differ and an appellate court ought not to interfere unless it is satisfied that the judge's conclusion is outside the bounds within which reasonable disagreement is possible.
>
> Thus, in the absence of a legal error by the trial judge, which might be asking the wrong question, failing to take account of relevant matters, or taking into account irrelevant matters, the Court of Appeal would be justified in differing from a trial judge's assessment of obviousness if the appellate court were to reach the view that the judge's conclusion was outside the bounds within which reasonable disagreement is possible. It must be satisfied that the trial judge was wrong.'

This elaboration of what constitutes an 'error of principle' and the characterisation of this concept as something distinct from a strict error of law suggests a broadening of

45. *Actavis v. ICOS Corporation* [2016] EWHC 1955 (Pat) at [343].
46. *Actavis v. ICOS Corporation* [2016] EWHC 1955 (Pat) at [335].
47. *Actavis v. ICOS Corporation* [2017] EWCA Civ 1671 at [152].
48. *Actavis v. ICOS Corporation* [2017] EWCA Civ 1671 at [171].
49. See the oft-cited remarks of Lord Hoffman in *Biogen v. Medeva* [1997] R.P.C. 1, 45.

scope for appellate courts to overturn first instance findings in relation to obviousness. Whilst not going so far as to suggest appellate courts can revisit primary findings of fact, secondary findings of fact (such as the statutory question of obviousness) based on an evaluation of the matrix of primary facts now appear to be fair game in circumstances where the primary judge's finding falls outside of the margins within which, on an assessment of the logical consequences of the primary findings, there would be scope for reasonable minds to differ.

Ultimately the Supreme Court agreed with the Court of Appeal that the judge's failure to appreciate the logical consequences of the finding that it was very likely that the skilled team would continue the testing down to 5 mg was an error of principle which allowed an appellate court to carry out its own evaluation.[50]

Although, as noted above in §9.04[C], the Supreme Court stressed that there is no policy reason why a novel and inventive dosage regime should not be rewarded by a patent, the reverberations of this judgment in practice and the consequences it has for the validity of dosage regime patents (generally, as well as those for antibody treatments) remains to be seen. Equally, time will tell whether the decision will embolden parties to increasingly seek to overturn secondary 'evaluative' findings of fact on appeal, as 'errors of principle', including in relation to obviousness, and how successful such attempts will prove to be.

The overriding influence of expert evidence on the ultimate outcome of UK patent litigation (including in relation to inventive step) should also be noted. In contrast to other fora where the role of the expert is more circumscribed and/or limited to written evidence, or where experts are appointed directly by the court to provide wholly independent assistance, the performance of experts in a UK trial (in the form of oral evidence and responses to cross-examination) will often be determinative.

[B] Particularities Regarding Claims to Antibodies

The State of the Art

Many of the particular issues regarding the inventiveness of different forms of antibody claims are discussed above at §9.02. As previously discussed, it will be important to bear in mind the likelihood that the UKIPO and UK courts will consider many processes involved in the production of antibodies to now be entirely routine and uninventive, unless a case can be made in respect of some unusual feature or particular difficulty that had to be overcome in relation to a particular functional feature of a claim to an otherwise known antibody (or antibody to a known antigen). Of course many of those processes that are now routine were once inventive, cutting edge techniques that were the subject of patents themselves. This is illustrative of an issue that is common to the state of the art in any field, but which one must be particularly mindful of in respect of fast-moving fields like biotechnology.

What was once inventive or would have constituted an undue burden to perform can now become absolutely routine in a mere matter of years. The journey of CRISPR-Cas9 gene editing from new invention in 2012 to regular laboratory use

50. *Actavis v. ICOS Corporation* [2019] UKSC 15 at [86].

by about 2015/16 is a good illustration of this point. This rapid pace of development in the biotechnology field re-emphasises the importance of closely digging in to the state of the art at the priority date with experts, including using contemporaneous resources like textbooks and review articles to help re-orientate them as to the prevalent mindset and common general knowledge at the relevant time.

Experiments

In spite of the fact that many of the processes involved in the production of antibodies are now regarded as routine from an inventive step perspective, the fact remains that, in a relative sense, compared to small molecule medicines for example, antibody inventions involve highly technical and complex subject matter. Furthermore, the functional claim features often found in antibody claims (and discussed at §9.02 above) are rather more complex than those found in other fields, and may require the performance of some kind of assay or experiment to assess (e.g. cross-competition, affinity, specificity).

Accordingly, there may be an increased role for the use of experiments in the course of antibody patent litigation (assuming those experiments are successful and show what they were intended to show) in order to cut through some of the complexity and uncertainty that can be associated with highly technical subject matter. They may also play an influential role in supporting an obviousness attack. Notably, in *Eli Lilly v. Genentech*[51] in which Eli Lilly sought to clear the path for its Taltz (ixekizumab) recombinant humanised anti-IL17-A antibody product for the treatment of plaque psoriasis and psoriatic arthritis, extensive experiments[52] based on murine monoclonal antibodies to IL17-A/A that were known in the prior art were performed in order to demonstrate that the working of the IL-17A/A prior art would inevitably yield the claimed invention.[53] Ultimately, although Eli Lilly seemed to present their case based on these experiments primarily as a novelty attack and only secondarily as an obviousness attack, Arnold J found the claims in dispute to be obvious over the IL17A/A prior art, but not anticipated by it. The successful strategic use of experiments in this case may see an increased interest in the use of experiments in UK patent litigation, at least in cases of sufficient value.

A broader discussion of the potential role for experiments in UK antibody patent litigation is below in section §9.06.

§9.06 ENFORCEMENT AND SCOPE OF PROTECTION

The enforcement of a granted patent in national litigation raises a host of practical, procedural and evidentiary issues not present in prosecution and opposition

51. [2019] EWHC 387 (Pat).
52. Taking over six months of laboratory time and costing over GBP 600,000.
53. Essentially the point was to show that any humanised anti-IL-17A/A antibody generated from prior art murine anti-IL-17A/A antibodies using the techniques available at the priority date would also bind and neutralise IL-17A/F. The specific binding to and inhibition of the activity of IL-17A/F by antibodies of the claimed invention was alleged to the key contribution of the patent in suit over the prior art.

proceedings before the Patent Office. The UK has an adversarial legal system based on common law principles, in which it is up to the parties to define the scope of the dispute and the relevant law to be applied comprises not only statute but also case law precedent. This is of course true for any UK patent litigation, however due to the nature of antibodies and the patents that protect them, with claim formats such as those considered above, the enforcement of antibody patents raises a number of particular issues that are worthy of consideration.

It should be noted that, whilst the UK courts have had some opportunity to consider patents and claims protecting antibodies on a number of occasions over the last decade or so, the sample size of such cases remains small and many of the claim formats discussed above are yet to be the subject of judicial consideration. Accordingly, like in many other jurisdictions, the case law in respect of antibody patents and the various claim formats commonly employed to protect antibody inventions is still very much developing. The discussion in this section is based on observations and extrapolations from the case law in the area that we do have, as well as the authors' experience litigating in the UK more generally. It is not intended by any means to be a guide to litigating in the UK, but rather a spotlight on a number of issues of particular relevance to antibody patent litigation.

Establishing Infringement

It is trite law that in order to prove infringement of a patent claim, the onus is on the claimant (the patentee or their exclusive licensee) to demonstrate that the alleged infringer has performed each and every integer of that claim. Naturally, the more complex the claim in issue, with more integers and more limitations, the narrower the scope of the protection and the commensurately more difficult it will be to prove infringement. Additionally, the nature of some types of claim features means that they will in practice be more difficult to establish than others – for example, functional integers and those claiming a particular physicochemical property or binding interaction will be more difficult to prove than a simple structural feature. It will readily be apparent from the discussion of common antibody claim formats that many of these will potentially be quite challenging to establish without experimental evidence. The use of experimental evidence in UK patent litigation, and its specific utility in relation to antibody patent enforcement, is discussed further below.

Evidentiary Issues

Additionally, it should be observed that, the further upstream of the eventual product that the focus of the claims sought to be relied upon is, the less public information there will be about the alleged or suspected acts of infringement. This is often a particular challenge where process claims are in issue. Whereas some key information about a product will generally be publicly available from regulatory approval documents and other such mandatory disclosures, the upstream manufacturing processes employed to create the product are typically highly confidential and jealously guarded, such that very little public information about them will be available. Given the complex manufacturing processes involved in the production of antibodies (certainly relative to small molecule manufacturing), process patents covering aspects of that manufacturing will often form an important part of the portfolio of patents designed to protect an antibody product. However, the limited public information about the processes employed by a suspected infringer poses significant evidentiary challenges to the enforcement of such patents.

Pleading and Particularising the Infringement Claim

Notably, in commencing patent infringement proceedings in the UK a claimant is required to file statements of case, in the form of particulars of claim and particulars of infringement, which set out the key factual elements required to make out the claimant's cause of action and provide particulars of the facts, documents and other evidence that the claimant is at that time able to point to in order to support their contentions. The defendant's defence directly responds to the contentions of the claimant's pleadings, either admitting or denying each, and thus the scope of the dispute is defined by the interplay between the pleadings. This is a key procedural feature of UK litigation and is seen as a matter of procedural fairness and effective case management - one's case must be adequately pleaded in order to allow the other side to understand the case they must meet, and parties are not allowed to ambush their opponents with unpleaded arguments.

If a claim is not sufficiently pleaded and particularised it may be struck out under rule 3.4(2) of the Civil Procedure Rules (CPR), either upon the application of the other side, or of the court's own motion. Therefore, to avoid strike out the facts set out in the pleadings should disclose a legally recognisable claim against the defendant which is sufficiently well founded.[54] A claimant seeking to enforce a patent should have a sufficiently clear idea of their case and gathered sufficient evidence in support of the key factual elements of that case before commencing proceedings. As noted above, this will not always be easy for certain types of antibody claims.

Pre-action Disclosure and Inspection

In the UK, disclosure (also known as discovery in other jurisdictions) is available in litigation to redress the informational imbalance between parties by compelling a party in possession of documents relevant to the issues in dispute and/or which are required for the other party to understand the case they must meet to disclose those documents to the other side. As of 1 January 2019 a new pilot disclosure scheme[55] has entered into force in the UK and is due to run for an initial period of two years.

In certain circumstances a party may be able to apply for and obtain an order for 'pre-action disclosure' of specific documents or classes of documents before proceedings have started.[56] The conditions set out in CPR rule 31.16 must be complied with, and the court must be satisfied that disclosure before proceedings have started is desirable in order to: dispose fairly of the anticipated proceedings; assist the dispute to be resolved without proceedings; or save costs. In a similar vein, the

54. See paragraphs 1.4 and 1.5 of CPR Practice Direction 3A.
55. Set out in CPR Practice Direction 51U.
56. CPR rule 31.16(4)(a); section 33(2) *Senior Courts Act*.

High Court also has the power to order the inspection, taking of samples and carrying out of any experiment on or with property which may become the subject matter of subsequent proceedings in the High Court or as to which any question may arise in such proceedings.[57]

Pre-action disclosure or inspection allows a party to decide whether it has a viable cause of action and, if so, provides it with sufficient material to adequately plead and particularise its case. The availability of such orders for pre-action disclosure or inspection should be borne in mind in the context of antibody patent enforcement in the UK, given the practical evidentiary difficulties around antibody process patents discussed above. The new disclosure pilot scheme does not disturb the procedure set out in CPR rule 31.16 or 25.5.

The recent decision in *Boehringer Ingelheim v. Mylan*[58] illustrates the utility of a pre-action application for inspection of property and provision of samples for experimentation, and the High Court's willingness to grant such applications where the judge considers the order sought to be sensible and likely to have the effect of either avoiding proceedings altogether or, if an action for infringement does ensue, enabling the parties to focus on the correct issues in a timely manner. Notably, in exercising his discretion to grant the order sought by the applicant (in part at least) Henry Carr J:

1. accepted the applicant's evidence despite it being 'at a high level of generality';
2. considered that it was not appropriate to engage in a detailed analysis of the merits; and
3. did not accept that consideration of the merits is a particularly high hurdle to satisfy when it comes to this discretion.[59]

Experiments

It is possible in UK patent litigation for a party to perform experiments in order to attempt to generate data/evidence in support of their case. As discussed at §9.06[B] above, there may be a growing role for experiments to support obviousness attacks on antibody patents in UK litigation. Equally, given the evidentiary issues in establishing infringement, referred to above, experiments may be required for certain forms of claim (e.g. where a functional feature is defined by reference to a measurement using a particular assay). The procedure for parties seeking to establish any fact by experiment proof conducted for the purpose of litigation is set out in paragraph 7 of CPR Practice Direction 63.

Despite the availability of experiments as a means by which to supplement/generate evidence in a case, the use of experiments in UK litigation has been relatively limited. It is often perceived as a high risk, high reward strategy and UK practitioners have historically been somewhat hesitant to avail themselves of this mechanism unless truly necessary.

57. CPR rule 25.5; section 33(1) *Senior Courts Act*.
58. [2019] EWHC 584 (Ch).
59. [2019] EWHC 584 (Ch) at [14].

However, in the right circumstances and for the right case, a simple and well-designed experiment has the ability and potential to establish facts that might otherwise be impossible to bring into the case, and which could prove crucial to its outcome. As the volume of antibody patent litigation increases, in which experiments may in fact be the best or only way to, on the one hand, prove infringement of certain claim types or, on the other, demonstrate anticipation or obviousness based on the prior art, this historical reluctance may be changing. Eli Lilly's use of experiments to support its successful obviousness attack on Genentech's patents in the Taltz (ixekizumab) case[60] referred to above is a good example of this. Whilst the use of experiments will not make sense in every case, or even in the majority of cases, practitioners should be alive to its availability (for either side) and increasing relevance.

Injunctive Relief

The courts in the UK have demonstrated flexibility in tailoring injunctive relief to the specific facts and circumstances of each case. At the interim stage public interest factors and the respective loss to each party will be weighed in determining where the balance of convenience lies (as per the classic *American Cyanamid*[61] test), however there is scope for flexibility even in respect of final injunctions where the public interest is involved. This is particularly the case where the product to be enjoined is a life-saving medicine or medical device and serious clinical consequences will ensure from preventing its sale.

In the recent decision of *Edwards Lifesciences v. Boston Scientific*,[62] the defendant was found to infringe a valid patent for transcatheter heart valves in circumstances where the patentee had a directly competing product on the market. However, it was found that specific training was required in order to use a given transcatheter heart valve, such that clinicians only trained to use the infringing device would need to be retrained with the patentee's product. Further, a subset of patients existed who could not be treated with the patentee's product. In light of those factors the Court: (i) stayed the final injunction for a 12-month period to allow time for clinicians to be retrained to use the patentee's product; and (ii) carved out a non-time limited exception to the injunction to allow supply of the infringing device to patients for whom there was no other suitable treatment.

Where an infringing product is catering to a clinical need that would otherwise go unmet (e.g. where the patentee does not have a competing product available to patients or a particular subpopulation thereof), or there are other public interest factors mitigating against the imposition of an unqualified injunction, courts in the UK may decline to grant injunctive relief, or limit the injunction to cater appropriately for the interests of the patient. These public interest factors are likely to play a role in antibody patent litigation, which in recent times has seen an increase in innovator vs. innovator disputes in respect of popular clinical targets (see e.g. *Merck v. Ono*[63]

60. *Eli Lilly v. Genentech* [2019] EWHC 387 (Pat).
61. *American Cyanamid v. Ethicon Limited* [1975] AC 396.
62. [2018] EWHC 1256 (Pat).
63. [2015] EWHC 2973 (Pat).

in relation to PD-1; *Eli Lilly v. Genentech*[64] in relation to anti-IL-17 (Taltz); *Amgen v. Sanofi/Regeneron*[65] in the US in relation to PCSK9).

Target/Antigen claims and Supplementary Protection Certificates

It has been held by the High Court that a broad claim to antibodies that bind to a novel antigen can provide the basis for a Supplementary Protection Certificate (SPC). In yet a further action between Eli Lilly and HGS (*Eli Lilly and Company v. Human Genome Sciences Inc.*[66]), a specific anti-neutrokine α antibody, tabalumab, developed by Lilly and which had received a marketing authorisation, was considered 'protected by a basic patent' as required by Article 3(a) of the SPC Regulation by virtue of antibody claim 13 of the neutrokine α patent. An SPC could thus be granted. The case confirms that in the UK an antibody claim with at least a functional definition of the antibody can be regarded as specific enough protection for a medically approved antibody for the patent to deserve extension by an SPC.

[A] Biosimilars

In the UK there is no statutory regime that governs disclosure and/or litigation pursuant to a regulatory approval of a biosimilar product (i.e. no equivalent to the US 'patent dance' under the Biologics Price Competition and Innovation Act). Nor does the UK have a patent linkage system or Hatch-Waxman equivalent. Therefore, biosimilar litigation in the UK procedurally resembles traditional small molecule innovator vs. generic litigation.

However, from a commercial perspective the development of a biosimilar product represents a far more expensive and therefore riskier undertaking than a small molecule generic medicine. From the originator's perspective, those biologic products likely to generate biosimilar completion are mega-blockbuster products with multi-billion dollar yearly sales revenue, often comprising a substantial proportion of the total revenue of the originator company, and protected by a suitably robust portfolio of patents to maintain exclusivity. Strategically these practical and commercial differences cast biosimilar disputes in a rather different light to traditional small molecule generic litigation.

It is notable that instances of biosimilar vs. biosimilar litigation have recently emerged in both the UK and the US, in each case in relation to biosimilar versions of adalimumab (Humira®), the world's best selling drug. In the US Coherus BioSciences has claimed Amgen's biosimilar product Amgevita infringes a number of its adalimumab-related formulation patents, whilst in the UK Samsung Bioepis and Biogen have sought to clear the way for their biosimilar product Imraldi by invalidating a Fresenius Kabi adalimumab formulation patent.

Although generic companies often possess portfolios of such formulation patents, generic vs. generic litigation in the small molecule arena has been rare. The

64. [2019] EWHC 387 (Pat).
65. *Amgen Inc. v. Sanofi*, 872 F.3d 1367 (Fed. Cir. 2017).
66. [2014] EWHC 2404 (Pat).

different economics at play in the biosimilar sphere, with higher barrier to entry, less competition, significantly larger sunk development costs and the potential to differentiate the product from the competition (given they are by definition not identical), may encourage biosimilar developers to enforce their own patent portfolios against biosimilar competitors. At present it is too early to say whether the *Coherus v. Amgen* and *Samsung Bioepis and Biogen v. Fresenius Kabi* suits are an isolated, exceptional incidents or indicative of a future biosimilar vs. biosimilar trend.

Arrow Declarations

We observed above that the commercial value and importance of biologic products are such that, in practice, those products will likely be protected by substantial patent portfolios, probably consisting of multiple patent families and possibly including pending divisional patent applications. It is therefore a significant challenge for a prospective biosimilar entrant to navigate the web of granted and pending patents and clear the way for their product, particularly given the ability of the patentee to amend their claims.

An innovative mechanism that has developed in the UK courts to address this is the so-called '*Arrow* declaration', so-named after the *Arrow Generics Limited v. Merck & Co. Inc.*[67] case in which a claim for this type of declaration was first sought, and found by Kitchin J to be arguable. It is a declaration that a product (i.e. the generic/ biosimilar product sought to be launched) was old (i.e. not novel) or obvious at a particular date (i.e. a date the same as or earlier than the priority date of the relevant patent(s) or patent application(s)).

The utility of an *Arrow* declaration lies in providing the biosimilar entrant with de facto protection against a future infringement action in circumstances where a revocation action is not able to be brought to clear the way (i.e. where a pending application likely to cover the product has yet to be granted). By obtaining an *Arrow* declaration in respect of its product, a party is effectively employing a pre-emptive form of '*Gillette*'[68] defence - i.e. an argument that, as the product is old or obvious at the priority date, if it infringes a patent then the patent is also old or obvious and therefore invalid.

In *Fujifilm Kyowa Kirin Biologics v. AbbVie Biotechnology Ltd* ,[69] the Court of Appeal upheld Henry Carr J's finding at first instance, reaffirming the existence of the court's discretionary power to grant declarations of the *Arrow* kind. The claimants in those proceedings had sought *Arrow* declarations in respect of their biosimilar versions of adalimumab (marketed by *Abbvie* as Humira®), in circumstances where the patentee had abandoned/de-designated several patents that would otherwise have been in suit but divisional applications claiming essentially the same subject matter were being prosecuted to grant in the EPO. Henry Carr J ultimately granted the declarations sought,[70] applying the factors relevant to the court's exercise of its discretionary power he had identified earlier:

67. [2007] EWHC 1900 (Pat).
68. *Gillette Safety Razor Co v. Anglo-American Trading Co Ltd* (1913) 30 RPC 465.
69. [2017] EWCA Civ 1.
70. *Fujifilm Kyowa Kirin Biologics v. AbbVie Biotechnology Ltd* [2017] EWHC 395 (Pat).

a) Would the declaration sought serve a useful purpose?
b) Is the underlying issue sufficiently clearly defined to make it properly justiciable?
c) Are there special circumstances why the court should not grant the declaration sought?
d) Justice to the parties.

The importance of a UK nexus to the useful purpose test is illustrated in *Pfizer Limited v. F. Hoffmann-La Roche AG.*[71] In that case, Pfizer had sought *Arrow* declarations to clear the way in the UK for the launch of its biosimilar version of bevacizumab (marketed by Roche as Avastin®), in circumstances where the patentee had no relevant UK patent and had abandoned any prospect of obtaining such a relevant UK patent in future by de-designating the UK from all pending European applications in the relevant families. Notably, the de-designation of pending European applications in respect of two of the relevant patent families occurred after the action had been filed by Pfizer but prior to the filing of Roche's defence.

Pfizer argued that Roche had engaged in deliberate 'shielding' of its portfolio from scrutiny by the English court and maintained that the declarations would serve the useful purpose of removing any uncertainty in the UK and having persuasive effect in other EPC contracting states including Belgium, from where Pfizer planned to supply the UK market. Notably, in response Roche declined to advance any positive case on the technical issues of novelty/obviousness and instead focused its response of the threshold question of the exercise of the Court's discretion.

Despite agreeing with Pfizer that Roche had engaged in 'shielding' behaviour, that a reasoned judgment giving rise to an *Arrow* declaration in the UK would in general be taken into account in Belgium, and that such a declaration would be of real commercial value for Pfizer, Birss J ultimately held that the declarations sought by Pfizer would serve no useful purpose. Given the complete absence of the possibility of UK rights in the future, there was no outstanding certainty at all relating to UK rights regarding bevacizumab – the commercial value to Pfizer of an *Arrow* declaration was in the utility it might have in helping Pfizer to defend itself against suits brought by Roche in other European countries.[72] If there had been any pending UK applications in any of the families, Birss J indicated that it would have been a plain case for an *Arrow* declaration, however, as things stood, the foreign utility of a declaration was not considered enough.

The availability of *Arrow* declarations in the UK is a good example of the flexible and creative approach UK courts are willing to take to the resolution of disputes and the provision of commercial certainty to parties. Whilst it seems apparent from the judgments of Henry Carr J and the Court of Appeal in *Fujifilm v. AbbVie* and Birss J in *Pfizer v. Roche* that *Arrow* declarations will only be appropriate in particular exceptional cases, they are potentially a powerful tool for biosimilar developers in the right circumstances, as they proved to be for the claimants in *Fujifilm v. AbbVie.*

71. [2019] EWHC 1520 (Pat).
72. [2019] EWHC 1520 (Pat) at [118].

[B] Equivalence

With the UK Supreme Court decision in *Actavis UK Limited v. Eli Lilly and Company*,[73] the UK courts for the first time acknowledged the existence of a doctrine of equivalents in UK patent law. Prior to that decision, the preferred UK view, as addressed in the previous leading authority of *Kirin-Amgen Inc v. Hoechst Marion Roussel Ltd*,[74] was that the infringement of an immaterial variant of a patented invention should be determined as a matter of purposive construction of the claims rather than by way of a separate doctrine of equivalents that extended protection beyond the terms of those claims. The *Improver* questions[75] (aka the 'Protocol questions') were viewed as simply guidelines for applying the principle of purposive construction to equivalents, which would be more useful in some cases than in others.

The unanimous judgment of the UK Supreme Court in *Actavis v. Lilly*,[76] penned by Lord Neuberger, has expressly reversed that position. Rather than approaching infringement as purely a matter of claim interpretation, Lord Neuberger embraced a two-step approach to the 'proper approach to infringement claims': (i) does the variant infringe any of the claims as a matter of normal interpretation (i.e. purposive construction, not literal);[77] and, if not, (ii) does the variant nonetheless infringe because it varies from the invention in a way or ways which is or are immaterial? At [56] Lord Neuberger stated that:

> 'However, I have concluded that that nettle needs to be grasped, because, so long as the issue is treated as one of interpretation, it will lead to a risk of wrong results in patent infringement cases and it will also lead to a risk of confusing the law relating to the interpretation of documents. In my opinion, issue (ii) involves not merely identifying what the words of a claim would mean in their context to the notional addressee, but also considering the extent if any to which the scope of protection afforded by the claim should extend beyond that meaning. As Sir Hugh Laddie wrote in his instructive article Kirin-Amgen – The End of Equivalents in England? (2009) 40 IIC 3, para 68, "[t]he Protocol is not concerned with the rules of construction of claims" but with "determining the scope of protection".'

To guide the approach to the new UK doctrine of equivalents for immaterial variants (as required by part (ii) of the approach outlined by Lord Neuberger), a reformulated version of the *Improver* questions was adopted by the Supreme Court (at [66]):

> 'i. Notwithstanding that it is not within the literal [read as "normal"][78] meaning of the relevant claim(s) of the patent, does the variant achieve substantially the same result in substantially the same way as the invention, i.e. the inventive concept revealed by the patent?

73. [2017] UKSC 48.
74. [2005] RPC 9.
75. *Improver Corpn v. Remington Consumer Products Ltd* [1990] FSR 181.
76. [2017] UKSC 48.
77. As interpreted by later courts applying the judgment – see e.g. Arnold J in *Generics (U.K.) Limited and others v. Yeda Research and Development Company Limited and others* [2017] EWHC 2629 (Pat) at [135]-[138].
78. Per Kitchin LJ in *Icescape v. Ice-world* [2018] EWCA Civ 2219 at [60] and [66].

ii. Would it be obvious to the person skilled in the art, reading the patent at the priority date, but knowing that the variant achieves substantially the same result as the invention, that it does so in substantially the same way as the invention?
iii. Would such a reader of the patent have concluded that the patentee nonetheless intended that strict compliance with the literal meaning of the relevant claim(s) of the patent was an essential requirement of the invention?

In order to establish infringement in a case where there is no literal infringement, a patentee would have to establish that the answer to the first two questions was 'yes' and that the answer to the third question was 'no'.

Actavis v. Lilly also raised the question of the use of the patent office file in the construction of patent claims and considering the scope of protection afforded by the doctrine of equivalents. Historically, unlike some jurisdictions where 'file wrapper estoppel' is common, the courts of the UK, Germany and the Netherlands have discouraged if not actually prohibited reference to the patent office file in aid of construction (as observed by Lord Hoffman in *Kirin Amgen* at [35]). Whilst far from advocating for a wholesale change to that position, Lord Neuberger did seem to acknowledge the utility of reference to the patent office file in certain cases, stating (at [87]) that 'it is appropriate for the UK courts to adopt a sceptical, but not absolutist, attitude to a suggestion that the contents of the prosecution file of a patent should be referred to when considering a question of interpretation or infringement' and noting (at [88]) that:

> 'While it would be arrogant to exclude the existence of any other circumstances, my current view is that reference to the file would only be appropriate where (i) the point at issue is truly unclear if one confines oneself to the specification and claims of the patent, and the contents of the file unambiguously resolve the point, or (ii) it would be contrary to the public interest for the contents of the file to be ignored. The first type of circumstance is, I hope, self-explanatory; the second would be exemplified by a case where the patentee had made it clear to the EPO that he was not seeking to contend that his patent, if granted, would extend its scope to the sort of variant which he now claims infringes.'

Since *Actavis v. Lilly*, practitioners and lower courts in the UK have been adapting to the existence of the new doctrine of equivalents. We are still in the early days of seeing how the new principles will be applied in practice in first instance courts. The early signs are that the scope of protection of claims has indeed been significantly expanded by the application of the reformulated *Improver* questions (as compared to the previous purposive construction approach), and that the sceptical attitude to 'file wrapper estoppel' arguments against the assertion of a particular construction of a claim and/or the scope of protection it affords by operation of the doctrine of equivalents continues to prevail in the UK.

The recent decision of HHJ Hacon in *Regen Lab SA v. Estar Medical Limited*[79] is a clear illustration of how far beyond the terms of the claims the scope of protection has been expanded by the operation of a doctrine of equivalents. That case involved

79. [2019] EWHC 63 (Pat).

a claim to a process for the preparation of a cell composition that involved, inter alia, centrifugation of whole blood in a separator tube containing a polyester-based thixotropic gel and buffered sodium citrate solution at 0.10M. Despite finding that the defendant's process used a non-polyester based gel and used 0.136M sodium citrate, HHJ Hacon found that, had the patent been valid, it would have been infringed, on the basis of his application of the reformulated *Improver* questions. The decision indicates a shift in emphasis away from protection of the invention (as expressed in the claims) to the 'inventive concept' or 'inventive core' (which may yield broader protection).[80]

The expansion in scope of protection is also apparent from the Court of Appeal's decision in *Icescape v. Ice-world*,[81] in which the Court indicated that, had it been valid, a claim that had been interpreted as being to an arrangement of pipes in parallel would have been infringed by an arrangement of pipes in series.

As many of the claim formats common to antibody patents have yet to be considered by UK courts, it is difficult to predict how they may be interpreted even as a matter for 'normal' purposive construction, much less how far beyond the terms of the claims the scope of protection will extend as a result of the new doctrine of equivalence. However what is clear is that the potential scope of protection for patent claims in the UK has never been broader. The application so far of the reformulated *Improver* questions suggests that the second and third questions are unlikely to prevent a finding of infringement. Thus antibody developers would be well advised to focus on demonstrating that their product or process achieves a different result to the inventive concept of the patent and/or does so in a different way – i.e., showing it is a material variant that should not be captured by the doctrine of equivalents.

80. See *Regen v. Estar* at [221]-[222] and *Icescape* at [74].
81. [2018] EWCA Civ 2219 [50].

Chapter 10

Israel

David Gilat & Mirit Lotan

§10.01 ANTIBODIES AS PATENTABLE SUBJECT-MATTER

[A] Legal Framework

The Israeli Patents Law 5727-1967 ('the Patents Law') does not contain specific exclusions for inventions which are antibodies, and the provisions applicable to antibody patents are the general provisions prescribed in sections 3 and 7 of the Patents Law.

Section 3 of the Patents Law concerns patentable subject-matter, and stipulates as follows:

> 'An invention, whether a product or a process in any field of technology, which is new, useful, and has industrial application and involves an inventive step, is a patentable invention'.

Although not explicitly specified, it is established case law that patents may not be granted on abstract ideas, products of nature, natural phenomena or mental steps.

Section 7 of the Patents Law specifically excludes from patent protection a method of therapeutic treatment of the human body (section 7(1)), and new varieties of plants or animals, except microbiological organisms not derived from nature (section 7(2)).

The Israeli Patent Office Manual for Patent Examination Procedure (MPEP) is used as guidance for patent examiners when examining patent applications.

The Israeli MPEP does not yet include a chapter on the examination of antibodies. However, in March 2019 the Israeli Patent Office (ILPTO) published its objectives for the year 2019, which included an intention to update the MPEP so as to incorporate therein specific guidelines for the examination of inventions concerning antibodies. Currently, the patentability of antibodies is referred to in the Israeli MPEP draft only in the context of section 7(1) (Appendix c, section 3.5) where it is stated that injection of a target protein for producing antibodies in a host will not be considered as a method of therapeutic treatment, and thus a process for preparing and isolating antibodies for manufacturing a medicament would not fall within the definition of therapeutic treatment.

[B] General Amenability or Exclusion of Antibodies from Patentability

Generally, antibodies are not excluded from patentability and are thus amenable to patent protection.

[C] Required Distinction from Naturally Occurring Antibodies

Notwithstanding the rule that 'products of nature' do not qualify for patent protection, it has been held that a patent may be granted with respect to bacteria used in the manufacturing of a 'product of nature', since such bacteria (e.g. Streptomyces which produced antibiotics) were found to be different from products of nature in purity and concentration.

Similarly, antibodies are not considered products of nature as such. Thus, for example, despite them being natural products of the immune system, isolated polyclonal antibodies may be patentable. Patentability of monoclonal antibodies is not in dispute, as these are artificially produced.

Both mammalian and non-mammalian host cells can be claimed; and a 'microbiological organism' objection would not be raised also where the host cell is non-mammalian, e.g. a bacterium or yeast.

§10.02 ACCEPTABLE CLAIM FEATURES FOR DEFINING ANTIBODIES

There are not yet specific formal requirements for defining antibodies and the only available guidelines are the general requirements for sufficiency of disclosure and clarity of claims as delineated in Sections 12 (enabling disclosure) and 13 (support to scope of the claim) of the Patents Law and in Regulation 20(a)(3), which, *inter alia*, include the requirement of claim clarity.

Antibodies have a unique molecular structure that enables the 'lock and key' matching of such biological molecules to their target, namely the epitope to which the antibody binds. Consequently, there are various ways to define an antibody; whether by its own structure which is determined by the amino acid sequence of the binding portions of the antibody ('structural features'), or by the structure of the target molecule that it recognizes, namely the epitope. In addition, antibodies may in certain cases be defined by their function.

It is sufficient to define an antibody by merely specifying those structures within the antibody's variable region which are responsible for the binding activity, termed CDRs (complementarity determining regions).

A CDR is a portion of the antibody that recognizes and binds to a portion in the antigen namely, the target epitope. The binding characteristics of an antibody to its target epitope are multifaceted and these unique characteristics can also serve to define the antibody molecule. Such unique binding characteristics are also referred to as 'functional features'.

According to the practice of the ILPTO both structural and functional features may be used in the claims to define an antibody, depending on the type of disclosure in the patent application.

It should be noted however that most antibodies are defined by their CDR structure, i.e. the amino acid sequence of their complementary determining regions.

It should also be noted that regardless of the way by which the antibody is defined (structurally or functionally), the target is always recited in the claim.

[A] Functional Features

[1] Target/Antigen

A claim defining an antibody by its target may cover various types of antibodies, e.g. a polyclonal antibody, monoclonal antibody as well as a fragment thereof.

Defining the antibody by the target is possible when the target is a newly described polypeptide. In such case, the claim may recite the entire sequence of the target polypeptide, e.g.:

> 'A polyclonal or monoclonal antibody or fragment that specifically binds to an *"antigen X" polypeptide of SEQ ID NO: 1'*;

or recite specific regions of the target molecule by their sequence, e.g.:

> 'An antibody capable of recognizing *a region of "antigen X"* wherein the region comprises the amino acid sequence AAA as shown in SEQ ID NO:1 or a fragment thereof.'

[2] Mode of Binding: Target Affinity, Binding Specificity, Epitope, Definitions via Reference Antibodies and Competitive Binding

Mode of Binding: Target Affinity, Binding Specificity, Epitope

As indicated above, an antibody may be defined through unique functional features of its binding to the target, namely its mode of binding. In such case, the definition usually combines two or more functional features. Examples of functional features through which an antibody may be defined are provided below.

One such feature is the antibody's *affinity* to its target. An antibody's affinity refers to the strength with which the antibody (through its antigen binding site) associates with the specific epitope on the target. High affinity antibodies bind relatively strongly to the antigen, while low affinity antibodies, by contrast, bind relatively weakly to the antigen.

The affinity of the antibody-target binding may be measured quantitatively and is defined by Kd (dissociation constant) value. Where the antibody is defined by its affinity to the target, a specific Kd value must be provided in the claim, optionally in conjunction with the measuring assay, e.g. 'wherein said antibody binds to the "target protein" with a Kd less than or equal to 10^{-10} M'.

Another functional feature is the antibody's binding *specificity* to the target. An antibody's specificity refers to the selective binding of the antibody to its specific target. Selective binding can manifested itself in various fashions, for example:

- binding to a specific isoform of the protein. A protein isoform is a protein variant which is a member of a set of highly similar proteins that originate from a single gene or gene family as a result of various cellular processes, e.g. alternative RNA splicing. If an antibody has specificity to a certain isoform and not to another, this can be used as a defining functional feature;
- binding only when the target is complexed/not complexed with another polypeptide;
- binding with specific selectivity to certain regions in the polypeptide. The antibody may be defined as binding a specific domain in the target polypeptide, or may be defined using negative language, namely wherein the antibody does not bind to a specific domain in the target polypeptide, e.g. the N-terminus of the protein;
- binding to specific cell types e.g. binding certain cancer cells and not binding other cell types'binding specificity can also be defined through the ability of certain compounds to inhibit the binding (e.g. the ability of oligosaccharides to inhibit binding in the case of a carbohydrate epitope);
- binding specificity may also be affected by the chemical composition of the medium in which the binding takes place, namely cation-dependent or cation-independent binding, or binding that takes place under certain pH values.

Mode of binding can also be defined using specific features of the epitope (other than the sequence of the epitope as described above). Such features include, for example a phosphorylated epitope on the identified target polypeptide, optionally emphasizing differential binding properties to the phosphorylated *versus* non-phosphorylated versions of the epitope. An epitope can also be defined as being a carbohydrate epitope.

An additional feature that may be used to define the epitope is by recitation of a particular domain of the target antigen in which the epitope resides, e.g. the K2 domain of the polypeptide TFPI (Tissue Factor Pathway Inhibitor), as well as indicating the presence of certain specific amino acids in particular positions in the epitope.

Mode of Binding: Definitions via Reference Antibodies and Competitive Binding

An antibody can also be defined indirectly, in relation to a competing known antibody ('reference antibody') which binds to an epitope. There are no formal rules or guidelines as to how the reference antibody should be defined. Thus, the reference antibody may be defined using amino acid sequences or functional features. The competing assay may be recited in the claim, and optionally the degree of competition is defined (e.g. more than 75%).

In addition, other functional features may be used, such as effect on the target, specificity for a certain protein isoform or configuration, or other characteristics of the epitope as described above.

[3] *Effect on Target*

An antibody can be defined by its effect on the target. The following are types of effects that can be used as part of the antibody's definition:

- induction of cell death/apoptosis;
- induction of cell proliferation;
- induction of a certain activity, for example: inhibition of cell adhesion, inhibition of T cell-mediated immune response, increasing complement dependent cytotoxicity (CDC) or antibody dependent cell mediated cytotoxicity (ADCC);
- modulation of the target polypeptide's levels;
- inhibition of the target's association with another polypeptide;
- inhibition of an enzyme's activity.

For example:

> 'A *monoclonal antibody* that binds "antigen X" wherein the antibody reduces "antigen X" activity in a particular assay'; or

> 'A *monoclonal antibody* or a functional fragment thereof, each of which binds to "antigen X" and inhibits the function of "antigen X" to increase the intracellular level of a 'marker Y'.

The antibody can be defined as an 'antagonist antibody', however the definition of the antibody always requires additional features either structural or functional.

[B] Structural Features

[1] *Molecular Topology: Antibody Types, Fragments and Antibody Constructs*

Antibody Types

All types of antibodies may be claimed. Examples for antibodies are:

- a monoclonal antibody;
- a polyclonal antibody (usually defined by target);
- a chimeric antibody (e.g. murine-human);
- a humanized antibody;
- a human antibody;
- a murine/rat/rabbit/camel antibody;
- the antibody isotype may also be recited, e.g. 'IgM' or 'IgG4 isotype' 'IgG1';
- a single chain antibody molecule (optionally bispecific) or any type of functional (namely binding) fragment of the antibody.

Fragments

An antibody fragment may be claimed to the extent that it preserves the binding activities of the complete antibody. Such fragments may include for instance Fab,

$F(ab')_2$, scFv etc. Thus, when claiming a fragment of an antibody it must be recited in the claim that the fragment can perform the binding and/or functional activity of the complete antibody.

The following language may be used to describe a fragment. For example:

> '[An antibody] ... or a fragment of an antibody that binds (or "specifically" binds) to the target'

> '[An antibody] ... or a part of an antibody having the same biological activity as the entire antibody'

> '[An antibody] ... or a functional fragment of the antibody which has the same antigen-binding activity as the antibody'

> '[An antibody] ... or divalent functional fragment thereof'

> '[An antibody] ... or a derivative thereof which is capable of binding to the target'

General features such as 'a variant [of an amino acid sequence]', without indicating the specific amino acid residues subjected to deletions/substitutions/additions, as well as their number and location in a sequence, are generally not accepted by the examiners, since they are regarded as encompassing any mutations with any number of any amino acid residues, and thus relate to an unlimited number of polypeptides.

Antibody Constructs

It is possible to claim antibody constructs, for example:

- antibody-drug conjugates (e.g. an antibody bound to a cytotoxic agent);
- fusion proteins comprising an antibody;
- immunoliposome complexes comprising a liposome and an antibody or antibody fragment and optionally an additional compound;
- – bi-specific, bivalent antibodies (directed to two different targets and composed of two different antibodies or antigen binding sites);
- tetrameric immunoglobulins composed of two (identical) heavy chains and two (identical) light chains.

[2] Amino Acid Sequences

Most antibodies are claimed through referencing a particular amino acid sequence of the antibodies' binding regions. Framework sequences may be included but are not obligatory. Furthermore, it is not necessary to combine sequence-based definitions of the antibodies with functional features, however such claims are common.

Where the novelty or inventive step reside in non-binding regions, reciting such sequences is obligatory. For example, an antibody can be defined by the sequence of the hinge region or be defined by having an Fc domain with a mutated IgG2 constant region. In such case the specific mutations should be defined in the claim.

The nucleic acid molecule encoding the antibody can also be claimed by reciting its sequence as well as host cells which include the nucleic acid molecule.

[a] *Full-Length Sequences of Antibodies*

It is not needed to recite in the claim the full sequence of an antibody, and reference may be limited to specific sequences only, e.g. CDRs or variable region.

[b] *Sequences of Fragments, CDRs and Framework Regions*

Antibody claims in which the antibody is defined by the sequence of the six CDRs (three heavy chain CDRs and three light chain CDRs) are accepted. For example:

> 'An antibody or antigen binding fragment thereof that binds to '"antigen X"', said antibody comprising
>
> a heavy chain variable region having
>
> a. a CDRH1 sequence comprising SEQ ID NO: 1 or as set forth in SEQ ID NO: 1,
> b. a CDRH2 sequence comprising SEQ ID NO: 2 or as set forth in SEQ ID NO: 2, and
> c. a CDRH3 sequence comprising SEQ ID NO: 3 or as set forth in SEQ ID NO: 3; and
>
> a light chain variable region having
>
> d. a CDRL1 sequence comprising SEQ ID NO: 4 or as set forth in SEQ ID NO: 4,
> e. a CDRL2 sequence comprising SEQ ID NO: 5 or as set forth in SEQ ID NO: 5, and
> f. a CDRL3 sequence comprising SEQ ID NO: 6 or as set forth in SEQ ID NO: 6.'

It is important to include the sequences of all six CDRs. An antibody defined by less than six CDRs is not accepted on the ground of lack of clarity, or sufficient disclosure or utility, unless otherwise shown in the specification.

Antibody claims in which the antibody is defined by the sequence of the variable region of both the heavy and the light chain are also accepted, for example in the form:

> 'An antibody which binds "antigen X" having a light chain wherein the variable domain of the light chain comprises the sequence given in SEQ ID NO:1 and the variable domain of the heavy chain comprises the sequence given in SEQ ID NO: 2.'

It is necessary to include the sequences of *both* variable light and variable heavy chains.

There are instances where only one of the variable chains is recited in the claims, but in such cases the claimed compound should not be defined as an 'antibody' (which according to Israeli practice is defined by having two chains), but rather as a 'specific binding member'.

For example, as follows:

> 'A specific binding member which binds to "antigen X", comprising an antigen-binding portion of an antibody, wherein said antibody comprises a heavy

chain comprising the amino acid sequence of "antibody Y" Variable Heavy domain (SEQ ID NO: 1).'

[3] Chemical Modifications, Conjugation and Glycosylation

Modified antibodies and methods for antibody modifications can be claimed including amino acid modifications and chemical modifications.

Amino acid modifications, namely the substitution of specific amino acids at specific positions, can be claimed. The numbering of the positions should be indicated in the claim as well as a recitation of the numbering system on which the designation is based, e.g. according to the EU index or Kabat numbering.

Chemical modifications may be included in a claim as part of the general definition of the antibody, for example:

- a 'glyco-engineered' antibody that is further defined by its sequences and effect on the target (e.g. increased ADCC);
- an antibody may be defined as being aglycosylated;
- an antibody may also be defined as having certain chemical attachments.

[C] Cell Line Deposits and Process of Production

A hybridoma can be claimed by specifying its accession number with a depository authority. The deposit must be made under the Budapest treaty and prior to filing the PCT application.

An antibody can be defined as being produced by the hybridoma, or as having the CDRs of the antibody produced by the hybridoma.

Process of Production

An antibody production process may be patentable if it includes novel and non-obvious steps. Normally, the preparation of an antibody is considered routine practice. Nonetheless, processes for improving affinity/specificity/activity of an antibody, or for reducing the immunogenicity of the antibody (e.g. by humanization) may be patented, for example where such steps include the introduction of specific substitutions at certain amino acid positions to achieve a desired effect. Such substitutions should be exemplified in the specification and must be shown to have an unexpected effect on the antibody characteristics to be considered inventive.

§10.03 BREADTH OF CLAIMS AND SUPPORT BY EXAMPLES

[A] Acceptable Breadth of Claims to Antibodies

Claims with respect to antibodies directed to a newly identified target molecule or to such molecule regarding which it has previously proven difficult to raise an antibody, or with respect to antibodies directed to a target epitope whose importance was previously unknown or to a target epitope that was known to be inaccessible, may be allowed. In such cases, the claims may be defined in a broad manner, solely in terms of the target. Such claims cover a wide range of antibodies (polyclonal, monoclonal, chimeric, humanized, etc.), and practically, 'any antibody which binds to antigen X'.

Typically, it is not necessary to provide evidence showing that an antibody has actually been produced if the target is susceptible to routine methods of antibody production. However, it is preferable to include at least one working example of an antibody directed against the novel target (e.g., any binding assay of the antibody to its newly defined epitope should suffice). Post filing data submitted during the prosecution may suffice.

Broad antibody claims may be acceptable also when the target is found to have a previously unappreciated role in a disease. That is, the target is found to be associated with a new medical use. In such cases, the antibody may be defined by reference to the target bound *and* the new medical use (e.g., 'an antibody directed against target X *for use* in the treatment of Y'). No further structural definition of the antibody is required in the claims or the specification. However, in such case the claim would be directed to an *antibody for use* and not to the antibody *per se*.

In this scenario it is recommended to include at least one working example for such antibody. It will also be necessary to establish that it is at least plausible that an antibody binding to the target will have a therapeutic effect.

In vitro functional data will likely be sufficient, particularly if derived from a disease model or other assay relevant to the indication.

[B] Required Experimental Support for Claims to Functionally Defined Antibodies

It is necessary for an application to include sufficient information so as to enable a person of skill in the art to generate antibodies which meet the functional definition recited in the claims.

Ideally, at least some direct experimental evidence of the functional characteristic(s) should be provided in the patent application, for at least one exemplary antibody. Under some circumstances it may be possible to rely upon supplementary data filed later, but there must be a connection to the characteristic(s) shown in the application. The characteristic(s) relied upon must be at least plausible at the filing date.

[C] Required Experimental Support for Claims to Structurally Defined Antibodies

If the antibodies are structurally defined in the claims, the amino acid sequences of the regions determining the antibody binding site (namely the amino acid sequence of the CDRs and/or the heavy and light variable chains) must be provided in the specification. These sequences may appear in the text, and/or the figures but they must be included also in a sequence listing. If antibodies to the same target are already known in the art, it is preferable to show that the structurally claimed antibodies have certain functional advantages in order to avoid obviousness objections. In most cases applicants provide a significant amount of structural information (primary amino acid sequences) in the patent application. Examiners often insist that minimal structural detail be provided to define the target binding region of an antibody. It may alternatively be possible to meet such a requirement by reference to a biological deposit of, for example, hybridoma cells producing the claimed antibodies.

§10.04 SPECIFIC MEDICAL APPLICATIONS AND OTHER FOLLOW-UP INVENTIONS

As elaborated above, claims directed to methods of treatment of the human body are excluded from patentability according to section 7(1) of the Patents Law. However, products for use in therapeutic treatment of humans may be patented.

[A] Treatment of Specific Diseases

Therapeutic applications of antibodies can be claimed via three main formats:

1. Claims directed to pharmaceutical compositions comprising the antibodies;
2. Claims directed to antibodies for use in treating a certain disease (also acceptable format for second medical use claims); and
3. Claims directed to antibodies for use in a method of treating a certain disease (also acceptable format for second medical use claims).

[B] Mode of Administration

New modes or routes of administration and new patient groups may be deemed eligible of patent protection if formulated in the manner specified under [A] above. In practice such claims have been granted by the ILPTO.

[C] Dosage Regimens

According to the Israeli MPEP (Appendix c, section 6), a dosage regimen that leads to unexpected results may be patented if presented as a technical feature in a product claim. Such claim will not be classified as a 'method for treating the human body', since it is a manufacturer's instruction not intended to limit the discretion of the treating physicians. Like any other invention, a dosage regimen must satisfy the requirements for subject-matter eligibility, otherwise the patent will not be granted.[1]

[D] Specific Patient Groups

The patentability of claims relating to new 'patient groups' has not yet been discussed in the Israeli case law. However, a medicament useful for new patient groups may be deemed eligible of patent protection if formulated in the manner specified under [A] above.

---

1. Decision of the Registrar of Patents re Opposition to Patent Application No. 153109 *Teva Pharmaceutical Industries Ltd. v. Merck & Co. Inc.* (5.8.2010); LCA 6837/12 *Merck Sharp & Dohme Corp. v. Unipharm Ltd.* (28.4.2013).

[E] Specific Mode of Action

Specific Mode of Action may not in general be claimed per se, however it may be included as a functional feature of the antibody together with additional defining features.

[F] Combinations with Other Active Ingredients

Combinations with other active ingredients are acceptable. Claims directed to such combinations may generally be phrased as 'A pharmaceutical composition comprising a combination', or 'An antibody (or pharmaceutical composition) for administration in combination with'.

Additional secondary inventions relating to antibodies may include stabilized solutions (or pharmaceutical formulations) comprising the antibody. Such stabilized solutions are characterized by predefined concentrations of the various components of the formulation. An enabling description in the specification is required to support the claimed range.

[G] Specific Diagnostic Applications

Diagnostic applications are not considered methods of treatment and therefore section 7(1) of the Patents Law does not form an obstacle to patentability.

§10.05 ASSESSMENT OF INVENTIVENESS

[A] General Approach

Inventive Step

Section 5 of the Patents Law defines *inventive step* as follows:

> 'An inventive step is a step which to an average man of the art does not appear obvious in the light of information published, prior to the application date, in the ways indicated in section 4.'

Assessment of Inventive Step/Non-Obviousness

In general, when assessing whether a claimed invention is based on a step that would seem obvious to a person of ordinary skill in the art, the examiner shall proceed in the following order:[2]

1. Identify the inventive concept of the invention in question;
2. Establish the relevant prior art for the invention in question and the extent of an average skilled person's knowledge;

---

2. See Patent Registrar decision on Israeli patent application 123976 of *CompuCraft Ltd.*

3. Identify the differences, if any, between the prior art and the concept at the basis of the invention in question;
4. Determine whether the differences found in (3) would have seemed obvious to an average skilled person, without introducing new knowledge from the invention in question.

Combining Publications

When examining inventive step, two or more publications may be combined for procuring a full picture, on the condition that such combination was obvious, intuitive and routine to a skilled person at the relevant date.[3] However, section 5.2 of Appendix G to the Israeli MPEP states that a need to combine more than three prior publications casts doubt over obviousness, and such doubt increases as the number of combined prior publications increases in order to deny inventive step.

Unexpected advantage

Inventive step can be based on an unexpected advantage even when the elements defining the invention are obvious on the basis of prior art (e.g., when the invention is very similar to the prior art such that the difference is obvious, or an invention that deals with dosage regimen). For this purpose, the applicant must demonstrate, by means of comparative data, that there is an unexpected advantage over the closest prior art. It should be established that the advantage stems from a new feature (or a new combination of features) that is common to the entire scope claimed, so it can be assumed that this advantage exists in all the individuals of the claimed group.

Obvious-to-try test

Patent applications may be rejected on the footing of lack of inventive step also when the prior art does not explicitly teach the invention claimed. Cases of this sort include inventive concepts which were obvious to an average skilled person at the effective date to try and execute in the same manner outlined in the application with reasonable expectation of success, i.e. achieving the result/advantage promised in the application.

The obvious-to-try test is a standard one in Israeli law for examining inventive step.

To establish whether it was obvious to attempt a performance as laid out in the application, the examiner needs to check whether the following three conditions were met at the effective date:[4]

1. there was a known problem in the field requiring a solution;
2. the components of the experimental process for achieving a solution to the problem were known;

3. See 345/87 *Hughes Aircraft company v. State of Israel*, 44 (4) 45, 108 (1990).
4. See patent registrar decision on Israeli patent application 136294 of *Pharmacia & UpJohn AB*; patent registrar decision on Israeli patent application 136532 of G.D. Searle & Co.

3. a person of ordinary skill in the art would have carried out the experiment for achieving the solution with a reasonable expectation of success.

Notable points with respect to biotechnology:

1. Cloning and identifying sequences similar to a known sequence by hybridizing nucleotide sequences is considered obvious. When there is difficulty implementing hybridization, one should consider that it is possible to identify similar sequences by using computational methods utilizing sequence libraries or a complete genome.
2. Orthologous sequences are *per se* known sequences. Preparing an orthologous sequence from a source, namely a species, sex or other type, may be considered obvious, since there exist methods, based on hybridization, cloning and isolation, which allow for finding sequences having considerable structural similarity to a known sequence. Inventive step can be established when the source, i.e. the species, sex or other type, was unknown or when there is a significant difference between the sequences and there is no considerable structural similarity allowing the orthologous sequence to be prepared.
3. Identifying sequences within known sequences and identifying gene activity by homologous comparison to gene(s) with known activity is generally considered obvious. Bioinformatics tools usually allow for identifying such sequences (an area also known as 'information mining'). Publicly available service software on the NCBI website, e.g. BLAST, allows for identifying sequences in known sequences. The same is true for identifying gene activity by homologous comparison to a gene or genes with known activity. Inventive step in these cases will be recognized with respect to claims that link between the sequence or gene and the non-obvious functionality.
4. Combinations of micro-arrays and probes. For a unique combination of micro-arrays to be recognized as having inventive step, it must have an unexpected advantage, for example, more accurate detection of disease than using each and every micro-array separately (this is in fact an example for synergistic effect).

[B] Particularities Regarding Claims to Antibodies

The issue of inventive step is most relevant in cases where the claimed antibody is directed to a known target for which there are pre-existing antibodies. In such case it would be necessary in addition to provide the sequence data (CDRs and/or entire variable region) to demonstrate unexpected functional characteristics of the claimed antibody that could not have been predicted from the prior art.

§10.06 ENFORCEMENT AND SCOPE OF PROTECTION

[A] Biosimilars

There is no case law or guiding authority as to the scope of protection afforded to biosimilars of antibodies or the enforcement of patents on biosimilars in general.

[B] Equivalence

Section 49 of the Patents Law provides that also absent literal infringement, a patent is infringed by exploiting the essence of the inventions as transpires from the claims.

> '49(A) A patentee is entitled to prevent any other person from exploiting without consent or unlawfully the invention for which the patent has been granted, either in the manner prescribed in the claims or in any manner which involves the essence of the invention subject matter of the patent, in light of the definition in such claims (hereafter – infringement).'

This section was interpreted as adopting the concept of the doctrine of equivalents as enunciated in *Graver Tank*,[5] which set out the rule that in order to infringe the patent the accused product or method must perform substantially the same function of the claimed invention in substantially the same way to obtain substantially the same result.

5. *Graver Tank & Manufacturing Co. v. Linde Air Products Co.*, 339 U.S. 605 (1950).

Chapter 11

United States of America

Michele M. Wales & John C. Todaro

§11.01 ANTIBODIES AS PATENTABLE SUBJECT-MATTER

[A] Legal Framework

The United States does not have specific laws that control the patentability of antibodies. Instead, the standard statutory provisions of patentable subject-matter and utility,[1] written description, enablement, and definiteness,[2] novelty,[3] and obviousness[4] that apply to all inventions also apply to antibodies.

For example, under US patent law, for an invention to be patentable it must have utility. 35 U.S.C. §101 provides that a patent is authorized to an inventor of 'any new and useful process, machine, manufacture, or composition of matter, or any new and useful improvement thereof'. In *In re Brana*, 51 F.3d 1560 (Fed. Cir. 1995), the CAFC commented that in the context of pharmaceutical inventions, the utility standard does not require proof that the compound would be approved by the FDA. Rather, 'proof of an alleged pharmaceutical property for a compound by statistically significant tests with standard experimental animals is sufficient to establish utility'.[5] The CAFC stated that '[u]sefulness in patent law ... in the context of pharmaceutical inventions, necessarily includes the expectation of further research and development'.[6]

1. 35 U.S.C. § 101.
2. 35 U.S.C. § 112.
3. 35 U.S.C. § 102.
4. 35 U.S.C. § 103.
5. *In re Brana*, 51 F.3d 1560 (Fed. Cir. 1995) at 1567.
6. *Id.* at 1568. In a 1992 decision, the Board of Patent Appeals and Interferences commented on the utility requirement in the context of pharmaceutical or medical inventions: 'Case law ... is receptive to early filing of applications in the biomedical field so long as the patent applicant, when properly challenged by the examiner, can provide evidence showing

The first paragraph of section 112 of title 35 of the United States Code provides the basis for the enablement and written description requirements of all US patents. As explained further in §11.03, these requirements are of particular significance in the patenting of antibodies.

The statute provides:

> The specification shall contain a written description of the invention, and of the manner and process of making and using it, in such full, clear, concise, and exact terms as to enable any person skilled in the art to which it pertains, or with which it is most nearly connected, to make and use the same, and shall set forth the best mode contemplated by the inventor or joint inventor of carrying out the invention.

The CAFC has interpreted 35 U.S.C. § 112 as presenting two separate requirements for patentability – 'enablement' and 'written description.[7]

A patent claim is enabled, under section 112, first paragraph, if the patent contains a description of 'the manner and process of making and using' the claimed invention, 'in such full, clear, concise, and exact terms as to enable any person skilled in the art to which it pertains, or with which it is most nearly connected, to make and use the same'.

A patent claim satisfies the written description requirement if the patent contains a written description of the invention such that a person of ordinary skill would understand that the inventor had possession of the invention at the time of filing.[8] While the statute does not expressly require that the claims recite specific examples of a generic invention, the claims must be sufficient so that the disclosure 'allows one skilled in the art to visualize or recognize the identity of the subject-matter purportedly described'.[9]

As explained in §11.01[B] and §11.03[A], case law has evolved in the United States that governs how these statutes are to be applied to antibody inventions.

A patent claim must also be novel and non-obvious. See, §11.05 for a discussion of these requirements as applied to antibody claims.

[B] General Amenability or Exclusion of Antibodies from Patentability

The relevant question in the US for patent eligible subject-matter of biologics focuses on whether the biologic is identical to a product that can be found in nature ('natural products'). If the biologic is identical to a natural product, the biologic cannot be patented.[10] However, if the biologic has *any* structural or functional differences,

---

substantial activity in screening tests customarily used and accepted as predicative of human activity for the type of chemical tested.' *In re Aggarwal*, 23 U.S.P.Q.2d 1334 (Bd. Pat. App. Int. 1992).

7. See *Vas-Cath, Inc. v. Maharkar*, 935 F.2d 1555, 1563 (Fed. Cir. 1991).
8. See *Ariad Pharmaceuticals, Inc. v. Eli Lilly and Co.*, 598 F.3d 1336, 1351 (Fed. Cir. 2010).
9. See *Allergan v. Sandoz*, 796 F.3d 1293, 1308 (Fed. Cir. 2015) (quoting *Enzo Biochem Inc. v. Gen-Probe Inc.*, 323 F.3d 956, 968 (Fed. Cir. 2002).
10. In *Association for Molecular Pathology v. Myriad Genetics, Inc.*, 569 U.S. 576 (2013), the United States Supreme Court held that naturally occurring isolated genes were not

then the antibody can be patented.[11] Thus, rejections involving whether an antibody qualifies as patent eligible subject-matter can usually be overcome.

First, because of the nature of the immune system and of the way 'self-antibodies' are eliminated during development, the existence of an antibody to a self-antigen (such as, for example, an antibody that binds to a human protein) is unlikely to occur in nature. Moreover, the US examiner cannot just allege that there is a 'mere possibility' that the antibody exists in nature. Instead, the examiner must provide evidence suggesting the existence of the antibody in nature.[12] Therefore, antibodies to naturally occurring self-proteins are unlikely to exist and are therefore patentable.

Secondly, most antibodies made in the laboratory are artificial and would not be found in nature. For example, antibodies directed to a human protein yet made in a mouse hybridoma will not be found in nature, just as human antibodies directed to a drosophila protein will also not occur in nature. Similarly, chimeric, humanized and antibody fragments are also not naturally occurring. Thus, attorneys drafting applications directed to these types of antibodies should highlight these structural differences to avoid patent eligible subject-matter rejections.[13]

---

patentable. The Court ruled that the naturally occurring genes were within the judicial exception to patentable subject-matter: 'Laws of nature, natural phenomena, and abstract ideas are not patentable.' *Id.* at 589 (citing *Mayo Collaborative Services v. Prometheus Laboratories, Inc.* 566 U.S. 66 (2012).

11. USPTO Examination Guidelines call for a three part test: Step 1: confirm that the claim covers the patentable subject-matter of 35 U.S.C. § 101, i.e. a process, machine, manufacture of composition of matter; Step 2A: determine whether the claim is directed to a judicial exception to patentable subject-matter; and Step 2B: determine 'whether the claim recites additional elements that integrate the exception into a practical application of that exception.' USPTO 2019 Revised Patent Subject Matter Eligibility Guidance, 7 January 2019. According to the Guidelines, a practical application of the subject-matter 'will apply, rely on, or use the judicial exception, such that the claim is more than a drafting effort designed to monopolize the judicial exception.' The Guidelines provided the following examples:
    - an improvement in the functioning of a computer, or an improvement to other technology or technical field;
    - an additional element to effect a particular treatment or prophylaxis for a disease or medical condition;
    - a transformation or reduction of a particular article to a different state or thing.
12. MPEP § 2106.07, entitled 'Formulating and Supporting Rejections for Lack of Subject Matter Eligibility,' states that 'the initial burden is on the examiner to explain why a claim or claims are ineligible for patenting clearly and specifically, so that applicant has sufficient notice and is able to effectively respond.' Section 2106.07(a) further states that 'if the claim is directed to a law of nature or a natural phenomenon, the rejection should identify the law of nature or natural phenomenon as it is recited (i.e., set forth or described) in the claim and explain using a reasoned rationale why it is considered a law of nature or natural phenomenon.'
13. Although mouse, chimeric, and humanized antibodies that bind to a human protein may be easier to protect from a patent standpoint, these types of antibodies are often less desirable from a therapeutic standpoint as there are concerns of increased antigenicity from the FDA. Thus, the US courts have created conflict between encouraging pharmaceutical companies to invent in the safest antibodies (e.g., a fully human antibody directed to a human protein) vs. antibodies that can be patent protected.

Thirdly, manufacturing methods can alter the overall structure of an antibody. For example, glycosylation patterns can differ depending on the type of host cell used to produce the antibody. Thus, if the primary, amino acid structure of an antibody is found in nature, patentable claims can still be obtained if the recombinant antibody has a different glycosylation pattern. However, these claims will likely be narrow and limited to the specifically described glycosylated antibody.

Finally, even if an antibody is found in nature, patentable method claims can still be obtained. For example, if an antibody sequence is found in nature, new uses of that antibody, such as for example therapeutic or diagnostic uses, may be an avenue for patent protection.

However, unlike other jurisdictions, the addition of 'purified' or 'isolated' to antibody claims is unlikely to overcome patentable subject-matter rejections. In the United States, the *Myriad* decision makes it clear that 'purified' or 'isolated' language will not transport an antibody found in nature to patent eligible subject-matter.[14]

[C] Required Distinction from Naturally Occurring Antibodies

As explained in the §11.01[B], so long as there is some structural difference (e.g., a difference in amino acid sequence or glycosylation pattern), a new use, or credible argument that the antibody cannot be found in nature, the antibody will overcome the patentable subject-matter hurdle in the United States.

However, please see §11.03 for a discussion regarding the other statutory provisions that have higher hurdles that must be met in order to obtain patentable antibody claims in the United States.

§11.02 ACCEPTABLE CLAIM FEATURES FOR DEFINING ANTIBODIES

[A] Functional Features

[1] Target/Antigen

As explained in §11.03, claiming antibodies based solely by the target/antigen to which the antibody binds is increasingly difficult and is no longer the standard in the United States, resulting in a dramatic shift in antibody protection.

[2] Mode of Binding: Target Affinity, Binding Specificity, Epitope, Definitions via Reference Antibodies and Competitive Binding

As explained in §11.03, obtaining patentable antibody claims using functional language is increasingly difficult in the United States and will require substantial 'representative number of species' disclosed in the specification.

---

14. See USPTO Nature Based Product Examples 9–18, from 6 December 2014 USPTO Subject Matter Eligibility Guidelines.

[3] *Effect on Target*

As explained in §11.03, obtaining patentable antibody claims in the United States using functional language (e.g., such as an agonist or antagonist) will require substantial 'representative number of species' disclosed in the specification.

[B] Structural Features

[1] *Molecular Topology: Antibody Types, Fragments and Antibody Constructs*

As explained §11.03, obtaining patentable antibody claims in the United States to different structures of antibodies (chimeric, humanized, fully human antibodies, bispecific, fragments, etc.) will require a 'representative number of species' actually disclosed in the specification to the satisfy written description requirement. In other words, it may no longer be possible to obtain allowable antibody claims to chimeric antibodies, for example, without the disclosure (by amino acid sequence) of a specific chimeric antibody in the specification.

[2] *Amino Acid Sequences*

[a] *Full-Length Sequences of Antibodies*

Assuming that the antibody is not found in nature (see discussion in §11.01), the best way to ensure patent protection in the United States for an antibody (for example a therapeutic antibody that will be registered as an active ingredient) is by disclosing and claiming the antibody amino acid sequence (e.g., by SEQ ID NO:).

For example, a representative claim in the United States to a full-length antibody heavy chain (SEQ ID NO: 1) or light chain (SEQ ID NO: 2) would be:

> 'An antibody comprising the amino acid sequence of SEQ ID NO: 1 *or* SEQ ID NO: 2.'

In this example, any antibody that contains either the heavy or light chain identical to SEQ ID NO: 1 or SEQ ID NO: 2 would be covered by the claim. In contrast, a representative claim covering antibodies having both heavy *and* light chains would be:

> 'An antibody comprising the amino acid sequence of SEQ ID NO: 1 *and* SEQ ID NO: 2.'

This claiming strategy is ideal if one is trying to protect a commercial antibody. These claims are essentially 'picture' claims and are intended to capture bio-similar antibodies that are identical in sequence. However, one single amino acid change in either SEQ ID NO: 1 or 2 will avoid literal infringement. Therefore, antibodies are also claimed in the United States as described in §11.02[B][2][b] to capture efforts to design around.

[b] *Sequences of Fragments, CDRs and Framework Regions*

Although at first it may seem counter-intuitive, claims reciting fewer rather than more amino acids are broader in scope. For example, a claim directed to an amino acid sequence of 10 amino acids is broader than a claim directed to amino acid sequence of 100 amino acids. This is because an alleged infringer must use all 100 amino acids in their composition as compared to using only 10 amino acids.

Moreover, antibody specificity to a target is determined mainly by the complementarity determining regions (CDRs). Thus, one of the broadest ways to claim antibodies in the United States is to claim the antibodies by the CDR sequences. For example, an antibody claim to the heavy and light chain CDRs (in this example identified as SEQ ID NO: 3–8) can be drafted as:

> 'An antibody comprising SEQ ID NO: 3–8.'

Or

> 'An antibody comprising HCDR1, HCDR2, HCDR3, LCDR1, LCDR2, and LCDR3 wherein HCDR1 comprises SEQ ID NO: 3, HCDR2 comprises SEQ ID NO: 4, HCDR3 comprises SEQ ID NO: 5, LCDR1 comprises SEQ ID NO: 6, LCDR2 comprises SEQ ID NO: 7, LCDR3 comprises SEQ ID NO: 8.'

Note that the USPTO is unlikely to grant claims to a single CDR as the single CDR will lack utility on its own. Instead, the USPTO takes the position that all six CDRs are necessary to create a functional antibody. By claiming antibodies in this manner, scope of protection can be gained as the backbone or framework region can be varied while the CDRs are maintained.[15]

Another approach for claiming antibodies is to claim fragments of the full-length antibody sequence. For example, antibody fragments comprising the variable regions or a single-chain (scFV) antibodies can also be claimed and allowed by the USPTO. These claims will be narrower than the CDR claims described above but broader than the claims reciting the full-length antibody sequence.

However, with any of these approaches, the amino acid sequence of the antibody must be described in the application as filed.

[3] *Chemical Modifications, Conjugation and Glycosylation*

If chemical modifications of the antibody can be specifically described, then one can successfully claim these chemically modified antibodies in the United States. For example, if an antibody has a unique glycosylation pattern which happens to extend the half-life of the antibody, and that pattern and improved function is described in the specification as filed, the USPTO will likely grant claims to that specific antibody structure.

---

15. Please note, that we are beginning to see an increasing number of rejections by the US examiners that antibody binding is controlled by both the CDRs and the framework sequences. Thus, the USPTO may begin to require that the claims specify both the framework regions as well as the CDRs, unless applicants can provide evidence showing that framework sequences are not relevant to the antibody's activity.

However, claims to such chemically modified antibodies will be even narrower than claims directed to the full-length antibody sequence, as infringers must use both the recited antibody sequence and the specified chemical modifications. Therefore, due to the ability to easily design around these claims, this approach is best used when the chemical modification provides substantially improved antibody function (such as increased antibody half-life and/or reduced antigenicity) and/or reduces antibody manufacturing costs.

[C] Cell Line Deposits and Process of Production

In the United States, one way to satisfy the written description requirement for an antibody when the antibody sequence is unknown, is to deposit the antibody in a public depository.

The Federal Circuit has held that depositing a biological sample with a public depository will satisfy the written description requirement.

Specifically, in *Enzo Biochem, Inc. v. Gen-Probe Inc.*,[16] the plaintiff sued for infringement of a patent covering nucleic acid probes that could hybridize to a bacterium that causes a strain of gonorrhoea. The patentee had deposited the biological material in a public depository, in accordance with the Budapest Treaty on the Deposit of Biological Materials. The District Court found the patent invalid for lack of written description. On appeal, the CAFC reversed, finding that the deposit 'constitutes an adequate written description of the deposited material sufficient to comply with the written description requirement'.[17]

However, two main downsides exist for depositing antibodies. First, costs associated with depositing a single antibody can be substantial. For example, to deposit a single antibody sample with ATCC depository costs over USD 2,500. In contrast, sequencing of the antibody will both be cheaper and provide a better written description as being both more comprehensive and providing the ability to vary claiming strategies. For example, the presence of the antibody sequence in the specification may permit the applicant to obtain broader claims, that cover fragments (such as the CDRs).[18] The applicant may also be able to claim the recited sequence and other sequences having a high percent homology.

Secondly, the deposited antibody sample must be capable of reproduction. For antibodies, this requirement often results in the depositing of a cell line capable of producing the antibody. Thus, care must be taken to not deposit a sample of the master cell bank that is used to commercially produce the antibody. Instead, an earlier, progenitor cell line should be deposited. Otherwise, by depositing the master cell bank, biosimilars manufacturers could then readily obtain and produce the originator's antibody.

Thus, although depositing of a cell line that produces the antibody can satisfy written description in the United States, providing the sequence of the antibody is preferred.

---

16. 323 F.3d 956 (Fed. Cir. 2002).
17. *Id.* at 965.
18. See §11.02[B].

§11.03 BREADTH OF CLAIMS AND SUPPORT BY EXAMPLES

[A] Acceptable Breadth of Claims to Antibodies

In the United States, enablement/sufficiency is generally not a key rejection for antibody claims in view of the enablement standard established in *In re Wands.*[19] Here, a patent applicant appealed a decision of the USPTO Patent Board of Appeals rejecting an application claiming an assay using a monoclonal antibody on the grounds that the applicant had not enabled the invention. The Board had determined that the specification did not teach one skilled in the art how to make the monoclonal antibodies recited in the claims. The CAFC reversed the PTO Board, stating that enablement 'is not precluded by the necessity for some experimentation', provided that the required experimentation is not 'undue'.[20] The Court then considered what constitutes undue experimentation. The CAFC stated that the test 'is not merely quantitative, since a considerable amount of experimentation is permissible, if it is merely routine, or if the specification in question provides a reasonable amount of guidance with respect to the direction in which the experimentation should proceed'.[21]

The CAFC identified eight factors that should be considered in determining whether the amount of experimentation is undue:

(1) the quantity of experimentation necessary;
(2) the amount of direction or guidance presented;
(3) the presence or absence of working examples;
(4) the nature of the invention;
(5) the state of the prior art;
(6) the relative skill of those in the art;
(7) the predictability or unpredictability of the art; and
(8) the breadth of the claims.

In view of the settled case law on enablement, most applicants claiming antibodies are able to provide an enabling specification of the claimed invention.

However, written description is now a key issue for antibody claims in the United States as the Federal Circuit in 2017 fundamentally changed the standard by which antibody claims could satisfy the description requirement, previously established in *Noelle v. Lederman.*

In *Noelle v. Lederman,*[22] the plaintiff patent applicant Noelle appealed a decision in an interference, finding no interference-in-fact with the defendant Lederman's patent. The count of the interference was for an antibody defined functionally rather than structurally. For example, representative claim 51 read:

> 'A monoclonal antibody or fragment thereof which specifically binds CD40CR.'

CD40CR is a specific antigen found on T cells. The claims notably did not recite any of the antibody structure. In addressing whether the claimed invention satisfied the

19. 858 F.2d 731 (Fed. Cir. 1988).
20. *Id.* at 737.
21. *Id.*
22. 355 F.3d 1343 (Fed. Cir. 2004).

written description requirement, the Court noted that the claims recited only function and not structure, and that in prior cases (including *Regents of the University of California v. Eli Lilly and Co.*),[23] the Court had found that claiming genetic material 'only by a statement of function or result may be insufficient to meet the written description requirement'.[24]

However, the *Noelle* Court cited the PTO's own guidance on antibody claims, which stated that 'any antibody which is capable of binding to antigen X' would have sufficient support in a written description that disclosed '*fully characterized* antigens'.[25] The PTO guidance relied on the 'well defined structural characteristics' of antibodies. Thus, in *Noelle*, the CAFC concluded that 'as long as an applicant has disclosed a "*fully characterized* antigen", either by its structure, formula, chemical name, or physical properties, or by depositing the protein in a public depository, the applicant can then claim an antibody by its binding affinity to that described antigen'.[26]

The fully characterized antigen theory of claiming was in sharp contrast to prior written description case law established for small molecules, which required that a generic claim in the chemical field included some structure of the invention.[27] As explained by the Court, the claims in *Ariad* covered 'the use of all substances that achieve the desired result of reducing the binding of NF kappa B to NF kappa B recognition sites'.[28]

The Federal Circuit in *Ariad* ruled that the claim was invalid, as lacking written description support. The Court stated that 'a sufficient description of a genus ... requires the disclosure of either a representative number of species falling within the scope of the genus or structural features common to the members of the genus so that one of skill in the art can 'visualize or recognize' the members of the genus.'[29] According to the CAFC, 'an adequate written description requires a precise definition, such as by structure, formula, chemical name, physical properties, or other properties, of species falling within the genus sufficient to distinguish the genus from other materials'.[30] The Court found that in order to satisfy the written description requirement, the specification needs to show that the inventors possessed the claimed methods by sufficiently disclosing molecules capable of reducing NF- kappa B activity so as to 'satisfy the inventor's obligation to disclose the technologic knowledge upon which the patent is based, and to demonstrate that the patentee was in possession of the claimed invention'.[31]

---

23. 119 F.3d 1559 (Fed. Cir. 1997).
24. *Id.* at 1347.
25. Synopsis of Application of Written Description Guidelines, at 60, available at http:// www.uspto.gov/web/menu/written.pdf (last visited Jan. 16, 2003) (emphasis added).
26. *Id.* at 1349. The Court in *Noelle* ultimately concluded that the applicants' claims did not meet the written description requirement, because the applicant did not provide a sufficient description of the antigen, as the antigen was not well isolated or characterized.
27. See, e.g., *Ariad Pharmaceuticals, Inc. v. Eli Lilly and Company*, 598 F.3d 1336 (Fed. Cir. 2010) (en banc).
28. *Id.* at 1341.
29. *Id.* at 1350 (quoting *Regents of the University of California v. Eli Lilly*, 119 F.3d 1559, 1568–1569).
30. *Id.*
31. *Id.* at 1355 (quoting *Capon v. Eshar*, 4128 F.3d 1349, 1357 (Fed. Cir. 2005).

Following the *Noelle* decision, the biotech industry relied upon the 'well characterized antigen' standard for satisfying written description for antibodies for over ten years. Innovative biotech companies obtained many patents with claims reciting only function (such as antigen binding properties), and not reciting structure. Then, the CAFC abruptly eliminated this theory of claiming antibodies in their decision of *Amgen v. Sanofi*.[32]

In *Amgen*, the plaintiff Amgen sued Sanofi and its partner Regeneron for an injunction, seeking to stop Sanofi and Regeneron from marketing their anti-PCSK9 antibody, marketed as Praluent™. Amgen asserted that Praluent™ infringed their granted claims which covered a genus of anti-PCSK9 antibodies. A representative claim from the patents asserted by Amgen is below:

> 'An isolated monoclonal antibody, wherein, when bound to PCSK9, the monoclonal antibody binds to at least one of the following residues: S153, I154, P155, R194, D238, A239, I369, S372, D374, C375, T377, C378, F379, V380, or S381 of SEQ ID NO:3, and wherein the monoclonal antibody blocks binding of PCSK9 to LDL[-]R.'

The claims did not recite any structure of the antibody, but instead recited solely a functional limitation (the capacity to bind to certain residues of the PCSK9 target). The trial court jury found that the patent was valid and satisfied the written description requirement. The court had instructed the jury as follows on the written description standard:

> 'In the case of a claim to antibodies, the correlation between structure and function may also be satisfied by the disclosure of a newly characterized antigen by its structure, formula, chemical name, or physical properties if you find that the level of skill and knowledge in the art was such that production of antibodies against such an antigen was conventional or routine.'

On appeal, the CAFC reversed, concluding that the patent was invalid and lacked written description. The Court stated that to satisfy the written description requirement, the specification 'must contain enough information about the actual makeup of the claimed products – "a precise definition, such as by structure, formula, chemical name, physical properties, or other properties, of species falling within the genus sufficient to distinguish the genus from other materials," which may be present in "functional" terminology "when the art has established a correlation between structure and function".'[33]

The CAFC noted that commentators have disputed whether in fact 'knowledge of the chemical structure of an antigen gives the required kind of structure-identifying information about the corresponding antibodies'.[34] The CAFC stated that the 'newly characterized antigen' test 'flouts basic legal principles of the written description

32. 872 F.3d 1367 (Fed. Cir. 2017) (cert. denied), 2019 WL 113092 (7 Jan. 2019).
33. *Id.* at 1378 (quoting from *Ariad*, 598 F.3d at 1350).
34. *Id.*

requirement'.[35] The Court stated that Congress 'has not created a special written description requirement for antibodies as it has, for example, for plant patents'.[36]

Thus, the Federal Circuit remanded the question of whether Amgen's specification satisfied the written description requirement based purely on disclosure of a representative number of species of antibodies and not whether the antigen is well defined. In February 2019, a jury in the US District Court for the District of Delaware upheld the validity of Amgen's patents. As of the time of this writing, Sanofi and Regeneron were pursuing legal challenges to the jury verdict.

Note that Amgen's patent specification disclosed the amino acid sequence for 22 different human anti-PCSK9 antibodies which met the functional limitation of the claim – namely the ability to block the binding of PCSK9 to LDL-R. Amgen's scientist identified these 22 antibodies by screening over 3,000 potential antibody candidates which were subsequently narrowed to 85 antibodies for further processing and testing. Such an extensive disclosure of antibody sequences is not typical for patent applications filed by relying on the 'well characterized antigen' theory of patentability, and therefore, many applications already on file may not satisfy this new heightened antibody hurdle.

Following the *Amgen* decision in February 2018, the USPTO issued a memorandum warning that the examples in its 2008 Written Description Training Materials are 'outdated and should *not* be relied upon as reflecting the current state of the law regarding 35 U.S.C. §§ 101 and 112' for antibodies. Specifically, the memorandum instructs examiners that the disclosure of a fully characterized antigen can no longer provide written descriptive support of an antibody to that antigen, and that these examples in the training materials should be ignored.

Thus, it is unlikely that antibody claims will be allowable by the USPTO unless the specification has described a sufficient number of antibodies (by amino acid sequence or by deposit) that meet *all* of the limitations of the claims. Moreover, if the claims recite more complex functional limitations (such as agonistic activity and/or antibodies that bind to specific epitopes) written description will not be satisfied unless antibodies are described (by amino acid sequence or deposit) that possess these specific functional attributes.

Finally, the *Amgen v. Sanofi* decision can be applied retroactively. Thus, licensees should consider evaluating whether currently in-licensed antibody portfolios are still valid if patentability was originally based on the 'well-characterized' antigen standard. Under the *Amgen* decision, patents that do not specifically exemplify antibodies arguably will no longer meet the written description requirement in the United States. It is therefore possible that a licence would no longer be necessary for these patents. However, before such a decision is made, licensees should discuss whether to terminate such a licence only after consultation with their attorneys.

35. *Id.*
36. See, e.g., 35 U.S.C. § 162 (exempting plant patents from § 112 'if the description is as complete as is reasonably possible').

[B] Required Experimental Support for Claims to Functionally Defined Antibodies

As more fully explained in §11.03[A], the United States (unlike other jurisdictions) no longer recognizes that the disclosure of a fully characterized antigen will satisfy the written description requirement for antibodies that bind to the antigen. Thus, it is unlikely that antibody claims will be allowable by the USPTO unless the specification has described a sufficient representative number of antibodies (by amino acid sequence or by deposit) that meet *all* of the limitations of the claims. Moreover, if the claims recite more complex functional limitations (such as agonistic activity and/or antibodies that bind to specific epitopes) written description will not be satisfied unless antibodies are described (by amino acid sequence or deposit) that possess these specific functional attributes.

[C] Required Experimental Support for Claims to Structurally Defined Antibodies

As more fully explained in §11.03[A], the United States (unlike other jurisdictions) no longer recognizes that the disclosure of a fully characterized antigen will satisfy the written description requirement for antibodies that bind to the antigen. Thus, it is unlikely that antibody claims will be allowable by the USPTO unless the specification has described a sufficient representative number of antibodies (by amino acid sequence or by deposit) that meet *all* of the limitations of the claims. Moreover, if the claims recite more complex functional limitations (such as agonistic activity and/or antibodies that bind to specific epitopes) written description will not be satisfied unless antibodies are described (by amino acid sequence or deposit) that possess these specific functional attributes.

§11.04 SPECIFIC MEDICAL APPLICATIONS AND OTHER FOLLOW-UP INVENTIONS

[A] Treatment of Specific Diseases

In an application claiming and disclosing a novel antibody, if all other statutory provisions are met (see, e.g., §11.01[A]-[B] and §11.03[A]), claims directed to the treatment of a specific disease will be allowable with the disclosure of at least *in vitro* data that reasonably correlates with the disease being treated. Clinical data supporting such treatment is not necessary.

[B] Mode of Administration

In an application claiming and disclosing a novel antibody, if all other statutory provisions are met (see, e.g., §11.01[A]-[B] and §11.03[A]), claims directed to a specific mode of administration will be allowable. The need for *in vitro* data will depend on how specific the mode of administration is claimed. Clinical data supporting such mode of administration is likely unnecessary.

[C] Dosage Regimens

In an application claiming and disclosing a novel antibody, if all other statutory provisions are met (see, e.g., §11.01[A]-[B] and §11.03[A]), claims directed to specific dosage regimens will be allowable. The need for *in vitro* data will depend on how specific the dosage regimen is claimed and clinical data supporting such dosage regimen is likely unnecessary.

However, practically, one does not uncover a patentable dosage regimen without clinical data. Unfortunately, at this point, the clinical trial will have already been completed, which arguably places the dosage regimen in the public domain (undermining the novelty of the dosage regimen). Therefore, if a dosage regimen is being investigated in a clinical trial, patent attorneys should file on this dosage regimen when the clinical trial is being designed and not after the trial has completed.

[D] Specific Patient Groups

In an application claiming and disclosing a novel antibody, if all other statutory provisions are met (see, e.g., §11.01[A]-[B] and §11.03[A]), claims directed to specific patient groups will be allowable.

However, practically, one does not uncover a patentable 'patient group' without clinical data. Unfortunately, at this point, the clinical trial will have already been completed, which arguably places the 'patient group' in the public domain (undermining novelty of the 'patient group'). Therefore, if a particular 'patient group' is being investigated in a clinical trial, patent attorneys should file on this 'patient group' when the clinical trial is being designed and not after the trial has completed.

[E] Specific Mode of Action

In an application claiming and disclosing a novel antibody, if all other statutory provisions are met (see, e.g., §11.01[A]-[B] and §11.03[A]), claims directed to a specific mode of action will be allowable with the disclosure of at least *in vitro* data that reasonably correlates with the claimed mode of action. Clinical data supporting such mode of action is not necessary.

[F] Combinations with Other Active Ingredients

In an application claiming and disclosing a novel antibody, if all other statutory provisions are met (see, e.g., §11.01[A]-[B] and §11.03[A]), claims directed to combination therapies will be allowable with the disclosure of at least *in vitro* data that reasonably correlates with the claimed combination therapy. Clinical data supporting such combination therapy is not necessary.

[G] Specific Diagnostic Applications

If all other statutory provisions are met (see, e.g., §11.01[A]-[B] and §11.03[A]), claims directed to specific diagnostic applications will be allowable with the disclosure of at least *in vitro* data that reasonably correlates with the claimed diagnostic application. Clinical data supporting such diagnostic application is not necessary.

However, claims to diagnostic methods in the US are often subject to rejection on grounds of lacking patentable subject-matter (see §11.01[A]). These rejections should be easier to overcome in view of the January 2019 Guidance Document provided by the USPTO stating that the practical application of a natural law is patent eligible subject-matter.

§11.05 ASSESSMENT OF INVENTIVENESS

[A] General Approach

In the United States, like most jurisdictions, a claim is patentable if it is both novel and non-obvious. The novelty provision of US patent law is found in 35 U.S.C. § 102 (a), which states that an applicant will be entitled to a patent 'unless the claimed invention was patented, described in a printed publication, or in public use, or on sale, or otherwise available to the public before the effective filing date of the claimed invention'. Anticipation requires that a single prior art reference disclose every limitation of the claimed invention, either expressly or inherently.[37] Note that anticipation requires a two-step analysis: first, the claims must be construed; second, the prior art must be compared to the claims, to determine whether every limitation of the claims is disclosed.[38]

Even if an invention is found novel, it still must be non-obvious. Under 35 U.S.C. § 103 a patent is unpatentable under the US law of obviousness, when 'the differences between the claimed invention and the prior art are such that the claimed invention as a whole would have been obvious before the effective filing date of the claimed invention to a person having ordinary skill in the art to which the claimed invention pertains'.[39] Factors to be considered when evaluating obviousness include:

- the scope and content of the prior art;
- the differences between the prior art and the claims at issue;
- the level of ordinary skill in the art; and
- objective indicia of non-obviousness, which includes commercial success, any long felt but unsolved need, and copying.

Unlike other jurisdictions, a motivation to combine references need not be explicit and an 'obvious to try' rationale may be sufficient to render a patent claim obvious. In *KSR Int'l Co. v. Teleflex, Inc.*,[40] the US Supreme Court specifically rejected the Federal Circuit's 'rigid' application of the teaching, suggestion, or motivation to combine (TSM) test, in favour of an 'expansive and flexible' approach it considers consistent with the 'broad inquiry' set forth in *Graham v. John Deere*. This decision has made it substantially easier for patents to be held obvious in the United States.

37. See *Eli Lilly and Company v. Los Angeles Biomedical Research Institute*, 849 F.3d 1073 (Fed. Cir. 2017).
38. See *In re Cruciferous Sprout Litigation*, 301 F.3d 13431347-49 (Fed. Cir. 2002).
39. See *Graham v. John Deere Co.*, 383 U.S.1 (1966).
40. 127 S. Ct. 1727 (2007).

[B] Particularities Regarding Claims to Antibodies

With the decision of *Amgen* (see, §11.03[A]) a new type of 112/103 squeeze is created – not as it relates to enablement, but for written description. In the United States, the publication of an antigen will render obvious all antibodies. However, the discovery of a new antigen will no longer provide written description to support claims directed to all antibodies that bind to that antigen. Thus, a gap of protection exists in the United States unlike other jurisdictions, such as Europe. Now, generic claims directed to all antibodies that bind to a particular antigen are unlikely to be granted.

§11.06 ENFORCEMENT AND SCOPE OF PROTECTION

[A] Biosimilars

The United States established a legal and regulatory pathway for an abbreviated approval of biosimilar drugs in the Biological Price Competition and Innovation Act (BPCIA),[41] which was enacted as part of the Affordable Care Act of 2009. The pathway includes a scheme for resolving patent issues prior to market entry, which was designed as a large molecule counterpart to the Orange Book patent linkage system established in the United States for small molecule drugs.

Under the BPCIA patent scheme, which has become known as the 'patent dance', within 20 days after an application for a biosimilar is filed with the FDA, the biosimilar applicant must provide counsel for the reference product sponsor with access to the biosimilar application, including manufacturing information.[42] The reference product owner then has 60 days to provide the biosimilar applicant with a list of its patents that would be infringed by the manufacture or sale of the biosimilar drug, and the identification of any patents which would be available for a licence. The biosimilar applicant then has 60 days to respond, for example by submitting a detailed explanation of why the referenced patents would not be infringed by the biosimilar drug, or alternatively why the patents are invalid or unenforceable. The reference product sponsor has 60 days to respond to the biosimilar applicant's submission. Thereafter, the statute calls for the parties to negotiate and decide on a list of patents to be litigated, and for the reference product sponsor to begin patent litigation.[43] This is the 'first phase' of patent litigation contemplated by the BPCIA.

In addition, the statute also states that the biosimilar applicant must notify the reference product sponsor 180 days before commercial marketing of the biosimilar.[44] The reference product sponsor may then seek an injunction based on any patent not included in the agreed patent list, such as a patent granted after the list created by the exchange of patent information. This is the 'second phase' of patent litigation contemplated by the BPCIA.

The enactment of the BPCIA led to the development of a biosimilar industry in the United States, and several companies have pursued biosimilar product approvals

41. Codified at 42 U.S.C. § 262(k)-(l).
42. See 42 U.S.C. § 262(l)(1)-(2).
43. 42 U.S.C. §262(l) (3)-(5).
44. See 35 U.S.C. § 242(l)(8)(A).

in recent years. At the time of this writing, biosimilars have been approved for at least nine reference drugs, including such antibody drugs as Remicade, Humira and Avastin.

Despite the extensive statutory provisions of the BPCIA, the legal pathway for approval of biosimilars has proven to be complex, with extensive patent litigation and patent validity challenges, and litigation concerning regulatory procedures.

One reason for the complexity is that the US courts have determined that a biosimilar applicant can effectively 'opt out' of the BPCIA patent dance. The US Supreme Court, in *Sandoz, Inc. v. Amgen, Inc.*,[45] ruled that a court may not issue an injunction requiring the biosimilar applicant to follow the statutory scheme by making its submission available to the innovator. As a result, biosimilar applicants can choose not to follow the 'first phase' litigation statutory scheme and may proceed without disclosing information about its product to counsel for the reference product owner. If the biosimilar applicants opt out, then the reference product owner can seek a declaratory judgment in the courts that the biosimilar will infringe its patents.[46]

Nevertheless, the Court found that the biosimilar applicant may provide notice of commercial marketing not later than 180 days before the date of commercial marketing, thus starting the 'second phase' BPCIA litigation. The Supreme Court in *Sandoz* did not decide or comment on whether the innovator could expect an injunction against the biosimilar applicant that fails to comply with the 180-day notice provision.

Other issues regarding BPCIA are still being decided. For example, whether a third party, who will benefit from the sale of a biosimilar product, can be sued for infringement even though they are not the biosimilar applicant is being considered by the courts.[47] Additionally, biosimilar parties, having their own IP estate are now asserting these estates against other third parties, including other biosimilar parties.[48]

In addition to the litigation, biosimilar applicants have challenged patents covering approved antibody products under the US PTO's Inter Partes Review (IPR) procedures. IPRs have proceeded at the same time as patent litigation.

Since the enactment of the BPCIA, there has been biosimilar litigation and accompanying IPR challenges.[49] For AVASTIN, at least ten IPRs have been filed, challenging five Genentech patents. First, Genentech sued the biosimilar applicant Amgen, trying to compel it to follow the BPCIA procedure. The suit was dismissed. Later, Amgen sued Genentech, the marketer of AVASTIN, on the grounds that more than 20 patents were invalid or not infringed by its biosimilar. The case is currently pending.

As described in §11.03[A], the *Amgen v. Sanofi* decision eliminated the ability to rely on the 'well characterized antigen theory' for patentability. This will likely result in even more patents covering commercial antibodies being invalidated.

---

45. 137 S.Ct. 1664 (2017).
46. See 42 U.S.C. § 262(l)(9).
47. See *Amgen Inc. and Amgen Mfg., Ltd. v. Adello Biologics, LLC, Amneal Pharmaceuticals, LLC and Amneal Pharmaceuticals, Inc.*, C.A. No. 2:18-cv-03347-CCC-MF (D.N.J.).
48. See, e.g., *Coherus v. Amgen*, No. 19-139 (D. Del. Jan. 24, 2019), in which Coherus asserted that Amgen's US manufacture of its EU approved biosimilar for adalimumab infringes three Coherus patents on stable aqueous pharmaceutical compositions of adalimumab.
49. In practice, some biosimilar applicants have complied with the BPCIA statutory scheme and exchange of information, while others have not.

In addition to patent protection, biologics products in the United States are given 12 years of data exclusivity from the date of first approval. No biosimilars may be filed for four years from approval of the innovator's reference product, and no biosimilar can be approved until 12 years from the date of approval.

In view of the complex litigation and IPR processes, biosimilar applicants in the US are advised to obtain excellent counsel early in the process, and to explore the various strategies for proceeding.

[B] Equivalence

In the US, subject-matter that does not literally infringe may still be found to infringe a claim under the doctrine of equivalents. One test for determining the doctrine of equivalents is known as the 'function/way/result test'. Under this approach, a product or method may be found to infringe a patent if the accused activity 'performed substantially the same function as the claimed invention, in substantially the same way, to achieve substantially the same result'.[50] However, the CAFC has noted that the function way result test may be more suitable for mechanical inventions, and an insubstantial differences test may be more appropriate for chemical and biological inventions.[51] According to this test, the relevant question is 'whether the accused product or process is substantially different from what is patented'.[52]

In any event, courts have cautioned on the scope of the doctrine of equivalents. According to the US Supreme Court, '[e]ach element contained in a patent claim is deemed material to defining the scope of the patented invention, and thus the doctrine of equivalents must be applied to individual elements of the claim, not to the invention as a whole'.[53] Further, the doctrine of equivalents is limited by the concept of prosecution history estoppel – that a patentee is not entitled to cover subject-matter under the doctrine of equivalents, if that subject-matter was surrendered during prosecution for reasons related to patentability.[54]

---

50. *Graver Tank & Mfg. Co. v. Linde Air Products Co.*, 339 U.S. 605, 608 (1950).
51. *See Mylan Institutional LLC v. Aurobindo Pharma Ltd.*, 857 F.3d 858, 866–867 (Fed. Cir. 2017).
52. *Id.* at 867 (citing *Graver Tank*, 339 U.S. at 608–609.
53. *Warner-Jenkinson Co., Inc. v. Hilton Davis Chemical Co.*, 520 U.S. 17 (1997).
54. *Id.*, at 30–34.

Chapter 12

Argentina

Martín Bensadon & Cristian D. Bittel

§12.01 ANTIBODIES AS PATENTABLE SUBJECT-MATTER

[A] Legal Framework

The patentability of biotechnological inventions is governed by the Argentine Constitution, the TRIPS agreement (approved by Law No. 24,425), the Patent Law, its Regulatory Executive Order and Guidelines of the Argentine Patent Office (AR PTO).

Observing the hierarchical order of legal rules, Article 17 of the Argentine Constitution provides as follows:

> '*Any* author or inventor is the exclusive owner of his/her work, invention or discovery during the term established by law' (emphasis added).

On the other hand, Article 27(1) of TRIPS provides as follows:

> 'patents shall be available *for any inventions*, whether products or processes, *in all fields of technology*, provided they are new, involve an inventive step and are capable of industrial application' (emphasis added).

A similar provision is included in section 1 of the Patent Law:

> 'Inventions, *in all types and branches of production* shall grant its authors the rights and duties specified in this law' (emphasis added).

Both the letter and the spirit of the Argentine Constitution, TRIPS and the Patent Law allow inferring the general principle in favour of the patentability of inventions.

Pursuant to the provisions of the Argentine Constitution and the TRIPS Agreement (a treaty with higher legal hierarchy than the laws, according to Article 75(22) of the Argentine Constitution), as long as the requirements of novelty, inventive step and industrial application are met, a patent must be granted in all fields of technology.

Upon establishing the general principle, in favour of patentability, TRIPS authorizes Member States to exclude certain inventions from the protection granted by the patent system.

In this sense, section 6(g) and section 7(b) of the Patent Law provide as follows, in full accordance with the provisions of the TRIPS Agreement:

> 'Section 6(g):
>
> For the purposes of this law, the following items shall not be deemed inventions
>
> ...
>
> (e) *Methods of diagnosis or surgical or therapeutic treatment*, applicable in the human body, and those related to animals;
>
> (g) *Any class of living material* and substances *pre-existing in nature*' (emphasis added).

On the other hand, section 7(b) provides:

> 'No patent shall be granted to ...b) the biological and genetic material existing in nature or any replication thereof, in the biological processes involved in animal, plant and human reproduction, including the genetic processes related to the material capable of self-replication in ordinary and free conditions, as it happens in nature.'

Furthermore, part C of chapter IV, paragraph 2.1.7 of the Guidelines of the AR PTO provides:

> 'Any living material and substances pre-existing in nature are not inventions pursuant to the Patent Law of Patents. Living material and substances pre-existing in nature, even if purified, isolated and/or characterized, are discoveries and, therefore, they are not patentable ...'

[B] General Amenability or Exclusion of Antibodies from Patentability

As a consequence of the legal rules governing patentability, it can be concluded that antibodies constitute patentable subject-matter as long as they are not preexisting in nature.

[C] Required Distinction from Naturally Occurring Antibodies

The AR PTO considers that polyclonal antibodies, which are produced by a living organism upon exposure to an antigen, are naturally occurring molecules. According to the Patent Office, polyclonal antibodies are not the result of human intervention, but a natural reaction of the immune system and therefore not patentable.

In this regard, it must be noted that the current Guidelines on patentability state that

> 'Living material and substances pre-existing in nature, even if purified, isolated and/or characterized, are discoveries and, therefore, they are not patentable ...'

Therefore, for Argentine standards, the mere isolation of an antibody from a polyclonal pool of antibodies does not render it patentable, as it is considered to be a mere discovery.

However, it is considered that other well defined antibodies such as monoclonal, humanized, chimeric or engineered antibodies are not naturally occurring. In these cases, obtaining the antibody is a consequence of human intervention. Only after human manipulation of cells, sequences, etc., can these species be obtained. Therefore, these antibodies are patentable according to Argentine standards.

§12.02 ACCEPTABLE CLAIM FEATURES FOR DEFINING ANTIBODIES

[A] Functional Features

As a rule, functional definitions are not acceptable in Argentine practice. This is not a limitation in certain fields of technology but a general principle that is applied to all patent applications.

However, it should be noted that Part A, Chapter III, paragraph 3.12 of the AR PTO's Guidelines provides that:

> 'd) In the case of claims of physical entities, these must define and characterize the physical structure of the object to be protected and the interrelation between its parts, avoiding as far as possible functional expressions or indicative of the purpose to be achieved'.

[1] Target/Antigen

An antibody must de defined structurally. Defining the desired target or antigen it recognizes is considered as the result to be obtained, and not the technical solution to the problem. This is not circumvented by defining the antigen structurally. This means that even if the antigen is defined by its full sequence or by the sequence of a particular epitope, the antibody itself would not be properly defined.

[2] Mode of Binding: Target Affinity, Binding Specificity, Epitope, Definitions via Reference Antibodies and Competitive Binding

An antibody must de defined structurally. Defining the desired target affinity, specificity or its capabilities to compete with other known antibodies for a target or epitope is considered as the result to be obtained, and not the technical solution to the problem. The Argentine Patent Office considers that if a certain antibody shows such desirable binding/competing properties, these are a consequence of the particular sequence of said antibody.

[3] Effect on Target

As mentioned above, an antibody must de defined structurally. Defining the desired effect on the target is considered as the result to be obtained, and not the technical solution to the problem.

[B] Structural Features

[1] *Molecular Topology: Antibody Types, Fragments and Antibody Constructs*

Antibodies must be defined by their relevant sequences.

[2] *Amino Acid Sequences*

[a] *Full-Length Sequences of Antibodies*

Antibodies must be defined structurally. Defining an antibody by the complete sequences of its two amino acid chains is one of the acceptable ways of doing so. It must be noted that according to the guidelines on Patentability of Biotechnological inventions issued by the Patent Office in October 2015, no identity percentage language is allowed in the claims. Thus, only the specific sequences that are disclosed in the specification can be claimed. This results in limited scope for such claims. For this reason, it is usually advisable to define antibodies by their complementarity determining regions (CDRs) or other relevant shorter sequences.

[b] *Sequences of Fragments, CDRs and Framework Regions*

In addition to its full sequence, an antibody can be defined by the sequence of its variable regions, which are responsible for specificity since the CDRs are included in these fragments.

It is also possible to define an antibody by specifying its six CDRs. It must be noted that all six CDRs must be part of the definition, as it is considered that only in the presence of all of them is the specificity disclosed in the specification fulfilled.

In some cases, for example if inventiveness depends on the presence a specific framework region, such sequences can be part of the definition, but always in addition to the recitation of the six CDRs.

[3] *Chemical Modifications, Conjugation and Glycosylation*

Whenever chemical modifications introduced to an antibody are relevant in its technical properties, they can be used as part of the definition in the claims, so as to distinguish them from the prior art. However, it must be noted that such definitions must be specific and supported by the specification, i.e. the particular substituent(s) and the particular amino acid(s) that are modified must be specified. It is usually difficult to define glycosylation patterns so as to comply with this requirement, but in the case a proper characterization is included in the specification, this can be included in the claims.

[C] Cell Line Deposits and Process of Production

Another acceptable definition for an antibody is the provision of the hybridoma producing it. In practice, this means depositing hybridoma cells with a depositary institution recognized by the Budapest Treaty before the filing date and declaring said deposit at the time of filing the application. In the case the depositor is different from the applicant of the Argentine application, an authorization issued by the depositor in favour of the applicant must be filed, since the deposit must be publicly available upon publication of the Argentine application.

Although uncommon, defining an antibody in this way would allow the applicant to claim a given antibody even if its sequence is unknown.

§12.03 BREADTH OF CLAIMS AND SUPPORT BY EXAMPLES

[A] Acceptable Breadth of Claims to Antibodies

As discussed previously, acceptable definitions for antibodies are: a deposit of the hybridoma producing it, the full amino acid sequence of both chains, the variable regions of both chains or its six CDRs. No identity language is allowed. Thus, the broadest possible scope is obtained by defining an antibody by its six CDRs.

[B] Required Experimental Support for Claims to Functionally Defined Antibodies

As discussed previously, functional definitions are not allowed. Therefore, there are no specific requirements in this regard.

[C] Required Experimental Support for Claims to Structurally Defined Antibodies

The specification must include complete information on the sequences defining the antibody and a full characterization thereof. It must be clear from the specification that the inventor did obtain the antibody and that the antibody shows the required specificity.

It must be noted that if the antibody is defined by its CDRs, the particular CDRs claimed must be disclosed in the specification, so it is not possible to define a CDR as 'a CDR present in SEQ ID NO: X' wherein SEQ ID NO: X corresponds to the variable region of the light chain. Similarly, it is not possible to define a CDR by reference to Chotia, Kabat or other standard numbering schemes. Each CDR must be identified in advance and its sequence must be disclosed specifically in the specification as filed. In line with the current guidelines of the Patent Office, it is not possible to include identity language in the definition of CDRs. If one or more substitutions are allowed for a given position, they must be supported by the examples and all these variants must be specifically disclosed.

§12.04 SPECIFIC MEDICAL APPLICATIONS AND OTHER FOLLOW-UP INVENTIONS

[A] Treatment of Specific Diseases

According to section 6(e) of the Argentine Patent Law, methods of therapeutic treatment applicable to the human body or animals are not held to be inventions.

Regarding uses, the Patent Office has ruled recently that use claims are not acceptable. The Patent Office bases this on the text of section 4 of the Patent Law, which states that

> 'Inventions of products or processes shall be patentable, provided they are new, involve an inventive activity, and are applicable in industry …'

As a consequence of these legal rules, it is not possible to obtain direct protection on the treatment of specific diseases with known antibodies.

[B] Mode of Administration

As a consequence of the non-patentability of methods of treatment and uses, claims directed to particular modes of administration are not accepted as these are considered to be directed to methods of treatment applicable to the human body. Any reference to a mode of administration in the wording of a claim results in an objection on these grounds.

[C] Dosage Regimens

Applying the same rationale as with different modes of administration, claims directed to dosage regimes are not accepted as these are considered to be directed to methods of treatment. In general, any reference to a dose in a claim will result in an objection based on the non-patentability of methods of treatment.

[D] Specific Patient Groups

The Patent Office considers that defining the use of an antibody based on the intended population in which it will be effective equates to claiming a method of treatment applicable to the human or animal body, and therefore is not patentable. Additionally, it has argued that identifying a particular subset of individuals on which a known antibody has a particular effect can be considered as a discovery. The Argentine Patent Office does not differentiate between a discovery and a mere discovery and considers them both non-patentable.

[E] Specific Mode of Action

As with Specific Patient Groups, the Patent Office considers that identifying the mode of action of a known antibody is a discovery, as said mode of action in inherent to the antibody once administered to a patient. Since there is no distinction between a discovery and a mere discovery, such claims are not allowed.

[F] Combinations with Other Active Ingredients

In the case of new combinations with other active ingredients, if such combination occurs in the human or animal body (i.e. both drugs are administered separately), this would be considered as method of treatment. However, if both drugs are part of the same composition, and said composition fulfils the inventiveness requirement, claims directed to the composition would be allowable.

[G] Specific Diagnostic Applications

Specific diagnostic methods are allowable, as long as they are not performed in the human or animal body. Typically, an in vitro diagnostic method is allowable. Such methods must exclude any reference to the patient and must exclude the step of obtaining a sample.

§12.05 ASSESSMENT OF INVENTIVENESS

[A] General Approach

Section 4 is one of the essential rules of the Patent Law since it specifies and defines the basic requirements for patentability: novelty, inventive step and industrial application. When referring to the requirement of inventive step, item (d) sets forth as follows:

> 'There will be inventive step when the creative process or the results thereof may not be evidently deduced from the state of the art by a person with average skill in the corresponding technical field.'

A patent is considered to involve an inventive step when the creative process or its results cannot be deduced from the state of the art in a way that is obvious for a person normally skilled in the relevant technical field (section 4(d) of the Patent Law).

In other words, this norm requires that, in order to demonstrate that a patent application does not meet the inventive step requirement, what the Examiner must prove is that the object to be protected or its results would have been obvious to an expert in the art based on the knowledge that could be considered public on the filing date of such application.

It should be noted that neither the Patent Law nor its regulatory decree require that the patent application demonstrate the advantages over the prior art. Indeed, section 12(b)(3) of the regulatory decree establishes that the Applicant must include, among other aspects, the following information:

> 'b) A technical description of the invention, headed by the title of the patent, coinciding with that in the application, which must contain: ...
>
> 3) a detailed and complete description of the invention, highlighting the advantages with respect to the known state of the art, understandable to a person skilled in the art ...'

As can be seen, what is required is that the advantages of the invention be emphasized in relation to the prior art, that is to say, that the merits of the object to be protected are mentioned and highlighted, as compared to what was known in the state of the art, but not that they are demonstrated.

It should be pointed out that the Examiner not only demands advantages be demonstrated when this is not a legal requirement, but also that the applicant performs useless comparative tests, which proves once again the unlawfulness of the appealed decisions.

[B] Particularities Regarding Claims to Antibodies

The general rules for assessing inventiveness are usually applied to antibodies with no major considerations.

When an antibody having the same specificity is already known in the art, the new antibody must show surprising or improved effect over that of the known antibody in order to comply with the inventiveness requirement.

§12.06 ENFORCEMENT AND SCOPE OF PROTECTION

[A] Biosimilars

There is no case law related to the enforcement of biosimilars and/or antibodies.

[B] Equivalence

The doctrine of equivalents has never been applied in an antibody claims case in Argentina. In fact, the doctrine of equivalents is not well developed in Argentina as no specific test has been brought before the courts to decide when such doctrine would be applicable to a specific case.

In any event, we believe that the Doctrine of Equivalents would be applicable to antibody claims in the same way as in other cases. In this respect, there have been lawsuits where the court found that there was no literal infringement, but that the patent was still held to be infringed because the defendant had introduced obvious variations of some elements of the invention in the product.

A decision rendered on 5 December 1967 by the Federal Court of Appeals (*Lavandera v. Arabia*) reads as follows:

> 'Notwithstanding the above-mentioned differences, it is to be noticed that the proven similarity of the mechanism in question with the patented mechanism has beyond any doubt a bearing on the result distinguishing the invention and which result is an objective fundamental factor, since the utilization of all the essential means employed in the combination or 'new application' of means protected by Patent No. 107.562 is involved (in the infringing mechanism). In addition, in this field the protection comprises within its reach the means positively claimed and also those which the doctrine calls technical 'equivalents' and which are to be regarded as such in relation to the function performed by these means within the patented combination since in the species such means

> perform the same function and contribute to accomplish the same result. Therefore, one arrives at the conclusion that the accused mechanism employs all the means protected by the patent.'

In the above case the patent apparently described and claimed as one of the parts of a given mechanism a hollow shaft with adjusting means housed therein while the infringer used for the same purpose a solid shaft and adjusting means arranged adjacent the shaft.

In another court ruling, dated 14 February 1967 of the Federal Court of Bahia Blanca in the case of *Nopco Chemical Company v. Monterrey, S.R.L.*, in reference to the nullity of defendant's patent it was decided that:

> 'the process of Argentine Patent No. 123,307 is neither original nor novel; that as a particular case all of its steps may be included within those of the general method protected by Patent No. 115,232. From this the conclusion is that although there are different devices for the process patented by the defendant for vitamin preparation, the differences thereof are not the essence of the problem. The verification effected ratifies the technical equivalency.
>
> ... said process in spite of not being absolutely identical to the one appearing in the specification of Patent No. 123,307, is nevertheless (identical) in substance to the one protected by plaintiff's patent ... it is therefore decided that Patent No. 123,307 is null in terms of invention ...'

With respect to the existence of infringement of plaintiff's patent the ruling stated as follows:

> 'the Supreme Court has already decided that the owner of a patented invention has the right to request compensation of damages against whoever employs the same invention to obtain the same effects proposed by the inventor, without said right being impaired by virtue of alterations of details employed in the application (of the invention), if the same is equal in its fundamental principles ...'

The Court apparently reasoned in the two cases above that there will be infringement when a different means performs within a particular combination of elements the same function and leads to the same final result or purpose of the patented invention. In short, while Argentine courts have not expressly adopted the Doctrine of Equivalents, it may be expected that in certain cases an Argentine court will establish the scope of protection afforded by a patent to cover not only the express wording of the claims of the patent, but also what the patent as a whole teaches or intends to teach as a new means for achieving a given result.

Chapter 13

Andean Community: Bolivia, Colombia, Ecuador, and Peru

Andres Rincon & Sergio Arboleda

§13.01 ANTIBODIES AS PATENTABLE SUBJECT-MATTER

[A] Legal Framework

The Andean Community provides member countries with a common Industrial Property Regime that excludes naturally occurring biological matter or processes from patentability. However, modified variations of subject-matter found in nature is patent-eligible.

Andean Decision 486 (2000), which is the equivalent to an EU Regulation and, at least in theory, does not require (or allow) any national implementation, and certainly nothing in an internal legislation of a member country can contradict it. That understanding certainly applies in practice for countries like Colombia and Peru but has not prevented Ecuador from issuing its own internal legislation (*Código de Ingenios*) providing specific rules for that country. The situation with Bolivia is different, to the extent it does not have internal legislation on the matter, but it does have a User's Manual for Invention Patents and Utility Model Patents issued by SENAPI (Bolivian Patent Office) as recently as 2017. Although these guidelines, at least in theory, allow modified variations of biotechnological subject-matter, in practice the SENAPI certainly does not grant patents over biological matter or processes claiming modified variations of natural phenomena.

Although in relation to biotechnology, the *Código de Ingenios* does not contradict the possibility to claim modified variations of subject-matter found in nature, it clearly adds that traditional knowledge is not patent-eligible subject-matter. In fact, our guess is that this slight modification of local IP Law extracted from Decision 486 comes as a result of more than 120 patent applications filed worldwide including genetic material from endemic species of Ecuador. Moreover, Article 268(2) of the *Código de*

Ingenios of 2016, consider that naturally occurring organisms or parts thereof such as isolated fragments, genes, proteins, genome or germplasm from any living being will not be considered an invention. Although biotechnological patent applications are, in theory, susceptible to be granted in Ecuador if they comply with the novelty, inventive step and industrial applicability requirements, it is a different story from an enforcement procedures standpoint. In fact, compulsory licences on medicines for the treatment of illnesses or diseases of the general population were installed in 2009 by Presidential Decree 118 (2009). Ever since, ten compulsory licences out of 32 patented products have been granted and thus patents reciting biotechnological products have been of open access. This paints a gloomy picture for biotechnology companies seeking to introduce themselves into the Ecuadorian market and seeking protection via the patent system. Besides, there is no record of new biotechnological inventions being granted in Ecuador since 2009, meaning that in practice, having antibody patents in that country is unfortunately not an option right now.

[B] General Amenability or Exclusion of Antibodies from Patentability

Antibodies are patent-eligible subject-matter yet they must be defined by their essential structural features, i.e., their amino acid sequence in one or various forms: light and heavy complementarity determining regions (CDRs) and/or light and heavy variable chains and/or light and heavy full chain sequences.

Variations of naturally occurring antibodies are also patentable in Colombia as long as their structure is not exactly the same as that found in nature. Furthermore, claims reciting antibodies may also recite results to be achieved such as the epitope or the antigen which it binds to, but said binding site should also be structurally defined.

[C] Required Distinction from Naturally Occurring Antibodies

Antibodies must be defined by their essential structural features. In fact, the Colombian and Peruvian Patent Offices allow for antibodies to be defined, at least, by their six CDRs or combinations of multiple CDRs as long as they are duly supported in the specification. Other more restrictive embodiments such as variable chains are also allowed and advisable in depending claims; as well as full light and heavy chains defined by their specific SEQ ID NOs. The first claim drafting option, i.e., CDRs, must further comply with unity of invention requirements. Antibodies are defined in terms of six CDR options: three from the heavy chain and three from the light chain. Each class of CDRs 1, 2 and 3 (either light or heavy) may have multiple structures but these should maintain a close structural relationship, i.e., having a high degree of homology.

Andean IP Law excludes naturally occurring biological matter or processes from patentability. However, modified variations of subject-matter found in nature is patent-eligible.

§13.02 ACCEPTABLE CLAIM FEATURES FOR DEFINING ANTIBODIES

[A] Functional Features

[1] Target/Antigen

Functional features in antibody claims are accepted by Colombia and Peru as long as the antibody is defined in terms of its essential structural features. That is, if the antibody is defined in any acceptable format (CDRs, variable chains or full chains), functional language is accepted. In fact, such drafting clarifies the object of the invention since it specifies its target. Moreover, antibody claims may also recite results achieved such as K_D values, biological effects and the like.

[2] Mode of Binding: Target Affinity, Binding Specificity, Epitope, Definitions via Reference Antibodies and Competitive Binding

Antibodies, as mentioned above, may be further defined by their function or activity. In fact, the Colombian and Peruvian Patent Offices allow for antibodies to be defined by their target, their affinity, binding specificity, epitope (as long as it is structurally defined) and all other biological effects provided by the antibodies themselves. However, the greater part of the antibody's definition is by its structural features which, in the broadest of terms, is by its six CDRs.

[3] Effect on Target

The effect on the target, such as its binding affinity, competitiveness and the like are accepted as long as the claimed antibodies are defined by their structural features such as their CDRs, light and heavy variable domain chains or light and heavy full chains; each defined by its amino acid sequence.

[B] Structural Features

[1] Molecular Topology: Antibody Types, Fragments and Antibody Constructs

Antibodies must be defined in terms of their essential structural features and these may be of any kind and for any type of application, be it for human or animal use. Thus, antibodies such as are monoclonal, chimeric or humanized, and derivatives thereof such as constructs are acceptable under local practice in Colombia and Peru, with the proviso that they do not correspond to naturally occurring biological matter comply with unity of invention standards, are defined by their structural features, and are novel and inventive.

[2] *Amino Acid Sequences*

[a] *Full-Length Sequences of Antibodies*

Antibodies are patentable subject-matter in light of Article 14 of Andean Decision 486 (2000) since they correspond to products. However, and as mentioned above, these may not correspond to naturally occurring antibodies. One of the most restrictive forms of claiming antibodies in Colombia and Peru is by their full-length sequences. The latter is because it would correspond to a picture claim of the developed antibody. When it comes to various antibodies, these must hold a certain high structural correlation (i.e., identity or homology) such that they are encompassed within the same inventive concept and are not rejected on the grounds of unity of invention. Nonetheless, antibody picture claims are accepted under local practice, yet any slight variation therefrom would escape any enforcement procedures and thus such embodiments are suggested to be drafted in dependent claims from broader claims.

In all cases, at least in theory, homology, identity and similarity language is not accepted when it comes to nucleotide or amino acid sequences since it can be understood as unclear or verbose.[1] Nonetheless, when provided with evidence showing that the aforementioned properties are, in fact, supported by bioinformatics software and that the claimed sequences hold certain degrees of homology, identity and/or similarity, the examiner may accept such claims. Notwithstanding the exceptions, common practice usually indicates that such language should be avoided.

[b] *Sequences of Fragments, CDRs and Framework Regions*

CDRs are, as is widely known in the field, the six fragments responsible for the antigen-binding activity of an antibody. As such, they correspond to the most important part of the antibody; while all other remaining structures are scaffolds that allow for the CDRs to correctly interact with the antigen which it binds to. As such, the most important fragment that must be structurally defined by its amino acid sequences is the six CDRs of the claimed antibody. Other fragments and features such as hinge regions, disulfide bonds, framework region and constant regions may also be recited in antibody claims. The most straightforward option to draft and prosecute claims in Colombia and Peru is initially by its six CDRs (and slight variations of each CDR), then light and heavy variable domain chains, and finally by its full-length chains; all of the aforementioned structurally defined by its amino acid SEQ ID NO.

[3] *Chemical Modifications, Conjugation and Glycosylation*

Antibody derivatives such as glycosylated, pyruvylated, fucosylated, PEG-ylated and the like, are also acceptable as long as they are properly drafted in terms of their CDRs,

---

1. User's Manual Invention Patents and Utility Model Patents, SENAPI (Bolivian Patent Office), 2017; Guidelines for Patent and Utility Model Examination, SIC (Colombian Patent Office), 2014; Manual for the Training of Patent Examiners in Peru, INDECOPI (Peruvian Patent Office), 2012.

light and heavy variable chains or full light and heavy chains, are duly supported in the specification and comply with patentability requirements.

[C] Cell Line Deposits and Process of Production

Other embodiments acceptable are nucleotide sequences, vectors such as plasmids and modified cell lines that allow the production of the claimed antibodies. Moreover, composition claims comprising any of the aforementioned embodiments are also accepted by the Colombian and Peruvian Patent Offices. These must not necessarily be defined in terms of their specific sequences or ingredients and ratios thereof since they correspond to preferred embodiments of the inventive concept developed to which the applicant is also entitled. Specific cell line deposits must be mentioned such as the ATCC number for specific cell lines and, in any case, should allow the person having ordinary skill in the art to fully replicate the object of the invention.

Lastly, biological processes *per se* correspond to non-patent eligible subject-matter according to Article 15 of Andean Decision 486 (2000). However, processes for the production of antibodies wherein biological materials are used among other human-involved specific procedures are eligible for patenting. These processes must also comply with the patentability requirements of novelty, inventive step, and industrial applicability; as well as a description of how said process is executed in terms that any person having ordinary skill in the art may replicate.

§13.03 BREADTH OF CLAIMS AND SUPPORT BY EXAMPLES

[A] Acceptable Breadth of Claims to Antibodies

An antibody cannot be defined only in terms of the antigen to which it binds. The claim cannot be defined solely by functional features or results achieved. As mentioned above, claims reciting antibodies should be defined, in the broadest of cases, in terms of their six CDRs; a preferred embodiment could recite the full light and heavy variable domain chains and an even more preferred embodiment may recite the full light and heavy chains. These must be fully supported in the specification and must be included within the sequence listing.

[B] Required Experimental Support for Claims to Functionally Defined Antibodies

Working examples of such antibodies must, at least, have been developed and described in the specification. Additional information such as binding affinity, stability, freeze-thaw and other routine experimental data are very useful during prosecution, especially when arguing the inventiveness of the application. It is worth noting that the inventiveness of an application is defined as the non-obviousness of the structural features of the antibody, the biological effect or enhanced properties when compared to that disclosed in the prior art is not necessary, yet highly advisable. The latter because although the structure must not be obvious in light of the teachings of the prior art, it must show a technical effect which is provided by experimental data and analysis, which is generally in the form of working examples.

[C] Required Experimental Support for Claims to Structurally Defined Antibodies

Article 30 of Andean Decision 486 states that the claims shall be clear and concise and entirely supported by the specification. If no structural definition of the antibody is provided in the specification, the claim 'any antibody which binds to antigen X' would be rejected due to lack of support. The Peruvian Patent Office has a very strict position regarding the support requirement.

§13.04 SPECIFIC MEDICAL APPLICATIONS AND OTHER FOLLOW-UP INVENTIONS

[A] Treatment of Specific Diseases

Andean Decision 486 states in Article 20(d) that diagnostic, therapeutic, and surgical methods for human or animal treatment are not patentable. Moreover, use claims in all forms are also considered as unpatentable subject-matter. Nonetheless, section 2.2 of the Colombian Patent Examination Guidelines states that amendments may be made to applications directed to methods of treatment wherein said applications may be converted into composition claims with the proviso that they are fully defined in terms of their ingredients and ratios.

[B] Mode of Administration

Given the depositions of Article 20 from Decision 486, modes of administration when related to a method of treatment are not patent-eligible subject-matter. Nonetheless, when it comes to administration embodiments for product claims such as pharmaceutical compositions, these must be defined in terms of their structural features. That is, a composition comprising the antibody wherein the composition is in the form of an injectable, oral or rectal formulation, or similar.

[C] Dosage Regimens

Claim drafting in terms of dosages is not allowed. The Colombian and Peruvian Patent Offices struggle with inventions defined in terms of dosages since, by definition, dosages relate to the frequency of administration of a pharmaceutical product and thus it is considered as unpatentable subject-matter.

[D] Specific Patient Groups

Given that method of treatment claims are not patentable subject-matter, any language within the claim directed to specific patient groups is objected to, since Andean IP Law states that methods of treatment or diagnostics are excluded from patentability.

[E] Specific Mode of Action

Specific modes of action may be protected indirectly. Namely, antibody claims may recite results to be achieved (such as specific modes of action) by means of binding language, inhibitory features and the like, with the proviso that said antibody is defined by its essential structural features.

[F] Combinations with Other Active Ingredients

Combination therapy is allowed. However, the standards related to the patentability for combination therapy are quite strict. Namely, combination therapy must involve a surprising and unexpected technical effect. In fact, one of the key and most frequently required features that combination therapy must show in order to prove non-obviousness is synergy.

[G] Specific Diagnostic Applications

Patent applications directed to a medical or veterinarian diagnosis are not allowed in light of Article 20(d), which states that, as mentioned above, diagnostic, therapeutic, and surgical methods for human or animal treatment are not patentable.

§13.05 ASSESSMENT OF INVENTIVENESS

[A] General Approach

Inventiveness, as in any other field of technology in the Andean Community, is determined as a solution to an existing technical problem through a set of claims that cannot be obviously derived from the prior art. The closest prior art is a document that lies in the same technical field that tries to solve the same or a similar problem. It is usually the one that has more characteristics in common with the invention or presents slight structural variations yet having the same function or purpose.

[B] Particularities Regarding Claims to Antibodies

Determining the difference between the invention and the prior art

Compare the essential technical characteristics of the invention with those of the closest prior art in the form of a matrix showing how each feature is disclosed or how the differential feature is absent from the prior art.

Defining the technical effect associated to the differential element

The analysis must focus on the differences between the claimed invention and the prior art, and how said structural differences are related with the technical effect.

Deducing the objective technical problem

The technical problem should be drafted as 'How to modify or amend the closest prior art in order to obtain a desired effect', whereby the desired effect is that caused by the difference identified earlier. The definition of the technical problem is based on the facts of the prior art and on the results achieved by the invention.

The expression 'technical problem' should be interpreted broadly; as it does not imply that the solution constitutes a technical improvement in relation to the prior art; since it may be that the problem consists of a replacement solution in a known device or procedure that produces identical or similar effects.

Evaluating whether the claimed invention, starting from the closest prior art and the technical problem, would have been obvious for the person having ordinary skill in the art

This stage consists in answering the question of whether there is a second document that contains a teaching that indicates or guides the person having ordinary skill in the art (not only that it could indicate, but does indicate that), when faced with the technical problem, to modify or adapt the closest prior art in such fashion that he/she would evidently arrive at the claimed invention.

If the answer is affirmative, the invention is considered obvious, and therefore it is concluded that it has no inventive step. But if the answer is negative, the invention is not obvious, and it is considered to have an inventive step.

The Colombian Patent Examination Guidelines further emphasize in section 5.3.2 that inventions in the biotechnological field are inventive when the claimed subject-matter has a surprising technical effect (e.g., a recombinant protein), when compared to that of the naturally occurring or already known modified version thereof.

§13.06 ENFORCEMENT AND SCOPE OF PROTECTION

Antibody patents are fully enforceable in the Andean Community whenever there is a patent granted in that field. However, due to the limited scope of protection restricted to essential structural features, there is no case law available for enforcement analysis in practice, nor cases where the validity of antibody patenting has been maintained in contentious proceedings in Colombia, Ecuador, Peru or Bolivia.

[A] Biosimilars

Colombia and Peru have very recent regulations for marketing authorizations (MA) for products of biological origin. Ecuador and Bolivia do not have regulations in this regard, nor patents covering products or processes for biotechnological products, especially not for antibodies.

In Colombia, Decree 1782 (2014), enforceable since 2016, establishes the pathway for MA for biologic and biosimilars in Colombia basically through three different pathways: 1. Complete pathway, for innovative products wherein all clinical studies showing safety and efficacy should be provided; 2. Comparative pathway, for biosimilar products wherein heath to heath studies in comparison with the innovator should be provided; and 3. Abbreviated pathway, wherein it is not mandatory to provide clinical studies and the dossier requesting the MA could include publicly available information either from the innovator or from any other highly similar active ingredient.

In practice, monoclonal antibodies do obtain MA in Colombia after safety and efficacy is proven and up to this moment no biosimilars of monoclonal antibodies have been approved so far through the third 'abbreviated' pathway. However, there are approvals for monoclonal antibodies following the second 'comparative' pathway. None of the innovative products from which biosimilars were obtained was covered by a granted patent.

Peru also issued Law 29459 (2016) with MA regulations for biosimilars, which is more strict, and own clinical studies are required in order to demonstrate safety and efficacy. Before this regulation was in place, biosimilars attempting to enter the Peruvian market were stopped through preliminary injunctions from Peruvian regulatory authorities, but this was done through unfair competition and not through industrial property actions.

Antibody patenting is relatively a new trend in the Andean Community countries and the products including patent protected technologies have not yet reached the market, meaning there are no cases of patent enforcement against biosimilar antibodies. Those cases are expected to come in the near future.

[B] Equivalence

Since there are no products or processes for antibodies covered by a granted patent in the Andean Community, there is no case law available showing direct infringement or infringement by equivalence. However, nothing in the Andean legislation voids the possibility of having infringement by equivalence rulings issued by the judiciary in the future.

Chapter 14

Brazil

Maria Carmen de Souza Brito & Pedro Henrique Borges de Figueiredo

§14.01 ANTIBODIES AS PATENTABLE SUBJECT-MATTER

[A] Legal Framework

The legal framework applicable to the patentability of antibodies in Brazil consists of the Brazilian Industrial Property Law (the IP Law) and the patent examination Guidelines provided by Instituto Nacional da Propriedade Industrial (INPI, the Brazilian Patent and Trademark Office).

INPI's Guidelines consist of several Resolutions, which, despite some small overlap, are directed to specific aspects of the examination of patent applications and technical fields.

The following Resolutions are relevant to the examination of antibody related inventions:

Resolution No. 124/2013 – General Examination Guidelines (Block I): Applicable to all technical fields, contains provisions regarding sufficient disclosure, support by the specification, clarity and unity of invention.

Resolution No. 169/2016 – General Examination Guidelines (Block II): Applicable to all technical fields, contains provisions regarding novelty and inventive step.

Resolution No. 144/2015 – Examination Guidelines for Patent Applications in the Field of Biotechnology: Contains provisions regarding eligibility exemptions, sufficient disclosure, support by the specification, and clarity in the field of biotechnology.

Resolution No. 208/2017 – Examination Guidelines for Patent Applications in the Field of Chemistry: Contains provisions regarding eligibility exemptions, sufficient disclosure, support by the specification and clarity in the field of chemistry and pharmaceutical technology.

[B] General Amenability or Exclusion of Antibodies from Patentability

Generally, any type of invention meeting the patentability requirements of novelty, inventive step and industrial applicability are deemed amenable to patentability under Article 8 of the IP Law:

> 'Article 8 – The invention that meets the requirements of novelty, inventive step and industrial applicability is patentable.'

Articles 10 and 18 of the Brazilian IP Law provide the relevant eligibility exemptions to antibody related inventions:

> 'Article 10 – The following are not considered to be inventions or utility models
>
> ...VIII operating or surgical techniques and therapeutic or diagnostic methods, for use on the human or animal body;
>
> IX Natural living beings, in whole or in part, and biological material, including the genome or germplasm of any natural living being, when found in nature or isolated therefrom, and natural biological processes'

> 'Article 18 – The following are not patentable:
>
> ...(III) – living beings, in whole or in part, except transgenic microorganisms meeting the three patentability requirements – novelty, inventive step and industrial application – provided for in article 8 and which are not mere discoveries;
>
> Sole Paragraph – For the purposes of this law, transgenic microorganisms are organisms, except the whole or part of plants or animals, that exhibit, due to direct human intervention in their genetic composition, a characteristic that cannot normally be attained by the species under natural conditions.'

Product claims

Biological molecules, including antibodies, are deemed to be 'biological materials' according to item 4.1 of Resolution No. 144. Therefore, the exemption from patent eligibility of Article 10(IX) of the Brazilian IP Law is deemed to be applicable to naturally occurring antibodies according to Resolution No. 144.

However, according to item 4.2.1 of Resolution No. 144, the examiner is required to provide 'unequivocally clear' evidence that the claimed product occurs in nature, which may be a post-filing document.

Specifically regarding antibodies, polyclonal antibodies are deemed natural biological products (non-patentable under Article 10(IX)), whereas monoclonal antibodies are not deemed natural biological products according to item 6.4.6 of Resolution No. 144. Likewise, chimeric and humanized antibodies are eligible to protection in view of item 6.4.6.3 of Resolution No. 144.

Method/use claims

Since the provisions of Article 10(VIII) are limited to methods applied to the human or animal body, said provisions are not deemed to be applicable to diagnostic methods carried out *in vitro* or on a sample (item 1.41 of Resolution No. 169).

A method is deemed to be therapeutic if said method involves 'curing and/or preventing a disease or malfunction of the human body or an animal, or the relief from symptoms of pain, suffering and discomfort, with a view to re-establish or maintain the normal health functions' (items 1.27 and 1.28 of Resolution No. 169).

Although the provisions of Article 10(VIII) are not deemed to apply to methods of treatment which do not have a direct connection between the treatment and a therapeutic effect (items 1.30 and 1.31 of Resolution No. 169), if the non-therapeutic effect is indissociably linked to a therapeutic effect, or even if it is only a secondary consequence of therapy, the provisions of Article 10(VIII) are deemed to be applicable (item 1.34 of Resolution No. 169).

[C] Required Distinction from Naturally Occurring Antibodies

Product claims

According to item 4.2.1.1 of Resolution No. 144, only a product's composition/ structural features would be relevant for the assessment of the exemptions of Article 10(IX) of the IP Law. Therefore, qualifiers such as 'isolated', 'chimeric', 'humanized' or 'monoclonal' *per se* are not useful for overcoming the exemption of Article 10(IX) as even a product produced by synthetic means but containing a composition/ structure identical to that of natural origin is not deemed patentable under Article 10(IX) of the IP Law. This is also true for fragments of biological molecules in view of the provisions of item 6.4.3 the Resolution No. 144.

In view of the above, in order to be deemed patentable under the current Guidelines, a claim directed to an antibody *per se* must define a hybridoma or structural features which are not present in naturally occurring antibodies.

Although claims directed to naturally occurring products *per se* are not deemed acceptable, claims directed to a composition comprising a naturally occurring product in combination with an artificial product are deemed allowable according to item 4.2.1.1.1 of Resolution No. 144.

Method/use claims

The language deemed allowable for either first or second medical use claims is the Swiss-type language (items 3.75 and 3.76 of Resolution No. 124 and item 1.29 of Resolution No. 169). Therefore, Swiss-type claims are useful not only for obtaining protection for second medical use inventions, but also to first medical use inventions involving naturally occurring biological products.

The intended use is not deemed to confer patentability on an otherwise non-patentable product (item 3.74 of Resolution No. 124). Therefore, use-restricted product claims (EPC 2000, 'product for use' claims) are not useful for overcoming objections under Article 10(VIII) and (IX).

Future developments

On 6 February 2019 INPI published proposed amendments to Resolution No. 144 for public debate. Interested parties could submit comments and proposals up to 6 April 2019.

The amendments proposed by INPI to Resolution No. 144, indicate that polyclonal antibodies may not always be deemed natural since the antibody may not exist without significant human intervention, such as the use of adjuvants in order to activate specific cells for immune response. On the other hand, the proposed amendments also indicate that polyclonal antibodies would lack sufficient disclosure, clarity and support since, regardless of how specifically the process for obtaining such antibodies is defined in the application, the final product would always be different each time such process is carried out. The proposed amendments also explicitly state that claims directed to the process of producing polyclonal antibodies would be patentable as long as said claims exclude natural biological methods and therapeutic methods.

A further amendment proposed by INPI to Resolution No. 144 regarding antibodies intends to clarify that 'fully human' antibodies are not necessarily naturally occurring, as said nomenclature is also used for recombinant antibodies and are not deemed natural unless their sequence has been shown to occur in nature.

Although INPI's above intended amendments are known, it is hard to predict at this time whether such amendments or any other amendments proposed by interested parties will be included in the final version.

§14.02 ACCEPTABLE CLAIM FEATURES FOR DEFINING ANTIBODIES

[A] Functional Features

[1] Target/Antigen

INPI has adopted the position that only the embodiments shown to achieve the technical effect of the invention by experimental results would be sufficiently disclosed and supported by the specification so as to comply with the provisions of Articles 24[1] and 25[2] of the Brazilian IP Law.

This position is usually based on item 2.15 of Resolution No. 124 which defines that in order to provide sufficient disclosure, the application should contain enough

1. Article 24 – The specification must describe the subject matter clearly and sufficiently so as to enable a person skilled in the art to carry it out and to indicate, when applicable, the best mode of execution.
   Sole Paragraph – In the case of biological material essential for the practical execution of the subject matter of the application, which cannot be described in the form of this article and which is not accessible to the public, the specification will be supplemented by a deposit of the material in an institution authorised by INPI or indicated in an international agreement.
2. Article 25 – The claims must be based on the specification, characterising the particularities of the application and defining clearly and precisely the subject matter to be protected.

technical information to enable a person skilled in the art to put the invention into practice, just as it is claimed, without undue experimentation (which is deemed to be any additional experimentation).

Therefore, claims which define antibodies only in terms of function, such as target/antigen, regardless of the precision of the definition of the antigen, epitope or effect on target, are objected as lacking sufficient disclosure, clarity and support by the specification based on the allegation that the skilled technician would have to carry out undue experimentation to verify which of the embodiments covered by the broad claims would in fact achieve the technical effect of the invention.

This does not mean that functional definitions are not acceptable. In addition to structural definitions, functional definitions do not impart lack of clarity according to item 3.13 of Resolution No. 124 and item 6.1 of Resolution No. 208. However, such definitions are not usually given any weight with regard to patentability.

[2] Mode of Binding: Target Affinity, Binding Specificity, Epitope, Definitions via Reference Antibodies and Competitive Binding

INPI adopts the same position regarding definitions based on target/antigen, as discussed in §14.02[A][1], to definitions based on mode of binding.

[3] Effect on Target

INPI adopts the same position regarding definitions based on target/antigen, as discussed in §14.02[A][1], to definitions based on effect on target.

[B] Structural Features

[1] Molecular Topology: Antibody Types, Fragments and Antibody Constructs

In view of INPI's position regarding sufficient disclosure, clarity and support by the specification, antibodies are only deemed to be sufficiently disclosed and clearly defined if defined by at least all the six CDR sequences or their deposited hybridoma (Examples 35 and 37 of Resolution No. 144).

The standard for antibody fragments is essentially the same. Claims which recite any fragments of a given antibody, regardless of functional definitions, are not deemed to be sufficiently disclosed, clearly defined or supported by the specification. However, antibody fragments defined by comprising the structural features shown to achieve the technical effect of the invention (CDR set or VL and VH regions) are deemed allowable according to item 6.4.6.4 of Resolution No. 144.

It is possible however to submit post-filing experimental data as evidence that the technical effect of the invention is in fact achieved by the claimed embodiments according to item 9.1.3 of Resolution No. 208. Obviously, the effect must be qualitatively defined in the application as filed.

INPI's Guidelines only specifically address inventions corresponding to antibodies with new antigen-binding regions. In the absence of clear guidelines for other types of innovations, such as fusion with other proteins, modifications in the constant regions, chemical modifications, it is at the examiner's discretion whether to rely on either the general provisions for proteins of item 6.4.1 of Resolution No. 144 or the specific provisions for antibodies and evaluate which structural features would be required in order to comply with said requirements.

[2] Amino Acid Sequences

[a] Full-Length Sequences of Antibodies

As mentioned above, antibodies are only deemed to be sufficiently disclosed and clearly defined if defined by at least all the six CDR sequences or their deposited hybridoma (Examples 35 and 37 of Resolution No. 144). There is no bar to further defining full-length sequences of antibodies.

[b] Sequences of Fragments, CDRs and Framework Regions

As mentioned above, the definition of all the six CDR sequences is the broadest definition for antibodies or antibody fragments currently deemed acceptable according to INPI's Guidelines. There is no bar to further defining framework regions.

[3] Chemical Modifications, Conjugation and Glycosylation

There are no specific rules regarding chemical modifications, conjugation and glycosylation. The abovementioned general provisions regarding antibodies and antibody fragments still apply to chemically modified, conjugated and glycosylated antibodies.

[C] Cell Line Deposits and Process of Production

Since the provisions of Article 18(III) of the Brazilian IP Law are not limited to naturally occurring living beings, transgenic plants and animals are also not deemed patentable.

According to item 4.1 of Resolution No. 144, 'part of living beings' would refer to any portion of living beings, such as organs, tissues and cells. Therefore, general claims to host cells are not deemed allowable due to encompassing plant and animal cells.

Although hybridomas are deemed a 'transgenic microorganism' under item 6.4.6.2 of Resolution No. 144, there are no such provisions for any other type of modified plant/animal cells, which are not deemed patentable under Article 18(III).

The process of production of antibodies by culturing host cells and isolating the antibodies are generally patentable.

Therefore, although product claims directed to mammalian host cells are not deemed allowable, methods of producing antibodies by culturing mammalian host cells are deemed allowable.

The deposit of biological material 'essential for the practical execution of the subject matter of the application', which cannot be clearly and sufficiently defined so as to enable a person skilled in the art to carry it out and which '*is not accessible to the public*' is explicitly required by the sole paragraph of article 24 of the Brazilian IP Law.

Item 2.2.1.2 of Resolution No. 144 exemplifies microorganisms selected from random mutagenesis and which genetic alterations which result in a differential effect are not defined in the application as a case wherein deposit would be required.

On the other hand said item also provides that 'deposit of the material does not necessarily apply to all and every biological material involved in a certain invention, since, for example, polynucleotides and polypeptides shall be described by way of their nucleotide and amino acid sequences' and that 'deposit of the biological material is not necessary when the inventive characteristic can be achieved by various strains or species of microorganisms available using the methodology described in the application'.

Item 2.2.1.2 of Resolution No. 144 provides that the deposit must be performed prior to the filing date of the patent application or to or by the date of the claimed priority, if applicable, and also requires that a simple copy of the deposit receipt is submitted.

Article 24 of the Brazilian IP Law provides that the deposit must be performed 'in an institution authorised by INPI or indicated in an international agreement'. Although Brazil is not a Budapest Treaty assignee, item 2.2.1 of Resolution No. 144 acknowledges Budapest Treaty deposits as acceptable to comply with the provisions of the sole paragraph of Article 24.

§14.03 BREADTH OF CLAIMS AND SUPPORT BY EXAMPLES

[A] Acceptable Breadth of Claims to Antibodies

As previously mentioned, the breadth of antibody claims is narrow due to the requirement to specify at least all the six CDR sequences or deposited hybridoma.

Since INPI has adopted the position that only the embodiments shown to achieve the technical effect of the invention by experimental results would be sufficiently disclosed and supported by the specification, patent applications without any experimental results usually face objections regarding lack of sufficient disclosure and support.

It is possible to submit post-filing experimental data as evidence that the technical effect of the invention is in fact achieved by the claimed embodiments under item 9.1.3[3] of Resolution No. 208. Obviously however, the effect must be qualitatively defined in the application as filed.

Although there is no specific provision regarding the type of experimental support required, it is usually required that the experimental results show that the claimed antibodies achieve the inventive effect, which can vary for each application.

3. 9.1.3 According to paragraph 3.89 of the Guidelines for the Examination of Patent Applications, Block I, the burden of demonstrating the claims are supported by the specification is on the applicant and, for that purpose, additional proof is accepted in the course of the technical examination, provided that it is exclusively intended to supplement the information already provided in the application as originally filed.

Since satisfying the abovementioned sufficient disclosure and clarity requirements with regard to the definition of the antibody itself can significantly restrict the scope of the claims, an alternative to try to achieve a more effective scope for inventions directed to post-translational modifications is by method of production claims. In this sense, it is relevant to bear in mind that a patent confers on its owner the right to prevent third parties from manufacturing, using, offering for sale, selling or importing for such purposes without his consent product directly obtained by a patented process according to Article 42(II) of the Brazilian IP Law.

A further option is to pursue 'product-by-process' claims. However, such claims also face a significantly high bar. For instance, a product is not considered novel simply because it is produced by means of a novel process. Therefore, the product must contain novel technical features. Furthermore, such claims are only deemed acceptable if the product *per se* cannot be adequately defined by other features besides the manufacture process.

INPI's current Resolutions also have a *sui generis* position regarding the definition of polynucleotides. The definition of polynucleotides by encoding amino acid sequences is not deemed acceptable according to item 6.1 of Resolution No. 144. Therefore, it is usually necessary to restrict polynucleotide/vector claims to specific nucleotide sequences.

It is also questionable whether it would be acceptable to define polynucleotide claims by a specific nucleotide sequence SEQ ID NO 'or degenerated nucleotide sequences thereof encoding the same amino acid sequences' under the provisions of item 6.1 b) of Resolution No. 144 as some examiners have adopted the position that literal disclosure and support by experimental results of each of such sequences would be required in order to render such language acceptable.

[B] Required Experimental Support for Claims to Functionally Defined Antibodies

There are no specific provisions in INPI's Guidelines regarding experimental support for claims to functionally defined antibodies since the definition solely by functional features is not deemed acceptable.

[C] Required Experimental Support for Claims to Structurally Defined Antibodies

There are no specific provisions in INPI's Guidelines regarding qualitative or quantitative experimental support for structurally defined antibodies. However, item 2.13 of Resolution No. 124 requires that '[t]he specification shall contain sufficient conditions that will guarantee reduction of the invention to practice'. Such provision is usually interpreted to mean that the application should contain experimental results which support the technical effect of the invention. Therefore, examiners usually require that the application contains experimental results showing that the surprising technical effect of the invention can be achieved by the claimed antibody. As also mentioned above, it is possible to submit post-filing experimental data as evidence that the technical effect of the invention is in fact achieved by the claimed embodiments under item 9.1.3 of Resolution No. 208. Obviously however, the effect must be qualitatively defined in the application as filed.

§14.04 SPECIFIC MEDICAL APPLICATIONS AND OTHER FOLLOW-UP INVENTIONS

[A] Treatment of Specific Diseases

As previously mentioned, the only language deemed allowable for either first or second medical use claims is the Swiss-type language (items 3.75 and 3.76 of Resolution No. 124 and item 1.29 of Resolution No. 169).

However, INPI's Guidelines set a very high standard for acknowledging sufficient disclosure and support by the specification of second medical use claims.

According to items 9.1.3 and 9.1.4 of Resolution No. 208, only specific compounds and diseases supported by experimental results are deemed to be sufficiently disclosed and clearly defined. Claims reciting Markush formulas and general disorders are not deemed acceptable.

[B] Mode of Administration

INPI's Guidelines have adopted a position which essentially renders inventions regarding mode of administration, dosage regimens, specific patient groups, and specific modes of action unallowable.

According to item 9.1.1 of Resolution No. 208, a new medical use would only be novel if the application discloses the use of a pharmaceutical product already known to produce a medicament for treating or preventing a disease other than that for which this product has already been employed in the prior art.

> 'Characteristics related to the use of the compound, such as the therapeutic regimen (dosage, via administration/application, dosage interval) and/or group of patients do not provide novelty on the known use of the compound. For example, if the prior art discloses the "use of compound X to the manufacture of a medicament for treating disease Y" and the application claims the "use of compound X to the manufacture of a medicament for treating disease Y in diabetic patients", the claimed use is not considered novel.'

Definitions regarding mode of administration on Swiss-type claims are also deemed to lack clarity under item 9.1.4 of Resolution No. 208.

It is debatable however whether such provisions would also apply to dependent claims if the independent claim already complies with the provisions of items 3.75 and 3.76 of Resolution No. 124 and item 1.29 of Resolution No. 169.

[C] Dosage Regimens

As mentioned above, INPI's Guidelines have adopted a position which essentially renders inventions regarding dosage regimens unallowable. It is debatable however whether such provisions would also apply to dependent claims if the independent claim already complies with the provisions of INPI's Guidelines.

[D] Specific Patient Groups

As mentioned above, INPI's Guidelines have adopted a position which essentially renders inventions regarding specific patient groups unallowable. It is debatable however whether such provisions would also apply to dependent claims if the independent claim already complies with the provisions of INPI's Guidelines.

[E] Specific Mode of Action

As mentioned above, INPI's Guidelines have adopted a position which essentially renders inventions regarding specific modes of action unallowable. It is debatable however whether such provisions would also apply to dependent claims if the independent claim already complies with the provisions of INPI's Guidelines.

[F] Combinations with Other Active Ingredients

Resolution Nos. 169 and 208 contain several provisions regarding combination inventions. According to item 5.25 of Resolution No. 169, the test for assessing inventiveness of combinations contains the following steps:

(i) whether the combined technical characteristics integrate functionally;
(ii) whether it is difficult or easy to carry out the combination;
(iii) whether there is any motivation to make the combination; and
(iv) the technical effect resulting from the combination.

Item 5.30 of said Resolution also provides that inventiveness is acknowledged '[i] f the combined technical characteristics functionally interact with each other and produce an unexpected technical effect or, in other words, if the technical effect after the combination is different from the sum of the technical effects of individual characteristics'.

Furthermore, item 7.18 of said Resolution also provides that inventiveness is acknowledged if 'the interaction between the active substances associated with the combination produces an unexpected technical effect different from that provided, for example, a synergistic or supra-additive effect, which does not correspond to the mere sum of the individual effects of each active substance composing the association (additive effect), reduction of unwanted effects, among others'.

However, item 7.19 of said Resolution also provides that 'the existence of a synergistic effect does not necessarily confer inventive step to the invention as it might already be provided for a certain class of compounds'.

Resolution No. 169 also establishes a restrictive position regarding the scope of the claims for such inventions. For instance, if 'the prior art comprises compositions containing the components of interest, even though no synergistic effect among them is observed/described or if there is evidence of incompatibility between these components in the broad range of concentration claimed, the claims should be defined qualitatively and quantitatively, clearly specifying what are the desired proportions of the components present, limited to those that are supported in the specification provided there is an unexpected technical effect'.

Claims which do not quantitatively define the components are deemed allowable according to item 7.21 of said Guidelines if (i) the combination of known products for the same application in any proportions has not been provided in the prior art; (ii) the synergistic effect is demonstrated for various contents of the two compounds; and (iii) the synergistic effect may be observed in any proportions of products involved.

Again, post-filing experimental results may be submitted in order to evidence the effect originally described in the application as filed according to item 5.16 of the said Resolution.

[G] Specific Diagnostic Applications

There are no provisions specifically directed to diagnostic applications involving known antibodies.

§14.05 ASSESSMENT OF INVENTIVENESS

[A] General Approach

The general test for assessment of inventive step is provided by item 5.9 of Resolution No. 169: '(i) establishing the closest prior art; (ii) defining the distinguishing features of the invention and/or the technical problem to be solved by the invention; and (iii) determining whether, before the considered technical problem, and starting from the closest prior art, the invention is or not obvious for a person skilled in the art.'

[B] Particularities Regarding Claims to Antibodies

There are no provisions specifically directed to the assessment of inventive step of antibodies. Therefore, the general provisions are applicable.

§14.06 ENFORCEMENT AND SCOPE OF PROTECTION

[A] Biosimilars

Agência Nacional de Vigilância Sanitária (ANVISA, the National Health Surveillance Agency) defines biosimilar products as 'biological products registered by the comparative development route, which is the regulatory route used by a biological product to obtain registration in which the comparability exercise was used in terms of quality, efficacy and safety, between the product developed to be comparable and the reference biological product'.

Therefore, biosimilars must share the same production route as the reference medicament and the applicant for a biosimilar must provide comparative studies between the biosimilar and the reference biological product containing sufficient information to predict whether differences detected in quality attributes between products result in adverse impacts on the safety and efficacy of the biosimilar.

In view of the above, claims to the methods for producing the antibody may be quite useful in the enforcement of antibody patents.

Regarding product claims, unless post-translation features are required in the main claims and shown to not be present in the biosimilar, general antibody claims should be enforceable.

There is however, no case law regarding the enforcement of antibody patents.

[B] Equivalence

Infringement by equivalence is explicitly provided in Article 186 of the Brazilian IP Law.

However, although the Brazilian IP Law does not contain specific provisions related to prosecution history 'estoppel', it has been applied. In fact, the courts have been applying a general legal concept called *venire contra factum proprium* which, in a nutshell, provides that parties cannot take contradictory courses during prosecution either in the Patent Office or the courts. Therefore, patentees cannot argue one way to have the patent granted and, thereafter, enforce the rights with opposing arguments.

Chapter 15

Canada

Graeme Boocock & Charles Boulakia

§15.01 ANTIBODIES AS PATENTABLE SUBJECT-MATTER

[A] Legal Framework

The legal requirements for patenting antibodies in Canada have not been extensively tested in court. Instead, the practical requirements for examination have been determined by a series of Commissioner's Decisions (CD), rendered by the Patent Appeal Board (PAB), which the Canadian Intellectual Property Office (CIPO) has used to set its examining policies. These decisions have tended to at first restrict, and then to incrementally allow over time claims to non-exemplified antibodies of progressively specialized subtypes. Guidelines for examiners are contained in CIPO's Manual of Patent Office Practice (MOPOP). Although based on forgoing CD, the guidelines do not reflect all nuances of local practice.

From 1995 to 2010, CIPO's examining policies for antibodies was largely guided by the decision of the Commissioner of Patents in *Re Institut Pasteur*, in which claims to non-exemplified monoclonal antibodies, and hybridomas secreting them, were denied.[1] The PAB found that written description and enablement requirements were not met, stating that methods of preparing monoclonal antibodies were not routine. Although the application considered in *Pasteur* was filed in 1987, this decision was applied subsequently by CIPO examiners to reject any claim that covered an antibody that had not been made, despite vast changes in the state of the art since 1987.

It was not until 2008 that the PAB acknowledged the precedential problems with *Pasteur* for enablement, faced with a critical affidavit from a scientist whose out-of-context textbook passages had been relied on in the decision.[2]

1. *Re Institut Pasteur Patent Application*, 76 CPR 3d 206 (PAB 1995) [*Pasteur*].
2. *Re Central Sydney Area Health Service Patent Appn No 605,609*, Commissioner's Decision 1283 (PAB 2008) [*Central Sydney Harbour*].

In 2009, in the *Sloan-Kettering* decision, the PAB allowed claims to non-exemplified chimeric antibodies, but refused to allow similar claims to humanized antibodies.[3] The application described a murine monoclonal antibody and referenced a biological deposit for a hybridoma producing it. Sequence information for the complementarity determining regions (CDRs) was not provided in the application. The PAB noted this, and stated that the process for producing humanized antibodies was 'considerably more involved' than for chimeric antibodies.[4] This decision was subsequently and consistently applied by CIPO examiners subject to reject claims to non-exemplified humanized antibodies, even when complementarity determining region (CDR) sequences for a corresponding non-human monoclonal were provided.

In 2010, the PAB allowed, for the first time, claims to non-exemplified monoclonal antibodies in an application that described the target epitope.[5] Once the antigen was in hand, the work that followed did not, in the Board's view, involve undue experimental burden. The Board indicated that a target polypeptide could be 'fully characterized' by providing a complete amino acid sequence.[6] The decision changed CIPO's examination practices, but only for monoclonal antibodies. The PAB cautioned that claims to antibodies having special functional attributes, such as diagnostic or therapeutic antibodies, may require 'correspondingly detailed support'.In 2016, the PAB allowed claims to non-exemplified humanized antibodies, even in the absence of sequence information for the relevant CDRs of the murine monoclonal antibodies (mAbs) made by the inventors.[7] The Board stated that:

> [Sloan-Kettering] leaves open the possibility that a humanized antibody can be described in ways other than by providing the amino acid sequences of the CDRs ... In line with the law and practices of other leading jurisdictions, Canadian examination practice with respect to antibodies has also evolved since [Sloan-Kettering]. For example, a previous decision of the Commissioner held that a mouse monoclonal antibody can be adequately described through reference to the antigen to which it specifically binds, provided the antigen has been fully characterized (e.g., through the provision of an amino acid sequence, see [Immunex] at para 68). We are of the view that the same principle may apply, by extension, to humanized antibodies.[8]

The Board concluded:

> In our opinion, [Sloan-Kettering] cannot impose a rigid rule that sequence information of the variable regions of a number of humanized antibodies must be provided in order to adequately describe and enable claims more generally

3. *Re Sloan-Kettering Institute for Cancer Research Patent Appn No 2,072,017*, 82 CPR 4th 33 (PAB 2009), Commissioner's Decision 1296 [*Sloan Kettering*].
4. *Ibid.* at para. 54.
5. *Re Immunex Corporation Patent Application No. 583,988*, 89 CPR 4th 34 (PAB 2011), Commissioner's Decision 1302 [*Immunex*].
6. *Ibid.* at page 35.
7. *Re Chugai Seiyaku and Kabushiki Kaisha*, Commissioners Decision 1398 (PAB 2016) [*Chugai Seiyaku*].
8. *Ibid.* at para. 37.

reciting humanized versions of various murine antibodies that may bind to various epitopes of the same antigen.[9]

The PAB acknowledged the dynamic state of the art and indicated that CIPO examiners cannot be bound by static policy, thus overturning longstanding examining practices, both for humanized antibodies, and antibodies generally.

CIPO then carried out internal examiner training in September 2016, and guidance for claiming antibodies in CIPO's MOPOP was expanded and revised in 2017.[10] The updated guidelines endorse a more flexible approach, responsive to changes in the state of the art.

Although many elements of Canadian practice are now quite favourable to patentees, there remain restrictive, historical elements that do not always align with scientific realities. Certain quirks of local practice are only evident with experience of the system.

Prospective patentees should be mindful that, with no specific jurisprudence on point for patents concerning antibodies, examiner determinations for antibody claims based on CIPO examining policies may be particularly susceptible to challenge, either in an appeal proceeding initiated by an applicant, or in a post-grant validity challenge undertaken by a third party.

[B] General Amenability or Exclusion of Antibodies from Patentability

Antibodies are considered patent-eligible subject matter in Canada provided that standard criteria for patentability are met. Subject matter exclusions do exist for certain follow-on applications (see §15.04).

[C] Required Distinction from Naturally Occurring Antibodies

The question of distinguishing an antibody over a naturally occurring counterpart is not one that arises frequently in Canadian practice.

There is no general requirement to claim antibodies in an isolated state during examination, except in rare circumstances in which an examiner requires it, for example, by raising an anticipation argument versus pre-existing natural antisera. In those instances, the term 'isolated' or 'monoclonal' is generally sufficient to differentiate over natural antisera. Given that selection patents have been upheld in Canada,[11] an argument is available, at least in principle, that pre-existing natural antisera comprising a mixture of many different antibodies do not constitute an enabling disclosure of a specific antibody.

9. *Ibid.* at para. 38.
10. Anik Marquis, *MOPOP Chapter 17 – Antibodies*, https://ipflyonthewall.files.wordpress.com/2017/01/a-2016-00719_0001-english.pdf#page=6 (updated September 2016); *Supra* note 1 at §17.07.
11. *Sanofi-Synthelabo v. Apotex*, 69 CPR 4d 251 (SCC 2008).

§15.02 ACCEPTABLE CLAIM FEATURES FOR DEFINING ANTIBODIES

Antibodies may be defined, in part, by functional features, though there is a general requirement that the definition also includes a structural element. For CIPO, requisite 'structure' can be provided either by defining the key binding portion of the antibody (e.g., the CDRs) or by defining the antigen or epitope.

Combinations of structural and function features are permitted. While there are certain accepted minimal requirements for antibodies defined by structure, there is no set standards for claims involving combinations of both types of features.

[A] Functional Features

[1] Target/Antigen

Antibodies may be defined by the antigen to which they bind. MOPOP states:

> 'Generally, a claim to an antibody specific for antigen X will be considered supported by a specification provided:
>
> i. antigen X itself has been fully characterized; and
> ii. either antiserum has been prepared, or where antiserum has not been prepared, there is neither anything peculiar about the antigen nor any indications that would lead a person of skill in the art to question the likelihood of success if that person desired to produce an antibody to the antigen.'[12]

The ability to claim is this way flows from the 'functional identity' between paratope and epitope acknowledged by the PAB in *Immunex*:

> 'A specific structural description of a monoclonal antibody can be accomplished by providing particular structural information of the antigen binding regions … Likewise it is possible to structurally describe a corresponding epitope … it is not possible to deduce structural information of one from the other. However, there is specific and meaningful functional identity (specific immunoreactivity) between the two a fact that is exploited during the apparent routineness of the preparation of monoclonal antibodies.'[13]

Claims that define the antibody in terms of the target antigen alone will not be available, however, if the antigen itself was previously disclosed. MOPOP cautions that:

> 'If antigen X is known or obvious in view of the prior art then an antibody reactive with that antigen would generally be considered obvious.
>
> Where the prior art discloses and enables antibodies reactive with a close structural relative of antigen X, then a claim to an antibody reactive with antigen X (e.g. an antibody "capable of binding" or "that specifically binds" to antigen

12. *Supra* note 1 at §17.07.
13. *Supra* note 6 at para. 67.

> X) will be anticipated if the claim, upon a purposive construction, is construed to encompass cross-reacting antibodies of the prior art.'[14]

[2] Mode of Binding: Target Affinity, Binding Specificity, Epitope, Definitions via Reference Antibodies and Competitive Binding

Epitope

Pursuant to *Immunex*, claims to non-exemplified monoclonal antibodies can be obtained if an epitope is adequately characterized, for example, by providing its full sequence. The PAB stated:

> 'the skilled person would appreciate that monoclonal antibodies can be adequately described based on a combination of a structural description of the antigen, functional identity [that is, specific immunoreactivity] between the antibody and antigen, and knowledge of predictable production methods.'[15]

Accordingly, when an application describes a novel epitope, monoclonal antibodies can be claimed without any requirement for the antibody to have been actually produced. The decisions of the PAB in *Sloan-Kettering* and *Chugai Seiyaku* extend this rationale to chimeric and humanized antibodies, respectively.[16]

Claims to an epitope on a known antigen may be required to show an unexpected advantage, or evidence that it is, in fact, a new epitope as compared to prior art antibodies.

Claims involving discontinuous or conformational epitopes may pose challenges during examination if an examiner does not believe that a complete definition of the epitope is provided (examiners are most accustomed to handling continuous, linear epitopes). Arguments against such objections may be successful if it can be shown that the identified residues are sufficient to define and distinguish the binding region.

Competitive Binding

Although not codified in MOPOP, CIPO indicated in a 2016 training session for examiners that antibodies may be defined by competition with a well-defined reference antibody for specific binding to a target.[17] This marked a reversal of previous practice. In the training example, the reference antibody is defined as produced by a hybridoma having a particular accession number. However, reference antibodies can also be defined by sequence. It is quite common for CIPO to require the reference antibody to be very narrowly defined. Typically, the definition of complete set of CDR sequences will suffice as a structural definition. A narrow definition for the reference antibody in effect defines a test condition, and should not adversely impact the scope of the claimed competing antibody.

14. *Supra* note 1 at §17.07.
15. *Ibid.*
16. *Supra* note 4; *supra* note 8.
17. *Supra* note 11 at p. 33, see Example 2 – claim 3.

CIPO tends to require such antibody claims to define binding to the target, or competition with the reference antibody, as being 'specific'. The underlying rationale appears to be that an antibody lacking such a feature could be completely non-specific in its binding preference.

Other Functional Features

Antibodies may also be defined by other functional features such as target affinity and potency.

The Federal Court decision in *AbbVie Corporation v. Janssen* is a rare example in which antibody technology was considered by a Canadian court.[18] The main claims were to uses of an anti-IL12 antibody, defined by minimum affinity and potency values, for treatment of psoriasis. The affinity and potency features had been challenged for indefiniteness, but the Federal Court found that the claims were adequately clear.[19] The decision was subsequently overturned on a point of procedure and is therefore, strictly speaking, non-precedential, though the decision does indicate the court's intent.[20] Indeed, shortly thereafter, CIPO appears to have ceased its former practice of objecting to functional features defined by minimum values – the very features considered and upheld by the FC in *AbbVie Corporation v. Janssen*.

Claims involving functional features beyond epitope binding and competitive binding will be closely scrutinized during examination for support and utility requirements (see [3] below). Such features may be objected to as 'desired results' if the specification is found to be lacking.

[3] ***Effect on Target***

It is possible to define antibodies having particular effects on a target. In these cases, MOPOP states that 'more detailed support' may be required:

> 'where the applicant is claiming a particular monoclonal antibody reciting particular functional characteristics that go beyond the simple interaction with the target antigen binding, e.g., where the monoclonal antibody is asserted to have agonist, antagonist or neutralizing activity, specificity for a particular epitope, or a remarkably high affinity constant…'[21]

Such feature may also garner scrutiny from the perspective of utility requirements. MOPOP states:

> 'In cases where the utility requires the antibody to possess not only binding capacity to the target antigen but also functional activities, such as antagonist (i.e., blocking), agonist (i.e., activating) or neutralizing activity, the description would likely require more than a disclosure of the binding capacity to the target antigen to establish utility. The provision of a working example of the claimed

---

18. *AbbVie Corp v. Janssen Inc*, 116 CPR 4th 399 (FC 2014).
19. *Ibid. at* paras. 181–182.
20. *Janssen Inc v. AbbVie Corporation*, 131 CPR 4th 128 (FCA 2014).
21. *Supra* note 1 at §17.07.02a.

antibody and in vitro *or* in vivo *data showing the antibody has the required activity may be sufficient to demonstrate utility. In the absence of demonstration, the applicant must be in a position to soundly predict the additional functional activity necessary for the utility.'*[22]

Requirements for sound prediction are described in more detail in §15.03[A].

[B] Structural Features

[1] Molecular Topology: Antibody Types, Fragments and Antibody Constructs

Antibody Types

Claims can be successfully pursued for a variety of antibody subtypes, and CIPO will adjust its examination parameters depending on the core structural architecture of the particular class or fragment type.

Fragments

Claims to particular types of antibody fragments can be obtained. If it is self-evident that the defined fragment includes the paratope (e.g., in the case of an Fab fragment), no further qualification is necessary. However, when a 'fragment' of an antibody is claimed without technical limitation, CIPO will require the claim to be amended to specify the functional limitation – that the fragment has binding specificity to the antigen or epitope thereof.

Antibody Constructs

Claims to constructs may be obtained. For inventive antibodies linked to other moieties, claims can usually be obtained without exemplary support in the absence of significant technical hurdles to production.

In the case of nucleic acid constructs encoding antibodies, CIPO will tend to insist that heavy and light chain sequences be encoded by the same molecule. Likewise, it is common for CIPO to object to claims to sequences that encode *only* a heavy or a light chain sequence. CIPO views both types of claims as encompassing something less than the entirety of the patentable antibody.

22. *Supra* note 1 at §17.07.05.

[2] *Amino Acid Sequences*

[a] *Full-Length Sequences of Antibodies*

Claims to full-length antibody sequences can be obtained, but are not required if the CDRs are defined. Sequence variation can usually be claimed without exemplary support, provided that it is excluded from the CDRs (see below under [b]).

Where an antibody sequence is known, a separate, independent claim to the full-length antibody sequence may be recommended, since it may be helpful in a determination of infringement, and since it may be more difficult to invalidate. Note that in Canada, there are no excess claims fees or limits on the number of independent claims in a patent.

[b] *Sequences of Fragments, CDRs and Framework Regions*

Sequences of Fragments

Claims to sequences of fragments may be obtained, provided that the CDRs are encompassed. When a fragment class is well-known, such as in the case of an Fab or $F(ab)_2$ fragment, there is no need to define the full sequence.

CDR Sequences

For antibodies to be defined exclusively by their structure (as opposed to that of the epitope), a full set of unmodified CDR sequences (or sequences comprising them) must be defined in the claims. Modifications to the CDR sequences are generally not tolerated, unless exemplified. Even then, CIPO will tend to limit applicants quite strictly to the scope of the exemplified sequence variation.[23]

This requirement is so strictly applied that CIPO will sometimes require a subsequent dependent claim defining sequence variation to explicitly rule out modifications in the CDRs, even when the dependent claims reference a foregoing claim reciting fixed CDRs.

CIPO's view – reflected in highly standardized objection language – is that modifications to CDR sequences can abrogate binding, and that their effects are not readily discernible. It may be the case that CIPO examiners perceive difficulties in identifying a core invention if CDR sequences are accepted as modifiable.

Claims identifying an antibody by its CDR regions, but characterizing less than all six CDR regions, are routinely objected to unless there is concrete evidence in the patent that the claimed CDR regions are sufficient for binding.

---

23. For a detailed review of CIPO's practices with respect to CDRs, see G.R.B. Boocock, *Antibody Examination Practice at the Canadian Patent Office: Immune to Change?*, 29:2 CIPR 225, §3.1 (2013) https://ssrn.com/abstract=2368817.

Framework and Constant Regions

It is generally not required to define framework or constant regions, and modifications in these sequences are more easily claimed without exemplary support.

[3] Chemical Modifications, Conjugation and Glycosylation

Claims to antibodies that are chemically modified, glycosylated, or conjugated to another moiety are readily available, and are not unduly scrutinized if the core, unmodified antibody is inventive. These appear to be acceptable in most cases as dependent claims, without specific exemplification in the specification.

[C] Cell Line Deposits and Process of Production

Claiming by Reference to a Biological Deposit

Antibodies may be claimed by reference to a biological deposit made under the Budapest Treaty. The Canadian Patent Act indicates that:

> 'the deposit shall be considered part of the specification and, to the extent that subsection 27(3) [which defines disclosure requirements] cannot otherwise be complied with, the deposit shall be taken into account into consideration in determining whether the specification complies with that subjection.'[24]

As discussed under §15.02[A][2], reference to a biological deposit may also be used in claims to antibodies that compete with a reference.

At the time of writing, however, examiners continue to object to claims that reference CDR sequences of an unsequenced biological deposit. CIPO's view is that reference to a biological deposit is not a substitute for disclosure of sequences. This is curious. The PAB has allowed claims to a non-exemplified humanized antibody when considering an application describing murine monoclonal antibodies that had neither been sequenced nor deposited.[25] In such a situation, the notional skilled person would have to go back to the antigen/epitope to produce an antibody and then humanize it. Compared to this, mere sequencing of a deposited hybridoma appears, to the authors, to be much more straightforward. Thus, there appears to be a disparity between what the PAB considered to be adequately descriptive and enabling, and the standard applied during examination.

When such objections arise, applicants may wish to include claims to antibodies that compete with the hybridoma, given that such claims would necessarily include antibodies having the same CDRs as the hybridoma.

24. *Patent Act*, RSC 1985, c P-4 s 38.1(1).
25. *Supra* note 8.

Process of Production

A request for access to a biological deposit can be made only once the application is open to public inspection, at which point the deposit is also considered 'available to the public'. The request must be made to the Commissioner of Patents using a form that accords with Rule 11.3(a) of the Regulations under the Budapest Treaty.[26] A letter of undertaking must also be provided, in which the requester agrees not to make the sample, or any culture derived from the sample, available to any other person nor to use the sample, or any culture derived from the sample, for any purpose other than experiments that relate to the subject-matter of the application.[27] These provisions apply until the patent is issued or the application is refused, withdrawn, or irrevocably lapsed.

An applicant is entitled to restrict access to an independent expert nominated by the Commissioner of Patents.[28] Such a request must be made by the applicant before the application is open to public inspection. The restriction lasts until the patent is issued, or the application is refused, withdrawn, or irrevocably lapsed. The independent expert is required to provide a letter of undertaking, as a third party would if no restriction were in place.[29]

§15.03 BREADTH OF CLAIMS AND SUPPORT BY EXAMPLES

[A] Acceptable Breadth of Claims to Antibodies

Claim breadth is assessed on a case-by-case basis from the perspectives of the general enable and written description requirements prescribed by the Patent Act and the Patent Rules.[30]

MOPOP provides the following non-exhaustive list of considerations for the determination of enablement, taken from the earlier PAB decision in *Re Central Sydney Harbour*:

- whether the applicant actually prepared a monoclonal antibody;
- where a monoclonal antibody had not been prepared,
    - whether the target antigen to which the monoclonal antibody specifically binds was fully characterized,
    - the availability and/or ease of production of the antigen,
    - whether there is an absence of any indications that the applicant was unable to produce a monoclonal antibody or that one of skill in the art would be unable to reproducibly make a monoclonal antibody to the target antigen, or

26. *Patent Rules*, SOR/96-423 s 107(1); *supra* note 1 at §17 and Appendices 1 and 2.
27. *Patent Rules*, *supra* note 27, s. 108.
28. *Patent Rules*, *supra* note 27, s. 104(4).
29. *Ibid.*
30. *Supra* note 25, s. 27(3)(b); *Patent Rules*, *supra* note 27, s. 84.

  - whether there is an absence of any indications that undue experimentation or undue adaption of known core steps would be necessary for preparing a monoclonal antibody;
- whether the scope of an antibody claim in respect to the antigen is appropriate.[31]

MOPOP also provides a non-exhaustive list of considerations for determining if the description is correct and full, also taken from *Re Central Sydney Harbour*:

- whether there was a full characterization of the target antigen to which the monoclonal antibody specifically binds;
- if not, whether the applicant actually prepared the monoclonal antibody and provided a full characterization thereof;
- if not, whether the applicant prepared a monoclonal antibody and deposited a hybridoma which produces the antibody, in accordance with the *Patent Rules*, on or before the filing date of the application; and
- whether the scope of an antibody claim with respect to the antigen is appropriate.[32]

In making these assessments, CIPO is, in principle, newly responsive to the state of the art at the filing date. CIPO's 2016 training presentation for examiners acknowledges that monoclonal, human, and humanized antibodies could be routinely produced as of 1992, 2000, and 2002, respectively.

Claims will also be scrutinized from the perspective of utility requirements established under the Patent Act.[33]

The SCC has recently affirmed the general principle that a mere scintilla of utility will suffice.[34] Where utility has been demonstrated at the time of filing, there is no requirement to disclose that utility in the application.[35] However, when claims cover embodiments for which utility has not been demonstrated at the time of filing, the utility of the full scope of the claim must have been 'soundly predicted' by the inventors at filing.[36] In order to be considered a sound prediction, there must be adequate 'factual basis' and a 'sound line of reasoning' for inferring the claim scope therefrom.[37] Therefore, at the drafting stage, it can be important to rationalize any extrapolations as far as Canada is concerned. The SCC has affirmed that sound prediction does not require certainty, as it presupposes that further work remains to be done.[38] However, sound prediction cannot be based on speculation alone.[39] The Federal Court of Appeal (FCA) has stated that sound prediction can be 'based on

31. *Supra* note 1, s. 17.07.02a.
32. *Ibid.*
33. *Supra* note 25, s. 2.
34. *AstraZeneca Canada Inc v. Apotex Inc*, 147 CPR 4th 79, para. 50 (SCC 2017).
35. *Teva Canada Ltd v. Pfizer Canada Inc*, 106 CPR 4th 161, paras. 36 to 43 (SCC 2012).
36. *Apotex Inc v. Wellcome Foundation Ltd*, 21 CPR 4th 499, para. 56 (SCC 2002).
37. *Ibid.* at para. 70.
38. *Ibid.* at para. 62.
39. *Ibid.* at para. 69.

knowledge forming part of the common general knowledge and on a line of reasoning which would be apparent to the skilled person'.[40]

During examination, questions of utility, written description, and enablement tend to be conflated, as examiners ultimately scrutinize the specification for the required factual basis and line of reasoning. Post-filing evidence may not be relied on to establish a sound prediction, though may be persuasive if presented as merely confirmatory of material in the specification.

[B] Required Experimental Support for Claims to Functionally Defined Antibodies

Provided that a novel epitope is described in an application, CIPO will allow claims to antibodies directed to this epitope without further experimentation.

Other types of functional limitations will garner scrutiny for fulfilment of written description, enablement, and utility requirements, which includes scrutiny of experimental data (see previous section 15.05[A]).

[C] Required Experimental Support for Claims to Structurally Defined Antibodies

Claims to structurally defined antibodies are somewhat more straightforward, perhaps owing to the assumption that the antibody was made if the inventors were in a position to define its CDR sequences.

It is not possible to claim sequence variation in the CDRs unless variants have experimentally verified binding activity. Sequence variation elsewhere in the antibody tends to be permissible without supporting experiments, provided that the description contemplates such variation.

§15.04 SPECIFIC MEDICAL APPLICATIONS AND OTHER FOLLOW-UP INVENTIONS

[A] Treatment of Specific Diseases

Methods of medical treatment are not patent-eligible in Canada.[41] Claims to corresponding medical 'uses' have been upheld by the SCC, and are available when a known molecule was found to be amenable to novel and inventive therapeutic application.[42]

Given Canada's flexible basis for amendment, conversion of claims from 'method' to 'use' format during examination is usually straightforward. Such claims may be presented in the Canadian-style format ('A use of antibody X for treatment of disease Y'), the Swiss-style format ('A use of antibody X for preparation of a medicament for treatment of disease Y'), or the EPC2000 format ('An antibody, X,

---

40. *Bell Helicopter Textron Canada Ltee v. Eurocopter*, 120 CPR 4th 394, para. 155 (FCA 2013).
41. *Tennessee Eastman Co et al. v. Commissioner of Patents*, 8 CPR 2d 202 (SCC 1972).
42. *Supra* note 37.

for use in treatment of disease Y'). Claims to more than one format may be included in an application.

It is longstanding practice that such claims must avoid active language (e.g. a step of 'administering'), steps requiring the professional skill of a physician, or define therapeutic effects beyond the 'for' clause.

While the SCC has upheld broad medical 'use' claims that notionally cover all manner of application, the Federal Court of Canada (FCC) has struck down 'use' claims with more specific limitations, for example, dosage ranges, as patent-ineligible subject matter.[43] The Federal Court's reasoning was that such claims prevent physicians from exercising professional skill or judgement (e.g., in the case of a known drug used for known treatment in a new dosage range) or that the skill or judgement of a physician is required to select the appropriate amount. Accordingly, the dosage range is viewed as transforming an otherwise patentable 'use' claim into a patent-ineligible method of medical treatment. Note, however, that there is varying practice among examiners and courts on this point, since a dosage range could be interpreted as a limitation on the effective dose range (i.e. all dosages within the range work) - which should be permissible - versus a dosage range from which a doctor should determine a treatment - which should not.

These two strands of precedent - allowing broad 'use' claims but denying certainly, more limited claims - stand in tension to one another.

CIPO has set forth guidance concerning medical 'use' claims for its examiners in Practice Notice PN2015-01 and its attendant examples.[44] The Practice Notice provides an overview of the practicalities of examination, though not all of its guidance has a clear legal basis.

[B] Mode of Administration

According to CIPO, uses involving a novel mode of administration for a pre-existing antibody would be considered patent-eligible subject matter.[45] In such cases, it would be typical to define the use utilizing passive language (e.g. as 'for topical administration') or to state the antibody is, for example, 'formulated for oral delivery'.

[C] Dosage Regimens

Uses involving fixed dosage amounts are patent-eligible.[46] However, those involving dosage ranges are impermissible because the professional skill of a physician is required to select a precise dosage from within the range.[47] On similar rationale, fixed

43. See e.g. *Axcan Pharma Inc v. Pharmascience Inc*, 50 CPR 4th 321 (FC 2006); *Janssen Inc v. Mylan Pharmaceuticals ULC*, 88 CPR 4th 359 (FC 2010); *Bayer Inc v. Cobalt Pharmaceuticals Company*, 121 CPR 4th 14 (FC 2013).
44. Government of Canada, *Patent Notice: Revised Examination Practice Respecting Medical Uses - PN 2015-01*, https://www.ic.gc.ca/eic/site/cipointernet-internetopic.nsf/eng/wr03916.html (updated 18 March 2015).
45. *Ibid.*
46. *Ibid.*
47. *Ibid.*; *supra* note 44.

time intervals pose no problem to examination, whereas those involving ranges are problematic.[48]

Notably, CIPO will object to ranges in an independent claim, but will permit them in dependent claims. For the purposes of enforcement of a dependent claim so limited, it should be noted that Canadian courts may not make the same distinction.

Applicants may choose to include multiple independent claims to specific, fixed dosage amounts, preferably in alignment with their regulatory approvals and/ or commercial products.

[D] Specific Patient Groups

Claims to medical uses involving application of a known antibody to a new patent group are available.[49] However, CIPO takes the position that a claim to treatment of a patient *subgroup* (i.e., a defined group within a previously treated, larger group) is inherently anticipated and does not qualify as a selection. This appears to be a policy decision with no clear basis in law.

[E] Specific Mode of Action

Claims to antibodies may define the antibody in terms of a mode of action. Such claims may also be distinguishable if the use is new. However, 'use' claims that are distinguished merely by previously unknown mechanistic details that were already in effect will face inherency issues if the purpose of the 'use' is the same.

[F] Combinations with Other Active Ingredients

Claims to combinations with other active ingredients are permitted, and are fairly non-contentious in the case of an inventive antibody. Combinations of two known ingredients may also be permissible if they yield unexpected results.

[G] Specific Diagnostic Applications

Claims to medical diagnostics have, since 2015, faced challenges from the perspective of patent-eligible subject matter in view of CIPO's Practice Notice PN2015-02, which endorses a mode of claims construction and assessment subject matter that appears to be at variance with SCC and FCA jurisprudence.[50] This policy was written into MOPOP in November 2017.[51]

According to this policy, when an analyte or means for its measurement is 'common general knowledge' (CGK) as CIPO defines it, the 'essential elements' of a

48. *Supra* note 45.
49. *Ibid.*
50. Government of Canada, *Patent Notice: Examination Practice Respecting Medical Diagnostic Methods – PN 2015-02*, https://www.ic.gc.ca/eic/site/cipointernet-internetopic.nsf/eng/wr03945.html (updated 29 July 2015).
51. *Supra* note 1 at §17.03.04.

diagnostic claims are limited to patent-ineligible mental steps, i.e., the correlation to disease. The physical steps of acquiring data about the analyte are considered to be non-essential, and are excluded from analysis. Thus, if an antibody was previously known, its application in a new diagnostic method may not be sufficient for the method to pass CIPO's subject matter eligibility requirements.

In the case of an independently inventive antibody or analyte - or at least one that was 'non-CGK' as CIPO understands it - a diagnostic method would meet CIPO's requirements.

CIPO's approach to medical diagnostics has little basis in case law, and has been widely criticized, including in the national press.[52] That said, it appears to be universally followed by examiners at the time of writing, and presumably until further guidance is received from the courts.

§15.05 ASSESSMENT OF INVENTIVENESS

[A] General Approach

In order to render a claim obvious, cited prior art references must lead a skilled person in the art 'directly and without difficulty' to the claimed invention without the use of any inventive ingenuity.[53] The SCC has articulated the following four-part test for obviousness:

(1) (a) Identify the notional "person skilled in the art";
    (b) Identify the relevant common general knowledge of that person;
(2) Identify the inventive concept of the claim in question or if that cannot readily be done, construe it;
(3) Identify what, if any, differences exist between the matter cited as forming part of the "state of the art" and the inventive concept of the claim or the claim as construed;

52. G.R.B. Boocock, *Haunted by the Spirit of the Invention: Recent Examination Guidelines from the Canadian Intellectual Property Office for Medical Diagnostics Channel the Spectre of Contribution Analysis*, 32:1 CIPR 71, (2016) https://ssrn.com/abstract=2809891; I. McMillan and C. Gale, *Go your own way: Canadian Patent Office instructs examiners to disregard Supreme Court of Canada precedent in construing claims*, https://www.bereskinparr.com/doc/go-your-own-way-canadian-patent-office-instructs-examiners-to-disregard-supreme-court-of-canada-prec (updated 4 April 2017); R.C. Owens, *Going Rogue at the Patent Office*, National Post, https://www.pressreader.com/canada/national-post-latest-edition/20171213/282067687280727 (updated 13 Dec. 2017); N. Siebrasse, *Diagnostics Methods at CIPO*, Sufficient Description, http://www.sufficientdescription.com/2018/01/diagnostic-methods-at-cipo.html (updated 8 Jan. 2018); G. Galloway, *Diagnostic patents denied to researchers who link known body chemicals to disease*, The Globe and Mail, https://www.theglobeandmail.com/politics/article-diagnostic-patents-denied-to-researchers-who-link-known-body-chemicals/ (updated 25 April 2018).
53. *Beloit Canada et al v. Valmet Oy*, 8 CPR 3d 289, 294 (FCA 1986).

(4) Viewed without any knowledge of the alleged invention as claimed, do those differences constitute steps which would have been obvious to the person skilled in the art or do they require any degree of invention?[54]

If an antigen or epitope was previously disclosed, CIPO takes the view the claims to a general antibodies directed thereto, without further structural limitation, will be obvious. Likewise, if the CDRs of non-human monoclonal antibody were disclosed, CIPO's position is that a claim to general humanized antibodies derived therefrom will be obvious. Claims to specific antibodies having particular sequences may still be available under these circumstances.

[B] Particularities Regarding Claims to Antibodies

As the PAB has incrementally accepted the 'routineness' of making particular types of antibodies, the benchmark for inventiveness during examination has correspondingly increased. Some applicants have faced lack of enablement objections for claims drawn to general antibodies targeting a known epitope in one Office Action, only to face obviousness allegations in the next.

It is generally possible to secure claims to *specific* antibodies (i.e. defined by CDR sequences) in view of previous disclosure of an epitope. A claim to a general humanized antibody may be alleged to be obvious in view of a disclosure of CDR sequences of a corresponding non-human monoclonal, whereas claims to *specific* humanized antibodies may still be available. In some cases, the availability of such claims may depend on the unpredictable properties of the specific antibody in question.

§15.06 ENFORCEMENT AND SCOPE OF PROTECTION

There has been very little, if any, jurisprudence regarding antibody patents in Canada. Accordingly, there is very little court-considered guidance on enforcement. In general, however, a good strategy for claiming in Canada is to claim embodiments separately and explicitly, and to provide clean, independent claims for enforcement. Canada benefits from a regime with no excess claims fees, at any point in the process, and virtually no limit on the number of claims one can present in an application; accordingly, 'picture' claims, and separate, independent claims to each embodiment, are recommended, in addition to the usual and typical claim set.

One significant point of frustration in prosecution and litigation is the damage caused by 'double patenting' – anticipatory *and* obviousness-type double patenting is a common ground for invalidation, regardless of whether the double patenting results in term extension or whether the expiration dates are coterminous. Canada has no provision for terminal disclaimers to overcome double patenting situations.

A useful prosecution strategy is to have all potential claims examined in the parent application; if the Patent Office issues a unity of invention objection, it can typically quite convincingly be used to rebut a double patenting objection by the Office, and is likely to be helpful in rebutting an invalidity attack in litigation. The

54. *Sanofi-Synthelabo v. Apotex*, 69 CPR 4d 251, 272 (SCC 2008).

Supreme Court of Canada has found that there can be no double patenting when the division was forced by CIPO during examination.[55]

Note that recently proposed legislation will make file wrapper estoppel relevant to litigation proceedings; this may have significant effect on both prosecution and enforcement strategy.

Canada also has linkage regulations in the Patented Medicines (Notice of Compliance) ('PMNOC') Regulations (similar to Hatch Waxman in the US) which can significantly affect enforcement strategy. Claims must be crafted carefully to comply with listing eligibility requirements; even when claims are listable, recent changes to the PMNOC Regulations make it important to consider whether to list a patent on the Patent Register (which links the patent to the generic regulatory approval). There are strictly held and short timelines for listing a patent, which are related to both the timing of regulatory filings and to the issue date of the patent.

[A] Biosimilars

The question of whether a claim to an antibody would cover a biosimilar, and under what circumstances, has not yet been tested in court. Such a claim would likely be treated like a claim to any other compound. The question of scope would be a matter of claims construction and factual analysis of the biosimilar product.

As of December 2018, there have been ten biosimilars approved in Canada. Four of these were approved in 2018. Seven of these approvals are for antibodies or antibody-fusion proteins (etanercept (x2); adalimumab; infliximab; bevacizumab; infliximab (x2)).

[B] Equivalence

The SCC has stated that the exercise of claims construction may identify some elements of a claim that are non-essential. The non-essential elements are defined as those that 'may be substituted or omitted without having a material effect on either the structure or the operation of the invention described in the claims.'[56] The Court determined that there may be infringement if a non-essential element is substituted or omitted.[57]

Accordingly, claims may be cover equivalents – termed 'variants' by the SCC – in some circumstances. The SCC reiterated a three-part test this determination taken from *Improver v. Remington*:[58]

'(i) Does the variant have a material effect upon the way the invention works? If yes, the variant is outside the claim. If no: –

(ii) Would this (i.e.: that the variant had no material effect) have been obvious at the date of publication of the patent to a reader skilled in the art? If no, the variant is outside the claim. If yes: –

55. *Consolboard Inc v. Macmillan Bloedel (Saskatchewan) Ltd*, 56 CPR 2d 145, 169 (SCC 1981).
56. *Free World Trust v. Électro Santé Inc.*, 9 CPR 4th 168, para 20 (SCC 2000).
57. *Ibid.* at para. 31.
58. *Improver Corp v. Remington Consumer Products Ltd*, [1990] FSR 181, 182 (Pat Ct 1990).

(iii) Would the reader skilled in the art nevertheless have understood from the language of the claim that the patentee intended that strict compliance with the primary meaning was an essential requirement of the invention? If yes, the variant is outside the claim.'[59]

These questions have not yet been decided in a case involving an antibody claim.

To the extent that it is possible to capture variants and biosimilars within the literal wording of a claim, applicants should always endeavour to do so during examination. There are no excess claims fees and claim amendments are permitted provided that they are reasonably to be inferred from the originally filed specification. Accordingly, there is a good deal of flexibility to pursue claims of differing scopes in Canada.

59. *Supra* note 57, at para. 55.

Chapter 16

Chile

Rodrigo Marré Grez & Allison Ortega del Valle

§16.01 ANTIBODIES AS PATENTABLE SUBJECT-MATTER

[A] Legal Framework

The patentability of antibodies in Chile is regulated by the general patent legal framework, that is, the Industrial Property Law No. 19,039 (IPL), as well as by its corresponding Regulation (RIPL).

Additionally, the patentability of antibodies is also subject to the Guidelines for the Examination and Procedure of Patent Registration ('Guidelines'). Even though the Guidelines are not legally binding for the Instituto Nacional de Propiedad Industrial (which is the Chilean PTO, INAPI), in practice they are very relevant as they detail several aspects that are not mentioned in the IPL neither in the RIPL and which serve as the guiding manual for examiners.

[B] General Amenability or Exclusion of Antibodies from Patentability

By definition, an antibody is a type of glycoprotein, also called immunoglobulin (Ig), and produced by B lymphocytes, which binds to antigens, often with a high degree of specificity and affinity. The basic structural unit of an antibody is composed of two identical heavy chains. The N-terminal variable regions of the heavy and light chains form the antigen-binding sites, while the C-terminal constant regions of the heavy chains interact with other molecules of the immune system. Each individual has millions of different and specific antibodies, each with a unique antigen binding zone.

Antibodies are produced naturally by the body in response to infectious microbes or foreign substances, namely macromolecules, proteins, polysaccharides and small chemical substances, through the complex activation of the immune system.

In this context, and according to Article 37(f) of the IPL, a patent application that attempts to protect an antibody that has only been isolated from an organism, will be considered as a matter excluded from patentability.

Article 37 of the IPL:

'Not considered an invention and excluded from the patent protection of this law:

a) Discoveries, scientific theories and mathematical methods.
b) Plants and animals, except for microorganisms that keep to the general conditions of patentability. Plant varieties will only enjoy protection in accordance with the provisions of Law No. 19,342 on the Breeders' Right of New Plant Varieties. Essentially biological processes for the production of plants and animals are not patentable, except microbiological procedures. For these purposes, an essentially biological procedure is one that consists entirely of natural phenomena, such as crossing and selection.
c) The systems, methods, principles or economic, financial, commercial, business plans or simple verification and inspection; and those related to purely mental or intellectual activities or game matters.
d) The methods of surgical or therapeutic treatment of the human or animal body, as well as the diagnostic methods applied to the human or animal body, except for the products destined to implement one of these methods.
e) The new use, the change of form, the change of dimensions, the change of proportions or the change of materials of articles, objects or elements known and used for certain purposes. Notwithstanding the foregoing, the new use of known articles, objects or elements may constitute an invention susceptible to protection, provided that said new use resolves a technical problem without an equivalent prior solution, complies with the requirements referred to in Article 32 and requires of a change in the dimensions, proportions or materials of the article, object or element known to obtain said solution to said technical problem. The new claimed use must be accredited by experimental evidence in the patent application.
f) Part of living beings as they are found in nature, natural biological processes, and biological material existing in nature or that which can be isolated, including genome or germplasm. However, procedures that use one or more of the aforementioned biological materials and the products directly obtained by them, provided that they satisfy the requirements established in Article 32 of this law, that the biological material is adequately described, will be susceptible to protection and that the industrial application of the same be explicitly included in the patent application.'

The reason for this exclusion is based on the fact that our law considers that the mere fact of isolating an antibody does not correspond to an inventive activity, as it is considered a routine activity, therefore it would not meet the requirements of patentability and therefore, would not be patentable.

Based on the above, in order for an antibody to be patentable it is necessary to define what type of antibody is being patented and it should correspond to one that does not normally occur in nature. Accordingly, 'monoclonal antibodies', 'humanized antibodies', 'chimeric antibodies' among others could be patentable if they meet the patentability standards. The corresponding specification should describe whether the modifications of the antibody are structural and/or functional. A deep and detailed description of the procedure by which they were obtained should be provided as well.

Consequently, there are different definitions of the antibodies that are accepted by our local practice as shown below:

a) Monoclonal antibody: Corresponds to an antibody that is specific against an antigen and is produced by a hybridoma of B lymphocytes (a cell line derived from the fusion of a single normal B lymphocyte and an immortal B lymphocyte tumour line).
b) Humanized antibody: Corresponds to a monoclonal antibody encoded by a recombinant hybrid gene and composed of the antigen binding sites of a murine monoclonal antibody and the constant region of a human antibody.
c) Chimeric antibody: corresponds to an antibody whose origin is from the merger of genes from two different species, for example of murine and human origin.

Likewise, all biological materials (molecules, proteins, fragment of the genome, chemical substances) that are different and inventive (according to Articles 33, 35 and 36 of the IPL, respectively) will be patentable in comparison with any existing in nature.

Said articles expressly state:

> Article 33 of the IPL: 'An invention is considered new, when it does not exist before in the state of the art. The state of the art will include everything that has been disclosed or made accessible to the public, anywhere in the world, through a publication in tangible form, sale or commercialization, use or any other means, before the date of presentation of the patent application in Chile or the priority claimed according to Article 34. Also included in the state of the art, the content of national applications for patents or utility models as they were originally presented, whose filing date is prior to that indicated in the preceding paragraph and which were published on that date or at a later date.'

> Article 35 of the IPL: 'An invention is considered to have an inventive level, if, for a person normally versed in the corresponding technical matter, it is not obvious or would not have been derived in an obvious way from the state of the art.'

> Article 36 of the IPL: 'It is considered that an invention is susceptible of industrial application when its object can, in principle, be produced or used in any type of industry. For these purposes, the expression industry will be understood in its broadest sense, including activities such as: manufacturing, mining, construction, crafts, agriculture, forestry, and fishing.'

In connection to the possibility of patenting procedures and methods to modify an antibody it should be borne in mind that the IPL excludes them from patentability if said methods or procedures are surgical, therapeutic and diagnostic of the human or animal body. In this regard any methodology made '*in vivo*' will be considered as a non-patentable therapeutic, surgical or diagnostic method.

Notwithstanding the foregoing, methods or procedures that are not surgical, therapeutic or diagnostic, or those products that allow putting into practice said methods or procedures are patentable.

[C] Required Distinction from Naturally Occurring Antibodies

In the case of the protection of antibodies that are highly similar to the antibodies found in nature, a detailed description should be made in order to differentiate them and fulfil the requirements of novelty and inventive step.

Additionally, according to Article 39 of the RIPL, a detailed description of the invention and at least one example of embodiment of the same must be provided, in such a way as to make the invention reproducible.

Article 39 of the RIPL:

> 'The description of the invention must be presented in text forming a separate body and shall include a description of what is known in the material, a description of the drawings (if any), a description of the invention and an example of application, when appropriate.
>
> The description of what is known in the art will begin by introducing the preferred field of application of the invention, citing the technical problem that it tackles and will make a reference to the solutions given to said problem, ensuring that these solutions are as close and current as possible – from the technological point of view – highlighting its disadvantages or technical disadvantages. The description of the invention is a detailed and clear explanation of the invention in reference to the numbered parts or parts of the drawings if they exist and must be complete enough so that any person specialized in the industrial sector to which it refers may reproduce the invention. When the invention comprises a living biological material, including virus, or its method of obtaining, in such a way that the invention cannot be fully reproduced in the specification, the INAPI may request that said material be deposited with an internationally recognized body for such purposes effects, indicating the institution and the respective registration number. The application example of the invention will consist of a detailed description of at least one embodiment of the invention and may be supported or illustrated with the help of the drawings, if any, in such a way as to make the invention reproducible.'

In connection to second uses, in the case that it is discovered that a natural antibody has a different use or a second use, according to Chilean law it could be protected, as long as its use is not evident to an examiner in the field and also complies with the requirements of patentability mentioned above.

A second use, according to the Guidelines, is understood as a

> 'new use that *resolves a technical problem without previous equivalent solution*, which complies with the requirements, referred to in article 32 of the IPL and *requires a change in the dimensions*, in the proportions or in the materials of the object or known element to obtain said solution to said technical problem. The new claimed use must be accredited by experimental evidence in the patent application.'

For example:

> 'Use of an isolated antibody X or an antigen binding fragment that binds to Factor P, according to claim 1, CHARACTERIZED in that it is useful to inhibit the proliferation of cancer cell lines X.'

In this context, in order to comply with the guidelines and legal requirements it is necessary to fully describe the second use of the antibody and inventive step justifications in the specification.

For example, in order to comply with the change of dimension requirement in the case of a natural antibody, it could be demonstrated that a relevant different concentration of the same produces the unexpected effect which constitutes the second use. This change in the concentration should be duly described and experimentally evidenced in the specification.

§16.02 ACCEPTABLE CLAIM FEATURES FOR DEFINING ANTIBODIES

According to Article 43 bis of the IPL, claims shall define the subject matter for which protection is sought and they must be clear and concise and be based on the specification. Additionally, it is important to consider that according to the abovementioned article, the description shall be sufficiently clear and complete for an examiner or a person skilled in the art to reproduce the invention without need of any other information.

Article 43 bis of the IPL:

> 'The summary shall have an exclusively technical purpose and may not be considered for any other purpose, not even for the determination of the scope of protection requested. The claims define the object for which the protection is requested. These should be clear and concise and should be based on the specification. The specification should be clear and complete in order to allow an examiner or expert in the matter to reproduce the invention without needing other background information.'

Based on the above, patent applications shall comply with the requirement of sufficiency of the description (sufficient description or technical sufficiency), describing the technology that is sought to be patented by means of the detailed technical description of the invention. Otherwise, the request will be rejected for lack of sufficiency of the specification.

In this context, the Chilean IPL accepts the description of an antibody based on:

a) Functional characteristics (in exceptional cases);
b) Structural characteristics; and/or
c) Mode of production or obtaining the antibodies.

All three options above are acceptable, provided that they comply with the patentability requirements established by the IPL.

[A] Functional Features

Although the Chilean IPL does not generally accept the description of an antibody based on its functional characteristics, there are exceptions in those cases where the antigen is unknown. For example, in the following case:

> 'Use of an isolated antibody X or an antigen binding fragment that binds to Factor P, according to claim 1, CHARACTERIZED in that it is useful to prepare a drug to inhibit the alternative complement pathway'

In this case, for the description to be accepted by INAPI, the description of the antibody must meet three requirements simultaneously:

1. The antigen must be unknown.
2. The antigen-antibody binding must generate a technical effect.
3. Several different antibodies must show that they cause the same technical effect.

[1] Target/Antigen

Based on what has been mentioned above, and considering that an antigen is defined as a molecule that binds to an antibody or a TCR (T cell receptor), and that all kinds of molecules are covered, it is necessary that said antigen be different from the diverse existing molecules in nature and that its composition or structural conformation is not evident in the light of the state of the art.

In this context, if the antigen is unknown, it is probable that the antibodies that bind to it are also unknown and, therefore, could be considered new and inventive, provided they demonstrate a technical effect. On the contrary, in the case that the antigen is known but the antibody is unknown, the invention could be considered new but not inventive.

[2] Mode of Binding: Target Affinity, Binding Specificity, Epitope, Definitions via Reference Antibodies and Competitive Binding

Additionally, in order to be able to claim an antibody based on its functional characteristics, it must be experimentally demonstrated that the epitope-antibody binding generates an unexpected technical effect, an unexpected therapeutic effect, or a synergistic effect. For example, if the antigen is unknown, it could be demonstrated that the epitope-antibody binding generates a greater specificity than expected, it generates an *unexpected* physiological or therapeutic activity, or it generates an unusually high affinity.

The following claim would probably be excluded because it is not self-sufficient:

> 'An epitope, CHARACTERIZED in that it binds specifically to antibody X.'

In this case, it is suggested that said type of claims be worded as follows:

> 'An epitope of binding to antibody X CHARACTERIZED in that the binding specificity of the epitope by the antibody is X %, since the K_A is X [M^{-1}] and K_D is Y [M].'

In this case, the value of X% must be significantly better than that known in the state of the art and must be demonstrated experimentally throughout the specification, in order to meet the requirement of inventive step.

[3] *Effect on Target*

As in the previous case, the protection of an antibody based on the effect it causes on its target, whether agonist or antagonist, would be acceptable, if and only if:

a) The target of the antibody is clearly identified;
b) The applicant shows several examples of different antibodies that have the same target and that produce the same effects.

In this case, it is required that the technical effect of the invention be demonstrated experimentally and in detail, as reproducibility is fundamental.

For example, the following claim would be excluded as it is not self-sufficient:

> 'An (isolated/monoclonal/chimeric/humanized) antibody CHARACTERIZED in that it is used as a drug that produces an agonist/antagonistic effect.'

In this context, it is suggested that said type of claims be worded as follows:

> 'Use of an (isolated/monoclonal/chimeric/humanized) antibody CHARACTERIZED in that it has an agonist/antagonist effect on the X cells.'

Therefore, if an antibody meets all the above-mentioned requirements, namely: the antigen is unknown, the antigen-antibody binding generates a technical effect, and it is shown that several different antibodies cause the same technical effect, it could be considered patentable.

On the contrary, if said antibody does not meet the above-mentioned requirements, the request will be objected due to lack of inventive step, among other objections.

[B] Structural Features

When defining an antibody, the strongest characteristics are the structural features of the antibody. In this context, antibodies must be defined based on their six complementarity determining regions (CDRs) or sequences that contain them. Additionally, they can be defined based on: type, fragments, and constructs of an antibody, as will be detailed below.

[1] *Molecular Topology: Antibody Types, Fragments and Antibody Constructs*

Regarding the definition based on the type of antibody, this can be claimed for example as 'monoclonal antibodies', 'humanized antibodies', or 'chimeric antibodies', among others. However the specification must define antibodies not only on the basis of said terms, but rather the specification must define them based on the characteristics of the procedures by which said antibodies were obtained, indicating this procedure in detail and the experimental studies that support the results obtained.

For example, the following claim would probably be rejected by the examiner due to lack of self-sufficiency:

> 'A human monoclonal antibody, CHARACTERIZED in that it is directed against the surface antigen X, for use in the treatment of patients with Y.'

In this context, it is suggested that said type of claims be drafted as a Swiss-type claim, as follows:

> 'Use of a human monoclonal antibody, directed against the antigen X CHARACTERIZED in that said antibody is obtained from a hybridoma cell line deposited under No. YXY (ATCC 00000002) because it is useful to prepare a drug to inhibit the alternative complement pathway'

Another correct way to define an antibody is based on the characterization of the antibody fragments (Fab). The Fabs correspond to a proteolytic fragment of an IgG antibody molecule comprising a complete light chain paired with a heavy chain fragment containing the variable domain and only the first constant domain.

Therefore, to the extent that the Fab complies with the patentability requirements and is defined based on its nucleotide and/or amino acid sequences and structures, the antibody can be protected.

For example, the following claim would probably be rejected by the examiner due to lack of self-sufficiency:

> 'A fragment of antibody X CHARACTERIZED in that it binds specifically to factor Y.'

In this context, it is suggested that said type of claims be written as Swiss-type claims in the following way:

> '1. An antibody fragment X that binds specifically to the P-factor CHARACTERIZED in that the antigen binding comprises heavy and light chain variable regions that have amino acid sequences with SEQ ID NO: 175 and 176; SEQ ID NO: 7 and 8; SEQ ID NO: 189 and 190; SEQ ID NO: 203 and 204; SEQ ID NO: 217 and 218; or SEQ ID NO: 231 and 232, respectively.
>
> 2. Use of an antibody X fragment, according to claim 1, CHARACTERIZED in that it is useful to prepare a drug to inhibit the alternative complement pathway'

Likewise, the antibody constructs can also be protected, as long as they are defined based on the modifications of the nucleotide or amino acid sequences of the antibodies, and as long as they comply with the patentability requirements.

For example, the following claim would be rejected by the examiner due to lack of self-sufficiency:

> 'A DNA construct, CHARACTERIZED in that it comprises a first part encoding a variable domain having an amino acid sequence substantially identical to the amino acid sequence, starting with the amino acid in position 1, and ending with the amino acid in position 117.'

In this context, it is suggested that said type of claims be drafted in the following manner:

> 'A DNA construct, CHARACTERIZED in that it comprises:

a) a first part coding for a light chain comprising the: CDR 1 whose amino acid sequence corresponds to the sequence SEQ ID NO: 1; CDR 2 whose amino acid sequence corresponds to the sequence SEQ ID NO: 2; CDR 3 whose amino acid sequence corresponds to the sequence SEQ ID NO: 3;
b) a second part encoding a heavy chain comprising the: CDR 1 whose amino acid sequence corresponds to the sequence SEQ ID NO: 4; CDR 2 whose amino acid sequence corresponds to the sequence SEQ ID NO: 5; CDR 3 whose amino acid sequence corresponds to the sequence SEQ ID NO: 6.'

[2] Amino Acid Sequences

Another correct way to define an antibody corresponds to its definition based on its nucleotide or amino acid sequences. In this context, the sequences coding for said antibody should be disclosed in detail, indicating the six CDRs that make up the antibody and their respective sequences, whether they are amino acids or nucleotides.

For example, the following claim would be rejected by the examiner due to lack of self-sufficiency and lack of definition of the structural characteristics in a clear and detailed manner:

> 'An isolated antibody or fragment thereof which binds to X, wherein the antibody or fragment comprises a heavy chain CDR 3 selected from the group consisting of SEQ ID NO: 9, 34, 54, 72 and 79.'

In this context, it is suggested that said type of claims be worded as follows:

> 'An isolated antibody or fragment thereof that binds X, CHARACTERIZED in that the antibody or antigen-binding fragment thereof comprises:
> a) a light chain comprising the: CDR 1 whose amino acid sequence corresponds to the sequence SEQ ID NO: 1; CDR 2 whose amino acid sequence corresponds to the sequence SEQ ID NO: 2; CDR 3 whose amino acid sequence corresponds to the sequence SEQ ID NO: 3;
> b) a heavy chain comprising the: CDR 1 whose amino acid sequence corresponds to the sequence SEQ ID NO: 4; CDR 2 whose amino acid sequence corresponds to the sequence SEQ ID NO: 5; CDR 3 whose amino acid sequence corresponds to the sequence SEQ ID NO: 6.'

Also, in the case of antibodies containing specific modifications in their amino acid sequences, the modifications must be detailed and their position specified.

[a] Full-Length Sequences of Antibodies

In relation to the size of the nucleotide or amino acid sequences, the IPL does not define a certain size, since it will depend on the region or the chain of the antibody. However, it is required that the disclosure of the sequence allows the invention to be reproduced by a third party without the need for additional background information. In this context, it is sufficient to indicate the complete sequences corresponding to the six CDRs and to attach the list of claimed sequences.

[b] *Sequences of Fragments, CDRs and Framework Regions*

For an adequate description of an antibody it is required that it be defined at least based on its six CDRs, three CDRs of the heavy chain and the three CDRs of the light chain, or on the basis of the variable region of the heavy chain and the variable region of the light chain, or specific combinations of the variable regions of the light chain/heavy chain, or of the heavy and light chain CDR1/CDR2/CDR3.

For example, the following claim would probably be objected by examiner, because it is not self-sufficient and does not define clearly and in detail its structural characteristics:

> 'An (isolated/monoclonal/chimeric/humanized) antibody or antigen-binding fragment CHARACTERIZED in that it contains a CDR1, CDR2, CDR3, and where the variant has at least one to four amino acid changes in one of CDR1, CDR2 or CDR3.'

In this context, it is suggested that said type of claims be worded as follows:

> 'An (isolated/monoclonal/chimeric/humanized) antibody or antigen-binding fragment CHARACTERIZED in that the antibody comprises:
>
> a) a heavy chain variable region comprising a CDR1 complementarity determining region of SEQ ID NO: 1; CDR2 of SEQ ID NO: 2; CDR3 of SEQ ID NO: 3; and a light chain variable region comprising a CDR1 of SEQ ID NO: 4; CDR2 of SEQ ID NO: 5; and CDR3 of SEQ ID NO: 6; or
> b) a heavy chain variable region comprising a CDR1 complementarity determining region of SEQ ID NO: 7; CDR2 of SEQ ID NO: 8; CDR3 of SEQ ID NO: 9; and a light chain variable region comprising a CDR1 of SEQ ID NO: 10; CDR2 of SEQ ID NO: 11; and CDR3 of SEQ ID NO: 12.'

[3] ***Chemical Modifications, Conjugation and Glycosylation***

Naturally, during the synthesis of the protein chains of the antibodies, there are post-translational modifications consisting, for example, of glycosylation reactions, where saccharides are added to the peptide chain of the crystallizable fragment (Fc).

Said glycosylation process is responsible for the heterogeneity of the Fc region, which depends on the random presence of symmetric and asymmetric glycoform pairs bound to the antibody Fc and which determines the structural and functional characteristics of the antibody.

Therefore, the definition of an antibody determined on the basis of the glycosylations it contains in its Fc region would be considered a correct description according to the Chilean IPL, since they correspond to structural characteristics of said antibody, consequently they comply with the requirements of patentability. In this context, the amino acid position where the glycosylation is found and the region in which it is located should be specified.

Additionally, the antibodies can be modified using a wide variety of chemical techniques, which seek to increase the specificity and selectivity of an antibody, and which consequently modify the structural and functional characteristics thereof. In this sense, those antibodies can be claimed that have modifications that allow them to be differentiated from those antibodies disclosed in the state of the art and that their modification is not evident to a person skilled in the art.

For example, the following claim would probably be rejected by the examiner, since it is not self-sufficient and does not define clearly or in detail its structural characteristics:

> 'An antibody comprising an Fc region containing several chains of saccharides linked to the Fc region.'

In this context, it is suggested that said type of claims be worded as follows:

> 'An antibody CHARACTERIZED in that in its Fc region it contains a chain of saccharides "X" linked to the Fc region in the "Y" nitrogen of the amine group of asparagine.'

[C] Cell Line Deposits and Process of Production

Chile is party to the Budapest Treaty, therefore, when the invention comprises living biological material, including bacteria, viruses or cell lines, or a method of obtaining it, the Patent Office requires that such material be deposited with an internationally recognized organization in accordance with the Budapest Treaty, to comply with the sufficiency of the specification.

In this context, in the event that an invention comprises living biological material which has not been properly deposited in an internationally recognized organization in accordance with the Budapest Treaty, the patent application will be rejected.

Notwithstanding the foregoing, the Patent Office allows such deposit to be made during prosecution of the patent application, provided that it does not involve an extension of the claimed material.

In the case of antibodies, technical sufficiency is fulfilled by making the deposit of the hybridoma that allows the production of said antibody.

For example, the following claim probably would be rejected by an examiner due to lack of self-sufficiency:

> 'A monoclonal antibody CHARACTERIZED in that it is produced by an X-cell hybridoma.'

In this context, it is suggested that this type of claim be drafted as follows:

> 'A monoclonal antibody CHARACTERIZED in that it is produced by the hybridoma deposited with accession number ATCC HB 10709 in the American Type Culture Collection (ATCC).'

§16.03 BREADTH OF CLAIMS AND SUPPORT BY EXAMPLES

[A] Acceptable Breadth of Claims to Antibodies

The scope or amplitude of the claims will depend on the technology to be protected, on what is disclosed in the state of the art, and on the experimental data that support the technical effect generated by the antibody.

In the case of an antibody that has not been previously disclosed and its structure and sequences being unknown, it may be claimed in the broadest possible manner, as long as its technical effect is demonstrated experimentally, meets the requirements of patentability and is not within the exclusions of patentability.

[B] Required Experimental Support for Claims to Functionally Defined Antibodies

As mentioned above, claims that protect antibodies based on their functional characteristics are acceptable under the Chilean IPL as long as the following is evidenced:

- the antigen is unknown;
- the antibody-antigen binding generates a technical effect; and
- many different antibodies cause the same technical effect.

In this context, each claim must be supported in the specification by means of examples, experimental data that demonstrate its specificity, affinity and selectivity, among others.

[C] Required Experimental Support for Claims to Structurally Defined Antibodies

In the same way, the protection of an antibody based on its structural characteristics must be supported in the specification where the technical effect generated by the antibody is experimentally demonstrated.

In both cases, whether for the protection of an antibody based on its functional or structural characteristics, the patent application must give a detailed explanation of the invention and the technical effect generated by the antibody, in at least one embodiment of the invention.

Based on the foregoing, according to Chilean IPL, at least one embodiment of the invention is required in this type of technology. It is desirable that the inventive activity be demonstrated experimentally, in such a way as to allow the invention to be reproduced by a third party, without the need for additional information.

Additionally, we must emphasize that said example must demonstrate the technical and pharmacological effect that the antibody possesses; in such a way as to support the inventive level of the invention.

§16.04 SPECIFIC MEDICAL APPLICATIONS AND OTHER FOLLOW-UP INVENTIONS

[A] Treatment of Specific Diseases

In the case that an antibody has already been protected by a patent application, but a new mode of use of said antibody has been identified for the treatment of another disease very different from the initial one, a new patent application would be possible according to Chilean IPL, provided that said new use resolves a technical problem without a previous equivalent solution, generates a surprising and experimentally demonstrable technical effect, complies with the requirements referred to in Article 32 and requires a change in the dimensions, proportions or materials of the article, object or element known to obtain said solution to said technical problem. In this context, the new use of the claimed antibody must be accredited by experimental evidence in the patent application.

[B] Mode of Administration

In the case that it is determined that an antibody can be administered in a manner other than that originally claimed, said new mode of administration may be protected by a patent application, provided that the new administration mode solves a technical problem without a previous equivalent solution, generates a surprising and experimentally demonstrable technical effect, is not evident in the light of the state of the art and meets the requirements of patentability. In this case, it is necessary to take special care at the time of writing such claims so that they are not interpreted as a treatment method, since it would be considered excluded from patentability according to Chilean IPL.

For example, the following claim would probably be excluded from patentability by an examiner, since it refers to a therapeutic treatment:

> 'A composition CHARACTERIZED in that it comprises the administration of said composition to the patient with disease X.'

In this context, it is suggested that this type of claims be worded as follows:

> 'A composition containing a monoclonal antibody, CHARACTERIZED in that it is used in the preparation of an injectable composition intraperitoneally.'

In this example, it would be necessary to demonstrate experimentally in the specification of the patent application that said composition serves to be administered intraperitoneally.

[C] Dosage Regimens

According to Chilean IPL, in the case that it is determined that an antibody can be administered in a new dose different from that originally claimed, said dose may not be protected by a patent application due to exclusion of patentability.

[D] Specific Patient Groups

In the case that it is determined that an antibody can be administered to a new age group different from that originally claimed, said antibody can be protected by means of a patent application, as long as the antibody resolves a technical problem without a previous equivalent solution, for example, a pharmaceutical composition comprising an antibody for the control of a disease only in infants or only in older adults. In this case and according to Chilean IPL, it is necessary to demonstrate experimentally that said composition has a technical advantage in relation to other drugs for a specific age group.

[E] Specific Mode of Action

According to Chilean IPL, in the case that it is determined that an antibody has a new mode of action other than that originally claimed, this new mode of action may be protected by a patent application, as long as said new mode of action solves a technical problem without a previous equivalent solution, generates a surprising, experimentally demonstrable technical effect, is not obvious and complies with the requirements of patentability.

In this case, special care must be taken in that it could be considered that said new mode of action corresponds to a discovery, which would be considered excluded from patentability according to Chilean IPL.

[F] Combinations with Other Active Ingredients

In the case that it is determined that an antibody can be administered in conjunction with another component or active ingredient in proportions different from those originally claimed, said new composition may be protected by means of a patent application, as long as the new combination solves a technical problem without a previous equivalent solution, generates a surprising and experimentally demonstrable technical effect, is not evident in light of the state of the art and complies with the requirements of patentability.

[G] Specific Diagnostic Applications

According to the Chilean IPL, diagnostic methods are excluded from patentability when they are intended to be applied to the human body or to animals.

Based on the foregoing, it is possible to protect a diagnostic method as long as it is not applied to the human body or animals, such as for example a diagnostic method to determine the presence of a certain antibody in an isolated or *ex vivo* sample. In this case, it must be explicitly stated that said diagnostic method is not performed on the human body or an animal, but outside of it.

Additionally, it is possible to protect products intended to implement a diagnostic method, such as a device, or a composition.

In this context, said method of *ex vivo* diagnosis or products intended to implement said method may be protected by means of a patent application, provided that said methods or products solve a technical problem without a prior equivalent solution, generate a surprising and experimentally demonstrable technical effect, are not evident in light of the state of the art and meet the requirements of patentability.

§16.05 ASSESSMENT OF INVENTIVENESS

[A] General Approach

As mentioned throughout this chapter, any invention must comply with the patentability requirements, namely novelty, inventive step and industrial application. In general terms, the most difficult requirement to satisfy corresponds to the inventive step, which is understood as solving a technical problem without a solution, in a way that is not obvious to a person having ordinary skill in the art.

In addition to the patentability requirements mentioned above, Chilean IPLestablishes that patent applications must clearly define the invention and its essential characteristics in the specification, claims should be supported in said document, they must comply with the requirement of unity of invention and appropriate link between the claims, and finally, the patent must not claim any matter excluded from patentability.

[B] Particularities Regarding Claims to Antibodies

In this context, and specifically related to the protection of antibodies, the claims will be analysed by an examiner of the Patent Office, in order to determine whether the application meets formal, substantive and the requirements of patentability.

Regarding the aspects of formal presentation, the claims must be structured as follows:

Where the 'preamble' will contain what is known or disclosed in the state of the art, the word 'CHARACTERIZED' must be uppercase, in such a way as to separate the known from the new and inventive, and finally the 'inventive activity' must contain the description in a clear and self-sufficient manner, said structural characteristics and sequences that define the antibody.

Regarding the background aspects, the examiner will analyse whether the antibody complies with the requirements set above, namely, if it is well defined in terms of its structural characteristics and sequences, and will determine based on an exhaustive search of the state of the art whether said antibody meets or not the requirements of patentability.

§16.06 ENFORCEMENT AND SCOPE OF PROTECTION

[A] Biosimilars

According to the Chilean RIPL, a biosimilar pharmaceutical product is defined as a biotechnological medicine product that has proven to be comparable in quality, safety and efficacy to the reference biotechnological product, based on its exhaustive characterization by means of comparability studies under equal conditions, constituted by quality studies and non-clinical and clinical studies, all of them comparative.

In this context and given the nature of a biosimilar medicine, they will most probably contain a biotechnological material which will be slightly different from that included in the pharmaceutical product of reference protected by a patent.

Based on the above, the success of a potential infringement action will depend on the scope of protection of the set of claims of the patent that protects the product of reference.

Finally, the Chilean IPL does not have an express regulation from the point of view of the patents in connection to biosimilar goods. In addition, case law in connection with this matter is almost non-existent in Chile.

[B] Equivalence

The Chilean law does not expressly consider the doctrine of equivalents. Therefore, the plausibility of successfully invoking this theory would have to be analysed on a case-by-case basis. In any case and based on the characteristics of the Chilean civil law tradition system the successful application of this theory may prove to be very challenging.

The Chilean IPL does not expressly regulate equivalent infringements. Accordingly, the determination of whether a claim that protects an antibody may or may not be infringed by the commercialization of an equivalent one will depend on the criteria applied by the judge in each specific case. In this regard it must be borne in mind that the Chilean legal and judicial systems are of civil law tradition, thus case law and precedents are not binding for judges.

In this regard, Chilean doctrine (books and papers) are not in agreement as to the applicability of the doctrine of equivalents on the Chilean system, neither is there relevant case law on the matter.

Chapter 17

Mexico

Hector E. Chagoya-Cortes & Israel Jiménez

§17.01 ANTIBODIES AS PATENTABLE SUBJECT-MATTER

[A] Legal Framework

Mexican law does not have specific provisions related to eligibility of antibodies as such by statute or judicial decisions. The Mexican Industrial Property Law (IPL) is the main body of law that includes the requirements for patentable subject matter. The relevant provisions of Mexican IPL regarding patentable subject are described below.

The most powerful tool of Mexican law in order to assess eligibility of any invention is the definition of invention as such included in the IPL, which reads as follows (emphasis added):

> '§15. It shall be considered an invention any *human creation* that allows transforming matter or energy as existing in nature, for the benefit of mankind in satisfying its concrete needs.'

> '§16. *There shall be patentable* those *inventions* that are new, resulting from an inventive step and susceptible of industrial application under the terms of this Law, *except*:
>
> I. Essentially biological processes for the production, reproduction and propagation of plants and animals;
> *II. Biological and genetic material as existing in nature;*
> III. Animal breeds;
> IV. The human body and the living parts comprising it;
> V. Plant varieties.'

> '§19. *There shall not be considered inventions* for the purposes of this Law:
>
> I. Scientific or theoretical principles;
> II. Discoveries *consisting of discovering or uncovering something that already existed in nature, even if it was formerly unknown to mankind*;

III. Schemes, plans, rules and methods for performing mental acts, games or business and the mathematical methods;
IV. Computer programs;
V. Forms for presenting information;
VI. Aesthetic creations and artistic or literary works;
VII. Diagnostic, therapeutic or surgical treatment methods applicable to human body and those related to animals; and,
VIII. The juxtaposition of known inventions or mixtures of known products, its *variation of use, form, dimensions or materials*, unless the combination or fusion is in a way such that they cannot work separately or that *the characteristic features or functions of the same are modified in order to obtain a non-obvious industrial result or use* for those skilled in the art.'

Regarding the breadth of the claims directed to antibodies and the amenability of certain claim drafting it is important to consider also the provisions related to sufficiency of disclosure under Mexican law, which are contained in §47 Mexican IPL and the corresponding regulations of the same, as follows (emphasis added):

'§47. The patent application shall be accompanied by:

I. *The description of the invention, which shall be clear and complete enough for a full comprehension of the same and, in such a case, for guiding to put it into practice by a person with skills and regular knowledge in the subject matter*. Furthermore, it shall include *the best mode* known to the applicant to practise the invention, when this is not clear from the description of the invention, as well as include the information exemplifying the industrial application of the invention.
In the case of biological material for which the description of the invention cannot be detailed as such, the application should be complemented by a deposit certificate of such material in an institution so recognized by the Institute, according to the regulations of this Law;
II. The drawings that are required for the comprehension of the description;
III. One or more *claims that shall be clear and concise* and shall not exceed the contents of the description; and
IV. A summary of the description of the invention that shall serve only for publication purposes and as technical information element.'

In turn, the Regulations of the IPL establish the following (emphasis added):

'§28. The description shall be drafted subject to the following rules:

I. It shall indicate the denomination or title of the invention as described in the application;
II. It shall precise the technical field to which the invention refers to;
III. It shall indicate the background known to the applicant about the prior art to which the invention pertains and shall cite, preferably, those documents reflecting such art;
IV. *It shall specify the invention, as claimed, in clear and exact terms that allow the comprehension of the technical problem, even if such problem is not designated expressly as such, and shall provide the solution to the same, and shall expose the advantageous effects of the invention, if any, with regard to the prior art.*

The description shall be concise but as complete as possible, and there shall be avoided digressions of any kind. In the description there shall be noted the differences of the disclosed invention with respect to similar known inventions;

V. *When the deposit of biological material is required as mandated by §47 subsection I second paragraph of the Law, it shall mention that such deposit has been made and shall indicate the name and address of the deposit institution, and shall describe, to the extent possible, the nature and features of the deposited material in what is pertinent for the disclosure of the invention*;

VI. It shall contain the numbering of the different figures comprising the drawings by referencing to them and the different parts constituting the same;

VII. It shall indicate the best method known or the best way foreseen by the applicant in order to put in practice the claimed invention. When appropriate, the indication shall be made by means of practical examples or specific applications of the invention, provided that they are not unrelated to the invention described and with reference to the drawings, if any; and,

VIII. *It shall indicate explicitly, if and when it is not evident from the description or the nature of the invention, the way in which it can be produced or used, or both.*'

The description shall follow the form and order established in this section, except when due to the nature of the invention, a different form or order allows a better comprehension and a more practical presentation.

Every part of the description to which subsections II to VII above refer, shall be preceded by a heading.'

'§29. The claims shall be drafted according to the following rules:

I. The number of claims shall correspond to the nature of the claimed invention;

II. When several claims are filed, they shall be numbered consecutively with Arabic numbers;

III. They shall not contain references to the description or drawings, unless it is absolutely necessary;

IV. *They shall be drafted according to the technical features of the invention*;

V. If the application includes drawings, the technical features mentioned in the claims may be followed by reference signs, related to the corresponding parts of such features in the drawings, if they facilitate the comprehension of the claims. Such reference signs must be placed between parentheses;

VI. The first claim, which shall be independent, shall refer to the essential feature of a product or process for which protection is mainly claimed. When the application comprises more than one category of claims to which §45 of the Law refers to, it shall include at least one independent claim per category. The dependent claims shall comprise all the features of the claim from which they depend and specify the additional features that keep a congruent relationship with the independent or related dependent claims. The claims depending on two or more claims shall not serve as a base for any other claim that, in turn, depends on two or more claims; and,

VII. Any dependent claim shall include the limitations contained in the claim or claims from which it depends.'

[B] General Amenability or Exclusion of Antibodies from Patentability

From §15 of the Mexican IPL, it follows that antibodies will be eligible subject matter under Mexican law if and only if they are a result of some kind of transformation by human intervention (human creation), which means that naturally occurring antibodies will not be patentable unless it is proven that there is something that the inventor did in order to obtain them.

Because patents are only granted to inventions, this provision applied to antibodies implies that naturally occurring antibodies should not be considered inventions because they would not be a human creation. This is further reinforced by the provisions of §16 subsection II and §19 subsection II of the same IPL, which in both cases refer as non-eligible biological material as existing in nature and naturally occurring materials even if they were unknown to mankind.

An additional guidance for patentability of antibodies is found in §19 subsection VIII of the IPL, whereby it could be considered that, if the inventor has modified the nature of the claimed antibody, varied its use, form or materials in a way that falls into the exception of subsection VIII of §19 of the IPL, it could be considered an invention and, therefore, should be eligible.

[C] Required Distinction from Naturally Occurring Antibodies

According to what was discussed earlier in this section, the level of intervention of a person in obtaining the features of the antibody is of the essence in order to determine if it is eligible for patent protection.

Therefore, a humanized antibody could always be considered patent eligible since by definition a humanized antibody refers to an antibody that was obtained from cells of a different species that then has been subject to a process by intervention of a person, that humanized it by changing its sequence. Likewise, a chimeric antibody is by definition one that was obtained artificially and therefore should be patent eligible.

However, a monoclonal antibody may occur naturally or not, and the fact that it is monoclonal might not be enough to make it patent eligible, whereas isolated antibodies may not be patentable in Mexico per §15, 16 subsection II and/or 19 subsection II, *unless they have been modified, changed or combined* so that they fall into the exception of § 19 subsection VIII and because of such modification, change or combination have now an inventive feature such as increased stability or effectiveness to treat a disease. In such a case, however, the claim should not be limited to the antibody as such only, but must include such modification, change or combination that gave rise to the non-obvious result.

§17.02 ACCEPTABLE CLAIM FEATURES FOR DEFINING ANTIBODIES

[A] Functional Features

The Mexican IPL and its regulations do not expressly prohibit the drafting of antibody-related claims based on function. However, it can be said that claims drafted by referring only to functional features are not likely to be allowed under Mexican law and might be actually rejected by the Mexican Patent Office, unless such functional features refer to new uses of structurally known antibodies. The reason is that such claims are not considered to contain all the features necessary for those skilled in the art to reproduce the invention and therefore render it undefined and unclear, thus contravening § 29 of the Regulations of the IPL and the IPL itself under § 47 subsection III.

[1] Target/Antigen

The definition of an antibody by the target or the antigen is not considered clear because the features of the antibody, particularly the CDRs and other features that are necessary in order to bind to such target or antigen are not clearly defined and therefore the invention cannot be reproduced by those skilled in the art. Under Mexican practice, the ability of an antibody to bind to the target or antigen is the problem to be solved and therefore it does not constitute a technical feature in the context of § 29 of the Regulations of the IPL.

[2] Mode of Binding: Target Affinity, Binding Specificity, Epitope, Definitions via Reference Antibodies and Competitive Binding

Just like defining by the target or antigen, a functional definition alone related to the affinity, specificity of the binding, or the result in cases of competitive binding or behaviour regarding reference antibodies are not considered a technical feature of the antibody, but a technical problem to be solved and an effect of the actual structure of the antibody. Therefore, under the current Mexican patent practice such kind of definitions are not allowable unless they are complemented by a structural feature that leads to such function. Therefore, this kind of claim is typically rejected by the Mexican Patent Office for lack of compliance with § 29 of the Regulations of the IPL.

[3] Effect on Target

This is also considered a technical problem to be solved and not a technical feature of the antibody, which therefore is also rejected by Mexican examiners for lack of compliance with § 29 of the Regulations of the IPL, because the effect of an antibody on the target is considered to be the result of its structure and therefore examiners do not consider such effect as a technical feature of the claimed invention.

[B] Structural Features

As opposed to functional features, structural features of the antibodies are generally accepted by examiners as technical features in claims, very often accompanied by the effects or functional features in order to differentiate the antibodies with respect to other similar antibodies known in the prior art, which is particularly useful when the function is what provides the antibody as structurally defined with inventive step. Actually, the strongest antibody claims are those structurally defining the antibody and then providing the effect in terms of the function achieved by providing such structure.

[1] Molecular Topology: Antibody Types, Fragments and Antibody Constructs

All of the features regarding the molecular topology of the antibody can be used to define it, but patentability of each will depend on the prior art and the effect of the topology on the effects of the antibody.

[2] Amino Acid Sequences

Amino acid sequences are extremely important in defining antibody structures under Mexican practice. The need to provide the full-length or not will depend on the claimed features and their effects.

[a] Full-Length Sequences of Antibodies

As antibody studies become increasingly available in the scientific community, the need to refer to the specific sequences will depend on the level of novelty of the claimed antibody. For well-known sequences it might be enough to make reference to the published sequence, but in terms of the definition of the claim all the relevant sequences differentiating the antibody from the prior art must be included in the specification, and of course the specific sequences must be included if they are going to be claimed as a technical feature (see next section).

[b] Sequences of Fragments, CDRs and Framework Regions

As explained before, the sequences of any fragments or regions of an antibody will be necessary in the specification if they are relevant in order to define the full structure of the antibody and/or such structure is an essential feature that will be claimed as such in the claims by referring to the sequence.

The described and/or claimed regions as defined by their sequences can range from the heavy or light chains and the variable or constant regions of the immunoglobulin domains, and may be as specific as the sequences of the CDR, Fab, Fc hinge or paratopes, depending on the specific region that provides the novelty and inventiveness to the claimed antibody.

An example of this kind of claim as allowed in Mexico is as follows:

> 'An antagonist antibody or a fragment thereof binding to [TARGET] comprising a heavy chain CDR1 comprising the amino acid sequence SEQ ID NO: [X], a heavy chain CDR2 comprising the amino acid sequence SEQ ID NO: [Y] and a heavy chain CDR3 comprising the amino acid sequence SEQ ID NO: [Z]; and further comprising a light chain CDR1 comprising the amino acid sequence SEQ ID NO: [X']; a light chain CDR2 comprising the amino acid sequence SEQ ID NO: [Y'] and a light chain CDR3 comprising the amino acid sequence SEQ ID NO: [Z']'

As may be seen, in addition to the sequences the target and type of antibody are relevant for claiming the antibody.

[3] Chemical Modifications, Conjugation and Glycosylation

When a chemical modification is made to an antibody, the best thing to do is to structurally describe the antibody that is obtained through such modification by defining the obtained sequence and structure. However, when this kind of modification occurs, including conjugation or glycosylation of antibodies, it is very often not possible for the inventor to particularly describe the obtained structure and in such cases, if the experimental data available is enough, it might be possible to claim the obtained antibody if the starting structure is clearly defined and the specific conditions of the chemical change are also clearly described and the resulting product is specifically tested functionally. This kind of claim and description may face objections by Mexican examiners but upon the impossibility of defining it structurally examiners may accept an indirect claim if all the technical features necessary for obtaining it are clearly defined including the starting material.

[C] Cell Line Deposits and Process of Production

Because of the biological complexity of the interaction of antibodies with the antigens, hybridoma cell lines may be claimed as such based on the description of the antibody and often are not deposited if the process for obtaining them is clearly described in the specification and they are tied to the antibody structure as claimed. However, it might be necessary to deposit the cells under the Budapest Treaty whenever they are designed and necessary for obtaining the antibody and they are not obtained through known techniques as part of the compliance with the requirement of sufficient disclosure (Art. 47 of Mexican IPL).

As for the processes, all the conditions of a process including culture media, growth conditions and purification and isolation steps can all be claimed if and when they provide an improved result even for known antibodies. As with all processes, the steps must be defined properly. The description of the process is typically a must, at least in the specification, for complying with Art. 47 of the Mexican IPL regarding sufficient description for the best mode to put into practice the invention.

§17.03 BREADTH OF CLAIMS AND SUPPORT BY EXAMPLES

[A] Acceptable Breadth of Claims to Antibodies

As explained above, there might be scenarios in which antibodies could be claimed as such based on the functionality. This of course limits the breadth of the subject matter for which it is possible to claim in antibody technology in Mexico. However, for well-known antibodies that are found a new use, claims of European Patent Convention (EPC) type may be used in order to claim such new use or functional effect if the same was previously unknown, such as:

> 'An agent consisting of an antibody or a CDR thereof with specificity for [TARGET] for use in the treatment of [NEW DISEASE] wherein [SPECIFIC CONDITIONS FOR USE].'

The breadth of the claims and the specified conditions will depend on the experimental evidence and the actual functional effects of the antibody whenever the same were not originally described in the prior art and must be assessed case-by-case as explained below.

[B] Required Experimental Support for Claims to Functionally Defined Antibodies

As explained above, these functional features of antibodies may be claimed only for modified antibodies or new uses of known antibodies where the contribution is not the antibody itself.

Mexican examiners try to limit the scope of the claims strictly to the embodiments actually provided in the examples or experimental evidence of the patent specification.

Accordingly, it is important to take into account when drafting antibody claims the fact that modifications or new uses of known antibodies are, as a general rule, not patentable. This is unless an unexpected or synergistic effect is proven, according to the provisions of § 19 subsection VIII of the Mexican IPL. Therefore, for this kind of claim the allowed breadth of the claim would be dependent on whether the evidence of such modification or variation of use is shown for a variety of embodiments. Otherwise the invention will be rendered obvious because those skilled in the art would expect antibodies to behave technically in a certain way and, if the antibody itself is not new, the non-obvious effect must be experimentally proven in order to be patentable under Mexican IPL.

[C] Required Experimental Support for Claims to Structurally Defined Antibodies

When an antibody is claimed by its structure, it is assumed that the antibody itself is new and inventive. Accordingly, the requirement for support would be complied with by providing the sequence, which is the most effective way to claim an antibody. As also explained, when the antibody is claimed as a modification of a known antibody the structure of which is already known, the description of the modification would be enough for the claim.

As a general rule, however, it must be taken into account that the requirement of Mexican IPL is to provide the best mode known to the applicant for practising the invention (Art. 47 of Mexican IPL) and that therefore there is no statutory or legal obligation to provide experimental evidence of every possible embodiment of the claimed invention.

This means, however, that for a new structure of an antibody the specification must provide support for obtaining it in terms of and purification process, including techniques, cell lines and even testing techniques for identifying the same. This kind of information, in addition, may also serve in support of claims related to modified antibodies, when an antibody cannot be structurally defined by the applicant.

§17.04 SPECIFIC MEDICAL APPLICATIONS AND OTHER FOLLOW-UP INVENTIONS

Under § 19 subsection VIII of the Mexican IPL there is a general statement that juxtaposition of inventions or a variation in use, form, dimensions or materials is not patentable. The same section provides an exception whenever known inventions are combined such that they cannot work separately (synergistic effect) or whenever such change or use is such that provides a non-obvious result for those skilled in the art.

Second medical uses, compositions comprising known antibodies and all kinds of follow-up inventions are therefore patentable if and only if experimental information proving synergistic or non-obvious effects of the claimed subject matter is provided.

Accordingly, the comments below assume that proper experimental evidence is provided to comply with the requirements of Mexican IPL regarding the synergistic or non-obvious effect of the claimed invention.

[A] Treatment of Specific Diseases

Treatment of specific diseases can be claimed based on experimental evidence and the format for such claims may be EPC2000 or Swiss-style. Please note that the Mexican practice for this kind of claims obliges drafting the claim directed to the manufacturer and user in the structure:

> 'The use of antibody [FULL IDENTIFICATION] for the manufacture of a pharmaceutical composition for treating [DISEASE].'
>
> 'An antibody [FULL IDENTIFICATION] for use in treating [DISEASE].'

[B] Mode of Administration

Mode of administration claims can also be allowable ideally as a composition claim, and when the mode of administration has a new therapeutic effect also as EPC or Swiss style claims.

[C] Dosage Regimens

Dosage regimens may be claimed also in EPC2000 and Swiss style claims according to the latest practice of the Mexican Patent Office.

[D] Specific Patient Groups

The use of an antibody in specific patient groups must include means for identifying the patients and may be claimed in the same fashion as dosage regimens when the antibody is already known and used for the same disease.

[E] Specific Mode of Action

Specific mode of action alone may not be patentable as something that consists of making known something that was previously unknown to mankind, an exception to patentability under § 19 of Mexican IPL, unless there is a human intervention so that the antibody acts in a way that would otherwise not happen naturally.

[F] Combinations with Other Active Ingredients

A combination of antibodies with other active ingredients may be claimed as a composition of matter.

[G] Specific Diagnostic Applications

Diagnostic applications are commonly drafted in the same fashion as treatment of diseases claims, but most commonly in EPC2000 style. Only the invasive steps of diagnosing methods are excluded from patentability, and therefore, if such steps are excluded from the claim and the diagnosis is still achieved, the claims can be valid. If the diagnostic application happens to be *in vitro*, process or method claims may be included considering that the restriction of patentability is for diagnostic methods applied directly on the human or animal body, which is interpreted in Mexico as a restriction to *in vivo* methods.

§17.05 ASSESSMENT OF INVENTIVENESS

[A] General Approach

In general, Mexican examiners use the problem-solution approach for examining inventive step. Under Mexican law an invention has inventive step when the results of the invention cannot evidently be deducted from the prior art for those skilled in the art.

Therefore, the prior art must provide premises enough for a deductive logical process so that such deductive process would result in the claimed invention for solving the same problem. This means that references in the prior art must be such that guide those skilled in the art towards the invention clearly based on specific premises of the prior art and not only speculative or hindsight conclusions.

[B] Particularities Regarding Claims to Antibodies

It is extremely important to define in the description the problem that is solved through the claimed antibody, and particularly, for variations of antibodies (either structural or functional), it is of the essence to provide the experimental evidence proving that the change made to the antibody or to its use is such that an unexpected result is achieved with regard to the prior art.

In other words, those skilled in the art would expect to achieve a certain result by the use of the antibody as known, and therefore, the experimental evidence should be such that proves that a different result is obtained by using or modifying the antibody according to the claims.

Without proper experimental evidence, the invention very likely will be considered not-inventive or not patent-eligible as an obvious variation of a known invention.

§17.06 ENFORCEMENT AND SCOPE OF PROTECTION

[A] Biosimilars

Biosimilar drugs in Mexico nowadays have a higher regulatory burden than regular generic drugs, considering that the chemical equivalence is not enough for demonstrating that an antibody (and in general any biotechnology drug) acts in the same way as another.

Mexico has a system linking patents covering drugs with the health approval system which operates differently than the FDA's Orange Book but serves the purpose of avoiding the grant of health approvals for patented drugs.

The system, unlike the FDA's, is based on a publication made by the Mexican Institute of Industrial Property (IMPI), as the Mexican Patent Office, where the patents are listed according to their active principle. Currently all patents covering an active principle and formulations are readily published and there is still litigation related to second medical use patents.

The linkage system establishes that whenever a patent is published in the so-called Linkage Gazette by IMPI, the health authorities will not grant an approval of such drug. Antibodies and biotechnology drugs are eligible to be published in the Gazette.

Significantly for antibodies, process patents are expressly excluded from the linkage system. The reason is that the system was designed for chemical entity-based drugs, where the production process has little or no impact in the final performance of the drug. However, for antibodies it is well known that the process might determine certain features affecting affinity and even safety of the drug, and that therefore, the process patents are also extremely important for this matter.

Accordingly, for process patents, in the absence of a patent claiming the product or formulation specifically, the linkage system is not applicable.

[B] Equivalence

The doctrine of equivalents is not well established in Mexico and therefore only literal infringement is recognized in practice by the Mexican Patent Office. However, under Mexican practice, whenever a claim is drafted in a two-part form with a prior art features section preceding the characterizing section of the claim, it is considered that the novel and inventive features are those recited after the characterizing section. Therefore, if the prior art features are not exactly found in an allegedly infringing product but the novel features are, it could be argued that there could be an equivalence with the subject matter that is claimed.

In the case of antibodies it would be extremely difficult to demonstrate equivalence because of the complex nature of their biological behaviour, which would not necessarily lead to the same result and therefore the same basis to say that an antibody must not be biosimilar makes it difficult to apply a doctrine such as equivalents for antibody cases in Mexico.

Chapter 18

China

Gesheng Huang

§18.01 ANTIBODIES AS PATENTABLE SUBJECT-MATTER

[A] Legal Framework

Article 5 and Article 25 of the Chinese Patent Law ('the Law', unless indicated otherwise) provide relevant legal provisions governing patentable subject matter in China.

Article 5 of the Law sets forth a general provision for amenability to patentability, which excludes the following from patent protection: 'contrary to the laws of the State or social morality', 'detrimental to public interest', and 'relying on genetic resources illegally obtained'.

Article 25 of the Law, on the other hand, specifically lists the subject matter that is excluded from patent protection:

(1) scientific discoveries;
(2) rules and methods for mental activities;
(3) methods for the diagnosis or for the treatment of diseases;
(4) animal and plant varieties;
(5) substances obtained by means of nuclear transformation;
(6) any design of pattern, colour or their combination on plane printed articles and mainly have labelling functions.

In addition, the Patent Examination Guidelines of China's National Intellectual Property Administration (CNIPA) ('Guidelines') give further interpretation and explanation on how to apply Article 5 and Article 25 of the Law in patent examination.

With respect to patentability of biotechnical and pharmaceutical related inventions, the relevant provisions and stipulations under the Guidelines are cited and/or summarized below.

For inventions against 'social morality' under Article 5, the Guidelines state in Part I, Chapter 1, Section 3.1.2 that:

> 'An artificial sexual organ or its substitute not for medical use, or a method of mating a human-being with an animal, a process for modifying the germ line genetic identity of human beings or a human being thus modified, a process for cloning human beings or a cloned human being, use of human embryos for industrial or commercial purposes, and a process for modifying the genetic identity of animals which is likely to cause them suffering without any substantial medical benefit to human beings or animals, are contrary to social morality and thus shall not be granted patent rights.'

Furthermore, in Part II, Chapter 10, Section 9.1.1 of the Guidelines, 'use of human embryos for industrial or commercial purposes' is interpreted as including 'both an embryonic stem cell of human beings and a preparing method thereof' and 'the human body, at the various stages of its formation and development, including a germ cell, an oosperm, an embryo and an entire human body'.

For 'Scientific discoveries' under Article 25, the Guidelines state in Part I, Chapter 1, Section 4.1; Part II, Chapter 10, Section 2.1 and 9.1.2.2, that a natural substance found in nature and existing in its natural state is merely a discovery and thus is unpatentable. Similarly, a microorganism, gene or DNA fragment found in nature and existing in its natural state is also regarded as a 'scientific discovery' rather than an invention, thus no patent rights shall be granted.

However, the Guidelines further stipulate in Part II, Chapter 10, Section 2.1 that:

> 'If a substance is isolated or extracted from nature for the first time, of which the structure, the morphology or other physical/chemical parameters are unknown in the prior art and can be precisely characterized, and if it can be exploited industrially, the substance per se and the process for obtaining it are all patentable under the Patent Law.'

Furthermore, the Guidelines explicitly apply the same criteria of distinguishing inventions from scientific discoveries to biological materials such as genes, DNA fragments as well as to microorganisms.

For 'a method for the diagnosis or for the treatment of diseases' under Article 25 of the Law, the Guidelines illustrate in Part II, Chapter 1, Section 4.3, and Part II, Chapter 10, Section 4.5.2 numerous examples to identify whether an invention belongs to a method for the diagnosis or treatment of diseases or not. As exceptions to this unpatentable subject matter, it is stipulated that:

(1) Instruments or apparatus for implementing these methods of diagnosis or treatment, or substances or materials for use in such methods is subject matter for which patent right can be granted; and
(2) Medical use in forms such as 'use of substance X for the manufacturing of a medicament', 'use of substance X for the manufacturing of a medicament for the treatment of a disease' and so on, are patentable.

[B] General Amenability or Exclusion of Antibodies from Patentability

From the legal framework as summarized above, it is quite clear that, although the patentability issue of an antibody is not specifically prescribed either in the Law or in the Guidelines, the principles and criteria on patentability of natural substances and biological materials such as genes or DNA fragments are also applicable to antibodies. That is to say, all types of antibodies are amenable to patentability under Chinese patent practice.

[C] Required Distinction from Naturally Occurring Antibodies

As outlined in §18.01[A] above, natural substances are regarded as a patentable subject matter under certain circumstances and the same patentability criteria also apply to naturally occurring antibodies. Therefore, a naturally occurring antibody is still regarded as patentable subject matter provided that:

(1) it is isolated or extracted for the first time from nature (no need for this to be recited in the claims, but it should be described in the specification);
(2) its structure (for example, amino acid sequences) or other features are unknown in the prior art and can be clearly characterized (and need to be defined in the claims);
(3) it can be exploited industrially (no need for this to be recited in the claims, but it should be described in the specification).

§18.02 ACCEPTABLE CLAIM FEATURES FOR DEFINING ANTIBODIES

[A] Functional Features

[1] Target/Antigen

Frankly speaking, the current Guidelines do not give detailed stipulations on how to define antibodies in the claims, including which technical features are admissible, and whether a feature alone suffices or has to be used in combination with other features. Therefore, the discussion in this section is mainly based on current practice.

Generally, antibody claims solely defined by target/antigen/epitope are rarely accepted by Chinese examiners, and are likely to be rejected as being unclear or too broad to be supported by the specification. If a target/antigen is already known in the prior art, such claims may further be rejected for lack of inventive step.

Under certain circumstances, for example, if an antigen is novel and inventive, or if a specific epitope of a known antigen is identified and characterized for the first time, and the antigen/specific epitope is structurally defined clearly in the claims (for example, by amino acid sequence of the epitope or the novel antigen), it might be possible to define antibodies solely by the target/antigen/epitope feature. However, even in these cases, methods for the preparation and identification of antibodies and specific examples of antibodies obtained by said method should be disclosed in the specification, unless antibodies to such target/antigen/epitope can be obtained by routine methods, so as to meet the sufficient disclosure requirement.

As to the question of whether a definition of target/antigen is always required for a claim directed to antibodies, it depends on the essence of the claimed invention. If the invention is directed to a molecular topology and/or modification of antibodies, it is not required to define the specific target/antigen of the antibody in the claims. On the other hand, if the invention is directed to an antibody against a novel and specific antigen/target, said target/antigen needs to be further defined in the claims, either alone or in combination with other features of the antibodies.

Examples of claims defined by antigen or epitope are provided in the following:

ZL98801808.X, granted on 27 July 2005

Granted claims 17 and 18:

17. An IFNAR1 binding protein, having the sequence of SEQ ID NO:2 or SEQ ID NO:8.
18. A molecule, comprising antibody or antigen binding region that is specific to the IFNAR1 binding protein of claim 17.

ZL201080048573.1, granted on 22 August 2017

Granted claim 1:

1. An antibody or binding fragment thereof, directed against E1 extracellular loops of a human sodium channel, wherein the human sodium channel is Na v1.7, wherein the antibody or fragment thereof binds the following amino acid sequence selected from SEQ ID NO: 128 and 129.

[2] Mode of Binding: Target Affinity, Binding Specificity, Epitope, Definitions via Reference Antibodies and Competitive Binding

'Mode of binding' is regarded as a functional feature, and it is frequently used by applicants in the claims to define antibodies, with the expectation that such a definition can give a broad scope of protection.

However, as to limitation effects of such features, it is stipulated in the Guidelines, Part II, Chapter 3, Section 3.2.5, when judging the novelty of a claim on a product comprising functional features, it should be considered whether such functional feature(s) imply that the claimed product has a structure and/or composition distinct from that of the product disclosed in the prior art. If based on such functional features, a person skilled in the art cannot distinguish the claimed product from the known product, it can be presumed that the claimed product is identical with the known product. In such case, it is usually deemed that such a functional feature has no limitation effect on the claims.

Therefore, under current Chinese patent practice, if a claim defines an antibody by functional feature(s) alone, such claim is usually deemed as lack of novelty. In addition, such claim may also be deemed as too broad to be supported by the specification or as unclear.

In view of the above, a claim defining antibodies only with 'mode of binding' is rarely accepted under the Chinese patent practice. Such features should be used to define claims in combination with other features, such as structural feature(s), for example, amino acid sequences of the claimed antibodies.

[3] Effect on Target

Similar to 'mode of binding', an 'effect on target' is also deemed as a functional feature, and cannot be used to define an antibody in the claims alone. It should be in combination with other features, such as structural feature(s), for example, amino acid sequences of antibodies.

[B] Structural Features

[1] Molecular Topology: Antibody Types, Fragments and Antibody Constructs

Any molecular topology, including specific antibody types, fragments and antibody constructs, can be used to define antibodies, as long as they can clearly define the claimed antibodies and distinguish them from antibodies known in the art.

Regarding antibody types, applicants can define an antibody based on its structure type, for instance, by 'single chain antibody (for example, heavy chain antibody)', or with its creation type, for instance, by 'humanized antibody' or 'chimeric antibody'. Moreover, antibodies can also be defined by its specificities, such as monoclonal antibody, bi-specific antibody or multi-specific antibody. If an antibody type is firstly discovered, the specific antibody type can be used alone to define an antibody. However, in most cases, antibody types are known in the prior art, so antibody type should be used to define antibodies in combination with other features of an antibody, such as sequences of an antibody.

Similarly, antibody fragments can also be used to define antibodies, and in most cases, they need to be used in combination with other features in the claims.

Unlike the antibody fragment or antibody type, an antibody construct may be unique and can distinguish an invention from the prior art. In such cases, applicants can use the specific construct alone to define an antibody. For instance, if an antibody is a bispecific antibody with a specific construct (for example, with domain/chain exchange, see also granted claim 1 in ZL200880121900.4 as follows), applicants can define the construct alone in the claims and do not need to define other features such as the sequence of the chain/domain, or even the antigen of the antibody.

Examples of claims defined by molecular topology are provided in the following:

ZL200880121900.4, granted on 17 July 2013

Granted claim 1:

1. Bivalent bispecific antibody, comprising:
   A) light and heavy chains of an antibody that specifically binds to a first antigen; and
   B) light and heavy chains of an antibody that specifically binds to a second antigen, wherein the variable domains VL and VH exchange with each other.

ZL 201180040675.3, granted on 28 September 2016

Granted claim 1:

1. A bi-specific antibody comprising
   a) a full length antibody specifically binding to a first antigen and consisting of two antibody heavy chains and two antibody light chains;
   b) a Fv fragment specifically binding to a second antigen comprising a VH^2 domain and a VL^2 domain, wherein both domains are connected via a disulfide bridge, and wherein the Fv fragment is fused via the N-termini of the VH^2 domain and the VL^2 domain to the both C-termini of the heavy chain of the full length antibody specifically binding to a first antigen via a first and second peptide linker, or via the C-termini of

the VH^2 domain and the VL^2 domain to the both N-termini of one heavy and one light chain of the full length antibody specifically binding to a first antigen via a first and second peptide linker,

characterized in that one of the linkers comprises a protease cleavage site, which is cleavable by furin, wherein said protease cleavage site cleavable by furin is SEQ ID NO:13 or SEQ ID NO:14, and the other linker does not comprise a protease cleavage site; or in that one of the linkers comprises a protease cleavage site, which is cleavable by Prescission protease, wherein said protease cleavage site cleavable by Prescission protease is SEQ ID NO:15, and the other linker does not comprise a protease cleavage site.

[2] *Amino Acid Sequences*

[a] *Full-Length Sequences of Antibodies*

It is allowable to define antibodies with full-length sequences of the antibodies, either alone or in combination with other features such as antigen in the claims. However, if such a claim is drafted as an independent claim, rather than as a dependent claim, it will narrow down the scope of protection.

[b] *Sequences of Fragments, CDRs and Framework Regions*

As one of the major structural features of antibodies, amino acid sequences can be used to define antibodies in the claims. In fact, in most cases, Chinese examiners will normally ask applicants to define antibodies by amino acid sequences, either the full sequences of antibodies or sequences of some fragments of antibodies.

Where an invention is directed to a specific fragment of antibodies, which is unrelated to antigen specificity and can be applied generally to most of the antibodies (for example, specific FR sequence), the sequence of said fragment can be used to define the antibody alone, without defining the specific target/antigen of the antibody.

Where an invention is directed to an antibody to a specific antigen/target, the antibody should be defined with sequences of CDRs or fragments comprising CDRs, in combination with its specific target/antigen. In this case, the applicant can choose one or more of the following ways to define the antibody in an independent claim:

(1) Sequences of six intact CDRs;
(2) Sequences of variable regions of both heavy chain and light chain;
(3) Sequences of heavy chain and light chain.

Examples of claims defined by amino acid sequences are provided in the following:

Definition by six CDRs:

ZL 201380073489.9, granted on 19 December 2017

Granted claim 1:

1. An isolated antibody which specifically binds to human NTB-AJ, comprising CDR-H1 amino acid sequences represented by SEQ ID NO: 5, CDR-H2 amino acid sequences represented by SEQ ID NO: 6, CDR-H3 amino acid sequences

represented by SEQ ID NO: 7, CDR-L1 amino acid sequences represented by SEQ ID NO: 8, CDR-L2 amino acid sequences represented by SEQ ID NO: 9, CDR-L1 amino acid sequences represented by SEQ ID NO: 10.

ZL201110411417.3, granted on 2 March 2016

Granted claim 1:

1. An anti-NGF antibody or a fragment thereof, comprising:
   (a) three CDRs from a heavy chain variable region represented by SEQ ID NO:1; and
   (b) three CDRs from a light chain variable region represented by SEQ ID NO:2,

   wherein the CDR is a Kabat CDR or Chothia CDR,
   wherein the fragment is Fab, Fab', F(ab')2 , Fv and a ScFv.

Definition by VH + VL:

ZL 201710130518.0, granted on 13 March 2018

Granted claim 1:

1. An anti-VEGFR-2 monoclonal antibody, characterized in that the amino acid sequence of the heavy chain variable region of the antibody is SEQ. NO: 4, and the amino acid sequence of the light chain variable region of the antibody is selected from SEQ. NO: 1, SEQ. NO: 2 or SEQ NO: 3.

ZL 200980132989.9, granted on 26 November 2014

Granted claim 8:

8. An antibody or antigen-binding fragment thereof, wherein the antibody comprises a heavy chain variable region comprising the amino acid sequence of SEQ ID NO: 13 and a light chain variable region comprising the amino acid sequence of SEQ ID NO: 14; or comprises the heavy chain variable region comprising the amino acid sequence of SEQ ID NO: 33 and the light chain variable region comprising the amino acid sequence of SEQ ID NO: 14, and wherein the antibody neutralizes influenza A virus Group 1 subtype and Group 2 subtype.

Definition by HC + LC:

ZL201380042094.2, granted on 22 December 2017

Granted claim 8:

8. An antibody agent, with a heavy chain being or comprising the amino acid sequence set forth in SEQ ID NO: 21 and a light chain being or comprising the amino acid sequence set forth in SEQ ID NO: 22.

[3] Chemical Modifications, Conjugation and Glycosylation

Should inventions be based on chemical modification, conjugation or glycosylation of antibodies, relevant features of chemical modification, conjugation or glycosylation of antibodies can be used to define the antibodies in the claims of the inventions.

In this case, if the original antibodies to be modified are known in the art, the claimed antibodies can be defined solely by chemical modification, conjugation or glycosylation. Otherwise, both the antibodies to be modified and the chemical modification, conjugation or glycosylation of the antibodies should be defined in the claims.

Examples of claims defined by chemical modifications, conjugations or glycosylations are provided in the following:

ZL200480039946.3, granted on 20 May 2015

Granted claim 1:

1. A humanized Fc-glyco engineered II type anti-CD20 antibody, comprising i) a heavy chain variable region of SEQ ID NO: 32 or 40; ii) a light chain variable region of SEQ ID NO: 76, wherein as Fc-glyco engineered result, the antibody has increased ADCC, wherein the Fc region has an increased proportion of bisected, non-fucosylated oligosaccharides.

ZL 201380073311.4, granted on 16 November 2018

Granted claim 1:

1. A glycan-modified anti-CD4 antibody, comprising one or more engineered N-linked glycosylation sites in a light chain variable region, wherein the antibody has a heavy chain amino acid sequence and a light chain amino acid sequence, the heavy chain amino acid sequence comprises the three CDRs contained in SEQ ID NO: 2, the light chain amino acid sequence comprising the three CDRs contained in SEQ ID NO: 3 and one or more engineered N-linked polyglycosylation site(s), which are located in the amino acid sites in SEQ ID NO: 3 selected from the group consisting of the 54th amino acid (30E Gln) of SEQ ID NO: 3, the 77th amino acid (52Ser) of SEQ ID NO: 3, the 78th amino acid (53Thr) of SEQ ID NO: 3, the 79th amino acid (54Arg) of SEQ ID NO: 3, the 85th amino acid (60Asp) of SEQ ID NO: 3, the 90th amino acid (65Ser) of SEQ ID NO: 3, the 92nd amino acid (67Ser) of SEQ ID NO: 3 and the 101st amino acid (76Ser) of SEQ ID NO: 3.

[C] Cell Line Deposits and Process of Production

As to cell line deposits, the Guidelines state in Part II, Chapter 10, Section 9.3.1.7 that 'A claim directed to a monoclonal antibody may be defined by specifying hybridoma which produces it'.

Therefore, a cell line deposit alone can be used to define an antibody. However, it is not clear how the judges will interpret the scope of an antibody claim defined by a cell line deposit in legal proceedings, it shall only protect an antibody produced by the same cell line as defined or can extend to antibodies that can be produced by different methods but have the same structure and properties with that produced by the defined cell line? Therefore, under current Chinese patent practice, it is recommended to define antibodies in such a way as 'antibodies with the same CDRs, VH and VL, or specific epitope as that of the monoclonal antibody produced by a deposited hybridoma cell line', which can make the scope of protection of the claim be not limited to antibodies only produced by the same cell line, but extended to other antibodies that have the same CDRs, VH and VL, or specific epitope with the antibody produced by said cell line (see also granted claim 1 in ZL201180024312.0 as follows).

With regard to 'process of production', the Guidelines state that if a polypeptide could not be defined by its structural features, it can be defined by its process of production. As an antibody is also a polypeptide, and thus 'process of production' can also be used to define it, either alone or in combination with other feature(s).

Examples of claims defined by the process of production are provided in the following:

ZL03811524.7, granted on 21 March 2007

Granted claims 1 and 10:

1. A method of preparing a humanized antibody, comprising the steps of
   (a) replacing each amino acid residue in the complementarity determining region (CDR) of the heavy and light chain variable regions of the murine monoclonal antibody with alanine to generate a transformant, selecting a transformant having a lower affinity (K_D) to human antigen compared with the original murine antibody, and determining that the substituted amino acid residue in the transformant is a specificity determining residue (SDR); and
   (b) the SDR is grafted to at least one corresponding amino acid sequence in the variable region of a human antibody.
10. A humanized antibody prepared by the method according to any one of claims 1 to 9, which has an antigenic affinity higher than 8.2×10^{-9} M and inhibits HAMA (human anti-mouse antibody) reaction to a higher extent, compared with the antibody prepared by CDR-grafting method.

Examples of claims defined by cell line deposits are provided in the following:

ZL200480015677.7, granted on 10 February 2010

Granted claim 1:

1. An isolated monoclonal antibody prepared by the hybridoma cell line deposited with the ATCC as Accession Number PTA-5065.

ZL201180024312.0, granted on 26 December 2017

Granted claim 1:

1. An isolated antibody or antigen-binding fragment thereof, which:
   (a) specifically binds to C. difficile toxin B and comprises the CDR1, CDR2, CDR3 of the VH of the monoclonal antibody produced by the hybridoma cell line deposited under ATCC Accession No. PTA-9693, and the CDR1, CDR2, CDR3 of the VL of the monoclonal antibody produced by the hybridoma cell line deposited under ATCC Accession No. PTA-9693; or
   (b) specifically binds to C. difficile toxin B and comprises the CDR1, CDR2, CDR3 of the VH of the monoclonal antibody produced by the hybridoma cell line deposited under ATCC Accession No. PTA-9692, and the CDR1, CDR2, CDR3 of the VL of the monoclonal antibody produced by the hybridoma cell line deposited under ATCC Accession No. PTA-9692; or
   (c) specifically binds to C. difficile toxin B and comprises the CDR1, CDR2, CDR3 of the VH of the monoclonal antibody produced by the hybridoma cell line deposited under ATCC Accession No. PTA-9694, and the CDR1,

CDR2, CDR3 of the VL of the monoclonal antibody produced by the hybridoma cell line deposited under ATCC Accession No. PTA-9694; or

(d) is the monoclonal antibody PA-41 produced by the hybridoma cell line deposited under ATCC Accession No. PTA-9693 or a Fab, $F(ab')_2$, Fv or scFv antigen binding fragment thereof; or

(e) is a monoclonal antibody selected from the group consisting of: (i) a monoclonal antibody PA-39 produced by a hybridoma cell line of ATCC Accession No. PTA-9692 or a Fab, $F(ab')_2$ Fv or scFv antigen binding fragment thereof; (ii) a monoclonal antibody PA-50 produced by a hybridoma cell line of ATCC Accession No. PTA-9694, or a Fab, $F(ab')_2$, Fv or scFv antigen binding fragment thereof; or (iii) the monoclonal antibody PA-38 produced by the hybridoma cell line of ATCC Accession No. PTA-9888 or a Fab, $F(ab')_2$, Fv or scFv antigen binding fragment thereof.

§18.03 BREADTH OF CLAIMS AND SUPPORT BY EXAMPLES

[A] Acceptable Breadth of Claims to Antibodies

As summarized above, under current Chinese patent practice, it is usually possible to define antibodies by one or more of the following definitions:

(1) an antigen or a specific epitope on an antigen;
(2) structure(s) of an antibody by reference to particular sequence(s);
(3) deposited hybridoma with a specific deposition number; and
(4) a method for production of an antibody.

Regarding item (1), if an antibody is solely defined with a novel and inventive antigen, the antigen itself should be defined according to the stipulations in the Guidelines, Part II, Chapter 10, Section 9.3.1.5 regarding a protein/polypeptide claim:

(a) A polypeptide or protein may be defined by specifying an amino acid sequence or a base sequence of structural gene encoding said amino acid sequence.

(b) Where the amino acid sequence of the polypeptide or protein is set forth in the 'Sequence Listing' or drawing of the description, reference may be made to the sequence by use of the sequence identifier in the 'Sequence Listing' or the number of the drawing.

(c) Where a protein has a special function, for example, it has the activity of enzyme A, the protein may be defined by a combination of the terms 'substitution, deletion or addition' and functions of the protein.

(d) When the above-mentioned expressions (1)-(3) cannot be used, a polypeptide or protein may be described by specifying functions, physiochemical properties, origin or source of said polypeptide or protein, a process for producing said polypeptide or protein, etc.

In this case, the antibody claim can be defined only by its antigen, such as 'an antibody that binds to antigen X, wherein the antigen X…'.

If an antibody is directed to an epitope, usually it is necessary to define the epitope by structural feature(s), such as the sequences and/or the modifications (if modification is essential to the epitope's function, for example, its binding to the antibody). Since an epitope is usually a comparatively short peptide and a single variation may destroy its function, variations of epitopes are rarely accepted and usually specific sequence should be defined for the epitope.

Once such a claim defined with an antigen/epitope is granted, it can cover all antibodies (including monoclonal antibodies or polyclonal antibodies) against the antigen/epitope.

Regarding item (2), usually an antibody can be defined by one of the following ways:

(a) Sequences of six intact CDRs;
(b) Sequences of variable regions of both heavy chains and light chains;
(c) Sequences of heavy chain and light chains.

For items (a) to (c) above, it is usually required that, in an independent claim, each and all of the six CDRs, both VH and VL, or both HC and LC should be defined by their specific full sequences with close-ended term (for example, CDR consisting of a sequence represented by SEQ ID NO: X); Definitions with open-ended term (for example, VH comprising a sequence represented by SEQ ID NO: X) or with identity percentage (for example, HC comprising a sequence having X identity with SEQ ID NO: Y) are rarely accepted under current practice, especially with respect to the item (a) where the sequences of CDRs are comparatively short.

In addition, under current Chinese patent practice, it is difficult to define antibodies by CDR with variations, since the CNIPA usually believes that the specific CDRs are critical to the function of antibodies, and thus even a change on one amino acid in the CDR will influence the function of the antibodies.

In the case that six CDRs are defined with specific sequences in an independent claim, it is allowed to define variable region(s) or heavy/light chain(s) comprising the CDRs with variations, identities or open-ended definitions in dependent claims.

[B] Required Experimental Support for Claims to Functionally Defined Antibodies

As indicated in §18.02[A][1] above, even in the case that an antibody is solely defined by an antigen/epitope in a claim, it is still necessary to disclose at least one method for the preparation and identification of the antibodies in the specification to meet the sufficient disclosure requirement. To have such functionally defined antibodies granted, it is suggested to disclose and verify as many antibodies as possible in working examples. In addition, it is necessary to disclose experimental results for at least one property/function of these antibodies in the specification.

For an antibody defined by other functions or uses, such as affinity or therapeutical use in the claims, it is necessary to disclose experimental results/data to prove the claimed functions or uses, unless those functions or uses of the claimed antibody can be easily deduced from the prior art.

[C] Required Experimental Support for Claims to Structurally Defined Antibodies

For structurally defined antibodies, if the structural feature is deemed to be applied generally to most of the antibodies (for example, topology structure, chemical modifications), it is suggested to disclose and verify as many antibodies as possible in working examples. In addition, it is better that the antibodies are those with different antigen specificities.

If antibodies are defined by six specific CDRs (or the region comprising CDRs, such as variable regions or the heavy/light chains), at least one antibody comprising the six claimed CDRs should be exemplified and its effects should be verified in the specification.

Usually, it is necessary to provide experimental data in the original specification to show a claimed antibody has effect(s) better than known antibodies directed to the same antigen (which is required for inventive step issue, as outlined in Section §18.05[B]).

§18.04 SPECIFIC MEDICAL APPLICATIONS AND OTHER FOLLOW-UP INVENTIONS

[A] Treatment of Specific Diseases

Therapeutic use of an antibody should be claimed in so-called Swiss style format, such as 'Use of an antibody for preparing a medicament for the treating disease X'.

[B] Mode of Administration

Under current practice, it is commonly held by examiners that 'mode of administration' merely exists in the course of administration and thus has no limitation on preparation of a medicament. Therefore, a Swiss-style medical use claim solely defined by mode of administration is hard to have granted in China.

However, if an applicant could prove that the feature of 'mode of administration' implies the obtained medicaments have a different and non-obvious structure or composition, e.g. a specific dosage form, the feature will be deemed as having limitation on the medicament and thus such a medical use claim is likely to be accepted.

[C] Dosage Regimens

It is commonly held by the CNIPA and the Chinese courts that 'dosage regimen(s)' merely exist in the course of administration and thus have no limitation on the preparation of a medicament. Therefore, a Swiss-style medical use claim solely defined by dosage regimen(s) is hard to have granted in China.

[D] Specific Patient Groups

Similar to mode of administration, a Swiss-style medical use claim solely defined by specific patient groups is hard to have granted in China.

However, if applicant could prove the feature of 'specific patient groups' makes the disease to be treated different from that in the prior art, such a feature will be deemed as having a limitation on the disease and thus can be used to define the medical use.

[E] Specific Mode of Action

If applicant could prove that a feature of 'specific mode of action' makes an indication recited in the claims different from that in the prior art, such a feature will be deemed as having a limitation on the disease, thus can be used to define a medical use claim.

[F] Combinations with Other Active Ingredients

Similar to a pharmaceutical composition, an antibody can also be protected by a product claim in the form of 'combinations of the antibody with other active ingredients'.

[G] Specific Diagnostic Applications

Diagnostic use of an antibody should be claimed in Swiss-style claims such as 'Use of an antibody for preparing an agent to diagnose disease X'.

§18.05 ASSESSMENT OF INVENTIVENESS

[A] General Approach

According to Article 22 of the Chinese Patent Law, inventions should have novelty and inventive step.

The Guidelines further explain standards of the inventive step of an invention in Part II, Chapter 4. Generally speaking, an invention with inventive step means that, compared with the prior art, it is non-obvious to a person skilled in the art, and can produce an advantageous technical effect, and a so-called 'three steps' approach should be applied in assessing inventive step of a claimed invention.

[B] Particularities Regarding Claims to Antibodies

With respect to the inventive step of claims to antibodies, the Guidelines provide some specific provisions in Part II, Chapter 10, Section 9.4.2.1:

> 'If an antigen is known and it is clearly known that the antigen has immunogenicity (for example, said antigen clearly has immunogenicity because a polyclonal antibody of the antigen is known or the antigen is a polypeptide with a large molecular weight), the invention of a monoclonal antibody of the antigen does not involve an inventive step. However, if the invention is further defined by other features, and hence has unexpected technical effects, the invention of that monoclonal antibody involves an inventive step.'

In general, the inventive step of a claimed antibody may lie in one or several of the following aspects: (1) it is directed to a novel and inventive antigen, (2) it is structurally different from the antibodies known in the prior art, and (3) it is of some unexpected use/effects as compared with the antibodies known in the prior art.

In addition, there is no specific standard on what kinds of effects of antibodies can be deemed as 'unexpected'. In our experience, for example, if the affinity constant of a claimed antibody increases by an order of magnitude, such an increase can be deemed as unexpected.

§18.06 ENFORCEMENT AND SCOPE OF PROTECTION

[A] Biosimilars

For patent enforcement with respect to biosimilars, there are rare court decisions. In fact, as far as we know, there is no court decision up to now on patent infringement for antibodies. Therefore, in this part, we can only briefly summarize some of the general principles and doctrines in judging patent infringement in China, which of course shall be applicable to possible future cases on infringing antibody patents.

In China, laws comprise statutes and judicial interpretations from the Supreme People's Court of the People's Republic of China ('the Supreme Court'). On the other hand, with the current judicial reform, precedents will play a more and more important role in practice, although they are not a source of laws.

With respect to patent enforcement and protection, the basic statute is of course the Patent Law, which stipulates the general and fundamental provisions. In parallel, the judicial interpretations from the Supreme Court stipulate more detailed and specific provisions in guiding how to apply the general provisions of the Patent Law. Up to now, the Supreme Court has issued three major judicial interpretations on patent various issues, namely (1) Several Provisions of the Supreme People's Court on Issues Relating to Application of Law to Adjudication of Cases of Patent Disputes (enacted in 2001 and revised in 2015) ('SPC's Provisions'), (2) Interpretation of the Supreme People's Court on Issues Concerning the Application of Law in the Trial of Disputes over Infringement of Patent Rights (enacted in 2009) ('Interpretation I'), and (3) Interpretation of the Supreme People's Court on Issues Concerning the Application of Law in the Trial of Disputes over Infringement of Patent Rights (II) (enacted in 2016) ('Interpretation II').

To summarize the relevant provisions of the Law and judicial interpretations of the Supreme Court, some major principles and doctrines on judging patent infringements are provided below:

> **Acts of Patent Infringement**
>
> After the grant of the patent right for an invention or utility model, except where otherwise provided for in this Law, no entity or individual may, without the authorization of the patentee, exploit the patent, that is, make, use, offer to sell, sell or import the patented product, or use the patented process, and use, offer to sell, sell or import the product directly obtained by the patented process, for production or business purposes. (Article 11 of the Law)

Interpretation of Patent Claims

The extent of protection of the patent right for inventions or utility models shall be determined by the terms of the claims. The description and the appended drawings may be used to interpret the terms of the claims. (Article 59 of the Law)

Acts Deemed not Constituting Patent Infringement

None of the following shall be deemed as infringement of the patent right:

...

(4) Where any person uses the patent concerned solely for the purposes of scientific research and experimentation.

(5) Where any person manufactures, uses or imports a patented drug or patented medical device for the purpose of providing information that is necessary for regulatory approval, or any other person manufactures or imports a patented drug or patented medical device solely for him to provide such information. (Article 69 of the Law)

Doctrine of Equivalents

The extent of protection of a patent right should be determined by all technical features stated in the claims, including the extent as determined by the features equivalent to the technical features.

The equivalent features refer to the features which use substantially the same means, perform substantially the same function and produce substantially the same effect as the stated technical features and which can be contemplated by an ordinarily skilled person in the art without inventive labour at the time when the alleged infringement act occurs. (Article 17 of SPC's Provisions)

Doctrine of File Wrapper Estoppel

In the procedure leading to a grant or an invalidation of a patent right, where the patent applicant or the patentee abandons a technical solution by amendments to the claims, the description or via the observations, the incorporation of the abandoned technical solution into the scope of protection of the patent right by the patent holder in a patent infringement lawsuit shall not be supported by the courts. (Article 6 of Interpretation I)

Doctrine of Donation

For a technical solution which is only depicted in the description or the appended drawings but not recited in the claims, the incorporation of such a technical solution by the patent holder in a patent infringement lawsuit into the scope of protection of the patent right shall not be supported by the courts. (Article 5 of Interpretation I)

[B] Equivalence

As summarized in §18.06[A] above, the doctrine of equivalents is available in enforcing a patent in China, though the doctrine of file wrapper estoppel and the doctrine of donation shall be applied at first before the doctrine of equivalents is applied.

Moreover, Interpretation II also specifies some specific situations in determining the scope of protection of a patent claim. Applying these specific provisions to antibody inventions, we may conclude that:

(1) for a claim defined with close-ended definition, such as 'an antibody, wherein its CDR/variable region is consisted of a specific sequence', if the CDR/ variable region in an accused antibody not only comprises such specific sequence, but also comprises additional sequences, the court is likely to determine that the accused antibody does not fall within in the scope protection of the claim (see also, Article 7 of Interpretation II).

(2) for an antibody claim defined with manufacturing process, if the manufacturing process of the accused antibody is neither identical with nor equivalent to the manufacturing process recited in a claim, such accused antibody will be deemed as not falling within the scope of protection of the patent (see also, Article 10 of Interpretation II).

(3) for an antibody claim defined with a functional or other feature (for example, dosage feature in a medical use claim), these features will still be considered by the court when determining the scope of protection of such claim, even if they are deemed as having no limitation effects on the claims in the substantial examination or invalidation procedure.

Although no real infringement case with respect to antibodies has been reported in China, a typical case in the Supreme Court in 2012 for a pharmaceutical composition patent (*Shanxi Zhendong Taisheng Pharmaceutical Co., Ltd.* and *Shandong Telier Marketing Planning Co., Ltd. Pharmaceutical Branch v. Xiaoquan HU*, the Supreme People's Court Retrial Judgment No. 10 (2012)) can give us some help in understanding how the court interprets the scope of protection of a claim with a close-ended term and how the doctrine of equivalents applied.

This case relates to a patent named 'adenosine disodium triphosphate and magnesium chloride for injection', patent number ZL200410024515.1, and the related claim 2 reads as:

> '2. A disodium adenosine triphosphate magnesium chloride lyophilized powder injection for injection, which is characterized in that it consists of disodium adenosine triphosphate and magnesium chloride, and the weight ratio of the two is 100 mg to 32 mg.'

During the trials, both parties acknowledged the accused infringing product, in addition to disodium adenosine triphosphate and magnesium chloride, also had arginine.

In the first retrial of the case by the Shandong Higher People's Court, the Court held that the excipient 'sodium bicarbonate and arginine' in the accused infringing product are not the essential components, but just adjuvants. From the claims and specifications of the patent in question, other adjuvant ingredients cannot be excluded from the claim. Therefore, the close-ended definition in the claim should not be interpreted as excluding the adjuvant ingredients. Although the accused infringing product comprises two excipients not included in the claimed composition, it still falls within the scope of protection of claim 2 of the patent in question.

Taisheng Company and Telier Branch refused to accept the first retrial judgment, and required a second retrial at the Supreme Court.

Upon the retrial of this case, the Supreme Court held that, for close-ended claims, it shall be explained that structural components or steps and procedures which are not defined in the claims are excluded from the scope of protection; for a close-ended claim of a composition, it shall be explained that the composition only comprises the defined components to the exclusion of all other components, however, impurities in appropriate amount can be included in, and the excipients do not belong to the impurities.

In addition, the Supreme People's Court has also made some comments about application of Doctrine of Equivalents in infringement cases involving close-ended claims. The Supreme People's Court indicated that choosing to use a close-ended term in a claim means that other undefined structural components or steps and procedures are excluded from the scope of protection, it is not proper to reincorporate such structural components or steps and procedures into the scope of protection by applying the Doctrine of Equivalents.

Chapter 19

India

Mamta Rani Jha

Mamta Rani Jha

§19.01 ANTIBODIES AS PATENTABLE SUBJECT-MATTER

Patent Law in India has undergone tremendous change over the years, making it possible to patent antibodies which are not naturally occurring and synthesized artificially, subject to fulfilling the requirements under the Patents Act, 1970 (hereinafter 'the Act'). In India, prior to 2005, only process patents were granted in respect of inventions relating to food, drug, medicines and 'substances produced by chemical processes' which included bio-chemical, biotechnological and microbiological processes.[1] Post 2005 amendments to the Act in compliance with India's TRIPS obligations, product patents became possible subject to meeting the criteria laid down under the Act.

Until 2002, the Indian Patent Office (IPO) did not grant process patents for inventions relating to (a) living entities of natural or artificial origin, (b) biological materials or other materials having replicating properties, (c) substances derived from such materials and (d) any processes for the production of living substances/ entities including nucleic acids. The 2002 *Dimminaco AG v. Controller of Patents and Designs*[2] decision opened doors for the grant of process patents to inventions where the final product of the claimed process contained living microorganisms.

[A] Legal Framework

In India, product and process patents are possible for antibodies, subject to inventions fulfilling the three criteria of (1) novelty (2) inventive step and (3) industrial application.

The biggest challenge faced by the patentee in India is section 3 of the Act, which deals with inventions which are not patentable'. The relevant provisions under

1. *See* section 5, Patents Act, 1970, omitted *vide* Patents (Amendments) Act, 2005
2. IPLR 2002 July 255

section 3 while examining claims *qua* antibodies are section 3(c), 3(d), 3(e), 3(i) and 3(j). The relevant extracts thereof are:

> **Section 3(c):** 'The mere discovery of any living thing or non-living substance occurring in nature.'
>
> **Section 3(d):** 'The mere discovery of a new form of a known substance which does not result in the enhancement of the known efficacy of that substance or the mere discovery of any new property or new use for a known substance or of the mere use of a known process, machine or apparatus unless such known process results in a new product or employs at least one new reactant.'
>
> Explanation—For the purposes of this clause, salts, esters, ethers, polymorphs, metabolites, pure form, particle size, isomers, mixtures of isomers, complexes, combinations and other derivatives of known substance shall be considered to be the same substance, unless they differ significantly in properties with regard to efficacy.'
>
> **Section 3(e):** A substance obtained by a mere admixture resulting only in the aggregation of the properties of the components thereof or a process for producing such substance.
>
> **Section 3(i):** Any process for the medicinal, surgical, curative, prophylactic, diagnostic, therapeutic or other treatment of human beings or any process for a similar treatment of animals to render them free of disease or to increase their economic value or that of their products.
>
> **Section 3(j):** Plants and animals in whole or any part thereof other than micro organisms but including seeds, varieties and species and essentially biological processes for production or propagation of plants and animals.

[B] General Amenability or Exclusion of Antibodies from Patentability

The general objections and amenability are discussed below with reference to provisions of section 3 (see above).

Products such as antibodies, microorganisms, nucleic acid sequences, proteins, enzymes and compounds, which are directly isolated from nature (naturally occurring substances) are not patentable. However, antibodies which are not naturally occurring or synthesized in a laboratory, and processes of isolation of antibodies are patentable provided they meet the triple test of novelty, inventive step and industrial application.

Generally, the examiners interpret section 3(c) in a very narrow sense. It is their perspective that any antibody/polypeptide – even if it is a truncated part of some naturally occurring antibody/polypeptide – if has 100% similarity to the original, is construed as naturally occurring. Examiners usually allow modified or recombinant moieties. Thus, to counter the said objection, it needs to be demonstrated that the claimed antibody/polypeptide or nucleotide sequences are not naturally occurring and are modified using human intervention.[3] It is also important to demonstrate or

3. *See* Prosecution History of Patent No. 302196 [Application No. 5040/CHENP/2012 titled '*Antibody Binding to Human CSF-IR*', available publicly at www.ipindia.nic.in

distinguish a claimed antibody by highlighting the modifications by way of mutations or conjugation, for example.

In order to overcome the objections under section 3(c), following illustrative aspects may be part of the specification and claims:

- The invention relates to new monoclonal antibody, whose generation involves human intervention and it is not isolated from nature;[4]
- The combination of the light and heavy chain and constant regions are not to be found in nature;[5]
- The claimed combination of complementarity-determining regions (CDRs) in the monoclonal antibody are an unnatural construct formed by human intervention;
- The claim is for an isolated polynucleotide encoding the light and/or heavy chain of an antibody which is an unnatural construct formed by human intervention.

Section 3(d)

Section 3(d) is peculiar *sui generis* provision under Indian law, under which any new use of a known substance is not patentable unless there is enhanced known efficacy over the known substance. The Supreme Court of India in *Novartis v. UOI & Ors.*,[6] interpreted section 3(d) and held that enhanced known efficacy over the known substance has to be enhanced therapeutic efficacy and clarified that mere increase in bioavailability may not necessarily lead to an enhancement of therapeutic efficacy to overcome section 3(d).

While dealing with objections under section 3(d) of the Act, it has to be borne in mind that section 3(d) does not *ipso facto* apply to all chemical or pharmaceutical inventions. To apply section 3(d), it has to be established that the invention is a 'new form of a known substance' meaning that there has to be a known substance and the examiner has to identify the same. Although examiners frequently raise objections under section 3(d), if it is not a case thereunder, then an appropriate reply explaining how there was no known substance or derivative and thus section 3(d) is not applicable may be submitted.

However, if the invention does fall under section 3(d), then enhanced therapeutic efficacy data of a modified/derivative antibody over the prior known antibody should be provided. Examiners generally accept comparative data showing improved efficacy of the new substance/method *vis-à-vis* the closest prior art.[7] The IPO usually accepts

4. *See* Prosecution History of Patent No. 297285 [Application No. 797/DELNP/2012 titled '*Human Monoclonal Antibody Against S. Aureus Derived Alpha-Toxin and its Use in Treating or Preventing Abscess Formation*', available publicly at www.ipindia.nic.in
5. *See* Prosecution History of Patent No. 284359 [Application No. 171/MUM/2012 titled '*Anti-RHD Monoclonal Antibodies*' available publicly at www.ipindia.nic.in
6. AIR 2013 SC 1311
7. *See* Prosecution History of Patent No. 291864 [Application No. 4132/KOLNP/2009 titled '*Polypeptides, Antibody Variable Domains and Antagonists*', available publicly at www.ipindia.nic.in; Prosecution History of Patent No. 302148 [Application No. 2884/CHENP/2011

additional comparative data submitted during prosecution to overcome the objection under Section 3(d).

Section 3(e)

Typical objections under section 3(e) from the IPO are with regard to a composition comprising a combination of antibodies or an antibody with integers such as carriers or other substances.

A composition claim comprising an antibody is usually of two types. First, the composition may comprise the antibody as the only active ingredient along with inactive excipients. Secondly, the composition may comprise two active ingredients with an antibody being one of them.

Examiners routinely raises objections to composition claims construing prima facie composition claims to be mere admixtures resulting only in aggregation of properties.

In cases where there is only one active component in the composition, there could be scope to argue that such a composition is not contemplated under section 3(e).[8] However, where there are two active ingredients, which may fall under section 3(e), such objection can be overcome by submitting experimental data establishing that the claimed composition exhibits synergistic or unexpected properties[9] (i.e. a surprising effect beyond the sum of their individual effects). Further, the examiner may also ask for the ratio ranges of the individual components of a composition to make the claim more definitive.[10]

Section 3(i)

Although there is a prohibition under section 3(i) for processes for medicinal, surgical, curative, prophylactic, diagnostic, therapeutic or other treatment of human beings or animals, there is no bar for patenting a surgical, therapeutic or diagnostic instrument or apparatus.

Generally, the objections raised by the examiner pertain to the patentability of claims directed to a method of administration of antibody to treat a disease or detection of a disease. The case for a method of detection of a disease can be argued as long as it can be shown that such a technique is carried out *in vitro* and *ex vivo* and is only directed to detection of the disease and not towards rendering a human or an animal free of the said disease. A method of prognosis which is essentially the prediction of the occurrence of a disease based on presence or absence of certain markers can overcome the objection under section 3(e). Likewise, an antibody used

---

titled '*High Affinity Human Antibodies to Human IL-4 Receptor*', available publicly at www.ipindia.nic.in

8. *See* Prosecution History of Patent No. 302196 [Application No. 5040/CHENP/2012 titled '*Antibody Binding to Human CSF-IR*', available publicly at www.ipindia.nic.in
9. *See* Prosecution History of Patent No. 296780 [Application No. 1358/CHENP/2012 titled '*A Composition Comprising an Afucosylated ANTI-CD20 Antibody and Bendamustine*', available publicly at www.ipindia.nic.in
10. *Ibid.*

purely for research for detection of a protein using a molecular biology technique, for example, cannot be construed to be directed to rendering a human or animal free of disease and thus does not fall within the ambit of section 3(i).

Section 3(j)

Although, microorganisms are excluded from the non-patentability list, a conjoined reading with section 3(c) of the Act implies that only *modified* microorganisms, which do not constitute discovery of a living thing occurring in nature, are patentable subject matter under the Act.

Thus, any transgenic plant or animal that can be used to make antibodies is not patentable. Examiners are very rigid regarding the patentability of animal or plant derived cells. However, it may be argued that the established mammalian cell lines are propagated *in vitro* and not derived from an animal.

Biodiversity related issues

All intellectual property including patents based on research or information *qua* biological resources obtained from India can be granted only with the approval of the National Biodiversity Authority (NBA) established under The Biological Diversity Act, 2002. Under section 10(4) of the Act, disclosure of the source and geographical origin of a biological material used in an application for a patent is mandatory. Section 10 further requires that the microorganisms *qua* the invention be deposited at an International Depository Authority (IDA) under the Budapest Treaty before filing of the Indian application.

India being a party to the Budapest Treaty requires that in the particular case of inventions involving microorganisms, a deposit of biological material must be made in a recognized depository institution. The applicant need only deposit the biological material at one such institution, recognized by the IPO. Hence, to meet the sufficiency of disclosure requirement, in cases where the invention relates to biological material wherein it is not possible to describe the invention in a sufficient manner and further where it is not available to the public, the applicant shall deposit the material to an IDA. The deposit of the material shall be made no later than the date of filing of the application in India and a reference of the deposit shall be given in the specification within three months from the date of filing of the patent application in India.

[C] Required Distinction from Naturally Occurring Antibodies

As stated above, under section 3(c) of the Patents Act 'discovery of any living thing or non-living substances occurring in nature' is barred from patentability. However, there is no judicial pronouncement on the nature and quantum of human intervention/ modification – genetic and/or morphological – required to differentiate a living thing from one that already exists in nature. The argument as to whether isolation of biological material after extensive processing and technical intervention renders it outside the purview of 'living thing occurring in nature' and thus barred under section 3(c) is still to be settled.

There is no guidance whether usage of any term or qualifier aids or facilitates in the antibody patent prosecution. However, few best practices can be discerned from studying prosecution history and examiners' decisions, as stated above.

§19.02 ACCEPTABLE CLAIM FEATURES FOR DEFINING ANTIBODIES

[A] Functional Features

Functional antibody claims are claims that are directed to antibodies which have not necessarily been invented or created, but have been discovered or simply isolated without substantial human intervention and are capable of being used to perform alternative functions. Claims such as these are viewed differently in India primarily in view of section 3(c) of the Act. Therefore, if an isolated antibody binds to a target which is known in the art, such an antibody – in order to be patentable – might be considered to further fulfil the requirements of section 3(d) of the Act. In order to prove that a new form of a known substance has led to the actual enhancement of the known efficacy of such a substance, substantive test results and/or experimental data – evidencing surprising results and/or some especially desirable property of the known substance over the nearest prior art – has to be adduced as extrinsic evidence or otherwise. The only proviso is that there has to be a specific reference to the enhancement of efficacy of, for example, an antibody bound to a known target being claimed in the disclosure of the complete specification over related prior art. Such data can be submitted as extrinsic evidence and can help applicants in rebutting objections under this section.[11]

Therefore, a product or an antibody when defined by a functional feature is construed to fall under the 'use' category of claims as per the current patent practice. Examiners usually ask for structural features of the product to primarily characterize an antibody. However, functional features may further be included in the body of a claim as a further characterizing feature, especially in dependent claims.

[1] Target/Antigen

If a new protein has been discovered and a therapeutic use thereof has been disclosed, the IPO may in some cases grant claims related to a putative antibody against the said protein, particularly when an exemplification of such an antibody has been provided in the specification. Claims of this type would obviously have the broadest scope, as they encompass all future antibodies against the said target put into practice later on. The IPO's rationale is that the provision of a novel protein X enables a skilled person to produce an antibody against said protein.

Antibodies can have functional properties which are target-independent. The development of such a new functional property can thus give rise to a patent, the

11. Kumar, Swarup, *Patentability of Biological Material(s) – Essentially, Therapeutic Antibodies – In India* (2008) SCRIPT-ed, Vol. 5, No. 3, 2008 available at https://ssrn.com/abstract=1578224

scope of which extends to all antibodies having such property, irrespective of the target they bind.

As regards a composition claim wherein the composition comprises a monoclonal antibody binding to antigen X, such a claim comprising a monoclonal antibody is mostly narrower than a claim that may cover a polyclonal antibody which has a wider ambit. The standard of interpretation of such claims is to primarily look at the intrinsic evidence or the disclosure in the specification. If the specification is unclear or silent as to the interpretation of a claimed feature, extrinsic evidence such as scientific definitions and common knowledge possessed by the skilled person at the priority date of the invention would apply.

Epitope targeted antibody claims

A patent can also be sought in respect of a second generation antibody by claiming specificity against a given epitope, or subdomain, of a target, provided that the said epitope has not yet been described as clinically relevant.

[2] *Mode of Binding: Target Affinity, Binding Specificity, Epitope, Definitions via Reference Antibodies and Competitive Binding*

Antibody based claims may also be defined by the mode of binding of antibody paratope with the epitope on antigen. Such type of claims may be drafted in the following manner: 'An antibody capable of binding X and blocking the binding of X to X-receptor.'

[3] *Effect on Target*

Another way to seek patent protection for a second generation antibody is to specify the latter through target-dependent functional properties, e.g., binding affinity against a given target, or competitive binding.[12] Such claims may be allowed by the IPO subject to meeting section 3 and require support with respect to sufficiency of disclosure.

Amongst other effects of the antibody on the target, the following types of effect may be defined in the claims:

- antagonistic/blocking or agonistic
- opsonising, neutralising
- monomeric or multimeric (dimeric, pentamer, etc)
- bispecific (binding two different types of antigens)

When defining the functional features in an antibody claim, it is not necessary to define a specific method of measurement for certain functional features in the claims. However, requisite support defining such functional features must be present in the specification along with the working example of the antibody with the said functional features and experimental support (if any).

12. U. Storz et al., *Intellectual Property Issues, Springer Briefs in Biotech Patents*, DOI: 10.1007/978-3-642-29526-3_1, The Author(s) 2012

[B] Structural Features

An antibody is primarily defined in the patent claims by its structural features and several levels of structural definition are possible.

[1] Molecular Topology: Antibody Types, Fragments and Antibody Constructs

In the case of a conventional antibody, the antibody can be defined by CDRs, which determine binding; by its light and heavy variable regions; or by its entire antibody sequence.

If the inventiveness of the antibody is based solely on the antibody having a higher binding affinity to the antigen than other known antibodies, the IPO may require the structural features, in particular, heavy and light variable domains to be specified in the claim because it recognizes that the choice of framework region residues can influence the antibody's final affinity. Regarding fragments, it has to be clearly established that they don't fall within the purview of 'naturally occurring substance' under section 3(c). Antibody construct based structural claims are also acceptable by the IPO.

[2] Amino Acid Sequences

[a] Full-Length Sequences of Antibodies

Structural claims reciting the full length sequences of antibodies are allowed by the IPO subject to section 3(c) of the Act.

[b] Sequences of Fragments, CDRs and Framework Regions

Sequence of fragments and framework region based structural claims may be allowed by the IPO subject to section 3(c) of the Act. As regards CDR based claims, as a rule, the IPO requires all six CDRs in the claim.[13]

[3] Chemical Modifications, Conjugation and Glycosylation

Apart from structurally defined antibody claims based on sequence listing, claims may also be defined by various chemical modifications[14] such as conjugation and glycosylation,[15] which have also found to be acceptable by the IPO.

---

13. *See* Prosecution History of Patent No. 293079 [Application No. 3392/DELNP/2011 titled '*Improved Anti-CD19 Antibodies*', available publicly at www.ipindia.nic.in
14. *See* Prosecution History of Patent No. 305455 [Application No. 5305/DELNP/2012 titled '*Fusion Polypeptide Against EB Virus-Induced Tumor and Colicin IA Mutant*', available publicly at www.ipindia.nic.in
15. *See* Prosecution History of Patent No. 299247 [Application No. 8361/DELNP/2010 titled '*Methods and Compositions for Making Antibodies and Antibody Derivatives with Reduced*

[C] Cell Line Deposits and Process of Production

The deposition of a cell line, e.g. a hybridoma cell line or a transfected host cell line, may be an adequate way of specifying an antibody in order to avoid sequencing errors and typographical errors, or to provide enabling information for features which relate to post-translational modifications (e.g. unusual glycosylation patterns). The language of such antibody claims simply refers to the deposition nomenclature of the deposited cell line. Such claims are drafted in the following manner: 'The antibody produced by the hybridoma deposited under Accession No. 12345'.

As stated above, in the case of inventions involving microorganisms, a deposit of biological material must be made in a recognized depository institution. Further, in accordance with the Budapest Treaty, the applicant needs only to deposit the biological material at an IDA, recognized by the IPO.

§19.03 BREADTH OF CLAIMS AND SUPPORT BY EXAMPLES

Section 10(5) of the Act provides a general requirement that the claim(s) must be clear and succinct and fairly based on the matter disclosed in the specification. There is no special practice or threshold that has been adopted for examination of antibody claims. Thus, antibody claims are examined on a case by case basis, according to the aforementioned yardstick.

[A] Acceptable Breadth of Claims to Antibodies

Claims that define an antibody by sequence supported by the description generally fulfil the requirement of clarity and conciseness of claims mandated under the Act.

Generally, sufficiency requirements are met so long as at least one method for performing the invention covering the whole subject-matter claimed in the claims (not only a part thereof) is capable of being carried out by a skilled person in the relevant art without the burden of an undue amount of experimentation or the application of inventive ingenuity.[16]Antibody claims with therapeutic or diagnostic potential should be supported by defining their role for the target protein in a specific disease and should be substantiated by sufficient data. For specifications disclosing a wide range of unrelated diseases as the potential therapeutic target of a claimed gene or encoding protein, evidence should be provided to prove the claimed therapeutic or diagnostic use of the encoding protein.[17]

As regards the disclosure requirement vis-à-vis biological material, the specification should disclose the source and geographical origin of the biological resource used in the invention. Further, inventions using biological resources that are unavailable to the public, the same should be deposited in a depository authority listed on the website of the IPO. Additionally, the reference of the source of the biological material

---

Core Fucosylation', available publicly at www.ipindia.nic.in

16. *Raj Praksh v. Mangatram Chowdhury*, AIR 1978 Del 1
17. Bakhru, Rachna, Pandey, Suvarna, '*A Review of Recent Patent Opposition Cases*' publicly available at http://www.managingip.com/IssueArticle/3485799/Supplements/A-review-of-recent-patent-opposition-cases.html?supplementListId = 94724

should be made in the specification. The specification can be amended to include the source of biological material-during the prosecution as well.[18]

[B] Required Experimental Support for Claims to Functionally Defined Antibodies

As far the issue of disclosure is concerned (of specific amino acid sequences of the claimed antibodies), this requirement is something that is, more often than not, insisted upon by the IPO. Describing antibodies with respect to merely physical or chemical parameters (molecular weight or physical characteristics associated with such antibodies, for example) is generally not accepted by the IPO.[19]

The objection of lack of sufficient disclosure in case of functionally defined claims to antibodies may be met by referring to one to two examples along with relevant figures and experimental data, if necessary.

[C] Required Experimental Support for Claims to Structurally Defined Antibodies

It is generally insisted upon by the IPO that a specific reference to sequences of antibody chains, proteins or amino acids be included with the claims. The specific sequence IDs of the antibodies or nucleotide sequences being claimed must have been described sufficiently in the description so as to enable a person skilled in the art to identify and work upon such material. Otherwise, the 'lack of support' issue as well as enablement objections could be raised. Additionally, it must also be kept in mind that reference to more than one sequence IDs in the main claim is not accepted by the IPO unless it is possible to establish unequivocally that the multiple sequence IDs are correlated with another so that they constitute a *single inventive concept.*[20]

As far as the extent of disclosure of the variable chains of an antibody is concerned, it will depend on what is claimed, for example if a full length variable region is claimed and only a part of such a claim has been disclosed in the description, the claim will certainly be considered unsupported by the description. Similarly, it is preferred that the description includes a reference to both the heavy as well as the light chain CDR, even if it is only a heavy chain CDR that is claimed, so that a clear distinction can be brought out between them if necessary.

Examiners usually ask for the amino acid/nucleotide sequences and so on for antibody claims. Any experimental data that would support the claimed structural feature would be accepted by examiners such as sequencing data, DNA/protein modification data, X-ray diffraction data. Examiners usually look for the functional data for establishing superior technical effect.

---

18. http://www.mondaq.com/india/x/799164/Patent/Patenting+Antibodies+in+India
19. Kumar, Swarup, *Patentability of Biological Material(s) – Essentially, Therapeutic Antibodies – In India* (2008) SCRIPT-ed, Vol. 5, No. 3, 2008 available at https://ssrn.com/abstract=1578224
20. *Ibid.*

§19.04 SPECIFIC MEDICAL APPLICATIONS AND OTHER FOLLOW-UP INVENTIONS

As mentioned in section §19.01[A], claims involving medical applications have to overcome the bar under section 3(i). Given the overarching scope of the said section, claims for medical applications are often objected to and not granted.

[A] Treatment of Specific Diseases

In India there is a bar to patentability for method of treatment claims under section 3(i). Any method directed to rendering a human or an animal free of disease falls under the purview of this statute.

[B] Mode of Administration

Even the mode/method of administration of a drug/biologic is usually construed to be a method directed to rendering a human or animal free of disease. Hence, the examiner may raise an objection under section 3(i) to such a claim.

[C] Dosage Regimens

The dosage regimen or the method of dosing *per se* would not be allowed in India under section 3(i). However, a product, composition or a combination that crosses the threshold of patentability may further be characterized by the dosage regimen in a dependent claim. Some examiners may allow it and not raise an objection under section 3(i). However, patent practice in India varies from examiner to examiner and depends on each examiner's interpretation of the provisions.

[D] Specific Patient Groups

The method of treating a specific patient group using a claimed antibody would be objected to by most examiners under section 3(i).

[E] Specific Mode of Action

A product in India is defined by its essential technical features that are usually construed to be the structural features. The mode of action may be described in a dependent claim or as a secondary characterization in the body of the claim.

[F] Combinations with Other Active Ingredients

Combinations are allowed in India, subject to a higher patentability threshold. The examiner may raise an objection to a combination under section 3(d). To overcome this objection, the applicant has to show an enhanced therapeutic efficacy as compared to when the product is used alone. If the combination is formulated together, the examiner may further raise an objection under section 3(e), construing the claims as a mere admixture. In such a case, the applicant shall have to show synergistic effect associated with such a combination when both the drugs are used in tandem.

[G] Specific Diagnostic Applications

Most examiners would raise a prima facie objection to a diagnostic application and bring it under the purview of section 3(i). However, it may be argued that the diagnostic application is carried out *in vitro* and *ex vivo*. Hence, there is no interaction with the patient and that the diagnostic application is not used *per se* in rendering a human or animal free of disease.

Only product and process claims are allowed in India and 'use' claims are generally not allowed. These include direct use claims, Swiss-type claims and second medical use claims. Second medical use claims worded in any form (Swiss-type, use claims or method of treatment claims) are not granted by the Indian Patent Office. Also, new use of known substances is clearly barred from patentability under section 3(d) of the Patents (Amendment) Act, 2005.

As regards 'kit' claims, such claims are usually not objected to since they are directed to a tangible entity in contradistinction to a method of treatment. The only further requirement with respect to such claims could be that of the inclusion of further 'constructional' features of the claimed kit. Further, there should be proper support for such constructional features in the accompanying description. Examiners sometimes object to kit claims and further construe them as a mere admixture and usually raise an objection preliminarily under section 3(e). Thus, any kit claim comprising an antibody and further components for putative treatment or diagnosis purpose may be objected to under section 3(e).[21] However, it may be argued that the kit *per se* is not an admixture as the components of a kit do not interact and produce any effect, if the components are packaged separately and further are submitted for consideration of the kit as a first application of a novel invention.

§19.05 ASSESSMENT OF INVENTIVENESS

The general principles regarding assessment of inventiveness are applicable to antibody patents equally and each case may be dealt with on its own description and supporting technical data.

[A] General Approach

Inventive step has been clearly defined in the Act by way of section 2(1)(ja):

> '"inventive step" means a feature of an invention that involves technical advance as compared to the existing knowledge or having economic significance or both and that makes the invention not obvious to a person skilled in the art.'

21. *See* Prosecution History of Patent No. 297285 [Application No. 797/DELNP/2012 titled '*human monoclonal antibody against s. aureus derived alpha-toxin and its use in treating or preventing abscess formation*', available publicly at www.ipindia.nic.in

Accordingly, the test for inventive step is two pronged i.e. the claimed invention should involve technical advancement or qualification over the prior art and such technical advancement must not be obvious to the person skilled in the art as on the priority date.

Furthermore, the test of inventive step has been refined over time by the Indian courts. In one landmark decision in pharmaceutical patent litigation case involving *Roche and Cipla*,[22] the division bench at Hon'ble Delhi High Court laid down the following five-step test to determine whether an invention involves inventive step:

Step No. 1	To identify an ordinary person skilled in the art.
Step No. 2	To identify the inventive concept embodied in the patent.
Step No. 3	To impute a normal skilled but unimaginative ordinary person skilled in the art of common general knowledge at the priority date.
Step No. 4	To identify the differences, if any, between the matter cited and the alleged invention and ascertain whether the differences are ordinary application of law or involve various steps requiring multiple, theoretical, and practical applications.
Step No. 5	To decide whether those differences, viewed in the knowledge of alleged invention, constituted steps which would have been obvious to the ordinary person skilled in the art and rule out a hindsight approach.

[B] Particularities Regarding Claims to Antibodies

In context of claims pertaining to antibodies, if the claimed invention relates to a polynucleotide/polypeptide having mutation(s) in a known sequence of polynucleotides/polypeptides, which does not result in an unexpected property whatsoever, then the claimed subject-matter lacks inventive step.[23] Therefore, it is essential to submit technical, experimental data to establish unexpected technical advantages/ properties of the mutated sequence of such polypeptides.

It is seen that even when an antibody is described by its structural features, which are different from those of any known antibody, it may not be considered to be inventive. This is because the IPO considers it to be routine to prepare a polyclonal or monoclonal antibody (mAb) against any known antigen. Therefore, an antibody is considered inventive by the IPO only if it is unexpected that the antibody could be produced at all (e.g., if there are difficulties with isolation), or if the claimed antibody has unexpected, advantageous properties such as higher binding affinity, an unexpected antagonistic or agonistic effect, low cross-reactivity, or differential

22. *F. Hoffmann-La Roche Ltd & Anr. v. Cipla Ltd.* (2016) 65 PTC 1
23. *Guidelines for Examination of Biotechnology Applications for Patent*, 2013, as released by the IPO and available publicly at http://www.ipindia.nic.in/writereaddata/Portal/IPOGuidelinesManuals/1_38_1_4-biotech-guidelines.pdf

binding to monomer vs. dimer. However, the unexpected, advantageous property may depend on what is already known.[24]

§19.06 ENFORCEMENT AND SCOPE OF PROTECTION

There are hardly any cases regarding enforcement of antibody patents in India and therefore there is not much clarity on the scope of antibody protection. The litigation *qua* biosimilars is still awaiting resolution.

[A] Biosimilars

So far, Indian jurisprudence has not evolved any precedents on the scope of protection of antibody patents, particularly in context of biosimilars. However, the Hon'ble Delhi High Court, in the case of *Roche Products (India) Pvt. Ltd. & Ors. v. Drugs Controller General of India & Ors.*[25] had the occasion to elucidate upon the enforcement of biosimilars. The case in question pertains to the drug Trastuzumab, a monoclonal antibody used primarily in the treatment of HER 2 positive breast cancer, which was patented by Roche and marketed under the brands Herceptin, Herclon and Biceltis. After the expiry of Roche's patent in 2013, the defendants, Biocon, Mylan Inc. and Mylan Pharmaceuticals Pvt. Ltd., applied for and obtained marketing authorization for an alleged biosimilar of trastuzumab, namely, bmab/CANmab. Roche brought a court action against the alleged biosimilars in 2014. Roche was granted a secondary, formulation patent in relation to trastuzumab from the Controller General of Patents, in India, which lapsed on 3 May 2013. The plaintiff in this case sought an injunction against launching or introducing the drug by the defendants, an injunction from representing the impugned products as bio-similar until appropriate tests and studies were conducted including guidelines on similar biologics and an injunction from relying upon or referring to the plaintiff's trademark claiming similarity of the two drugs. However, the plaintiff did not allege infringement of its trade mark or its rights in respect of the expired patent in 2013. Its main concern was that without establishing the safety and efficacy as required under the Drugs & Cosmetics Act, Rules and Biosimilar Guidelines 2012, the defendants were not entitled to claim that it is a biosimilar drug of the innovator and would not be entitled to use the data of the plaintiff and give references in its package insert, carton and publicity materials by making the false statement and misrepresentation. The Court in this case upheld Roche's claims and restrained the Defendant companies from marketing their drugs as biosimilar of Roche's drugs pending the judgment of the trial.

---

24. *See* Prosecution History of Patent No. 302273, Application No. 2250/DELNP/2011 titled '*A Multivalent, Dual Specificity Antibody Fusion Protein*', available publicly at www.ipindia.nic.in; *See* Prosecution History of Patent No. 302887, Application No. 6768/CHENP/2011 titled '*Anti-Human α9 Integrin Antibody and Use Thereof*', available publicly at www.ipindia.nic.in; *See* Prosecution History of Patent No. 293079 Application No. 3392/DELNP/2011 titled '*Improved Anti-CD19 Antibodies*', available publicly at www.ipindia.nic.in.
25. 2016 SCC Online Del 2358

The decision of the Single Judge has been challenged in appeal to the Division Bench, which has permitted the defendants to sell the alleged biosimilars in respect of Metastatic Breast Cancer, Early Breast Cancer and Metastatic Gastric Cancer and also maintain accounts. A final decision is awaited, and in any event a challenge to the Supreme Court is inevitable.

Interestingly, as a counterblast to the litigation, the defendants filed a complaint[26] in 2016 before the Competition Commission of India (CCI) alleging abuse of dominance by Roche and its affiliates in prohibiting entry of the bmab biosimilar in the market. Particularly, the defendants claimed that Roche was entering into vexatious litigations and writing frivolous communications to various authorities claiming that the bmab/CANmab biosimilar was hazardous to health, thereby impeding entry of the defendants in the market. In an order dated 21 April 2017, the CCI held that prima facie Roche's conduct was anti-competitive and directed an enquiry into the allegations. The same has since been challenged in appeal before the Delhi High Court by Roche. However, it is surely an interesting point for right-holders to be aware of when contemplating biosimilar litigation.

[B] Equivalence

There has been, so far, no ruling by the Indian courts on the interpretation of 'equivalents' of the claimed subject-matter which may be embraced by antibody claims.

26. *Biocon & Anr. v. Roche and Ors.*, Case No. 68 of 2016

Chapter 20

Japan

Takashi Fujita & Osamu Yamamoto

§20.01 ANTIBODIES AS PATENTABLE SUBJECT-MATTER

[A] Legal Framework

The first sentence of Article 29 (1) of the Japan Patent Act, states as follows: 'An inventor of an invention that is industrially applicable may be entitled to obtain a patent for the invention.' From this statement it can be read that inventions that are not industrially applicable are not patentable. However, the Japan Patent Act does not state what kind of inventions are not industrially applicable. Rather, the *Examination Guidelines for Patent and Utility Models* (https://www.jpo.go.jp/tetuzuki_e/t_tokkyo_e/1312-002_e.htm) state that 'a method of surgery, treatment, or diagnosis of a human is not an industrially applicable invention.' Thus, under Japanese patent law and practice, parts of living things found in nature are not per se excluded from patentability.

[B] General Amenability or Exclusion of Antibodies from Patentability

The *Examination Handbook for Patent and Utility Models* summarizes practice and points out what examiners need to consider when conducting examinations. In the Handbook, Chapter 2 is entitled 'Biological Inventions,' as stated in Annex B of the Examination Handbook for Patent and Utility Models (hereafter, referred to as Examination Handbook 'Biological Inventions': http://www.jpo.go.jp/tetuzuki_e/t_tokkyo_e/files_handbook_sinsa_e/app_b2_e.pdf). It is stated that naturally occurring molecules that have been isolated by technical means from their biological environment are eligible for patent protection, even if the structure of that element is identical to that of a natural element. Eligibility is predicated on the necessity for human intervention in the isolation and preparation of the naturally occurring molecules; and it follows that not only antibodies, but also other proteins and genes are thus patent eligible.

Practical utility of naturally occurring molecules should be identified in the specification. In this regard, Examination Handbook 'Biological Inventions' states that 'Inventions of a gene, a vector, a recombinant vector, a transformant, a fused cell, a recombinant protein and a monoclonal antibody whose utility is not described in a specification or cannot be inferred, do not meet the requirements set forth in the first sentence of the Japan Patent Act, Article 29(1).'

[C] Required Distinction from Naturally Occurring Antibodies

There is no requirement to recite a term 'isolated' or the like in a claim. This practice applies not only to antibodies but also to other proteins, genes, and other products of nature.

§20.02 ACCEPTABLE CLAIM FEATURES FOR DEFINING ANTIBODIES

[A] Functional Features

In practice, while recitation of a structural element in a claim, e.g., a sequence, may be of use in obtaining allowance, under some circumstances it is sufficient to define an antibody merely by referring to functional feature(s). Functional feature(s) may relate to competing for binding to another antibody, cross-reacting with multiple antigens, or selectively binding to one antigen rather than another. To satisfy clarity and industrial application requirements, the specification must include an assay method that can be used for measuring such functional feature(s).

[1] Target/Antigen

In Japan, it is possible to define antibodies by their target/antigen. For example, the phrasing 'An antibody which binds to antigen X' constitutes acceptable claim language so long as antigen X is new, and is structurally described as a substance.

As for support and industrial application requirements, a patent will be granted for an antibody to a new antigen without production of an actual antibody, provided that the antigen is structurally described and has been ascribed a particular function. Thus, it is generally not necessary to disclose specific examples or embodiments of a claimed (monoclonal) antibody, since the Japan Patent Office (JPO) considers that generation of an antibody to a new antigen is no more than a routine matter for a person skilled in the art. As no structural definition of an antibody is required to be set out in the claims or in the specification, the claims can cover a very wide range of antibodies (e.g., polyclonal, monoclonal, chimeric, humanized etc.), in fact, practically 'any antibody which binds to antigen X.'

As for novelty, Examination Handbook 'Biological Inventions' in section 5.2(1)(b) states as a case – antigen A is partially modified from publicly known antigen A' – and a claim reciting 'a monoclonal antibody to antigen A.' The explanation given in Examination Handbook 'Biological Inventions' is that 'If antigen A is novel, a monoclonal antibody to the antigen A is generally considered novel. However, if a monoclonal antibody to a publicly known antigen A' is itself publicly known, and if the antigen A has the same epitope as that of A' because the antigen A is partially modified from the publicly known antigen A' or the like, a monoclonal antibody to antigen A' will also bind to antigen A. In such a case, the claimed invention of "a monoclonal antibody to antigen A" is not novel.'

On the other hand, in a case that the antigen is known, Examination Handbook 'Biological Inventions' in section 5.3(1)(c) states that 'If antigen A is publicly known and it is clear that the antigen A has immunogenicity (for example, antigen A clearly has immunogenicity because a polyclonal antibody to the antigen A is publicly known or because the antigen A is a polypeptide with a large molecular weight, etc.), the claimed invention of "a monoclonal antibody to the antigen A" does not have inventive step. However, if the claimed invention is further specified by other features, etc. leading to an advantageous effect that a person skilled in the art could not foresee, the claimed invention has inventive step.' To obtain a patent, it is generally required that the antibody be structurally defined with inclusion of at least six complementarity determining region (CDR) sequences, in addition to having a feature of binding to an antigen.

[2] Mode of Binding: Target Affinity, Binding Specificity, Epitope, Definitions via Reference Antibodies and Competitive Binding

Features that may be required to be present in a claim for an antibody to secure patentability will always depend upon what already exists in the prior art.

Examination Handbook 'Biological Inventions' in section 2.1(1)(c) states as an example 'A monoclonal antibody which binds not to antigen B but to antigen A,' noting that it is necessary to define antigen A and antigen B by specifying them as substances. As for the novelty of such a claim, Examination Handbook 'Biological Inventions' in section 5.2(1)(b) states that 'the claimed invention of a monoclonal antibody specified by a cross-reactivity, such as "a monoclonal antibody which binds not to antigen B but to antigen A" is not novel, if a monoclonal antibody to antigen A is publicly known and if there is no particular technical significance in specifying the monoclonal antibody described by such a cross-reactivity (e.g., when it is clear that the publicly known monoclonal antibody to antigen A does not bind to antigen B either, because antigen B has no similarity to antigen A in its function, structure, etc.).' Accordingly, an applicant must show a difference in claimed antibodies relative to the prior art based on binding features.

A claim may define an antibody by its ability to bind to a particular epitope. In the majority of cases an epitope must be defined by its exact sequence. The definition should be as precise as possible, and may include information on structural features that contribute to epitopic properties, including glycosylation, where relevant, and whether the epitope is linear or conformational. Otherwise, a claim may be open to objection on ground of lack of clarity or industrial application. Further, it will typically be necessary to demonstrate that an unexpected, advantageous property is associated with the epitope. An example of claiming antibodies by epitope without reciting sequences of the antibodies is given below.

> JP 6286590
>
> Claim 1: An isolated anti-tau antibody or an antigen-binding fragment thereof, which is capable of binding to tau in one or more of the minimal epitopes selected from the group consisting of HQPGGG (SEQ ID NO: 223), HVPGGG (SEQ ID NO: 154), and HKPGGG (SEQ ID NO: 224).

It is also possible to draft a claim with reference to an antibody, as in:

> 'An antibody specific to target X having a same epitope as an antibody produced by a hybridoma deposited under ATCC —.'

Examination Handbook 'Biological Inventions' cites the following as Case 27 relating to the industrial application requirement.

> Claim 1: A monoclonal antibody binding to protein A, having a dissociation constant of 10^{-13} M or more and 10^{-12} M or less.
>
> Note: In the description, it is stated that only one strain, "hybridoma HK," producing the monoclonal antibody having 5.6 10^{-13} M in the dissociation constant, was obtained. However, in this case, the deposition of "hybridoma HK" is not stated in the original description. Accordingly, the case is rejected since it is not deemed that the description sets out the invention clearly and sufficiently to enable a person skilled in the art to carry out the invention claimed in Claim 1.

It is stated in Examination Handbook 'Biological Inventions', however, that the reason for refusal may be overcome by proving, based on specific and objective evidence in a written opinion or the like, that it would not be necessary for a person skilled in the art to carry out unreasonable trial and error, and/or complicated and sophisticated experimentation to obtain the monoclonal antibody according to Claim 1 with reproducibility at a time of performing an additional test. In practice, examination results will vary depending on individual facts (on a case by case basis).

In the *Amgen Inc. v. Sanofi* cases (Hei 29 Gyo-ke 10225, Hei 29 Gro-ke 10226, and Hei 29 wa 16468), the point at issue was 'whether it is acceptable to define an antibody merely by reference to a functional feature', as is discussed in §20.03 and §20.06.

[3] Effect on Target

Broad antibody claims may be acceptable when a target is found to have a previously unappreciated role in a disease, etc. Various forms of claim language regarding the effect of an antibody on its target, including functional mechanism, are accepted. That is, if the target is found to be associated with a new medical use, a typical example of claim language would be:

> 'A pharmaceutical composition for treating a disease X, which comprises an antibody directed against target Y.'

In many cases, no further structural definition of the antibody would be required to be included in the claims; although the specification should include at least one working example showing that binding of such an antibody to the target Y has a treatment effect on disease X. In this regard, *in vitro* functional data will likely be sufficient, on condition that the data derives from an established disease model or other assay relevant to the disease.

[B] Structural Features

[1] Molecular Topology: Antibody Types, Fragments and Antibody Constructs

As stated above, under Japanese patent law and practice, parts of living things found in nature are not per se excluded from patentability, and therefore it follows that antibodies are a patentable subject-matter. This means that humanized or chimeric antibodies, as well as fragments, are also patentable, insofar as they meet the requirements of patentability concerning novelty, inventive step and industrial application.

Examination Handbook 'Biological Inventions' in section 2.1(1)(c) cites an example:

> 'Example 5: A single domain antibody to an antigen A.
>
> Note: It is necessary to describe an antigen A by specifying it as a substance. As for a fragment of an antibody, it is necessary to recite that the fragment has antigen binding ability.'

[2] Amino Acid Sequences

As stated above, if the antigen is not new, an antibody defined solely by the antigen to which it binds is not patentable. However, in most cases, an antibody directed to a known target may be claimed by structurally defining the antibody with reference to a particular sequence. The extent of a sequence that is required to be defined varies depending on the case at issue; for example, a definition may be required that refers to a full length, to whole variable regions, or to all CDR sequences.

[a] Full-Length Sequences of Antibodies

Reciting both a variable and constant region primary sequence in full will suffice to establish novelty of an antibody, assuming uniqueness, but as for inventive step it will be necessary to show that a new antibody to a known target provides 'an unexpected effect'. In Japan, a structural difference over prior art antibodies is not sufficient in itself to meet inventive step requirements.

[b] Sequences of Fragments, CDRs and Framework Regions

When a structure of an antibody must be provided, it is often necessary to define six CDR sequences in a claim. In many cases, an antibody is defined by referring to its six CDRs and binding target X.

Examination Handbook 'Biological Inventions' in section 2.1(1)(c) cites an example:

'Example 4: A monoclonal antibody in which each amino acid sequence of CDRs 1 to 3 of a heavy chain is represented by SEQ ID NO: 1 to 3 and each amino acid sequence of CDRs 1 to 3 of a light chain is represented by SEQ ID NO: 4 to 6.'

However, defining the six CDRs will not suffice if the framework regions are considered to play a role in binding affinity, or if they are otherwise relevant to one or more characteristics that are relied upon. It is of note here that the relevance of framework regions for target binding is increasingly appreciated, with the result that there is a trend in the JPO towards requiring that framework regions also be specified in claims.

[3] Chemical Modifications, Conjugation and Glycosylation

It is well known that a structure of a sugar chain plays an important role in a function of human antibodies. Further, it is well known that it is possible to increase the function of an antibody by changing the structure of the sugar chain. For example, the correlation between removing fucose and improving ADCC is well known. However, in reality, structures of sugar chains are various and complex, and therefore if an important structure for a function is identified, a claim should be drafted by inclusion of the important specific identified structure. In this regard, a number of patent applications directed to a method for chemically modifying an antibody have been filed in Japan.

[C] Cell Line Deposits and Process of Production

According to Examination Handbook 'Biological Inventions' in section 2.1(1)(c), a claim directed to a monoclonal antibody may be defined by specifying a hybridoma that produces the antibody. In this case, the hybridoma should be deposited and its accession number should be described in the specification as filed, except where the hybridoma can be created by a person skilled in the art with reference to the description in the specification. Thus, if sufficient description exists for a method of reproducibly obtaining such a hybridoma, it is not necessary for the hybridoma to be deposited.

In Japan, product-by-process claims satisfy clarity requirements only where it is impossible to determine a structure or property of the product as of the filing date (Case Nos. 2012(ju)1204 and 2012(ju)2658). In this context, a case proceeded to appeal where the point at issue was whether the claim 'Antibody or antigen binding fragment thereof, which is produced by the hybridoma deposited as the number of FERM BP-11110 or FERM BP-11111' satisfies clarity requirements (Fufuku 2014-017732). The Board of Appeal at the JPO decided that the claim satisfies clarity requirements, stating that the claimed antibody can be produced by use of the deposited hybridoma, and it would take an unreasonable length of time to otherwise identify the structure of the antibody.

§20.03 BREADTH OF CLAIMS AND SUPPORT BY EXAMPLES

[A] Acceptable Breadth of Claims to Antibodies

As explained in §20.02, various forms of claim language can be used for defining an antibody. The number of examples and evidence from experiments required to support a broadly defined antibody may also vary depending on the case at issue. The number of examples must be sufficient to enable a person skilled in the art to carry out the invention in its full scope as claimed without undue burden. It is usually required to disclose a representative number of species falling within the scope of a genus common to antibodies covered by the genus, such that a person skilled in the art is able to envision members of the genus.

[B] Required Experimental Support for Claims to Functionally Defined Antibodies

As described above, a claim may define an antibody by its functions, for example, by an ability to compete for binding to a structurally defined reference antibody.

Experimental support for claims to functionally defined antibodies is required to be sufficient to enable a person skilled in the art to carry out the invention in its full scope as functionally claimed without undue burden. In this regard, there have been recent cases involving an antibody that is functionally defined; for example, the *Amgen Inc. v. Sanofi* cases. In these cases, one of the points of dispute was 'whether it is sufficient to define an antibody merely by reference to functional features'.

The specification of the Amgen patent discloses two reference antibodies named 21B12 and 31H4; the first divisional patent JP 5705288 (hereafter, referred to as Patent 1) recites reference antibody 21B12, and the second divisional patent JP 5906333 (hereafter, referred to as Patent 2) recites reference antibody 31H4. Sanofi filed invalidation trials against Patent 1 (Invalidation Trial No. 2016-800004) on 18 January 2016, and against Patent 2 (Invalidation Trial No. 2016-800066) on 31 May 2016 before the JPO. In both cases, the reasons for invalidation alleged by Sanofi related to lack of support, industrial application, clarity, and inventive step. Decisions on both cases were issued on 10 August 2017. Patent 1 was maintained with a correction being made to Claims 1 and 9, and cancellation of the remaining claims. Corrected Claim 1 reads as follows:

> 'Claim 1: An isolated monoclonal antibody, which can neutralize binding of PCSK9 and LDLR protein, and which is competitive for binding to PCSK9 with the antibody including a heavy chain variable region consisting of an amino acid sequence shown as SEQ ID NO: 49, and a light chain variable region consisting of an amino acid sequence shown as SEQ ID NO: 23.'

Patent 2 was maintained with correction of Claims 1 and 5, and cancellation of the remaining claims. Corrected Claim 1 reads as follows:

> 'Claim 1: An isolated monoclonal antibody, which can neutralize binding of PCSK9 and LDLR protein, and which is competitive for binding to PCSK9 with the antibody including a heavy chain variable region consisting of an amino acid

sequence shown as SEQ ID NO: 67, and a light chain variable region consisting of an amino acid sequence shown as SEQ ID NO: 12.'

The cases were brought before the IP High Court on 8 December 2017. The High Court handed down decisions on both cases on 27 December 2018 (Hei 29 Gyo-ke 10225, Hei 29 Gro-ke 10226), upholding the JPO decisions.

As for support and industrial application requirements, in both cases Sanofi argued that the descriptions in each of the corrected Claim 1 were merely functional or characteristic definitions, and therefore the claimed invention encompassed an enormous number of antibodies or a wide variety of structures; while in the specification only a limited number of antibodies is disclosed. In both cases, Amgen argued that the specification includes detailed descriptions of how to prepare the claimed monoclonal antibody based on results of experiments, and that it was common technical knowledge at the filing date that desired antibodies can be obtained by a screening test based on known characteristics. The IP High Court accepted Amgen's position.

In view of the relatively strict practice deployed in this technical field, these decisions appear to be lenient on the patentee. However, where a person skilled in the art can obtain the claimed antibodies by following screening tests described in the specification, it is worth drafting a claim that is defined only by functional features.

[C] Required Experimental Support for Claims to Structurally Defined Antibodies

As described in §20.02[B][2], indication of all six CDRs in a claim has been usually required for defining antibodies directed to a known target. In this regard, it will be necessary to show that such defined antibody provides 'an unexpected effect' by experimental data, since a structural difference over prior art antibodies is not sufficient in itself to meet inventive step requirements.

As for sequence changes, it is common for examiners to state that given the sequences of the six CDRs are responsible for a specific binding of an antibody to its antigen, small changes to those sequences may significantly and unpredictably alter binding specificity and affinity. In this regard, it is generally not permissible to claim sequence variation in the six CDRs unless variation has been experimentally exemplified in the specification.

If the framework regions are considered to perform a role in binding affinity, or if they are otherwise relevant to a characteristic(s) that is relied upon, defining the six CDRs will not suffice. In such cases, it will be required to include a certain extent of framework limitation unless an applicant successfully shows that the framework regions do not substantially perform the role with reasonable explanation or experimental data.

§20.04 SPECIFIC MEDICAL APPLICATIONS AND OTHER FOLLOW-UP INVENTIONS

After developing an invention directed to an antibody per se, various types of follow-up inventions may be pursued.

[A] Treatment of Specific Diseases

In the Examination Handbook, Chapter 3 is titled 'Medical Inventions' in Annex B (hereafter, referred to as Examination Handbook 'Medicinal Inventions': https://www.jpo.go.jp/e/system/laws/rule/guideline/patent/handbook_shinsa/document/index/app_b3_e.pdf). Examination Handbook 'Medical Inventions' states that: 'when the claimed invention is "a medicine for disease Z comprising an active ingredient A," and a cited invention is "a medicine for disease X comprising an active ingredient A," the claimed medicinal invention involves novelty if it becomes evident that disease X and disease Z are different diseases in light of common general technical knowledge as of the filing.' Claims such as 'A pharmaceutical composition of matter for the treatment of cancer comprising an effective amount of an antibody against X' are allowed.

[B] Mode of Administration

The Examination Handbook 'Medicinal Inventions' at (3-2-2) states as follows:

> 'Even if the compounds etc. of the claimed medicinal invention do not differ from those of the cited invention, and there is also no difference in a disease to which the invention is applied, the claimed medicinal invention involves novelty when there is a difference between the claimed medicinal invention and the cited invention in medicinal use in which the invention is applied to the specific disease in a specific dosage or administration based on the attribute of the compounds etc. thereof.'

As for inventive step, Examination Handbook 'Medicinal Inventions' states that 'optimizing a dosage or an administration in order to solve the problem well known to a person skilled in the art, such as to increase a drug effect, to reduce a side effect, or to improve compliance, is an exercise of ordinary creativity of a person skilled in the art,' and also states that 'a favourable effect compared with the cited invention being remarkable by surpassing the extent that can be predicted from the state of the art as of the filing, the claimed medicinal invention involves an inventive step.'

Claims such as 'A medicine for the treatment of immune thrombocytopenic purpura comprising anti-CD20 antibody, wherein the anti-CD20 antibody is intravenously administered at a dose of 375mg/m^2 on 1st, 8th, 15th, and 22nd days' have been allowed.

[C] Dosage Regimens

As mentioned in §20.04[B] above, dosage regimens may also be recited in a claim to distinguish the claim from the cited invention.

[D] Specific Patient Groups

Even though the current version of Examination Handbook 'Medicinal Inventions' does not state concrete cases involving a specific patient group, the previous version of the Examination Guidelines included a hypothetical allowable claim directed to 'A pharmaceutical composition comprising a compound A as an effective component for the treatment of a hepatitis C patient having an alpha-type genotype, which is administered at an initial dose of 5.0mg/kg to 10.0mg/kg, followed by a dose of 0.3mg/kg to 0.5mg/kg on alternate days.' With regard to the hypothetical case it is explained that the higher amount of administration to the specific patient group made it possible to effectively treat the specific group of patients, and therefore the claimed invention has inventive step.

Various similar claims with a format limited to a specific patient group have been granted.

[E] Specific Mode of Action

If a specific mode of action provides a new medical use, the specific mode of action would provide a basis of novelty and inventive step for the claim limited by the specific mode of action. Claims such as 'A monoclonal antibody binding to FND1 of AXL and having activity to inhibit cell growth' have been granted.

However, attention should be directed to the Examination Handbook 'Medicinal Inventions' in which it is stated to the effect that novelty of a claimed medicinal invention shall be denied when the medicinal use of the claimed medicinal invention is merely expressed as a newly discovered working mechanism in place of the medicinal use of the cited invention.

[F] Combinations with Other Active Ingredients

In Examination Handbook 'Medicinal Inventions' it is stated to the effect that a claimed combination medicinal invention has inventive step when an advantageous effect, such as synergistic effects, is produced by the combination medicinal invention in comparison with each effect of the publicly known medicinal components.

Claims such as 'A pharmaceutical composition for the treatment of a stomach cancer in a patient comprising an effective amount of an antibody binding to VEGFR2 comprising light chain variable region (LCVR) amino acid sequence of SEQ ID NO: 1 and heavy chain variable region (HCVR) amino acid sequence of SEQ ID NO: 2, and an effective amount of a compound or its pharmacologically acceptable salt represented formulae (i) below', have been granted.

[G] Specific Diagnostic Applications

Various claims for diagnostic applications have been granted. An example of an allowed sample claim recites 'A method for detecting sepsis or systemic infection similar to sepsis comprising measuring procalcitonin 3-116 in a serum of a patient.'

§20.05 ASSESSMENT OF INVENTIVENESS

[A] General Approach

In essence, the current Examination Guidelines state that the following should be considered in examination of an inventive step of a claimed invention:

- selecting the prior art most suitable for the reasoning as 'the primary prior art' (note: A prior art document is a document that is most suitable for use as a basis for reasoning to deny inventive step, and such prior art need not necessarily be a closest reference.),
- determining whether it is possible to reason that a person skilled in the art would easily arrive at the claimed invention from the primary prior art by following the steps (1) to (4):
  (1) The examiner determines whether or not the reasoning is possible based on the various factors in support of the non-existence of an inventive step for the differences between the claimed invention and the primary prior art by adopting other pieces of prior art or considering the common general knowledge.
  (2) If the examiner determines that the reasoning is impossible based on the above step (1), the examiner determines that the claimed invention involves an inventive step.
  (3) If the examiner determines that the reasoning is possible based on the above step (1), then the examiner determines whether the reasoning is possible by comprehensively assessing various factors which includes factors in support of the existence of an inventive step, such as 'advantageous effects', 'obstructive factors', and 'teach away'.
  (4) If the examiner determines that the reasoning is impossible based on the above step (3), the examiner determines that the claimed invention involves an inventive step. If the examiner determines that the reasoning is still possible based on the above step (3), the examiner determines that the claimed invention does not involve an inventive step.

Factors in support of the non-existence of an inventive step include 'motivation,' mere alteration of a design or a plan, and mere aggregation. In determining motivation, there should be taken into account commonality among technical fields, a problem to be solved, a function or action, and suggestions in relevant references.

[B] Particularities Regarding Claims to Antibodies

For assessment of inventive step of an antibody against an antigen defined by six CDRs where another antibody against the same antigen is already known, other factors should be considered for the assessment of inventive step. Differences in epitope or binding sites or other advantageous or unexpected effects might be considered. Advantageous effects or unexpected effects would include, for example, specific neutralizing effects against disease-causing antigen, cross reactivity, or unexpectedly higher affinity.

Simple differences in CDRs associated with new or different binding sites would not constitute sufficient indication of inventive step, for example, as set out below, in a case that the difference is not associated with advantageous effects disclosed in the description.

Binding Sites or Epitope

In Appeal No. 2016-8151 decided on 6 July 2017, claims 1–4 are directed to four isolated antibodies, and each of the antibodies is defined by specificity to TAT425 and six CDRs.

Claim 1 reads

> 'An isolated antibody that binds TAT425 comprising:
> (a) a CDR-L1 sequence of SEQ ID NO: 10;
> (b) a CDR-L2 sequence of SEQ ID NO: 13;
> (c) a CDR-L3 sequence of SEQ ID NO: 16;
> (d) a CDR-H1 sequence of SEQ ID NO: 19;
> (e) a CDR-H2 sequence of SEQ ID NO: 23; and
> (f) a CDR-H3 sequence of SEQ ID NO: 27, wherein the TAT 425 comprises amino acid sequence of SEQ ID NO: 2 or its extracellular domain.'

Cited document 1 discloses the same antigen TAT425 sequence along with other TATs including TAT430 and refers to an isolated antibody that binds to TAT polypeptides including TAT 425. Example 11 discloses preparation of a monoclonal antibody against TAT 430.

The Appeal Board decided that no particular difficulty exists in preparation of various antibodies against TAT425, and the claimed invention is merely defined by CDRs and provides no superior effect, and thus lacks inventive step.

The patent applicant/appellant argued (1) none of the cited documents discloses an antibody defined by CDRs, and (2) the Examples show that the claimed antibodies were bound to different extracellular epitopes, and Example 6 confirms that the claimed antibodies against TAT425 actually bound to both primary human prostate cancer and metastatic prostate cancer.

Against the above arguments, the Board found that (1) it was routine to analyse the amino acid sequence of an antibody, and it would be an easy matter for a person skilled in the art to produce antiTAT425 monoclonal antibody, and thus simple identification of an amino acid sequence does not provide inventive step; (2) as the TAT425 is a larger polypeptide, having 1325 amino acids, it is not surprising that the TAT425 comprises a plurality of epitopes that do not compete for binding to a plurality of antibodies; and, (3) the cited documents also disclose that both primary human prostate cancer and metastatic prostate cancer showed positive for expression of TAT 425, and thus it would be within reasonable expectation of a person skilled in the art that the antibody against TAT 425 disclosed in the cited document 1 would bind to both primary human prostate cancer and metastatic prostate cancer.

Appeal No. 2017-4625 can be cited as another example, which relates to a claim directed to an isolated antibody or its fragment defined by six CDRs. The claimed antibody was different from the antibody disclosed in cited documents in its binding capability to HD-1 domain. However, the Appeal Board decided that the claimed invention lacked inventive step, stating that it is customary for a person skilled in the art to obtain another antibody having characteristics different from those of a known antibody, and the application does not provide other such advantageous characteristics.

Types of Advantageous Effects Associated with Antibody

A difference at a binding site or an epitope alone is unlikely to suffice to establish inventive step, but if that difference gives rise to particular advantageous effects, the difference could be persuasively asserted in support of inventive step. In the following two cases, inventive step was admitted.

In Appeal No. 2011-10160 decided on 30 May 2014, Pat No.5570681, the patent application relates to an antibody against human soluble BAFF raised by using amino acid residues of 134-146. At the time of the Appeal, amended Claim 1 read as follows: 'An antibody against AVQGPEETVTQDC (amino acid sequence represented by one letter code), which is an amino acid sequence from the 134th amino acid to the 146th amino acid of human BAFF (B cell activating factor belonging to the TNF family) protein.'

Cited document 1 disclosed an antibody against a full-sequence of amino acid residue 134 to 285 of soluble human BAFF. The Appeal Board found that the N terminal portion of amino acid residue 134-141 was known *not* to reside inside its three dimensional structure, and thus deemed it preferable as an antigen.

Against the Notice of Rejection issued by the Appeal Board, the appellant introduced into the claims a limitation that the monoclonal antibody has activity in suppressing production induction of IgG, INF-gamma, and TNF-q by peripheral blood lymphocytes stimulated by anti-CD3 antibody; and the appellant asserted that the amended invention produced unexpected effects that are supported by the Examples in the specification. The appellant further argued that the monoclonal antibody can inhibit activation of peripheral blood lymphocytes by BAFF, and a person skilled in the art would understand that the monoclonal antibody may contribute to treatment of autoimmune disease mediated by hyper-activation of BAFF.

The Appeal Board revoked the examiner's rejection and issued a patent for the application.

Similarly, in Appeal No. 2012-20040, the Appeal Board revoked the examiner's decision to reject the patent application, and issued a grant of patent for the application. The claim in question related to a monoclonal antibody specific to NKG2A, a NK cell surface receptor. The cited documents disclosed antibodies against NKG2A, but its CDRs are different. In response to the inquiry from the Appeal Board the appellant argued that known antibodies against NKG2A disclosed in the cited documents are not selectively specific to NKG2A, but bind also to NKG2C or NKG2E, and explained that blocking NKG2C would reduce a capability of NK cells to respond to infection because NKG2C is expressed in the subset of NK cells reactive to virus infection.

Evaluation of Unexpected Result: 'Treatment of Post Filing Data'

In many cases, the issue of inventive step hinges on an assessment of advantageous or unexpected effects, and thus on what data such advantageous effects are deemed to derive from is an important factor to be taken into account. A recent IP High Court judgment touched on this issue.

At present, the JPO accepts relatively widely late-filed experimental data in support of inventive step over cited documents, so long as the effects shown by the data can be inferred from descriptions in the specification. However, the decision outlined below may result in a less lenient approach being adopted.

Hei 29 Gyo-ke 10106 was decided on 22 October 2018. The case is an appeal against a decision issued by the Appeal Board in Invalidation Trial No. 2016-800021.

Claim 1 reads as follows:

> 'A medicament for the treatment of a human patient diagnosed as having a breast tumour expressing ErbB2 protein comprising a therapeutically effective amount of humanized 4D5 anti-ErbB2 antibody, wherein the treatment comprises the following sequential step of (1) treating the patient with the medicament, (2) surgically removing the tumour, and (3) treating the patient with the medicament or chemotherapeutic agent.'

One of the issues concerning patentability is inventive step, in particular the unexpected effects produced by the claimed medicament.

Both the Board of Appeal and the IP High Court found that Claim 1 differs from Exhibit A 1, which is a package insert for Herceptin, in that Exhibit A 1 is silent on the sequential steps (1) to (3) recited above, but found that the sequential steps could readily have been conceived of by a person skilled in the art based on Exhibits A 1–4.

Both the Appeal Board and the IP High Court then considered whether unexpected effects are produced by the claimed invention.

The Appeal Board found that the above difference does produce the effects referred to in the specification, that is: 'Patients treated according to the above therapeutic regimen will display improved overall survival and/or reduced time to tumor progression (TTP)' at [0119] and the effects are substantiated by other Exhibits detailing experimental data not mentioned in the application, thus the effects should be taken into consideration.

On the other hand, the IP High Court disagreed with the Appeal Board's assessment of the late-filed experimental data.

The IP High Court found that the application discloses its effects at best at the above cited portion only, but fails to mention what other regimen and to what extent the claimed invention will produce an improved survival rate and/or reduced TTP. The patentee/defendant asserted that the late-filed documents disclosing experimental data should be taken into consideration. The IP High Court considered the data could be considered only to the extent indicative of qualitative effects, and declined to consider data beyond the extent of qualitative effects. Thus, the IP High Court determined that the invention lacked inventive step. Hence, the IP High Court rescinded the JPO Appeal Board's decision to reject the demand for invalidation.

§20.06 ENFORCEMENT AND SCOPE OF PROTECTION

General

As regards interpretation of scope of protection, Article 70 of Patent Law stipulates as follows:

> Article 70 (Scope of patented invention)
>
> (1) The scope of a patented invention shall be determined based upon the terms in the claims attached to the application.
>
> (2) In the case of the preceding paragraph, the meaning of each term used in the claims shall be interpreted in consideration of the descriptions in the specification and drawings attached to the application.
>
> (3) In the case of the preceding two paragraphs, descriptions in the abstract attached to the application shall not be taken into consideration.

To interpret a scope of protection of claims, the prosecution file history is also taken into consideration.

[A] Biosimilars

We are unable to find any court decision involving a biosimilar of an antibody medicine in a strict sense, that is, a case involving an antibody medicine having exactly the same amino acid sequence.

The recent lower court cases referred to below show how the scope of the claims is interpreted in an antibody related patent. In those cases, the District Court looked at the specification and drawings to interpret the claim language. In case (1), the Court construed a functional limitation recited in claim restrictively in line with the descriptions in the specification; but in case (2) the Court found no need to narrowly construe functional language.

Hei 28 wa 11475 decided 31 March 2018

The patentee lodged a patent infringement suit seeking an injunction based on Patent No. 4313531.

The claim is directed to 'an antibody against factor IX or IXa, or its derivatives, wherein the antibody increases the procoagulant activity, provided antibody clone ----- are excluded.'

The allegedly infringing product is a non-symmetric bispecific antibody IgG having two binding sites, one of which binds to active type factor IX and the other of which binds to factor X.

The patentee argued that a person skilled in the art may work, without undue effort, an antibody against factor IX or IXa, wherein the antibody increases procoagulant activity, or its derivative derived from the antibody while maintaining its activity. A bi-specific antibody is derived from a mono-specific antibody, and thus is covered by the claim.

The defendant/alleged infringer argued that the limitation of 'wherein the antibody increases the procoagulant activity' should be construed based on technical knowledge concretely disclosed in the specification, because the limitation is a purpose or problem to be solved by the invention, and hence the claim is broadly drafted. The defendant also argued that the bi-specific antibody was developed by application of technical knowledge completely different from the technical knowledge disclosed in the specification of the patent. The specification discloses that an increase in the procoagulant activity was assayed using chromogenic assay, and the ratio to negative control is over three, thus the claimed antibody should be construed as covering only an antibody showing a ratio to negative control of over three, as determined by use of chromogenic assay.

The Tokyo District Court found that the limitation 'wherein the antibody increases the procoagulant activity' in the claim only describes the purpose or effects of the invention, and the limitation fails to clarify any concrete constitution or structure that would achieve the purpose or effect of the invention. The gist of the Court's response is as follows. The monopoly right based on the patent right is offered as compensation for disclosing a new and inventive patent invention to the public. Thus, regarding a functional claim, if it is to be construed that any possible embodiments that could achieve the function are included in the scope of the invention, it would mean that a monopoly right based on the patent right is given for an invention including a technical idea not disclosed in the specification. Such an interpretation would not be permitted because it is contrary to the purpose of the patent system of granting a monopoly right as compensation for the disclosure of the invention.

The Court continued by stating that the scope of the invention cannot be clarified only by the statement in the claim, where the claims are described using abstract and functional expressions. The Court held that the scope of the patented invention should be determined, by taking into consideration the descriptions in the specification and drawings, based on the technical idea shown in the concrete constitutions disclosed therein. However, the Court cautioned that the foregoing is not intended to limit the scope of the patented invention to specific examples. A constitution may be included in the scope so long as it can be worked by those skilled in the art based on the descriptions in the specification and drawings.

Then, the Court looked at the specification and common technical knowledge available in the art as of the filing, and found that a 'bi-specific antibody that increases the procoagulant activity' should be included within the scope of the claim as a derivative derived from an antibody.

Next, the Court considered the meaning of 'antibody that increases the procoagulant activity' in the claim, and found that in the specification an antibody having an ability to increase procoagulant activity 1.7 times or 2 times over negative control in the chromogenic assay was not evaluated as 'positive.' In consideration of these findings, the Court stated that antibodies within the scope of the claims should be those having an ability to increase procoagulant activity by more than about 2 times in chromogenic assay. The Court found that the alleged infringing product shows an ability to increase procoagulant activity by 1.36 to 1.48 times over negative control by chromogenic assay, and thus the product is *not* covered by the scope of the claimed invention, and hence does *not* infringe the patent.

H29 wa 16468 decided on 17 January 2019

This infringement case relates to the same patents as discussed in §20.03, and the alleged infringed product relates to the trade name 'Praluent'. The alleged infringer/defendant asserted that the scope of the claims should be interpreted as being within the enabled scope, and therefore the claimed antibody should be limited to the antibodies concretely disclosed in each of the two specifications, or antibodies having a substitution of one or more amino acids at specifically defined sites; and accordingly, the defendant's products do not fall within this scope.

Responsive to the above argument, the Tokyo District Court found that the specifications disclose, for the purpose of identifying and obtaining antibody neutralizing binding of PCSK9-LDLR, a method for preparation of an immunized mouse in accordance with an immunization procedure and schedule, a method for preparation of hybridoma, a screening method, and an epitope binding assay method. The Court found that in accordance with the methods described, antibodies competing with reference antibodies other than those concretely disclosed in the specifications can be conceived of by a person skilled in the art, and thus the claimed antibody is *not* limited to the antibodies concretely disclosed in each of the specifications, or to the antibodies having a substitution of one or more amino acids at the specifically defined sites.

The defendant also argued to the effect that (i) it is not possible to infer that the specifications disclose technical ideas that antibodies competing with the reference antibodies may neutralize binding between PCSK9 and LDLR; and, (ii) it cannot be said that a huge number of antibodies competing with reference antibodies are all antibodies that neutralize PCSK9-LDLR binding based on 3 or 2 groups of antibodies disclosed in the examples, and moreover, the specifications do not disclose grounds as to why such a huge number of antibodies competing with reference antibodies are all antibodies that neutralize PCSK9-LDLR binding.

The Court studied the specifications and noted the facts that in Table 2, 24 antibodies are those that neutralize PCSK9-LDLR binding and compete with the reference antibodies among the 30 antibodies identified by the above screening method: and, in Table 37.1, at least 20 antibodies are those that neutralize PCSK9-LDLR binding and compete with the reference antibodies among the 16 and 2 and 7 antibodies in BIN 1, 2, and 3 respectively.

Hence, the Court found that there are plural antibodies disclosed in the specifications that compete with the reference antibodies among antibodies obtained by the specific screening method, and which also neutralize PCSK9-LDLR binding.

Furthermore, the Court stated that no additional concrete antibody is presented that competes with the reference antibodies but does not neutralize binding between PCSK9 and LDLR, thus it is not clear that the ratio of antibodies that do not neutralize PCSK9-LDLR binding among those competing with the reference antibodies is high.

[B] Equivalence

The doctrine of equivalents is applicable in Japan. In 1998, the Supreme Court rendered a decision (Hei 6 wo 1083) that clarified requirements for applicability of the doctrine of equivalents as follows:

> 'Even if there exists a part of elements in the accused product which differs from the part recited in the claims, the accused product is considered to fall within the scope of the patented invention if the following five requirements are fulfilled:
>
> Requirement 1: the part is not an essential part of the patented invention;
>
> Requirement 2: even if the part is replaced in the accused product, the object of the patented invention can be attained with the same meritorious effect;
>
> Requirement 3: a person skilled in the art could have easily conceived of the replacement of the part at the time the product was made;
>
> Requirement 4: the accused product is not identical to publicly known technology at the time of filing, and a person skilled in the art could not have easily conceived of the accused product from publicly known technology at the time of filing; and
>
> Requirement 5: there are no particular circumstances, for example, to exclude the accused product from the claims in the prosecution of the application.'

Whether an accused antibody infringes a patent under the doctrine of equivalents should be judged under the principle mentioned above.

Chapter 21

Singapore

Khoo Kian Hoe

§21.01 ANTIBODIES AS PATENTABLE SUBJECT-MATTER

[A] Legal Framework

The Singapore Patents Act (Cap. 221) and the Patent Rules provide the legislative framework for the patent system in Singapore. Patent applications may be filed at the Registry of Patents at the Intellectual Property Office of Singapore (IPOS). IPOS also has the authority to issue administrative decisions in relation to revocation and restoration of patents. Any contentious infringement matters may be brought before the High Court, while appeals from decisions of the High Court can be made to the Court of Appeal of Singapore. Certain decisions of IPOS may be appealed to the High Court.

Jurisprudence under the Patents Act is not yet well developed. However, the Patents Act is based closely on the UK Patents Act 1997. As such, the courts in Singapore tend to consult UK jurisprudence when considering equivalent provisions under the Singapore Patents Act. They may also consult EPO case law.

The Patents Act was significantly amended in 2014 to abolish the previous 'self-assessment' system and to introduce a new 'positive grant' system. Under the new system, applications may only proceed to grant based on fully positive examination results where patentability requirements for novelty, inventive step and industrial applicability are met. This is unlike the old 'self-assessment' system where an application may proceed to grant even though there are one or more patentability objections that are outstanding in the examination report.

Two forms of examination are possible. Substantive examination is a full assessment of substantive patentability requirements. Supplementary examination[1]

1. The supplementary examination route will no longer be available in Singapore for patent applications with a filing date (such as a national or international filing date) on or after 1 January 2020.

allows applicants to rely on the positive examination results of a corresponding international application or a corresponding foreign application. Under supplementary examination, only certain prescribed matters[2] are considered by the Examiner as it is presumed that the quality of examination carried out in the foreign offices is such that no further examination as to novelty, inventive step or industrial applicability is required on the application in Singapore. These prescribed matters include a) whether each claim is supported by the description, b) whether each claim is related to a claim of a corresponding foreign application that has been examined to be novel, inventive and industrially applicable, c) whether each claim relates to excluded subject-matter, d) whether there is any double patenting issue, and e) whether the application contains any added matter.

Section 13(1) of the Patents Act lists the requirements of a patentable invention as follows:

> 'Subject to subsection (2), a patentable invention is one that satisfies the following conditions:
>
> (a) the invention is new;
> (b) it involves an inventive step; and
> (c) it is capable of industrial application.'

Section 16(2) of the Patents Act provides that an invention of a method of treatment of the human or animal body by surgery or therapy or of diagnosis practised on the human or animal body shall not be taken to be capable of industrial application.

In other words, methods of treatment of the human or animal body by surgery or therapy or of diagnosis practised on the human or animal body are statutorily excluded from patentability in Singapore.

Subsection (3) further provides that subsection (2) shall not prevent a product consisting of a substance or composition from being treated as capable of industrial application merely because it is invented for use in any such method.

Section 14(7) of the Patents Act also states the following:

> 'In the case of an invention consisting of a substance or composition for use in a method of treatment of the human or animal body by surgery or therapy or of diagnosis practised on the human or animal body, the fact that the substance or composition forms part of the state of the art shall not prevent the invention from being taken to be new if the use of the substance or composition in any such method does not form part of the state of the art.'

Hence, antibodies may be made the subject of medical or diagnostic use claims, and may be drafted in the form of a first medical use claim[3] (e.g. antibody X for use in therapy), or a Swiss-style second medical use claim[4] (i.e. use of antibody X in the manufacture of a medicament for the treatment of disease Y).

2. Rule 2A(3) of the Patent Rules.
3. Examination Guidelines for Patent Examination at 8.114 (https://www.ipos.gov.sg/docs/default-source/resources-library/patents/examination-guidelines-for-patent-applications-at-ipos_2017-oct.pdf).
4. Examination Guidelines for Patent Examination at 8.139 (https://www.ipos.gov.sg/docs/default-source/resources-library/patents/examination-guidelines-for-patent-applications-

Section 25(4) requires that the specification discloses the invention in a manner which is clear and complete for the invention to be performed by a person skilled in the art. This may also be referred to as the requirement for 'enabling disclosure' or 'sufficiency'. Failure to meet the requirement under section 25(4) is a ground of revocation under section 80(1) of the Patents Act.

Section 25(5) also requires that the claims to:

'(a) define the matter for which the applicant seeks protection;
(b) be clear and concise;
(c) be supported by the description; and
(d) relate to one invention or to a group of inventions which are so linked as to form a single inventive concept.'

These are grounds of substantive examination but not of revocation.

[B] General Amenability or Exclusion of Antibodies from Patentability

Inventions directed to antibodies *per se* and their applications are generally patentable in Singapore, provided that the requirements for novelty, inventive step and industrial applicability under section 13(1) are met.

[C] Required Distinction from Naturally Occurring Antibodies

In *Merck & Co, Inc v. Pharmaforte Singapore Pte Ltd*,[5] a patent directed to a purer form of Lovastatin (an anti-hypercholesteremic agent) was challenged for lack of inventiveness based on evidence that standard techniques could be used to purify Lovastatin. In the assessment of inventive step, the Court of Appeal distinguished between a discovery and an invention and stated the following at [63]:

> 'In this regard, we must also point out that the fact that a discovery is made does not mean there is an invention. The latter does not necessarily follow from the former. This distinction was brought out by Lindley LJ in Lane Fox (supra) at page 429 where he said:
>
> > "An invention is not the same thing as a discovery. When Volta discovered the effect of an electric current from his battery on a frog's leg he made a great discovery, but no patentable invention. Again, a man who discovers that a known machine can produce effects which no one before him knew could be produced by it, may make a great and useful discovery; but if he does no more, his discovery is not a patentable invention: ... He has added nothing but knowledge to what previously existed. A patentee must do something more; he must make some addition, not only to knowledge, but to previously known inventions, and must so use his knowledge and ingenuity as to produce either a new and useful thing or result, or a new and useful method of producing an old thing or result."'

---

at-ipos_2017-oct.pdf).

5. *Merck & Co, Inc v. Pharmaforte Singapore Pte Ltd* [2000] SGCA 39.

The Court of Appeal concluded at [65]:

> 'We would agree that a person, skilled in the art, faced with impurities in a compound would naturally use those techniques to reduce the impurities. In our opinion, what the appellants have achieved in the alleged patent is a discovery. It does not amount to an invention.'

As a consequence, the patent was invalidated for lack of inventive step.

The Examination Guidelines for Patent Applications at IPOS ('Examination Guidelines') explain that section 13(1) contains the word 'invention' and the subject-matter of a patent must therefore be for an invention.[6] This threshold requirement has not been judicially considered save for the distinction between discoveries and inventions in the *Merck* case.

The patentability of naturally occurring antibodies has not yet been considered in a Singapore court. The Examination Guidelines were, however, amended in 2017 to clarify the distinction between inventions and discoveries for isolated materials or microorganisms that are found in nature. The revised Examination Guidelines state the following:[7]

> 'To find a material or microorganism that pre-existed in nature would represent a discovery and therefore an isolated or purified material or microorganism from nature is not an invention. However, if a new use of the isolated or purified material or microorganism is found, then the new use can be claimed.'

In view of the revised Examination Guidelines, a naturally occurring antibody that is isolated or purified from nature (such as one that is directly isolated from human serum) may be considered by an Examiner to be a discovery, which is not patentable. However, if a new use of the naturally occurring antibody is found, the new use may be claimed such as in the form of a first or second medical use claim.

The Examination Guidelines[8] further explain:

> 'If the contribution made by the claimed subject-matter goes beyond isolating or purifying the material or microorganism that pre-existed in nature, such as to include modification of an isolated natural material or microorganism in order that the isolated natural material or microorganism can be adapted for a specific use, then both the modified material or microorganism and the specific use of the modified material or microorganism are considered inventions. The same consideration also applies to a claim to a composition or a combination comprising an isolated or purified materials or microorganism that pre-existed in nature. If the contribution made by the claimed composition or combination

6. Examination Guidelines for Patent Examination at 8.1 (https://www.ipos.gov.sg/docs/default-source/resources-library/patents/examination-guidelines-for-patent-applications-at-ipos_2017-oct.pdf).
7. Examination Guidelines for Patent Examination at 8.12 (https://www.ipos.gov.sg/docs/default-source/resources-library/patents/examination-guidelines-for-patent-applications-at-ipos_2017-oct.pdf).
8. Examination Guidelines for Patent Examination at 8.14 (https://www.ipos.gov.sg/docs/default-source/resources-library/patents/examination-guidelines-for-patent-applications-at-ipos_2017-oct.pdf).

> resides merely in combining the isolated or purified material or microorganism that pre-existed in nature with another product (e.g. a container), then the claim is not considered an invention. However, if the contribution of the claimed composition or combination goes beyond just putting the composition or combination together, such as resulting in a specific useful application, then the claimed composition or combination would be an invention.'

It follows that if an isolated or purified antibody that pre-existed in nature now includes a modification that adapts it for a specific use, then both the modified antibody and the specific use of the modified antibody may be patentable. For example, a chimeric or humanised version of a mouse antibody may reduce its immunogenicity in humans and adapt it for use in treating a disease in a human. Such an antibody is likely to be considered non-natural and therefore patentable. An isolated or purified antibody that pre-existed in nature can also be a patentable invention when combined with another product (such as an excipient), if the combination results in a specific useful application (such as having an improved pharmacokinetic property for administering to a patient).

§21.02 ACCEPTABLE CLAIM FEATURES FOR DEFINING ANTIBODIES

[A] Functional Features

Rule 19(7) states that the definition in the claim of the matter for which protection is sought shall be in terms of the technical features of the invention which may be expressed in structural, functional or mathematical terms. The Examination Guidelines explain that functional claims are generally broader than claims reciting structural features, and the Examiner will typically require that the claims are neither ambiguous nor unduly broad.[9] The technical contribution of the invention and whether the claim goes beyond that contribution will also be considered by the Examiner.

The Examination Guidelines[10] describe how Lord Hoffmann, in *Biogen Inc v. Medeva Plc* [1996] UKHL 18 considered there is more than one way in which the breadth of the claim could exceed the technical contribution to the art of the invention (at paragraph 71):

> 'The patent may claim results which it does not enable, such as making a wide class of products when it enables only one of those products and discloses no principle which would enable others to be made. Or it may claim every way of achieving a result when it enables only one way and it is possible to envisage other ways of achieving that result which makes no use of the invention.'

9. Examination Guidelines for Patent Examination at 5.107 (https://www.ipos.gov.sg/docs/default-source/resources-library/patents/examination-guidelines-for-patent-applications-at-ipos_2017-oct.pdf).
10. Examination Guidelines for Patent Examination at 5.85 (https://www.ipos.gov.sg/docs/default-source/resources-library/patents/examination-guidelines-for-patent-applications-at-ipos_2017-oct.pdf).

The Examination Guidelines further explain[11] that some types of claim are more likely to involve consideration of whether there is sufficient support. This includes broad claims, claiming by result, claims in which features are defined by function, and reach through claims, which are construed as per any other type of claim.

Antibody claims that are defined solely in functional terms are often considered by Examiners to be ambiguous and unduly broad. Such claims may be required by Examiners to be limited to recite additional structural features such as variable heavy and light chain sequences or complementarity determining region (CDR) sequences.

[1] Target/Antigen

An antibody may be defined functionally in terms of the target or antigen that it recognises, provided that the requirements for patentability under section 13(1) are satisfied. Such broad claims are typically directed to antibodies that bind to a newly discovered target or antigen that is disclosed for the first time in a patent application. Such claims were more common in the past at a time when new targets or antigens were still regularly being discovered. However, the question of validity of such claims has not yet arisen for consideration before a Singapore court. In particular, there has not yet been judicial consideration as to whether such claims meet the requirements for clear and complete disclosure under section 25(4).

[2] Mode of Binding: Target Affinity, Binding Specificity, Epitope, Definitions via Reference Antibodies and Competitive Binding

An antibody may be defined functionally in terms of its target affinity or binding specificity, or via reference antibodies and competitive binding. As mentioned above, the Examination Guidelines require that the claims are neither ambiguous nor unduly broad. The Examiner will also assess whether the claims go beyond the technical contribution of the invention.

There are no guidelines with regard to any specific techniques that should be used for determining binding affinity or avidity in antibody claims. However, techniques such as surface plasmon resonance (e.g. using a BIAcore) have been accepted as being able to determine binding affinity or avidity constants.[12]

[3] Effect on Target

An antibody that is defined functionally in terms of its effect on a target may be regarded as a claim that is defined in terms of desirable results. In such instances, the specification will need to provide enough instruction for the skilled person to make each product that is encompassed by the claim, without undue burden or the need

11. Examination Guidelines for Patent Examination at 5.80 (https://www.ipos.gov.sg/docs/default-source/resources-library/patents/examination-guidelines-for-patent-applications-at-ipos_2017-oct.pdf).
12. *Lonza Biologics Tuas Pte Ltd v. Genpharm International Inc* [2015] SGIPOS 13 at [56]-[67], a copy of which is downloadable from https://www.ipos.gov.sg/resources/hearing-mediation.

for further invention.[13] The Examiner will also consider whether the specification enables the full scope of the claim and whether the claims encompass matter that owes nothing to the teaching of the invention.

[B] Structural Features

[1] Molecular Topology: Antibody Types, Fragments and Antibody Constructs

An antibody may also be defined in terms of its molecular topology, such as in terms of antibody type (e.g. IgG, IgM or IgA) or fragment or construct (e.g. F(ab), $F(ab)_2$, Fv, Fc, scFV or diabodies). This may help to provide some structural definition to the claim to avoid the issues encountered by claims that are defined functionally. The structural definition may also help to distinguish the antibody from other antibodies that are disclosed in the prior art.

[2] Amino Acid Sequences

[a] Full-Length Sequences of Antibodies

An antibody may be characterised structurally by defining the full-length sequence of the antibody (or shorter sequences such as variable heavy and light chain sequences or the six CDRs of the antibody). This again provides a narrower structural definition to the claim and avoids the issues that are encountered by functionally defined claims.

[b] Sequences of Fragments, CDRs and Framework Regions

An antibody may be defined structurally in terms of the sequence of the antibody fragment or framework regions. It is also common to recite at least the sequences of the six CDRs of an antibody to define the parts that confer specificity on the antibody and to distinguish the antibody from the prior art.

[3] Chemical Modifications, Conjugation and Glycosylation

An antibody may also be defined structurally in terms of chemical modification or conjugation to another molecule (such as to a toxin or label). An antibody may also be engineered to have a novel glycosylation pattern.

[C] Cell Line Deposits and Process of Production

A cell line deposit (such as a hybridoma or transfected host cell line) can be made at an International Depositary Authority to meet the requirements for disclosing

13. Examination Guidelines for Patent Examination at 5.98 (https://www.ipos.gov.sg/docs/default-source/resources-library/patents/examination-guidelines-for-patent-applications-at-ipos_2017-oct.pdf).

the invention in a manner which is clear and complete enough for the invention to be performed by a person skilled in the art.[14] A claim directed to, for example, an antibody produced by the cell line, may refer to the cell line deposit by stating the accession number of the deposit.

§21.03 BREADTH OF CLAIMS AND SUPPORT BY EXAMPLES

A claim to an antibody would need to meet the requirement for clear and complete disclosure under section 25(4) and support under section 25(5)(c). However, as noted above, lack of support is not a ground of revocation.

[A] Acceptable Breadth of Claims to Antibodies

Clear and Complete Disclosure

As mentioned above, section 25(4) of the Patents Act requires that the specification of an application discloses the invention in a manner which is clear and complete for the invention to be performed by a person skilled in the art.

A two-step approach was used in *First Currency Choice Pte Ltd v. Main Line Corporate Holdings Ltd*[15] to determine whether a specification meets the requirements for a clear and complete disclosure. The first step is to ascertain what the invention is, while the second step is to ascertain whether the directions provided by the patent are sufficiently enabling for a person with practical interest in the subject-matter of the patent to arrive at the invention after following the directions.

As stated in *First Currency Choice Pte Ltd v. Main Line Corporate Holdings Ltd*:[16]

> 'The two-stage test as laid out above can be supplemented by two further considerations. First, the specification of the patent must embrace an embodiment of the invention asserted in each of the claims with sufficient particularity to enable the invention to be understood and carried into effect by those in the industry without making further inventions or prolonged study of the matter. The specification must be set out clearly and fairly so that any individual desirous of carrying out the invention may obtain full knowledge of its practical aspects. But, it is not necessary that the specification be so detailed that this notional individual can perform the invention without any trial or experiment at all. Second, the description of the invention should not be unnecessarily difficult to follow, and must not contain any traps or seriously misleading statements which the reader cannot correct ...'

14. Section 114 of the Patents Act, Rule 20 and Fourth Schedule of the Patent Rules.
15. *First Currency Choice Pte Ltd v. Main Line Corporate Holdings Ltd* [2008] 1 SLR(R) 335 at [61].
16. *First Currency Choice Pte Ltd v. Main Line Corporate Holdings Ltd* [2008] 1 SLR(R) 335 at [62].

Support

Section 25(5)(c) of the Patents Act states that the claim or claims shall be supported by the description. The Examination Guidelines explain that this is taken to mean that:[17]

> '(a) the scope of the claims should be justified by the disclosure provided by the description, drawings and sequence listing, and in particular "*should not extend to subject matter which, after reading the description, would still not be at the disposal of the person skilled in the art*" (*Generics (UK) Ltd v. Lundbeck A/S* [2009] RPC 13 at [36]; and
>
> (b) the specification must provide a disclosure that enables the invention to be performed across the breadth of the claims. (Asahi Kasei Kogyo KK's Application [1991] RPC 485).'

As further explained by the Examination Guidelines[18]:

> 'Most claims will represent a generalisation of the inventive concept. The extent to which that generalisation is supported will vary from case to case. Thus, as stated by Lord Hoffmann in *Biogen Inc v. Medeva Plc* [1996] UKHL 18:
>
> > "... if the patentee has hit upon a new product which has a beneficial effect but cannot demonstrate that there is a common principle by which that effect will be shared by other products of the same class, he will be entitled to a patent for that product but not for the class, even though some may subsequently turn out to have the same beneficial effect: see May & Baker Ltd v. Boots Pure Drug Co Ltd (1950) 67 RPC 23, 50. On the other hand, if he has disclosed a beneficial property which is common to the class, he will be entitled to a patent for all products of that class (assuming them to be new) even though he has not himself made more than one or two of them."'

[B] Required Experimental Support for Claims to Functionally Defined Antibodies

Claims directed to functionally defined antibodies will have to meet the requirements under section 25(4) and 25(5)(c) as mentioned above. The specification should provide sufficient information for the skilled person to determine whether or not they have achieved the desired result without undue experimentation and without exercising any inventive ingenuity.[19]

---

17. Examination Guidelines for Patent Examination at 5.76 (https://www.ipos.gov.sg/docs/default-source/resources-library/patents/examination-guidelines-for-patent-applications-at-ipos_2017-oct.pdf).
18. Examination Guidelines for Patent Examination at 5.77 (https://www.ipos.gov.sg/docs/default-source/resources-library/patents/examination-guidelines-for-patent-applications-at-ipos_2017-oct.pdf).
19. Examination Guidelines for Patent Examination at 5.29 (https://www.ipos.gov.sg/docs/default-source/resources-library/patents/examination-guidelines-for-patent-applications-at-ipos_2017-oct.pdf).

In a revocation proceeding at IPOS in *Lonza Biologics Tuas Pte Ltd v. Genpharm International Inc.*,[20] an application was filed by Lonza Biologics Tuas Pte Ltd to revoke Singapore Patent No. 51905 on the basis of several grounds, including an alleged lack of sufficiency in claims 1 and 10. These claims were directed to antibodies defined by a lower limit of their binding affinity constants (at least 2 x 10^9 M^{-1} in claim 1 and at least 1 x 10^{10} M^{-1} in claim 10) to a predetermined human antigen. It should be noted that during the initial stage of the proceeding, the proprietor (Genpharm International Inc.) had attempted to correct several occurrences of 'affinity' with 'avidity' and 'affinity constant' with 'avidity constant'.[21] The proposed corrections were objected to by the applicant and only the corrections to the title of Table 17 and an occurrence of 'affinity' in the specification (which refers to Table 17) were found to be allowable. Other proposed corrections, including proposed replacements of 'affinity' with 'avidity' in claims 1 and 10, were disallowed.

The Registrar subsequently found claims 1 and 10 to lack sufficiency as there were no instructions (in view of the correction to Table 17) that a reasonably skilled technician may follow in order to achieve the affinity values of the magnitude that were claimed (i.e. at least 2 x 10^9 M^{-1} in claim 1 and at least 1 x 10^{10} M^{-1} in claim 10). There was also no data supporting the claim that the disclosed method could achieve affinity binding constants beyond the lower limits that were claimed. Lastly, the Registrar found that while claims 1 and 10 are directed to targeting a 'predetermined human antigen', the specification does not clearly disclose targeting all types of human antigens but only provides data for targeting CD4 human globular protein.

The Registrar also found claims 1–13 to lack an inventive step, which is discussed further in §21.05[A] below.

[C] Required Experimental Support for Claims to Structurally Defined Antibodies

Claims directed to structurally defined antibodies will also have to meet the requirements under section 25(4) and 25(5)(c) as mentioned above.

Rule 19(5)(e) requires at least one embodiment of the invention to be fully described. The Examination Guidelines further explain that if the claims themselves provide an enabling disclosure and are supported by the description, then this may provide a sufficient disclosure.[22]

---

20. *Lonza Biologics Tuas Pte Ltd v. Genpharm International Inc* [2015] SGIPOS 13, a copy of which is downloadable from https://www.ipos.gov.sg/resources/hearing-mediation.
21. *Lonza Biologics Tuas Pte Ltd* [2014] SGIPOS 9, a copy of which is downloadable from https://www.ipos.gov.sg/resources/hearing-mediation.
22. Examination Guidelines for Patent Examination at 5.27 (https://www.ipos.gov.sg/docs/default-source/resources-library/patents/examination-guidelines-for-patent-applications-at-ipos_2017-oct.pdf).

§21.04 SPECIFIC MEDICAL APPLICATIONS AND OTHER FOLLOW-UP INVENTIONS

[A] Treatment of Specific Diseases

As discussed above, claims directed to the method of treatment of the human or animal body are not patentable in Singapore under section 16(1). Second or subsequent medical uses directed to the treatment of specific diseases may be claimed in the form of Swiss-type claims in Singapore (e.g. 'use of antibody X in the manufacture of a medicament in the treatment of disease Y').

It should be noted that the validity of Swiss-type claims for the protection of second or subsequent medical uses has not yet been fully considered by a Singapore Court. In *Warner-Lambert Company LLC v. Novartis (Singapore)*,[23] the Court of Appeal noted in orbiter that Swiss-type claims are currently allowable by IPOS and does not disagree with the validity of such claims at this stage. The Court of Appeal, however, commented that if a broader and more purposive interpretation is conferred on section 14(7) of the Patents Act, protection of a new use of a known substance via purpose limited product claims may be allowable and it may therefore no longer be necessary to rely on Swiss-type claims for the protection of second and subsequent medical uses. IPOS is currently studying the Court of Appeal's position and may issue revised examination guidelines in the near future. In the meantime, Swiss-type claims will continue to be accepted for the protection of second or subsequent medical uses at IPOS.

[B] Mode of Administration

Second medical use claims may be defined in part by their modes of administration which can serve as a distinguishing feature over the prior art. The Examination Guidelines[24] explain that in the EPO Technical Board of Appeal decision T51/93 SERONO, the subcutaneous administration of human chorionic gonadotrophin for treating male sexual disorders or infertility was considered to be novel over the cited prior art documents, which disclosed administration via an intramuscular route. In this case, the applicant showed that subcutaneous administration provided the advantages of reduced nerve lesions and the option of self-administration.

[C] Dosage Regimens

Second medical use claims which are distinguished from the prior art documents based on the dosage regime used are patentable. This is provided that the claimed dosage regime is novel and inventive. The Examination Guidelines[25] refer to *Actavis*

23. *Warner-Lambert Company LLC v. Novartis (Singapore) Pte Ltd* [2017] SGCA 45.
24. Examination Guidelines for Patent Examination at 8.151 (https://www.ipos.gov.sg/docs/default-source/resources-library/patents/examination-guidelines-for-patent-applications-at-ipos_2017-oct.pdf).
25. Examination Guidelines for Patent Examination at 8.152 (https://www.ipos.gov.sg/docs/default-source/resources-library/patents/examination-guidelines-for-patent-applications-

v. Merck [2008] RPC 26, in which a second medical use claim directed to a new dosage regime for treating androgenic alopecia was found to allowable.

[D] Specific Patient Groups

A second medical use claim may rely solely on the patient group to be treated, for the purposes of novelty and inventive step, despite the known association between the claimed substance or composition and the disease to be treated. The Examination Guidelines[26] provide the following guidance from the EPO Technical Board of Appeal in T 233/96 MEDCO RESEARCH:

> '(1) the new patient group must be clearly distinct from the patient group treated in the prior art and these 2 groups must not overlap;
>
> (2) the distinction must not be arbitrary and must be based on a functional relationship between the physiological or pathological characteristics of the new group and the therapeutic effect.'

[E] Specific Mode of Action

Second medical use claims that are directed to the same therapeutic purpose as the prior art but distinguished solely by a different mechanism of action or technical effect will be considered to lack novelty. The discovery of the new mechanism of action or technical effect will have to be associated with some other feature of the treatment to distinguish it from the prior art (e.g. new specific disease or patient group).

[F] Combinations with Other Active Ingredients

A second medical use claim directed to the use of a composition comprising two or more agents for the treatment of a disease is novel if the stated combination has not previously been used for the specified disease or condition.

[G] Specific Diagnostic Applications

Methods of diagnosis practised on the human or animal body are not patentable in Singapore. However, if the methods of diagnosis are performed *in vitro* on a tissue sample obtained from the body, then these claims would be patentable in Singapore.

---

at-ipos_2017-oct.pdf).

26. Examination Guidelines for Patent Examination at 8.155 (https://www.ipos.gov.sg/docs/default-source/resources-library/patents/examination-guidelines-for-patent-applications-at-ipos_2017-oct.pdf).

§21.05 ASSESSMENT OF INVENTIVENESS

[A] General Approach

Section 15 of the Patents Act states that an invention shall be taken to involve an inventive step if it is not obvious to a person skilled in the art having regard to the relevant state of the art.

Section 14 of the Patents Act also provides a definition in relation to the state of the art:

> '(2) The state of the art in the case of an invention shall be taken to comprise all matter (whether a product, a process, information about either, or anything else) which has at any time before the priority date of that invention been made available to the public (whether in Singapore or elsewhere) by written or oral description, by use or in any other way.
>
> (3) The state of the art in the case of an invention to which an application for a patent or a patent relates shall be taken also to comprise matter contained in an application for another patent which was published on or after the priority date of that invention, if the following conditions are satisfied:
> (a) That matter was contained in the application for that other patent both as filed and as published; and
> (b) The priority date of that matter is earlier than that of the invention.'

Under section 14(4)(a)-(d), a grace period of 12 months prior to the date of filing of a patent application is available for disclosures made in breach of confidence, disclosures by the inventor at international exhibitions and disclosures by or with the consent of the inventor before a learned society. Under section 14(e), a grace period of 12 months prior to the date of filing of a patent application is also available for disclosures made to the public by the inventor, or by a person who obtained the matter directly or indirectly from the inventor under other circumstances not described above. Section 14(e), however, does not cover instances where an earlier patent application filed with the same subject-matter is published, unless the earlier application was i) filed without the consent of the inventor, ii) published in error or iii) published earlier than provided under the law or treaty governing the application. It should also be noted that section 14(e) only applies to disclosures made after 30 October 2017.

The first step in the assessment of inventive step involves determining the relevant state of the art for the invention. This is followed by comparing the invention with the state of the art to determine if the invention is obvious to the person skilled in the art.

Singapore courts have adopted the four-step 'Windsurfing' approach[27] in the assessment of inventive step:

27. *Windsurfing International Inc v. Tabur Marine Ltd* [1985] RPC 59 at 73, which has been adopted in a number of Singapore Court decisions including: *V-Pile Technology (Luxembourg) SA and Others v. Peck Brothers Construction Pte Ltd* [2000] 3 SLR 358; *Merck & Co Inc v. Pharmaforte Singapore Pte Ltd* [2000] 3 SLR 717; *Genelabs Diagnostics & Anor v.*

> '1) Identify the claimed inventive concept;
>
> 2) Assume the mantle of the normally skilled but unimaginative addressee in the art at the priority date and impute to him what was, at that date, common general knowledge of the art in question;
>
> 3) Identify what, if any, differences exist between the matter cited as being "known or used" and the alleged invention; and
>
> 4) Decide, without any knowledge of the alleged invention, whether these differences constitute steps which would have been obvious to the person skilled in the art or whether they require any degree of invention.'

In *Lonza Biologics Tuas Pte Ltd v. Genpharm International Inc.*[28] (*see* also §21.03[B] above), the Registrar applied the 'Windsurfing approach' in relation to the assessment of inventive step of claims 1–13 in an antibody patent, Singapore Patent No. 51905, during a revocation proceeding. The Registrar identified in step 1 that the inventive concept is the provision of fully human antibodies with high affinity constant that are produced by the introduction of human transgenes into a mouse. In step 2, the Registrar found that the prior art document D8 (US 209,741) teaches the introduction of human YAC genetic material into a mouse which produces transgenic antibodies of affinity binding values in the range of $9 \times 10^7 M^{-1}$ and $8 \times 10^7 M^{-1}$. In step 3, the Registrar found that Singapore Patent No. 51905 does not support the levels of affinity binding strength that were claimed and that the disclosed affinity binding values were within the range that was claimed in D8. It was noted that an additional difference existed in Singapore Patent No. 51905 from D8 in that the KCo5 mouse (which has human light chains) was crossed with the HC2 mouse (which has human heavy chains). In step 4, it was concluded that crossing a KCo5 mouse with a HC2 mouse would have been an obvious step for a reasonably skilled technician to increase diversity. Accordingly, claims 1–13 were found to lack an inventive step.

There are various considerations that are also useful in assessing whether an invention is obvious over the prior art. For example, a claim that is a 'mere workshop improvement' over the prior art will lack an inventive step as the invention would be obvious to a person skilled in the art. The evidence of a long-felt want or commercial success may also be a consideration for inventive step. Overcoming a technical prejudice may also be an indication of inventiveness.

[B] Particularities Regarding Claims to Antibodies

There are no specific requirements with regard to claims to antibodies in Singapore.

Institut Pasteur & Anor [2001] 1 SLR 121; *Ng Kok Cheng v. Chua Say Tiong* [2001] 3 SLR 487; *Peng Lian Trading Co v. Contour Optik Inc & Ors* [2003] 2 SLR 560; *Trek Technology (Singapore) Pte Ltd v. FE Global Electronics Pte Ltd* [2005] 3 SLR(R) 389; *First Currency Choice Pte Ltd v. Main-Line Corporate Holdings Ltd and Another Appeal* [2007] SGCA 50; and *Martek Biosciences Corporation v. Cargill International Trading Pte Ltd* [2012] SGHC 35.

28. *Lonza Biologics Tuas Pte Ltd v. Genpharm International Inc* [2015] SGIPOS 13, a copy of which is downloadable from https://www.ipos.gov.sg/resources/hearing-mediation.

§21.06 ENFORCEMENT AND SCOPE OF PROTECTION

Section 66(1) of the Patents Act states the following:

> 'Subject to the provisions of this Act, a person infringes a patent for an invention if, but only if, while the patent is in force, he does any of the following things in Singapore in relation to the invention without the consent of the proprietor of the patent:
>
> (a) where the invention is a product, he makes, disposes of, offers to dispose of, uses or imports the product or keeps it whether for disposal or otherwise;
>
> (b) where the invention is a process, he uses the process or he offers it for use in Singapore when he knows, or it is obvious to a reasonable person in the circumstances, that its use without the consent of the proprietor would be an infringement of the patent;
>
> (c) where the invention is a process, he disposes of, offers to dispose of, uses or imports any product obtained directly by means of that process or keeps any such product whether for disposal or otherwise.'

There are also various defences to acts done under section 66(2) which are exempt from infringement. These include, for example, an act done privately and for non-commercial purposes, an act done for experimental purposes; or an act that consists of the extemporaneous preparation of a medicine that has been prescribed for an individual. Other defences include an act done to support an application for marketing approval for a pharmaceutical product (i.e. the 'Bolar' defence).

[A] Biosimilars

Under the Health Products Act, all therapeutic products (such as biosimilar products) must be registered at the Health Sciences Authority (HSA) before they can be supplied in Singapore. An applicant for registration of a therapeutic product is required to make a declaration on whether the therapeutic product for which registration is sought is subject to a subsisting patent and will be required to notify the relevant patent proprietor where necessary.[29] This provides the patent proprietor an opportunity to initiate legal proceedings to block the registration of the therapeutic product.

[B] Equivalence

Singapore courts have endorsed and applied the purposive approach to claim construction developed in the UK Courts in *Catnic Components v. Hill & Smith* [1982] RPC 183 and *Improver Corporation v. Remington* [1990] FSR 181. The 'purposive approach' is also codified under section 113 of the Patents Act, which states the following:

> 'For the purposes of this Act, an invention for a patent for which an application has been made or for which a patent has been granted shall, unless the context otherwise requires, be taken to be that specified in a claim of the specification of the application or patent, as the case may be, as interpreted by the description

29. Regulation 23 of the Health Products (Therapeutic Products) Regulations.

> and any drawings contained in that specification, and the extent of the protection conferred by a patent or application for a patent shall be determined accordingly.'

In a recent case in *Lee Tat Cheng v. Maka GPS Technologies Pte Ltd*,[30] the Court of Appeal rejected the doctrine of equivalence adopted by the UK Supreme Court in *Actavis UK Limited and others v. Eli Lilly and Company.*[31] The Court of Appeal held that the approach taken in *Actavis* is not consistent with Singapore law as it allows the extent of protection as conferred by a patent to go beyond the scope of the claims in the patent, when purposively construed. The Court held that it is fair for a patentee to be bound by the language that he chooses to frame the claims of his patent. Lastly, the Court stated that applying *Actavis* imports the doctrine of equivalence, which may give rise to undue uncertainty in Singapore.

30. *Lee Tat Cheng v. Maka GPS Technologies Pte Ltd* [2018] SGCA 18.
31. *Actavis UK Limited and others v. Eli Lilly and Company* [2017] UKSC 48.

Chapter 22

South Korea

Min Son

§22.01 ANTIBODIES AS PATENTABLE SUBJECT-MATTER

[A] Legal Framework

In Korea, patent eligibility is generally governed by the following two provisions of the Korean Patent Act (KPA):

> Art. 29.1: industrial applicability
>
> 'An industrially applicable invention is amenable to patent protection...'
>
> Art. 32: exclusions from patentability under public order or morality
>
> 'Inventions that are likely to contravene public order or morality or to injure public health shall not be patentable'

There are no other particular provisions in the Patent Act that specifically address patent eligibility of biological molecules including antibodies; however, KIPO's Patent Examination Guidelines provide practical guidance for applying the above general provisions to biological molecules and their therapeutic or diagnostic applications, as follows.

Industrial Applicability (Art. 29.1)

The Examination Guidelines set forth two requirements under Art. 29.1: i) the subject-matter shall fall under the statutory invention, which is defined as 'creation of technical ideas utilizing the law of nature' under Art. 2.1; and ii) the invention should have 'industrial applicability'.

With regard to subject-matter which shall not be regarded as inventions, the Examination Guidelines provide a non-exhaustive exemplary list as follows:

(a) laws of nature;
(b) discoveries of laws of nature or natural phenomena;
(c) ideas contrary to the laws of nature (e.g., a perpetual motion machine);
(d) personal skills obtainable by practice (e.g., a method for playing a musical instrument);
(e) mere presentation of information;
(f) aesthetic creations; and
(g) computer programming languages or computer programs *per se*.

Issues may arise with regard to antibody inventions as well as inventions of other biological molecules, namely whether they would fall under item (a) or (b), for which the Examination Guidelines provide the following guidance:

> 'Mere discovery per se of natural products, natural phenomena, etc. shall not be regarded as inventions. However, if a method of artificially isolating certain material from natural products is developed, the method and the isolated chemical substances or microorganisms, etc., can be recognized as inventions.
>
> Use inventions, which are derived from discoveries of properties of naturally occurring substances, thereby resulting in new uses of the substances based on the discovered properties, are distinct from mere discoveries ... can be acknowledged as inventions if there are non-obvious, inventive efforts therein.'

Further, the Korean courts ruled that in order for naturally existing molecules such as genes to be industrially applicable, in addition to the discovery of their existence, their utility, i.e., the specific and substantial utility, must be proved in a credible manner (Patent Court Case Nos. 2011Heo7645 and 2007Heo5116). For example, claiming hypothetical sequences derived from a sequence database is usually considered to be insufficient for this purpose, and it is usually required to show at least some kind of function associated with the claimed sequences. This rule will apply to inventions claiming nucleotide sequences of antibodies.

Many commercially important antibodies have therapeutic functions, and therefore claiming medical use of an antibody is as important as patenting the antibody itself as a product. Antibodies are patentable as a component of pharmaceutical compositions, but when their medical use is claimed as a method claim, some limitations exist in Korea. A method for treating a human, such as a surgical, therapeutic, or diagnostic method practised on a human body, is regarded as non-patentable subject-matter in Korea. Diagnostic methods which, for example, comprise steps such as assaying, analysing, comparing, and measuring may be non-patentable, but will become patentable if they exclude a clinical judgment step. This limitation is specific to humans, so if claims are explicitly limited to a surgical, therapeutic, or diagnostic method practised on a non-human subject, such methods are patent eligible (Supreme Court Case No. 90Hu250).

Exclusions under Public Order or Morality (Art. 32)

The Examination Guidelines exemplify inventions that are excluded from patent protection under Article 32. Parts that may in any sense be relevant to antibody inventions are as follows:

- Process for cloning human beings;
- Process for modifying the germ line genetic identity of human beings, and the product thereof;
- Transformant not excluding human beings.

[B] General Amenability or Exclusion of Antibodies from Patentability

Under the legal framework above, any substances isolated as products of nature, even from a human body, or otherwise produced by means of a technical process, including tissues, cells, genes, etc., may constitute a patentable invention, as long as the specific and substantial utility thereof is proved in the specification. As such, all types of antibodies are, in principle, amenable to patentability in Korea. Therefore, in order to avoid exclusion from patentability, it is not absolutely necessary to use terms such as 'isolated', 'chimeric', 'humanized', or 'monoclonal' in the claims.

As discussed above, methods of treatment or diagnostic methods for human beings are not patentable in Korea. The issue can be circumvented by drafting claims directed to 'a pharmaceutical composition for treating disease Y, comprising an antibody X', 'an *in vitro* method', or 'a method for providing information for diagnosis of disease Y, with no clinical judgment steps' or by excluding a human from the claims.

[C] Required Distinction from Naturally Occurring Antibodies

When an antibody recognizes antigens that are naturally present, it may be required to distinguish the claimed antibodies from the naturally occurring antibodies. In Korea, this is not yet a common rejection, so it is not absolutely required to delimit the claims from antibodies that are or may be present in nature in the context of novelty under current practice. However, in a situation where the antibodies are directed to common, well-known prior art antigens, and where there have been many reports about the presence of antibodies recognizing the same antigens, the examiner may raise the issue and ask the applicant to distinguish the claimed antibodies from those already present in nature.

§22.02 ACCEPTABLE CLAIM FEATURES FOR DEFINING ANTIBODIES

[A] Functional Features

[1] Target/Antigen

In Korea, it is possible to claim an antibody by reference to an antigen/target to which the claimed antibody binds, without reciting sequences or other structural features of the antibody if the target/antigen is novel and inventive. In this case, the structure of target or antigen must be clearly definable.

When a target/antigen is novel and inventive, 'the type of antibody (e.g., monoclonal or polyclonal)' does not necessarily need to be included in the claim, and, for example, '[a composition comprising] an antibody binding to antigen X' would be acceptable.

[2] *Mode of Binding: Target Affinity, Binding Specificity, Epitope, Definitions via Reference Antibodies and Competitive Binding*

An antibody may be claimed by reference to its target affinity, binding specificity, and competitive binding to different antibodies, but antibodies are usually defined together with some of their structural features. Antibodies may be defined by reference to an epitope alone as long as the epitope is novel and inventive. For this purpose, if the epitope is a protein, a linear epitope works fine, but it is not yet certain whether a conformational epitope would also be sufficient. There are cases where antibody claims have been allowed when solely defined via reference antibodies.

Epitope

An antibody may be defined by reference to an epitope. There are enough examples of cases allowed with antibodies defined solely by epitopes. In many such cases, epitopes were defined with structural terms, most typically with their sequences or chemical modifications.

It is not yet certain whether epitopes can be defined functionally, for example, by conformational epitopes. There are allowed cases, but these have not yet been confirmed by the court.

Definitions via Reference Antibodies

If a reference antibody is clearly defined, it is possible to claim antibodies by a reference antibody.

For example, while clearly specifying a reference antibody Y produced from a hybridoma deposited under a particular accession number, it is possible to claim the antibody in the following manners: (i) antibodies binding to the same epitope that the reference antibody Y binds to; or (ii) antibodies comprising the variable regions of the reference antibody Y.

Target Affinity, Binding Specificity, and Competitive Binding

These elements may be recited in the claims to define antibodies, but usually they are claimed together with other elements that define antibodies; target affinity, binding specificity, or competitive binding to known molecules alone would probably not be accepted unless there are special circumstances. Most commonly, affinities or specificities are expressed as a K_D value. Reciting an actual method used to measure affinity, specificity, or binding characteristics may be required depending on the circumstances.

[3] *Effect on Target*

It is not yet certain if an antibody can be defined solely by its effect on a target. Even if this is possible, it would be very difficult to have such claims granted. However, the effects of antibodies are frequently used in claims to define antibodies together with other elements; for example, antibodies that are defined with their partial amino acid or nucleotide sequences can be claimed with functional features such as an effect on the target.

[B] Structural Features

[1] Molecular Topology: Antibody Types, Fragments and Antibody Constructs

If a novel structure of an antibody (e.g., engineered structure of antibody) is newly created or developed, the antibody can certainly be claimed by *solely* disclosing such structural features.

For example, the CrossMAb platform, a bispecific antibody format, was granted in Korea only based on the structural features of the antibody format as described below:

> 'Claim 1. A bivalent, bispecific antibody, comprising: a) the light chain and heavy chain of an antibody specifically binding to a first antigen; and b) the light chain and heavy chain of an antibody specifically binding to a second antigen, wherein the variable domains VL and VH are replaced by each other, and wherein the constant domains CL and CH1 are replaced by each other.'

[2] Amino Acid Sequences

[a] Full-Length Sequences of Antibodies

In the case of a monoclonal antibody, it is not necessarily required to specify the antibody with its full-length sequences, and defining antibodies with six CDR sequences or variable region sequences would be sufficient as described below.

[b] Sequences of Fragments, CDRs and Framework Regions

According to the Examination Guidelines, the variable region sequences are required to be cited in their entirety in the monoclonal antibody claims. In practice, however, the KIPO accepts antibody claims defined by six CDR sequences and does not demand further specifying to a framework region. Even sequence homologies are allowed when there are sufficient examples disclosed.

In addition to specifying antibodies by six CDRs, it is possible to claim more broadly in the following manners:

(i) Claim antibodies by reference to the combination of six CDR sequences
(ii) Claim antibodies by reference to the sequence identity (%) to the (reference) CDR sequences

In the case of antibody claims specified with a sequence, the replacement or modification of one of the claimed residues with another residue which is not claimed may avoid literal infringement of the antibody sequence claims, even though the modified antibody still retains the function of the claimed antibodies. Therefore, it is recommended to have sufficient examples to claim an antibody more broadly than by simply using six CDRs.

In Korea, the claim scope may be expanded by the doctrine of equivalents under certain conditions, but it is important to note that the application of the doctrine of equivalents may be ruled out if the scope of the claims is narrowed or changed intentionally by amendments and/or arguments during the prosecution.

[3] Chemical Modifications, Conjugation and Glycosylation

Chemical Modification

When antibodies feature a particular chemical modification (e.g., PEGylation), it is possible to claim the antibodies by indicating the type of specific chemical modification. For example, antibodies may be further defined by the site, number, or type of PEGylation.

Conjugation

If an antibody is characterized in a manner of conjugating an antibody with other substances (e.g., radionuclides, drugs, toxins, enzymes, proteins), for instance, an antibody, which has a novel conjugation structure providing special benefits (e.g., improving preparation yield, physical/physiological advantages), has been developed, such antibody conjugate can be claimed by specifying the conjugation structure between the antibody and the substances. If there are essential structural features of the antibody for such conjugation (e.g., conjugation site or functional group for conjugation), it is recommended to describe such features in the claim.

Glycosylation

In the case of characterizing the content of glycosylation/deglycosylation of a group of prepared antibodies, it can be claimed in the form of 'a group of antibodies' or 'composition' comprising multiple antibodies.

When the adjustment of glycosylation content is achieved by a fermentation or purification method, an antibody can be specified by such a method. However, as described in §22.02[C] below, the preparation method is considered only as a means for defining the structure or properties of a substance. Even if the preparation method is novel and inventive, the antibody defined by such method is not necessarily considered as being novel and inventive. Therefore, the prepared antibodies should have their own characteristics to be distinguished from known antibodies.

If an antibody is characterized by its amino acid sequence modification via glycosylation or deglycosylation, the Examination Guidelines recommend specifically defining the site and type of such modification.

[C] Cell Line Deposits and Process of Production

Cell Line Deposits

An antibody can be specified by a cell line producing the antibody such as a hybridoma. In this case, except when one of ordinary skill in the art can easily obtain such microorganism (e.g., the microorganism is commercially available, or can be reproducibly produced according to the method described in the specification), it should be deposited at a depositary authority (Art. 2.1 of the Enforcement Decree of the KPA). In Korea, the deposition of a microorganism should be carried out prior to filing the patent application.

Process of Production

In Korea, an antibody can be claimed by specifying it by a production method in the form of product-by-process (PBP) claim, and such specified antibodies are considered as being clearly defined.

However, under Korean patent practice, the preparation method in such a PBP claim would be considered as a means of defining the structure or properties of a final product, and the novelty and inventiveness of an antibody is determined only based on the features of the antibody itself, i.e., the final product, and not a process. A similar principle is applied for determining the scope of a PBP claim in the patent infringement thereof, but claims can also be construed to be limited to the preparation method when not doing so would be clearly unreasonable due to excessively broad claim scope (Supreme Court Case No. 2013Hu1726, 2015.2.12.).

§22.03 BREADTH OF CLAIMS AND SUPPORT BY EXAMPLES

[A] Acceptable Breadth of Claims to Antibodies

The acceptable breadth of claims is substantially affected by the support and enablement requirements. According to the KPA, i) the claims should be supported by the specification (Art. 42.4(i); support requirement) and ii) the specification should be described in a clear and detailed manner so as to enable one of ordinary skill in the art to easily carry out the claimed invention (Art. 42.3(i): enablement requirement).

Claims do not have to be literally supported; the support requirement is satisfied when the claimed invention is implied in the specification so as to be understood by one of ordinary skill in the art. In this context, if the disclosures of the specification cannot be generalized or expanded to the scope of claims in light of common general knowledge as of the filing date, the claims may not be deemed to be supported by the specification (Supreme Court Case No. 2004Hu1120).

In order to satisfy the enablement requirement, it is required that one of ordinary skill in the art would be able to accurately understand and reproduce the claimed invention based on the disclosure of the specification and in light of common general knowledge as of the filing date, without undue trial and error or experimentation (Supreme Court Case Nos. 97Hu2477, 2004Hu3362).

Antibody claims are also subject to the above general standards. In this light, in order to ensure a broader scope for antibody claims, a reasonable number of representative examples are usually required in the specification. Under Korean patent practice, broader antibody claims may be prone to rejections or invalidations for lacking enablement and/or support, and submission of post-filing date evidence may not be very effective in addressing such rejections or invalidations as compared to rejection or invalidation based on lack of an inventive step. Thus, during prosecution, broader antibody claims may often suffer being made narrower.

In Tables 1 to 3, examples are listed of various types of antibody claims which are generally regarded as acceptable in Korea.

Table 22.1: Antibodies defined with functional terms

	Defined by	*Exemplary Claims*
a.	Target or antigen	An antibody Y that binds to antigen X.
b.	Epitope (sequence)	An antibody binding to an epitope present in an antigen X, wherein the epitope has an amino acid sequence represented by SEQ ID NO: 1.
c.	Epitope (functionally defined by reference to the binding of a different antibody)	An antibody binding to an epitope present on protein X to which an antibody M binds.
d.	Conformational epitope + function	An antibody binding to only an epitope present in an activated protein C (APC) which is generated by proteolytic cleavage of unactivated protein C, wherein said antibody does not bind to or inhibit activation of unactivated protein C, and wherein said antibody inhibits anticoagulant activity but does not inhibit cytoprotective effects of APC.
e.	Reference antibodies	An antibody comprising the variable regions (or CDRs) of reference antibody Y which is produced from a hybridoma deposited under accession number XXX.
f.	Cross-reactivity with different proteins*	An antibody which binds to a human protein X but not to a mouse homologue X'; or An antibody which binds to an isotype 1 but not to an isotype 2 of protein family A protein.
g.	Target affinity, binding specificity, competitive binding, or effect on target (in combination with acceptable claim features such as antibody sequence or epitope)	An antibody comprising a variable region of an amino acid sequence represented by SEQ ID NO: 1, wherein: (i) the dissociation constant for antigen X is Y; (ii) the antibody competitively inhibits antibody Y; or (iii) the antibody is an allosteric antagonist for antigen X. An antibody which competitively inhibits reference antibody Y that comprises a variable region of an amino acid sequence represented by SEQ ID NO: 2.

* While this type of claim was easy to patent in the past, it has become difficult in recent times.

Table 22.2: Antibodies defined with structural terms

	Defined by	*Exemplary Claims*
a.	Molecular topology	A bivalent, bispecific antibody, comprising: a) the light chain and heavy chain of an antibody specifically binding to a first antigen; and b) the light chain and heavy chain of an antibody specifically binding to a second antigen, wherein the variable domains VL and VH are replaced by each other, and wherein the constant domains CL and CH1 are replaced by each other. (see Claim 1, KR 1265912)
b.	Sequence (one variable region)	A monoclonal antibody which comprises a variable region comprising an amino acid sequence represented by SEQ ID NO: 1.
c.	Sequence VH and VL	A monoclonal antibody which comprises a VL domain comprising an amino acid sequence represented by SEQ ID NO: 1, and a VH domain comprising an amino acid sequence represented by SEQ ID NO: 2.
d.	Sequence six CDRs	An antibody specific for Y…, wherein a VL domain comprises (i) CDR1 selected from a, d, and g; (ii) CDR2 … b, e, and h; and (iii) CDR3 … c, f, and i; and a VH domain comprises (i) CDR1 … A, D, and G; (ii) CDR2 …; and (iii) CDR3 …
e.	Sequence identity	An antibody specific for Y…, wherein a VH chain comprises (i) CDR1 which comprises a region that is at least 90% identical to R1, R2, or R3; (ii) CDR2 …; and (iii) CDR3 …, and a VL chain comprises (i) CDR1 …; (i) CDR2 …; and (iii) CDR3 …
f.	Chemical modification	A functionalized antibody, in which A of a compound represented by Formula 1 is linked to a thiol group formed by the reduction of a disulfide group in the Fc domain of the antibody, wherein the reduction is performed using a reducing agent at a molar ratio of 1:500 to 1:1000 (antibody : reducing agent): [Formula 1] R-L-A wherein, in Formula 1 above, R is a C_{6-30} alkene group …, L is a bond, …, A is a functional group of maleimide, … C_{5-12} alkyl halide. (see KR 919427)
g.	Conjugation	An antibody-drug conjugate wherein an antibody is linked to a drug having Formula I. (see KR 1941758) An antibody-drug conjugate comprising an antibody linked to a drug, wherein the antibody comprises a variable region comprising an amino acid sequence represented by SEQ ID NO: 1.

h.	Glycosylation	An antibody composition produced by CHO cells, ..., wherein among the total complex N-glycoside-linked sugar chains bound to the Fc region in the composition, the ratio of a sugar chain in which fucose is not bound to N-acetylglucosamine in the reducing end in the composition is 20% or higher. (see KR 0877676)

Table 22.3: Antibodies defined by cell line deposit and/or process

	Defined by	*Exemplary Claims*
a.	Hybridoma	An antibody obtainable by the hybridoma cell deposited under KCTC XXX. An antibody comprising a variable region (or CDRs) of the antibody obtainable by the hybridoma cell deposited under KCTC XXX.
b.	Product-by-process	An antibody obtainable by the method of claim 1.

[B] Required Experimental Support for Claims to Functionally Defined Antibodies

In principle, the specification must include some sort of experimental data that discloses: (1) *how to make* an antibody (e.g., a preparation method of an antibody-producing cells (hybridomas) such as an access/preparation process of an immunogen, an immunization method; and a selection/collection method of an antibody, etc.) and (2) *how to identify* the antibody (e.g., reactivity and non-reactivity with antigens) so as to enable one of ordinary skill in the art to produce the antibody (Examination Guidelines, Part for Biotechnological Invention).

In one case (Patent Court Case No. 2006Heo2158), a claim to 'a therapeutic agent comprising an anti-arthritogenic peptide antibody' was ultimately rejected on the ground that the functionally defined expression 'anti-arthritogenic peptide antibody' is not supported by an enabling disclosure. The Court concluded that the claim is overly broad for the reason that i) whereas, in view of the specification, the anti-arthritogenic peptide means 'a protein comprising a rheumatoid arthritis (RA) susceptibility sequence', and the anti-arthritogenic peptide antibody means all antibodies which specifically bind thereto, ii) the specification merely discloses several RA susceptibility sequences, and iii) one of ordinary skill in the art cannot easily recognize other RA susceptibility sequences and antibodies specifically binding thereto.

However, in general, when the specification discloses working examples of monoclonal (e.g., mouse monoclonal) or chimeric antibodies, it may be possible to broadly claim an 'antibody' covering other types of antibodies (e.g., humans, chimera, scFv) even without disclosing working examples thereof, as long as the production of such antibodies has become routine.

Antibodies Defined by Targets/Antigens

In the case where an antigen itself is patentable, in order to claim 'any antibody which binds to the antigen', it is not necessary to disclose working examples of the antibody, with the proviso that (i) the specification sufficiently discloses the antigen to the extent that one of ordinary skill in the art can easily work the antigen, and (ii) one of ordinary skill in the art can easily prepare and use the antibody specific for the antigen based on the disclosure of the specification (Examination Guidelines, Part for Biotechnological Invention). In this case, it is necessary to describe the utility of the antigen (e.g., physical, chemical, or biological characteristics of the protein) in the specification because the antigen is novel.

Antibodies Defined by Epitopes

In order to claim an antibody defined by an epitope, experimental disclosure on identification, activity, functions, and/or properties of the epitope should be described in the specification (Examination Guidelines, Part for Biotechnological Invention).

In the case where the epitope is a novel and inventive peptide, claims to an antibody defined by the epitope alone may be acceptable even without disclosure of the working examples in the specification, as long as the new target epitope is sufficiently disclosed and one of ordinary skill in the art can understand how to produce the antibody by routine and conventional methods. In this case, the peptide (epitope) may also be claimed.

Antibodies Defined by Functional Features in Addition to Structures

The specification should include additional experimental disclosure on additional functional features (e.g., cross-reactivity, neutralization) of the antibody.

[C] Required Experimental Support for Claims to Structurally Defined Antibodies

The specification should include the experimental disclosure in the same manner as required for claiming functionally defined antibodies above. Additional disclosure may be required for the antibodies defined as shown below.

Antibodies Defined by CDR Sequences

Antibody claims defined by fewer than six CDRs may not be acceptable for lacking enablement and/or support. In Supreme Court Case No. 2008Hu3179, the Court held that claims to antibodies defined by two CDRs from each of the heavy and light chains are not supported, since the specification fails to provide experimental disclosure showing that such antibodies have their antigen specificity regardless of whether any sequences are selected for remaining CDRs.

Antibodies Defined by Sequence Identity (%) to a Reference Sequence

According to precedents, a claim to a protein (e.g., antibody) or polynucleotide having a sequence identity (%) to a reference sequence can be acceptable if the specification provides a sufficient number of examples and a specific basis showing that variants having such sequence identity have the same function as the protein (e.g., antibody) or polynucleotide having the reference sequence (Patent Court Case No. 2009Heo4261).

Others

For claims to antibodies defined by hybridoma, an access/preparation method and/or accession number of the hybridoma should be disclosed in the specification. The hybridoma cell lines should be deposited before filing an application, except in cases where the microorganism can easily be obtained by one of ordinary skill in the art (e.g., the microorganism is commercially available or can be reproducibly produced according to the method described in the specification).

§22.04 SPECIFIC MEDICAL APPLICATIONS AND OTHER FOLLOW-UP INVENTIONS

Medical use of antibodies can be patented in Korea like any other therapeutic substance or biological material. Thus, the general principles regarding medical use inventions also apply to antibodies.

Under current Korean patent practice, for medical use inventions, the *original* specification must disclose *pharmacological data* for a specific active ingredient so as to demonstrate the medical utility.

[A] Treatment of Specific Diseases

If an antibody is effective in treating specific diseases, such medical use can be claimed as a composition claim in the form of 'A pharmaceutical composition for treating or preventing [specific diseases] comprising [an antibody] as an active ingredient'. Unlike some other jurisdictions, in Korea, specific disease names must be included in the pharmaceutical composition claims, even if the active ingredient (i.e., antibody) is a novel molecule.

According to the Examination Guidelines, a method for treating a human disease, such as a surgical, therapeutic, or diagnostic method practised on a human body, i.e., medical conduct, is not considered patentable subject-matter as it lacks industrial applicability. Therefore, a claim directed to a treatment method is not patentable in Korea unless a human being is explicitly excluded from the subject to be treated.

[B] Mode of Administration

A mode of administration is patentable subject-matter in Korea. Therefore, if the technical feature is finding a new mode of administration, the invention will be patentable as long as it satisfies other requirements. An important aspect of this type of claim is demonstrating a remarkable technical effect of the invention, particularly when the antibody already exists and is used for treatment.

[C] Dosage Regimens

In *en banc* Supreme Court Decision 2014Hu768, decided on 21 May 2015, the Court made it clear that dosage regimens (such as an administration route, a dosing interval, and a dosing frequency) are recognized as *patentable* technical features of medical use inventions.

In this regard, the Patent Court's position is that 'merely optimizing' a dosage regimen to reduce toxicity or improve efficacy is considered a common goal in the pharmaceutical industry, and thus this lacks technical difficulty. In this light, in determining the inventive step of a dosage regimen, the Patent Court tends to focus on advantageous effects which cannot be predicted from the prior art.

The Patent Court indicated that a dosage regimen may be acknowledged to have an inventive step when (i) the specific dosage regimen improves therapeutic effects, or minimizes toxicity or side effects ('remarkable known effect, or different effect'), and (ii) such effects cannot be expected from the prior art ('unpredictable effect') (Patent Court Case No. 2015Heo7889 rendered on 3 February 2017, which was upheld by the Supreme Court).

[D] Specific Patient Groups

A pharmaceutical composition for treating a specific subpopulation of patients is considered as *patentable* under Korea patent practice *if* the specific patient group is distinguishable from the previously known group of patients.

Although there is no case law directly addressing the patentability of a specific patient group, it seems that selecting a specific patient group is treated in a similar manner to a selection invention. Therefore, an invention specifying a patient sub-group would be acknowledged to have inventiveness where the active ingredient exhibits beneficial effects in the specified sub-group when compared to the remaining patient group having the same disease.

[E] Specific Mode of Action

A newly discovered mode of action, i.e., the pharmacological mechanism, of an antibody is not considered as an independent patentable subject-matter, but rather as *an inherent property, unless* it leads to a novel therapeutic use (see, e.g., Supreme Court Case Nos. 2012Hu238 and 2012Hu3664 rendered on 16 May 2014, and Patent Court Case No. 2012Heo1590 decided on 26 October 2012). From the newly discovered mechanism, an inventive screening method may be derived, and in such case, the mechanism may be patentable as method claims.

[F] Combinations with Other Active Ingredients

If an antibody in combination with other active ingredients is effective in treating a specific disease, it is possible to obtain a patent, most typically as a pharmaceutical composition claim.

[G] Specific Diagnostic Applications

According to the Examination Guidelines, a method for diagnosing a human disease, which involves the human body, is not considered patentable subject-matter as it lacks industrial applicability. In this light, diagnostic applications can be claimed in the form of a diagnostic composition, diagnostic kit, or method for providing information for diagnosis, or by excluding a human from the claims.

§22.05 ASSESSMENT OF INVENTIVENESS

[A] General Approach

In general, inventiveness is determined by assessing three factors: (i) the purpose, (ii) the technical constitution (technical feature), and (iii) the effect (Supreme Court Case Nos. 97Hu2224, 97Hu1085, etc.). In unpredictable arts such as chemistry and life sciences, the remarkable technical effect may be a particularly important factor.

When assessing inventiveness, the level of ordinary skill in the art as of the filing date and the ordinary creativity of those skilled in the art should be considered. Further, hindsight bias is prohibited in judging inventiveness (Supreme Court Case Nos. 2007Hu3660, 2010Hu2698, etc.).

[B] Particularities Regarding Claims to Antibodies

Antibodies Defined by Functional Features

According to the Examination Guidelines, the inventive step of an antibody defined by an antigen or epitope (an antibody Y that binds to antigen X or epitope X) is determined on the basis of the following standards:

(i) a monoclonal antibody specific to a novel and inventive antigen (or epitope) is basically considered as having an inventive step;
(ii) an invention which merely substituted a known polyclonal antibody with a monoclonal antibody is considered as lacking an inventive step; and
(iii) if a monoclonal antibody specific to a known antigen is specified by a distinctive technical feature or exhibits a remarkable effect, the antibody is considered as having an inventive step.

The distinctive technical features or remarkable effects indicated in item (iii) above may include a unique structural feature, reactivity with an antigen, physiological function, a preparation method, efficacy of treatment, etc.

Antibodies Defined by Structural Feature

Molecular Topology

If a novel type of antibody (e.g., antibodies having a novel engineered structure) is claimed, its inventive step will be determined by the above general principles.

Amino Acid Sequence

For an antibody specified by amino acid sequences, if its CDR sequences are different from those of known antibodies, the inventive step at issue is likely to be acknowledged. However, merely sequencing CDR sequences may not be sufficient to show an inventive step.

Chemical Modifications, Conjugation, and Glycosylation

The above general principles are applied in determining the inventive step of an antibody engineered by chemical modification, conjugation, or glycosylation, e.g., an antibody-drug conjugate (ADC).

Antibodies Defined by Process (Product-by-Process Claims)

Under Korean patent practice, a product-by-process claim is, in principle, deemed to claim a product itself, and the inventive step of such product-by-process claim is determined based on the features of the claimed antibody itself as a final product. Sometimes, antibodies can be more clearly definable by the preparation method rather than its sequences, or other structural limitations. This is the case, for example, when different antibodies having a certain profile of post modifications are generated. In such case, it may be advisable to detail the preparation method in the specification so that it could be used as a basis to distinguish the claimed antibodies with other known antibodies.

Antibody Formulations

Claims to antibody formulations also follow the general approach in assessing inventiveness, as mentioned above.

In a recent case, the Patent Court recognized the inventive step of a 'stable lyophilized formulation of human or humanized IgG antibody', featuring using a surfactant as a protein stabilizer, on the ground that four prior art references teach a way of using surfactants in protein stabilization. However, the Supreme Court reversed the Patent Court decision and ruled that the Patent Court erred in judging inventiveness. The Supreme Court found that there are other prior art references that teach using surfactants in protein stabilization and noted that the Patent Court cherry-picked or overly generalized certain teachings of the prior art references (Supreme Court Case No. 2016Hu1529, rendered on 13 December 2018).

§22.06 ENFORCEMENT AND SCOPE OF PROTECTION

[A] Biosimilars

Since 2009, a regulatory framework for biosimilars in Korea has been established by the Ministry of Food and Drug Safety (MFDS). Starting with Remsima, the first biosimilar of the blockbuster drug Remicade (infliximab), which was approved in 2012, Celltrion has been continuously developing other biosimilars for the world's top-selling biologics. Subsequently, other domestic biopharmaceutical companies such as Samsung Bioepis, Hanwha Chemicals, LG Chem, GC Green Cross, Chong Kun Dang, CJ Healthcare, and Dong-A ST have also been involved in the biosimilar market. As of 2018, more than ten biosimilars for blockbuster biologics, such as etanercept, trastzumab, rituximab, adalimumab and darbepoetin alpha, have been approved in Korea. With the entry of biosimilars into the market, biosimilar patent litigation continues to rise in Korea.

Basically, patent holders may enforce their patents for the infringements arising from manufacturing, using, transferring, importing, etc. of patented inventions by civil and criminal remedies under the KPA. In Korea, personal use of an invention does not infringe a patent, and only an act done for business purposes constitutes patent infringement (Art. 94). An act of (i) manufacturing, using, transferring, leasing, importing, or offering for transfer or lease of a patented product, (ii) using of a patented method; and (iii) manufacturing, using, transferring, leasing, importing, or offering for transfer or lease of a product manufactured by a patented method, by unauthorized persons may be deemed to constitute patent infringement (direct infringement). Further, any unauthorized business acts of manufacturing, transferring, leasing, importing, or offering for transfer or lease of (i) articles 'used exclusively' for producing a patented *product*, or (ii) articles 'used exclusively' for the practice of a patented *process*, may be deemed to constitute patent infringement (indirect infringement, Art. 127).

As civil remedies against an accused patent infringer, a patentee (or exclusive licensee) may file (i) a preliminary or permanent injunction action (Art. 126); (ii) an action for seeking compensation for damages (Art. 128); and (iii) a request for restoration of injured business credit or reputation (Art. 131) (e.g., advertisement of notice of apology by the infringer). As to criminal remedies, a patent infringer may be liable to an imprisonment for up to seven years or a fine of up to KRW 100 million (Art. 225)

Korea has a bifurcated system for patent litigations. In the first instance, while an infringement action should be filed in one of five specialized District Courts (Seoul Central, Daejeon, Daegu, Busan, and Gwangju), the accused infringer may bring an invalidation action at the IPTAB (Intellectual Property Tribunal and Appeal Board) within KIPO as a defence against the patent infringement. Both District Court decisions and IPTAB decisions are appealed to the Patent Court, and then to the Supreme Court.

In addition to the court actions, the patent may be enforced through banning imports or exports of infringing products by the Korea Trade Commission or Korean Customs Service.

According to the recent revision of the KPA (revised on 9 January 2019, effective 9 July 2019), Korea has provisions to promote more effective patent enforcement: (i) *punitive damages:* damages for wilful infringement may be awarded within a maximum of three times the amount of actual damages (Art. 128.8 and 128.9); (ii) *shifting burden of proof:* in patent infringement action, to deny the alleged infringing acts an accused infringer should present evidence showing his/her own specific acts (Art. 126bis.1), and if the accused infringer fails to present evidence without justification, the court may accept the alleged infringing acts to be true (Art. 126bis.4); and (iii) *reasonable royalty*: a patentee (or exclusive licensee) may demand the payment of a 'reasonable' royalty for infringement damages, instead of a standard royalty (Arts. 65.2, 128.2, 128.5, and 207.4).

Further, the Korean patent-linkage system effective 2015, a similar version to the US Hatch-Waxman regime, applies to biologics as well as small molecule drugs. Thus, antibody patents may also be enforced by using the patent-linkage system. In order to use the patent-linkage system, patents covering the originator's product should be listed on the Green List (similar version to the US FDA's Orange Book), with the product-related claims being indicated. If patentees of the listed patents receive a notification that a competitor's regulatory process for biosimilar products was initiated, they can file a patent litigation within 45 days of the date of receipt, together with a request for a nine-month stay on sales of biosimilars, which is an administrative process by the MFDS.

Due to patent barriers, including the first-generation antibody compound patents followed by follow-on patents, such as cultivation methods, therapeutic uses, dosage and combination drugs, market entry of biosimilars is not easy even after expiration of the first-generation patents. For that reason, most biosimilar patent litigation in Korea has been focused on the invalidation cases challenging follow-on patents, e.g., *Celltrion v. Biogen* (rituximab, Truxima vs. Rituxan), *Samsung Bioepis v. Abbvie* (adalimumab, Hadlima vs. Humira), and *Celltrion v. Roche* (trastuzumab, Herzuma vs. Herceptin). To date, Biogen's four patents (KR1092171, KR1155957, KR1063278, and KR1023367), and Abbvie's two patents (KR1283877 and KR1378873) were finally and conclusively invalidated. Further, in an invalidation case, *Celltrion v. Roche*, the Supreme Court recently overturned the Patent Court's Judgment recognizing the validity of KR514207, which is related to the freeze-dried formulation of Herceptin (Supreme Court Case No. 2016Hu1529, 13 December 2018).

[B] Equivalence

Interpretation of Scope of Claims

Although there is no noteworthy case law specifically dealing with the issue of interpreting antibody claims in Korea, the following general rules apply to antibody patents as well.

The Korean courts consider that when the claim language is clear, the scope of claims should, in principle, be determined solely by the *claim language per se*, and cannot be narrowly interpreted by taking the disclosure of the specification into account; however, when interpreting the claims literally is considered obviously unreasonable in light of the other description of the specification (e.g., when a part of the literally interpreted matters is not supported by the specification, or falls under the applicant's conscious exclusion from the scope of claims), it is possible to interpret the claim scope *narrowly* (Supreme Court Case No. 2001Hu2856). Therefore, if the scope of claims is considered as overly broad in view of the contribution of the invention disclosed in the specification, the scope may be narrowly construed to the extent that the specification provides support.

As to selection inventions, the Korean courts state that when an invention (species invention) covered by a generic claim of a patent (generic invention) exhibits a remarkably improved technical effect which is not present in the patented generic invention, such an invention is different from the patented generic invention, and thus it can be considered as *not* falling under the scope of the patent (Supreme Court Case No. 90Hu960).

As to patent term extension (PTE), which is allowed based on market approval of a drug, the scope of an extended patent is *limited* only to the working of the patented invention with respect to the drug whose approval was the basis for PTE (Art. 95). In this regard, the Supreme Court recently ruled that the scope of an extended patent shall be interpreted based on whether the accused product is identical to the patentee's approved product in terms of *the active ingredient, treatment effect, and utility*; though the accused product is different from the patentee's approved product in terms of a salt form, if (i) *a person skilled in the art could easily have selected* the modified salt; and (ii) *the treatment effects* would be *substantially identical* between the two products, it is recognized that the accused product is covered by the scope of the extended patent (Supreme Court Case No. 2017Da45798). In this case, the Court held that the accused product (solifenacin fumarate) falls under the scope of the patent for which PTE was granted based on market approval of solifenacin succinate, since solifenacin fumarate can be easily selected by one of ordinary skill in the art, and the therapeutic effect thereof is substantially identical to that of solifenacin succinate.

Doctrine of Equivalents and Estoppel

An infringement action against biosimilars can be brought under the doctrine of equivalents as well as literal infringement.

Literal infringement has limitations in that an alleged biosimilar must include all elements of a patent claim to be infringed. Further, when there is a minor variation in the biosimilar from the patent claim, it will be useless. Therefore, it will be a more powerful strategy to combine infringement under the doctrine of equivalents, i.e., DOE infringement.

In order for an accused product or process to fall within the scope of the patented invention, each of the claimed elements and the systematic links between the claimed elements must be included in the accused product or process.

Where an element of the patented invention is modified in the accused product or process, a finding of infringement under the doctrine of equivalents requires that:

(i) the essence of the technical concepts or principle to solve the problem of the patented invention and the accused invention be the same or common;
(ii) the modified element in the accused invention perform substantially the same function in substantially the same way to obtain substantially the same result of the patented invention; and

(iii) such modification be obvious to an ordinarily skilled person in the art.

However, the doctrine of equivalents shall not be applicable in the circumstances where

(iv) such modification was already known to skilled persons in the art at the time of filing an application and
(v) the modified element was excluded from the claimed invention during prosecution.

The courts stated that when determining whether or not the two inventions (the patented invention and the accused product or process) have an identical problem-solving principle (the above requirement (i)), the essence of the technical concept (upon which the special technical solution of the patented invention over the prior art is based) should be substantially examined and determined in view of the specification and the prior art at the time of filing (Supreme Court Case No. 2012Hu1132).

An alleged infringer can use an offensive/defensive option known as 'prosecution history estoppel' to counter the DOE infringement claim. In order to apply the estoppel, the examiner's opinion and the applicant's intention expressed in the amendments and/or arguments during prosecution shall be considered in determining whether the alleged infringing product was consciously excluded from the patent claim (Supreme Court Case Nos. 2001Hu171, 2006Da35308). The estoppel can be based on all amendments related to obtaining patentability such as clarity, enablement, support, novelty, and inventive step (flexible bar). Further, the arguments without any amendments during prosecution can be a basis for the estoppel (Supreme Court Case No. 2014Hu638).

For example, in a trial case seeking confirmation that CJ's method for preparation of erythropoietin (EPO) does not fall under the scope of Genetics' patent (*CJ v. Genetics Institute*), CJ's estoppel defence was defeated, and the DOE infringement was acknowledged (Supreme Court Case No. 2001Hu171). In this case, the Court held that the two methods are equivalent for the reason that: (i) EPO genes (*2.4kb* EPO gDNA), vectors, promoters, host cells, and culture media used in CJ's method are equivalent to those of Genetics' claimed method, the use of LTR enhancers in CJ's method is a mere addition of a known element, and the effects of the two methods are not differentiated only by the difference in yield; and (ii) the estoppel is not applied since it cannot be assured that the equivalents were consciously excluded by the claim amendments from 'a method … EPO gDNA sequence or a part thereof' to 'a method … *3.4kb or 2.9kb* gDNA sequence' during prosecution, considering that the applicant argued that the amended claims specifying the base sequence are novel and inventive since the prior art fails to disclose any base sequence and it is recognized that the prior art has no disclosure directly related to the added sequence.

Chapter 23

Australia

Michael Christie

§23.01 ANTIBODIES AS PATENTABLE SUBJECT-MATTER

[A] Legal Framework

Australia's Patents Act 1990 (Cth)[1] does not expressly deal with the patentability of biological molecules. Rather, it provides that an invention is patentable if, so far as claimed in any claim, the invention is a manner of manufacture within the meaning of section 6 of the Statute of Monopolies.[2] That provision has left much of the heavy lifting to the courts when it comes to defining patentable subject-matter.

In *NRDC v. Commissioner of Patents*,[3] the High Court of Australia described a manner of manufacture as 'an artificially created state of affairs' which provides 'an economically useful result'. In doing so, the High Court established a test that could be applied to new technology as it is developed. Under this test, and until recently, biological molecules such as nucleic acids and antibodies were considered to be patentable subject-matter provided they were distinct from molecules that occurred in nature. Terms like 'isolated' or 'recombinant' were routinely used in claims to render a biological molecule distinct from a possible naturally occurring counterpart.

However, in 2015, the practice of patenting biological molecules changed significantly when the High Court in *D'Arcy v. Myriad Genetics Inc*[4] ruled that isolated nucleic acids encoding certain polymorphic forms of BRCA1 are not patentable subject-matter. Overturning the unanimous decision of the Full Federal Court below it, the High Court found that the substance of the disputed claims was the information embodied in the sequence of the isolated nucleic acids. Since that information was the

1. 'Patents Act'.
2. Patents Act s 18(a)(a).
3. (1959) 102 CLR 252. ('*NRDC*').
4. [2015] HCA 35. ('*Myriad*').

same as that which occurs in nature, the High Court considered that it had not been 'made' by human action and could not be the subject of a valid claim. Following the *Myriad* decision nucleic acid molecules, whether DNA or RNA, human or non-human, synthesised, isolated or recombinant, are no longer patentable in Australia if they merely replicate the genetic information of a naturally occurring organism.

Yet despite the High Court's decision, certain nucleic acids remain patentable in Australia. The Patent Office has handed down a number of decisions since *Myriad* confirming that including interfering RNAs,[5] codon-optimised nucleic acids[6] and gene combinations[7] are still considered to be patentable subject-matter. While the act of isolating or synthesising is no longer sufficient to render a nucleic acid patentable subject-matter, isolated products of nature which do not embody naturally occurring information may still be the subject of a valid claim.

[B] General Amenability or Exclusion of Antibodies from Patentability

It remains to be seen what affect the *Myriad* decision will have on the patentability of biological molecules more broadly. But its affect on the patentability of antibodies appears to be fairly limited. Therapeutic or diagnostic antibodies are still considered to be patentable subject-matter by the Australian Patent Office provided the claims which define them do not encompass naturally occurring antibodies. Patents directed to therapeutic antibodies may even be eligible for an extension of term. The Patents Act provides an extension of up to five years beyond the normal 20 year term of a patent when the following three requirements are met:

i. one or more pharmaceutical substances *per se* (or one or more pharmaceutical substances when produced by a process that involves the use of recombinant DNA technology) is in substance disclosed in the patent specification and in substance falls within the scope of the claims;
ii. goods containing, or consisting of, the substance are included in the Australian Register of Therapeutic Goods (ARTG); and
iii. the period beginning on the effective filing date of the patent application and ending on the first regulatory approval date for the substance is at least five years.[8]

Although the term of the patent as a whole is extended, exploitation of any form of the invention that is not a pharmaceutical substance, and exploitation of the pharmaceutical substance for non-therapeutic uses, does not constitute infringement of the patent during the extended term.

While antibodies remain patentable following *Myriad*, the situation regarding nucleic acids is less clear. An isolated or recombinant nucleic acid molecule encoding an antibody fragment is unlikely to be considered patentable if the nucleic acid merely embodies naturally occurring information.

---

5. *Arrowhead Research Corporation* [2016] APO 70.
6. *Cargill Incorporated v. Dow AgroSciences LLC* [2016] APO 43.
7. *Commonwealth Scientific and Industrial Research Organisation v. BASF Plant Sciences GmbH* [2016] APO 83.
8. Patents Act s 70.

[C] Required Distinction from Naturally Occurring Antibodies

Therapeutic or diagnostic antibodies are still considered to be patentable subject-matter by the Australian Patent Office provided the claims which define them do not encompass naturally occurring antibodies. The guiding principles established by the High Court in *NRDC* are still applied today, and in that regard, terms like 'isolated', 'recombinant' or 'chimeric' can be sufficient to render an antibody an 'artificially created state of affairs'.

§23.02 ACCEPTABLE CLAIM FEATURES FOR DEFINING ANTIBODIES

There are many ways to define an antibody including by reference to its structural features, such as its complementarity determining regions (CDRs), and to its functional features, such as its binding properties. But before we explore those in greater detail, it should be noted that recent amendments to Australia's Patents Act[9] have significantly changed the disclosure requirements for patent specifications and, consequently, the practice of claiming antibodies in Australia. The new disclosure requirements remain to be tested by Australian courts and so this section will largely be based on: i) the Explanatory Memorandum[10] which explains the purpose of the 'new' Patents Act; ii) a small number of Patent Office decisions that have dealt with the new disclosure requirements (although these decisions do not directly concern antibodies); iii) the Australian Patent Office Manual of Practice and Procedure; and iv) Patent Office practice under the new Patents Act. Here, we will focus on different ways that antibodies may be claimed in Australia. In the next section, we will discuss the level of disclosure that may be required to enable such claims.

[A] Functional Features

[1] Target/Antigen

Under Australian practice, functional features may be used to define an antibody without reference to structural features, but only under certain conditions. A claim which defines an antibody solely by reference to its target-binding specificity may be sufficiently enabled provided the target is new and the specification sufficiently describes the epitope and has shown that antibodies can be raised against it. The Australian Patent Office Manual of Practice and Procedure provides that a claim to an antibody that specifically binds to a particular epitope would be fully enabled where the applicant had disclosed the epitope and had shown that antibodies can be raised against it.[11] To enable such a claim, the specification need only disclose one such antibody. This approach is taken because, in the view of the Patent Office,

9. Intellectual Property Laws Amendment (Raising the Bar) Act 2012 (Cth).
10. Intellectual Property Laws Amendment (Raising The Bar) Bill 2011 (Cth), Explanatory Memorandum.
11. The Australian Patent Office Manual of Practice and Procedure, s 2.11A Annex A.

raising antibodies to a defined epitope is a principle that can be generally applied to produce antibodies over the whole scope of the claim.

[2] *Mode of Binding: Target Affinity, Binding Specificity, Epitope, Definitions via Reference Antibodies and Competitive Binding*

The Australian Patent Office also allows claims which define an antibody by its ability to compete for binding with a reference antibody. For example, the Patent Office has accepted claims in the following format:

> Claim 1: An isolated or recombinant antibody or antigen-binding fragment thereof which binds to [target antigen] and comprises [six CDR sequences].
> Claim 2: An isolated or recombinant antibody or antigen-binding fragment thereof which competes for binding to [target antigen] with an isolated or recombinant antibody or antigen-binding fragment thereof according to claim 1.[12]

Similarly, an antibody may be defined as having the same epitope specificity as a reference antibody. In *Alethia Biotherapeutics Inc. v. Daiichi Sankyo Company, Limited*[13] – a case decided under the previous, more lenient, disclosure provisions of the Patents Act – the Delegate of the Commissioner of Patents provided clarity on the scope of such claims, observing that:

> '[t]he concepts of epitope specificity and competition between antibodies were well understood in the art before the priority date. Antibodies with the same epitope specificity bind the same epitope (target site) on a protein/peptide of interest. Competitive antibodies compete with each other for binding to a target protein, and bind either the same epitope or closely sited epitopes.'[14]

The Delegate also noted that a claim which defines an antibody by its ability to compete with a reference antibody will be broader than a claim which defines an antibody as having the same epitope specificity as a reference antibody.[15] Incidentally, in a rather creative submission, the opponent in that case argued that the skilled addressee would understand the reference to a 'competing' antibody to include commercial competition for sales. That, the Delegate bluntly observed, was 'an absurd construction'.[16]

[3] *Effect on Target*

Other binding properties such as association or dissociation constants can also be employed to further define an antibody. An antibody can also be defined as 'inhibitory', 'antagonistic' or 'agonistic' on a particular target or biological pathway.[17]

---

12. See, for example, Australian Patent No. 2015202353.
13. [2015] APO 59.
14. *Alethia Biotherapeutics Inc. v. Daiichi Sankyo Company, Limited* [2015] APO 59, [32].
15. *Alethia Biotherapeutics Inc. v. Daiichi Sankyo Company, Limited* [2015] APO 59, [33].
16. *Alethia Biotherapeutics Inc. v. Daiichi Sankyo Company, Limited* [2015] APO 59, [35].
17. See, for example, Australian Patent No. 2016210867 which was granted with claims defining an antibody as an 'agonist' of its target, and with reference to its association rate constant

Again, the validity of such claims will largely depend on the accompanying disclosure in the specification. But in *Alethia Biotherapeutics Inc. v. Daiichi Sankyo Company, Limited,*[18] the Delegate found that the techniques used to screen antibodies and identify those with inhibitory activity are routine in the art.[19]

[B] Structural Features

[1] Molecular Topology: Antibody Types, Fragments and Antibody Constructs

An antibody that has been developed against a known target will typically be defined by its structural features rather than by its binding specificity. For example, such antibodies may be defined by the sequence of their six CDR sequences or by the sequence of their light and heavy chain variable regions or, even more narrowly, by the sequence of their full heavy and light chains.

Antibodies can take a variety of different forms and may be defined more broadly, for example, as an antibody 'fragment' or an 'antigen binding protein'. The Patent Office has accepted claims which use the preamble 'An isolated or recombinant antibody or antigen binding fragment thereof …'[20] and 'An isolated antigen binding protein …'.[21] But the validity of such claims will, of course, depend on their scope vis-à-vis the disclosure of the specification. If, for example, the 'fragment' is defined by its CDR sequences, then all of its CDR sequences should be defined in the claim. An antibody fragment defined by a single CDR is unlikely to be allowed for the same reason that a claim to an antibody defined in the same way is unlikely to be allowed.

[2] Amino Acid Sequences

[a] Full-Length Sequences of Antibodies

Antibodies may be defined in a claim by the sequence of their full heavy and light chains. They may also be defined by reference to a biological deposit which has been made by the applicant at a recognised International Depositary Authority.

---

and dissociation constant. No support or sufficiency objections were raised against a claim of Australian App. No. 2016262656 which recited 'An isolated neutralizing antigen binding protein that binds to a PCSK9 protein comprising the amino acid sequence of SEQ ID NO: 1, wherein the neutralizing antigen binding protein decreases the LDLR lowering effect of PCSK9 on LDLR'. Similarly, in Australian App. No. 2016219676 no support or sufficiency objections were raised against a claim which recited 'An isolated antibody, or an antigen binding fragment thereof that specifically binds to a cysteine knot region of human activin A, said region spanning amino acids C11-S33 and amino acids C81-E111 of the sequence set forth in SEQ ID NO:255, and which inhibits binding of human activing A to human activin A receptor'.

18. [2015] APO 59.
19. *Alethia Biotherapeutics Inc. v. Daiichi Sankyo Company, Limited* [2015] APO 59, [127].
20. See, for example, Australian Patent No. 2015202353.
21. See, for example, Australian Patent No. 2016210867.

[b] Sequences of Fragments, CDRs and Framework Regions

Under the 'old' Patents Act, it was possible to define an antibody by a single heavy and light chain CDR – typically CDR3 – and argue that that CDR is the most important determinant of antigen specificity. However, under the new disclosure requirements, such arguments are unlikely to be persuasive. The Australian Patent Office now takes the position that an antibody or antibody fragment defined by less than six CDRs places an undue burden on the person skilled in the art tasked with performing the invention as claimed.[22] The Patent Office will, however, accept claims which define an antibody by reference to its six CDR sequences provided that sufficient disclosure is provided in the specification.

As described above, the Patent Office may allow claims which define an antibody solely by reference to its novel target-binding specificity. However, further defining the antibody by reference to 'one or more' of six disclosed CDRs may render the claim insufficiently enabled. The Patent Office takes the view that the disclosure of the epitope is not a principle of general application that can be applied to generate the antibodies in the claimed subset, to the exclusion of other antibodies not encompassed by the claim.[23] In performing the claimed invention, a person skilled in the art would have to raise antibodies against the epitope and then perform an additional sequencing step to identify those that fall within the claimed subset. This, in the Patent Office's view, would place an undue burden on the person skilled in the art.

What represents an 'undue burden' will depend on the facts of the case. If the specification relates to the production of a fully defined library of antibodies, it may be expected that the skilled addressee would generate a large number of antibodies and then sequence all of them.[24] In considering what represents an undue burden, regard should be had to the nature of the invention and the abilities of the person skilled in the art.[25] This topic will be explored further in the following section.

Antibodies can also be defined by reference to the sequence of their light and heavy chain variable regions. As will be discussed in the following section, a certain level of sequence variability (e.g., 90% identity to a defined V_H and V_L sequence) may be permitted provided that: i) the invention is deemed plausible across the full scope of the claim; and ii) the invention could be performed across the full scope of the claim without undue burden.

[3] Chemical Modifications, Conjugation and Glycosylation

Structural modifications such as conjugation, glycosylation and other chemical modifications can also be features of a claim to an antibody provided the specification sufficiently describes antibodies having such modifications.

22. The Australian Patent Office Manual of Practice and Procedure, s 2.11A Annex A.
23. The Australian Patent Office Manual of Practice and Procedure, s 2.11A Annex A.
24. The Australian Patent Office Manual of Practice and Procedure, s 2.11A Annex A.
25. The Australian Patent Office Manual of Practice and Procedure, s 2.11.3.4.3A.

[C] Cell Line Deposits and Process of Production

The Budapest Treaty provides a further mechanism for enabling claims directed to an antibody or a group of antibodies. In the absence of a written description that would enable a skilled person to generate a claimed antibody, the applicant can make a deposit of reproducible biological material such as a hybridoma with a recognised International Depositary Authority. A claim may define an antibody which is produced by a deposited cell line, or it may define an antibody which competes for binding with, or binds to the same epitope as, an antibody produced by a deposited cell line.

§23.03 BREADTH OF CLAIMS AND SUPPORT BY EXAMPLES

As noted in the previous section, recent amendments to Australia's Patents Act have significantly changed the disclosure requirements for patent specifications. The amendments are intended to import the standards of sufficiency and support from European and United Kingdom law.[26] With that in mind, the reader is encouraged to consider this chapter in the context of chapters in this book which deal with European jurisdictions.

[A] Acceptable Breadth of Claims to Antibodies

Under Australia's new disclosure requirements, a claim's scope must be commensurate with the patentee's technical contribution to the art, and the patent specification must provide sufficient information to enable a person skilled in the art to perform the invention over the entire scope of the claims without undue burden or the need for further invention. The skilled person may carry out ordinary methods of trial and error and may use their common general knowledge to supplement the information contained in the patent specification.[27] Where the subject-matter of the invention is inherently complex – antibody engineering may be one such example – a substantial amount of work may be required, and indeed expected, for a person skilled in the art to perform the invention. The level of disclosure required to enable a claim will therefore depend on the nature of the invention, the teachings provided by the specification and the identity of the hypothetical person skilled in the art.

A claim which defines an antibody solely by reference to its target-binding specificity may be enabled provided the target is new and the specification sufficiently describes the epitope and has shown that antibodies can be raised against it. The specification need only disclose one such antibody since raising antibodies against the epitope is considered to be a principle that can be generally applied to produce antibodies over the whole scope of the claim.

Antibodies that have been developed against a known target, however, will typically be defined by reference to their structural features. A claim which defines an antibody by reference to its variable domains may encompass a certain degree

26. *Intellectual Property Laws Amendment (Raising The Bar) Bill 2011* (Cth), Explanatory Memorandum.
27. *Eli Lilly & Co v. Human Genome Sciences, Inc* [2008] RPC 29, [239]. *Evolva SA* [2017] APO 57, [24].

of sequence variability provided that: i) the invention is deemed plausble across the full scope of the claim; and ii) the invention could be performed across the full scope of the claim without undue burden. In *Evolva SA*,[28] the Patent Office considered the enablement of claims encompassing polypeptide sequences having 90% sequence identity to those specifically described in the specification. The decision is only the second to consider Australia's new disclosure requirements, and the first to look at these requirements in the context of a biological invention. The disputed application relates to methods and materials for glycosylating mogrol using uridine-5'-diphos-pho-dependent glycosyltransferases (UGTs). The specification describes five UGTs that glycosylate mogrol, but the claims encompass methods of using polypeptides having at least 90% sequence identity to any one of them. The examiner had rejected the claims, finding that the specification did not describe a principle of general application that would enable the invention to be performed across the full scope of the claims. The examiner contended that the skilled person would have to produce every polypeptide encompassed by the claim and then perform an assay on each to identify those which exhibited the desired activity.

Unsatisfied by the examiner's position, the applicant requested a hearing with the Australian Patent Office. In the absence of Australian authority on the new disclosure requirements, the Delegate of the Commissioner of Patents drew on authorities from Europe and the United Kingdom and provided the following two-step inquiry into whether the specification was sufficient to enable the invention to be performed across the full scope of the claims:

(a) Is it plausible that the invention can be worked across the full scope of the claim?
(b) Can the invention be performed across the full scope of the claim without undue burden?[29]

The answers to both questions will depend on the teachings provided by the specification, the specific technology at issue and the capabilities and background knowledge possessed by the notional person skilled in the art. On the issue of the person skilled in the art, the Delegate considered that a team, comprising biotechnologists and synthetic chemists, would be the 'person' to whom the specification is addressed.[30] The Delegate did not agree with the examiner's representation of the skilled person as being 'a single synthetic chemist, perhaps a PhD candidate'. Needless to say, the team of people described by the Delegate would have a much wider breadth of skills and knowledge at their disposal when it comes to assessing the plausibility of, and to performing, the invention as claimed. It was in this context that the Delegate considered the first question in the two-step inquiry, i.e., the question of plausibility. Given what was known about the structure and function of UGTs, the Delegate concluded that the skilled person would consider it plausible that functional variants to a level of identity of at least 90% could be identified and would be useful in the claimed methods.[31] On the issue of 'undue burden', the Delegate found that the

28. [2017] APO 57. ('*Evolva*').
29. *Evolva*, [45].
30. *Evolva*, [54].
31. *Evolva*, [62].

specification provided sufficient disclosure about the manner in which UGT variants may be generated and tested. Although such tests may involve time-consuming experimentation, they did not, it was found, present difficulties that would require the skilled person to undertake any prolonged research or experimentation that would be considered an undue burden in the relevant field of technology.[32]

The decision provides useful guidance for those seeking to patent antibodies in Australia. The degree of sequence variability that will be allowed in a claim to an antibody will depend on several factors including the extent of disclosure provided in the specification, the identity of the notional person skilled in the art, the purpose to which the antibody will be put (e.g., diagnostic or therapeutic), whether the claim also defines the antibody by its target binding specificity and, of course, the region of the antibody to which the sequence relates. One might expect, for instance, that an amino acid change within a CDR is more likely to affect the binding specificity of an antibody compared with an amino acid change within a framework region. (Although amino acid changes within the framework region can still impair the folding within, or the pairing between, the variable domains.) Given the significant role played by the CDRs in dictating binding specificity, the Patent Office may allow a greater degree of sequence variability within the variable domain than it would within the CDRs themselves. For claims which define an antibody solely by reference to the sequence of its heavy and light chain variable regions, the Patent Office has allowed up to 90% sequence identity.[33]

[B] Required Experimental Support for Claims to Functionally Defined Antibodies

Australian law does not prescribe a level of experimental data that must be disclosed in a specification in order to support a claim to an antibody. However, useful guidance was recently provided by the UK Supreme Court in *Warner-Lambert v. Generics (t/a Mylan) & Actavis*,[34] a case which concerned the validity and infringement of claims directed to the second medical use of the drug pregabalin. A key claim which had been asserted against Actavis identifies the medical condition as neuropathic pain and was found invalid for lack of sufficiency. While the disclosure of the specification supported claims which defined the treatment of inflammatory pain, the Court found that it was not plausible, based on the disclosure of the specification, that pregabalin would also be effective at treating both central and peripheral forms of neuropathic pain. The Court made clear that a bare assertion of efficacy would not be enough to establish plausibility. The specification should disclose a technical rationale - ideally, but not necessarily, in the form of experimental data - that makes the claimed effect plausible to a person skilled in the art. Remarking on the threshold for plausibility, Lord Sumption observed:

> 'the proposition that a product is efficacious for the treatment of a given condition must be plausible ... it is not made plausible by a bare assertion to

32. *Evolva*, [68].
33. See, for example, Australian Patent No. 2015242981.
34. [2018] UKSC 56. ('*Warner-Lambert*').

> that effect, and the disclosure of a mere possibility that it will work is no better than a bare assertion …
>
> the claimed therapeutic effect may well be rendered plausible by a specification showing that something was worth trying for a reason, i.e. not just because there was an abstract possibility that it would work but because reasonable scientific grounds were disclosed for expecting that it might well work. The disclosure of those grounds marks the difference between a speculation and a contribution to the art …
>
> although the disclosure need not definitively prove the assertion that the product works for the designated purpose, there must be something that would cause the skilled person to think that there was a reasonable prospect that the assertion would prove to be true …
>
> the effect on the disease process need not necessarily be demonstrated by experimental data. It can be demonstrated by a priori reasoning. For example, and it is no more than an example, the specification may point to some property of the product which would lead the skilled person to expect that it might well produce the claimed therapeutic effect; or to some unifying principle that relates the product or the proposed use to something else which would suggest as much to the skilled person …sufficiency is a characteristic of the disclosure, and these matters must appear from the patent. The disclosure may be supplemented or explained by the common general knowledge of the skilled person. But it is not enough that the patentee can prove that the product can reasonably be expected to work in the designated use, if the skilled person would not derive this from the teaching of the patent.'[35]

When it comes to second medical use claims, the Australian Patent Office also takes the position that a mere assertion in the specification that a pharmaceutical compound can treat a particular condition will not provide support for claims to a method of treatment. Even if the pharmaceutical compound *per se* is new, a claim to the therapeutic use of the compound will lack support in the absence of evidence of the therapy working over the whole scope of the use as claimed.[36] More broadly, though, the decision of the UK Supreme Court indicates that an abundance of experimental data is not a prerequisite for plausibility. Plausibility may be demonstrated by *a priori* reasoning.

For a claim which defines an antibody solely by reference to its novel epitope-binding properties, a single example may be sufficient to enable the claim. The Australian Patent Office Manual of Practice and Procedure provides that a claim to an antibody that specifically binds to a particular epitope would be fully enabled where the applicant had disclosed the epitope and had shown that antibodies can be raised against it.[37] To enable such a claim, the specification need only disclose one such antibody. In the view of the Patent Office, raising antibodies to a defined epitope is a principle that can be generally applied to produce antibodies over the whole scope of the claim.

35. *Warner-Lambert*, [37]-[39].
36. The Australian Patent Office Manual of Practice and Procedure, s 2.11.7.10A.
37. The Australian Patent Office Manual of Practice and Procedure, s 2.11A Annex A.

[C] Required Experimental Support for Claims to Structurally Defined Antibodies

Neither the courts nor the Patent Office has prescribed a level of experimental data that is required to enable a claim to an antibody, whether it is defined functionally or structurally. Obviously an abundance of experimental data can help to enable a claim which encompasses a large number of structurally defined antibodies. Such claims for instance might benefit from binding assays which employ antibodies spanning the breadth of the claim. But there is no requirement for an abundance of experimental data. The question to ask is whether, based on the disclosure of the specification, including any *a priori* reasoning provided therein, a person skilled in the art would find the claimed invention plausible and could work the invention across the full breadth of the claim.

§23.04 SPECIFIC MEDICAL APPLICATIONS AND OTHER FOLLOW-UP INVENTIONS

There are several ways to claim a therapeutic use in Australia. Method of treatment claims and Swiss-style claims are frequently employed to claim both first and second medical uses. In Europe, second medical uses are often claimed using the EPC2000 format which defines the pharmaceutical substance 'for use' in a particular treatment. Although such claims are also permitted in Australia, they do not share the same scope. The term 'for' does not limit the claim to the specified treatment, but rather, simply renders the pharmaceutical substance *suitable for* that treatment. Such a claim would therefore be construed as defining the pharmaceutical substance *per se*.

[A] Treatment of Specific Diseases

So called second medical use claims (i.e., claims directed to a new use of a known substance) can be drafted in a method of treatment format or in a Swiss-style format; both are permitted in Australia. Different approaches are taken by the courts when it comes to determining infringement of each type of claim. Whereas method of treatment claims are directly infringed by a practitioner who administers the pharmaceutical substance, Swiss-style claims can be infringed by a person offering to supply the manufactured pharmaceutical substance for the claimed therapeutic use.[38] Both types of claim are therefore commonly employed when protecting a therapeutic use in Australia.

[B] Mode of Administration

Subsequent improvements to a medical use may form the basis of a valid claim in Australia. A new mode of administration, for example, may confer novelty to a first or second medical use claim.

38. *Otsuka Pharmaceutical Co., Ltd v. Generic Health Pty Ltd (No 4)* [2015] FCA 634; *Apotex Pty Ltd v. Warner-Lambert Company LLC (No 3)* [2017] FCA 94.

[C] Dosage Regimens

Whether a particular dosage regimen will render a claim inventive (i.e., non-obvious) in light of the prior art will vary depending on the facts of each case. For example, in *AstraZeneca AB v. Apotex Pty Ltd*,[39] the High Court of Australia found that claims directed to methods of using low doses (5 or 10 mg) of rosuvastatin to treat hypercholesterolemia were obvious in light of a prior art document describing rosuvastatin as a potent statin. The High Court found that the skilled person would have been directly led as a matter of course to try rosuvastatin in the expectation that it might well be an efficacious treatment, and that it would then have been a routine step to test rosuvastatin at the lowest efficacious dose as part of a conventional treatment. By contrast, in *Apotex Pty Ltd v. ICOS Corporation*,[40] the Federal Court held that claims relating to particular daily dosages of tadalafil for oral administration were inventive in light of the prior art. In that case, the Court found that a development team would not, as a matter of course, be directly led to the claimed doses with an expectation of success because, as Besanko J observed:

> '[t]he nature of the condition, the nature of measurement tools available and the limits on the information available lead me to conclude that a dose ranging study at the claimed doses would not be undertaken as a matter of course and, even if a decision was made to carry out a study at the claimed doses, it would not be a decision made with the required expectation of success'.[41]

[D] Specific Patient Groups

The identification of specific patient groups for which a treatment is particularly effective may confer novelty to a first or second medical use claim. For example, a claim may define a method of treating a condition in a patient having a particular concentration of a biomarker present in their blood.

[E] Specific Mode of Action

Medical use claims may also be drafted with reference to a therapeutic target (e.g., 'A method of treating a disease mediated by protein X'). But merely reciting a mode of action in a claim will not confer novelty if that mode of action is inherent to previously described methods and would inevitably result from performing those earlier methods. In *Otsuka Pharmaceutical Co., Ltd v. Generic Health Pty Ltd*,[42] Beach J observed that 'novelty is not conferred merely by … explaining the scientific theory for the mechanism which underlines a use already described in the prior art'.[43]

39. *AstraZeneca AB v. Apotex Pty Ltd; AstraZeneca AB v. Watson Pharma Pty Ltd; AstraZeneca AB v. Ascent Pharma Pty Ltd* [2015] HCA 30.
40. *Apotex Pty Ltd v. ICOS Corporation (No 3)* [2018] FCA 1204.
41. *Apotex Pty Ltd v. ICOS Corporation (No 3)* [2018] FCA 1204, [465].
42. *Otsuka Pharmaceutical Co., Ltd v. Generic Health Pty Ltd (No 2)* [2016] FCAFC 111.
43. *Otsuka Pharmaceutical Co., Ltd v. Generic Health Pty Ltd (No 2)* [2016] FCAFC 111, [176].

[F] Combinations with Other Active Ingredients

New formulations, combinations of known compounds and the therapeutic uses thereof can also form the basis of valid claims under Australian practice. An inventive step may be found, for example, where the formulation or combination has a new and unexpected property or therapeutic effect.

[G] Specific Diagnostic Applications

While the ability to patent diagnostic methods has become increasingly difficult in the United States, claims directed to diagnostic methods – performed directly or indirectly on a human body – are allowable in Australia, even if those methods involve an association between a 'natural phenomenon' and a particular condition. Australian courts have not directly considered the patentability of diagnostic methods involving antibodies, but in *Meat & Livestock Australia Limited v. Cargill, Inc*,[44] the Federal Court confirmed that methods of genetic testing can be validly claimed in Australia. The principal claims in that case are directed to methods of identifying a trait in a bovine subject which make use of naturally occurring single nucleotide polymorphisms. Relevantly, the Court found that the invention as claimed involved the practical application of a naturally occurring phenomenon to a *particular use*. In the words of Beach J, the claims are 'within the plain vanilla concept of manner of manufacture'.[45]

§23.05 ASSESSMENT OF INVENTIVENESS

[A] General Approach

Inventive step is determined under Australian law by asking whether a claim would have been obvious to a person skilled in the art in light of the common general knowledge as it existed (whether in or out of Australia) before the priority date of the claim, where that knowledge can be considered together with any single piece of prior art information or a combination of two or more pieces of prior art information that the person skilled in the art could, before the priority date of the claim, be reasonably expected to have combined.[46]

There are several tests for inventive step which have been applied by Australian courts. One test is whether the skilled addressee, faced with the same problem, would have taken, as a matter of routine, whatever steps might have led from the prior art to the invention, whether they are the steps of the inventor or not.[47] The Cripps Question has been endorsed by the High Court and involves asking whether the person skilled in the art would have been directly led as a matter of course to try the

44. *Meat & Livestock Australia Limited v. Cargill, Inc* [2018] FCA 51.
45. *Meat & Livestock Australia Limited v. Cargill, Inc* [2018] FCA 51, [428].
46. Patents Act s 7.
47. *Wellcome Foundation Ltd v. VR Laboratories (Aust) Pty Ltd* (1981) 148 CLR 262, 286.

claimed invention in the expectation that it might well produce a useful result.[48] In the rosuvastatin case discussed above,[49] the High Court adopted the Cripps question considered by the Full Federal Court below it, namely 'whether the notional skilled person would have directly been led as a matter of course to try the invention as claimed in the expectation that it might well produce a better method of treating a patient suffering from hypercholesterolemia than existing statins and doses'.[50] In the remainder of this section, we will discuss how inventive step has been applied in the context of antibody claims.

[B] Particularities Regarding Claims to Antibodies

In *Daiichi Sankyo Company Limited v. Alethia Biotherapeutics Inc.*,[51] the disputed claims define antibodies by reference to their target, Siglec-15, a protein with established roles in bone metabolism. Specifically, the claims define an antibody by reference to: i) the sequence of Siglec-15; and ii) its ability to impair an activity of Siglec-15 in osteoclast precursor cells or in osteoclasts. The claims were opposed on the ground of obviousness in light of a prior art document that did not specifically disclose the nucleic acid or polypeptide sequences of Siglec-15. However, it did disclose a polynucleotide sequence sharing two regions of homology with the nucleic acid sequence encoding Siglec-15, albeit outside the regions that the prior art document explicitly identified as the protein-coding region. That disclosure was not enough to deprive the claims of an inventive step. The Delegate of the Commissioner of Patents found that the disclosure of the prior art would not directly lead the person skilled in the art as a matter of course to raise antibodies against a polypeptide encoded by either of the two homologous regions disclosed in the prior art document with a reasonable expectation that this would provide a useful agent in the context of abnormal bone remodelling and associated disorders.[52]

In *Alethia Biotherapeutics Inc. v. Daiichi Sankyo Company, Limited*,[53] the Delegate again considered claims which define anti-Siglec-15 antibodies by reference to the sequence of Siglec-15 and by the functionality of the antibodies. The claims were opposed on the ground of obviousness in light of a prior art document which disclosed the identification of new therapeutic targets for the amelioration of symptoms of bone remodelling disorders. Siglec-15 was among the targets identified in the prior art, but no specific antibodies targeting Siglec-15 were described. After consideration of expert evidence from both sides, the Delegate of the Commissioner of Patents found that the steps taken to proceed from the prior art to the claimed antibodies were of a routine nature which the person skilled in the art would directly

48. *Olin Mathieson v. Biorex* (1970) RPC 157, 187; *Aktiebolaget Hassle v. Alphapharm P/L* (2002) 212 CLR 411.
49. *AstraZeneca AB v. Apotex Pty Ltd; AstraZeneca AB v. Watson Pharma Pty Ltd; AstraZeneca AB v. Ascent Pharma Pty Ltd* [2015] HCA 30.
50. *AstraZeneca AB v. Apotex Pty Ltd; AstraZeneca AB v. Watson Pharma Pty Ltd; AstraZeneca AB v. Ascent Pharma Pty Ltd* [2015] HCA 30, [40].
51. [2015] APO 88.
52. *Daiichi Sankyo Company Limited v. Alethia Biotherapeutics Inc.* [2015] APO 88, [146].
53. [2015] APO 59. ('*Alethia*').

be led to as a matter of course to try, with an expectation of producing a useful result.[54] The Delegate acknowledged that many steps would be involved in producing anti-Siglec-15 antibodies based on the disclosure of the prior art, but considered them to be a matter of routine:

> 'I am satisfied that the evidence as a whole establishes that in seeking to develop new compounds to inhibit or prevent abnormal bone metabolism, the person skilled in the art would, as a matter of routine, first identify a potential target; conduct validatory experiments to confirm its role in bone metabolism and determine the appropriate targeting strategy; before proceeding to prepare inhibitors. Furthermore, that in the case of inhibitory antibodies, antibodies generated against the validated target must be screened to identify those with inhibitory activity and this effect confirmed in vivo. The evidence establishes that the manner and sequence in which these steps are carried out and the techniques used (where not explicitly disclosed by [the prior art document]) are routine in the art.'[55]

The Delegate went on to find that claims which define an antibody by reference to the sequence of Siglec-15, and by its ability to inhibit osteoclast formation and/or osteoclastic bone resorption, lacked an inventive step. Further, claims which define an antibody by its ability to compete with one of two reference antibodies - the reference antibodies being defined by reference to two deposited hybridoma lines - and claims which define an antibody as binding to the same epitope as one of those reference antibodies were also found to lack an inventive step. On those claims, the Delegate observed:

> 'it is reasonable to conclude that in screening for inhibitory antibodies in an antibody pool, the person skilled in the art would, as a matter of course, identify those that bind the same epitope as, or which would compete for binding with, the monoclonal antibodies produced by Daiichi's deposited hybridomas.'[56]

While the Delegate in *Alethia* may appear to have characterised rather extensive experimentation as routine and thereby set a high threshold for an 'undue burden', it is worth noting that the Applicant in *Alethia* did not adduce evidence of the difficulties, dead ends or unexpected results that may have been encountered in producing inhibitory antibodies against Siglec-15.[57] In that regard, Australian courts have observed that an inventive step may be demonstrated in situations demanding complex and laborious work, or where there is no predictability of success. In *Aktiebolaget Hassle v. Alphapharm Pty Ltd*,[58] the High Court found that:

> 'The tracing of a course of action which was complex and detailed, as well as laborious, with a good deal of trial and error, with dead ends and the retracing

54. *Alethia*, [132]
55. *Alethia*, [127].
56. *Alethia*, [135].
57. *Alethia*, [130].
58. [2002] HCA 59.

> of steps is not the taking of routine steps to which the hypothetical formulator was taken as a matter of course.'[59]

Quoting Judge Rich *In re O'Farrell*,[60] High Court also observed that:

> '[F]or many inventions that seem quite obvious, there is no absolute predictability of success until the invention is reduced to practice. There is always at least a possibility of unexpected results, that would then provide an objective basis for showing that the invention, although apparently obvious, was in law nonobvious.'[61]

Evidence of difficulties, dead ends or unexpected results that may have been encountered when raising or testing antibodies can therefore support a case for inventive step, although when pursuing such a case, one should always be mindful of the tension that may arise with the requirement for sufficiency.

§23.06 ENFORCEMENT AND SCOPE OF PROTECTION

[A] Biosimilars

Given the often complex methods used to produce biologics, innovators seeking to obtain broad patent protection for their biologics will often include process claims. Enforcing such claims against the manufacturer of a biosimilar can be difficult, however, if the manufacturer does not disclose their production methods. In these circumstances, a patentee concerned about possible infringement of their patent may need to seek an order for preliminary discovery, compelling the suspected infringer to disclose information about their production methods. In *Pfizer Ireland Pharmaceuticals v. Samsung Bioepis AU Pty Ltd*,[62] the Full Federal Court considered an application by Pfizer for preliminary discovery of documents relating to its biologic medicine, etanercept, after Samsung Bioepis listed a biosimilar product on the Australian Register of Therapeutic Goods. Pfizer sought access to documents which had been filed with the Therapeutic Goods Administration in order to form a view as to whether the processes that Samsung Bioepis had used to manufacture its biosimilar infringed one or more of its patents. In the first instance decision, the Federal Court dismissed Pfizer's application, finding that evidence provided by Pfizer's expert witness did not provide a reasonable basis for Pfizer's belief in patent infringement, but instead amounted to a mere suspicion.[63] On appeal, however, the Full Federal Court overturned the first instance decision and granted Pfizer preliminary discovery. The Full Federal Court turned to the language of the relevant provision in the Federal Court Rules,[64] placing less emphasis on the factual correctness of the expert evidence and observing that

---

59. *Aktiebolaget Hassle v. Alphapharm Pty Ltd* [2002] HCA 59, [58].
60. 853 F 2.d 894, 908 (1988).
61. *Aktiebolaget Hassle v. Alphapharm Pty Ltd* [2002] HCA 59, [74].
62. [2017] FCAFC 193.
63. *Pfizer Ireland Pharmaceuticals v. Samsung Bioepis AU Pty Ltd* [2017] FCA 285.
64. Rule 7.23(1).

> '[t]he relevant question posed by the rule is whether the applicant reasonably believes that it may have the right to obtain relief. It is not whether one scientific view is more or less persuasive than another. In the field of science, expert views may differ about important scientific aspects that can be seen to bear upon a question. If the applicant has a belief that is founded on considerations or views reasonably open (even if contested as incorrect by others) that may well found a conclusion that the applicant has a relevant reasonable belief.'[65]

The Court criticised the tendency for preliminary discovery applications to descend into 'mini-trials'. Instead, the appropriate question is whether the applicant reasonably believes that it may have a right to relief. The decision is good news for patentees of biological processes who believe their rights are being infringed, but require further information before deciding whether to sue for infringement.

In further good news for biologic innovators, the Federal Court recently granted for the first time an interlocutory injunction restraining the threatened launch of a biosimilar product.[66] The decision concerned four Roche patents relating to the therapeutic use of rituximab, and Sandoz's intended launch of two biosimilar products. Sandoz had obtained regulatory approval for their product and had applied to have their products listed on Australia's Pharmaceutical Benefits Scheme (PBS), a government program that provides subsidised prescription drugs, including several biologics. Concerned that the PBS listing would cause irreversible damage, Roche sought an interlocutory injunction to restrain Sandoz from launching its biosimilar products. In deciding whether to grant an interlocutory injunction, Australian courts will make the following two inquiries:

i. has the applicant established a *prima facie* case; and
ii. does the balance of convenience favour granting the injunction?

With regard to the first question, Sandoz had accepted that its proposed activities would infringe Roche's patents, but argued that the relevant claims were invalid for lack of an inventive step. The Court acknowledged that the question of inventive step was difficult to answer at the interlocutory stage, but nevertheless concluded that although Sandoz's case for invalidity was arguable, it was not possible to conclude that it was strongly arguable.[67] On the question of balance of convenience, Roche submitted that the launch of Sandoz's biosimilar product would cause irreversible harm that could not be easily calculated, including a mandatory 16% price drop following PBS listing. Sandoz submitted that the difficulties calculating such losses were overblown and that if an injunction were granted and then overturned at final hearing, it would be much more difficult to calculate the harm suffered by Sandoz. Ultimately the Court found that the balance of convenience favoured granting an injunction against Sandoz. The injunction restrains Sandoz from supplying for use, offering for supply or sale, supplying or selling its biosimilar product until 11 August 2019, the date when the first of Roche's patents is set to expire.

65. *Pfizer Ireland Pharmaceuticals v. Samsung Bioepis AU Pty Ltd* [2017] FCAFC 193, [69].
66. *F. Hoffmann-La Roche AG v. Sandoz Pty Ltd* [2018] FCA 874.
67. *F. Hoffmann-La Roche AG v. Sandoz Pty Ltd* [2018] FCA 874, [153].

[B] Equivalence

A patent will be infringed when a person exploits a claimed invention without the authorisation of the patentee.[68] Where the invention is a process, 'exploit' includes, *inter alia*, using the process or making, hiring, selling or importing a product resulting from the process. Where the invention is a product, 'exploit' includes, *inter alia*, making, hiring, selling or importing the claimed product, and offering to make, hire or sell the product.[69]

The question of whether listing a medicine on Australia's PBS amounts to an infringement was recently considered by the Full Federal Court in *Apotex Pty Ltd v. Warner-Lambert Company LLC (No 3)*.[70] The Court confirmed that applying for listing on the PBS does not involve an offer to supply and does not constitute an infringement *per se*. Rather, applying for PBS listing was found to be a mere preparatory step to enable the exploitation of the invention at a later point in time.

Australia's Patents Act recognises indirect or 'contributory' infringement where a person supplies non-infringing goods to another for use in a way that could infringe a patent.[71] Supply of an antibody with instructions for use in a method or treatment can, for example, constitute indirect infringement of a claim directed to the method of treatment.[72] In contrast, importation, marketing or supply of an antibody for the claimed therapeutic use can amount to direct infringement of a Swiss-style claim.[73] Given the additional burden imposed on patentees to demonstrate contributory infringement as opposed to direct infringement,[74] both types of claim are commonly employed when protecting first and second medical uses in Australia.

As described in the first section of this chapter, the term of a patent directed to a pharmaceutical substance such as a therapeutic antibody can, in certain circumstances, be extended by up to five years. If the term of a patent is extended, exploitation of any form of the invention that is not a pharmaceutical substance, and exploitation of pharmaceutical substances for non-therapeutic uses, does not constitute infringement of the patent during the extended term.[75]

The basic test for infringement involves asking whether the alleged infringer has taken all of the features from a claim of the patent. If the answer is yes, then there has been infringement, subject to the defences available under the Patents Act. However, claims are not given a purely literal construction in Australia. Rather, they are construed purposively from the perspective of a person skilled in the art as to what such a person would have understood the patentee to be using the language of the claim to mean.[76]

---

68. Patents Act s 13.
69. Patents Act sch 1 (definition of 'exploit').
70. [2017] FCA 94.
71. Patents Act s 117.
72. *Bristol-Myers Squibb Co v. F H Faulding & Co Ltd* [2000] FCA 316.
73. *Otsuka Pharmaceutical Co., Ltd v. Generic Health Pty Ltd (No 4)* [2015] FCA 634; *Apotex Pty Ltd v. Warner-Lambert Company LLC (No 3)* [2017] FCA 94.
74. Patents Act ss 117(2).
75. Patents Act s 78.
76. *ESCO Corporation v. Ronneby Road Pty Ltd* [2018] FCAFC 46, [144].

Non-literal infringement can occur, for example, where a feature of a claim, which has been omitted or substituted by the infringer, is deemed inessential to the claimed invention.[77] Infringement can also occur where an infringer takes the essence or the 'pith and marrow' of the claimed invention, but avoids doing or producing something that falls within the literal scope of the claims.[78] Such cases are rare, however, and purposive construction does not extend the patentee's monopoly to the 'ideas' disclosed in the specification.[79] Whether a simple structural modification to a claimed antibody, such as a conservative amino acid substitution, is sufficient to avoid infringement in Australia remains to be tested. Clearly, though, proving literal infringement of a claim is a more straightforward undertaking than proving infringement of a claim whose scope is different to that provided by the precise language of the claim. Where possible, then, antibodies are generally claimed in multiple ways, including structurally and functionally, to ensure that variants of equivalent function are directly captured by the patent.

77. *Root Quality Pty Ltd v. Root Control Technologies Pty Ltd* [2000] FCA 980.
78. *Commonwealth Industrial Gases Ltd v. MWA Holdings Pty Ltd* [1970] HCA 38; *Pharmacia Italia SPA v. Mayne Pharma Pty Ltd* [2005] FCA 1078.
79. *Australian Mud Company Pty Ltd v. Coretell Pty Ltd* [2011] FCAFC 121, [69].

Table of Cases

CANADA

CHINA

EUROPEAN PATENT OFFICE

EUROPEAN UNION

FRANCE

GERMANY

INDIA

ISRAEL

ITALY

JAPAN

THE NETHERLANDS

POLAND

SINGAPORE

SOUTH KOREA

SPAIN

SWITZERLAND

UNITED KINGDOM

UNITED STATES OF AMERICA

AIPPI LAW SERIES

1. Sanna Wolk, Kacper Szkalej (eds.), *Employees' Intellectual Property Rights*, second edition 2017 (ISBN 978-90-411-9230-1).
2. Jochen Bühling (ed.), *Patent Protection for Second Medical Uses*, 2016 (ISBN 978-90-411-8253-1).
3. Christopher V. Carani (ed.), *Design Rights: Functionality and Scope of Protection*, 2017 (ISBN 978-90-411-8864-9).
4. Eléonore Gaspar (ed.), *Genuine Use of Trademarks*, 2018 (ISBN 978-94-035-0563-3).
5. Jürgen Meier, Oswin Ridderbusch (eds.), *Antibody Patenting: A Practitioner's Guide to Drafting, Prosecution and Enforcement*, 2019 (ISBN 978-94-035-1073-6).

www.ingramcontent.com/pod-product-compliance
Lightning Source LLC
LaVergne TN
LVHW020646300926
849161LV00004B/840